Media and Mass Communication in a Digital Age

Media and Mass Communication in a Digital Age

Edited by Alley Webster

Clanrye International
www.clanryeinternational.com

Clanrye International,
750 Third Avenue, 9th Floor,
New York, NY 10017, USA

ISBN: 978-1-63240-719-1

Cataloging-in-Publication Data

Media and mass communication in a digital age / edited by Alley Webster.
p. cm.
Includes bibliographical references and index.
ISBN 978-1-63240-719-1
1. Mass media. 2. Communication. 3. Digital media. 4. Digital communications. I. Webster, Alley.
P90 .M43 2018
302.23--dc23

For information on all Clanrye International publications
visit our website at www.clanryeinternational.com

Clanrye International

Printed in China.

Contents

Preface

This book aims to highlight the current researches and provides a platform to further the scope of innovations in this area. This book is a product of the combined efforts of many researchers and scientists, after going through thorough studies and analysis from different parts of the world. The objective of this book is to provide the readers with the latest information of the field.

The advancement of science and technology has facilitated rapid progress of varied fields. Media and mass communication is one significant field with has majorly benefitted from the innovation in technology. Mass communication directly impacts the behavior and opinion of the people. Advertising, journalism, broadcasting and public relations are some of the sub-fields of mass communication. The objective of this book is to give a general view of the different areas of this field, and its applications. It includes some of the vital pieces of work being conducted across the world, on various topics related to mass communication. This book is a complete source of knowledge on the present status of this important field.

I would like to express my sincere thanks to the authors for their dedicated efforts in the completion of this book. I acknowledge the efforts of the publisher for providing constant support. Lastly, I would like to thank my family for their support in all academic endeavors.

Editor

1

The Finns Party: Euroscepticism, Euro Crisis, Populism and the Media

Juha Herkman

Department of Social Research, University of Helsinki, 00014 Helsinki, Finland; E-Mail: juha.herkman@helsinki.fi

Abstract

In many European countries, populist right-wing parties have been most noticeable representatives of Euroscepticism. In Finland, the Finns Party (Perussuomalaiset) has been a constant promoter of organisational Euroscepticism through its leader, Timo Soini. The party broke through in Finland's 'big bang elections' of 2011, when the most debated issue was the European economic crisis, which was dominated by Eurosceptic Soini. Research concerning the relationship between the media, populism and Euroscepticism usually focus on national or European Parliament elections. This study analyses the media portrayal of the Eurosceptic Finns Party during times other than elections, focusing on the Finland's overall Euro crisis press coverage in 2010–2012. The analysis shows that the populist Finns Party has been a minor player in that coverage, which was dominated by the Euro positive political and economic elites. Differences between newspapers indicate that journalistic routines and political context direct media coverage toward particular framings, even when the media proclaims itself politically independent and neutral.

Keywords

Euro Crisis; Euroscepticism; Finland; frame analysis; media; populism

Issue

This article is part of a multidisciplinary issue of *Media and Communication*, edited by Epp Lauk (University of Jyväskylä, Finland) and Raul Reis (Emerson College, USA).

---

1. Introduction

Opposition to immigration and ethnic minorities can be described as the main themes unifying extreme right movements, however, populist right-wing parties have also promoted Euroscepticism (Caiani & Conti, 2014; Mudde, 2007; Pirro, 2014). Hooghe, Marks and Wilson (2002) conclude this is because European integration combines several supposed threats—immigrants; external political and cultural influences; and European laws—which populist right-wing parties perceive as undermining national sovereignty (pp. 976–977). Thus, the European Union (EU) and its institutions constitute a symbolic enemy to right-wing populist movements (Caiani & Conti, 2014, pp. 186–188).

Taggart and Szczerbiak (2002, p. 31) noted that Eurosceptic parties are generally small and gain relatively low shares in national elections, making their political influence marginal. This might have been true at the beginning of the new millennium. However, since the expansion of the international financial crisis into a European debt and currency crisis in year 2008, Eurosceptic sentiment in many European countries has increased (Pew Research, 2013). The simultaneous increase in internal and external migrants in the EU has helped populist parties strengthen their political influence, allowing them into government in many countries.

Since the political and economic establishment has generally promoted the benefits of European integration, populist parties have been the most eager representatives of Euroscepticism in their domestic arenas. This is true for the Finns Party (Perussuomalaiset [PS], previously True Finns), a constant promoter of organisational Euroscepticism through its leader, Timo Soini. Even if there have been some exceptions depending on their government-opposition status of the moment, in general Finnish mainstream parties are favourable to European integration in comparison to their rank and file (Raunio, 2011, p. 204). Hence, PS's consistent Euroscepticism has been a defining image of the party.

The Nordic party system has been identified as 'enduring' (Sundberg, 1999), but the Euro currency crisis has challenged it in Finland. The crisis is purported to be a main reason behind the 'big bang election' of 2011 (Arter, 2012), in which PS gained 19.1 percent of the vote, becoming the third largest party in the Finnish parliament (see Borg, 2012). According to the research, the European economic crisis became the most important topic in election campaign debates (Railo & Välimäki, 2012a) and PS and Soini challenged the more established candidates, dominating agenda setting during the election campaigns (Pernaa, 2012, pp. 35-38; Railo & Välimäki, 2012b, pp. 120–135).

However, the election campaign was a specific period in the relationship between Finland's political parties and the media. Similar specific periods have been found throughout Europe because research into Eurosceptics has concentrated on electoral campaigns (Schuck et al., 2011; Silke & Maier, 2011; Strömbäck et al., 2011; Van Spanje & De Vreese, 2014), and therefore PS studies have focused precisely on the 'big bang election' of 2011 (Arter, 2012; Borg, 2012; Rahkonen, 2011; Wiberg, 2011). Additionally, PS gained success in the 2015 parliamentary elections, gaining 17.7 percent of the vote and entering into government for the first time.

EU issues are especially prominent during election campaigns in countries with Eurosceptic parties (see Silke & Maier, 2011), although media analysis of the Euro crisis coverage reveals the portrayal of the crisis is dominated by elites in favour of the Euro rather than Eurosceptics (Picard, 2015). To redress that focus on election periods, this study examines the role of PS's media coverage outside of electoral periods, namely the Euro crisis. Secondly, most studies indicate that media elites are generally more favourable to mainstream political parties upholding the political status quo, whereas the tabloid media is more 'populist' and promotes divisive politics (Leconte, 2010, p. 195; Mazzoleni, 2003, p. 8). Thus, it is worth exploring if there is difference between the quality and the tabloid media's portrayal of PS when referring to the Euro crisis.

The research questions (RQ) of the study are as follows:

RQ1. How has the Finns Party (PS) been portrayed in the Finnish press coverage of the Euro crisis?

RQ2. How does the portrayal differ compared to the coverage of the 'big bang elections' of 2011?

RQ3. What does the portrayal reveal about the relationship between the press and populist movements in general?

The data for the study has been collected as part of the large international research project that compared the press coverage of the Euro crisis in ten EU countries (Picard, 2015). The sample consists of 11 two-week periods between the years 2010 and 2012 and contains articles from the leading quality newspaper, the leading popular paper, the leading financial paper, and the most prominent regional paper in Northern Finland. The main study method is quantitative and qualitative frame analysis.

2. Euroscepticism and the Media

Even if Leconte (2010) has demonstrated in her book *Understanding Euroscepticism* that 'the perceptions of the EU are largely influenced by issues apparently unrelated to European integration, such as citizens' perception of national democracy, immigration, multiculturalism and so on' (pp. 246–247), Euroscepticism has most often been linked to doubts or distrust of the EU and its bodies and regulative power. The central position of the EU in Euroscepticism is because EU institutions and regulation are central to the debate over national sovereignty and European integration since the 1990s (Caiani & Conti, 2014, pp. 186–187). Populist radical right-wing movements have adopted Euroscepticism to critique globalisation (Mudde, 2007).

It is possible to classify different levels or dimensions of Euroscepticism (e.g. Leconte, 2010, pp. 43–67). If we accept the definition of Euroscepticism as being the distrust of the EU, Euroscepticism can become organised by political parties or movements critical of the EU, or it may appear as general dissatisfaction among EU citizens. Euroscepticism can also be either strong and principled—opposing EU membership or the union itself, or it can refer to weaker (soft) resistance on specific questions in which the interests of some member states conflict with EU regulation (Taggart & Szczerbiak, 2002).

Euroscepticism has been strong, for example, in the UK. Taylor (2008) has crystallised a common EU theme found in British discussions: EU is far too expensive, 'Eurocratic' and self-serving, which prevents a reasonable agricultural policy; meddles with subjects it should not, such as domestic employment, health and security policies; and increases undesired immigration, resulting in social tensions in member states (pp. 34–35). In general, British Euroscepticism has mostly been focused on European Monetary Union (EMU) (Lubbers & Scheepers, 2005, p. 228) and on immigration (Luedtke, 2005). Similar arguments have been presented in other EU countries too (Caiani & Conti, 2014), but in the UK attitudes against the EU led to Brexit in the July of 2016.

Therefore, Euroscepticism varies between countries (Leconte, 2010, p. 99). Whereas Euroscepticism has been strong in the UK both among citizens and policy-makers, France has traditionally been a 'Europhilic' country representing a positive attitude towards European integration. Euroscepticism has been strong in the Nordic countries, albeit weaker in Finland than in Sweden, Norway and Denmark—countries not in the EMU (Ekman, 2010, pp. 108–119). In addition to Eurosceptic and Europhile extremes, it is also possible to define 'critical Europeanist' countries such as the Netherlands in which the attitude towards European integration has been generally positive, although the attitude towards EU institutions is negative (Koopmans, Erbe, & Meyer, 2010, pp. 91–92).

According to various surveys, Euroscepticism among EU citizens has increased during the last twenty years (Eurobarometer, 2015; Leconte, 2010, p. 161; Pew Research, 2013). Support for the EU was highest in the early 1990s, but by the beginning of the new millennium support had declined remarkably, for example, in the Netherlands, France and Italy, where the attitude towards European integration had been very positive (Caiani & Conti, 2014, p. 184; Taylor, 2008, pp. 26–27). In many countries, distrust has confronted the attitudes of the establishment and ruling parties, which have generally promoted European integration. This, in turn, has created space for populist political parties that apply Eurosceptic rhetoric (Caiani & Conti, 2014, p. 184; Ekman, 2010, p. 92).

Taggart and Szczerbiak (2002) claim that Eurosceptic parties will likely succeed in countries with multi-polar competition between the parties than in countries with bi-polar competition because, in multi-polar systems, peripheral parties can benefit from second-order issues, such as European integration, when differentiating themselves from more established parties (pp. 34–35). In addition, Paloheimo (2012) emphasises that populist parties have been especially successful in countries traditionally reliant on consensus in policy-making because the establishment is easily labelled a 'corrupt elite' by populists (p. 329).

Finnish EU policy has been based on consensus among established political parties, even if conflicts within parties on EU questions have appeared (Raunio, 2011, p. 198). This has opened a door through which the populist PS can act as a Eurosceptic voice, seducing voters. In addition to the structural transformation of industries and scandals concerning election campaign funding in Finland, Euroscepticism, containing distrust of and protest sentiment against established parties, has been shown to be one of the main reasons for PS's success in the 'big bang elections' of 2011 (e.g. Borg, 2012; Grönlund & Westinen, 2012; Rahkonen, 2011).

Studies of the European Parliament (EP) elections of 2009 indicated that there is a correlation between the media portrayal of the EU and the election results: in countries with strong Eurosceptic parties, the negative portrayal of the EU has been more common than in other countries (Silke & Maier, 2011; Van Spanje & De Vreese, 2014). However, there were significant differences between the countries. In the 2009 EP election, the pro-EU frame dominated, for example, Italian, German and Finnish media coverage, whereas the anti-EU frame was strong in the Czech, Danish and UK media (Strömbäck et al., 2011, p. 171). In general, a negative tone on EU issues was more common than positive (Schuck et al., 2011, p. 177)—also in Finland and other Nordic countries (Schuck et al., 2011, p. 184). However, the EU was framed as beneficial in all other countries, except the UK, Austria and Czech Republic—the most prominent representatives of Euroscepticism (Schuck et al., 2011, pp. 186–187).

Thus, media coverage commonly portrays the EU as beneficial for the member states but regards EU institutions as reducing individual member state's democracy and sovereignty (Schuck et al., 2011, p. 193). This reflects discussions on the EU's 'democratic deficit', deriving from the disparity between Europe's institutional development and national public spheres as core arenas of political debate (Koopmans, 2007, p. 183; Leconte, 2010, p. 209; Schuck et al., 2011, p. 175). The European Commission has responded to the challenge with a strategic increase in transparency and public discussion (De Beus, 2010, p. 26; Heikkilä, 2007). However, as Hix (2008) reminds us, publicity strategies cannot bridge the gap between the European elites and European citizens if there are no real possibilities to challenge predominant policy-making at the EU level (p. 64).

The problem from the media's perspective has been that the mainstream European media have made the Euro elites their main source when discussing EU questions and issues, whereas the Eurosceptic views of those who have less political power have been marginalised (Koopmans, 2007). In Finland, journalists, on the whole, supported joining the EU more than the average citizen (Mörä, 1999). However, Finland has been an EU member state for over 20 years and the Euro crisis has seriously challenged the country's economy since 2012. Thus, the opinions and attitudes of journalists may have changed. In the coverage of the 2009 EP election the tone towards the EU was generally more positive in newer member states than in older ones, indicating that there is a 'honeymoon period' (Schuck et al., 2011, p. 185).

Trenz (2007) has demonstrated that the quality press has, in general, promoted European integration and been EU positive. However, soft versions of Euroscepticism are quite common also in the quality press (Leconte, 2010, pp. 197, 218). Several studies indicate that the tabloid media adopts a Eurosceptic discourse more eagerly than the quality media and repeats the so-called 'Euro myths', especially in countries as the UK and Austria, which are known from their strong Eurosceptic sentiment (Leconte, 2010, pp. 195, 203–204). It is also worth acknowledging that Web-based communication and social media play significant roles in today's Eurosceptic mobilisation (Leconte, 2010, pp. 206–208). This is especially true with right-wing populist movements, whose supporters eagerly link the mainstream media to the liberal and corrupt elites and therefore strengthen their group identities via their own social media sites (Herkman, 2016).

3. Materials and Methods

The data here derive from a large comparative research project 'The Euro Crisis, Media Coverage, and Perceptions of Europe within the EU' organised by the Reuters Institute for the Study of Journalism at the University of

Oxford (see Picard, 2015). The newspaper materials of the project were collected from ten EU countries: the UK, France, Germany, Spain, Italy, Greece, Netherlands, Belgium, Poland and Finland. The sample consists of articles that discuss the Euro crisis. The articles were gathered from four newspapers from each country during 11 two-week periods during 2010 to 2012. The selected newspapers included the leading liberal and conservative quality dailies, business or financial papers and tabloid or popular papers. The sampling periods were built around the 'key moments' of the crisis, including the EU summits in 2010, 2011 and 2012 as well as the Eurozone members' and the International Monetary Fund's agreement for the 100 billion euro loan for Greece on 2 May 2010 (Picard, 2015, pp. 269–273).

The sample included all journalistic articles such as news stories, editorials, interviews, feature stories, columns and commentaries published during the sample periods. However, letters to the editors were excluded from the sample. The coding book contained variables that considered the basic data of the articles, e.g., the size of the story, genre, author; the main topics and sources used in the articles; the main causes; responses; actors, winners and losers of the crisis—if there were any—as well as the geopolitical frame and portrayal of the EU institutions presented in the articles (Picard, 2015, pp. 273–293). In total, 10,492 articles were coded and analysed in the project.

In Finland, as in other Nordic countries, it is difficult to define newspapers according to the liberal/conservative axis since there is no such kind of political orientation in the Nordic newspaper field. Thus, Finnish dailies chosen for the sampling were the leading newspaper of the country *Helsingin Sanomat*, traditionally sympathetic towards European integration and Europhilic elites; the leading regional paper of northern Finland *Kaleva*, traditionally more critical towards EU and the Europhilic metropolitan elites; the leading business paper *Kauppalehti*; and the most popular tabloid *Ilta-Sanomat*. The Finnish sample contained 971 articles discussing the Euro crisis (see Harjuniemi & Herkman, 2013, p. 15). The coding of the sample was carried out by two trained research assistants, whose inter-coder reliability was 0.78 according to the Holsti formula.

The coding book was supplemented for this study by variables exploring how much and in what way PS was portrayed in Euro crisis articles (Harjuniemi & Herkman, 2013, p. 83). Only 61 Euro crisis articles, meaning six percent of the Finnish sample, mentioned PS. Two of the 61 articles did not actually discuss the expected topic and were thus excluded from the materials. Therefore, 59 articles remained from the larger sample of the Finnish Euro crisis coverage and were taken for qualitative frame analysis; 20 from *Kaleva*, 18 from *Helsingin Sanomat*, 15 from *Ilta-Sanomat* and only six from *Kauppalehti*.

The roots of frame analysis lay in Goffman's (1974) ideas on social experience, but since the 1980s the frame analysis has been applied by media studies and become one of the most popular methods of journalism studies (Borah, 2011). The definition of the 'frame' varies depending on the study, but usually it refers to the possible framings restricting or directing interpretations (Van Spanje & De Vreese, 2014, p. 327). In journalism studies, framing refers to the processes in which the media emphasises some parts of reality and hides others by putting certain views to the fore of an article, thereby endorsing a particular interpretation (Entman, 1993, p. 53).

The frame analysis separates media frames from audience frames. The former is framing that the media carries out in portraying various topics, actors and phenomena, whereas the latter is the way audiences receive and interpret media texts (De Vreese, Jochen, & Holli, 2001, p. 107). In political studies, the frame analysis is also used to comprehend the construction of political ideas and identities (e.g. Caiani & Conti, 2014, p. 185). In this study, the focus is solely on media frames that are studied with reference to how the Finnish press framed PS in the Euro crisis articles. The main frames are found by sifting through sentences in which PS or its representatives are mentioned and by reflecting on how PS was presented in comparison with the context of the whole article.

4. Finns Party and Coverage of the Euro Crisis

According to election studies, the economic crisis in the EU region became the most popular topic of television debates and newspaper articles during the campaigns of Finnish elections in 2011, a debate led by the Eurosceptic PS (Railo & Välimäki, 2012a, pp. 36, 53–57). However, debates on the Euro crisis appear to have had two phases. In the first phase, the media were highly critical of the EU institutions' and Finland's official policy during the crisis. However, after Portugal's government fell on 23 March 2011 because of the crisis, the Finnish media started to support Finland's official EU policy and sought a new economic consensus (Railo, 2012, p. 258–261). Thus, the significance of Euroscepticism faded during the campaigns once the crisis worsened.

The period of the 'big bang elections' and the collapse of Portugal's government are not included in the sample of this study. The sample contains the period before the spring of 2011, during which the EU Contract was changed on 16 December 2010, and the period after spring 2011, when the European Central Bank asked Italy for more austerity measures on 5 August 2011 (Picard, 2015, pp. 269–272). Therefore, the material here focuses on the coverage of the Euro crisis specifically from the point of view of the crisis not from the Finnish elections.

As mentioned, only six percent of the Euro crisis articles mentioned PS and not all of those articles promoted a Eurosceptic approach. Thus, it seems that PS gained only modest publicity at times other than elections. In contrast, the media coverage of the crisis was dominated by domestic and European political leaders, with economists often representing EU positive 'Euro elites' (Harjuniemi, Herkman, & Ojala, 2015; Herkman &

Harjuniemi, 2015). The leader of PS, Timo Soini, was often quoted in Finnish Euro crisis articles, but less than the Prime Minister and the Minister of Finance or the EU's Financial Commissioner, Olli Rehn, and economists and other EU officials (Harjuniemi & Herkman, 2013, pp. 21–29). Therefore, it is clear that PS did not define the Finnish media agenda during the Euro crisis.

However, since the 'big bang elections' made PS a legitimate debater on the Euro crisis, almost all the Euro crisis articles that mention PS were published after the 2011 elections. In fact, only six articles were published before the elections. Thus, PS's higher proportional share of media attention came after the election period. Furthermore, as the economic recession has become more topical since then, the continuing media spotlight on Euroscepticism has slightly strengthened (Harjuniemi & Herkman, 2013, p. 19).

The Finnish press discussed the Euro crisis mostly as an economic issue to be covered by the business or financial sections of the papers (Harjuniemi & Herkman, 2013, p. 24). This also explains why PS was mentioned so infrequently and mostly in a negative light by the business paper *Kauppalehti* (see Table 1). *Kauppalehti* approached the crisis as an economic issue and mostly used economists and bankers for its sources. The other papers mentioned PS three times more often in their Euro crisis articles than *Kauppalehti* because they discussed the political dimensions of the crisis. The leading daily, *Helsingin Sanomat*, mentioned PS in six percent of its Euro crisis articles and generally gave more visibility to PS than *Kauppalehti*. *Helsingin Sanomat* also approached PS quite neutrally in its news journalism.

As a percentage of all Euro crisis stories, PS was most often mentioned in *Ilta-Sanomat*, in which 12 percent of all Euro crisis stories discussed the party or Soini. In addition, *Ilta-Sanomat* was most positive in its portrayal of PS, since only two of its articles clearly criticised the party. This indicates that *Ilta-Sanomat* adopted the most visible Eurosceptic approach. The paper also gave increased visibility to PS by publishing impressive images of Soini. *Helsingin Sanomat* and *Kaleva* published fewer images of him. In many ways, *Kaleva* was the antithesis of *Ilta-Sanomat* in its portrayal of PS; even though *Kaleva* mentioned PS quite frequently, the party was repeatedly discussed in a negative light and even downplayed.

Different assessments can be partly explained by the article types. In *Kaleva* and *Kauppalehti* PS was mentioned quite often in editorials and commentaries—article types in which critical statements are common—whereas in *Helsingin Sanomat* and in *Ilta-Sanomat* PS was more often discussed in news stories that emphasise the more objective and neutral tone of factual reporting. However, political and ideological grounds can also be found, especially for *Kaleva*'s critical portrayal of PS.

Since PS was portrayed so infrequently in Finnish Euro crisis articles, it is not possible to make any statistically reliable conclusions about the subject. However, a few recurring frames was possible to identify from the data. The material found in 59 articles introduced ten frames in which the interpretations of PS were delimited by the media. Some of these frames were very specific concerning, for example, Soini's candidacy for the 2012 presidential elections. When these kinds of specialties and overlaps between the frames were eliminated, three main frames could be defined, namely: (1) PS as a representative of the opposition, (2) PS as a representative of populism, and (3) PS as a representative of Euroscepticism (see Table 2).

A single article might employ several frames, but usually one frame dominated the portrayal of PS. The most common primary frame was that of 'opposition'. The 'populism' frame was the second most popular, and 'Euroscepticism' came third. However, 'Euroscepticism' was evidently most common as a secondary frame. Thus, one can argue that PS was usually presented as a representative of opposition or populist politics, although these presentations were frequently accompanied by the Euroscepticism frame. The opposition frame was complemented by the Euroscepticism frame especially in news stories, whereas editorials and commentaries favoured a populist frame with a critical assessment of PS. Each frame will be next introduced in more detail.

Opposition Frame. This frame emphasized PS as a representative of domestic opposition politics. In opposition frame PS was seen typically as a contender or challenge to government rather than as a proponent of its own

Table 1. Finns Party (PS) in Euro crisis articles (n = 971).

Newspaper	PS in articles (total amount of articles)	Share from all articles (%)	Visibility of PS in articles	Assessment of PS in articles
Kauppalehti (business paper)	6 (309)	2%	Minor	Negative
Helsingin Sanomat (leading daily, capital area)	18 (312)	6%	Modest	Neutral
Kaleva (regional daily, Northern Finland)	20 (228)	9%	Minor/modest	Negative
Ilta-Sanomat (popular paper)	15 (122)	12%	Sizeable	Positive

agenda. The party was thus defined by what it is not (i.e. a government participant). In consensus democracies such as Finland government/opposition division is one of the most important dimensions structuring the party field and, therefore, it is not a surprise that this frame was most common and used by all newspapers included to the study, because PS was an opposition party during all sample periods of 2010–2012.

Opposition frame was most common in news stories published by dailies. Especially *Helsingin Sanomat* favoured this framing that was used also in such story headlines as 'Opposition accuses the government for increasing the charges of Finland' (3 August 2011) or 'Opposition scolded the Prime Minister Katainen' (3 July 2012). Opposition frame appeared several times in *Helsingin Sanomat* news stories as neutral mentions of PS (e.g. 8 May 2010; 3 August 2011).

However, quite often the opposition/government division was dramatized by using metaphors known from sports and conflict narratives (cf. Joris, Puustinen, Sobieraj, & d'Haenens, 2015). This was common also in *Helsingin Sanomat*, in which the opposition was 'furious' with the schedule of parliamentary processing of collateral agreement with Spain (19 July 2012) or when the Prime Minister Katainen had to time after time 'deny allegations' (3 August 2011). Dramatization was even more typical in other papers, in which 'the government and the opposition clashed' (*Kauppalehti* 18 June 2012) or the leader of PS Soini 'attacked the government very hard' (*Kaleva* 9 November 2011). Usually attacker was the opposition and the government was defender (e.g. *Ilta-Sanomat* 7 October 2011).

Even if the opposition frame was most common in the news stories, it was also used in other story types highlighting the differences between the papers. Whereas popular paper *Ilta-Sanomat* presented PS and its leader Soini quite often positively as the representatives of the opposition, regional paper *Kaleva* made usually completely different evaluations. This can be explained by the fact that even if *Kaleva* is announced to be politically independent the strong position of the Centre Party in the region *Kaleva* is distributed has implications to the alignments of the paper. In *Ilta-Sanomat* PS was a snappy opposition party, whose leader's Eurosceptic blog writings were repeated almost as they were (28 November 2011), but in *Kaleva* PS was just a secondary opposition party 'accompanying Centre Party in its EU criticism' (3 August 2011). Thus, according to *Kaleva* the Centre Party was the primary opposition party (10 August 2011), and PS was often portrayed in negative or critical light (e.g. 21 July 2012).

Populism Frame. Populism as such is a slippery concept. Populism has been historically linked to very different left- and right-wing movements, totalitarian and democratic systems as well as nationalist and liberalist approaches (see Taggart, 2000). In many political cultures and languages the term 'populism' carries rather negative connotations (cf. Canovan, 2005, p. 75), even though the etymological background of the word, deriving from the Latin noun 'populus' meaning 'the people', gives it an emancipative or empowering signification (cf. Williams, 1988, p. 66). Pejorative meanings of 'empty talk' are common in accusations of someone being a 'populist', but other kinds of usages with more positive connotations of democracy have also been connected to populism (e.g. Canovan, 1999).

Mostly negative meanings of populism appeared in populism frame of PS. Surprisingly, the positive meanings of populism and PS representing 'the people' were also sometimes used in newspapers that generally were critical against the party. For example, in a commentary writing of *Kauppalehti*, PS was presented as fresh air in EU politics between the people and the elites (17 August 2011), and also dailies noted Soini as a defender of democracy when the Finnish government rushed the parliamentary decision of EU loan programme for Spain during parliament's recess period (*Kaleva* 19 July 2012; *Helsingin Sanomat* 19 July 2012).

However, positive approaches of populism frame were most common in *Ilta-Sanomat* that quite often presented Eurosceptic PS as a representative of 'the real people' opposing Europhilic political and economic elites. *Ilta-Sanomat*, for example, published a web survey asking if the support Finland pays for Greece is too much or not (3 May 2010). It was not a surprise that 94 percent of over 50,000 respondents thought that the amount of money was too much. In addition to the survey results, Soini promoted his Eurosceptic views in the article. Positive framing of populism was used also in other articles of *Ilta-Sanomat* presenting PS as a mediator of 'the people' and challenger of the Euro elites (e.g. 7 November 2011). Contradiction compared to *Helsingin Sanomat* was striking: the leading quality paper of the country almost avoided using the populism frame.

The reason why populism frame was used so rarely in *Helsingin Sanomat* derives from the most popular meanings of the term in Finnish language. The term is used often pejoratively, combining the meanings of populist

Table 2. Main frames of Finns Party (PS) in Euro crisis articles (n = 59).

Frame	As a primary frame	As a secondary frame	Total
Opposition frame	24	5	29
Populism frame	16	7	23
Euroscepticism frame	10	24	34
Total	50	36	86

rhetoric or style to ideological emptiness. To call someone a 'populist' has been a negative statement in Finnish political discourse. This kind of pejorative use of populism frame was popular in editorials and commentaries of *Kaleva* and *Kauppalehti*, in which PS was most often discussed as a troublemaker on the Finnish political field. Especially *Kaleva* seemed to accuse PS of 'populist' Euro policies in its editorials and commentaries (4 and 17 August 2011; 13 November 2011; 26 June 2012; 21 July 2012). *Kauppalehti* also promoted this kind of approach to PS (18 August 2011; 31 October 2011; 18 June 2012).

Also in the 'big bang election' media coverage especially editorials and commentaries presented PS as a protest channel through which the voters could project their disappointments. However, EU policy and anti-immigration strategies of PS were criticized in these articles as 'populist rhetoric' (Hatakka, 2012, pp. 297–301), and some writers thought that PS might even threat the very functionality of Finnish political system (Hatakka, 2012, p. 317). In Euro crisis coverage these kinds of evaluations were common especially on editorials and commentaries published by *Kaleva* and *Kauppalehti* in 2010–2012.

Euroscepticism Frame. Euroscepticism frame goes naturally hand in hand with PS because, as mentioned earlier, the party has represented most consistently Eurosceptic approach in Finnish political field during the twenty-first century (Raunio, 2011). Therefore, in Euroscepticism frame media echoed the self-definitions of PS. Again, popular paper *Ilta-Sanomat* applied most commonly the positive approach to Euroscepticism and PS—the stance indicated by an opinion poll asking if joining to EMU had been a mistake or not (1 June 2012). According to the poll, only the supporters of PS thought that Finland should not have been joined the EMU. Soini was commenting the result in a story so that he was glad if PS was the one and only Eurosceptic party in Finland.

Euroscepticism as a primary frame was most popular in *Ilta-Sanomat*, which gave in all most positive and notable publicity to PS (cf. Harjuniemi & Herkman, 2013, p. 59). Thus, PS and its leader Soini promoted in Ilta-Sanomat directly their political agenda, which was not oppressed by opposition or populism frames. Soini argued in *Ilta-Sanomat* that he had been right all the time when warning about the support of the European banks (30 June 2012) or when the 'Europhilic government' had to explain away their EU policies (11 August 2011; 12 July 2012). The paper also quoted some other Eurosceptic commentators, such as economist Stefan Törnqvist from Ålandsbanken, who predicted the breakdown of the Eurozone.

In other newspapers the Euroscepticism frame was approached usually more neutrally than in *Ilta-Sanomat*. In *Helsingin Sanomat* news stories, for example, also other PS representatives than Soini, such as MP Vesa-Matti Saarakkala (28 October 2011) and MEP Sampo Terho (29 September 2011), criticised the government's EU policies. However, majority of Euroscepticism framings were secondary to the opposition frame that was the primary frame of PS in *Helsingin Sanomat*. Thus, first and foremost PS was presented as an opposition party which criticises the government about its EU policies.

The use of Euroscepticism frame commonly as a secondary frame in *Helsingin Sanomat* and in some news stories of *Kaleva* also can be explained partly by the sampling. The sample focusing solely on articles discussing Euro crisis emphasizes Euroscepticism as central topic of PS' opposition politics. In articles discussing PS outside the Euro crisis, other topics would have probably dominated. Critique of the campaign financing of the more established parties, but also immigration, were common issues in 'big bang election' coverages and promoted especially by PS and its leader Soini (Railo & Välimäki, 2012a). These typical topics with a populist movement did not come out so much in media coverage of the Euro crisis.

5. Discussion and Conclusions

To answer RQ1, the role of the Eurosceptic PS turned out to be rather modest in determining media coverage of the 2010–2012 Euro crisis: only six percent of the Euro crisis articles mentioned PS or its representatives. In those articles, PS was primarily framed as a representative of the opposition or populism meaning a negative or neutral tone accompanied its portrayal. However, Euroscepticism was a common secondary frame and especially accompanied the opposition frame, indicating the significance of PS as a public representative of Finnish Euroscepticism.

The differences between the framings demonstrate differences between newspaper types. The business paper did not grant much attention to PS because it mostly discussed the Euro crisis as an economic issue, thus favouring economists and bankers as news sources (cf. Arrese & Vara, 2015). In its rare articles that mentioned PS, the party was usually presented as a populist troublemaker. In daily newspapers, PS was given more visibility and discussed in a more neutral manner, even if the amount of articles was not very substantial and PS was portrayed negatively, especially in *Kaleva*.

The most significant difference between the newspaper types was that between the quality newspapers and the tabloid, which was the only newspaper to portray PS positively and adopt a Eurosceptic approach. The visibility given to PS was also remarkably greater in the tabloid than in other papers: PS was mentioned in 12 percent of all Euro crisis articles and often portrayed through flamboyant images of the party leader, Soini. Therefore, this study supports previous studies indicating that the tabloid media serves populist and Eurosceptic audiences more eagerly than quality newspapers (Jungar, 2010, pp. 215–216; Leconte, 2010, pp. 203–204; Mazzoleni, 2003, p. 8).

Compared to the media coverage of the big bang elections 2011 (RQ2), the attention given to PS appeared completely different: PS and Timo Soini were visible in election campaigns in defining the media agenda (Railo & Välimäki,

2012a), but the agenda setting power of the party turned out to be rather modest during the Euro crisis issue, although the visibility of PS seemed to increase slightly after the elections. Generally, the Euro crisis coverage was dominated by Euro-positive political leaders, the government and economists, whereas representatives of civil society were seldom mentioned or used as story sources (Harjuniemi & Herkman, 2013, pp. 21–29). This accords with other studies of actors who 'inhabit the European public sphere' (Koopmans, 2007, pp. 203–206).

The sample period of this study ends in 2012. The consequences of the Euro crisis have since that struck Finland extremely hard. Thus, the archive of *Helsingin Sanomat* indicates that there might be more room for Euroscepticism in Finnish media coverage after 2013. Keynesian approaches and other alternatives to austerity have been discussed more often than during the sample period—when the Euro elite dominated debates. However, there is no evidence that PS would have gained more attention in those debates either. Since that PS has been profiled rather by its public criticism of immigration and by scandals that some of their representatives have faced.

Therefore, the study implies that the relationship between the populist movement and the media (RQ3), depends on many other variables than thematic issues such as Euroscepticism, which seems to be still quite marginal in Finnish mainstream media (cf. Taggart & Szczerbiak, 2002). The most important factor in this relationship is the position of the populist party in a domestic political field. Thus, it is necessary to consider if the party is marginal or not in the political arena, whether it is in opposition or in government, in its insurgent phase or established—all these factors impact heavily on the overall media attention given to it (see Herkman, 2015). Therefore, it is probable that the dominant frames of opposition and populism have changed when PS became established and joined the government after the 2015 elections.

The media factor itself is another major variable defining the relationship between the populist party and the media. Obviously, the tabloid media adopts Eurosceptic sentiment more eagerly than quality media. Criticism for and against Euroscepticism is also more common in commentaries, editorials and columns than in news stories that tend to be more neutral. However, political affiliations between the media and domestic political parties appear to direct media coverage toward particular framings, even if the news media proclaims to be politically independent. For instance, the commitment to the Centre Party in *Kaleva*'s editorials and commentaries indicates the strong impact of the party in the region in which the paper is published. Hence, the audience addressed by the particular media organisation may also greatly explain media frames regarding Euroscepticism and populism.

However, even more important media factor derives from journalistic routines. Several studies in Finland and elsewhere have indicated that the media attention emphasizes leading politicians, such as key Ministers, explaining why PS was not a prominent agent in Euro crisis coverage during its opposition period (see Bos, Van der Brug, & De Vreese, 2011; Suikkanen, Holma, & Raittila, 2012). More specifically, as Bennett's (1990) 'indexing hypothesis' supposes, the mainstream media organizations usually adopt the hegemonic views of government debate, and challenging viewpoints are therefore introduced merely insomuch as they are emerged in these 'official circles' (p. 106). This is especially true in such countries as Finland whose media can even today be called 'politics friendly' (cf. Van Dalen, 2012).

The explicit difference between the Euro crisis coverages during the election campaign and times other also support the indexing hypothesis, which is intended to apply the everyday news accounts rather than coverage of such specific events as elections 'that may have a normative-ritual order of their own' (Bennett, 1990, p. 107). Thus, during the election campaign, the conflict frame enabled PS to challenge the established Euro-positive political elites that in other times dominated the everyday news stream. Therefore, it seems that to become a prominent point of view in the news media, Euroscepticism has to be promoted by established government politicians who either challenge the other decision-making elites by this view or adopt Euroscepticism as their hegemonic idea on European issues. For the moment, this does not seem to be a probable option in Finnish public discourse.

Acknowledgements

This work was supported by the Academy of Finland (under grant 259393) and 'The Euro Crisis, Media Coverage, and Perceptions of Europe within the EU' project, organized by the Reuters Institute for the Study of Journalism at the University of Oxford; the Finnish sub-study was funded by the Helsingin Sanomat Foundation.

Conflict of Interests

The author declares no conflict of interests.

References

Arrese, Á., & Vara, A. (2015). Divergent perspectives? Financial newspapers and the general interest press. In R. Picard (Ed.), *The Euro crisis in the media* (pp. 149–175). London: I. B. Tauris.

Arter, D. (2012). 'Big Bang' elections and party system change in Scandinavia: Farewell to the 'Enduring Party System'? *Parliamentary Affairs*, *65*, 822–844.

Bennett, L. W. (1990). Toward a theory of press-state relations in the United States. *Journal of Communication*, *40*(2), 103–125.

Borah, P. (2011). Conceptual issues in framing theory: A systemic examination of a decade's literature. *Journal of Communication*, *61*(2), 246–263.

Borg, S. (2012). Perussuomalaiset. In S. Borg (Ed.), *Muutosvaalit 2011* (pp. 191–210). Helsinki: Oikeusministeriö.

Bos, L., Van der Brug, W., & De Vreese, C. (2011). How the media shape perceptions of right-wing populist leaders. *Political Communication*, *28*(2), 182–206.

Caiani, M., & Conti, N. (2014). In the name of the People: The Euroscepticism of Italian radical right. *Perspectives on European Politics and Society*, *15*(2), 183–197.

Canovan, M. (1999). Trust the People! Populism and the two faces of democracy. *Political Studies*, *47*(1), 2–16.

Canovan, M. (2005). *The People*. Cambridge: Polity Press.

De Beus, J. (2010). The European Union and the public sphere. In R. Koopmans & P. Statham (Eds.), *The making of a European public sphere* (pp. 13–33). Cambridge: Cambridge University Press.

De Vreese, C. H., Jochen, P., & Holli, S. A. (2001). Framing politics at the launch of the Euro: A cross-national comparative study of frames in the news. *Political Communication*, *18*(2), 107–122.

Ekman, J. (2010). Euroskepticism: Olika former av EU-kritik. In J. Ekman & J. Linde (Eds.), *Politik, protest, populism—Deltagande på nya villkor* (pp. 92–130). Malmö: Liber.

Entman, R. M. (1993). Framing: Toward clarification of a fractured paradigm. *Journal of Communication*, *43*(4), 51–58.

Eurobarometer. (2015). *Standard Eurobarometer 83*. Retrieved from http://ec.europa.eu/public_opinion/archives/eb/eb83/eb83_en.htm

Goffman, E. (1974). *Frame analysis: An essay on the organization of experience*. Cambridge, MA: Harvard University Press.

Grönlund, K., & Westinen, J. (2012). Puoluevalinta. In S. Borg (Ed.), *Muutosvaalit 2011* (pp. 156–190). Helsinki: Oikeusministeriö.

Harjuniemi, T., & Herkman, J. (2013). *Eurokriisi suomalaisissa sanomalehdissä 2010–2012*. Helsinki: Helsingin yliopisto, sosiaalitieteiden laitos.

Harjuniemi, T., Herkman, J., & Ojala, M. (2015). *Eurokriisin politisoituminen suomalaisissa sanomalehdissä. Media & Viestinta*, *38*(1), 1–22.

Hatakka, N. (2012). Perussuomalaisuuden kuva pääkirjoitus- ja kolumnijulkisuudessa. In V. Pernaa & E. Railo (Eds.), *Jytky. Eduskuntavaalien 2011 mediajulkisuus* (pp. 294–322). Turku: Turun yliopisto/Kirja-Aurora.

Heikkilä, H. (2007). Beyond 'in so far as' questions: Contingent social imaginaries of the European public sphere. *European Journal of Communication*, *22*(4), 427–441.

Herkman, J. (2016). Articulations of populism: The Nordic case. *Cultural Studies*. doi:10.1080/09502386.2016.1232421

Herkman, J. (2015). The life cycle model and press coverage of Nordic populist parties. *Journalism Studies*. doi:10.1080/1461670X.2015.1066231

Herkman, J., & Harjuniemi, T. (2015). Unity or heterogeneity: The promise of a European public sphere? In R. Picard (Ed.), *The Euro crisis in the media* (pp. 221–235). London: I. B. Tauris.

Hix, S. (2008). *What's wrong with the European Union and how to fix it*. Cambridge: Polity Press.

Hooghe, L., Marks, G., & Wilson, C. J. (2002). Does left/right structure party positions on European integration? *Comparative Political Studies*, *38*(8), 965–989.

Joris, W., Puustinen, L., Sobieraj, K., & d'Haenens, L. (2015). The battle for the Euro: Metaphors and frames in the Euro crisis news. In R. Picard (Ed.), *The Euro crisis in the media. Journalistic coverage of economic crisis and European institutions* (pp. 125–145). London: L. B. Tauris.

Jungar, A.-C. (2010). Populismens återkomst: Hot eller löfte? In J. Ekman & J. Linde (Eds.), *Politik, protest, populism—Deltagande på nya villkor* (pp. 202–224). Malmö: Liber.

Koopmans, R. (2007). Who inhabits the European public sphere? Winners and losers, supporters and opponents in Europeanised political debates. *European Journal of Political Research*, *46*(2), 183–210.

Koopmans, R., Erbe, J., & Meyer, M. F. (2010). The Europeanization of public spheres: Comparisons across issues, time, and countries. In R. Koopmans & P. Statham (Eds.), *The making of a European public sphere* (pp. 63–96). Cambridge: Cambridge University Press.

Leconte, C. (2010). *Understanding Euroscepticism*. Basingstoke: Palgrave Macmillan.

Lubbers, M., & Scheepers, P. (2005). Political versus instrumental Euroscepticism: Mapping Euroscepticism in European countries regions. *European Union Politics*, *6*(2), 223–242.

Luedtke, A. (2005). European integration, public opinion and immigration policy. *European Union Politics*, *6*(2), 83–112.

Mazzoleni, G. (2003). The media and the growth of neo-populism in contemporary democracies. In G. Mazzoleni, J. Stewart, & B. Horsfield (Eds.), *The media and neo-populism: A contemporary comparative analysis* (pp. 1–20). Westport: Praeger.

Mörä, T. (1999). *EU-journalismin anatomia. Mediasisältöjä muokanneet tekijät ennen kansanäänestystä 1994*. Helsinki: Helsingin yliopisto.

Mudde, C. (2007). *Populist radical right parties in Europe*. Cambridge: Cambridge University Press.

Paloheimo, H. (2012). Populismi Puoluejärjestelmän vedenjakajana. In S. Borg (Ed.), *Muutosvaalit 2011* (pp. 324–345). Helsinki: Oikeusministeriö.

Pernaa, V. (2012). Vaalikamppailu mediassa. In S. Borg (Ed.), *Muutosvaalit 2011* (pp. 29–42). Helsinki: Oikeusministeriö.

Pew Research. (2013). *The new sick man of Europe: The European Union*. Retrieved from http://www.pewglobal.org/2013/05/13/the-new-sick-man-of-europe-the-european-union

Picard, R. (Ed.). (2015). *The Euro crisis in media: Journalistic coverage of economic crisis and European institutions*. London: I. B. Tauris.

Pirro, A. (2014). Populist radical right parties in Central and Eastern Europe: The different context and issues of the prophets of the patria. *Government & Opposition, 49*(4), 600–629.

Rahkonen, J. (2011). Perussuomalaisten ruumiinavaus. Onko työväen protestipuolueen kannatus saavuttanut vielä ylärajaansa? *Yhteiskuntapolitiikka, 76*(4), 425–435.

Railo, E. (2012). Euroopan unionin talouskriisin julkisuus—kritiikistä konsensukseen. In V. Pernaa & E. Railo (Eds.), *Jytky. Eduskuntavaalien 2011 mediajulkisuus* (pp. 231–263). Turku: Turun yliopisto/Kirja-Aurora.

Railo, E., & Välimäki, M. (2012a). Vaalikevään media-agenda. In V. Pernaa & E. Railo (Eds.), *Jytky. Eduskuntavaalien 2011 mediajulkisuus* (pp. 32–66). Turku: Turun yliopisto/Kirja-Aurora.

Railo, E., & Välimäki, M. (2012b). Kamppailu julkisuuden hallinnasta. In V. Pernaa & E. Railo (Eds.), *Jytky. Eduskuntavaalien 2011 mediajulkisuus* (pp. 100–161). Turku: Turun yliopisto/Kirja-Aurora.

Raunio, T. (2011). Missä EU, siellä ongelma: Populistinen Eurooppa-vastaisuus Suomessa. In M. Wiberg (Ed.), *Populismi. Kriitinen arvio* (pp. 197–220). Helsinki: Edita.

Schuck, A., Azrout, R., Boomgaarden, H., Elenbaas, M., Van Spanje, J., Vliegenhart, R., & De Vreese, C. (2011). Media visibility and framing of the European Parliamentary elections 2009. In M. Maier, J. Strömbäck, & L. L. Kaid (Eds.), *Political communication in European Parliamentary elections* (pp. 175–196). Farnham: Ashgate.

Silke, A., & Maier, M. (2011). National parties as politicizers of EU integration? Party campaign communication in the run-up to the 2009 European Parliament election. *European Union Politics, 12*(3), 431–453.

Strömbäck, J., Negrine, R., Hopmann, D. N., Maier, M., Jalali, C., Berganza, R., . . . & Róka, J. (2011). The mediatization and framing of European Parliamentary election campaigns. In M. Maier, J. Strömbäck, & L. L. Kaid (Eds.), *Political communication in European Parliamentary elections* (pp. 161–174). Farnham: Ashgate.

Suikkanen, R., Holma, A., & Raittila, P. (2012). *Muuttumaton uutinen? Suomalaisen uutismedian vuosiseuranta 2007–2012*. Tampere: COMET.

Sundberg, J. (1999). The enduring Scandinavian party system. *Scandinavian Political Studies, 22*(3), 221–241.

Taggart, P. (2000). *Populism*. Buckingham: Open University Press.

Taggart, P., & Szczerbiak, A. (2002). Europeanisation, Euroscepticism and party systems: Party-based Euroscepticism in the candidate states of Central and Eastern Europe. *Perspectives on European Politics and Society, 3*(1), 23–41.

Taylor, P. (2008). *The end of European integration: Anti-Europeanism examined*. Abingdon and Oxford: Routledge.

Trenz, H.-J. (2007). '*Quo vadis Europe*?' Quality newspapers struggling for European unity. In J. E. Fossum & P. Schlesinger (Eds.), *The European Union and the public sphere: A communicative space in the making?* (pp. 89–109). Abingdon: Routledge.

Van Dalen, A. (2012). Structural bias in cross-national perspective: How political systems and journalism cultures influence government dominance in the news. *The International Journal of Press/Politics, 17*(1), 32–55.

Van Spanje, J., & De Vreese, C. (2014). Europhile media and Eurosceptic voting: Effects of news media coverage on Eurosceptic voting in the 2009 European Parliamentary elections. *Political Communication, 31*(2), 325–354.

Wiberg, M. (2011). Mitä populismi on? In M. Wiberg (Ed.), *Populismi. Kriitinen arvio* (pp. 11–21). Helsinki: Edita.

Williams, R. (1988). *Keywords: A vocabulary of culture and society*. London: Fontana.

2

Clipper Meets Apple vs. FBI—A Comparison of the Cryptography Discourses from 1993 and 2016

Matthias Schulze

International Relations Department, Friedrich-Schiller University Jena, 07743 Jena, Germany;
E-Mail: matthias.schulze@mailbox.org

Abstract

This article analyzes two cryptography discourses dealing with the question of whether governments should be able to monitor secure and encrypted communication, for example via security vulnerabilities in cryptographic systems. The Clipper chip debate of 1993 and the FBI vs. Apple case of 2016 are analyzed to infer whether these discourses show similarities in their arguments and to draw lessons from them. The study is based on the securitization framework and analyzes the social construction of security threats in political discourses. The findings are that the arguments made by the proponents of exceptional access show major continuities between the two cases. In contrast, the arguments of the critics are more diverse. The critical arguments for stronger encryption remain highly relevant, especially in the context of the Snowden revelations. The article concludes that we need to adopt a more general cyber security perspective, considering the threat of cyber crime and state hacking, when debating whether the government should be able to weaken encryption.

Keywords

Apple; cryptowar; discourse analysis; encryption; FBI

Issue

This article is part of the issue "Post-Snowden Internet Policy", edited by Julia Pohle (WZB Berlin Social Science Center, Germany) and Leo Van Audenhove (Vrije Universiteit Brussel, Belgium).

---

1. Introduction

One effect of the leaks by former National Security Agency (NSA) contractor Edward Snowden in 2013 was that both Apple and Google introduced encryption to their smartphones. Law enforcement and intelligence agencies protested that widespread, unbreakable encryption would make it harder to retrieve evidence from these phones in criminal investigations (Kehl, Wilson, & Bankston, 2015, p. 1). In early 2016, the Federal Bureau of Investigation (FBI) issued a court order to compel Apple to unlock an encrypted iPhone 5C that was used by the San Bernardino attacker in December 2015. The FBI wanted Apple to rewrite its iOS software, to disable encryption security features that would allow the enforcement agency to guess the correct passcodes in a trial and error fashion. Apple resisted and ignited a wider debate within the context of the presidential elections. For some observers, the Apple/FBI debate resembled another instance of the so-called crypto-wars, defined as technological debates about whether the government should have access to encrypted communication. The crypto-wars between national security actors, technology firms and Internet users emerged during the early days of the World Wide Web in late 1992 with the debate about the Clipper chip (Kehl et al., 2015). The aim of this contribution is to analyze whether these two crypto-war discourses are in fact similar. Are there any lessons that can be drawn for the current debate?

This paper builds broadly on the Copenhagen School (Buzan, Waever, & Wilde, 1997) in International Relations and the concept of securitization of technology (Barnard-Wills & Ashenden, 2012; Deibert & Rohozinski, 2010; Hansen & Nissenbaum, 2009), which provides a link to Science and Technology Studies. Securitization is understood as the social construction of security/insecurity, for example in the digital realm (cyber security). Actors compete in the discourse over the meaning of security, i.e. what counts as a threat and how these threats should be dealt with (Dunn Cavelty, 2013). Threat constructions are used for the legitimization of extraordinary security measures that would not be approved by a democratic audience in the absence of a threat. These measures include electronic surveillance, Internet censorship (Deibert, 2015), offensive computer-network-attack capabilities (Lawson, 2012) and exceptional access or state-regulation of encrypted communication, called crypto-politics (Moore & Rid, 2016).

Interestingly, the securitization framework has been rarely adopted to study cryptography discourses. Studies on the crypto-wars debate tend to be either technical (see Abelson et al., 2015; Dam & Lin, 1996) or historical (Kehl et al., 2015). Empirical securitization studies, which focus on digital technologies, tend to ignore the potential material impact of discourses, as Dunn Cavelty argues (Dunn Cavelty, 2015). The securitization of cryptography could have severe implications for cyber security but also for human rights in the digital age. Governmental access to otherwise secure cryptography could, in the worst case, substantially weaken these systems and thus threaten the safety of digital technologies like smartphones, which billions of people use.

The next section offers a short introduction to cryptography debates and outlines the two cases. These are then compared in a qualitative fashion, focusing on what the dominant arguments and actors are. I will concentrate on similarities first and then discuss the differences between the discourses. The final section offers a critical discussion of the arguments.

2. A Short History of the Crypto-Wars

Encryption is a century-old technique to scramble readable text, via mathematical algorithms, into unreadable cypher-text. Sender and recipient require a correct key or password to make the encrypted text intelligible again. The purpose of encryption is to avoid eavesdropping from third parties. Since 1976, a method called public-key encryption (Diffie & Hellman, 1976) promised easy-to-use, widespread encryption of electronic communication. The NSA recognized the potential danger to its global signals intelligence (interception of communication data) effort, if encrypted communication became a mainstream technology. Director of the NSA, Bobby Inman, warned that "unrestrained public discussion of cryptologic matters will seriously damage the ability of this government to conduct signals intelligence" (Inman, 1979, p. 130). Coinciding with the beginning of the personal computer revolution, the NSA argued that an important data source would be "going dark" if every new PC user were to use encrypted, digital communications. Thus, the entire sphere of digital communication could be metaphorically shrouded in darkness, unreadable to the NSA. The dilemma of how to resolve this issue was born.

In 1992, American Telephone and Telegraph (AT&T) began with the development of a consumer-market telephone that could encrypt voice communication between two parties. The NSA recognized that with the looming digital age, traditional, interceptable audio communication could be replaced by encrypted digital communication (Kaplan, 2016, p. 21). This led NSA Director Michael McConnell to rush into the development of the Clipper technology, which would set a standard for the emerging market. The proposal theoretically allowed user-friendly encryption based on a hardware chip called Clipper, which would be attached to devices like phones or computers. In contrast to other products on the market, it had a built-in security weakness: a copy of the encryption key would be stored in government databases. This key-escrow method gave law enforcement "exceptional access" to an otherwise secure technology. The NSA and FBI could thus eavesdrop on any Clipper-based phone call with a warrant because they could access a copy of the key. In February 1993, the newly elected Clinton–Gore Administration adopted the idea (Levy, 1994). On April 16th, 1993, the White House announced the launch of the voluntary Clipper initiative (White House, 1993). A strong public reaction across the political spectrum followed. Most computer experts, technology companies and a social movement of digital natives opposed it (Rid, 2016, pp. 333–337). A series of hearings were held to evaluate the technology. In early 1994, the Clipper program officially started, yet it never saw any widespread adoption. According to the National Research Council, only 10,000 to 15,000 Clipper-enabled phones have ever been sold, mostly to the government (Dam & Lin, 1996, p. 174). A CNN survey in 1994 found that roughly 80% of Americans opposed the initiative (US Senate, 1994). The death blow came when a cryptography expert discovered a security flaw within Clipper's algorithm, although the NSA and its supporters claimed the system was superior and more secure than anything else on the market (Brickel, Denning, Kent, Maher, & Tuchman, 1993). During the mid-1990s, the proposal was silently dropped. According to General Michael Hayden, the NSA "lost" this crypto-war: "We didn't get the Clipper Chip, we didn't get the back door" (Hayden, 2016a).

An outcome of the Clipper debate was that the US government relaxed its strict opposition to the widespread use of encryption. Laws like the Communications Assistance for Law Enforcement Act (CALEA) were adopted to prohibit the government from forcing companies to build government backdoors in their technology (Crawford, 2016). Over time, the US government relaxed its very strict export-regime that treated cryptographic products as dual-use goods. By the end of the 1990s, a widespread consensus (Kehl et al., 2015, p. 19) had been reached that "the advantages of more widespread use of cryptography outweigh the disadvantages" (Dam & Lin, 1996, p. 6). Scientists made the convincing case that key-escrow systems "enabling exceptional access to keys would be inherently less secure, more expensive, and much more complex than those without" (Abelson et al., 2015, p. 7).

The debate about governmental "exceptional access" reemerged in the summer of 2014, after Apple had decided to turn device encryption of its iPhones on by default. On October 10th, FBI Director James B. Comey warned that encryption was hindering evidence retrieval for law enforcement. Comey urged the government to adopt a legislative fix and companies to find a solution (Comey, 2014). In fall 2015, the Washington Post published internal communication from within the intelligence community complaining about a hostile legislative environment on the encryption matter "that could turn in the event of a terrorist attack or criminal event where strong encryption can be shown to have hindered law enforcement" (Nakashima & Peterson, 2015). This was a reference to President Obama who had indicated that his government would not pursue legislation on the matter. The debate resurfaced on February 16th, 2016, when an US Magistrate ruled—ex parte—that Apple must provide "reasonable technical assistance" to FBI investigators to unlock an iPhone 5C that belonged to the San Bernardino shooter of December 2015 (Volz & Menn, 2016). The judge issued the warrant based on the All Writs Act (AWA) from 1789, which becomes active only if there is no other governing law, thus bypassing CALEA (Tangri, Lemley, Feldman, & Landers, 2016). Apple indeed helped the FBI with this iPhone, but mistakes were made and normal unlocking procedures did not work. Apple CEO Tim Cook, the main protagonist of the counter-discourse, contested that the court order was "unreasonably burdensome" (Cook, 2016a). Because of the ongoing election campaign, multiple high profile politicians, intelligence professionals, media and tech companies began to publicly take side with or against Apple. According to a Pew survey, the public sided with the FBI initially, with around 51% arguing that Apple should help the FBI. However, later polls with diverse methodologies showed that the public sided with Apple (Elmer-Dewitt, 2016). The fierce discourse about encryption lasted until March, when a Brooklyn court ruled in Apple's favor that AWA did not govern the unlocking of an iPhone in a similar case (Lichtblau & Goldstein, 2016). The whole debate suddenly disappeared in March, when it became public that a third party could unlock the iPhone without Apple's help (Benner & Apuzzo, 2016). Two weeks later it was revealed that the phone did not include any valuable information (McGoogan, 2016) and the Department of Justice issued a filing that it would no longer need Apple's assistance (Novet, 2016).

3. Methodology

The paper analyses the Clipper discourse between 1993–1994 and the Apple/FBI case between 2014 and 2016, with a focus on the peak of the debate in February/March 2016. Using the snowball technique, a literature corpus (Apple/FBI N = 42, Clipper N = 22) was assembled that contains official statements, newspaper or internet coverage, congressional hearings and some scientific literature of the respective debates. Documents repeatedly mentioned in the corpus were analyzed more deeply using content analysis techniques (Mayring, 2000). The first step was to identify the different discursive positions (opponents, proponents and middle ground). Then the arguments of the respective positions were inductively identified and coded throughout the corpus in an iterative fashion (Keller, 2007). Some codes were deduced from the securitization framework, namely *threats*, *threatened referent* objects and *extraordinary measures* that are demanded to remedy the threat and that go beyond established social norms and procedures (Buzan et al., 1997, pp. 23–24). Another aim was to find out which characteristics, whether negative or positive, were being attributed to encryption. Finally, the frequencies of individual codes were counted and collected in a table to provide some (limited) quantitative insights and to assess what the most dominant arguments were in each debate. Of course, these findings are not generalizable and serve more as an ideal type (Weber, 1973) to gauge the general content of other potential cryptography discourses in the future.

During the Clipper discourse in 1993, only 27% of Americans owned a computer and 2% used the Internet (World Bank, 2016). The Apple/FBI discourse on the other hand happened at a time when 87% of Americans used the Internet (World Bank, 2016), 73% had a computer and 68% a smartphone (Anderson, 2015). In contrast to 1993, cyber security issues like hacking, data theft and state-sponsored cyber attacks were ubiquitous in 2016, with encryption being one line of defense against these issues. This means that in 2016, potentially more customers were affected by the encryption debate. Additionally, the Apple/FBI case stands in the context of the Snowden leaks of 2013 which uncovered the extensive Internet surveillance capacities of the NSA and its targeted operations against encryption systems. NSA programs like Bullrun allegedly implanted software backdoors in HTTPS encryption used for secure web-browsing and also utilized hardware backdoors for exceptional access to Internet routers (Ball, Borger, & Greenwald, 2013). Other Snowden leaks indicate intense NSA efforts to gain access to encrypted Virtual Private Network connections, often used by large corporations to offer secure access to files from afar (Goodin, 2015), or even the Onion Router or TOR network, that utilizes multiple layers of encryption and thus is highly resistant to eavesdropping (Sayer, 2014). Thus, the Snowden leaks increased public awareness of data security, encryption and concerns about government surveillance programs (Rainie & Maniam, 2016).

4. Comparing Two Crypto-War Discourses

4.1. Similarities between Clipper and Apple vs. FBI

The discursive positions in the two discourses are somewhat similar. Law enforcement (FBI), intelligence actors

(NSA) and politicians (predominantly, but not exclusively conservatives) argue for governmental regulation of encryption and providing exceptional access for legitimate law enforcement inquiries. In both discourses, this group produces a relatively homogenous set of arguments. Technology companies, cryptography experts, scientists and a mix of civil-libertarians and tech enthusiasts argue for widespread, public use of encryption. This group is more heterogeneous and uses a huge variety of arguments. In both instances, there is a middle ground, recognizing the needs of both groups and arguing for a compromise (which is technologically difficult to achieve).

When comparing the two discourses, it becomes immediately obvious that the law enforcement perspective is very similar in both cases. The general argument is that "encryption threatens to significantly curtail, and in many instances, preclude, effective law enforcement" (Sessions, 1993), which resembles the NSA's warning from 1979. This is the main argument (uttered 27x) within the debate and a center-piece of the "going dark" metaphor. It is supported by and often combined with a legalistic justification that with a court order or a warrant, the government should have access to encrypted communication (39x). This is the extraordinary measure demanded. It is extraordinary in the sense, that the government wants access to communication intended for no-one else except the communicating parties and demands from companies to change their technology to meet wiretapping needs, effectively influencing hard and software development (Lessig, 2006, p. 66). In other words, the crypto-war discourse is about establishing/contesting the norm of government control over cryptography vs. the right of every user to communicate privately (Levy, 1994).

How are these extraordinary capabilities and powers legitimized? Proponents argue that "criminals" (27x) and "terrorists" (31x) cannot be caught if they use encryption. Interestingly, the Clipper discourses highlights "drug-traffickers", whereas the Apple/FBI discourse is more about "terrorists" and "child molesters". These are framed by law enforcement as the main threats. Closely connected to the argument is the frame that "law enforcement must keep pace" (9x) with malign actors. It creates the impression that the highly trained and equipped, multi-million dollar law enforcement apparatus is falling behind. The referent objects that need to be protected from these threats are mentioned in statements like the following: "Successful conduct of electronic surveillance is crucial to effective law enforcement, to the preservation of the public safety, and to the maintenance of the national security" (15x) (Sessions, 1993). This clearly indicates a national-security perspective. Widespread encryption itself is presented as a threat or at least as a problem to national security (7x). The key description here is that encryption is presented (10x) as a "dual-edge sword: encryption helps to protect the privacy of individuals and industry, but it also can shield criminals and terrorists" (White House, 1993). The dilemma is that in both cases, the government recognizes the positive effects of encryption for privacy and the protection of intellectual property (12x). Therefore, the key metaphor is the demand for the rightful balance between privacy and (national) security (11x). In sum, the negative effects of encryption and threats to national security outweigh the benefits. The argument can be found in its entirety in the press release following the official announcement of the Clipper initiative in 1994: "if encryption technology is made freely available worldwide, it would no doubt be used extensively by terrorists, drug dealers, and other criminals to harm Americans both in the US and abroad. For this reason, the Administration will continue to restrict export of the most sophisticated encryption devices, both to preserve our own foreign intelligence gathering capability and because of the concerns of our allies who fear that strong encryption technology would inhibit their law enforcement capabilities" (White House, 1994).

Whereas the government predominantly uses national security-related arguments, the counter-discourse is more heterogeneous. There are three types of argument. Technical arguments state that government access makes encryption systems less secure and are mostly put forward by the technology and science community. Economic arguments argue against government interference in the market and the costs of the proposal. Finally, there are civil liberty arguments that revolve around privacy and mistrust of the expansion of state power and are uttered by libertarians. There are also several other arguments that overlap or do not necessarily fall into either group. Their common denominator is that the government wants to interfere with the products of private companies (24x) in terms of hardware with Clipper and software with Apple. The metaphor of choice is that the government wants to create a "backdoor" (25x) in an otherwise secure system. Libertarians see this as an expansion of government authority, or with the words of Apple CEO Tim Cook as "government overreach" (20x) and thus as a potential threat (Cook, 2016a). Business actors are more afraid of the potential future effects of the government regulating encryption, which might result in the widespread use of inferior technology (15x).

These diverse groups share a relatively similar perspective on encryption. Cryptography is a privacy-enhancing technology (19x) and seen in an exclusively positive way (13x). This explains why any government interference is seen as problematic. The referent objects in this discourse are privacy and civil liberties in particular (24x) and, more implicitly, American identity and values, which are prominently present in the Apple/FBI discourse. The argument in both cases is that control of encryption technology is a norm of authoritarian regimes and police states and therefore inappropriate in democracies (14x). The technological principles of encryption must be understood to make sense of this frame. The fewer parties have access to a system, the more secure it gets. Ideally, public key encryption only has two parties, the sender and receiver. With key-escrow, a third party (the government) is introduced, which creates security risks. The threat in both cases is that the method for exceptional access could fall into the wrong hands (21x) and thus could potentially be misused. In the case of Clipper, the key-escrow database could be stolen, and with the Apple/FBI case, the source code for bypassing iOS security could be hacked, for example by foreign states.

However, there is also a general critique against the government mandating which encryption products to use. In both discourses, technical experts point to the fact that those with malign interest will find a way around government mandated encryption (17x). The key question that comes up in congressional hearings is: Which bad actor would use a technology that he/she knows the government is using to listen in (12x)? Ultimately, law-abiding citizens would be forced to use an inferior technology, while bad actors could use encryption without US backdoors from the international market. This argument is particularly brought forward by critics in the Apple/FBI case (11x), but also existed in a slightly different form in 1993. The reference to foreign crypto-products or the "off-shoring" of cryptography, as former Director of NSA Michael Hayden calls it, is a compelling argument in both cases (Hayden, 2016b). It creates the overall risk that cryptography evolves outside the US market where the government has even less control. This would create a competitive disadvantage for American tech firms. The economic damage of regulating cryptography to American business is a key argument in the Clipper discourse (21x), but not so much in the Apple/FBI case (1x).

The general argument put forward by critics in both cases is that the government should look at the bigger picture (33x), recognizing the general interest of the people and corporations that need encryption, both for privacy reasons but also for business interests and data security. Cryptography is no longer a state monopoly but a matter for citizens (5x) and therefore the government should not prioritize the particular interests of the NSA and FBI. In other words, the general positive effects outweigh the negative effects for a greater audience. This ultimately reflects the legal and discursive consensus that was reached during the mid-1990s.

4.2. Differences

Clipper and the Apple vs. FBI cases differ in some aspects. The Clipper initiative is a government attempt at standard-setting using a NSA-developed chip. It is also a voluntary technology initiative and not a law per se. This means that the government utilizes a range of arguments to "sell" their product to the skeptical audience by arguing Clipper is far superior to anything else on the market (22x), that Clipper does not weaken, but enhances, privacy (9x) and generally that Clipper strikes the right balance between security and privacy (6x). These arguments are particularly highlighted in White House briefing documents from the FBI/NSA and indicate that the Clinton–Gore Administration must have been aware of a potential backlash (Sessions, 1993). Another indicator for this anticipation is the fact that this initiative is not a law, but described as a "voluntary" tech initiative (7x).

Critics contest these arguments. The tech community argues that the NSA developed Clipper (7x) and its encryption algorithm in secrecy (11x), which goes against industry best practices of public code evaluation and the law because the National Institute for Standards would be legally in charge (9x). Others criticize the enormous cost of several million dollars annually that it would take just to maintain the key-escrow infrastructure and the cost of the Clipper chip itself, which would increase hardware prices (8x). Because of these technical facts, the initiative is described as premature, rushed and not thought through (9x). A CNN poll of the time indicates that a majority of 80% is not convinced of the government's arguments (US Senate, 1994). The fact that almost all technology companies and experts are against the Clipper initiative is an important point (17x). To understand this, one must consider the strong skepticism vis a vis government interference in the market (12x).

This is different in the counter-terrorism and post-Snowden context of 2016. The first theme of the Apple vs. FBI discourse is that encryption and its potential weakening is not about the singular San Bernardino case but a *general matter*. Apple systematically argues that government mandated exceptional access is a "threat to millions of customers worldwide" and not just in the US (30x). For Apple, the debate is not about one particular iPhone, but a general case that affects potentially every phone today and in the future (40x). The FBI wants to interfere with Apple's hard/software design (24x) to mandate the construction of a backdoor (25x). Apple calls it the "software equivalent of cancer" (Cook, 2016b). If the courts allowed this, it would create a dangerous legal precedent (26x), which the FBI repeatedly denies (although Comey testifies that the FBI has around 600 other iPhones to be unlocked) (C-Span, 2016). Apple repeatedly argues that in the encryption debate we need to look at the bigger picture, beyond law enforcement interests (33x). The bigger picture includes the cyber security landscapes and new threats: from cyber attacks (20x), data-theft (14x) and hackers (15x). Backdoors resemble weaker encryption which itself is represented as a threat (19x). Backdoors would introduce vulnerabilities to all iPhones, which would represent an enormous public safety risk (16x) because iPhones are used in areas like government agencies and critical infrastructures. These areas would become vulnerable to hacking. Weak encryption would make the entire digital infrastructure less secure (10x). Apple also fears a potential future spillover: weakening encryption now will harm the US digital infrastructure in the future (9x), because exploits could be stolen, and thus fall into the wrong hands (15x). The powerful technical argument that there is no backdoor that could be exploited just by the good guys is put forward (11x). Moreover, other agencies might dig up cases to mandate companies to build in backdoors for more trivial reasons than fighting terrorism, a phenomenon called function creep (10x).

The second discursive feature is an identity or moral narrative. Apple argues that the referent objects are not just millions of customers or privacy and civil liberties but American identity in general (23). "This is not who we are", says Tim Cook (Cook, 2016b). If Western Democracies follow authoritarian regimes in their control of private communication (via government access), it would create a soft-power precedent (10x). Dictatorships would feel legitimized in their surveillance of citizens. Likewise, the FBI uses moralizing statements like "It is about the victims and justice. Fourteen people were slaughtered and many more had their lives and bodies ruined....We can't look the survivors in the eye, or ourselves in the mirror, if we don't follow this lead" (Comey, 2016b). However, most of the FBI's argument is rather legalistic, focusing on the argument that there should be no "warrant-proof" spaces (Comey, 2016a).

In sum, the FBI and Apple recognize each other's good intentions and need for cooperation to resolve this problem. Both parties argue that there needs to be a broad public discussion about this difficult issue (22x). Policymakers in general favor strong encryption with exceptional, warrant-based access while the tech community replies that the mathematics either support secure encryption without government backdoors or exceptional access with significantly less security. The combination of both secure cryptography and governmental access represents wishful thinking or the search for a magic pony solution (Abelson et al., 2015).

5. Discussion

Whereas the Clipper discourse is focused mostly on the privacy/security dichotomy, the Apple/FBI case shows that in times of cyber crime and hacking, this dichotomy needs to be rethought. Traditionally, the two have been framed as an antagonism or a zero-sum game: more security means less privacy/liberty. This is not necessarily true anymore because encryption enhances both privacy and security, both individually but also collectively or globally. In an interconnected world, a vulnerability in one iPhone is a threat for every user, as the recent Pegasus spyware, which affected all 1 billion active iOS devices, shows. Encryption is crucial for the security of digital infrastructures (i.e. cyber security). The question we need to address is "whose security are we talking about"? The debate shows that there are two paradigms of security at work: a national security perspective with traditional, physical threats such as terrorism and a cyber security perspective, which considers the vulnerabilities of software and hardware in terms of hacking, cyber crime and state-sponsored cyber war. Former NSA Director Michael Hayden belongs to the latter and argues that considering the cyber threat, "America is simply more secure with unbreakable end-to-end encryption" (Hayden, 2016a).

The second element we need to discuss critically is the "going dark" metaphor, which creates a false dualism of light and shadow and thus another artificial zero-sum game. The metaphor ignores the fact that there are multiple sources of light. Wiretapping of conversations is just one stream of data among an increasing number of law enforcement tools like automated biometric recognition, DNA sampling, geo-location tracking or contact-chaining with social network analysis. Our "digital exhaust" as Michael Hayden calls it, the often unencrypted metadata we generate using smartphones and online services such as Facebook or Google, is in fact growing (Hayden, 2016b). Never before has there been so much private information about us in the open. The government has access to most of these new sources of data. The amount of data traversing global networks in 2016 makes the year 1993 appear like the dark ages of data and law enforcement. Arguing that we are currently "in the light" and the future will be dark is somewhat misleading. Just because content data is increasingly more encrypted and one channel of data collection might be "going dark", it does not mean that all other channels are going dark as well. The opposite is probably true.

The "going dark" metaphor creates a false technological-deterministic assumption that widespread cryptography will *automatically* lead to only one single outcome: a future of uninterceptable information. This scenario is unlikely. There is no such thing as unbreakable encryption. It might get more complicated but it is unlikely that it will ever be impossible to break. Even today, strong cryptography is circumvented by exploiting other weaknesses in the system, which probably is the reason why the FBI got into the San Bernardino iPhone without Apple's help (Benner & Apuzzo, 2016). Even if encryption was unbreakable, it would not be guaranteed that it would ever reach 100% user adoption. The technological barriers for users are still high and market mechanisms like ad-based, big-data business models stand in the way of widespread adoption. Practical reasons prohibit the adoption of encryption, which is the same reason why we do not whisper all the time to avoid eavesdropping. It is often too impractical and inconvenient. Even if everyone used encryption, people often make mistakes with the implementation which makes their systems vulnerable to attack (Gasser et al., 2016, p. 3).

Determinism overstates the effects of technology and ignores human response strategies. It is too easy to blame technologies when old strategies fail. To blame technology would be akin to the French blaming the invention of the tank for their inferior defense strategy against the German Blitzkrieg tactics in World War 2. There are always two components: technology and human agency. If encryption is indeed a problem, then law enforcement and intelligence agencies simply must adapt and change their operating strategies (Landau, 2016). For example, if electronic surveillance of a drug dealer is not feasible anymore because he/she uses encrypted phone calls, one way to resolve the problem would be to use human intelligence like surveillance personnel on the ground or even traditional acoustic surveillance bugs implanted in a car or house. Particularly the "Internet of Things (IoT)" with microphones in Smart TVs and loudspeakers and the trend of cloud-computing will offer new, unique capabilities that could be used in the traditional warrant process (Gasser et al., 2016, p. 10). At the same time, in the context of the growing vulnerabilities of a digitalized IoT infrastructure, safe systems and strong encryption are imperative. The old Clipper consensus that the widespread use of cryptography is the greater good is still valid, even though it is understandably harder to see in the current context of global terrorism.

As threatening as terrorism may be, cyber attacks from nation-states, cyber crime and digital espionage are growing rapidly and are costing millions of dollars annually. Richard C. Clarke, the senior counter-terrorism official during the Bush administration argued: "my point is encryption and privacy are larger issues than fighting terrorism" (Clarke, 2016). The ongoing securitization of cryptography in liberal democracies sets a normative precedent. Directly after the Apple/FBI debate, countries like Russia began to demand backdoors in cryptographic messengers like WhatsApp and Telegram by law and referred to the practices of Western democracies for justification (Howell O'Neill, 2016). Currently, France, Great Britain, Germany and others are pursuing similar legislation. Interestingly, the discourses in liberal and authoritarian countries rely on similar rhetorical figures, threat descriptions and referent objects identified in this article. To qualify this, further comparative research would be required. Authoritarian regimes will probably use exceptional access not to prosecute terrorists, but the political opposition or human rights NGOs. Besides this normative argument there is also a technical one: the more governments replicate this practice of actively punching holes in cryptography without disclosing them publicly, the less secure the worldwide IT-infrastructure gets.

Acknowledgements

Thanks to the anonymous reviewers for their positive and constructive feedback.

Conflict of Interests

The author declares no conflict of interests.

References

Abelson, H., Anderson, R., Bellovin, S. M., Benalo, J., Blaze, M., Diffie, W., . . . Weitzner, D. J. (2015). *Keys under doormats: Mandating insecurity by requiring government access to all data and communications* (Computer Science and Artificial Intelligence Laboratory Technical Report, MIT-CSAIL-TR-2015-026). Cambridge, MA: Massachusetts Institute of Technology.

Anderson, M. (2015). Technology device ownership: 2015. *Pew Research Center*. Retrieved from http://www.pewinternet.org/2015/10/29/technology-device-ownership-2015

Ball, J., Borger, J., & Greenwald, G. (2013). Revealed: How US and UK spy agencies defeat internet privacy and security. *The Guardian*. Retrieved from https://www.theguardian.com/world/2013/sep/05/nsa-gchq-encryption-codes-security

Barnard-Wills, D., & Ashenden, D. (2012). Securing virtual space: Cyber war, cyber terror, and risk. *Space and Culture*, *15*(2), 110–123.

Benner, K., & Apuzzo, M. (2016). US says it may not need Apple's help to unlock iPhone. *The New York Times*. Retrieved from http://nyti.ms/1UzGJTS

Brickel, E. F., Denning, D. E., Kent, S. T., Maher, D. P., & Tuchman, W. (1993). *Skipjack review: Interim report* (The SKIPJACK Algoritm). Retrieved from https://epic.org/crypto/clipper/skipjack_interim_review.html

Buzan, B., Waever, O., & Wilde, J. D. (1997). *Security: A new framework for analysis*. London: Lynne Rienner Publishers Inc.

C-Span. (2016). Apple iPhone encryption hearing. *C-Span*. Retrieved from https://www.c-span.org/video/?405442-1/hearing-encryption-federal-investigations

Clarke, R. (2016). Encryption, privacy are larger issues than fighting terrorism, Clarke says. *NPR.prg*. Retrieved from http://www.npr.org/2016/03/14/470347719/encryption-and-privacy-are-larger-issues-than-fighting-terrorism-clarke-says

Comey, J. (2014). Going dark: Are technology, privacy, and public safety on a collision course? *US Department of Justice*. Retrieved from https://www.fbi.gov/news/speeches/going-dark-are-technology-privacy-and-public-safety-on-a-collision-course

Comey, J. (2016a). Encryption tightrope: Balancing Americans' security and privacy. *US Department of Justice*. Retrieved from https://www.fbi.gov/news/testimony/encryption-tightrope-balancing-americans-security-and-privacy

Comey, J. (2016b). FBI director comments on San Bernadino matter. *US Department of Justice*. Retrieved from https://www.fbi.gov/news/pressrel/press-releases/fbi-director-comments-on-san-bernardino-matter

Cook, T. (2016a). *A message to our customers*. Retrieved from http://www.apple.com/customer-letter

Cook, T. (2016b). Apple CEO Tim Cook sits down with David Muir. *ABC News*. Retrieved from http://abcnews.go.com/WNT/video/exclusive-apple-ceo-tim-cook-sits-david-muir-37174976

Crawford, S. (2016). The law is clear: The FBI cannot make Apple rewrite its OS. *Backchannel*. Retrieved from https://backchannel.com/the-law-is-clear-the-fbi-cannot-make-apple-rewrite-its-os-9ae60c3bbc7b#.sa125j16z

Dam, K. W., & Lin, H. S. (1996). *Cryptography's role in securing the information society*. Washington, DC: National Research Council.

Deibert, R. J. (2015). Cyberspace under siege. *Journal of Democracy, 26*(3), 64–78.

Deibert, R. J., & Rohozinski, R. (2010). Risking security: Policies and paradoxes of cyberspace security. *International Political Sociology, 4*(1), 15–32.

Diffie, W., & Hellman, M. (1976). New directions in cryptography. *IEEE Transactions on Information Theory, 22*(6), 644–654.

Dunn Cavelty, M. (2013). From cyber-bombs to political fallout: Threat representations with an impact in the cyber-security discourse. *International Studies Review, 15*(1), 105–122.

Dunn Cavelty, M. (2015). Die materiellen Ursachen des Cyberkriegs Cybersicherheitspolitik jenseits diskursiver Erklärungen. *Journal of Self-Regulation and Regulation, 1*, 167–184.

Elmer-Dewitt, P. (2016). Apple vs. FBI: What the polls are saying. *Fortune*. Retrieved from http://fortune.com/2016/02/23/apple-fbi-poll-pew

Gasser, U., Gertner, N., Goldsmith, J., Landau, S., Nye, J., O'Brien, D. R., . . . Zittrain, J. (2016). *Don't panic. Making progress on the "Going Dark" debate*. Cambridge, MA: Berkman Klein Center.

Goodin, D. (2015). How the NSA can break trillions of encrypted Web and VPN connections. Researchers show how mass decryption is well within the NSA's $11 billion budget. *Ars Technica*. Retrieved from http://arstechnica.com/security/2015/10/how-the-nsa-can-break-trillions-of-encrypted-web-and-vpn-connections

Hansen, L., & Nissenbaum, H. (2009). Digital disaster, cyber security, and the Copenhagen School. *International Studies Quarterly, 53*, 1155–1175.

Hayden, M. V. (2016a). Hayden: The pros and cons of access to encrypted files. *Youtube*. Retrieved from https://www.youtube.com/watch?v=6HNnVcp6NYA

Hayden, M. V. (2016b). General Michael Hayden on the Apple FBI and data encryption. *AEIdeas*. Retrieved from https://www.aei.org/publication/gen-michael-hayden-on-apple-the-fbi-and-data-encryption

Howell O'Neill, P. (2016). Russia lawmakers pass sweeping spying law that requires encryption backdoors, call surveillance. *The Daily Dot*. Retrieved from http://www.dailydot.com/layer8/encryption-backdoor-russia-fsb-bill-passes

Inman, B. R. (1979). The NSA perspective on telecommunications protection in the nongovernmental sector. *Cryptologia, 3*, 129–135.

Kaplan, F. (2016). *Dark territory: The secret history of cyber war*. New York, NY: Simon & Schuster.

Kehl, D., Wilson, A., & Bankston, K. S. (2015, June). *Doomed to repeat history? Lessons from the crypto wars of the 1990s* (Report from the New America Foundation). Washington, DC: New America.

Keller, R. (2007). *Diskursforschung*. Berlin: Springer.

Landau, S. (2016). The real security issues of the iPhone case. Law enforcement needs 21st-century investigative savvy. *Sciencemag, 352*(6292), 1398–1399.

Lawson, S. (2012). Putting the "war" in cyberwar: Metaphor, analogy, and cybersecurity discourse in the United States. *First Monday, 17*(7). doi:10.5210/fm.v17i7.3848

Lessig, L. (2006). *Code: And other laws of cyberspace, version 2.0*. New York, NY: Basic Books.

Levy, S. (1994). Battle of the Clipper chip. *The New York Times*. Retrieved from http://www.nytimes.com/1994/06/12/magazine/battle-of-the-clipper-chip.html

Lichtblau, E., & Goldstein, J. (2016). Justice Dept. appeals ruling in Apple iPhone case in Brooklyn. *The New York Times*. Retrieved from https://www.nytimes.com/2016/03/08/technology/justice-dept-appeals-ruling-in-apple-iphone-case-in-brooklyn.html

Mayring, P. (2000). Qualitative content analysis. *Forum: Qualitative Sozialforschung, 1*(2). Retrieved from http://www.qualitative-research.net/index.php/fqs/article/view/1089

McGoogan, C. (2016). Terrorist's iPhone didn't turn up any useful information, FBI admits. *The Telegraph*. Retrieved from http://www.telegraph.co.uk/technology/2016/04/15/terrorists-iphone-didnt-turn-up-any-useful-information-fbi-admit

Moore, D., & Rid, T. (2016). Cryptopolitik and the darknet. *Survival, 58*(1), 7–38.

Nakashima, E., & Peterson, A. (2015). Obama faces growing momentum to support widespread encryption. *Washington Post*. Retrieved from https://www.washingtonpost.com/world/national-security/tech-trade-agencies-push-to-disavow-law-requiring-decryption-of-phones/2015/09/16/1fca5f72-5adf-11e5-b38e-06883aacba64_story.html

Novet, J. (2016). Apple vs. FBI: A timeline of the iPhone encryption case. *VB*. Retrieved from http://venturebeat.com/2016/02/19/apple-fbi-timeline

Rainie, L., & Maniam, S. (2016). Americans feel the tensions between privacy and security concerns. *Pew Research Center*. Retrieved from http://www.pewresearch.org/fact-tank/2016/02/19/americans-feel-the-tensions-between-privacy-and-security-concerns

Rid, T. (2016). *Maschinendämmerung: Eine kurze Geschichte der Kybernetik*. Berlin: Propyläen Verlag.

Sayer, P. (2014). Snowden docs show Tor, TrueCrypt, Tails topped NSA's 'most wanted' list in '12. *Computerworld*. Retrieved from http://www.computerworld.com/article/2863937/snowden-docs-show-tor-truecrypt-tails-topped-nsas-most-wanted-list-in-12.html

US Senate. (1994). *The administration's clipper chip key escrow encryption program: Hearing before the Subcommittee on Technology and the Law of the Committee on the Judiciary United States Senate*, Washington, DC: US Senate.

Sessions, W. S. (1993). *Leaked letter briefing document "Encryption: The threat, applications, and potential solutions"*. Retrieved from https://epic.org/crypto/clipper/foia/crypto_threat_2_19_93.html

Tangri, D., Lemley, M. A., Feldman, M. A., & Landers, A. L. (2016). Amicus Curiae Brief of law professors in support of Apple Inc. *Apple*. Retrieved from http://www.apple.com/pr/library/2016/03/03 Amicus-Briefs-in-Support-of-Apple.html

Volz, D., & Menn, J. (2016). Apple ordered to help FBI unlock data from San Bernadino shooter's iPhone. *Reuters*. Retrieved from http:// www.reuters.com/article/california-shooting-timcook-idUSKCN0VQ0YG

Weber, M. (1973). Die "Objektivität" sozialwissenschaftlicher und sozialpolitischer Erkenntnis. In J. Winckelmann (Ed.), *Gesammelte Aufsätze zur Wissenschaftslehre* (pp. 146–214). Tübingen: Mohr.

White House. (1993). *Statement by the press Secretary*. Retrieved from https://epic.org/crypto/clipper/white_house_statement_4_93.html

White House. (1994). *Statement by the press Secretary*. Retrieved from https://epic.org/crypto/clipper/white_house_statement_2_94.html

WorldBank. (2016). Internet users (per 100 people). *World Bank*. Retrieved from http://data.worldbank.org/indicator/IT.NET.USER.P2

3

Metadata Laws, Journalism and Resistance in Australia

Benedetta Brevini

Department of Media and Communication, The University of Sydney, Sydney, NSW 2006, Australia;
E-Mail: benedetta.brevini@sydney.edu.au

Abstract
The intelligence leaks from Edward Snowden in 2013 unveiled the sophistication and extent of data collection by the United States' National Security Agency and major global digital firms prompting domestic and international debates about the balance between security and privacy, openness and enclosure, accountability and secrecy. It is difficult not to see a clear connection with the Snowden leaks in the sharp acceleration of new national security legislations in Australia, a long term member of the Five Eyes Alliance. In October 2015, the Australian federal government passed controversial laws that require telecommunications companies to retain the metadata of their customers for a period of two years. The new acts pose serious threats for the profession of journalism as they enable government agencies to easily identify and pursue journalists' sources. Bulk data collections of this type of information deter future whistleblowers from approaching journalists, making the performance of the latter's democratic role a challenge. After situating this debate within the scholarly literature at the intersection between surveillance studies and communication studies, this article discusses the political context in which journalists are operating and working in Australia; assesses how metadata laws have affected journalism practices and addresses the possibility for resistance.

Keywords
digital resistance; journalists; metadata; surveillance

Issue
This article is part of the issue "Post-Snowden Internet Policy", edited by Julia Pohle (WZB Berlin Social Science Center, Germany) and Leo Van Audenhove (Vrije Universiteit Brussel, Belgium).

---

1. Introduction

The intelligence leaks from Edward Snowden in 2013 unveiled the sophistication and extent of data collection by the US's National Security Agency and major global digital firms prompting domestic and international debates about the balance between security and privacy, openness and enclosure, accountability and secrecy (Brevini, 2017). While many authors (Andrejevic, 2002, 2013; Lyon, 2014; Van Dijck, 2014) have warned about massive data collection by governments and businesses as a challenge to civil rights, there a need to encourage further public discussion around the world on the chilling effect that these data retention frameworks can have on freedom of the press, on journalists and on their ability to exert their traditional watchdog function (Lashmar, 2016). After situating this debate within the scholarly literature at the intersection between surveillance studies and communication studies, this article discusses the political context in which journalists are operating and working in Australia; assesses how metadata laws have affected journalism practices and addresses the violation of privacy for journalists and the emergence of a resistance.

2. From Surveillance Society to Resistance

Surveillance has been defined as the "collection and analysis of information about populations in order to govern their activities" (Ericson & Haggerty, 2006, p. 3) so the literature coming from surveillance studies becomes of great relevance in investigating the impact of metadata laws on journalism practices.

Yet, because of the unprecedented development of information and communication technologies, surveillance scholars have rightly pointed at the new ubiquitousness and embeddedness of surveillance in every aspects of life in current networked societies (Lyon, Haggerty, & Ball, 2012), going much beyond traditional and centralised institutional settings.

As a consequence of the accelerated development of a communication technologies, Mann and Ferenbok (2013) have also explored the possibility for "sousveillance" (Mann & Ferenbok, 2013, p. 19), surveillance from the bottom up, where the surveilled is empowered through technology to fight back and enact change from below through mutual watching and monitoring.

While digital surveillance practices have now been amply studied within surveillance studies, there is still great scope for development in the field of communication studies. In this article, I propose to investigate whether we can detect a space for resistance for journalists working within new metadata frameworks. This space is conceptualised as "field of struggles" (Bordieu, 1983)—a bourdieusian concept—that is helpful in investigating this space for agency.

In the launch edition of a new journal Big Data and Society, Couldry and Powell (2014) developed the argument that a question of agency is paramount to our understanding of big data, thus opening up a new research agenda for investigating not only dominant forms of data power, but also alternative forms of datafication emerging from civil society groups, community organisations, journalists .This study takes up this challenge by focusing specifically on the field of struggle (Bordieu, 1983) where journalists operate.

2.1. The Australian Context

Since the attacks of September 2001, there has been a steady increase in number of national security laws in Australia. Over fifty laws were passed to create new criminal offences, new detention, extended investigative powers for security and police officers, new tools to control people's movements and activities without criminal convictions (Ananian-Welsh & Williams, 2014). There is also a worrying tendency to limit courts' powers to review the legality of government action especially on matters of national security. At the same time, there is a clear trend towards an intensification of government secrecy and an extension of its own powers to limit the public's rights of access to information, thus making court reviews in these areas even more crucial (Human Rights Law Centre [HRLC], 2016).

In this context, the Snowden leaks (Brevini, 2017) and their challenges to state secrets can explain the haste that has characterised discussion and implementation of three major pieces of new national security laws in Australia between 2014 and 2015. As Attorney General George Brandis explained during the reading of the bill amending the Australian Security Intelligence Organisation Act 1979 (ASIO Act) and the Intelligence Services Act 2001 (IS Act), the reform is justified by a clear intent to curb whistleblowing activities:

> As recent, high-profile international events demonstrate, in the wrong hands, classified or sensitive information is capable of global dissemination at the click of a button. Unauthorised disclosures on the scale now possible in the online environment can have devastating consequences for a country's international relationships and intelligence capabilities. (Brandis, 2014)

The newly created metadata laws cannot be properly understood without considering the overall context of increased tightening of national security laws and investments in cybersecurity. In light of this, the Australian government announced in its 2015 budget that it will provide:

> $450 million to strengthen Australia's intelligence capabilities, including updating information technology systems and to counter extremist messaging. This includes $131 million to help the telecommunications sector upgrade its systems to retain metadata for two years. (Australian Government, 2015a)

As I will discuss later, the newly established framework is clearly at odds with a more recent tendency that is emerging in courts throughout Europe and the US and backed by international human rights mandates, where a clearly hostile attitude towards disproportionate digital surveillance is being displayed (see for example, Cannataci, 2016; Kaye, 2015).

3. Data Retention in Australia

The revised Telecommunications (Interception and Access, TIA) Act, passed in 2015, sought to specify "the types of data the telecommunications industry should retain for law enforcement and national security purposes or how long that information should be held". Rapid, ongoing changes occurring in the telecommunications environment have, apparently, "undermined" any systematic access to the tools and data that may be available (The Parliament of the Commonwealth of Australia, 2015a, p. 2). Recognising the variations that exist in the holding and maintenance of types of data in the telecommunications industry, the TIA Act demands the "standardisation" of such records for governmental use (The Parliament of the Commonwealth of Australia, 2015a). It is claimed that previous inconsistencies have impeded governmental efforts to "investigate and to prosecute serious offences" (The Parliament of the Commonwealth of Australia, 2015a).

Both houses have, therefore, passed this Bill, which oversees the implementation of a national data retention scheme. This scheme compels telecommunications service providers to "retain, for two years, particular types of telecommunications data" (The Parliament of the Commonwealth of Australia, 2015a).

The TIA Act cites several recommendations delivered by the Parliamentary Joint Committee for Intelligence and Security (PJCIS) as the basis for its framework, including that:

- the data retention obligation only applies to telecommunications data (not content) and internet browsing is explicitly excluded;
- service providers are required to protect the confidentiality of retained data by encrypting the information and protecting it from unauthorised interference or access;
- mandatory data retention will be reviewed by the PJCIS by three years after its commencement (The Parliament of the Commonwealth of Australia, 2015a, p. 3).

Telecommunications data, in this instance, has been largely characterised as metadata: that is data excluding "content" (The Parliament of the Commonwealth of Australia, 2015a, p. 7) such as the source and destination of a communication, subscribers' information, date, time and duration of a communication or connection to a service.[1]

The 2015–2016 Budget includes $153.8 million over four years to "support the implementation and ongoing management" of the data retention scheme, including $131.3 million over three years for telecommunications service providers (Australian Government, 2015b).

Access to citizens' metadata is therefore conferred without judicial oversight. No warrant is required by the 21 criminal law-enforcement agencies that have been permitted the capacity to requisition these records (Farrell, 2016; The Parliament of the Commonwealth of Australia, 2015a).

The explanatory memorandum for the TIA Act does, however, set out a "compatibility with human rights" statement, in accordance with the Human Rights (Parliamentary Scrutiny) Act 2011 (The Parliament of the Commonwealth of Australia, 2015a, p. 5). This statement, which is expanded upon over the course of 30 pages, includes certain caveats and safeguards to ensure the Act's compliance with the upholding of basic civil liberties. It therefore assures, among other things, that:

> The Bill...amends the TIA Act to bolster the privacy protections associated with the access to, and use of, telecommunications data. It achieves this by limiting the agencies which may authorise access to telecommunications data, and by providing that agencies' access to, and use of, telecommunications data is subject to comprehensive oversight by the Commonwealth Ombudsman. (The Parliament of the Commonwealth of Australia, 2015a, p. 6)

The statement asserts that the Bill "is compatible with human rights because it promotes a number of human rights". This is, however, followed by the disclaimer that "to the extent that (the Bill) may also limit human rights, those limitations are reasonable, necessary and proportionate" (The Parliament of the Commonwealth of Australia, 2015a, p. 36).

4. TIA Act and Its Impact on Journalists

In 2015, an amendment to the proposed TIA Act was put forward in the wake of concerns about how a data retention scheme might affect the media. It was recognised that a data retention scheme could "adversely affect" the media's capacity "to provide accurate and reliable information" (The Parliament of the Commonwealth of Australia, 2015b, p. 33) and leave sources vulnerable. The House of Representatives, thus, agreed to the implementation of a "journalist information warrant" regime, which prohibits agencies from "making authorisations to access journalists or their employers' data for the purpose of identifying a confidential source unless a journalist information warrant is in force" (The Parliament of the Commonwealth of Australia, 2015b, p. 33). This also means that journalists' metadata can always be accessed unless the agency is seeking data specifically for the purpose of identifying a journalist's source.

It is at the discretion of an "issuing authority" to issue or refuse the authorisation of a journalist information warrant, based on their understanding of the public interest (The Parliament of the Commonwealth of Australia, 2015a, p. 79). Issuing authorities are judicial officers approved by the minister or members of the Administrative Appeals Tribunal, or lawyers who are appointed by the minister.

It should also be noted that in the case of ASIO, it will be the minister that will issue the warrant. (The Parliament of the Commonwealth of Australia, 2015a, p. 33). According to the law, information warrants will be issued only when the "public interest in the issue of the warrant outweighs the public interest in maintaining the confidentiality of the source" (The Parliament of the Commonwealth of Australia, 2015a, p. 33).

The installation of (a) Public Interest Advocate(s) should be an additional measure by which the Act seeks to establish independence (The Parliament of the Commonwealth of Australia, 2015a, p. 33). The Public Interest Advocate can make submissions to requests for journalists' data, defending the need to maintain or discard

[1] In January 2016, Australian Privacy Commissioner Timothy Pilgrim appealed a decision of the Administrative Appeals Tribunal (Telstra Corp Ltd and Privacy Commissioner [2015] AATA 991 of 8 December 2015) that mobile phone metadata held by telecom provider Telstra were not "personal information" about its customers under the Australian Privacy Act 1988 This appeal has given the Federal Court a landmark opportunity to establish whether metadata constitutes personal information thus redefining data protection law in Australia. In 19 January 2017 the Federal Court has closed the case and delivered a groudbreaking decision that will have long lasting implications on how metadata is understood by Australians, and the access private citizens will be granted to their own data and digital trails: the Court decided that the mobile phone in question was not "personal information", effectively enshrining this interpretation into law and drastically narrowing the definition of "personal information" under the Privacy Act.

confidentiality, which the minister must consider as a part of the warrant's application. These may include conditions and/or restrictions (The Parliament of the Commonwealth of Australia, 2015a, p. 83). The Public Interest Advocate will, however, not be allowed to seek the advice of media entities, be it the journalist or the organisation, addressed in the journalist information warrant (Keane, 2015a). Indeed, the status of journalists and media organisations as parties subject to a warrant will not be permitted for disclosure (Keane, 2015a). It is so secret that there are two-year jail terms for disclosure, of the mere existence or non existence of a journalist information warrant, while journalists will not be informed of the request being pursued.

It is difficult not to see the flaws in this system and its detrimental effects on the practice of journalism. The journalist information warrant operates in secret, while journalists and their media organisation will never know if access was granted. It will still allow journalists' metadata to be accessed to identify a journalist's sources, while the public interest advocates won't be able to argue in defence of the public watchdog role of news organisation and their responsibility to protect the identity of a source. As journalist Laurie Oakes recalled: "metadata collection is the great press freedom issue of the internet age". The aggressive attitude towards whistleblowers means that governments "now hunt down those leakers with zeal and this means that metadata is their friend" (Oakes, 2015).

5. From Metadata Laws to Special Intelligence Operations Reform: Targeting Journalist's Sources

As discussed, the metadata retention scheme enforced by TIA 2015 has obvious consequences not only for journalists but for their sources, and whistleblowers. However, TIA, combined with another amendment of Australian National Security laws, specifically section 35P of the ASIO has even a greater detrimental impact on journalists' sources.

Under Section 35P of the ASIO Act 1979, those who have "disclosed information relating to a special intelligence operation" may be imprisoned for five to ten years (The Parliament of the Commonwealth of Australia, 2014, p. 71). A "special intelligence operation" can be understood as operations where ASIO agents are granted legal immunity for engaging in a range of otherwise criminal conduct. The most "basic" breach, in which information is simply disclosed, can result in a five-year penalty. Where a disclosure endangers "the health or safety of a person", the Act permits a penalty of ten years. This penalty applies regardless of whether the citizen or journalist in question is aware of an operation's status.

In a report commissioned by the Department of the Prime Minister and Cabinet (DPMC), the impact of this piece of legislation is suggested to be twofold: a gag order like 35P may instil a "chill effect" on publications about the activities of ASIO, and prevent "reprehensible conduct" by ASIO insiders from being susceptible to public scrutiny (DMPC, 2015). According to the report, such an impact is "unjustified" despite the need for secrecy in many ASIO operations. The inadequate protection of the rights of "outsiders", it argues, "infringes the constitutional protection of freedom of political communication" (DPMC, 2015). This new provision is concerning for a number of reasons. First, without an explicit verification from ASIO, it is extremely difficult for a journalist to know whether an ASIO operation is a special intelligence operation or not. Additionally, the new section criminalises both intentional and reckless disclosure, so journalists are likely to take a conservative approach to publication and avoid pursuing reporting of ASIO's activities for fear of being prosecuted. This will indeed lead to a progressive self-imposed censorship of journalists and a progressive lack of public reporting in formal publications or through anonymous disclosures and scrutiny of intelligence activities.

As the controversy around Australian asylum seekers policy arose, in 2015,[2] the Australian Government expanded secrecy laws frameworks and penalties for whistleblowers through the controversial Border Force Act. The legislation makes it unlawful for a Department of Immigration and Border Protection's employee or contractor, such as a social worker, a nurse, a doctor or welfare services provider, to disclose or record certain information obtained while carrying out their duties. The penalty for such a disclosure is up to two years in jail (HRLC, 2015).

As The Guardian's Paul Farrell commented:

> This is a move that should alarm all citizens. It's not an attack on any particular news outlet. It's an attack on those who have reported on matters of significant public interest in the increasingly secretive area of asylum seeker policy....These kind of attacks [sic] severely damage the confidence between reporters and their sources and pose a grave threat to effective and responsible journalism. When the federal police go knocking on the doors of a reporter's sources, sources will soon dry up. People will be scared. And that is exactly the point. (Farrell, 2015)

It is important to note that the Border Protection Act has been amended in October 2016 exempting health professionals from the definition of "immigration and border protection workers" following the pressures coming from the health professionals who challenged the Government in the High court (Hall, 2016). However, the current ban remains in place for others, such as child protection workers and teachers, who witnessed abuses in offshore detentions (Hall, 2016).

[2] For a good summary of controversial Australian Asylum policies and United Nations (UN) criticism please, see "Australia Asylum: Why Is It Controversial?" available at http://www.bbc.com/news/world-asia-28189608

6. A Look at the Current International Context

The newly established metadata scheme regime clearly posits new challenges not only for journalism practices but for the effectiveness of shield laws which are meant to prevent journalists from being forced to reveal their sources. It is also quite unclear how the current Australian national framework for data collection corresponds to, or addresses, existing international conventions, treaties or policies on free speech, political, economic and cultural inclusion. For example the European Court of Justice in April 2014 invalidated the EU's Data Retention Directive, which is very similar to the Australian scheme. In particular, "the Court held that the Directive entailed serious interference with the rights to privacy and personal data protection of individuals guaranteed by the Charter of Fundamental Rights, and also failed to establish limits on access by competent national authorities, such as prior review by a judicial or an independent administrative authority" (Data Retention Directive, 2014). The lack of safeguards around the access and use of metadata was a key reason for the directive to be in breach of the fundamental right to privacy.

Australia's attitude towards metadata frameworks is not unique in international settings. The first report issued by the UN rapporteur on privacy has noted that the country monitoring process of the last year has "revealed several examples of legislation being rushed through national parliaments in an effort to legitimise the use of certain privacy-intrusive measures by Security and Intelligence Services (SIS) and law enforcement agencies" (Cannataci, 2016, p. 6). Moreover, the report notes that there is a contradictory trend between governments and international attitude towards metadata regimes:

> The tensions between security, corporate business models and privacy continue to take centre stage but the last twelve months have been marked by contradictory indicators: some governments have continued, in practice and/or in their parliaments to take privacy-hostile attitudes while courts world-wide but especially in the USA and Europe have struck clear blows in favour of privacy and especially against disproportionate, privacy-intrusive measures such as mass surveillance or breaking of encryption. (Cannataci, 2016, p. 21)

The stand of the mandate of the International rapporteur on Privacy (Cannataci, 2016) is consistent with the indications of the UN, voiced by the former Rapporteur for Freedom of Information Frank La Rue.

> National data retention laws are invasive and costly, and threaten the rights to privacy and free expression. By compelling communications service providers to create large databases of information about who communicates with whom via a telephone or the Internet, the duration of the exchange, and the users' location, and to keep such information (sometimes for years), mandatory data retention laws greatly increase the scope of State surveillance, and thus the scope for infringements upon human rights. Databases of communications data become vulnerable to theft, fraud and accidental disclosure. (La Rue, 2013, p. 18)

The recommendations of the Rapporteur are clearly at odds with the newly approved Australian framework:

> Communications surveillance should be regarded as a highly intrusive act that potentially interferes with the rights to freedom of expression and privacy and threatens the foundations of a democratic society. Legislation must stipulate that State surveillance of communications must only occur under the most exceptional circumstances and exclusively under the supervision of an independent judicial authority. Safeguards must be articulated in law relating to the nature, scope and duration of the possible measures, the grounds required for ordering them, the authorities competent to authorize, carry out and supervise them, and the kind of remedy provided by the national law. (La Rue, 2013, p. 21)

7. Metadata Laws: Is There Room for Journalists' Resistance?

I have argued elsewhere (Brevini, 2017) that the revelations by whistleblower Edward Snowden triggered the birth of a new "new culture of disclosure" that has seen journalists, lawyers and software developers coming together to develop secure online protections and security of their sources. One of the most famous examples are Secure Drop and GlobaLeaks (Brevini, 2017) projects that aim at supporting the practice of whistleblowing by giving people the software tools necessary to start their own initiative. Unlike WikiLeaks (Brevini & Murdock, 2013), GlobaLeaks is an open-source software provider whose intentions are focussed on providing a platform for whistleblowers to use. GlobaLeaks does not handle any leaked documents but assists in the potential creation of whistleblowing sites such as OpenLeaks, MafiaLeaks, BalkanLeaks and BrusselsLeaks. However, there is also a more mainstream response to metadata laws: The New Yorker, the US not-for-profit investigative newsroom ProPublica, the Pierre Omidyar-backed start-up The Intercept and The Guardian are just a few examples of news providers that implemented a newly created open-source whistleblowing platform-SecureDrop to guarantee protections for their sources (Brevini, 2017).

In Australia,[3] the only platform of this kind is mediadirect.org, a platform that aims to encourage encrypted

[3] The paper adopted a multilayered methodological approach that combines policy and legal analysis with interviews with ten investigative Journalists in Australia that prefer to keep their anonymity.

disclosure by anonymous whistleblowers, thus protecting sources from the newly enhanced metadata laws. With a budget of about US$ 3,000 (Interview B)[4] the platform through encrypted interactions connects whistleblowers, who access it via the Tor network, and journalists (Keane, 2015b).

In light of the new metadata frameworks implemented in Australia, one would expect journalists rushing to demand an improved set of encryption tools, as well as formal training on anonymity mechanisms to protect their sources. However, our findings confirm not only a lack of knowledge of encrypting communications but also a lack of understanding of the risks of the newly established frameworks (Interview A, 2016).[5]

As one security consultant revealed:

> In a recent example, I just set them up to deal with the data, because they did not know how to deal with a major data leak. And when I got in there for the first meeting, one of the journalists said, "We'll print everything out". And I'm shocked: it's a million pages and hundreds of thousands of emails, how can we possibly print them? (Interview B, 2016)

Improving journalists' knowledge of encryption tools and their awareness of metadata laws should be a priority for media organisations, and perhaps one of the goals for Media Entertainment Alliance Australia.

Interviewees seemed to agree that the reasons for media institutions not to invest in security tools and training for their journalists has to do with the current financial crisis of journalism and the precarious conditions of reporters: when faced with the clear risk of losing their job, journalists are less keen to take risks and expose wrongdoings.

8. Conclusion

The newly established metadata scheme regime in Australia clearly undermines the work of journalists and the effectiveness of shield laws which were due to protect journalists from being forced to reveal their sources. As Crikey journalist Bernard Keane noted: "The threat arises from the existence and maintenance of data. That creates the chilling effect. You don't need a warrant to investigate a journalist if the agency can access the data of the whole department that the leak came from" (Keane 2015a).

The chilling effect on journalists and whistleblowers' activities are very consistent with findings of the scholarship in surveillance studies that have detected for example a similar pattern of "self censorship" on activists's or civil society groups' activities (see for example, Starr, Fernandez, Amster, Wood, & Caro, 2008).

There are obviously limits to what encryption and anonymity technologies can do to protect journalism practices, but the Australian case certainly shows that, aside from a few exceptions, journalists are currently not well equipped with the necessary know-how and awareness. In Bordieu's terms, journalists in the Australian context have not fully developed the resources or "capital" (Bordieu, 1983) to successfully oppose the collection and processing of personal data, thus developing a space for resistance to surveillance, radically different from "sousveillance" (Mann & Ferenbok, 2013).

It should also be noted that the findings of this study diverge from a recent study by Mills and Sarikakis (2016) that focused only on investigative journalists and found how investigative journalist in Western and non Western countries are engaging increasingly with technological and other communities to defend their work. Future research from Communication Studies perspective should engage with this recent scholarship to shed light on the crucial interplay between new metadata frameworks and journalism.

Conflict of Interests

The author declares no conflict of interests.

References

Ananian-Welsh, R., & Williams, G. (2014). New terrorists: The normalisation and spread of anti-terror laws in Australia. *The Melbourne University Law Review*, *38*, 362–408.

Andrejevic, M. (2002). The work of watching one another: Lateral surveillance, risk, and governance. *Surveillance & Society*, *2*(4), 479–497.

Andrejevic, M. (2013). *Infoglut: How too much information is changing the way we think and know*. Oxford: Routledge.

Australian Information Commissioner. (2015). Ben Grubb and Telstra Corporation Limited. *Austlii*. Retrieved from http://www.austlii.edu.au/au/cases/cth/AICmr/2015/35.html

Bourdieu, P. (1983). The field of cultural production, or: The economic world reversed. *Poetics*, *12*(4/5), 311–356.

Brandis, G. (2014). National Security Legislation Amendment Bill (No. 1) 2014, Second reading. *Parliament of Australia*. Retrieved from http://parlinfo.aph.gov.au/parlInfo/search/display/display.w3p;db=CHAMBER;id=chamber%2Fhansards%2F232fa1a8-d7e8-4b22-9018-1a99b5a96812%2F0116;query=Id%3A%22chamber%2Fhansards%2F232fa1a8-d7e8-4b22-9018-1a99b5a96812%2F0173%22

Brevini, B. (2017). WikiLeaks: Between disclosure and whistle- blowing in digital times. *Sociology Compass*, *1*(3), 1–11.

Brevini, B., & Murdock, G. (2013). Following the money: WikiLeaks and the political economy of disclosure. In

[4] Interview via Skype, 10 May 2016.
[5] Interview via Skype, 3 May 2016.

B. Brevini, A. Hintz, & P. McCurdy (Eds.), *Beyond WikiLeaks: Implications for the future of communications, journalism and society* (pp. 35–55). Basingstoke: Palgrave Macmillan.

Cannataci, J. A. (2016). Report of the special rapporteur on the right to privacy. *Human Rights Council*. Retrieved from www.ohchr.org/Documents/Issues/Privacy/A-HRC-31-64.doc

Couldry, N., & Powell, A. (2014). Big data from the bottom up. *Big Data & Society, 1*(2). doi:10.1177/2053951714539277

Data Retention Directive. (2014). *European Union: ECJ invalidates data retention directive*. Retrieved from http://www.loc.gov/law/help/eu-data-retention-directive/eu.php

Department of the Prime Minister and Cabinet. (2015). *Report on the impact on journalists of section 35P of the ASIO Act*. Retrieved from https://www.dpmc.gov.au/pmc/publication/report-impact-journalists-section-35p-asio-act

Ericson, R. V., & Haggerty, K. D. (2006). *The new politics of surveillance and visibility*. Toronto: University of Toronto Press.

Farrell, P. (2015). Journalism is not a crime. So why are reporters being referred to police? *The Guardian*. Retrieved from http://www.theguardian.com/commentisfree/2015/jan/22/journalism-is-not-a-so-why-are-reporters-being-referred-to-police

Farrell, P. (2016). Lamb chop weight enforcers want warrantless access to Australians' metadata. *The Guardian*. Retrieved from http://www.theguardian.com/world/2016/jan/19/lamb-chop-weight-enforcers-want-warrantless-access-to-australians-metadata

Hall, B. (2016). 'A huge win for doctors': Turnbull government backs down on gag laws for doctors on Naurus and Manus. *Sydney Morning Herald*. Retrieved from http://www.smh.com.au/federal-politics/political-news/a-huge-win-for-doctors-turnbull-government-backs-down-on-gag-laws-for-doctors-on-nauru-and-manus-20161019-gs6ecs.html

Human Rights Law Centre. (2016). *Safeguarding democracy*. Retrieved from http://www.bmartin.cc/dissent/documents/rr/HRLC16.pdf

Kaye, D. (2015). Report of the special rapporteur on the promotion and protection of the right to freedom of opinion and expression. *Human Rights Council*. Retrieved from http://www.un.org/en/ga/search/view_doc.asp?symbol=A/70/361

Keane, B. (2015a). Finally the Labor coalition surveillance deal revealed. *Crikey*. Retrieved from http://www.crikey.com.au/2015/03/19/finally-the-labor-coalition-surveillance-deal-revealed/?wpmp_switcher=mobile

Keane, B. (2015b). Media direct: Towards better security for whistleblowers. *Crikey*. Retrieved from https://www.crikey.com.au/2014/05/26/media-direct-towards-better-security-for-whistleblowers

La Rue, F. (2013). Report of the special rapporteur on the promotion and protection of the right to freedom of opinion and expression. *United Nations Human Rights*. Retrieved from http://ap.ohchr.org/documents/dpage_e.aspx?si=A/HRC/23/40

Lashmar, P. (2016). No more sources? The impact of Snowden's revelations on journalists and their confidential sources. *Journalism Practice*. doi:10.1080/17512786.2016.1179587

Lyon, D., Haggerty, K. D., & Ball, K. (2012). Introducing surveillance studies. In D. Lyon, K. D. Haggerty, & K. Ball (Eds.), *Routledge handbook of surveillance studies* (pp. 1–12). Oxford: Routledge.

Lyon, D. (2014). Surveillance, Snowden, and big data: Capacities, consequences, critique. *Big Data & Society, 1*(2), 1–13.

Mann, S., & Ferenbok, J. (2013). New media and the power politics of sousveillance in a surveillance-dominated world. *Surveillance & Society, 11*(1/2), 1–13.

Mills, A., & Sarikakis, K. (2016). Reluctant activists? The impact of legislative and structural attempts of surveillance on investigative journalism. *Big Data & Society, 3*(2), 1–13.

Oakes, L. (2016). *Speech delivered at the Melbourne Press Club, 27 September 2015*. Retrieved from http://www.melbournepressclub.com/wp-content/uploads/2015/09/150925_Melbourne_Press_Freedom_Dinner_Oakes_speech.pdf

The Parliament of the Commonwealth of Australia. (2014). National security legislation amendment bill (No. 1) 2014: Bill as passed by both houses. *Parliament of Australia*. Retrieved from http://www.aph.gov.au/Parliamentary_Business/Bills_Legislation/Bills_Search_Results/Result?bId=s969

The Parliament of the Commonwealth of Australia. (2015a). Telecommunications (Intercept and Access) Amendment (Data Retention) Bill 2015: Revised explanatory memorandum. *Parliament of Australia*. Retrieved from http://www.aph.gov.au/Parliamentary_Business/Bills_Legislation/Bills_Search_Results/Result?bId=r5375

The Parliament of the Commonwealth Australia. (2015b). Data Retention Bill: Budget Review 2015–16. *Parliament of Australia*. Retrieved from http://www.aph.gov.au/About_Parliament/Parliamentary_Departments/Parliamentary_Library/pubs/rp/BudgetReview201516/Telco

Australian Government. (2015a). *Budget 2015*. Retrieved from http://www.budget.gov.au/2015-16/content/highlights/nationalsecurity.html

Australian Government. (2015b). *Budget 2015–16* (Budget Paper no.2). Retrieved from http://www.budget.gov.au/2015-16/content/bp2/download/BP2_consolidated.pdf

Privacy Commissioner. (2015). Privacy Commissioner lodges appeal to Federal Court re Telstra Corporation Limited v Privacy Commissioner. *Office of the Australian Information Commissioner*. Retrieved from https://www.oaic.gov.au/media-and-speeches/state

ments/privacy-commissioner-lodges-appeal-to-federal-court-re-telstra-corporation-limited-v-privacy-commissioner

Starr, A., Fernandez, L. A., Amster, R., Wood, L. J., & Caro, M. J. (2008). The impacts of state surveillance on political assembly and association: A socio-legal analysis. *Qualitative Sociology*, *31*(3), 251–270.

Van Dijck, J. (2014). Datafication, dataism and dataveillance: Big data between scientific paradigm and ideology. *Surveillance & Society*, *12*(2), 197–208.

4

Participation in Social Media: Studying Explicit and Implicit Forms of Participation in Communicative Social Networks

Mikko Villi [1,*] and Janne Matikainen [2]

[1] Department of Communication, University of Jyväskylä, 40014 Jyväskylä, Finland; E-Mail: mikko.villi@jyu.fi
[2] Department of Social Research, University of Helsinki, 00014 Helsinki, Finland; E-Mail: janne.matikainen@helsinki.fi

* Corresponding author

Abstract
The diverse forms of participation in social media raise many methodological and ethical issues that should be acknowledged in research. In this paper, participation in social media is studied by utilising the framework of explicit and implicit participation. The focus is on the communicative and communal aspects of social media. The aim of the paper is to promote the reconsideration of what constitutes participation when online users create connections rather than content. The underlying argument is that research on social media and the development of methods should concentrate more on implicit forms of participation.

Keywords
connectivity; ethics; explicit participation; implicit participation; methods; social media

Issue
This article is part of the issue "Successes and Failures in Studying Social Media: Issues of Methods and Ethics", edited by Epp Lauk and Niina Sormanen (University of Jyväskylä, Finland).

---

1. Introduction

Participation in social media is multifaceted and, thus, methodologically challenging. In this paper, we shed light on the complexities of social media research by means of a literature review, building on the theoretical framework of explicit and implicit participation. The review of explicit and implicit participation can provide insights for research and methodology in the context of social media. In particular, we suggest that the review can aid in developing methods for studying implicit participation in social media.

First, it is necessary to examine the general concept of participation in social media. The word 'social' in the term 'social media' implies that these platforms facilitate communal activities. In the same sense, the term 'participatory' emphasises human collaboration (van Dijck, 2013, p. 11). However, all participation is not the same. Participation is an ambiguous concept that can take on many different forms, and it can even be seen as a problematic concept that is often overused and overstretched (Carpentier, 2011, pp. 351-353). One approach is to stress participation as a political-ideological concept that is intrinsically linked to power. Carpentier (2011) claims that participation is deeply embedded within our political realities and that it is therefore the object of long-lasting, intense ideological struggles. Carpentier also considers participation as structurally different from interaction. According to him, interaction remains an important condition of participation, but it cannot be equated with participation. Unlike participation, interaction has no such political meanings because participation entails power dynamics and interaction does not (Matikainen, 2015, p. 43).

Many other views on participation are less political and less occupied with notions of power; therefore, they may be closer to interaction. According to Jenkins (2006), participatory culture contrasts with older notions of passive media spectatorship and consumption. Rather than talking about media producers and consumers as occupying separate roles, we might see them interacting and collaborating. Jenkins refers to this as convergence culture. From this perspective, participation is associated more with acting together and communicating with each other and less with power, politics and struggle, although these elements still play a role.

The action within inter*action* is of essence. Former passive audiences turn into active participants and agents of cultural production on the Internet (Schäfer, 2011, p. 10). Thereby, audiences become participants or users. The term 'users' is often used to refer to people who are more or less active online. In this sense, 'users' is a better term than 'audience' to indicate interactive participants in social media. Being an audience only captures one segment of the contemporary media experience because an increasing part of online activity involves 'doing' things, such as messaging, sharing, tweeting, using Facebook, chatting, commenting, editing, posting and uploading (Merrin, 2009, p. 24).

Livingstone (2005) states that 'users' as a term does not work very well either. It is too broad, and it has less to do with communication. Users use computers when engaging online, but they also use, for example, washing powder, which does not have much to do with human interaction, communication or communality. Thus, Livingstone proposes that 'people' would be a good term to describe participants in the realm of social media.

It is important to acknowledge that being a user and being an audience member are not mutually exclusive roles. People can be online users and audience members simultaneously. The roles are not always defined by the level of activity, but the role can also be a question of attitude, i.e. how people themselves consider their positions in social media. In addition, the roles can depend on the platform, i.e. what kind of affordances different online platforms offer for interactivity. However, it is reasonable to question the significance of novel communication technology and platforms for participation in general. The presumption that new networked technologies lead to participation is rather generalising (Terranova, 2004; van Dijck, 2009). Nevertheless, users of 'old media' are often stereotyped as a passive audience, and users of digital, participatory media are equally stereotyped as hyperactive, co-creative people (Olsson, 2010, p. 101).

2. Explicit and Implicit Participation

To further examine participation, we will focus on explicit and implicit forms of participation (Schäfer, 2011). From the users' standpoint, explicit participation involves producing media texts and artefacts. Explicit participation has a 'pro' aspect, in the sense that it is about production, produsage and prosumerism and is closely linked with user-generated content (UGC). Explicit participation is also connected to co-creation when consumers are no longer satisfied with their traditional end-user roles, and they want to be involved in creating and developing digital products and services (Ramaswamy & Gouillart, 2010, pp. 3-6).

In contrast to explicit participation, implicit participation does not involve conscious production. Rather, it often comprises unacknowledged labour or even unconsciously performed labour. Implicit participation shows a trend towards automated user participation because it is channelled through easy-to-use interfaces and the automation of user activity processes (Schäfer, 2011, pp. 51, 78.). In implicit participation, the behaviour patterns, interests and consumption habits of users are turned into valuable data. For example, implicit participation occurs when a user connects his/her Spotify account with Facebook and information about music consumption is thereafter automatically communicated to his/her Facebook friends (Karppi, 2014, pp. 37, 72). Connections between users are essential to implicit participation. If UGC represents explicit participation, implicit participation is represented by user-generated behaviour (UGB) (Netzer, Tenenboim-Weinblatt, & Shifman, 2014, p. 625).

Most social media platforms are created to generate data about users for improved information management and targeted advertising (Schäfer, 2011, p. 78). In implicit participation, the actions of users and producers (as in produsage, see Bruns, 2012) do not necessarily blur; instead, the actions of users and information technology blur because the labour is performed by both the information system and the user (Schäfer, 2011, p. 78). An obvious example of this is Facebook. The social media platform connects users and technology (e.g. interface and platform infrastructure) to gather data from users. In this sense, implicit participation is closely related to the concept of connectivity (van Dijck, 2013), which we will return to shortly.

Implicit forms of user activity involve sustaining connections and togetherness rather than producing content. In this sense, implicit participation is connected to the ritual view of communication as defined by Carey (1989). Ritual communication concentrates on relationships between people and serves to maintain communality and community. The ritual view of communication exploits the mutual roots of commonness, communion, community and communication (Carey, 1989). However, many people might object to calling implicit online activities participation, at least in the sense that Carpentier has approached participation.

We adapt Schäfer's classification by replacing the dual construction of participation with a continuum or dimension of participation. Activities such as writing a blog post or contributing to a Wikipedia article lie at the explicit end of the continuum. In contrast, at the implicit end of the continuum, participation is non-productive from the users' point of view. Popular social media activities, such as sharing and liking content, lie between explicit and implicit participation on the continuum; however, in our view, they are closer to implicit participation.

2.1. Users of Users

Participatory social media users can be regarded, among others, as consumers, producers, distributors or products. We will now focus on the latter two roles, which represent more-implicit forms of participation on the continuum. First, we will discuss how participation can be regarded as a product or commodity. One well-known view associated with social media is that 'if you are not paying for it, you are not the customer, you are the product' (Noguera Vivo, Villi, Nyirő, de Blasio, & Bourdaa, 2013). From this view follows the argument that social media companies are *users of users* because the users and the data they provide about themselves are the products social media companies use in their business.

Van Dijck (2009, 2013) writes about this in a convincing manner. Many social media companies are less interested in selling paid memberships than they are in customers who do not pay anything for services. In exchange for free services, social media companies require the use of users' data. According to van Dijck (2009, p. 49), a user's role as a data provider is infinitely more important to social media companies than the user's role as a content provider. Personal data are turned into public, observable connections, such as liking something on Facebook. Privacy is the currency in social media.

Users profile themselves, e.g. by liking and using social plugins, while social media companies, which can also be called corporate social media (CSM), sell the resulting data to marketers and advertisers (Gehl, 2015). Likes and social plugins create new forms of connectivity between websites, generating a 'like economy' in which the acts integrate more objects into the social graph and enable social media companies to expand their activities throughout the Internet to monetise connections and data flows outside their own platforms (Gerlitz & Helmond, 2013; Langlois & Elmer, 2013, p. 9). Users willingly and often unknowingly provide important information about their profiles and behaviours to CSM companies (van Dijck, 2009, p. 47). This view is very much in line with Schäfer's conception of implicit participation. It can be argued that social media services are built on a double exploitation of explicit and implicit participation. First, social media companies thrive on the free labour of content creators (Terranova, 2004). Second, they exploit the labour of all site visitors, who generate valuable data about their interests and activities as they like and share content. This more-implicit user participation produces data that are valuable to marketers, who want to know what people are interested in and how those interests link to other interests (Gauntlett, 2011, p. 191).

In other words, in the context of participatory culture, users are a commodity sold by the media as eyeballs to advertisers, in the classic view of Smythe (1977), and also the communal activities of the audience, such as liking or distributing news stories, are a commodity (Fuchs, 2010). Social media users represent a labour power that produces attention to ads as well as data, which then feeds into the production of ads (Fisher, 2015, p. 65). Much of the user work or user labour in social media is associated less with production and more with communication and interaction. This also means that user work is described well by implicit forms of participation.

In relation to implicit participation, the role of connectivity has been emphasised as part of social media logic (van Dijck, 2013). Connectivity refers to how social media companies gather data from users and their connections and then exploit this data for their purposes, e.g. by selling that information to advertisers (van Dijck & Poell, 2013, p. 8). When engaged in social media, users are positioned within an algorithmic connectivity in which machine processes mine their data, which are then used to affect and engage other users (Karppi, 2014). Users produce a precious resource: connectivity (van Dijck, 2013, p. 16).

The term 'connectedness' is closely related to connectivity and implicit participation. In a sense, connectedness involves social media users connecting with each other in a multitude of ways. Commoditising relationships and connections to turn connectedness into connectivity is the essence of the business undertaken by social media companies (van Dijck, 2013). CSMs are less interested in co-creation or UGC than in users making connections, which yield valuable information about who the users are and what they are interested in (van Dijck & Nieborg, 2009, pp. 865-866). Accordingly, social media platforms record not only what is being said but also the more broad act of communication itself, including information about the profile of a user sending out a message, the users receiving that message and how users interact with a message by reading, liking and sharing it or not (Langlois & Elmer, 2013, p. 2).

Importantly, social dynamics on social media platforms depend on the platforms themselves (Gillespie, 2015; Helmond, 2015). Social media platforms have simplified the communication process and expanded potential communicative opportunities, but they have also been built to harness communication in an effort to monetise it (Langlois & Elmer, 2013, p. 2). Social media platforms are designed to enhance human connections and constant connectivity because smaller friendship networks and less communication would lead to less user data to market (Langlois, 2014, p. 7; Langlois & Elmer, 2013, p. 10). As Gillespie (2015) notes, 'Platforms matter...The platforms, in their technical design, economic imperatives, regulatory frameworks, and public character, have distinct consequences for what users are able to do, and in fact do'.

2.2. Sharing in User Communities

The context for connectedness can be labelled a 'user community'. When users in social media regularly communicate among themselves, they can be said to form an actual community; otherwise, impermanent, transient and atomised user structures simply represent a crowd (Bruns, 2012, p. 819). The traditional definition of a community, i.e. a spatially compact set of people with a high frequency of interaction, interconnections and a sense of solidarity, does not always fit well with user communities. Social media services in particular do not necessarily make people feel as if they belong to a community. Instead, social media can host sets of interlinked personal communities built on interpersonal commitments (Gruzd, Wellman, & Takhteyev, 2011, pp. 1296-1299). One way to illustrate a user community is to view it as connections between personal communities formed around friends, followers and other contacts in social media. Social networking services do not form mutually shared communities; instead, interaction takes place in many interlinked personal communities, such as one's Facebook friends. Overall, connectedness is significantly related to communality.

On the continuum of participation, sharing content can be placed at a position closer to implicit participation than to explicit participation. Sharing in social media involves connectedness and connectivity. Those who share content connect with their peers while also connecting with Facebook, Twitter and Google (van Dijck, 2013, p. 45). In general, the consumption of media content has gone from being an individual activity to one in which consumers have the opportunity to interact with others. In a sense, the consumption of content is a social experience (Villi, 2012, p. 627) and a networked practice (Jenkins, 2006, pp. 244–255). Thus, sharing is becoming central to the way in which people experience media content (Hermida, Fletcher, Korrell, & Logan, 2012, p. 7), such as when they read news stories recommended by others on Facebook. The word 'sharing' fittingly describes participation in social media at large: sharing can be an act of distribution, communication and consumption (Belk, 2010, p. 730; John, 2013). Sharing involves social exchange on the one hand and distribution and dissemination on the other (Wittel, 2011, pp. 3, 8).

We will now focus on sharing in the context of social media specifically from the viewpoint of user-distributed content (UDC). UDC describes the role of horizontal connections in disseminating media content; users take part in distribution processes by enclosing content with social relations (Villi, 2012; Villi & Matikainen, 2015). Users make personal referrals and guide their peers to consume content that they consider interesting and relevant by recommending the content on Facebook, tweeting links or sending messages through email or instant messaging applications. UDC involves sharing as a method of distribution. UDC refers to audience activities that serve to amplify the extent, visibility and impact of existing online media content. In this sense, it is possible to draw clear boundaries between UDC and user-generated content (UGC), which clearly involves producing new content.

Terms and concepts that closely relate to UDC include superdistribution, i.e. forwarding media through social networks (Anderson, Bell, & Shirky, 2013, p. 14), and social curation, which illustrates the networked distribution of media content by adding qualitative judgements and imbuing the content with personal and social significance (Villi, 2012, p. 615; Villi, Moisander, & Joy, 2012). Singer (2014, p. 68) has coined the term 'user-generated visibility', which is very close to UDC. The idea of friendcasting (Lee & Cho, 2011) is implicit in these approaches to social media use. User-copied content (UCC) can also be linked to UDC (van Dijck, 2013, p. 119).

UDC has the advantage of not being a very time-consuming activity for users. In many ways, UDC represents 'easy participation' (Newman & Levy, 2013, p. 70), consisting of simple, everyday actions (Jenkins, Ford, & Green, 2013, p. 199) that represent a light version of participation, i.e. 'participation lite'. Using a social plugin, such as pressing the Facebook recommend button placed next to a news item or another story, is less demanding than writing a post. In UDC, personal recommendations by online contacts, especially by friends, are of utmost importance; having media content recommended by a friend is very effective when deciding what content to consume (Enda & Mitchell, 2013; Matikainen & Villi, 2013). Influencers—people with large networks of connected followers and friends—are also important (van Dijck, 2013, p. 40). The term 'alpha distributors' can be used to refer to users who act as key nodes in social media and whose recommendations have an extensive reach and influence.

UDC involves connectedness in the sense that it entails communicative interactions and relationships between two or more individuals. At the same time, it represents connectivity because users lure their peers to consume media content, which then leads to data generating audience traffic. Users who distribute content in social media also engage in the work of advertisers and marketers by endorsing brands and their content (Napoli, 2010, p. 512) and mobilising themselves in the promotion of brands (Fisher, 2015, p. 50).

2.3. Participation and the Media

Explicit and implicit forms of participation can also be examined in the context of mass media and journalism.

Until now, UGC has been the most-recognised form of audience participation in journalism (Noguera et al., 2013), and legacy media organisations' strategies concerning audience participation have concentrated largely on UGC (Napoli, 2010; Netzer et al., 2014; Singer et al., 2011). However, an increasing number of media scholars have argued that for legacy media organisations, engaging, encouraging and assisting the audience in the circulation of media content is more important than having them participate in content production (Hermida et al., 2012; Singer et al., 2011). Naturally, these two ideas are interlinked in the sense that content in social media often acts as a social glue that connects people, such as when users view photographs on Instagram.

Marshall (2009) argued that the successful operation of the media industry in social media is as much related to content production as it is to facilitating the maintenance of social connections among its audience. In other words, the work of editorial teams is transformed from content production through creating platform concepts to coordinating, managing and nurturing audience communities (Malmelin & Villi, 2015).

Jönsson and Örnebring (2011) offer a simple distinction between a) features that require a low level of participation in the media, mainly addressing audience members as consumers; b) features that require a medium level of participation, addressing audience members as prosumers; and c) features that require a high level of participation, addressing audience members as producers. An example of the low level of participation is the use of the social media audience as a 'radar' (Villi, 2012, p. 616). Within the radar, journalists can observe which stories and content circulate the most in social media and make content decisions accordingly. Another term used to describe journalists watching what users discuss online is 'public sensor' (Heinonen, 2011, pp. 37–38). When users are monitored, the simple act of liking or sharing content can influence decision-making processes in mass media; thereby, users can take part in news selection and gatekeeping (Netzer et al., 2014, p. 628). Moving from a low level to a high level of participation correlates with the transition from implicit to explicit participation.

2.4. Methodological Challenges of Studying Implicit Participation

Now, we move on to discussing the methodological challenges of social media research. In connection to the continuum of explicit and implicit participation, a fundamental methodological challenge is the tension between human action and the data-based environment. As van Dijck and Poell (2013) demonstrated, programmability is an essential element of social media logic. Sociality is produced on social media platforms, and their code, data, algorithms, protocols and interfaces impose preconditions for social interactions and social being. The corpus is not just the product of people's participation; it is also crafted by social media platforms according to the logic of their algorithms, the imperatives of their business models and the enforcement of community guidelines (Gillespie, 2015).

Here, we can again refer to Schäfer's (2011) claim that in implicit participation, a user's actions and information technology are strongly interlinked. Therefore, there is both a human–social aspect and a data-based aspect of interaction and participation. When studying implicit participation, both of these aspects should be considered. However, the aspects are methodologically and pragmatically different. In most cases, user data are quantitative, but participation is human and social in nature; the human–social aspect of participation emerges in meanings and discourses.

To understand this context, Lessig (2001) has developed a useful specification. He presents three distinct layers of the Internet. The first layer is the physical layer, which is the basis of communication, i.e. computers and the wires that link computers. The physical layer, i.e. the hardware, enables operations in information networks. The second layer is the code layer, which makes the hardware run. This layer includes protocols and code. The third layer is the content layer, which is the visible part of the Internet, including images, texts and videos. Lessig's specification of the three layers helps us understand that implicit participation and participation in general operate on three levels, and the content layer is the only one visible to users.

In social media, the power of algorithms, i.e. the code layer, is stronger now than it has ever been. As Bucher (2012) notes, algorithmic architectures dynamically constitute certain forms of social practices. For example, Facebook's algorithms are based on the assumption that users are not equally connected to their friends. This assumption has two methodologically important consequences. First, explicit and implicit participation are partly constituted by the algorithm. Second, the data produced by algorithms is relevant when studying participation in social media.

A further methodological challenge involves determining how to gather research data, which in social media could be rather extensive. The data can be either user-based or platform-based, following the continuum from explicit to implicit participation. Traditionally, research data in social sciences have been gathered through surveys, interviews, observations and documentation, which are generally manual methods. Social media and the Internet in general generate a need for new forms of data analysis and software-supported data capture (Rieder, Abdulla, Poell, Woltering, & Zack, 2015), such as network analysis. For example, Facebook produces diverse, broad data, which can be gathered using computational techniques (Sormanen et al., 2016), such as an application programming interface (API). API-based data can highlight the role of administrators as connective leaders, measure the size and composition of the participating audience, engage in various types of periodisation and investigate issues that have been raised in comment sections (Rieder et al., 2015).

Even with new forms of data, interaction and participation in social media cannot be analysed fully using either qualitative or quantitative methods. The relationship between quantitative and qualitative methods is vague because they are based on different assumptions of reality and human action. The challenge is then to combine qualitative and quantitative methods in a sensible way. Quantitative and qualitative data also require various analytical skills, and multidisciplinary research is often necessary. In social media research, the lack of technical skills may lead to limited data and biased analysis (Weller, 2015). In addition, we should not become blinded by new data and methods. Big data and network visualisation can be impressive and imposing, but analytically, they are rather conventional. We as researchers must not only preserve analytical and critical thinking but also remain curious about new data and methods.

The challenge of data access and ownership of user data is of essence to research. As mentioned earlier, social media companies utilise user data as a product in their businesses. Thus, the data are commonly considered trade secrets. This causes many problems from a methodological perspective. At worst, research could be limited only to data that are freely available. This phenomenon is already evident, as shown in the amount of social media research focusing on Twitter due to the platform's comparatively easy and stable data access (Weller, 2015). Another point is that a majority of online participation is increasingly unreachable and hidden from researchers. The popularity of messaging apps, such as WhatsApp (Newman & Levy, 2014, p. 70), LINE and iMessage, in online communication is growing; however, data from these apps cannot be analysed in the same manner as traffic on Twitter.

2.5. Ethical Considerations

When conducting research on social media, ethical aspects should be considered. Implicit and explicit participation especially relate to the question of privacy, which depends on individual and cultural definitions and expectations (Markham & Buchanan, 2012, p. 6). These definitions are extremely complicated in the context of participation because users do not often perceive on their own whether their participation is implicit or explicit, or do not realise that their activity is participation at all.

As Sveningsson Elm (2009) notes, public and private are not univocal states; instead, they are based on users' perceptions. In this situation, researchers should be sensitive to users' rights and privacy. One essential notion is that like implicit and explicit participation, the concepts of public and private should be considered as a continuum and not a dichotomy (Sveningsson Elm, 2009). Many social media environments are semi-public, where some parts of the environment are public and some parts are not; in these cases, the definition of privacy is ambiguous. As Henderson, Johnson and Auld (2013, p. 550) stated, 'In the context of social media, it becomes increasingly difficult, if not impossible, to ethically claim a dichotomy of private or public'.

An important ethical aspect is the question of consent (Henderson et al., 2013, p. 549). If the research subject is identifiable, consent is needed. However, in the case of social media, from whom should consent be obtained and how should it be obtained? Consent is closely related to the above-mentioned dimension of private and public. Basically, consent is needed when content or communication is private. Because drawing the line between private and public in social media is challenging and sometimes even impossible, researchers should be extremely careful when gathering research data without consent. Often, the difficulty of obtaining consent adds to the challenge.

Research participants or subjects are regularly promised anonymity (Dawson, 2014). In social media, data are diverse because they also include information regarding people's preferences and social relationships, which is often a result of implicit participation. In relation to implicit participation, it should be noted that personal data in social media are also produced by platforms. Platform-based data can often reveal a user's identity easier than when the user makes an explicit decision to reveal or hide his or her identity.

One important question revolves around how researchers can penetrate social media, especially implicit forms of participation. Corporate social media companies are not shy about collecting information on implicit participation, and many users are not aware that they are leaving traces and collectable information. Can researchers be as straightforward and ethically blunt when digging into the forms and practices of implicit participation? How active as participants should the researchers themselves be? In relation to these questions, Markham (2013, p. 440) questions whether participation is always necessary for ethnographers working in online environments.

The ethical challenges are increased by the fact that children and young adults are remarkably active on social media. Scientific ethical rules emphasise that all humans, especially children, should be protected. It is interesting to note that despite many rules and guidelines related to research ethics, there are few empirical studies on ethics in online research (Dawson, 2014). Therefore, we suggest that in addition to concrete, detailed ethical rules concerning social media research, more meta-analysis of the fulfilment of research ethics in social media research is needed.

3. Conclusions

In this paper, we emphasised that implicit and explicit participation are the two ends of the continuum of participation. At the implicit end of the continuum lies fully automatic participation, as exemplified by the programmed publication of music listening habits on Facebook after listening to music on Spotify. At the explicit end lies writing a blog or publishing a picture on Instagram. Sharing and liking lie between the two ends of the spectrum, although they more closely represent implicit participation. Both explicit and implicit participation in social media are motivated at least partly by connectedness, and they benefit and support connectivity. Connectivity represents the relationship between the user and the information system or the platform (such as Facebook and Google), whereas connectedness represents the relationship between users.

We argue that the more-implicit forms of user participation in the communicative social networks of social media are of essence, especially for social media companies that offer services and platforms for interaction and that rely on connectivity in their businesses. We suggest that this is also increasingly the case for legacy media organisations. Therefore, we claim that when attempting to describe the instrumental participatory activities of users in a social media environment, discussion of UGC and other forms of more-explicit participation should be supplemented with discussion of more-implicit forms of participation. Accordingly, the development of methods should focus more on the study of implicit participation, which has not been the case in previous research.

The continuum of explicit and implicit participation should be considered as a theoretical, methodological, ethical and pragmatic phenomenon. Therefore, the elaboration of theoretical concepts is necessary but insufficient. We should remember that many methodological and pragmatic aspects can restrict the operationalisation of participation in social media and the nature of the data. For example, Langlois and Elmer (2013, pp. 10-11) argue that the promise that social media data offer a transparent trace of human behaviour is false because the behaviour is affected by the corporate logic of social media platforms. This leads to several challenges when studying modes of participatory culture on social media platforms, including access to data, the ethics of data research, the data, and what the data claim to stand for.

Conflict of Interests

The authors declare no conflict of interests.

References

Anderson, C. W., Bell, E., & Shirky, C. (2013). *Post-industrial journalism: Adapting to the present*. Retrieved from http://towcenter.org/wp-content/uploads/2012/11/TOWCenter-Post_Industrial_Journalism.pdf

Belk, R. W. (2010). Sharing. *Journal of Consumer Research*, *36*(5), 715-734. doi:10.1086/612649

Bruns, A. (2012). Reconciling community and commerce? Collaboration between produsage communities and commercial operators. *Information, Communication & Society*, *15*(6), 815-835. doi:10.1080/1369118X.2012.680482

Bucher, T. (2012). Want to be on the top? Algorithmic power and the threat of invisibility on Facebook. *New Media & Society*, *14*(7), 1164-1180. doi:10.1177/1461444812440159

Carey, J. W. (1989). *Communication as culture. Essays on media and society*. Boston: Unwin Hyman.

Carpentier, N. (2011). *Media and participation: A Site of ideological-democratic struggle*. Bristol, UK: Intellect.

Dawson, P. (2014). Our anonymous online research participants are not always anonymous: Is this a problem? *British Journal of Educational Technology*, *45*(3), 428-437.

Enda, J., & Mitchell, A. (2013). Friends and family—Important drivers of news. *The Pew Research Center's Project for Excellence in News Journalism*. Retrieved from http://www.stateofthemedia.org/2013/special-reports-landing-page/friends-and-family-important-drivers-of-news

Fisher, E. (2015). "You media": Audiencing as marketing in social media. *Media, Culture & Society*, *37*(1), 50-67. doi:10.1177/0163443714549088

Fuchs, C. (2010). Labor in informational capitalism and on the internet. *The Information Society*, *26*(3), 179-196. doi:10.1080/01972241003712215

Gauntlett, D. (2011). *Making is connecting: The social meaning of creativity, from DIY and knitting to YouTube and Web 2.0.* Polity Press: Cambridge, UK.

Gehl, R. W. (2015). The case for alternative social media. *Social Media + Society*, *1*(2). doi:10.1177/2056305115604338

Gerlitz, C., & Helmond, A. (2013). The like economy: Social buttons and the data-intensive web. *New Media & Society*, *15*(8), 1348-1365. doi:10.1177/1461444812472322

Gillespie, T. (2015). Platforms Intervene. *Social Media + Society*, *1*(1-2). doi:10.1177/2056305115580479

Gruzd, A., Wellman, B., & Takhteyev, Y. (2011). Imagining Twitter as an Imagined community. *American Behavioral Scientist*, *55*(10), 1294-1318. doi:10.1177/0002764211409378

Heinonen, A. (2011). The journalist's relationship with users: New dimensions to conventional roles. In J. B. Singer, D. Domingo, A. Hermida, A. Heinonen, S. Paulussen, T. Quandt, . . . M. Vujnovic (Eds.), *Participatory journalism: Guarding open gates at online newspapers* (pp. 34-56). Chichester, UK: Wiley-Blackwell.

Helmond, A. (2015). The Platformization of the web: Making web data platform ready. *Social Media + Society*, *1*(2). doi:10.1177/2056305115603080

Henderson, M., Johnson, N. F., & Auld, G. (2013). Silences of ethical practise: Dilemmas for researchers using socila media. *Educational Research and Evaluation*, *19*(6), 546-560.

Hermida, A., Fletcher, F., Korrell, D., & Logan, D. (2012). Share, like, recommend: Decoding the social media news consumer. *Journalism Studies*, *13*(5-6), 815-824.

Jenkins, H. (2006). *Convergence culture*. New York: NYU Press.

Jenkins, H., Ford, S., & Green, J. (2013). *Spreadable media: Creating value and meaning in a networked culture*. New York: New York University Press.

John, N. A. (2013). The Social logics of sharing. *The Communication Review*, *16*(3), 113-131. doi:10.1080/10714421.2013.807119

Jönsson, A. M., & Örnebring, H. (2011). User-generated content and the news: Empowerment of citizens or interactive illusion? *Journalism Practice*, *5*(2), 127-144. doi:10.1080/17512786.2010.501155

Karppi, T. (2014). *Disconnect.Me: User engagement and Facebook*. Turku: University of Turku.

Langlois, G. (2014). *Meaning in the age of social media*. New York: Palgrave Macmillan.

Langlois, G., & Elmer, G. (2013). The research politics of social media platforms. *Culture Machine*, *14*, 1-17.

Lessig, L. (2001). *The future of ideas: The fate of the commons in a connected world*. New York: Random House.

Livingstone, S. (2005). People living in the new media age: Rethinking "audiences" and "users". In *New approaches to research on the social implications of emerging technologies*. UK: Oxford Internet Institute.

Markham, A. N. (2013). Fieldwork in Social media what would malinowski do? *Qualitative Communication Research*, *2*(4), 434-446. doi:10.1525/qcr.2013.2.4.434.434

Markham, A. N., & Buchanan, E. (2012). *Ethical decision–making and internet research: Recommendations from the AoIR ethics working committee*. Retrieved from http://aoir.org/reports/ethics2.pdf

Marshall, D. P. (2009). New media as transformed media industry. In J. Holt & A. Perren (Eds.), *Media industries: History, Theory, and method* (pp. 81-89). Chichester, UK: Wiley-Blackwell.

Matikainen, J. (2015). Motivations for content generation in social media. *Participations: Journal of Audience & Reception Studies*, *12*(1), 41-58.

Merrin, W. (2009). Media Studies 2.0: Upgrading and open–sourcing the discipline. *Interactions: Studies in Communication and Culture*, *1*(1), 17-34. doi:10.1386/iscc.1.1.17/1

Napoli, P. M. (2010). Revisiting "mass communication" and the "work" of the audience in the new media environment. *Media, Culture & Society*, *32*(3), 505-516. doi:10.1177/0163443710361658

Netzer, Y., Tenenboim-Weinblatt, K., & Shifman, L. (2014). The construction of participation in news websites: A five–dimensional model. *Journalism Studies*, *15*(5), 619-631. doi:10.1080/1461670X.2014.895527

Newman, N., & Levy, D. A. L. (2013). Reuters institute digital news report 2013: Tracking the future of news. *Reuters Institute for the Study of Journalism*. UK: University of Oxford.

Newman, N., & Levy, D. A. L. (2014). Reuters institute digital news report 2014: Tracking the future of news. *Reuters Institute for the Study of Journalism*. UK: University of Oxford.

Noguera Vivo, J. M., Villi, M., Nyirő, N., de Blasio, E., & Bourdaa, M. (2013). The role of the media industry when participation is a product. In N. Carpentier, K. C. Schrøder, & L. Hallet (Eds.), *Audience Transformations: Shifting audience positions in late modernity* (pp. 172-190). New York: Routledge.

Olsson, T. (2010). From the ecology of broadcasting to the ecology of participation critical reflections. *Nordicom Review*, (2-3), 95-104.

Ramaswamy, V., & Gouillart, F. (2010). *The power of co-creation*. New York: Free Press.

Rieder, B., Abdulla, R., Poell, T., Woltering, R., & Zack, L. (2015). Data critique and analytical opportunities for very large Facebook Pages: Lessons learned from exploring "we are all Khaled Said." *Big Data & Society*, *2*(2). doi:10.1177/2053951715614980

Schäfer, M. T. (2011). *Bastard culture! How user participation transforms cultural production. culture.* Amsterdam: Amsterdam University Press.

Singer, J. B. (2014). User–generated visibility: Secondary gatekeeping in a shared media space. *New Media & Society*, *16*(1), 55-73. doi:10.1177/1461444813477833

Singer, J. B., Domingo, D., Hermida, A., Heinonen, A., Paulussen, S., Quandt, T., . . . Vujnovic, M. (2011). *Participatory journalism: Guarding open gates at online newspapers*. Chichester, UK: Wiley-Blackwell.

Smythe, D. W. (1977). Communications: Blindspot of Western marxism. *Canadian Journal of Political and Social Theory*, *1*(3), 1-27.

Sormanen, N., Rohila, J., Lauk, E., Uskali, T., Jouhki, J., & Penttinen, M. (2016). Chances and challenges of computational data gathering and analysis. *Digital Journalism*, *4*(1), 55-74. doi:10.1080/21670811.2015.1096614

Sveningsson Elm, M. (2009). How do various notions of privacy influence decisions in qualitative Internet research? In A. N. Markham & N. K. Baym (Eds.), *Internet inquiry: Conversations about method*. Los Angeles: Sage.

Terranova, T. (2004). *Network culture*. London: Pluto Press.

van Dijck, J. (2009). Users like you? Theorizing agency in user-generated content. *Media, Culture & Society*,

31(1), 41-58. doi:10.1177/0163443708098245

van Dijck, J. (2013). *The culture of connectivity: A critical history of social media*. Oxford: Oxford University Press.

van Dijck, J., & Nieborg, D. (2009). Wikinomics and its discontents: A critical analysis of Web 2.0 business manifestos. *New Media & Society*, *11*(5), 855-874. doi:10.1177/1461444809105356

van Dijck, J., & Poell, T. (2013). Understanding social media logic. *Media and Communication*, *1*(1), 2-14. doi:10.12924/mac2013.01010002

Villi, M. (2012). Social curation in audience communities: UDC (User-distributed content) in the networked media ecosystem. *Participations: The International Journal of Audience and Reception Studies*, *9*(2), 614-632.

Villi, M., & Matikainen, J. (2015). Mobile UDC: Online media content distribution among Finnish mobile Internet users. *Mobile Media & Communication*, *3*(2), 214-229. doi:10.1177/2050157914552156

Villi, M., Moisander, J., & Joy, A. (2012). Social curation in consumer communities: Consumers as curators of online media content. *Advances in Consumer Research*, *40*, 490-495.

Weller, K. (2015). Accepting the challenges of social media research. *Online Information Review*, *39*(3), 281-289. doi:10.1108/OIR-03-2015-0069

Wittel, A. (2011). Qualities of sharing and their transformations in the digital age. *International Review of Information Ethics*, *15*, 3-8. Retrieved from http://www.i-r-i-e.net/inhalt/015/015-Wittel.pdf

5

Free Software Beyond Radical Politics: Negotiations of Creative and Craft Autonomy in Digital Visual Media Production

Julia Velkova

Department of Media and Communication Studies, Södertörn University, 14189 Huddinge, Sweden;
E-Mail: julia.velkova@sh.se

Abstract

Free software development and the technological practices of hackers have been broadly recognised as fundamental for the formation of political cultures that foster democracy in the digital mediascape. This article explores the role of free software in the practices of digital artists, animators and technicians who work in various roles for the contemporary digital visual media industries. Rather than discussing it as a model of organising work, the study conceives free software as a production tool and shows how it becomes a locus of politics about finding material security in flexible capitalism. This politics is ultimately contradictory in that it extends creative and craft autonomy of digital artists but does not mobilise a critical project. Instead, it nurtures further precarious labour. Empirically, the article draws on ethnographically collected material from the media practices of digital artists and programmers who engage with two popular free software production tools, Blender and Synfig.

Keywords

Blender; craft autonomy; F/OSS; media tools; material politics; media industries; open source software; post-Fordism; Synfig

Issue

This article is part of the issue "Political Agency in the Digital Age: Media, Participation and Democracy", edited by Anne Kaun (Södertörn University, Sweden), Maria Kyriakidou (University of East Anglia, UK) and Julie Uldam (Roskilde University, Denmark).

---

1. Introduction

Media practices, such as free and open source software development, and the technological experiments of hackers have been broadly recognised as fundamental for the formation of political cultures that foster democracy in the digital mediascape. Their relevance for political agency today is expressed through the ability of actors who take part in these practices to reconfigure 'the material politics of cultural action' (Coleman, 2013, p. 185), primarily through introducing new 'entities' into the world (Söderberg, 2011, p. 23), and by making them public (Kelty, 2008). These entities can range from material objects that take the form of open hardware, such as self-made 3D printers (Söderberg, 2014), through writing an independent operating system (Coleman, 2013; Kelty, 2008), creating alternative institutions for intellectual property rights management, to experimenting with digital aesthetics and critical art projects (Morgan, 2013). In all these cases, politics is practised primarily through creatively engaging with building, modifying and maintaining technological equipment, an activity that resembles both public demonstrations of technical expertise and a way of arguing about technology with and through it (Kelty, 2008; Kubitschko, 2015).

Occasionally, the public entities and institutions that are brought to the world can inspire broader social groups to repurpose them for other goals and embed them in other practices, imbuing them with other meaning. Such cultural 'modulations' (Kelty, 2008, p. 242ff) of free software often represent forms of criticism, such as in the case of Indymedia, to make a case for alternative journalism (Atton, 2007; Lievrouw,

2011), its use by the open data movement (Baack, 2015), its use for creating alternative social media networks (Gehl, 2015) and the emergence of the Creative Commons licences for open cultural production (Coleman, 2013, p. 197ff). Free software also plays an important role among artistic minorities as a way to develop criticism of dominant regimes of ownership over digital 'materials', i.e. software used to make visual media (Morgan, 2013).

Despite the richness and importance of these studies, one of their limitations has been their focus on the uses of free software predominantly for political activism by social movements and creative minorities. However, free and open source software has also come to be increasingly integrated in the practices of corporate technological manufacturers like IBM, Google and Hollywood computer graphics giants Disney and Pixar. With regards to these developments, Kelty (2013) suggests that corporate use of free software threatens to make its critical potential 'sterile' by being equally easily put to use to mobilise counter-critical power that strengthens monopolies rather than to criticise them. At individual level, free software could also be used instrumentally for technical career advancement: 'for a great many software developers, toiling as they do in the richer veins of freelance precarity, it meant not having to rebuild the same damn thing over and over again with every upward career move' (Kelty, 2013). Kelty concludes that 'As open source becomes an instrumentalized kind of politics, the possibility of new beginnings fades'. Thus, the critical potential offered by free software seems to simultaneously flourish among activists, and get neutralised by its use in the media industries, converting it into a motor for new models of value creation (Barron, 2013).

This article seeks to broaden the scope of knowledge about the role of free software in the politics of digital media production by discussing its relevance for other actors, beyond activists, hackers or large media corporations. In particular it explores its value, use and development among computer graphics artists, designers and animators who work in a wide range of roles at small advertising agencies, visual effects and computer game and film production companies for the contemporary digital media industries, while occasionally engaging in projects on free culture and independent film making.

The material for this study comes from a large research project on the media practices of two free software computer graphics communities: those formed around the programs Blender for 3D animation and Synfig for 2D animation. The data has been collected through multi-sited ethnography and qualitative interviews with 35 visual media artists and developers. They were held between 2013 and 2015 and documented the use of these two programs for, predominantly, open and free cultural production (see Velkova, in press). As the large research project progressed, however, it became clear that the same producers who engage, for payment, in open cultural production and free software development also work in different roles for the media industries where they put the same media production tools to use. Some have worked on large projects such as the LEGO movie or Pixar's short films or for Rovio, who own the Angry Birds franchise. Others work for advertising agencies across Europe, develop animation for educational projects, or create independent and free culture films. Oscillating between two supposedly antagonistic fields of media production, by having a relation to the industries and to free culture projects, the empirical material that underpins this article represents a fruitful starting point to explore the broader value of free software as a media production tool beyond its uses for radical politics.

The approach I take here is to first briefly outline the work context in flexible capitalism using the overarching framework of Boltanski and Chiapello (2007) on the moral justifications that motivate society to engage in the ideology of capitalism. I then apply a narrow focus on digital media production and draw on Howard Becker's work on 'Art Worlds' (1982/2008) in order to discuss the role of materiality in creative practice, which I connect to the conditions of producing media in flexible capitalism.

The argument developed here is that free software for visual media production is conceived by media creators as a form of material capital that represents a source of creative emancipation and security in relation to their creative practice in the highly competitive media production environment. These forms of empowerment, however, are not mobilised to serve a broader critical political project, but represent individual pragmatic strategies to extend digital artists' creative autonomy in the media industries or establish links of equivalence with them while nurturing further precarity.

2. Media Production and Free Software in the New Spirit of Capitalism

Digital visual media production takes place today to a large extent in the context of post-Fordist work frameworks that promote 'creativity, reactivity and flexibility' (Boltanski & Chiapello, 2007, p. 90) as core cultural values. In their seminal work on the transformations of capitalism between 1960 and 1990, Luc Boltanski and Eve Chiapello advance the thesis that these values are not universal but rather manifestations of a new 'spirit' of capitalism. By 'spirit' they refer to a set of normative and moral rules that justify society's engagement in capitalism. These rules need to offer a promise of some form of autonomy and security for individuals while serving the common good. In terms of autonomy, Boltanski and Chiapello argue that there should exist an incentive for people to engage in the process of accumulation even if they will not necessarily enjoy the main benefits of it. Individuals also need to feel some form of security for themselves and their children, while participation in accumulation needs to be justified as serving 'the common good which contributes to producing for everyone' (p. 8) and being just.

The transition to post-Fordism in the 1980s and 1990s is regarded by Boltanski and Chiapello as a specific point in capitalism when its justification apparatus is radically redefined. In terms of autonomy, the core values become 'the development of oneself and one's employability' (p. 111). The former emerges through the paradigm of constant improvement of skills, reputation, being adaptable, self-organised, and participate in novel and exciting projects. To become employable, workers need to know how to engage in a project and to remain 'adaptable, physically and intellectually mobile' (p. 112). Enhanced by networked communications, qualities such as flexibility and adaptability are argued to emerge from *activity* and *autonomy*, rather than from obedience and belonging to hierarchical structures. In this way, personal development as an option for 'everybody' serves the ideal of the common good, while contributing to broader processes of value production and its accumulation.

This spirit is particularly identifiable in the contemporary media industries and in the debates about autonomy and control of media work. These industries carry a strong allure for young people and creators promising work of greater social status, autonomy, personal expression, flexibility and self-actualisation (Mayer, 2014). To stimulate their employees' creativity, many media companies adopt an anti-corporate work culture and on occasions enable creators to develop a reputation of being an 'auteur' (Deuze, Martin, & Allen, 2007), a celebrity (Hesmondhalgh, 2009), or a person with broader public recognition (Mayer, 2014). At the same time, the organisational frameworks of production are dependent on constant rationalisation of labour in order to accelerate production and reduce costs, thus constraining the autonomy of creators and adjusting it to market demands. They do so by, first, transferring ever greater responsibility for personal artistic and technical skill development to individual creators and, second, by embedding creators in institutions of employment and regulatory systems of intellectual property that detach creators from their creations, converting their labour into an object of value extraction (Deuze, 2007; Huws, 2014; Stahl, 2010). In the latter context, free software development has been acknowledged to have a potential to bring change in terms of offering more efficient and less alienating ways of organising and managing media production (Benkler, 2006). These alternatives have nonetheless been questioned in terms of their financial viability (Hesmondhalgh & Baker, 2010) and placed free software in the context of the free labour debates (Terranova, 2004), two issues that I have engaged with and nuanced extensively elsewhere (Velkova & Jakobsson, 2015).

In the context of digital media production, free labour has been discussed largely in terms of the unpaid work that media users perform by producing content in various online contexts, work that is valorised by the media industries (see for example Bolin, 2012; Hesmondhalgh, 2010; van Dijck, 2009). However, unpaid work has always been integral to certain spheres such as those of social reproduction (Jarrett, 2016) or cultural production (Hesmondhalgh, 2010, p. 277). In these spheres, free labour can be regarded not only in terms of paid or unpaid, but also as good and bad, just and unjust (Hesmondhalgh & Baker, 2010). For example, the internship systems in the media industries today are largely unjust, but unpaid labour as such has always been part of the process of developing skills, ranging from learning to play music instruments to programming, computer graphics and game development (Hesmondhalgh, 2010). Rather than being unjust, the latter forms of free labour stem from the dependency of cultural production on materiality and are addressed in part by Howard Becker (1982/2008) in his work on the sociology of art production. I will discuss this dependency later.

Free software producers are also able to engage in the valorisation of their products (Velkova & Jakobsson, 2015), something which, as Barron (2013) shows, has transformed it from a critical practice to a distilled form of the 'spirit' of contemporary capitalism. Converting technology into global software commons, free software enables autonomy and project mobility for everyone, serving the common good. What it falls short of, Barron concludes, is to guarantee security to those who engage in its development, thus paving the way for new forms of criticism.

Indeed, security is what Boltanski and Chiapello dismiss as the new 'spirit' of capitalism not offering enough solutions to. The main security that projects or companies can offer to individuals today is development of personal capital that could help employability in future projects and initiatives.

However, as I will argue, free software could represent a specific form of security, that of *material security*, that enables media creators who engage in using and developing it to also gain a form of creative autonomy, namely craft autonomy. In order to understand how this happens, we need to take a different perspective on free software and approach it as a *media production tool* rather than a *model of organising work*. This article therefore continues by exploring more deeply the relationship between technology and digital media creators rather than that between individuals and the broader organisational structures of media production.

3. Materials for Media Production

Employability and participation in media projects is largely predicated on the creativity and technical skills of creators, whose practice in turn develops in relation to the materials, or tools, available to them. In the current 'spirit' of flexible capitalism, media creators need to be adaptable and flexible not only in relation to the organisations or projects that they work on; their possibility to sell their work or develop criticism also depends on the flexibility and creative autonomy that the technologies they work with can offer them.

From this perspective, creators of media are not only integrated in structures of employment, nation state politics, or networks of peers, but also in the specific logics of technology with which they interact daily and in which they are embedded at multiple levels. The sociology of art proposed by Howard Becker (1982/2008) offers some insights into how to understand these entanglements in relation to creative autonomy. In his discussion of art as collective action, Becker emphasises that creators' choice of materials affects the work they do (p. 71). Materiality forms a crucial part of the production of artistic works:

> "Musical instruments, paints and canvas, dancers' shoes and costumes, cameras and film—all these have to be made and made available to the people who use them to produce art works." (Becker, 1982/2008, p. 3)

In the case of producing specialised media, e.g. digital visual media, creators need materials that are designed and manufactured specifically for them. Becker argues that since the manufacturing of specialised items is so technical a specialty, the artists who use them cannot in most cases produce the items themselves. Despite the fact that manufacturers try to be sensitive to the needs of the creators of a particular medium, they may fail to satisfy those who try to innovate in the medium: 'How much conventional materials constrain an artist depends on how monopolistic the market is', he argues (p. 73). Through this argument Becker establishes a link between technical innovation, creative autonomy and the frameworks of creation and distribution of materials. The fewer manufacturers that dominate the market, he argues, the more insensitive they become to what artistic minorities want or need. Occasionally, artistic minorities can revert to the craft of making their own materials, or of customising existing ones if faced with the threat of discontinuing the material against which creators have developed their skill, if they want more than the available materials can provide or if materials to satisfy a creative impulse are not available (Becker, 1982/2008, p. 71ff)

It is in this context, and rather pragmatic considerations about individual strategies to develop creative practice, that free software emerges as a tool of high value among media professionals, digital artists and aspiring media workers. The next section substantiates this point through a discussion of the emergence of two popular free software tools for computer graphics production, Blender and Synfig.

4. Crafting Technical Autonomy: The Blender and Synfig Free Software Projects

The free software discussed here, Blender for 3D animation and sculpting and Synfig for 2D vector animation, were conceived as digital tools that would enable their creators to exercise a greater degree of craftsmanship, innovation and autonomy in the medium. They also represent the free software alternatives for professional animation production to programs such as 3D Studio Max, Adobe After Effects, Anime Studio and Maya.

The 3D animation software Blender and the 2D Synfig were initiated by two industrial designers, one living in Europe and the other in the US, who had ambitions to make large-scale independent animation projects of Hollywood class. Despite having notable differences in their focus of specialisation, and being incepted at different points of time, with Blender having its roots in the late 1980s and Synfig in the mid-1990s, both were conceived as in-house programs developed within two small commercial animation studios. After facing bankruptcy in the early 2000s, both projects emerged as free software through very particular processes of de-commodification (Velkova & Jakobsson, 2015).

In the case of Blender, the need to start developing an independent program emerged from the ambition of its creator, Ton Roosendaal, to align with the industrial practices of 3D technological development:

> "3D is specialist...it is so specialist....any big studio who does animation—or visual effects—they depend for the most of it on their own, in-house software development. They are not going to buy all their applications—and even when they buy some stuff, they want to have the code. Because they can't depend on a software, submit a bug, then wait for two weeks for a bug fix to come in while a thousand people are waiting, right? That's kind of... at that level your IT, your information systems have to be under control...." (Ton Roosendaal, interview, 2014)

Blender emerged from its author's desire to have complete control over the development, changes to and possible extensions of a computer program, 'a digital tool' that would enable its creator to adapt it and mould it to his own creative ambitions.

Until the mid-1990s, software for computer graphics development was distributed as an add-on to very expensive hardware that media creators anyway needed to invest in. The computer industry restructured in the late 1990s. With computing power becoming cheaper and more ubiquitous, companies began developing business models around selling, and more recently renting specialised software for computer graphics production. The changes in the politics of distribution of software for computer graphics production have been experienced as constraining creativity, experimentation and large-scale projects by small studios and individual digital artists:

> "[In the 1990s] the hardware cost money, but once you had it, you could do anything—we were getting CDs with Silicon Graphics code! It was proprietary stuff, but it didn't prevent us from making things with it....Computer graphics is about openness, because you can build on everyone else's developments. Once you get a patent or close it—people find a way around it." (notes from informal conversation with Ton Roosendaal, May 2015)

Hence, the experiences of material constraints to continue experimenting with computer graphics led Blender's creator to find a way round them by relicensing his program as free software as a strategy to retain technological and creative independence and let the program grow by allowing other digital artists to contribute to it:

> "open source is about developing your own software. So the best model [to develop computer graphics]....OK, not the best, the Blender open source model is the in-house software model." (Ton Roosendaal, interview, August 2014)

Similar concerns drove the development of Synfig. Its founder Robert Quattlebaum wanted to rationalise one of the most laborious tasks in 2D animation creation, tweening, and adapt the software to his own creative ambitions:

> "Our goal was to write a tool that could be used for the production of feature-film quality 2D animation....In traditional animation, the senior animators use the storyboards to create the keyframes for each shot. The junior animators then use these keyframes as guides for making all of the frames in between—which is called tweening. Tweening is a time-consuming and labour-intensive (and thus expensive) process. However, it is also rather mechanical. So that was the original idea from day one—the elimination of the tweening process... While Synfig has been used in production, the animators using it had the benefit of having the primary developer sitting behind them. That counts for a lot." (OS News, 2006)

After its de-commodification in the mid-2000s, and conversion into a free software project, Synfig's development was driven forward primarily by one self-taught animator, Konstantin Dmitriev, from the city of Gorno-Altaysk in Southern Siberia, Russia. For him, Synfig, represented a technology that with some further development could fulfil his creative idea of making a large-scale independent feature-length animation film.

In search of style, his work had begun with proprietary programs such as 3D Studio Max but after some time he experienced a limitation in scale: 'the more I complicated a scene, the less controllable it became...', he explained. Facing in this way a constraint to innovate in the medium, instead of trying to adapt his practice to the technical limitations of the tool, he switched to experimenting with free software as a way to adjust technology to the scale of his creative ideas. Initially he tested Blender, an experience which he describes as largely affective:

> "What shocked me in Blender the first time I used it was that it had layers...layers existed in many other types of programs at that time, but not in 3D...this was so daring, to do layers in a 3D program, I had never seen such a thing before." (Konstantin, interview, January 2015)

While improving his skills in Blender, Konstantin also specialised in 2D animation in parallel with using proprietary programs until their development frameworks collided with his own work process. The manufacturer of the 2D animation program Moho discontinued its development under Linux, which had gradually become Konstantin's main platform. The impossibility to use this software as a production tool caused him great anxiety:

> "I liked the fact that everything (in Moho) was under my control. But nobody was supporting it...then I realised what dependencies proprietary software was creating. It is not about the cost, it is about the dependency." (Konstantin, interview, November 2014)

Since then he has focused his efforts on studying and developing the free software Synfig, which he integrated at the core of his creative practice, and multiple projects ranging from free-lancing work to education and independent free culture production (Velkova, 2014).

Both Konstantin's and Ton's choices to invest their time in developing Synfig and Blender respectively emerged out of explicitly pragmatic concerns related to the possibilities to create within frameworks of their own making and under their own control. This form of engagement with technology has been referred to, in the contexts of free software development and hacker cultures, as forms of establishing 'craft autonomy' (Coleman, 2016), one that fosters skill and expertise, but also sensibilities similar to pre-industrial, craft-like engagement with technology. The emergence of these two programs for visual media production is also an indication that constraints to creativity imposed by the politics of creation and distribution of media production tools continue to be a topic of high concern even in digital media contexts, and lead to reactions similar to those that have always been historically present in artistic practice (see Becker 1982/2008, pp. 71-77).

Despite the freedom of creative expression which developing autonomous media production tools granted to their creators, it also constrained their autonomy in new ways. In order to fulfil their ideas they needed to motivate more people to adopt these technologies and contribute to the free software projects in order to let them grow in functionality. Both Blender and Synfig faced the problem that, instead of developing art projects, they needed to develop frameworks to train or convince other people to use these technologies. As Becker (1982/2008, p. 74) points out, when creators go about developing their own materials, they need to spend time in developing their material precursors and knowledge frameworks instead of working on making art. There is no space in this article to discuss in detail the strategies employed in these cases, but for the present argument it is enough to say that Blender succeeded in creating a large user base on a greater scale than Synfig and is today embraced to a greater extent by animators, digital artists and technical artists who use it for a broad range of purposes. Uses range from experimental concept art projects through developing 3D printing models to experiments with novel forms of artistic collaboration; from open culture projects to the production of special effects, games, animation, and simulations for the media industries.

The variety of uses which it finds implies that the public nature of free software represents a source of value and craft autonomy for a broad range of actors and purposes. The next section discusses three main ways in which digital media artists find meaning in these tools and illustrates how they reconcile craft and creative autonomy with efficiency, independence, ultimately securing *materially* their creativity.

5. Sensibilities of Craft

Every media creator has a unique work process. The more creators develop their skill, the stronger the connection established to the tools they use, as this skill is shaped through practice which is anchored in the materialities of technologies, even in the case of digital ones.

French free-lancing illustrator and digital comic artist David Revoy recalls how he used to work with proprietary digital production tools such as Corel Painter, Manga Studio, Photoshop Elements and CS2. After upgrading to a newer computer and a newer version of a proprietary operating system, all these tools stopped working: 'I had to do a lot of horrible hack to make all my software run on it, but it wasn't [as] stable as it was on Xp anymore. I had to reboot almost twice a day' (Revoy, 2013). From a tool that automates and mediates creative expression, media production software can become an artifact with 'agential' (Paasonen, 2015) properties that may, for a time, leave the user powerless. Faced with the choice of either re-purchasing all his programs to match the new operating system and hardware, reverting to the older computer and operating system, or doing something completely different, Revoy (2013) chose to move to free software: 'I thought all of this circus couldn't work in the long term and wasn't happy.... I switched my machine to a full open-source system around 2009...thinking open-source could work on the long term.'

The result of this move was not explained in terms of economic gains, but in the qualitative difference related to a new degree of creative autonomy and security gained in relation to technology:

> "I really like the independence I get from it: I can install it on laptops, every machine, upgrade, downgrade, fine-tune it. This independence is gold. The con is that I'm now dependent on 'Linux' compatible [hardware]. Which is not easy to find and not well documented." (Revoy, 2013)

If, for David, free software was initially a way to reduce his material and creative dependency from technological frameworks out of his control, for other media producers switching to free software has been a way to increase their work efficiency.

Hjalti, an animator from Iceland who has worked for many years in the advertising industry, encountered Blender by chance after many years of using the popular package 3D Studio Max. He adopted Blender in his practice out of a desire to collaborate on a commercial campaign with a colleague of his who had it as a tool of his choice. He discusses his initial experience of learning Blender as an agony that has been worth it:

> "I was throwing my keyboard at the screen for the first couple of weeks or whatever, but once you get over it you start to realise why it makes sense. Why pressing G is already moving an object...instead of like having a widget that you press on...it's because it's faster. It just cuts a lot of steps out of the way. Which adds up. So you start doing things a little faster. And smoother. And then of course you can customise everything you want now after Blender 2.5. Which I do, a lot." (Hjalti, animator, interview, August 2014)

Later versions of Blender and Hjalti becoming more experienced with it allowed him to adapt it to his own work process in a way that increased his working speed. In practice this meant adjusting small details, such as the position of his hands which he wanted to keep static while working. Until moving to Blender, whenever he needed to change perspectives on the screen while animating, the program interface would require him to move his hand to the keypad on the right side of his keyboard. He experienced this as a constraint to be efficient:

"I am doing it every 10 seconds. And take one second to let go of my mouse, I am losing valuable time, you know, after 15 hours or whatever...and it also breaks your concentration. Because your eye, your thought process has to go into that motion instead of just keeping going, doing what you are supposed to be doing." (Hjalti, animator, interview, August 2014)

After version 2.5 of Blender it was easier for its users to customise their work processes to a great degree. Hjalti used this possibility to assign his own commands in such a way that he would no longer need to move his hands away from the keyboard while working. Such a seemingly minor detail was very important for him as regards experiencing a sense of craft:

"That's when it becomes really beautiful. When the tool itself doesn't become a hurdle, you are just doing something and it's an extension of you....So you can do something, you can adjust something, it's intuitive. It is muscle memory. Which is really awesome." (Hjalti, animator, interview, August 2014)

This example shows how free software as a production tool is conductive to frameworks of rationalising production, and personal skill development while maintaining a strong sense of autonomy among its users. This combination ultimately gives a competitive advantage in the media industries' labour market. Of course, possibilities for customisation exist in other software too yet, in line with Becker's argument about the constraints of materials, the limits to which free software allows creators to adapt technology to their everyday practice depends more on individual technical skill and creative ideas than on the production frameworks and affordances set by software manufacturers.

Besides reducing dependencies and increasing efficiency, many digital artists value free software for its infinite adaptability and extensibility. In the spring of 2014, a free-lancing animator and a technical artist from Costa Rica worked on a 4-second shot for the teaser for a larger free culture animation film project. The shot was supposed to show a green caterpillar blinking. The animator wanted the caterpillar's pupils to resemble the facial features of the main character in the animation film. They were using Blender for this production task and found that it did not have the technical capacity to animate the desired effect. The technical artist came up with a concept for how the problem could be solved and delved into the program code: 'I started hacking a python script to automate this ^_^. At about 3:00am it actually worked!'. He shared the script and the technical details online with the following comment:

"Beware it's a production script and as such it doesn't have a nice UI or anything and you might need to change a couple of names in the first few lines :)." (Salazar, 2014)

In this case, the animation process was very similar to hacking. Hackers, artists and free software developers have come to be described as 'craftspeople' who have resisted the general decline of craft in the Western that came with the dominance of Fordist styles of production (Coleman, 2016).

A common metaphor frequently used among the digital artists who were interviewed was to compare working with free software to the work of painters from pre-industrial craft production: 'It is more like the old painters who made their paint themselves. Mixing the ingredients and building their paint themselves', Timothée Giet, a comic illustrator explained. In these cases, the possibilities to craft and mould their own tools blur the separation between art and craft, techne and poiesis:

"Free software matches very good with the artistic idea because no artist wants to be locked into what they can do—a lot of the process of making art is about making the tools." (Bassam, animation director, archived blog post, 2014)

The above examples illustrate how free software strengthens feelings of creative autonomy in their users by being flexible and adaptable to individual needs for creativity, efficiency and material independence. In their totality, these experiences construct free software as a source of individual material security and capital that allows digital artists to gain competitive creative advantage in the post-Fordist media industry frameworks. With the increased transfer of responsibility over skills development to individual media creators, the choice of technology becomes an investment that can increase media producers' mobility and employability in different projects. At the same time, while free software stimulates a craft-like engagement with technology, it illuminates how the values of personal self-development, flexibility and security of the new 'spirit' of capitalism become embedded in digital artists' technological choices. The problem to which the latter leads is that the security and autonomy that controlling and extending free software digital tools gives may decrease criticism of some problematic aspects of the post-Fordist production frameworks, e.g. precarity of labour. As the next section will show, while digital artists strengthen their creativity and material security through free software, they further nurture precarity of work.

6. Tools Development as a Source of Precarity

Once digital artists identify free software as tools of value to them, they employ different strategies to attempt to further shape and adapt the programs to their individual needs. Those artists who are unable to code (and they constitute a majority), or do not want to dedicate time to code, resort to financial and rhetorical means to convince programmers to do the work for them. Below I discuss three dominant ways in which this can happen.

6.1. Hiring a Developer

The technical possibility to extend Blender for other purposes than those intended by its original creator emerged from a technical artist's need to rationalise his process of work at a wealthy media production company. He attempted to find a less costly and more flexible alternative to a professional 3D program that could satisfy the production needs of the company: 'I got Blender and I started extending it', he remembers. He admits that his programming skills were not good, so he hired a programmer from Canada to come to Australia to do the extension for him:

> "Well, no, I didn't know how to program, like—I was, I was artist, so—I was OK, making stuff with the mouse. But I knew some programmers so I got them to program...I hired them to program. I had one of the Blender developers come over to my house, doing internship with me, so I got him to program so it was like—the artist and developer thing happening." (technical artist, interview, 2014)

The functional extensions made at that time entered the core of Blender and made it possible for other artists to further develop the program. While representing a contribution to the common good, the possibility that free software opens for an artist to hire a developer changes the artist's status. From being a wage-earner who sells his or her work to the industry, the artist can become an employer who creates small, temporary jobs for programmers. By offering programmers temporary projects, digital artists mirror the frameworks of the media industries by outsourcing jobs with the promise of personal development, employability and a wage, for the common good. Hence, while free software represents a source of material security for artists, it becomes a source of work insecurity for developers, further nurturing precarity.

6.2. Becoming a Financial Patron of a Project

Another common strategy used by artists to influence the general direction of free software tools development is to become a financial patron of the project. This can happen by making small donations to the free software projects in order to buy developer time to develop the project in the direction they want.

A free-lancing animator from Sweden who specialises in cut-out animation which he sells to the Nordic advertising and film industries explained how he could make small financial donations to Synfig to push its development in the direction he needed. His principle has been to donate 3-4 per cent of his income from commercial projects to the free software projects he uses, with occasional higher donations in order to set a priority for the development of a specific feature. He remembered during a conversation we had how he once paid a few hundred euros to the project to speed up the development of a specific function in Synfig that he needed in his work for the industry.

This form of exercising influence over the broader technical development of the project turns digital artists into patrons who become connecting links between a media project (be it for the industry or not), the creative visions of an artist and the technical community that can be convinced to prioritise the development of a feature.

6.3. Motivating Developers

When artists do not have financial means to invest in a project, they resort to rhetorical means to motivate a developer to do the job for them for free, an approach that is the driver of major disputes in the communities formed around free software tools.

Digital artists can request features and extensions directly from the programs' main developers. Mobilising rhetoric and prototypes of unfinished media projects in order to illustrate the need to improve software in a particular direction, these interactions become the locus of many tensions and conflicts. In some cases, feature requests are welcomed and fulfilled, but in most cases they are ignored:

> "We get far, far more requests than we even have time to read. Also, these requests vary in quality. People may explain features in detail, which we already have....People ask for very specific stuff...'I'm using Blender for an interactive blah blah and it's draw modes don't work for me because...etc'.... People who use Blender for ten minutes and don't like colour also post..." (Blender developer, interview, December 2014)

This example illustrates the fact that despite gaining a greater technical autonomy, free software makes digital artists deeply embedded in the social dynamics surrounding the maintenance and development of their tools of choice. Those artists who manage to convince the developers of the importance of their request are usually those who are most active in the media industries and have concrete, urgent needs:

> "I was already doing graphics that were watched by millions, and I started falling in love with [Blender] because it is so versatile. And plus I really liked the idea that you could change the program....That's

what sold me on Blender. Wasn't the interface, wasn't the toolset, it was just the fact that you could change it. That made the case that even if you are not happy with it, if you argue for your case well, you can actually get changes to it." (Beorn, animator, interview by BlenderGuru.com, 2014)

Hence, a rhetorical approach anchored in a concrete project for the media industries can become the equivalent of a financial donation as its fulfilment may bring value for a broader range of digital artists while satisfying individual creative demands.

7. Conclusions

The empirical examples discussed in this article show that free software's role in the politics of digital media production should be understood as individual strategies to find material security and extend personal creative and craft autonomy through technological choices. Approaching free software as a tool, rather than as a form of organising work, allowed the degree to which digital media creators' creative autonomy is configured to be illuminated in relation to the affordances, mouldability and degree of control over the programs that they use in their everyday creative practice. The main issues which artists used to struggle with in the past, as described by Becker (1982/2008), such as dependency on materials and the frameworks of their production, changes in the politics of their distributions, and not least, their affordances, remain highly relevant in the contemporary digital mediascape.

Drawing on Becker, the article conceived free software as a strategy to develop one's own materials and independent frameworks of production in response to changes in the political economy of software distribution. In Becker's framework, such an approach has been commonly used by artistic minorities. This article has shown that free software can resemble this approach by becoming relevant for a broader range of users, beyond creative minorities, in particular those working in different roles for the contemporary media industries. Free software as a source of value for digital artists is thus about meaningful, and not ideological, self-realisation (cf Hesmondhalgh & Baker, 2010, p. 180ff). In the new 'spirit' of capitalism that promotes self-development and outsources the responsibility for skill development to media producers, the ability to shape technology according to distinct creative ideas becomes an individual strategy to remain flexible and competitive.

The specific ways in which artists find meaning from using free software as a production tool are in bringing their work to a form of pre-industrial craft, and saturating their work with an attitude described by Peter Dormer as: 'you get the best out of the computer and its software if you are able to drive the tool rather than being driven by it' (Dormer, 1997, p. 146). The senses of craft autonomy developed through free software are, importantly, not mobilised for a broader critical or political project for social change, but are rather pragmatic, rooted in strategies to influence technological development in ways that benefit one's individual work practice. As a consequence, digital artists inscribe further the values of the new 'spirit' of capitalism, embedding them in the free software tools that they use and develop.

Finally, in crafting security and autonomy for themselves, digital artists do not offset some of the negative effects of flexible capitalism, such as the shift of responsibility for skill, personal development and finding work onto individual creators. Rather, their practices further nurture precarity of labour by them becoming employers or patrons of other groups of creative workers, such as hackers and software developers. Further research could fruitfully explore the practice of media workers hiring developers to code functionality for them and study whether such engagements create new hierarchies or forms of exclusion, or whether they are a positive source of pleasure from digital work that enhances autonomy and creativity in the digital media industries.

Acknowledgements

This article has greatly benefitted from the comments and close readings of Patrik Åker, Göran Bolin, Johan Fornäs, Peter Jakobsson and Fredrik Stiernstedt, as well as the two anonymous reviewers. Special thanks go to Paško Bilić and Dina Vozab, the Croatian Sociological Association, as well as the ECREA Doctoral Summer School 2015 for providing me with a platform to develop the first drafts of this contribution.

Conflict of Interests

The author declares no conflict of interests.

References

Atton, C. (2007). Alternative media in practice: The Indymedia network. In K. Coyer, T. Dowmunt, & A. Fountain (Eds.), *The alternative media handbook* (pp. 71-78). New York: Routledge.

Baack, S. (2015). Datafication and empowerment: How the open data movement re-articulates notions of democracy, participation, and journalism. *Big Data & Society*, *2*(2).

Barron, A. (2013). Free software production as critical social practice. *Economy and Society*, *42*(4), 597-625.

Becker, H. S. (2008). *Art worlds*. London: University of California Press. (Original work published 1982)

Benkler, Y. (2006). *The wealth of networks how social production transforms markets and freedom*. New Haven: Yale University Press.

Bolin, G. (2012). The Labour of media use. *Information, Communication & Society*, *15*(6), 796-814.

Boltanski, L., & Chiapello, È. (2007). *The new spirit of capitalism*. London: Verso.

Coleman, G. (2013). *Coding freedom: The ethics and aesthetics of hacking*. Princeton: Princeton University Press.

Coleman, G. (2016). Hackers. In B. Peters (Ed.), *Keywords: A vocabulary of information society and culture*. Princeton: Princeton University Press.

Deuze, M. (2007). *Media work*. Cambridge: Polity.

Deuze, M., Martin, C. B., & Allen, C. (2007). The professional identity of gameworkers. *Convergence: The International Journal of Research into New Media Technologies, 13*(4), 335-353.

Dormer, P. (1997). *The culture of craft: Status and future*. Manchester: Manchester University Press.

Gehl, R. W. (2015). The case for alternative social media. *Social Media + Society, 1*(2), 1-12.

Hesmondhalgh, D. (2009). *The cultural industries* (2nd ed.). Los Angeles: Sage.

Hesmondhalgh, D. (2010). User-generated content, free labour and the cultural industries. *Ephemera, 10*(3/4), 267-284.

Hesmondhalgh, D., & Baker, S. (2010). *Creative labour: Media work in three cultural industries*. Abingdon: Routledge.

Huws, U. (2014). *Labor in the global digital economy: The cybertariat comes of age*. New York: Monthly Review Press.

Jarrett, K. (2016). *Feminism, labour and digital media: The digital housewife*. New York: Routledge.

Kelty, C. M. (2008). *Two bits: The cultural significance of free software*. Durham: Duke University Press.

Kelty, C. M. (2013). There is no free software. *Journal of Peer Production, 3*. Retrieved from http://peerproduction.net/issues/issue-3-free-software-epistemics/debate/there-is-no-free-software

Kubitschko, S. (2015). Hackers' media practices: Demonstrating and articulating expertise as interlocking arrangements. *Convergence: The International Journal of Research into New Media Technologies, 21*(3), 388-402.

Lievrouw, L. A. (2011). *Alternative and activist new media*. Cambridge: Polity.

Mayer, V. (2014). Creative work is still work. *Creative Industries Journal*. doi:10.1080/ 17510694.2014.892286

Morgan, T. (2013). Sharing, hacking, helping: Towards an understanding of digital aesthetics through a survey of digital art practices in Ireland. *Journal of Media Practice, 14*(2), 147-160.

OS News. (2006). Interview with Synfig's Robert Quattlebaum. Retrieved from http://www.osnews.com/story/13241

Paasonen, S. (2015). As networks fail: Affect, technology, and the notion of the user. *Television & New Media, 16*(8), 701-716.

Revoy, D. (2013, May 1). Why I use open-source? Retrieved from http://www.davidrevoy.com/article170/the-choice-of-open-source

Salazar, D. (2014). Caterpillar making of—Animating UVs. Retrieved from https://gooseberry.blender.org/caterpillar-making-of-animating-uvs

Söderberg, J. (2011). *Free software to open hardware: Critical theory on the frontiers of hacking* (Doctoral dissertation). Gothenburg: University of Gothenburg.

Söderberg, J. (2014). The cunning of instrumental reason: Reproducing wealth without money one 3D printer at a time. In J. Söderberg & S. Maxigas (Eds.), *Book of peer production* (pp. 46-58). Gothenburg and Århus: NSU Press.

Stahl, M. (2010). Cultural labor's 'democratic deficits': Employment, autonomy and alienation in US film animation. *Journal for Cultural Research, 14*(3), 271-293.

Terranova, T. (2004). *Network culture: Politics for the information age*. London and Ann Arbor: Pluto Press.

van Dijck, J. (2009). Users like you? Theorizing agency in user-generated content. *Media, Culture & Society, 31*(1), 41-58.

Velkova J. (2014). Two weeks in Siberia with Morevna Project, open-source animation tools, and Animé. Retrieved from http://phd.nordkonst.org/?p=84

Velkova, J. (in press). Ethnography of open cultural production: From participant observation to multi-sited participatory communication. In N. Wildermuth & T. Ngomba (Eds.), *Methodological reflections on researching communication and/for social change*. London: Palgrave Macmillan.

Velkova, J., & Jakobsson P. (2015). At the intersection of commons and market: Negotiations of value in open-sourced cultural production. *International Journal of Cultural Studies, August*, 1-17.

6

Mediatisation, Marginalisation and Disruption in Australian Indigenous Affairs

Kerry McCallum [1,*], Lisa Waller [2] and Tanja Dreher [3]

[1] News and Media Research Centre, Faculty of Arts and Design, University of Canberra, Bruce, ACT 2600, Australia; E-Mail: Kerry.mccallum@canberra.edu.au
[2] Faculty of Arts and Education, Deakin University, Burwood, VIC 3125, Australia; E-Mail: lisa.waller@deakin.edu.au
[3] School of Arts, English and Media, Wollongong University, Wollongong, NSW 2522, Australia; E-Mail: tanjad@uow.edu.au

* Corresponding author

Abstract

This article considers how changing media practices of minority groups and political and media elites impact on democratic participation in national debates. Taking as its case study the state-sponsored campaign to formally recognise Indigenous people in the Australian constitution, the article examines the interrelationships between political media and Indigenous participatory media—both of which we argue are undergoing seismic transformation. Discussion of constitutional reform has tended to focus on debates occurring in forums of influence such as party politics and news media that privilege the voices of only a few high-profile Indigenous media 'stars'. Debate has progressed on the assumption that constitutional change needs to be settled by political elites and then explained and 'sold' to Indigenous and non-Indigenous Australians. Our research on the mediatisation of policymaking has found that in an increasingly media-saturated environment, political leaders and their policy bureaucrats attend to a narrow range of highly publicised voices. But the rapidly changing media environment has disrupted the media-driven *Recognise* campaign. Vigorous public discussion is increasingly taking place outside the mainstream institutions of media and politics, while social media campaigns emerge in rapid response to government decisions. Drawing on a long tradition in citizens' media scholarship we argue that the vibrant, diverse and growing Indigenous media sphere in Australia has increased the accessibility of Indigenous voices challenging the scope and substance of the recognition debate. The article concludes on a cautionary note by considering some tensions in the promise of the changing media for Indigenous participation in the national policy conversation.

Keywords

mediatisation; Indigenous constitutional recognition; Indigenous media; participation; political communication

Issue

This article is part of the issue "Political Agency in the Digital Age: Media, Participation and Democracy", edited by Anne Kaun (Södertörn University, Sweden), Maria Kyriakidou (University of East Anglia, UK) and Julie Uldam (Roskilde University, Denmark).

---

1. Introduction

This article examines the mediatisation of Indigenous politics in Australia. Taking as its case study the state-sponsored campaign to formally recognise Indigenous people in the constitution, the article considers how the changing media practices of both Indigenous people and political and media elites impact on national policy debates. Our concern is the juncture between the mediation of political and policy issues by mainstream institutions of power, primarily established news media organisations, and the 'local' discussion of public affairs that is increasingly taking place through social media. In the media-focused policy process mainstream media continue to play a key role in reporting politics and are closely listened to by the politically powerful. Oppositional voices, such as the growing chorus of Indigenous opinion critiquing the very concept of recognition (Coulthard, 2014; Simpson, 2010), fight to be heard in the intimate relationship between policy and media (Davis, 2016; McCallum & Waller, 2013). At the same time, a changing media environment has enabled new players and platforms to execute political agency and challenge this established dynamic. We argue this has disrupted how political elites manage public debate, and the way public opinion is understood and acted upon.

The mediated political campaign for constitutional recognition provides an ideal lens to examine how processes of mediatisation operate in the context of core debates over national identity. The debate over constitutional recognition takes place in the context of Australia's complex racial history and the ongoing dispossession, colonisation and marginalisation of Indigenous people and communities (see Attwood & Markus, 2007; Davis, 2016; Davis & Williams, 2015; Dodson, 2012). Australia became a federation in 1901 at the height of racist thought and practice, and its constitution was deliberately drafted to exclude and discriminate against Aboriginal and Torres Strait Islander peoples. Australia's most successful referendum occurred in 1967, with 90.77% voting in favour of changing the constitution to enable the Commonwealth to make laws for all Australians and to take account of Aboriginal people in determining the population. Despite being held up as 'an outstanding expression of public sentiment' (Goot & Rowse, 2007, p. 27), since 1967 there have been persistent calls for further reform of the nation's framing document to recognise the status of Indigenous people and remove discriminatory clauses (Davis & Williams, 2015). At the same time a global movement and scholarly critique of the politics of recognition has emerged (e.g. Coulthard, 2014; McNay, 2008; Povinelli, 2002; Simpson, 2010). In the Australian context there have been growing calls to acknowledge unceded sovereignty, land rights and a treaty. Aileen Moreton Robinson stresses ongoing Indigenous sovereignty as fundamental, and welcomes 'a future in which Indigenous sovereignty is formally recognised and we are no longer treated as trespassers in our own lands' (2007, p. xi,). A series of government inquiries and committees have advised on the wording and process of the referendum (Australian Government, 2016), which by 2015 had cross-party support. As a key tenet of contemporary Indigenous politics, the referendum invokes unresolved questions at the very foundation of settler colonial Australia.

In 2015 Prime Minister Abbott oversaw a formal consultative process to bring on the referendum in 2017 to coincide with the 50th anniversary of 1967. This political process operated alongside an advocacy and awareness campaign run by the government-funded organisation Reconciliation Australia (*Recognise*, 2016). Together, these processes essentially took the complexity of settler colonial Australian race relations and reconstructed it as a simple political choice. Constitutional lawyer Megan Davis has observed that the common message from media and government has ignored an important facet of the debate:

> 'The mainstream media, by and large, uncritically report on referendum momentum and mostly obsess over any chinks in the bipartisan order of things. The subjects of recognition are all but erased from the process.' (Davis, 2016, p. 76)

However, the mediatised political campaign was challenged by the underlying multiplicity of views and perspectives on what might be changed by the referendum. Furthermore, by the end of 2015 Australia had a new prime minister, opposition to *Recognise* was increasingly vocal, and the move towards constitutional recognition had all but stalled.

This article builds on an ongoing research project that is investigating how changing media institutions, technologies and practices affect Indigenous participation in public debate (Dreher, McCallum, & Waller, 2016; Waller, Dreher, & McCallum, 2015). Here we consider how the media-related practices of Indigenous affairs policymaking, journalism and Indigenous participatory media intersect in an increasingly fragmented and abundant media environment. We first analyse the mediatised practices of government in the 2015 campaign for constitutional recognition. This is followed by a systematic examination of mainstream news reporting of policy debates and public opinion polls on the recognition issue. Finally, an analysis of social media-driven advocacy opposing or contesting *Recognise* demonstrates the breadth of political discussion and opinion formation taking place outside the dominant spheres of influence. We assess how Indigenous participatory media disrupted the mediatised development of the constitutional recognition campaign and argue that Indigenous resistance via social media had significant, if indirect, implications for policymakers and those seeking to harness public opinion in support of the referendum. Drawing on theories of public opinion, mediatisation and democratic participation, the article offers insights into the relationships between established forums of influence, new entrants to the Australian media landscape and local political engagement in Indigenous affairs.

2. Researching Political Discourse

Our research is broadly located in the fields of political

communication, Indigenous media and social movement studies. We acknowledge our status as non-Indigenous researchers working with the knowledge and innovation of Indigenous media practitioners. We see this article as contributing to our broader research paradigm that works with Indigenous researchers to challenge the colonial mindset and the prevailing discourse of deficit in Indigenous affairs (Fforde, Bamblett, Lovett, Gorringe, & Fogarty, 2013). In this article we emphasise Indigenous innovation in social media and use the mediatisation framework to focus attention, scrutiny, analysis and critique on non-Indigenous institutions and powerful elites.

Responding to criticism that the study of political communication has become too narrowly preoccupied with politics at the centre (Nielsen, 2014), our research approach considers the broad impacts of media on culture and society. We view politics as incorporating the everyday conversations and engagements with politics that take place outside the formal and traditional avenues of politics (Carey, 1975; Gamson, 1992; Tönnies, in Splichal, 1999). Herbst (1998) conceptualised public opinion as a discursive and contingent phenomenon that is constructed over time by the types of technologies and methodologies available for its assessment. In the late 20th century media content and opinion polls became the dominant technologies for 'knowing' public opinion about a topic. Herbst (1998, p. 138) identified a third understanding of public opinion, '...as something located in local community, something sewn into the fabric of interpersonal social networks' (see also Blumer, 1948; Salmon & Glasser, 1995, p. 452). The digital revolution means that 'reading' public opinion is more complex than ever. But we argue it is time to consider the conversations that take place in digital social networks, and their relationships with polls and news content.

In a 'hybrid media system' (Chadwick, 2013) political communication research is well placed to bridge the divide between a still-influential mainstream media and a burgeoning and transformative digital and social media sphere, where media consumption is increasingly individualised, networked and fragmented (Bennett & Iyengar, 2008; Bennett & Segerberg, 2013). This is not to imply news media are no longer important to opinion formation and change. We contend news media's framing of reality is crucial to the way policy issues are communicated in the post-mass media era. Our approach echoes calls for a more nuanced, rather than generalising, approach to political communication research to address the complex questions asked in public discourse, such as those about mediatised Indigenous policy. To that end we focus on three interrelated aspects of public discourse about constitutional reform—mediatised policymaking, news reporting, and oppositional campaigns in social networks—to shed light on the media-related processes of all players in this fundamental issue. We address the following research questions:

1. What were the media-related practices of the Australian government in the campaign for constitutional recognition?
2. What role did institutional news media play in reporting on constitutional recognition?
3. How did Indigenous participatory media engage with and disrupt the constitutional recognition campaign?
4. What are the implications of changing media environments for Indigenous people to engage with mainstream policy and media debates?

To address these questions we developed a project that analysed three bodies of intersecting mediated texts: official government material, news media reports, and Indigenous participatory media discussion. Texts were collected over the 12-month period 1 January to 31 December, 2015, by the chief investigator.

- We first recorded the media-related activities of the Abbott government and the *Recognise* campaign over 2015. We gathered all digitally available reports, media releases and statements emanating from the Department of Prime Minister and Cabinet in relation to constitutional recognition (Australian Government, 2016), as well as promotional material from the *Recognise* website (*Recognise*, 2016);
- Secondly, we mapped the dominant topics, themes, voices and media practices evident in news media coverage of constitutional recognition. Our dataset included 200 national news and opinion texts reporting on the constitutional recognition campaign. News sites included the Australian Broadcasting Corporation (online and television public broadcaster), *The Guardian* (Australia), Fairfax Media (*Sydney Morning Herald*, *Age*, *Canberra Times*), News.com (Herald Sun, Sydney Telegraph), *The Australian*, Sky News, Channel 9 News, and SBS News. We acknowledge a blurring of the boundaries between the online forums and 'mainstream', 'legacy' or 'institutional' media, with Twitter an essential tool of journalism, but contend that the crucial role played by commercial and public service news organisations in negotiating policy debate mean they remain a key site for investigation;
- Our final domain of media practice was Indigenous participatory media. We analysed the growing opposition to *Recognise* in a range of alternative news sites including New Matilda, Croakey and The Stringer, Indigenous media including NITV, National Indigenous Radio Service, Koori Mail, blogs such as IndigenousX and Rantings of

an Aboriginal Feminist, and social media discussion emanating from Twitter and Facebook. We are mindful of the potential risks of exploitation when working with readily available digital trace data, and the need to avoid 'extractive' research without informed consent, so have limited our analyses to publicly available blogs and news sites.

All texts were recorded and coded in a custom-built database to identify key features, and each body of data was analysed inductively using thematic analysis to identify the broad themes inherent in the text. The article concludes by considering the intersections between these three domains of media practice, with a particular focus on the role of new players in mainstream media such as *The Guardian* (Australia).

3. Constitutional Recognition as Mediatised Policymaking

Mediatisation theory helps us to understand how changes occurring in the media landscape were central to the way the constitutional recognition debate played out. Increasingly, the activities of political and oppositional actors are carried out within media and this is both opening up opportunities for a wider range of voices to be heard within the political process, and at the same time limiting opportunities for engagement. Mediatisation refers to the body of theory and research that considers the broad impacts of media on society. While it has been virtually ignored by the dominant US Political Communication journals (Nielsen, 2014) mediatisation has been embraced in European scholarship (Livingstone & Lunt, 2014; Lundby, 2014). Mediatisation relates to '...changes in practices, cultures, and institutions in media-saturated societies...' (Lundby, 2014, p. 3; Couldry & Hepp, 2013). The institutional approach to mediatisation concerns the transformations of institutions, like politics and religion, scrutinising when they adhere to the formats of media for their function and practices in society and culture (Hjarvard, 2014; Flew & Swift, 2015). This branch of scholarship emphasises the changing structural relationship between different spheres of society and micro processes such as 'news logic' whereby routines, priorities and practices of news media are internalised and embodied by policymakers (Thorbjørnsrud, Figenschou, & Øyvind, 2014). For example, the adoption of increasingly market-driven practices by bureaucracies, the reliance on easily consumed content such as polls and institutionally prepared media content can all be seen as the adoption of media logics in politics and policymaking. McCallum & Waller (in press) found the practices of bureaucrats working in the Indigenous affairs domain changed as the media environment changed and intensified. In major policy debates over Indigenous health and education the ear of senior political leaders and their bureaucrats was turned towards mainstream media, or attuned to a narrow range of Indigenous voices amplified through mainstream news institutions.

The case study of constitutional recognition builds on this body of research to explore the mediatised practices of political leaders and Indigenous people. Each of our three sites of evidence—policy, news reporting, and Indigenous participatory media activity—provide evidence of how media change—the central tenet of mediatisation—impacts on policy development. In addressing our first question we identify three elements of media-driven government policymaking during 2015: media events, government-funded advocacy, and the commissioning of opinion polls.

3.1. Media Events

Prime Minister Abbott made constitutional recognition a hallmark of his administration. Presenting the referendum process to mainstream political news media was a vital stage in gaining political legitimacy for a referendum. Throughout 2015 a series of high-profile events were held to gain maximum exposure. Standing with Australian of the Year, Indigenous sporting hero Adam Goodes, on Australia Day, the PM pledged in a nationally televised speech to:

> 'Work towards completing our constitution by recognising the first Australians. The spirit of generous inclusion has always marked our nation at its best.' (*The Guardian*, 2015a)

This statement demonstrates that, from the outset, the PM framed recognition as a way of containing Indigenous sovereignties via a politics of inclusion, rather than through an acknowledgement of Australia's ongoing colonial legacy. With bipartisan political support he pushed ahead with plans to confirm a question to take to the people. Debate progressed on the assumption that constitutional change would be settled by political elites and then explained and 'sold' to Indigenous and non-Indigenous voters. The report of a joint parliamentary committee[1] coincided with the Prime Minister calling a summit for July 6 to discuss the timing and the working of the referendum. Attended by a group of 40 secretly selected Indigenous leaders and held behind closed doors at the spectacular harbour-side Sydney residence of the Prime Minister (D. Parker, 2015), the summit was designed to achieve maximum media attention. During the second half of 2015 the PM was increasingly required to manage Indigenous calls for

[1] This followed a failed referendum to include a preamble in the constitution in 1999, the Report of the Expert Panel in January 2012, and the Joint Select Committee on Constitutional Recognition.

more consultation with Indigenous communities and growing evidence of widespread community scepticism about the proposal (Medhora, 2015c).

3.2. Government-Funded Advocacy

The Prime Minister was supported by the non-government organisation Reconciliation Australia through its $15 million *Recognise* awareness and advocacy program (Graham, 2016). *Recognise* is funded by government and private sponsorship to promote community understanding and acceptance of the need for constitutional reform. It worked in tandem with government as an arms-length public information tool; an outsourcing of political function in a form that adopted the logics of marketing to engage the electorate. Throughout 2015 *Recognise* engaged in a comprehensive social marketing program using advertising, publicity events, an interactive website and social media platforms. Public relations tactics included the production of news releases, editorials by the *Recognise* co-chairs, and third party endorsements from celebrities, sportspeople, and businesses elites (*Recognise*, 2016).

3.3. Opinion Polls and the Spectacle of Support

A final element of the campaign was the commissioning of opinion polls to gather quantifiable evidence and publicise public support for the referendum. In May 2015, Reconciliation Australia strategically released the results of a privately commissioned opinion poll that found the majority of Australians would support a change to the constitution to recognise Indigenous people (*Recognise*, 2015a; Sky News, 2015). As discussed later, this poll and others gained widespread, largely uncritical media coverage. Here we observe the commissioning of polls is an established mechanism for representing public sentiment about a policy issue. Polling has also been critiqued as a way of modelling public opinion on issues established by elite agendas in the absence of deliberation (Carey, 1995, p. 392; Lewis, 2001), with little consideration of significant minority groups' opinions. Using polls as quantified 'evidence' for media consumption (Herbst, 1998; Lewis, 2001) may provide the spectacle of community support, but it ignored vital voices in the process that ultimately worked against the campaign.

While it may seem self-evident that widespread community acceptance is a necessity in a census vote such as a referendum, the reliance on media and marketing logics calls for critical analysis. The increasingly commercialised and market-driven nature of government has long been of concern to critical political communication scholars (McChesney, 2015). *Recognise* critic Celeste Liddle (2014a) challenged *Recognise* for its collaboration with powerful commercial interests such as Qantas that have worked against Indigenous people. A more critical analysis comes from Treré (2016, p. 131) who takes the case of the 2012 Mexican elections to argue that political parties and governments deploy the same digital tools as political activists to 'manufacture consent' for government programs and 'sabotage dissent' against them. He argues 'the algorithmic construction of consent goes hand-in-hand with the undermining of critical voices' (2015, p. 131). While we do not contend that *Recognise* equates to the symbolic violence enacted against the populous in Mexico, we do observe parallels in the use of polling and social media to both model and mobilise Indigenous support. The upshot is that while Aboriginal and Torres Strait Islander people may have been highly visible in the campaign to bring the referendum to fruition, the full range of Indigenous voices was not heard or considered.

4. Reporting Constitutional Recognition

Our news media analysis identified three key features reinforcing the importance of political journalism in the communication of major policy developments: strong parallels between government and media agendas: broadly uncritical support for *Recognise*, and reliance on news subsidies driving news content.

4.1. Alignment of Media and Political Agendas

Over the first half of 2015 Australian journalists predominantly reported constitutional recognition as a political issue. News about the referendum process was decontextualised from reporting of Indigenous affairs more generally, and focused on the process of reaching an agreement on a question to bring to the people. From the Prime Minister's Australia Day speech through to the Kirribilli House meeting in July, national news media attended closely to the activities and priorities of Prime Minister Abbott and the machinations of the campaign with stories such as: 'Path for Indigenous recognition mapped out at historic meeting' (Tingle, 2015). In an article discussing growing frustration with the process of resolving the referendum question in late March, *The Guardian* reported:

> 'Divisions over Indigenous recognition fuels pressure for meeting with PM.' (Jabour, 2015)

As a result of *Recognise*'s advocacy efforts Indigenous faces and voices were highly visible in news media reports about recognition, but they belonged to a small number of high-profile spokespeople. *Recognise* co-chair Tanya Hosch was a prominent and widely quoted advocate, but the main focus of news reporting was on the two prominent leaders, Noel Pearson and Patrick Dodson, as representative of all Indigenous people to negotiate a referendum solution. News media's reliance on these two figures brought attention to the issue, but also allowed journalists to ignore a wider range of opinions. Journalists' sourcing practices are crucial to who and what gets listened to in Indigenous affairs (Waller, 2013). Journalists look to individuals who represent institutions, from the state to 'experts' and key community representatives, to both generate and verify stories about particular policy issues. When powerful decision-makers and powerful media look at Indigenous issues through the same frame, the range of policy problems to be addressed is limited, and so is the range of possible solutions.

4.2. A Good News Story for Non-Indigenous Australia

In what may appear a divergent finding from the extensive body of literature that shows Australian news media perpetuates racism and amplifies Indigenous failure in a discourse of deficit and negativity (Fforde et al., 2013; Hokowhitu, 2013; Meadows, 2001), our research demonstrates that constitutional recognition was generally framed as a 'positive' news story. News reporting framed recognition as an example of the non-Indigenous community's goodwill towards Indigenous people and readiness to amend a flaw in the founding document, rather than engaging with complex and challenging Indigenous demands, critique and dissent.

Major news outlets published news subsidies supplied by *Recognise* as an additional source of good news. Editorials by co-chair Tanya Hosch (*Telegraph*, 2016) and third party endorsements from high-profile sportspeople and political leaders featured in several news outlets. Conservative oppositional voices were largely portrayed as atypical of widespread community support for the referendum. However, this seeming contradiction supports a body of research that has found Australian news media has a long history of distancing itself from systemic racism by highlighting individual aberrant 'racist' acts while representing the white mainstream as 'tolerant' (Meadows, 2001). A potential outcome is that Indigenous people who oppose constitutional recognition are either silenced or shunned.

4.3. News Drivers, News Events and Polls

The July meeting at the PM's Sydney residence was the most widely reported topic in 2015, generating reports and commentary about constitutional recognition. Stunning imagery of Indigenous leader Pat Dodson in conversation with the prime minister on Sydney Harbour helped to frame the event as a constructive political process. The Australian Broadcasting Corporation (ABC) reported that:

> 'Political and Indigenous leaders are united in their support of Aboriginal and Torres Strait Islander recognition in the constitution, saying it is an "historical injustice" that needs to be addressed.' (ABC, 2015)

Noel Pearson, who attended the meeting, was scathing about the political spectacle, referring to the event as 'stage-managed' (Medhora, 2015b).

Survey research and opinion polls were prominent sources of news. Both government and media relied on poll results to reflect back to the population its support for the referendum. Hard news stories were driven by the release of polls commissioned by *Recognise* or media organisations. In May the ABC reported on a poll commissioned by *Recognise*:

> 'Australians would vote yes now to constitutional recognition: poll.' (Henderson, 2015)

Apart from the *Recognise* polls, journalists reported widely on an Australian National University ANUpoll (Gray & Sanders, 2015; Medhora, 2015a) and Fairfax Ipsos (Gordon, 2015). Each of these commissioned polls showed high rates of community acceptance for recognising Indigenous people in the constitution despite no question being settled on. Polls were strategically released to coincide with major political events. Ahead of the Kirribilli meeting, *The Australian* published an article based on an exclusive Newspoll:

> 'Two out of three back Indigenous recognition.' (Hudson, 2015)

As Australia's most established and newsworthy opinion poll, Newspoll generated substantial publicity for the *Recognise* campaign. This poll-driven news follows traditional political news values and formats that prioritise poll results as quantified evidence of public opinion (Lewis, 2001).

We conclude that the alignment of institutional news media coverage with the government's mediated policy approach left little room for other perspectives, limiting the range and agency of dissenting voices available to contribute to the conversation over constitutional recognition.

5. The Intervention of Indigenous Participatory Media

Our analysis to this point suggests the reconceptualisation of Indigenous recognition as an elite political issue worked to marginalise a wide range of Indigenous people from the mainstream political communication system. But close examination of the third domain of media practice—Indigenous participatory media—paints a different picture of public sphere activity in relation to the constitutional recognition debate. Throughout 2014 and 2015 an oppositional discourse to *Recognise* emerged through Indigenous-led, alternative and social media. Emanating in local social networks and communities, discussed via established social media networks and disseminated through the sophisticated Indigenous media sphere, this opposition both reflected and engaged with a national and global discourse challenging the very concept of constitutional recognition.

In recent years the digital and social media space has built on a long, rich and innovative Indigenous community media tradition (see Indigenous Remote Communications Association, 2016; Meadows, 2016). Social media has been crucial to promote Indigenous strength and showcase a diverse range of Indigenous voices (Sweet, Pearson, & Dudgeon, 2013). Indigenous Australians in urban, rural and remote settings are active in social media, with substantially higher rates of Facebook use than the general population (Balough, 2014; Carslon & Frazer, 2015). These networks operate with their own logics, largely outside of the mainstream media and policy spheres. But they have increasingly been used to enable engagement with political debate about local issues of concern. Indigenous media has harnessed political and social networks to express political opinion, engage with institutional media and perform protest, as part of a growing sphere of global social media activism (Bruns & Highfield, 2016; Cottle & Lester, 2011; Hutchins & Lester, 2015; Moscato, 2016; Waller et al., 2015). One significant new player is the media organisation IndigenousX. Established in 2012 as a rotating Twitter account to facilitate the unfettered exposure of a diverse range of Aboriginal and Torres Strait Islander people, IndigenousX has emerged as a fully integrated Indigenous owned and operated online media organisation (Pearson, 2015). Social media also provides a critical mechanism for Indigenous media activists to bridge private and public spheres and to bring a wider range of voices and perspectives to narrow political debates.

5.1. Anti-Recognise Campaigns in Social and Alternative Media

Facebook and Twitter were key sites of political activity as momentum built against the campaign for constitutional recognition. Several Facebook pages were opened including 'Facebook Anti*Recognise*' and 'Vote "NO" to Constitutional Recognition', each with widespread support (Dreher et al., 2016). With 20,000 followers, the Facebook page of Sovereign Union (2016) is an example of the melding of community forum and platform for activism, where opposition to *Recognise* has been debated and promoted. Twitter has also provided a forum for the diversity of Indigenous views about *Recognise*, with humour, advocacy and rapid responses to government activity, particularly through the influential #NoRespect hashtag. In addition, advocacy media such as *New Matilda* provided a crucial platform for the publication of the diversity of views on constitutional reform.

The July 2015 Kirribilli House Indigenous leaders event proved a catalyst for the growing opinion against the *Recognise* campaign and most Indigenous opposition took place via social media. In an article for IndigenousX and published in *The Guardian* titled:

> 'Indigenous community voices must be heard in the recognise debate.' (D. Parker, 2015),

@IndigenousX host Darren Parker captured the growing anger that Indigenous people were being excluded from decision-making processes. Parker's widely disseminated views indicated the level of mistrust in political institutions by Indigenous people. Davis (2016, p. 77) argues that 'Social media captured the overwhelming rejection of the campaign for recognition, and the growing resistance to being 'recognised' by the settler state.' By early 2016 *New Matilda* reported that 500 Indigenous people had openly rejected constitutional recognition at an historic Victorian government consultation, with the Victorian Aboriginal Affairs Minister, Natalie Hutchins, admitting that:

> 'Communities consistently express opposition to constitutional recognition.' (Graham, 2016)

Local communities have expressed desire for genuine consultation in plans for a referendum, and for the question to be posed in the context of their concerns. This response supports the First Nations writer Coulthard (2014, p. 152) who argued the cultural politics of recognition maintains rather than transforms the settler-colonial relationship between Indigenous nations and the (Canadian) state, and has advocated 'refusal' rather than recognition (see also Simpson, 2007, 2010).

5.2. The IndigenousX Poll

A significant intervention came with the publication of an online survey by IndigenousX. In response to a heavily publicised *Recognise* poll in May 2015 that found 87% of Indigenous people supported constitutional recognition, IndigenousX conducted an online, non-random sample survey of the Indigenous community. The results of the poll's 827 Indigenous respondents deviated significantly from four earlier surveys of community sentiment towards constitutional recognition. The survey found that just 25% of respondents supported *Recognise*, and the overwhelming majority of respondents (67%) would vote NO in a referendum if a question did not introduce specific measures against discrimination. Significantly, the poll showed Indigenous respondents felt most strongly about sovereignty and parliamentary representation—two issues that had been ignored in political and mainstream media representation (McQuire, 2015a, 2015b). Writing for *The Guardian*, blogger Celeste Liddle stated:

'87% of Indigenous people do not agree on recognition. You'd know if you listened.' (Liddle, 2015)

While the IndigenousX poll can be seen as advocacy polling (*Recognise*, 2015b), the exercise captured the otherwise unheard Indigenous public sentiment at the heart of the constitutional recognition question. Use of the established technology of polling for the measurement of public opinion, and publicity by alternative media such as *New Matilda*, helped move the anti-*Recognise* agenda onto the mainstream agenda. Here was clear, quantifiable evidence that Indigenous people were resisting the constitutional recognition process unless they could be part of it. Social media meant that IndigenousX had an established network to conduct the survey, the technologies to execute it online and the means to disseminate its findings both through its own networks and traditional media channels.

6. New Media Entrants and News Diversity

A key finding of our media analysis is the role played by new entrant to the Australian media landscape, *The Guardian* (Australia). Since it was launched in 2013, *The Guardian* (Australia) has made a concerted effort to listen out for and report diverse Indigenous stories. It provided a platform for the anti-*Recognise* movement through the publication of a series of invited columns by constitutional experts and vocal anti-*Recognise* advocates (e.g. Liddle, 2014a). As a result, its coverage painted a very different picture of the constitutional debate than found in other institutional news coverage. In a 2014 column for *The Guardian*, law expert Larrissa Behrendt identified a diversity of opinion in relation to how the constitution might be changed:

'Indigenous recognition: The concerns of those opposed must be taken seriously.' (Behrendt, 2014)

In April 2015 *The Guardian* reported Indigenous leader Kirsty Parker raising deep concerns. In a column titled 'Is Indigenous constitutional recognition salvageable? We have to hope so' she observed:

'Anyone plugged into conventional or social media over the past week could be forgiven for thinking Australia is on the cusp of settling the matter of appropriately recognising Aboriginal and Torres Strait Islander peoples in the nation's constitution.' (K. Parker, 2015)

In contrast to the favourable coverage of *Recognise* in the majority of mainstream news, *The Guardian* reported widespread disillusionment:

'Indigenous people fear being left out of recognition debate, academic says.' (*The Guardian*, 2015b)

The intersection between *The Guardian* and social media organisations such as IndigenousX is a crucial development in the changing media landscape. By reporting the stories of regular @IndigenousX hosts and publicising the IndigenousX poll, *The Guardian* amplified Indigenous voices, acted as a bridge between social and mainstream media, and provided a platform for otherwise unheard Indigenous perspectives. Its established relationship with *The Guardian* meant the results of the June 2015 IndigenousX poll permeated mainstream media, albeit with little acknowledgement from the legacy press who had, by this stage, lost interest in the campaign.

7. Discussion and Conclusions

This article has examined three interrelated elements of the mediatised campaign for constitutional recognition: the media-related practices of government; institutional media reporting and resistance to *Recognise* in Indigenous participatory media. We considered the implications of each of these for Indigenous people to engage with narrowly defined debates around constitutional recognition, and how the changing media environment is disrupting the exclusive domain of political communication.

The article provides evidence of the nature of mediatised political practice in the *Recognise* campaign and the centrality of pre-packaged news and political marketing to contemporary policymaking. Over the course of 2015 the Prime Minister led the government campaign to resolve the timing and question of the Indigenous recognition referendum. The government relied on a spectacle of community goodwill towards the recognition project, despite clear indications of diverse community opinion on the topic. The political project focused on ensuring that designated 'Indigenous leaders' reached agreement with government on the nature of the referendum question and its timing. It reconstructed constitutional recognition as a simple question of accepting the need for recognition in the constitution, rather than addressing fundamentally challenging questions around Indigenous sovereignties, rights and the legacies of colonialism. Events were designed to attract positive media attention while opinion polls were commissioned and publicised as a key indicator of widespread public support for *Recognise*.

Next we addressed the role of institutional media in reporting on the campaign and found support for the long line of political communication research pointing to the exclusive relationship between media and politics (Blumler, 2014; Voltmer & Koch-Baumgarten, 2010). Institutional news media embraced the 'good news story' of reforming the constitution. News agendas largely fell in line with political agendas in the media-driven campaign, with reporting focused on political priorities, debates over proposed models, and division in both Indigenous and non-Indigenous leadership. In short, Australia's established news media reported on this as a political story. Public opinion polls and media events generated by *Recognise* were a major source of news, reinforcing that established news organisations are increasingly reliant on subsidies from government-sponsored advocacy organisations. As political momentum for the grand symbolic change stalled in the second half of 2015, the campaign became enmeshed in a range of wider concerns about race relations. By 2016, in the absence of sustained political news, most media had lost interest.

Our third research question was: 'How did Indigenous participatory media engage with and disrupt the constitutional recognition campaign?' Drawing on a broad conceptualisation of politics we looked to local Indigenous social media networks and identified these as a vibrant site of social and political discussion about Indigenous sovereignties, rights, and the legacies of colonialism. We identified a powerful opposition that emerged to unsettle the *Recognise* campaign. As a result, this article addresses an aspect of political communication theory that has not been well thought through to date. It challenges the exclusive relationship between news media and politics that has been the focus of so much political communication theory, demonstrating how digital and social media have opened new spaces for Indigenous engagement in political processes from which they have typically been excluded.

An important finding was the role of new media entrant *The Guardian* in listening to and amplifying a wider range of Indigenous perspectives and voices. *The Guardian* (Australia)'s coverage raises a number of questions about the changing media environment in public discussion of Indigenous affairs. It suggests that its 'open journalism' approach has been an important intervention in the scene (Ingram, 2016). As a new player and an outsider to the legacy Australian political media, *The Guardian* was able to challenge the dominant routines and offer a wider range of perspectives on this national issue. It provides valuable evidence of how new media entrants have opened bridges between Indigenous participatory media and the mainstream. Given this amplification of diverse Indigenous voices, political leaders had ample opportunity to listen to the range of concerns over *Recognise*.

Our final question asked, 'what are the implications of changing media environments for Indigenous Australians to engage with mainstream policy and media debates?' While popular media celebrates the value of participatory media with terms such as 'Twitter revolution', our study resonates with the growing body of research that suggests a more complex picture (eg. Dencik & Leistert, 2015). Couldry (2012) sees evidence of successful politics of protest or disruption operating on certain temporalities, but what of enduring 'positive political action' (p. 116)? The multiplicity and interactivity of online politics is frequently associated with protest rather than a long-term fixed political project. Moreover, the transformations brought about by digital media benefit all political actors, so that both political elites and racist movements have enhanced opportunities for voice (Couldry 2012; Dencik & Leistert, 2015). State and corporate actors are well placed to mobilise the social media techniques and appearance of social movements (e.g. Curran, Fenton, & Freedman, 2012; Treré, 2016).

For our own study, we found the changing media environment included increased opportunities for diverse and dissenting Indigenous voices. The *Recognise* campaign was also able to mobilise a sophisticated social media strategy as well as established media advocacy techniques to enlist support and generate largely positive mainstream media coverage. We also found evidence of considerable disruption, whereby Indigenous media and new mainstream media entrants mobilised fundamental critique of the *Recognise* campaign. We argue that changes in the media environment are a significant factor in the increasing incapacity of formal political communication to manage such complex debates over Indigenous sovereignties, rights and the legacies of colonialism. However, longer-term research is required to address the argument that the social media environment enables a politics of protest and disruption, but does not necessarily produce longer-term political transformations.

Acknowledgements

We would like to acknowledge the many producers of Indigenous media whose work on participation and self-determination has inspired our analysis. Tanja Dreher's research for this article was supported by the Australian Research Council (FT140100515).

Conflict of Interests

The authors declare no conflicts of interest.

References

Australian Broadcasting Corporation. (2015, July 5). *In quotes: Indigenous constitutional recognition*. Retrieved from http://www.abc.net.au/news/2015-07-05/political-indigenous-viewpoints-on-constitutional-recognition/6594556

Attwood, B., & Markus, A. (2007). *The 1967 referendum: Race, power and the Australian constitution* (2nd ed.). Canberra: Aboriginal Studies Press.

Australian Government. (2016). *Constitutional recognition*. Retrieved from http://www.dpmc.gov.au/indigenous-affairs/constitutional-recognition

Bennett, W. L., & Segerberg, A. (2013). *The logic of connective action: Digital media and the personalization of contentious politics*. Cambridge: Cambridge University Press.

Bennett, W. L., & Iyengar, S. (2008). A new era of minimal effects? The changing foundations of political communication. *Journal of Communication*, *58*, 707-731.

Bruns, A., & Highfield, T. (2016). Is Habermas on Twitter? Social media and the public sphere. In A. Bruns, G. Enli, E. Skogerbo, A. Larsson, & C. Christensen (Eds), *The Routledge companion to social media and* politics (pp. 56-72). Milton Park: Routledge.

Balough, M. (2014). Indigenous media research: Matt Balogh, McNair ingenuity research. Retrieved from https://www.youtube.com/watch?v=_ZjcSsA5Yb8

Behrendt, L. (2014). Indigenous recognition: The concerns of those opposed must be taken seriously. *The Guardian*. Retrieved from http://www.theguardian.com/commentisfree/2014/sep/25/indigenousrecognition-the-concerns-of-those-opposed-must-be-taken-seriously#start-of-comments

Blumer, H. (1948). Public opinion and public opinion polling. *American Sociological Review*, *13*(5), 542-549.

Blumler, J. (2014). Mediatisation and democracy. In F. Esser & J. Strömbäck (Eds.), *Mediatisation of politics: Understanding the transformation of Western* democracies (pp. 31-41). London: Palgrave.

Carey, J. (1975). A cultural approach to communication. *Communication*, *2*(April), 173-191.

Carey, J. W. (1995). The press, public opinion and public discourse. In T. L. Glasser & C. T. Salmon (Eds.), *Public opinion and the communication of consent* (pp. 373-402). New York: Guilford Publications.

Carlson, B., & Frazer, R. (2015). 'It's like going to a cemetery and lighting a candle': Aboriginal Australians, Sorry Business and social media. *AlterNative: An International Journal of Indigenous Peoples*, *11*(3), 211-224.

Chadwick, A. (2013). *The hybrid media system: Politics and power*. Oxford: OUP.

Cottle, S., & Lester, L. (2011). *Transnational protests and the media*. New York, Peter Lang.

Couldry, N. (2012). *Media, society, world: Social theory and digital media practice*. Cambridge: Polity.

Couldry, N., & Hepp, A. (2013). Conceptualizing mediatisation: Contexts, traditions, arguments. *Communication Theory*, *23*(3), 191-202.

Coulthard, G. (2014). *Red skin, White masks. Rejecting the colonial politics of recognition*. Minneapolis: University of Minnesota Press.

Curran, J., Fenton, N., & Freedman, D. (2012). *Misunderstanding the internet*. Milton Park: Routledge.

Davis, M. (2016). Listening but not hearing: When process trumps substance. *Griffith Review*, *51*, 73-87.

Davis, M., & Williams, G. (2015). *Everything you need to know about the referendum to recognize Indigenous Australians.* Sydney: NewSouth.

Dencik, L., & Leistert, O. (2015). *Critical perspectives on social media and protest: Between control and emancipation*. Washington: Rowman & Littlefield.

Dodson, M. (2012). *Mick Dodson constitutional recognition of Indigenous Australians* (Senate Occasional Lecture Series, Parliament House). Retrieved from http://www.aph.gov.au/sitecore/content/Home/About_Parliament/Senate/Powers_practice_n_procedures/pops/pop57/c02

Dreher, T., McCallum, K., & Waller, L. (2016) Indigenous voices and mediatized policy-making in the digital age. *Information, Communication & Society*, *19*(1), 23-39.

Fforde, C., Bamblett, L., Lovett, R., Gorringe S., & Fogarty, W. (2013). Discourse, deficit and identity: Aboriginality, the race paradigm and the language of representation in contemporary Australia. *Media International Australia*, *149*, 162-173.

Flew, T., & Swift, A. G. (2015). Engaging, persuading, and entertaining citizens: Mediatisation and the Australian political public sphere. *International Journal of Press/Politics*, *20*(1), 108-128.

Gamson, W. (1992). *Talking politics*. Cambridge: CUP.

Goot, M., & Rowse, T. (2007). *Divided Nation? Indigenous affairs and the imagined public.* Carlton: Melbourne University Press.

Gordon, M. (2015, July 6). Recognition closer as Indigenous leaders meet. *Sydney Morning Herald*. Retrieved from http://www.smh.com.au/national/recognition-closer-as-indigenous-leaders-meet-20150517-gh3n61.html

Graham, C. (2016, February 8). *Recognise* rejected: Historic meeting of 500 Black leaders unanimously opposes constitutional recognition. *New Matilda*. Retrieved from https://newmatilda.com/2016/02/08/recognise-rejected-historic-meeting-500-black-leaders-unanimously-opposes-constitutional-recognition

Gray, M., & Sanders, W. (2015). *Australian public opinion on Indigenous issues: Injustice, disadvantage and support of recognition* (ANUpol Report No. 17). Canberra: School of Politics and International Relations, Australian national University.

Henderson, A. (2015, May 18). Constitutional recognition of Aboriginal and Torres Strait Islander people referendum has majority support, *Recognise* poll finds. *ABC*. Retrieved from http://www.abc.net.au/news/2015-05-18/majority-support-indigenous-recognition-in-constitution-poll/6476538

Herbst, S. (1998). *Reading public opinion: How political actors view the democratic process*. Chicago: University of Chicago Press.

Hjarvard, S. (2014). Mediatization and cultural and social change: An institutional perspective. In K. Lundby (Ed.), *Mediatisation of communication, handbooks of communication sciences* 21 (pp. 200-226). Mouton: De Gruyter.

Hokowhitu, B. (2013). Theorizing Indigenous media. In B.

Hokowhitu & V. Devadas (Eds.), *The fourth eye. Maori media in Aotearoa New Zealand* (pp. 101-123). Minneapolis: University of Minnesota Press.

Hudson, P. (2015, June 20). Two out of three back indigenous recognition. *The Australian*. Retrieved from http://www.recognise.org.au/wp-content/uploads/2015/06/200615_Two-out-of-three-back-indigenous-recognition_TheAus1.pdf

Hutchins, B., & Lester, L. (2015). Theorizing the enactment of environmental conflict. *The International Communication Gazette*, *77*(4), 337-358.

Indigenous Remote Communications Association. (2016). *History of the remote Indigenous media sector*. Retrieved from http://www.irca.net.au/sector/history-remote-indigenous-media-sector

Ingram, M. (2016, February 3). Do *The Guardian*'s losses mean 'open journalism' has failed? *Fortune Magazine*. Retrieved from http://fortune.com/2016/02/03/guardian-losses

Jabour, B. (2015, March 30). Divisions over Indigenous recognition fuels pressure for meeting with PM. *The Guardian*. Retrieved from http://www.theguardian.com/australia-news/2015/apr/13/divisions-over-indigenous-recognition-fuels-pressure-for-meeting-with-pm

Lewis, J. (2001). *Constructing public opinion: How political elites do what they like and why we seem to go along with it.* New York: Columbia University Press.

Liddle, C. (2014a). I don't want your *Recognise* campaign—It's nothing but a sham. *The Guardian*. Retrieved from http://www.theguardian.com/commentisfree/2014/aug/18/i-dont-want-yourrecognise-campaign-its-nothing-but-a-sham

Liddle, C. (2014b). *On diverse views of constitutional recognition. Rantings of an Aboriginal feminist*. Retrieved from http://blackfeministranter.blogspot.com.au

Liddle, C. (2015, July 19). 87% of Indigenous people do not agree on recognition. You'd know if you listened. *The Guardian*. Retrieved from http://www.theguardian.com/commentisfree/2015/jun/19/87-of-indigenous-people-do-not-agree-on-recognition-youd-know-if-you-listened

Lundby, K. (2014). Introduction. In K. Lundby (Ed.), *Mediatisation of communication. Handbooks of communication science*, *21* (pp. 3-35). Berlin: De Gruyter Moulton.

Livingstone, S., & Lunt, P. (2014) Mediatisation: An emerging paradigm for media and communication research? In K. Lundby (Ed.), *Mediatisation of communication. Handbooks of communication science,* 21 (pp. 703-723). Berlin: De Gruyter Moulton.

McCallum, K., & Waller, L. (in press). The dimensions of mediatized policymaking in Australian Indigenous affairs. *Communications: The European Journal of Communication*, *42*(2).

McCallum, K., & Waller, L. (2013). Media interventions in indigenous policymaking. *Media International Australia*, *149*, 139-149.

McChesney, R. W. (2015). *Rich media, poor democracy: Communication politics in dubious times.* New York: The New Press.

McNay, L. (2008). *Against recognition*. Cambridge: Polity.

McQuire, A. (2015a). Peak indigenous body acknowledges resistance to *Recognise* campaign. *New Matilda*. Retrieved from https://newmatilda.com/2015/02/20/peak-indigenous-bodyacknowledges-resistance-recognise-campaign

McQuire, A. (2015b). Online poll finds majority of black Australia opposed to *Recognise* campaign. *New Matilda*. Retrieved from: https://newmatilda.com/2015/02/20/peak-indigenous-bodyacknowledges-resistance-recognise-campaign

Meadows, M. (2001). *Voices in the wilderness: Images of Aboriginal people in the Australian media*. Westport: Greenwood.

Meadows, M. (2016). Dangerous dancing. A commentary on Australian Indigenous communication futures. *Media and Communication*, *4*(2), 33-37.

Medhora, S. (2015a, March 27). 73% of Australians want Indigenous recognition in constitution—Study. *The Guardian*. Retrieved from http://www.theguardian.com/australia-news/2015/mar/27/75-of-australians-want-indigenous-recognition-in-constitution-study

Medhora, S. (2015b, July 7). Noel Pearson claims Indigenous summit on referendum 'stage-managed'. *The Guardian Australia*. Retrieved from http://www.theguardian.com/australia-news/2015/jul/07/noel-pearson-claims-indigenous-summit-on-referendum-stage-managed

Medhora, S. (2015c, August 20). Tony Abbott changes mind, supports Indigenous meetings on recognition. *The Guardian Australia*. Retrieved from http://www.theguardian.com/australia-news/2015/aug/20/tony-abbott-changes-mind-supports-indigenous-meetings-on-recognition

Moscato, D. (2016). Media portrayals of hashtag activism: A framing analysis of Canada's #Idlenomore Movement. *Media and Communication*, *4*(2), 3-12.

Nielsen, R. (2014). Political communication research: New media, new challenges, and new opportunities. *MedieKultur*, *56*, 5-22.

Parker, D. (2015, July 6). Indigenous community voices must be heard in the recognise debate. *The Guardian*. Retrieved from http://www.theguardian.com/commentisfree/2015/jul/06/a-historic-indigenous-meeting-is-taking-place-why-dont-we-know-whos-at-it

Parker, K. (2015, April 20). Is Indigenous constitutional recognition salvageable? We have to hope so. *The Guardian*. Retrieved from http://www.theguardian.com/commentisfree/2015/apr/20/is-indigenous-constitutional-recognition-salvageable-we-have-to-hope-so

Pearson, L. (2015). *IndigenousX Constitutional recognition survey*. Retrieved from http://indigenousx.com.au/constitutional-recognition-survey

Povinelli, E. A. (2002). *The cunning of recognition: Indigenous alterities and the making of Australian multiculturalism*. Durham: Duke University Press.

Recognise. (2016). Retrieved from http://www.recognise.org.au

Recognise. (2015a, May 18). *An overwhelming 'Yes' if Recognise vote were held today*. Retrieved from http://www.recognise.org.au/wp-content/uploads/2015/05/5.-MR-ReadyTo*Recognise*18May2015.pdf

Recognise. (2015b). *We all have a responsibility to listen 24 July 2015*. Retrieved from http://www.recognise.org.au/blogs/polling

Salmon, C. T., & Glasser, T. L. (1995). The politics of polling and the limits of consent. In T. L. Glasser & C. T. Salmon (Eds.), *Public opinion and the communication of consent* (pp. 437-458). New York: Guilford.

Simpson, A. (2007). On ethnographic refusal: Indigeneity, 'voice' and colonial citizenship. *Junctures: The Journal for Thematic Dialogue*, *9*, 67-80.

Simpson, A. (2010). Under the sign of sovereignty: Certainty, ambivalence, and law in native North America and Indigenous Australia. *Wicazo Sa Review*, *25*(2), 107-124.

Sky News. (2015, May 18). Indigenous referendum would pass. *The Guardian*. Retrieved from http://www.theguardian.com/australia-news/2015/may/21/dont-rush-recognition-referendum-says-lnps-first-indigenous-senator

Sovereign Union. (2016). *Website*. Retrieved from http://www.sovereignunion.mobi

Splichal, S. (1999). *Public opinion: Developments and controversies in the twentieth century*. Lanham: Rowman & Littlefield.

Sweet, M., Pearson, L., & Dudgeon, P. (2013). @IndigenousX: A case study of community-led innovation in digital media. *Media International Australia*, *149*, 104-111.

The Guardian. (2015a, January 25). *Australia Day: Tony Abbott promises not to neglect Indigenous recognition*. Retrieved from http://www.theguardian.com/australia-news/2015/jan/26/tony-abbott-promises-indigenous-recognition-agenda

The Guardian. (2015b, May 25). *Indigenous people fear being left out of recognition debate, academic says*. Retrieved from http://www.theguardian.com/australianews/2015/may/25/indigenous-people-fear-being-left-out-of-constitutional-recognition-debateunsw-academic-says

Tingle, L. (2015, July 6). Path for indigenous recognition mapped out at historic meeting. *Australian Financial Review*. Retrieved from http://www.afr.com/news/politics/path-for-indigenous-recognition-mapped-out-at-historic-meeting-20150706-gi6847

Thorbjørnsrud, K., Figenschou, T., & Øyvind, I. (2014). Mediatization in public bureaucracies: A typology. *Communications: The European Journal of Communication Research, 39*(1), 3-22.

Treré, E. (2016). The dark side of digital politics: Understanding the algorithmic manufacturing of consent and the hindering of online dissidence. *IDS Bulletin*, *47*(1), 127-138.

Voltmer, K., & Koch-Baumgarten, S. (2010). Introduction: Mass media and public policy—Is there a link? In S. Koch-Baumgarten & K. Voltmer (Eds.), *Public policy and mass media: The interplay of mass media and political decision-making* (pp. 1-13). London: Routledge.

Waller, L. (2013). It comes with the territory: 'Remote' Indigenous reporting for mainstream Australia. *Australian Journalism Monographs*, *14*, 5-38.

Waller, L., Dreher, T., & McCallum, K. (2015). The listening key: Unlocking the democratic potential of Indigenous participatory media. *Media International Australia*, *154*, 57-66.

Political Participation and Power Relations in Egypt: The Scope of Newspapers and Social Network Sites

Mostafa Shehata

Department of Communication and Arts, Roskilde University, 4000 Roskilde, Denmark; E-Mail: shehata@ruc.dk

Abstract

The political use of media in Egypt post-2011 revolution brought about drastic transformations in political activism and power structures. In the context of communication power theory, this article investigates the effects of newspapers and social network sites on political participation and political power relations. The research employed a mixed methodology, comprised of a survey of 527 Egyptian youth and semi-structured interviews of 12 political activists and journalists. The results showed a significant relationship between reading newspapers and youth's political participation, but not between using social network sites and political participation. In addition, newspapers and social network sites were platforms for a series of conflicts and coalitions that emerged between pro- and anti-revolution actors. Despite the importance of social network sites as key tools for informing and mobilizing the public, they eventually failed to empower new political actors, and this was because old actors, supported by newspapers and other mainstream media, managed to obstruct the new actors' progress.

Keywords

communication power; Egyptian newspapers; Egyptian political actors; mediatization of politics; political participation; politicizing newspapers; power relations; social network sites

Issue

This article is part of a multidisciplinary issue of *Media and Communication*, edited by Epp Lauk (University of Jyväskylä, Finland) and Raul Reis (Emerson College, USA).

---

1. Introduction

The authoritarian nature of Mubarak's rule in Egypt substantially obstructed Egyptian youth's political participation (PP) for decades. In the last two parliamentary elections under his rule (held in 2005 and 2010), voter turnout did not exceed 23% and 15% respectively (Sika, 2012, p. 138). In contrast, youth protest activities considerably increased in the final years of his reign, culminating in the January 2011 revolution (25J) that managed to topple him on February 11th of the same year. In the wake of the revolution, Egyptians started to actively participate in politics in different respects. For example, voter turnout in the 2011 referendum and parliamentary election comprised 41% and 60% respectively (Abd Alsamad, 2014, paras. 2–4). However, PP was once again obstructed when the army seized power after ousting the Muslim Brotherhood (MB) affiliated president Mohamed Morsi on July 3rd, 2013. This obstruction was characterized mainly by repression of the revolution's advocates, in return for reinforcing its opponents (Khalifa, 2015, p. 216).

In addition to the rapid transformation of PP post-25J, the Egyptian political scene also witnessed a related transformation in the power structure of political actors. The fall of Mubarak's National Democratic Party in the wake of the revolution allowed for the emergence and rise of pro-revolution actors, such as revolutionary youth and the MB (Mason, 2013; Meier, 2011). Since that time, these actors have mostly collided with anti-revolution actors such as the army and remnants of the Mubarak regime. Consequently, a series of conflicts and coalitions have emerged between all these actors, and these have thwarted chances for a democratic transition.

In the midst of post-revolution political changes, Egyptian newspapers (both offline and online) and social network sites (SNS) have played a significant role in effecting changes in PP and power structures. On the one hand, the overall attitudes of newspapers toward the revolution's outcomes have substantially fluctuated (AlMaskati, 2012; Hamdy & Gomaa, 2012). In general, it can be said that newspapers, which have mostly been controlled by anti-revolution actors, have opposed the 25J, especially since July 3rd, 2013 (El-Adawy, 2014; Roll, 2014). On the other hand, SNS have largely been used by pro-revolution actors, both during and after 25J, as key mobilization platforms (Khamis, Gold, & Vaughn, 2012). For this reason, several scholars have considered SNS influential tools for changing societies (e.g. Aouragh, 2012; Aouragh & Alexander, 2012; ElNawawy & Khamis, 2012). In order not to overestimate their political effect, we can initially say that SNS have represented alternative platforms that have disclosed what traditional media have concealed (Abdulla, 2014, p. 1).

This article raises the question of how newspapers and SNS might have affected youth's PP and empowered revolutionary youth (as an emerging political actor) amidst other political actors following 25J. The first part of this two-sided question is addressed quantitatively, based on the definition of PP as the "activity that has the intent or effect of influencing government action—either directly by affecting the making or implementation of public policy or indirectly by influencing the selection of people who make those policies" (Verba, Schlozman, & Brady, 2002, p. 38). In this respect, PP is examined through the various kinds of political activities in which youth participated, such as voting, protesting, volunteering, and donating.

The second part of the research question, which focuses on the role of media in the power relations of political actors, is addressed qualitatively in the context of the theory of communication power. Conceptually, Manuel Castells (2009) defines power as: "the relational capacity that enables a social actor to influence asymmetrically the decisions of other social actor(s) in ways that favor the empowered actor's will, interests, and values" (p. 10). He also theorizes the relation between media and power by arguing that "power is primarily exercised by the construction of meaning in the human mind through processes of communication enacted in global/local multimedia networks of mass communication, including mass self-communication" (Castells, 2009, p. 416). In this context, this article investigates the nature of political relations between major political actors and the potential effects of newspapers and SNS in that regard. Hence, I argue that SNS cannot, in the long run, empower new political actor(s) especially if newspapers and other mainstream media are under the control of old actor(s).

2. Literature Review

2.1. Newspapers and Political Participation

The Egyptian newspaper landscape includes three major types: government-owned newspapers, which are loyal to the government; partisan newspapers, which enjoy some freedom in their handling of the government; and private newspapers, which are more free and professional (Allam, 2010, paras. 5–8). However, it is important to mention that the freedom of each type, which improved in the wake of the 25J, has considerably declined since July 3rd, 2013. Since this date, all newspapers have adopted and adhered to the country's official ideology (Abdulla, 2014, pp. 11–27).

The literature of PP has largely investigated whether reading newspapers relates to youth's PP. In this context, some studies have found no significant relationship between these variables (e.g. Gorsche, 2002; Wang, 2002; Wright-Phillips, 2010), while others have found a significant relationship between them (e.g. Bakker & De Vreese, 2011; Fawzy, 2008; Moeller, De Vreese, Esser, & Kunz, 2014; Shehata, 2010). Unexpectedly, findings of a relationship between newspapers and PP prove that newspapers are still able to affect youth, although youth have primarily become more interested in using SNS. Linking these results to the Egyptian case in the current study, we should expect the opposite results, as a large proportion of Egyptians have lost confidence in newspapers, which have become biased and loyal to the government.

With respect to newspapers' coverage of PP activities, a number of studies have found that Egyptian newspapers, in general, adopt negative attitudes toward protestors and participation (e.g. AlMaskati, 2012; Hamdy & Gomaa, 2012; Ibrahim, 2012; Youssef, 2012). The main exception to this is provided by Khamis (2011, pp. 1161–1162), who found that private newspapers kept people informed about negativities and protest activities, both before and during 25J. In general, the policies of Egyptian newspapers have changed several times, perhaps as a result of the four power transitions that have occurred over the last six years. In order to holistically understand the conditions of these changes, this article highlights the relationship between newspapers and political actors, which is expected to be a significant factor behind such changes.

2.2. Social Network Sites and Political Participation

Overall, SNS have provided Egyptian youth with a real opportunity to express themselves politically. SNS have also compensated for youth's absence from mainstream media, which have been inaccessible to them (Howard & Hussain, 2013, pp. 4–5). However, the political role of SNS in Egypt has been affected by government censorship, especially in the last three years. As SNS are no longer free in Egypt (as they were previously, in the wake of Mubarak's ouster), it is important to investigate the impacts of SNS censorship on PP and revolutionary youth's power.

With respect to the relationship between using SNS and PP, the literature has produced three different findings: (1) SNS play a key role in PP forms (e.g. Holt, Shehata, Strömbäck, & Ljungberg, 2013; Kamel, 2014;

Khamis & Vaughn, 2011; Meier, 2011; Rice, Moffett, & Madupalli, 2012; Schuster, 2013; Valenzuela, 2013); (2) the relationship is contingent upon a number of intervening variables, such as social and cultural background (Groshek, 2008), old media consumption (Budak, 2010), face-to-face communication (Vissers, Hooghe, Stolle, & Mahéo, 2012), membership in interest organizations (Gustafsson, 2012), dissatisfaction with the government (Harrebye & Ejrnæs, 2015), and socioeconomic status (Oser, Hooghe, & Marien, 2013); and (3) the relationship is doubtful (Dimitrova & Bystrom, 2013; Schlozman, Verba, & Brady, 2010).

As a result of the Arab Spring (AS) and similar movements in other countries, assessment of the effects of SNS on PP and power structures in the last years has been very optimistic. However, some very recent writings (e.g. Fenton, 2016) on this subject have re-assessed the effects of SNS in the light of the obstacles of the democratic transition in AS countries. Accordingly, in this article, SNS are handled as neither a main reason for PP nor a main source of empowerment for political actors. Rather, they are handled as platforms for participation and power relations, and the doubts raised about their effects are also considered.

2.3. Power Relations and Network Society

In his theory of communication power, Castells (2009) describes mass communication and Internet-based communication as processes through which power can be practiced, and he considers power, itself, as relations between different actors. In this context, Howard (2010, p. 12) claimed that technology can provide political actors new capacities and restrictions, but it cannot achieve political change. This claim was empirically supported by Meier (2011), who found that communication technology threatened the political regime in Egypt and shifted the balance of power in favor of civil society. However, it should be noted that the rise of civil society (including revolutionary youth) in Egypt did not last beyond June 2013; since that time, old actors have resurged. This article will further explain the conditions of this setback and the effects of newspapers and SNS in that regard.

The landscape of political actors in Egypt post-25J has diversified, according to El-Adawy (2014), into three major categories: formal institutions, informal societal actors, and executive authority. The latter has depended, as described by Roll (2014), upon three further main actors: Arab Gulf countries, the army, and the country's business figures. Among these actors, three major political coalitions were, as noted by El-Dine (2014), formed post-25J: (1) the army and the MB; (2) the army and the National Salvation Front, which were formed against the MB; and (3) the army, the business elite, the Salafist Nour party (the Light), and secular forces. In my opinion, a separation of formal institutions, executive authority, and the army, as suggested by El-Adawy (2014) and Roll (2014), does not apply to the Egyptian case, because the army has had the upper hand over all other institutions, including the government. Thus, in this article, the army will be handled as a major actor alongside the MB and revolutionary youth.

With respect to the relationship between the media and political actors, El-Adawy (2014) and Roll (2014) found that media outlets joined political forces to encourage people to demonstrate on June 30th, 2013 against the ousted president Morsi. In a similar context, Khamis et al. (2012) found that political activists used online and offline activism in their conflict with the post-Mubarak regime, which used both state-owned and social media. These results prove Castells' claim about the importance of communication networks for political power and counter-power (Castells, 2011, p. 783). They also raise the issue, which this article discusses, of the difference between the effects produced by traditional media versus those produced by new media on political actors, and the limitations of these effects.

3. Methodology

The empirical data of this study were collected through a mixed-method approach combining survey and semi-structured interviews using a convergent parallel design. Based on this approach, first, quantitative and qualitative data were collected concurrently to complement each other; later, the data were separately analyzed; and finally, points of analysis were synthesized to achieve the purpose of the study (Creswell & Plano Clark, 2011, pp. 77–81).

3.1. Survey

The survey was based on a face-to-face questionnaire (Foreman, 1991; Wimmer & Dominick, 2011) that was conducted in September and October 2015. The sample included 527 Egyptians aged 18 to 35. Only 400 questionnaires were used for a statistical analysis using the Statistical Package for Social Sciences, version 23 for Macintosh. The sample size was calculated by two methods described by Israel (1992, pp. 3–4), based on which the number of respondents was determined.

The respondents were chosen deliberately after using a proportional allocation considering gender (51% male and 49% female) and place of residence (57.75% from Cairo, 24.50% from Menoufia and 17.75% from Beni Suef). These governorates were specifically selected to represent three geographical and cultural aspects in Egypt. While Cairo is the capital and includes more urban and culturally modern inhabitants, Menoufia represents the northern part of the country, which is slightly culturally conservative, and Beni Suef represents the southern part of the country, which is more conservative. It is also noteworthy that a pre-test was applied in order to enhance the validity and relevance of the questionnaire.

In addition, the quantitative phase of this article developed three scales: newspaper readership, SNS exposure, and political participation. The first scale, newspaper readership, was modified from the scale described by Williams (2008, p. 163), which included two items: online and offline reading of eight of the most common Egyptian newspapers. In both items, each newspaper was rated on a four-point response format, where 0 = do not read it, 0.25 = read it a few times a year, 0.5 = once a month, 1 = a few times a month, 2 = once a week, 3 = a few times a week, and 4 = daily or approximately daily. Thus, the range of the total score was from 0.25 to 72. Respondents were classified into three categories on the basis of their scores (s): low reading ($s < 6$), moderate reading ($6 \leq s \leq 11$), and high reading ($s > 11$). Cronbach's α coefficient, which was adopted to test the internal consistency of the scale, was 0.727.

The second scale, SNS exposure, was modified from the commonly used scale of Ellison, Steinfield and Lampe (2007, p. 1150), and included three items. (1) The time consumed using three SNS (Facebook, Twitter and YouTube): this item was rated on a three-point response format for each website, where 0 = no time at all, 1 = less than 30 minutes, 1.5 = 30–59 minutes, 2 = 1 hour up to 2 hours, 2.5 = more than 2 hours up to 3 hours, and 3 = more than 3 hours. (2) The number of friends, followings and subscriptions: this item was also rated on a three-point response format for each website, where 0 = do not use it, 1 = fewer than 50, 1.5 = 50–149, 2 = 150–299, 2.5 = 300–449, and 3 = 450 or more. And (3) attitudinal relation to SNS: this item, which was examined by six sentences, was likewise rated on a three-point response format for each sentence, where 1 = strongly disagree, 1.5 = disagree, 2 = neutral, 2.5 = agree, and 3 = strongly agree. Before the overall score of this scale was calculated, the three items were statistically standardized, because they used different measurement units. Based on this process, the three items were converted to a *z* score, then a composite of *z* scores was computed (Anglim, 2009), and finally the composite score was converted to a scaled score (Richard, 2010, pp. 1439–1440). Accordingly, the range of the total score of this scale was from 1 to 19, based on which exposure to SNS was classified into three categories: low exposure ($s < 8,48$); moderate exposure ($8.48 \leq s \leq 11.44$); and high exposure ($s > 11.44$). In addition, Cronbach's α coefficient, based on the standardized items, was 0.791.

The third scale, political participation, consisted of three different sub-scales. (1) PP aspects, which was guided by Verba et al. (2002, pp. 544–545) and included the following eight political activities in which respondents might have participated in the two years preceding the survey (June 2013–June 2015):

- Voting in the last presidential or parliamentary elections;
- working in electoral campaigns in the last presidential or parliamentary elections;
- contacting government officials within the past year;
- taking part in protests, strikes or sit-ins within the past two years;
- working informally with others to solve community problems within the past year;
- being politically active through a voluntary association within the past two years;
- serving voluntarily in a local governmental board regularly within the past two years; and
- being a member of, or donating to, a political organization within the past year.

Each item was rated on a one-point format, where 0 = no and 1 = yes. (2) Interest in local politics and affairs. And (3) interest in national politics and affairs. These latter two sub-scales, which were also guided by Verba et al. (2002, p. 553), were rated on a three-point response format, where 3 = very interested, 2 = fairly interested, 1 = not very interested, and 0 = not at all interested. The score of each sub-scale was standardized using the same procedures that were described for the previous scale. Consequently, the range of the total score of this scale was from 1 to 19, based on which the levels of PP were classified into three categories: low participation ($s < 8,5$); moderate participation ($8.5 \leq s \leq 11$); and high participation ($s > 11$). Cronbach's α coefficient, based on the standardized items, was 0.574.

3.2. Semi-Structured Interviews

Initially, three online pilot interviews were conducted to develop an interview protocol guide. Following this, 12 semi-structured interviews were conducted in person in October 2015. The interviewees included four political activists and eight political journalists (two of whom could also be considered activists to a lesser degree). The categories of journalists and activists were particularly selected as those that were related to and informed about media and politics. The selection of interviewees drew mainly on a snowball sampling method, wherein early interviewees were asked to provide referrals to other relevant respondents (Blernackl & Waldorf, 1981, p. 141). This method facilitated reaching respondents especially political activists who had likely been placed under security surveillance.

The interview protocol guide included questions that were planned in advance to cover major points, such as PP developments post-25J, newspapers/SNS and PP, and the power relations of political actors. In addition, many further questions that emerged during the interviews were asked as well. It is noteworthy that a few number of newspaper clippings and SNS posts were shown to interviewees in order to enrich discussion of the study topic.

All interviews, which were conducted in Arabic, were transcribed and translated into English using NVivo software, version 11, for Macintosh. Following this, a grounded theory method was used for the analysis. This method did not aim to generate a theory, but to identify the key concepts and categories of the transcripts and to investigate the relationships between them. In this context, the method aimed to provide an in-depth understanding of the relationship between newspapers/SNS with PP and power relations over the previous six years. The results were used to complement and interpret the results of the quantitative phase of this study.

Data analysis was carried out in a three-step coding process. First, open coding was conducted line by line on all transcripts, in order to determine general points and themes. Second, axial coding was used to combine sets of codes in categories and sub-categories. This process was repeated until no new categories emerged. At this stage, all categories were constructed after their codes and concepts were read many times and it was certain that every category contained homogenous components. Third, selective coding was conducted to develop the categories and to identify core category(ies) (Corbin & Strauss, 1990, pp. 12–15; see also Glaser & Strauss, 1967, pp. 105–107; Strauss & Corbin, 1998, pp. 101–161). Alongside and after the coding process, many ideas were written down in memos in order to identify the relationships between themes and categories and to extract the explicit and implicit meanings of such relationships. This was important for eliciting and illustrating participants' views and forming a conceptual link between them (Charmaz, 2006, p. 72).

4. Results

4.1. Quantitative Analysis

Starting with the intensity of reading Egyptian newspapers (offline and online), the results found that about two-thirds (71%) of the respondents read newspapers, while less than a third (29%) did not read them. Among the readers, more than one-third (41.2%) achieved a high level of readership, about one-third (33.1%) had a moderate level, and about a quarter (25.7%) achieved a low level. These results indicate that Egyptian youth read newspapers in a relatively high rates; this can be ascribed to their high exposure to the Internet, as well as to the political polarization post-25J. With regard to PP levels, the results found that moderate participation came in the first place with 46.5%, followed by low participation with 28.2% and high participation with 25.3%.

More significantly, the correlation between reading newspapers and political participation was examined using a non-parametric test (Spearman's rho). As shown in Table 1, the results found a significant positive relationship between the two variables (r_s[284] = .131, p = .027): as reading newspapers increases PP increases, and as reading decreases PP decreases. These results agree with the findings of previous studies (e.g. Bakker & De Vreese, 2011; Fawzy, 2008; Moeller et al., 2014; Shehata, 2010), which have found a significant relationship between reading newspapers and PP. However, the findings disagree with some other studies (e.g. Gorsche, 2002; Wang, 2002; Wright-Phillips, 2010), which have found no such relationship between the variables.

With respect to the intensity of using SNS, the results indicated that the vast majority of respondents (97%) used SNS—especially Facebook, Twitter and YouTube—while only 3% did not use them. Among the users, exactly half of them (50%) used SNS at a moderate level, while slightly more than a quarter (25.5%) used them at a high level, and slightly less than a quarter (24.5%) used them at a low level. These results indicate that a relatively large proportion of Egyptian youth were highly exposed to SNS that were strong social and political platforms.

Furthermore, the correlation between SNS exposure and PP was examined using a non-parametric test (Spearman's rho). Unexpectedly, the results found no significant relationship between the two variables (r_s[388] = .081, p = .111) (Table 2). The Levels of using SNS were not associated with the levels of PP, which resulted in the elimination of the effects of SNS on youth's PP. These results agree with the results of previous studies (e.g. Dimitrova & Bystrom, 2013; Schlozman et al., 2010), though they disagree with the results of some other studies (e.g. Holt et al., 2013; Kamel, 2014; Khamis & Vaughn, 2011; Meier, 2011; Rice et al., 2012; Schuster, 2013; Valenzuela, 2013).

Comparing the relationships of both newspapers and SNS with youth's PP revealed that newspapers correlated significantly with PP, while SNS did not. The lack of a significant relationship between SNS and PP can be ascribed to the fact that participation was quantitatively examined for the two years preceding the questionnaire (June 2013 to June 2015), during this time period, all major political actions were undemocratic. SNS users were obvi-

Table 1. The relationship between newspaper readership and political participation.

			Levels of readership	Levels of PP
Spearman's rho	Levels of readership	Correlation coefficient	1.000	.131*
		Sig. (2-tailed)	.	.027
		N	284	284
	Levels of PP	Correlation coefficient	.131*	1.000
		Sig. (2-tailed)	.027	.
		N	284	400

*. Correlation is significant at the 0.05 level (2-tailed).

Table 2. The relationship between using SNS and political participation

			Levels of using SNS	Levels of PP
Spearman's rho	Levels of using SNS	Correlation coefficient	1.000	.081
		Sig. (2-tailed)	.	.111
		N	388	388
	Levels of PP	Correlation coefficient	.081	1.000
		Sig. (2-tailed)	.111	.
		N	388	400

*. Correlation is significant at the 0.05 level (2-tailed).

ously opposed to such actions. In contrast, the significant relationship found between reading newspapers and PP can be attributed to the fact that newspapers discourse was in line with undemocratic actions, which likely encouraged readers to participate.

Furthermore, political affiliation was examined to determine whether it yielded significant differences in PP levels. Using the non-parametric test of Kruskal-Wallis, the results found no significant differences between the two variables (χ^2 (2, N = 97) = .554, p = .758). This can be explained by three main factors: (1) most Egyptian youth do not tend to involve themselves in political parties or movements; (2) political parties and movements have been under government control for decades, and are also ineffective; and (3) the recent political actions in Egypt have been found to be connective actions (Shehata, 2017). According to Bennett and Segerberg (2012), most participants in connective actions tend to be unaffiliated, and these actions are likely moderated by communication technologies without interference from organizational actors (p. 755). This helps individuals (including youth) emerge as a political actor in the face of counteractors. In this way, SNS can empower political actors. This supports Castells' claim about the importance of mass media and Internet-based media for practicing power (Castells, 2009, p. 416). However, his is not an absolute claim, because the importance of SNS or even newspapers for structuring power relations and empowering political actors is contingent upon several factors, such as government repression and media censorship. In the following section, the discussion will seek more evidences to support or refute this claim.

4.2. Qualitative Analysis

The coding schemes of grounded theory yielded 803 codes, which represented the core ideas of the interviews transcripts. These codes were grouped into 33 categories and subcategories. Following this, two main categories were emerged from the analysis: fluctuation of PP; and power relations of political actors. Both categories were handled in relation to newspapers and SNS over the previous six years.

Starting with the fluctuation of PP, most interviewees pointed out that the youth's participation increased during and after 25J. This participation manifested in increased involvement in political parties, entities, and civil society organizations, and participating in protests and elections. However, since July 3rd, 2013, PP had been fundamentally thwarted by the governments. The lack of participation since then was best described and explained by the prominent political activist N. Abd Alhamid (personal communication, October 22nd, 2015), who told me in a despairing tone:

> Youth didn't run for elections; they didn't participate!
> You're talkin' about youth who have been distorted for two years!
> You're talkin' about the 25J that has been distorted for two or three years!
> You're talkin' about youth who have been excluded from political work!
> You're talkin' about jailed people!
> So, it is normal not to have a youth participation.

4.2.1. The Effects of Newspapers/SNS on Political Participation

Alongside the power transformations that occurred several times in post-25J Egypt, newspapers' attitudes toward the revolution and political actors rapidly changed. While newspapers supported the revolution and revolutionary youth in the wake of Mubarak's ouster, they turned against the revolution after July 3rd, 2013. This shift, as one interviewee stated, was normal in a context in which "media career in Egypt is subjected to two limitations: the extent of subordination to political authority; and, in a greater degree, the capital of the media" (A. Abdeen, personal communication, October 12th, 2015). This result agrees with Abdulla's study (2014), which also ascribed this shift to the changes in newspapers' freedom, which increased after 25J and declined after July 3rd, 2013.

Egyptian newspapers have suffered from both external and internal restrictions, especially since July 3rd, 2013. Whereas the former restrictions have manifested in security censorship, the latter restrictions have manifested in the self-censorship of editors-in-chief. Under these restrictions, many newspapers have suffered, according to the Freedom House (2016), from confiscation, banning issues, deterring writers from writing, and the imprisonment of journalists. Such restrictions have forced all newspapers to adopt a pro-government editorial policy, with very few exceptions, such as weak online newspapers such as *Bawabt Yanayer* (January Gate), *Albedaya* (The Beginning) and *Albadil* (The Alternative).

In a very significant testimony about the security interference, the journalist M. Al-kholy (personal communication, October 8th, 2015) revealed, "we received here in our newspaper a letter from the Defense Ministry stating that 'we'd like you not to publish any news about Sinai [the northeastern part of Egypt in which the army is fighting against terrorist groups] except the official statements issued by the Ministry's Department of Moral Affairs'." With regard to internal restrictions, the political activist and journalist S. Sayed (personal communication, October 20th, 2015), for example, talked about her personal experiment with newspapers' internal restrictions:

> I remember when I was working at Al-badil newspaper, I once uploaded a video and photos on Facebook entitled "MB demonstrations". In a very serious tone, my head of the department shouted at me and said "Don't you ever write the name of MB, you must append it with the term of terrorist group, this is an order for all newspapers."

In contrast to newspapers, SNS have been the main informational and mobilizational platforms for many political actions post-25J. In this regard, they have bridged the gap left by the government's control of mainstream media. However, the power transition since July 3rd, 2013 has negatively affected SNS. One such negative effect, for example, is that the use of SNS for opposition activities has increasingly become a case that might lead users to prison. As one interviewee noted, "there are more than one trial case, as published in newspapers, in which posting offensive content against the army or the country was between the seizures" (M. Al-kholy, personal communication, October 8th, 2015). As a result, the political effect of SNS has declined, although their ability to spread political awareness has increased (A. Dabbour, personal communication, October 15th, 2015).

In addition, most interviewees noticed that SNS had transformed from being platforms for political mobilization to being tools for political sarcasm and the defense of human rights. In this context, the prominent Journalist T. Abo Arab (personal communication, October 7th, 2015) noted:

> Now on Facebook there're no calls for protests, taking attitudes toward elections or overthrowing someone, because politics is no longer existent. The alternative is that SNS have become focusing on human rights and people's issues, and they've turned into a media channel that publishes what other media channels ignore.

The transformation of SNS from mobilization channels to human rights defenders adds a new dimension to the study of Alexander and Aouragh (2014), which found that online media are no longer primary platforms for transferring the activities and voices of specific revolutionary groups. More importantly, the transformations in attitudes of both newspapers and SNS toward PP coincided with and followed the transfer of political authority. Consequently, we can assume that the attitudes of newspapers and SNS toward PP related to authority transfer.

4.2.2. The Effects of Newspapers/SNS on Power Relations

The interviews had a special focus on the relationship of newspapers and SNS with the power relations of political actors post-25J. Initially, most interviewees agreed on the major actors, which included the army, the MB, revolutionary youth, remnants of the Mubarak regime, and, to a lesser degree, political parties. The prominent political activist S. Diab (personal communication, October 23rd, 2015) classified political actors into three groups:

> The political field in Egypt includes three sides: the country, not only the army but all institutions and those who belong to them; political Islam side, not only the Brotherhood but all Islamic actors; and civil side. Within every side there're influential and uninfluential actors....If two of these three sides allied against the third, they defeat it.

Based on the effectiveness of political actors, the previous six years could be divided, according to most interviewees, into three chronological stages: (1) from Mubarak's ouster on February 11th, 2011 to the beginning of 2012, when revolutionary youth, liberal actors, and leftist actors were a striking force in political activism; (2) from the beginning of 2012 to June 2013, when Islamic actors—including the MB and the Salafis—were a leading force in parliament and the presidency; and (3) after Morsi's ouster on July 3rd, 2013, when the army, remnants of the Mubarak regime, and business elite controlled all of the country's institutions.

Although it had only been a short period since the eruption of the revolution, political authority had been transferred several times, and with each transfer, the landscape of political coalitions and conflicts profoundly changed. During the revolution, a very short-term and spontaneous political coalition was formed between the revolutionary youth and the MB. This coalition cracked in March 2011, when the Brotherhood entered into an implicit coalition with the army. This new coalition completely broke down on June 30th, 2013, when the army joined a new coalition with the remnants of the Mubarak regime and a large portion of the civil forces and business elite. This latter new coalition managed to oust the MB from power on July 3rd, 2013, and following this, it massively repressed the MB and turned against revolutionary youth. Consequently, the three main actors (the army, the MB, and revolutionary youth) became separate and strongly conflicted. Accordingly, it can be said that the development of political relationships constructed the power and counter-power of political actors. In other words, political coalitions enabled allied actors to exert power over other actors. This analysis supports one of Castells' central claims that considers power as relationships between actors (Castells, 2009, p. 10).

Newspapers and SNS were indeed platforms upon which conflict and cooperation relationships were centered. On the one hand, newspaper ownership played a crucial role in shaping political discourse and affecting PP activities. According to the prominent activist I. Abd Al-fatah, newspapers that are owned or controlled by major political actors spark conflict relationships. While the army has almost controlled all types of newspapers, the MB-owned *Alhoriya Wa Aladala* (The Freedom and Justice), and the revolutionary youth have worked at some newspapers, through which they have expressed their views (I. Abd Al-fatah, personal communication, October 10th, 2015).

In addition, as most newspapers have been controlled by anti-revolution actors (the army, remnants of the Mubarak regime, and the business elite), their attitudes have been very negative toward the revolutionary youth and protest activities. This consequently has, as noted by M. Al-kholy (personal communication, October 8th, 2015), negatively affected newspapers' credibility for citizens, who no longer trust them. These results agree with those of some studies (e.g. Al-Maskati, 2012; Hamdy & Gomaa, 2012; Ibrahim, 2012; Youssef, 2012), which have found that newspapers have adopted negative attitudes toward protestors and participation activities.

On the other hand, SNS have been key tools for political information and mobilization. Revolutionary youth, in particular, have been superior in using them to organize protest activities. However other political actors have started to use SNS for counter-mobilization and shaping public opinion. In this context, T. Abo Arab (personal communication, October 7th, 2015) stated:

> Primarily, before the 25J, Facebook was mostly used by liberal activists, while the MB and the army were out of it. Straight after the revolution, the MB, followed by the army, started to use it intensively. The conflict between the MB and the army, therefore, moved to SNS. Both of the actors have had electronic teams that rivalled revolutionary youth online.

Going back to the argument of the inability of SNS to empower revolutionary youth in the long run, we can say, in light of this analysis, that SNS enabled the youth to transfer their voices, to provide different narratives of political actions, and to mobilize people for protests. As an emerging political actor, revolutionary youth could do this when they were the main users of SNS, which were also more free. But these conditions changed, and the ability of SNS to empower youth was affected by at least four determinants: access of other actors to SNS, the government's censorship of SNS, the government's control of mainstream media, and the political repression following July 3rd, 2013. As a consequence, the ability of SNS to give rise to revolutionary youth has considerably declined, leaving its ability to empower them in the long run very much in doubt.

This analysis disagrees with the results of some studies (e.g. Alexander & Aouragh, 2014, p. 892; Meier, 2011), which have shown that the Internet has shifted the power balance in favor of pro-revolution actors in Egypt. However, this does not necessarily mean that SNS have not been important for new political actors. Indeed, SNS and the Internet have been essential for playing, at least, two other roles: increasing tensions within the overall structure of power (Curran, 2002, p. 65) and making power (Castells, 2009, p. 416). These roles have not been maintained or translated into long-term empowerment by revolutionary youth.

5. Discussion

The quantitative analysis found that newspapers, but not SNS, related significantly with PP. The qualitative analysis supported these results and further indicated that both SNS and newspapers were crucial platforms for political actors, who were involved in a series of conflicts and coalitions over the last six years. While SNS gave rise to pro-revolution actors (especially revolutionary youth) and enabled them to topple Mubarak on February 11th, 2011, newspapers and other mainstream media enabled anti-revolution actors (especially the army) to restore authority on July 3rd, 2013. Thus, it can be said that SNS were not sufficient to empower the emergent force of revolutionary youth in the long-run in the face of anti-revolution actors.

The main reasons why the empowerment of revolutionary youth was obstructed, despite their strong access to SNS, are that anti-revolution actors controlled all mainstream media and practiced massive repression against opposition forces, and that SNS increasingly became available for anti-revolution actors (see, e.g., Castells, 2009, p. 414; Fenton, 2016, p. 176). These factors eventually led the anti-revolution actors to outweigh the revolutionary youth. Here, we can say that all aspects of the obstruction of PP by political regimes after July 3rd, 2013 undermined the emergence of new political actors and, at the same time, impaired the power of both revolutionary youth and the MB. Thus, it is reasonable to consider SNS a space for—not a holder of—power (Castells, 2007, p. 242). Nevertheless, this does not negate the importance of SNS and new political actors for the alteration of staging power relationships and decision making (Castells, 2009, p. 412; Curran, 2002, p. 65).

Furthermore, the quantitative analysis showed that Egyptian youth used newspapers and SNS in relatively high rates, and the qualitative analysis pointed out that political actors have overused both channels. Newspapers were exploited, especially by the army, for fighting political battles against opposition forces. As a result, the political discourse of newspapers became highly politicized and biased, and this consequently affected their credibility. In contrast, SNS were overused, especially by revolutionary youth, as a counter-platform for information and mobilization purposes. Many aspects of PP also shifted and were practiced through SNS. Especially right after the revolution, this made the logic of SNS more prevalent than the logic of political actions, which could be considered a type of mediatization of politics.

6. Conclusion

This article investigated the effects of newspapers and SNS on the political participation of youth and the power relations of political actors in Egypt following the 2011 revolution. In this context, I argued that SNS cannot, in the long run, empower new political actors, especially if newspapers and other mainstream media are under the control of old actors. In order to empirically validate this argument, a survey was applied on a sample of Egyptian youth and semi-structured interviews were conducted with a number of political activists and journalists.

The results found that newspapers, but not SNS, significantly related with youth's political participation. It was also found that both newspapers and SNS were decisive platforms for enabling pro- and anti-revolution actors, as powers and counter-powers, to achieve interim political goals. Both anti-revolution actors (supported by newspapers) and pro-revolution actors (supported by SNS) were involved in a series of cooperation and conflict relationships, which eventually ended up favoring the anti-revolution actors. Thus, SNS were not sufficient to empower revolutionary youth as a new political actor in the face of anti-revolution actors, primarily due to SNS censorship and political repression.

Acknowledgements

I am very grateful to my supervisor, Norbert Wildermuth, who guided me throughout the preparation of this article. I also thank the people who responded to the questionnaire and those who accepted the request for an interview despite the risks that might have entailed.

Conflict of Interests

The author declares no conflict of interests.

References

Abd Al-samad, R. (2014, January 17). Taqrir: MosharaKat Almasryeen fi kafat alentkhabat wa Alestifitaat baad thawrat 25 yanayr [Report: Egyptian's participation in all elections and referendums after the 25 January revolution]. *The Opinion*. Retrieved from: http://arrai.org/pages.php?option=browse&id=122832

Abdulla, R. (2014). *Egypt's media in the midst of revolution*. Washington, DC: Carnegie Endowment for International Peace.

Alexander, A., & Aouragh, M. (2014). Egypt's unfinished revolution: The role of the media revisited. *International Journal of Communication*, *8*, 809–915. doi:1932–8036/20140005

Allam, R. (2010). Media landscape: Egypt. *European Journalism Centre*. Retrieved from http://ejc.net/media_landscapes/egypt

AlMaskati, N. A. (2012). Newspaper coverage of the 2011 protests in Egypt. *International Communication Gazette*, *74*(4), 342–366. doi:10.1177/1748048512439820

Anglim, J. (2009). Calculating composite scores of ability and other tests in SPSS. *Jeromy Anglim's Blog: Psychology and Statistics*. Retrieved from http://jeromyanglim.blogspot.dk/2009/03/calculating-composite-scores-of-ability.html

Aouragh, M. (2012). Social media, mediation and the Arab revolutions. *Triple C*, *10*(2), 518–536.

Aouragh, M., & Alexander, A. (2012). The Egyptian experience: Sense and nonsense of the Internet revolution. *International Journal of Communication*, *5*, 1344–1358. doi:1932–8036/2011FEA1344

Bakker, T. P., & de Vreese, C. H. (2011). Good news for the future? Young people, Internet use, and political participation. *Communication Research*, *38*(4), 451–470. doi:10.1177/0093650210381738

Bennett, W. L., & Segerberg, A. (2012). The logic of connective action: Digital media and the personalization of contentious politics. *Information, Communication & Society*, *15*(5), 739–768. doi:10.1080/1369118X.2012.670661

Blernackl, B., & Waldorf, D. (1981). Snowball sampling problems and techniques of chain referral sampling. *Sociological Methods & Research*, *10*(2), 141–163.

Budak, A. (2010). *Facebook, Twitter and Barack Obama: New media and the 2008 presidential elections*. (Master Thesis, UMI No. 1474900). Georgetown University, Washington, USA.

Castells, M. (2007). Communication, power and counter-power in the network society. *International Journal of Communication*, *1*, 238–266. doi:1932-8036/20070238

Castells, M. (2009). *Communication power*. New York, NY: Oxford University Press.

Castells, M. (2011). A network theory of power. *International Journal of Communication*, *5*, 773–787. doi:1932–8036/20110773

Charmaz, K. (2006). *Constructing grounded theory: A practical guide through qualitative analysis*. London: Sage Publications.

Corbin, J. M., & Strauss, A. (1990). Grounded theory research: Procedures, canons, and evaluative criteria. *Qualitative Sociology*, *13*(1), 3–21. doi:10.1007/bf00988593

Creswell, J. W., & Plano Clark, V. L. (2011). *Designing and conducting mixed methods research* (2nd ed.). Thousand Oaks, CA: Sage Publications.

Curran, J. (2002). *Media and power: Communication and society*. New York, NY: Taylor & Francis.

Dimitrova, D., & Bystrom, D. (2013). The effects of social media on political participation and candidate image: Evaluations in the 2012 Iowa caucuses. *American Behavioral Scientist*, *57*(11), 1568–1583. doi:10.1177/0002764213489011

El-Adawy, A. (2014). Egypt's multiple power centers. *The Washington Institute for Near East Policy*. Retrieved from http://www.washingtoninstitute.org/policy-analysis/view/egypts-multiple-power-centers

El-dine, C. C. (2014). *Fragile alliances in Egypt's post-revolutionary order: The military and its partners*. Retrieved from https://www.files.ethz.ch/isn/185251/2014C46_chams_el_dine.pdf

Ellison, N. B., Steinfield, C., & Lampe, C. (2007). The benefits of Facebook "friends": Social capital and college students' use of online social network sites. *Journal of Computer-Mediated Communication*, *12*(4), 1143–1168. doi:10.1111/j.1083-6101.2007.00367.x

ElNawawy, M., & Khamis, S. (2012). Political activism 2.0: Comparing the role of social media in Egypt's "Facebook revolution" and Iran's "Twitter uprising". *CyberOrient*, *6*(1). Retrieved from http://www.cyberorient.net/article.do?articleId=7439

Fawzy, S. (2008). Taathir kol men alitsal algamahiry wa alshaksy ala alintmaat alhizbia wa almosharka alsyasya litolab algameat almesria bialtatbiq ala intikabat almagales almahlia (April 2008): Dirasa mashie ala tolab Gameat Alkahira [The effect of mass and personal communication on partisan affiliations and political participation of Egyptian university students, the case of local elections (April 2008): A survey on Cairo university students]. *The Egyptian Journal of Mass Communication Research*, *30*, 191–299.

Fenton, N. (2016). The internet of radical politics and social change. In J. Curran, N. Fenton, & D. Freedman (Eds.), *Misunderstanding the Internet* (2nd ed., pp. 173–202). New York, NY: Routledge.

Foreman, E. K. (1991). *Survey sampling principles*. New York, NY: Marcel Dekker.

Freedom House. (2016). *Egypt: Freedom of the press 2016*. Retrieved from https://freedomhouse.org/report/freedom-press/2016/egypt

Glaser, B. G., & Strauss, A. L. (1967). *The discovery of grounded theory, strategies for qualitative research*. New Brunswick: Aldine Transaction.

Gorsche, J. (2002). *Does newspaper reading still matter? Exploring the connection between the news: Media habits and political participation of Canadian youth* (Unpublished Master Thesis). The University of Calgary, Ottawa, Canada.

Groshek, J. (2008). *Freedom and new media: Examining the relationship between communication technologies and democracy cross-nationally from 1946 to 2003*. (Doctoral Dissertation, UMI No. 3319903). Indiana University, Bloomington, USA.

Gustafsson, N. (2012). The subtle nature of Facebook politics: Swedish social network site users and political participation. *New Media & Society*, *14*(7), 1111–1127. doi:10.1177/1461444812439551

Hamdy, N., & Gomaa, E. H. (2012). Framing the Egyptian uprising in Arabic language newspapers and social media. *Journal of Communication*, *62*(2), 195–211. doi:10.1111/j.1460-2466.2012.01637.x

Harrebye, S., & Ejrnæs, A. (2015). European patterns of participation: How dissatisfaction motivates extra-parliamentary activities given the right institutional conditions. *Comparative European Politics*, *13*(2), 151–174. doi:10.1057/cep.2013.7

Holt, K., Shehata, A., Strömbäck, J., & Ljungberg, E. (2013). Age and the effects of news media attention and social media use on political interest and participation: Do social media function as leveller? *European Journal of Communication*, *28*(1), 19–34. doi:10.1177/0267323112465369

Howard, P. N. (2010). *The digital origins of dictatorship and democracy: Information technology and political Islam*. New York, NY: Oxford University Press.

Howard, P. N., & Hussain, M. M. (2013). *Democracy's fourth wave, digital media and the Arab Spring*. Oxford: Oxford University Press.

Ibrahim, E. (2012). *Newspapers coverage of the Egyptian January 25 revolution: A framing analysis*. (Unpublished Master Thesis). The American University, Cairo, Egypt.

Israel, G. D. (1992, November). *Determining sample size* (PEOD6). Gainesville: University of Florida. Retrieved from http://www.psycholosphere.com/Determining%20sample%20size%20by%20Glen%20Israel.pdf

Kamel, S. H. (2014). The value of social media in Egypt's uprising and beyond. *The Electronic Journal of Information Systems in Developing Countries*, *60*(5), 1–7. Retrieved from https://www.ejisdc.org/Ojs2/index.php/ejisdc/article/view/1257

Khalifa, S. (2015). *Egypt's lost spring: Causes and consequences*. Santa Barbara, CA: Praeger.

Khamis, S. (2011). The transformative Egyptian media landscape, changes, challenges and comparative perspectives. *International Journal of Communication*, *5*, 1159–1177. doi:1932–8036/20111159

Khamis, S., & Vaughn, K. (2011). Cyberactivism in the Egyptian revolution: How civic engagement and citizen journalism tilted the balance. *Arab Media and Society*, *14*, 1-37.

Khamis, S., Gold, P. B., & Vaughn, K. (2012). Beyond Egypt's "Facebook revolution" and Syria's "YouTube uprising": Comparing political contexts, actors and communication strategies. *Arab Media & Society*, *15*, 1–30.

Mason, P. (2013). *Why it's kicking off everywhere*. London: Verso Books.

Meier, P. P. (2011). *Do liberation technologies change the balance of power between repressive states and civil society?* (Doctoral Dissertation, UMI No. 3499978). The Fletcher School of Law and Diplomacy, Medford, USA.

Moeller, J., De Vreese, C., Esser, F., & Kunz, R. (2014). Pathway to political participation: The influence of online and offline news media on internal efficacy and turnout of first-time voters. *American Behavioral Scientist*, *58*(5), 689–700. doi:10.1177/0002764213515220

Oser, J., Hooghe, M., & Marien, S. (2013). Is online participation distinct from offline participation? A latent class analysis of participation types and their stratification. *Political Research Quarterly*, *66*(1) 91–101. doi: 10.1177/1065912912436695

Rice, L. L., Moffett, K. W., & Madupalli, R. (2012). Campaign-related social networking and the political participation of college students. *Social Science Computer Review*, *31*(3), 257–279. doi:10.1177/0894439312455474

Richard, D. M. (2010). Standardized score. In N. J. Salkind (Ed.), *Encyclopedia of research design* (pp. 1437–1441). Thousand Oaks, CA: Sage Publications.

Roll, S. (2014). *Al-Sisi's development visions: Projects and power in Egypt* (SWP Comments 26). Berlin: Stiftung Wissenschaft und Politik. Retrieved from https://www.swp-berlin.org/fileadmin/contents/products/comments/2014C26_rll.pdf

Schlozman, K., Verba, S., & Brady, H. E. (2010). Weapon of the strong? Participatory inequality and the Internet. *Perspectives on Politics*, *8*(2), 487–509. doi:10.1017/S1537592710001210

Schuster, J. (2013). Invisible feminists? Social media and young women's political participation. *Political Science*, *65*(1), 8–24. doi:10.1177/0032318713486474

Shehata, A. (2010). Pathways to politics: How media system characteristics can influence socioeconomic gaps in political participation. *The International Journal of Press/Politics*, *15*(3), 295–318. doi:10.1177/1940161209360930

Shehata, M. (2017). Are people more connective than political actions? Toward an empirical approach for connective participants. *Interactions: Studies in Communication and Culture*. Manuscript in preparation.

Sika, N. (2012). Youth political engagement in Egypt: From abstention to uprising. *British Journal of Middle Eastern Studies*, *39*(2), 181–199. doi:10.1080/13530194.2012.709700

Strauss, A., & Corbin, J. M. (1998). *Basics of qualitative research: Techniques and procedures for developing grounded theory* (2nd ed.). Thousand Oaks, CA: Sage Publications.

Valenzuela, S. (2013). Unpacking the use of social media for protest behavior: The roles of information, opinion expression, and activism. *American Behavioral Scientist*, *57*(7), 920–942. doi:10.1177/0002764213479375

Verba, S., Schlozman, K. L., & Brady, H. (2002). *Voice and equality: Civic voluntarism in American politics* (4th ed.). Cambridge, MA: Harvard University Press.

Vissers, S., Hooghe, M., Stolle, D., & Mahéo, V. A. (2012). The impact of mobilization media on off-line and online participation: Are mobilization effects medium-specific? *Social Science Computer Review*, *30*(2), 152–169. doi:10.1177/0894439310396485

Wang, Y. W. (2002). *Talking, politics, and media: How does media use correlate with political talk and political participation?* (Master Thesis, UMI No. 1406955). California State University, Fullerton, USA.

Williams, A. E. (2008). *Engaging the electorate in an electronic age: Surveying citizens' use of digital newspapers during a presidential election*. (Doctoral Dissertation, UMI No. 3305105). University of Michigan, Ann Arbor, USA.

Wimmer, R. D., & Dominick, J. R. (2011). *Mass media research: An introduction* (9th ed.). Boston: Wadsworth.

Wright-Phillips, M. V. (2010). Mass media and political participation: Does news source matter? (Master Thesis, UMI No. 1482678). Southern Illinois University, Carbondale, USA.

Youssef, A. M. (2012). *A critical analysis on media coverage of the Egyptian revolution: The case of Al-Ahram, Al-Masry Al-Youm, The Telegraph and The Washington Post* (Unpublished Master Thesis). Örebro University, Örebro, Sweden.

8

Hazy Boundaries: Virtual Communities and Research Ethics

Helena Kantanen [1,*] and Jyri Manninen [2]

[1] Business School, University of Eastern Finland, 70211 Kuopio, Finland; E-Mail: helena.kantanen@uef.fi
[2] School of Educational Sciences and Psychology, University of Eastern Finland, 80101 Joensuu, Finland; E-Mail: jyri.manninen@uef.fi

* Corresponding author

Abstract
This paper examines ethical issues specific to research into virtual communities. Drawing on an empirical case with online forums of education experts, we identify the following key issues: publicity versus privacy of the community; the definition of human subjects research; participant recruitment; informed consent; and ethical questions associated with observing virtual communities, and with reporting and disseminating research results. We maintain that different research cultures in different countries can present challenges when studying global forums. Acknowledging the ephemeral characteristics of Internet contexts, this paper argues that ethical considerations should be more case-based, instead of relying on one model for all solutions. We suggest that local ethics committees or institutional review boards could, with their expert knowledge of ethics, provide valuable support for researchers operating in the complex and dynamic terrain of Internet research, as well as in fields and research settings where an ethical review is not a standard part of the research process.

Keywords
digital ethics; ethics; ethics committee; institutional review board; Internet research ethics; netnography; online communities; virtual communities

Issue
This article is part of the issue "Successes and Failures in Studying Social Media: Issues of Methods and Ethics", edited by Epp Lauk and Niina Sormanen (University of Jyväskylä, Finland).

---

1. Introduction

The ever-increasing popularity of social media platforms has made them alluring from the point of view of academic research. Researchers now have a unique and cost-efficient opportunity to examine and understand behaviours and beliefs in naturalistic contexts, and to reach populations which may be hard to reach otherwise (Madge, 2007; Moreno, Goniou, & Moreno, 2013). At the same time, the easy availability of research data made possible by social media raises new ethical questions such as what is public and what is private. Moreover, the prevailing ethical guidelines may not be applicable in all research settings. Therefore, the basic principles of ethical research conduct associated with respecting the autonomy of research subjects, avoiding harm, and protecting privacy and data, are extremely topical, and more discussion and understanding is needed about their implications in the context of relatively new electronic environments (Bruckman, 2006; Dennen, 2012; Finnish Advisory Board on Research Integrity, 2009; Hine, 2000; Kozinets, 2010; Markham & Buchanan, 2012; Zimmer, 2010).

This paper, written from the Finnish perspective, focuses on ethical issues related to the study of discussions on Internet forums—or, more specifically, virtual communities. Virtual communities, or online communities, are Internet-based communication forums or social networks where interaction is based on computer–mediated communication (Lakkala, 2010; Manninen & Nevgi, 2000). In these communities, participants typically have a common interest, like product development or the use of social media tools at work (Kosonen, 2009; Wasko & Faraj, 2005). These communities are also characterised by "public discussions long enough, with sufficient human feeling, to form webs of personal relationships in cyberspace" (Rheingold, 1993, p. 193).

During our ongoing research project (Kantanen, Manninen & Kontkanen, 2014), we have explored learning, communication and innovation generation, in both a national and global online community. During the different phases of our project, we have tackled several ethical issues. The questions we have asked have included, for example: Do we need an official ethical review when studying a global LinkedIn community, administered from the United States? Are we studying a public or private forum? Are community postings exempt? Does our study qualify as human subjects research? What would be an appropriate way to recruit research participants? How would we gain informed consent, and is it always necessary? How should we behave in an online forum when observing participants? How can we safeguard the confidentiality of participants' contributions when reporting the study?

Ethical questions are complicated in the real world but they are even more complex in the virtual environment. Such questions are related to the concepts of public and private, confidentiality, the integrity of data, reputational risks, intellectual property issues, and whether the research qualifies as human subjects research or not. Other issues include participant recruitment, disclosure of presence, and citing, anonymising and crediting when reporting and disseminating research results (Bassett & O'Riordan, 2002; Bruckman, 2006; Buchanan & Zimmer, 2013; Hine, 2000; Kozinets, 2010; Markham & Buchanan, 2012; Turtiainen & Östman, 2013; Walther, 2002).

The remainder of this paper is organised as follows: Section 2 clarifies different ethical questions concerning Internet research. Section 3 describes our study, the empirical case, and the ethical issues involved with it. Section 4 discusses these issues, and our conclusions follow in Section 5.

2. Internet Research Ethics

The Finnish Advisory Board on Research Integrity (2009) defines the ethical principles of research in the humanities and social and behavioural sciences in three regards: (1) respecting the autonomy of research subjects; (2) avoiding harm; and (3) privacy and data protection. Respecting the autonomy of research subjects means, before all, voluntary participation based on informed consent. Harm can be mental, financial or social, and can occur during the collecting of data, retaining of data, or during the publishing of research results. Privacy and data protection involve issues related to protecting research data and confidentiality, storing and destroying data, and publishing research results. The Advisory Board guidelines emphasise a balance between confidentiality and the openness of research.

Rosenberg (2010) shows how boundary work has challenged Internet researchers and revitalised the discussion about research ethics. For example, boundaries between private and public are often blurred. Rosenberg summarises the general principles of ethical matters: researchers should maximise benefits and minimise harm, people must be treated fairly and equally, research subjects should be treated as autonomous individuals, and those with diminished autonomy must be entitled to protection (Rosenberg, 2010).

One of the key issues in Internet research is whether to use the Internet as a practical research tool (e.g., online questionnaires, Internet–mediated research or online research practice), as a research data source (i.e., studies in the web), or as a research object (i.e., studies about the web) (Turtiainen & Östman, 2013). Turtiainen and Östman (2013) remind us that, often, all of these elements create a research environment that requires, for example, awareness of source criticisms, knowledge of cultural practices associated with the specific research environment, knowledge about how the data has been created, and an understanding of how research subjects perceive the publicity or privacy of their web presence.

Specific ethical questions related to virtual environments have become topical since 2000 (Turtiainen & Östman, 2013). Madge (2007) identifies five key issues discussed in the literature on online research ethics: informed consent, confidentiality, privacy, debriefing and netiquette. All of these issues will be discussed later from the point of view of our study. By netiquette, Madge refers to the often flexible codes of conduct or guidelines applied in Internet communication, including phenomena like flaming and online harassment. Tavani (2006) discusses ethical issues related to the increasing use of cybertechnology, which refers to a wide range of computing and communication systems. He calls for cyberethics as "a field of applied ethics that examines moral, legal, and social issues involving cybertechnology" (p. 19). According to Tavani, professional codes of conduct can often help to resolve professional ethics issues, which is also what the different ethical guidelines are meant for. To our knowledge, the most advanced recommendations and guidelines concerning Internet research come from the Association of Internet Researchers (AoIR) and its Ethics Working Committee. They outline general principles that are meant to guide decision-making in Internet research, regardless of rapidly changing technological contexts (Markham & Buchanan, 2012). Markham and Buchanan call for guidelines rather than a code of practice to ensure the flexibility of research and the usefulness of those guidelines in different research contexts. The major issues or considerations identified in the AoIR guidelines are: (1) questions of human subjects research; (2) publicity and privacy; (3) are we studying text or persons; and (4) top–down versus bottom–up approaches to ethics (Markham & Buchanan, 2012). Regarding the last tension, Markham and Buchanan refer to the need for researchers to balance between contextual, case–based requirements, and disciplinary, institutional, legal and cultural constraints.

McKee and Porter (2009a) developed an inquiry strategy to guide decisions about research ethics. They "believe that ethical decision-making for research must be systematic, deliberative, collaborative, and multidisciplinary in order to be valid" (p. 7), and offer a framework for those criteria. According to them, researchers must recognise the special circumstances of each case and be able to situate their case in proximity to other parallel cases and to community expectations in particular (McKee & Porter, 2009a). Instead of codes of practice or guidelines, they emphasise case-based processes that would help researchers with their decision-making in the ever-changing Internet environment (McKee & Porter, 2009b).

Ethnographic research has an interest in cultures and cultural meanings with an emphasis on the insider view, as well as in language and rhetoric (Eriksson & Kovalainen, 2016). Robert V. Kozinets coined the concept of *netnography*, which refers to ethnography conducted online. According to Kozinets (2010, p. 60): "Netnography is participant-observational research based in online fieldwork. It uses computer-mediated communications as a source of data to arrive at the ethnographic understanding and representation of a culture or communal phenomenon."

Kozinets (2010) maintains that "pure" ethnography studies communities or cultures, without important online elements, through face-to-face interaction and data collection, while "pure" netnography does the same, without important in-person elements, through entirely online interaction and data collection. Therefore, Kozinets challenges another pioneer of virtual ethnography, Christine Hine (2000, 2005), who maintains that online ethnography is always partial because the online experience is only one aspect of the social experience, and also because the culture or community studied does not have the field site needed for a holistic description of the culture.

The nature of our study in relation to netnography is examined further in the following section.

3. The Empirical Case and Its Ethical Challenges

In our project, our aim is to analyse learning, communication and innovation generation in virtual communities. Our data is derived from discussion threads published in online forums, as explained in Table 1.

In our pilot study (Kantanen et al., 2014), we examined a Finnish web-based community intended for those interested in using social media tools in teaching and learning (*Sometu*; http://sometu.ning.com). As of September 2013, that community, *Sometu*, had 4,828 members. The research question in our pilot study was: *What are the prerequisites of learning and innovation development in virtual communities of practice used by professionals?* In the more recent study (Kantanen & Manninen, 2014), the empirical data were collected from the international LinkedIn group Higher Education Teaching and Learning (HETL), founded in February 2010. As of January 2016, the group has 63,124 members. The HETL LinkedIn group is a network of professionals who participate by using their own names, job titles and photos. The research question of this study is: *How can discussions in virtual communities contribute to professional learning and development?* In addition to these studies, our project included Master's theses writers who use the HETL discussion threads as data. One completed thesis analysed the sense-making process in a discussion thread concerning the use of electronic devices in class (Tiiliharju, 2015).

This paper focuses on the ethical issues related to our HETL LinkedIn group study because its global nature allows more diverse ethical issues to be discussed than national forums. In 2010, at the advent of social media expansion, there was an exciting discussion thread in the HETL LinkedIn community. The opening question was: "Do you accept your students' invitations to connect on Facebook and other social networks?" The discussion continued over seven months and included about 280 discussants from over 190 organisations. Altogether, there were 508 replies. When printed out, the data were 135 pages long. We are interested in

Table 1. Virtual communities of practice project.

	Online Community	Practitioners Studied	Data	Approach/Methods
Pilot study	Finnish community Social Media Supporting Web-Learning (*Sometu*)	Higher education and business experts involved in the use of social media in education	Discussion threads	Qualitative content analysis (ATLAS.ti)
Current study	Global LinkedIn community, Higher Education Teaching and Learning (HETL)	Higher education and business experts involved in higher education and learning	Discussion threads, online observations, interviews	Qualitative content analysis (ATLAS.ti), Virtual ethnography (netnography)

both the process and the content of idea and innovation development in the forum. We have already studied *how* new ideas and innovations are developed on virtual forums, and *what* kinds of ideas and innovations are developed. In this paper, the focus is not on our research results, but on different ethical issues related to the study of this global virtual community of education experts.

Our study qualifies as Internet research because we utilise the Internet to collect data, study how people use the Internet through observing participation in virtual forums, utilise datasets available via the Internet, and employ content analysis to study the web (Markham & Buchanan, 2012). Drawing on Kozinets (2010), we can consider our study a netnography because we enter discussion forums as researchers, use discussion threads as natural data, observe participants on the forum, and also participate in the discussions ourselves. We are both members of the HETL group, and one of us also participated in the Facebook friending discussion thread. According to Kozinets (2010), netnographers should spend significant time interacting within and becoming a part of an online community. We see this participation as an advantage in our attempt to understand the innovation development process and communication of the group. Moreover, we claim that our thorough understanding of the context, culture and dynamics of the target forums contributed to the quality of our research because we were able to interpret our data from the point of view of our informants (Turtiainen & Östman, 2013).

3.1. Challenge 1: Ethical Review

We completed our literature review on virtual communities in early 2013 (Kantanen et al., 2014) and were ready to proceed to the data collection phase of our study. We thought that it would be a good idea to have the Committee on Research Ethics (equivalent to institutional review boards, or IRBs, in the U.S.) of our home university evaluate and approve our research plan. In our country, and in the field of the humanities and social and behavioural sciences, an ethical review is needed if the study involves an intervention in the physical integrity of subjects, deviates from the principle of informed consent, involves children under the age of 15, exposes research subjects to strong stimuli and evaluating possible harm requires expertise, has the potential to cause long-term mental harm, or poses a safety risk to subjects (Finnish Advisory Board on Research Integrity, 2009). None of these elements were involved in our planned project; however, we intended to study the global LinkedIn forum, HETL, operated from within the United States, and concluded that obtaining ethical approval would be advisable. The Chair of the Committee assured us that our national procedure is very cautious, and that the evaluation of ethical aspects of the research plan would be valid anywhere in the world.

Neither of us had previous experience with ethical reviews because, in our fields of business and adult education, the standard research process does not include ethical reviews—as it often does, for example, in the field of health research. Moreover, Finland has often been characterised as a high-trust society (e.g., Korhonen & Seppälä, 2005), which includes trust towards institutions, such as universities and their researchers. Therefore, many research environments have been accessible to our researchers without complicated application procedures.

Our first application was returned for revision, as was the second application. At this stage, however, we had come far enough that no Committee meeting was needed; but we nonetheless had to make final changes, which would then be evaluated and accepted—or rejected—by the Chair and the Secretary. In total, the process from the first application to the supporting statement took 1.5 years. There were several reasons for the delay. First, the instructions given and the structure and themes of the application form were poorly applicable to the type of Internet research we were planning. For this reason, we found it difficult to answer the questions as specifically as was required. Moreover, we were quite frustrated and not able to rewrite the application because of other duties. It was, indeed, very difficult to make decisions about possible ethical issues in advance of our study (Markham & Buchanan, 2012).

The HETL forum founder, who is the central gatekeeper when accessing the forum, accepted the ethical review from our home university, but it was a long process to gain the ethical approval. We obviously applied for the ethical review without fully thinking through the different aspects of Internet research ethics. Had we known then what we know now, our application would have been accepted in the first round. Our struggle with the ethics committee triggered a more profound understanding of the different and often complex dimensions of Internet research ethics. Because we have realised that both our students and fellow researchers sometimes have quite a nonchalant attitude towards ethical issues and Internet data, we wish to share what we have learned.

3.2. Challenge 2: Public or Private Forum

Like many other social media researchers, we pondered whether the HETL LinkedIn group was a public or private forum, or if it was a text more than it was a place. If it was a place, was it a public place? If it was a text, could it be quoted like a book? Or, could it be treated like the Letters to the Editor section in newspapers, where readers submit their input knowing that it will be made publicly available to all readers?

If the discussions can be considered a text, then the focus is totally different from the point of view of ethics than when dealing with human subjects. Could we observe LinkedIn discussants just as we would observe people in a public place? Or could we consider their inputs in the forum as texts? Does it make a difference if the discussion thread studied is several years old, as compared to a synchronous discussion?

McKee and Porter (2009b) make a distinction between a space and a place. If an Internet site is seen as a space, it is primarily a medium of publication, and the focus of research is mainly on what is published. If it is a place, people gather there to discuss and to share, and the focus of research is on people instead. The dominant view has long been that the Internet is a social domain, and this has led to "an imperative to apply restrictions from the human subjects model" (Bassett & O'Riordan, 2002, p. 234). The Internet is neither public nor private. It is neither a place (residence) nor a space (publication medium). As Kozinets (2010) explains, it is actually many types of social interaction, including chats, blogs, soundclips, and videos.

Private information is such that an individual can expect it to not be monitored or collected, or made publicly available. However, questions of publicity and privacy are complicated in virtual environments. Even on public forums, people may have expectations of privacy, or find it inappropriate that their inputs are read, collected or analysed by external parties (Dennen, 2012; Markham & Buchanan, 2012; Walther, 2002; Zimmer, 2010). Even with postings on public discussion forums, people do not expect that their inputs will be analysed. For example, in a public virtual world like Second Life, users consider their virtual homes to be private (Rosenberg, 2010). Also, public blogs have been considered to be a part of their writers' identity and should not be treated as publicly available data (Dennen, 2012; Markham & Buchanan, 2012). Dennen (2012) maintains that the only reliable way to evaluate a research subject's desire for privacy is to request his or her consent to participate in research.

In our case, our data, the Facebook friending thread in the HETL LinkedIn forum, can be considered as text because it was active several years earlier and is, therefore, archived material. Moreover, the question of publicity was clarified in the HETL Policy, which was published after we started our project. The Policy states that "The HETL LinkedIn discussion forum (i.e., global online community or practice) is considered a quasi-public group for the purpose of academic research and existing postings are therefore exempt. However, researchers must get approval from the HETL IRB before starting any research project involving this discussion forum data" (https://www.hetl.org/hetl-research/). The Institutional Review Board (IRB) was founded after we started our study, but the use of forum postings was approved by the HETL forum's founder, Dr. Patrick Blessinger, and we have committed to keeping him, as well as the Chair of the HETL Review Board, informed about the different phases of our project.

3.3. Challenge 3: Human Subjects Research—Or Not?

The definition of human subjects research matters because in many countries, like in the U.S., approval by the Institutional Review Board (IRB) is always required when researching human subjects (Bruckman, 2006). A study becomes human subjects research when the researcher deals and interacts with a living person (Bruckman, 2002). But do we interact with living persons when studying the LinkedIn group discussion threads?

"Human subjects research is research in which there is an intervention or interaction with another person for the purpose of gathering information, or in which information is recorded by a researcher in such a way that a person can be identified through it directly or indirectly" (U.S. Department of Health & Human Services, 2009).

The concept of human subjects research, which was originally related to the treatment of persons in medical experiments, still defines ethical research considerations (Markham & Buchanan, 2012). The concept has also been criticised by, for example, Bassett and O'Riordan (2002, p. 244), who claim that "research that positions the Internet as a social space containing cultural activity ripe for observation ignores the range of textual applications that the Internet supports." Bruckman (2002) suggests that, instead of human subjects, we should talk about "amateur artists" who use the Internet as a playground to create semi-published work.

According to the definition above, ethnographic Internet research (netnography) *is* human subjects research. However, research use of spontaneous conversations, gathered in a publicly accessible venue, is not human subjects research, according to the Code of Federal Regulations (2009) that governs Institutional Review Boards (IRBs) in the United States (Kozinets, 2010). The Association of Internet Researchers reminds us that because there are individual persons involved in digital information, researchers might need to consider principles related to research on human subjects (Markham & Buchanan, 2012).

Terms such as harmful, vulnerable, or personally identifiable information may be more relevant than the human subjects model, at least outside of the regulatory framework of research ethics (Markham & Buchanan, 2012). Instead of the spatial models behind the human subjects view, Bassett and O'Riordan (2002) suggest a hybrid model of relational ethics that would incorporate text, space and bodies and thus extend the limited application of the human subjects model. They argue that the human subjects research model is too narrow and does not consider the Internet as a cultural production of texts.

The conclusion is that research of publicly accessible conversations—or even semi-public conversations, like in our HETL case—is not human subjects research, but this does not exclude the need to consider ethical principles of avoiding harm and protecting privacy.

3.4. Challenge 4: Participant Recruitment and Informed Consent

When we discuss recruiting participants for research, we address two separate issues: first, under which conditions can we use the HETL discussions as research material; and second, what kind of process should be applied when recruiting HETL members for additional interviews.

In our study, we have thus far only been dealing with forum discussions. Because the HETL policy considers group postings exempt for academic research, we have not yet been involved in participant recruitment when studying forum postings. Also, Kozinets (2010) states that a netnographer's normal, asynchronous actions in online communities do not require informed consent. However, we are aware that there are different points of view about this. In the U.S., a utilitarian stance may prevail, meaning that benefits to society are weighed against potential risks; whereas in Central and Northern Europe, a deontological or communitarian stance that does not compromise confidentiality and anonymity may be taken (Markham, 2006, p. 48). Despite our Finnish background, we have adopted the Anglo-American view because the focal group for our study is an online forum administrated from the U.S.

The question of informed consent will become relevant at the next stage of our project because informed consent is always required for interviews. Also, the HETL Policy states that when collecting research data directly from research participants, researchers must first get approval from the HETL Institutional Review Board and receive informed consent from the research participants (https://www.hetl.org/hetl-research/). In the ethical review that we went through, the consent form that we made on the basis of Kozinets (2010, p. 194), as well as the process of electronic consent, was approved for our research purposes by our local ethics committee.

Enrolling research participants requires contact between the researchers and the study participants. Several sources consider informed consent to be a cornerstone of ethical research conduct (e.g., Buchanan & Zimmer, 2013). The process of informed consent involves the participants becoming aware, through conversations, of the purpose of the study, what rights and responsibilities participation involves, the risks and benefits of the study, possible compensation or costs, confidentiality and participant rights (Flicker, Haans, & Skinner, 2004; Kozinets, 2010). When studying virtual communities, all of this can be done online, and several authors advise gathering all relevant research information into a project website, and obtaining informed consent through a registration page (Bruckman, 2002, 2006; Kozinets, 2010). This process is recommended for adults and non-vulnerable populations, as well as when the research is not high risk.

According to our experience, online groups' Terms of Service and policies are very helpful when pondering the question of participant recruitment (see also Markham & Buchanan, 2012, p. 8). In our case, the HETL Policy requires HETL Institutional Review Board approval for any research project, as well as informed consent when collecting data directly from forum participants. The Policy also helped shape the public–private division and text–space discussion. Moreover, we advise researchers to identify different gatekeepers and to discuss their intentions openly with forum founders, administrators and group moderators. This is what we did with both our national and global group. Then, a statement can be added to the informed consent form that specifies that the study plan has been accepted by the forum administrator or owner.

One could also consider the timing of informed consent from a different point of view. Several authors (Markham & Buchanan, 2012; McKee & Porter, 2009b) suggest a process approach to research ethics. One may not need consent when collecting the data, but rather at the reporting and dissemination stage, if one wishes, for example, to quote a forum participant (Dennen, 2012). Many decisions at this stage pose ethical concerns; for example, which (if any) details to reveal about the study site and participants.

3.5. Challenge 5: Observing the Community

Much debate exists concerning how researchers should behave when observing a virtual community. The general rule should be to work as transparently as possible because, as Rutter and Smith (2005, p. 90) argue: "the ramifications of unethical disclosure are real and inescapable." However, not even the question of disclosing your presence is simple in the online environment. In our case, it was easy because we did not study synchronous discussions of the HETL LinkedIn group, but rather those that had become active several years earlier, and were already archived. However, during potential new phases of our study, these questions may become more important. We now have enough knowledge to face these questions in an ethical manner; that is, by disclosing our presence as researchers to the forum participants or to the discussants of a specific thread.

Kozinets (2010) advises netnographers to always disclose their presence, affiliations and intentions. Several authors are unequivocal about identity deception, such as Kozinets (2010): "Netnographers should *never, under any circumstances*, engage in identity deception" (p. 147). Identity deception may occur on the sites studied, but researchers should always identify themselves. There are different ways to do this, such as putting information about ongoing research on one's own personal profile (Bruckman, 2006).

There may be projects that would be unsuccessful if the researcher were to disclose his or her presence. Hudson and Bruckman (2004) studied how chatroom discussants responded to the researchers' presence and/or attendance in their forum and found that they reacted with hostility when they became aware of being studied. Therefore, the researchers considered the informed consent process to be impracticable. Sanders (2005) observed online communities of sex workers without disclosing her presence, as a so-called "lurker". She did not want the participants to alter their behaviour, nor did she want to harm the shared community or provoke hostility. Sometimes, this kind of anonymity may also protect the researcher. There may be some unwanted consequences if the researcher were to reveal his or her identity and affiliations to certain online groups (Sanders, 2005). It is possible that because hostile online behaviour is becoming more common (Jane, 2015), researchers might need to consider their own protection, even when studying relatively "safe" online forums—especially if discussed issues are sensitive, such as topical discussions revolving around asylum seekers. Bruckman (2006) gave an example of a student researcher who became the victim of racism on the site that he was studying. We know from our home university that hostile messages have been targeted at researchers working on issues related to immigration (Mikkonen, 2015).

3.6. Challenge 6: Reporting and Dissemination

Reporting and dissemination ethics apply to the various media in and through which research results are presented: academic journals and reports, conference presentations, websites, videos, press releases, interviews and information leaflets. Each of these reporting and dissemination mediums have their own distinct consequences. For example, writing about research methods transparently and in detail increases the credibility of a study.

It is obvious that there has been a delay in our research publication and reporting efforts because of the different ethical concerns we have experienced. The ethical questions at this phase of the study include, in our experience, questions of citing, anonymising, and crediting. Can we mention the HETL LinkedIn group and the specific discussion thread studied in our articles? Do the participants own copyright over their input in the discussion forum? If so, do we need to add author references for all cited input? And, if we delete all identifiers (like names and affiliations) to protect the informants' privacy, how do we give credit to those who contributed innovative ideas in the discussion thread?

Bruckman (2006, p. 91) states that "one of the thorniest problems concerns how to disguise names of people and sites." She asks how the researcher should balance the need to protect research participants with the need to give credit for their work (Bruckman, 2002). She uses the metaphor of "amateur artists", meaning that "all user-generated content on the Internet can be viewed as various forms of amateur art and authorship" (p. 229); consequently, these amateur artists deserve credit for what they have produced.

Bruckman (2002) proposes different levels of disguising, on a continuum from no disguise, to light and moderate disguise, to heavy disguise. In the case of no disguise, the report would have real names or pseudonyms of research subjects and the researcher would, therefore, respect the individual's copyright over his or her input. At the other end of the continuum, in the case of heavy disguise, the group studied would not be named and all identifying details would be changed. The report would include no verbatim quotes, and some false details might be introduced. It is worth noting that one cannot be careful enough with personal data. Zimmer (2010) explains a case where the researchers failed to anonymise their data with information about 1,700 college students' Facebook profiles. Even though all of the identifiers were deleted or encoded, the university in question was discovered and the privacy of research subjects' sensitive personal information was endangered.

Our case falls into the category of "light disguise" (Bruckman, 2002), where the community studied is named but participant names and some other identifying details like organisational affiliations are removed. We are also going to use verbatim quotes in our papers, even if they can be used to identify a group member with the help of search engines. For example, Moreno et al. (2013) advise against direct quotations to protect confidentiality. We do not consider this to be a problem because, as explained above, our study is not of high risk and, therefore, light disguise should be enough. Some authors have adopted the utilitarian approach to research ethics (Markham, 2006). For instance, Bruckman (2002) advises balancing the degree of risk against the benefits of the study, while Markham and Buchanan (2012) advise balancing the rights of subjects with the social benefits of the research and researchers' rights to conduct research.

McKee and Porter (2009b, p. 88) illustrate this issue of disguising by constructing a figure within which the necessity of informed consent can be assessed according to the following variables: Public vs. private, Topic sensitivity, Degree of interaction and Subject vulnerability. Each variable should be evaluated along the private–public or high–low scale. At the "low end" of the scale, consent may not be necessary; while at the "high end" of the scale, consent will most likely be required. The authors emphasise that these variables can be hard to determine and can also be culture–specific; in other words, a sensitive topic for one culture may not be sensitive at all for another. That said, our study occupies the "low end" of the scale in regards to all of these variables.

Importantly, our research question specifically examines verbatim quotes, not who said them, which thus eliminates the need to give credit to discussion participants. The main purpose of our study is neither to analyse what kind of innovations are generated in a discussion nor to examine the behaviour of those who generate them. Instead, the objective is to analyse online discussions and the internal logic of how text-based, delayed, asynchronous communication develops and proceeds in online communities (see Kantanen et al., 2014). In other words, we are not interested in *who* wrote *what*; rather, we are interested in the types of input (e.g., questions, experience sharing, reflections, etc.) generated in online discussions, as well as whether such discussions follow the five cycles of value creation (Wenger, Trayner & de Laat, 2011). As such, in this kind of analysis, verbatim quotes are important—even mandatory—because the research focus is on *how* text is written.

Bruckman (2002) suggests that if the study is low risk, the researcher could ask the research subjects if they want a pseudonym, real name, both, or neither to be used. If the study is high risk, it is not appropriate to list names or pseudonyms. Minimal risk means, by definition, "that the probability and magnitude of harm or discomfort anticipated in the research are not greater in and of themselves than those ordinarily encountered in daily life or during the performance of routine physical or psychological examinations or tests" (U.S. Department of Health & Human Services, 2009, Section 46.102). Our study falls into this category of minimal risk.

Ethical research conduct could and should also include the sharing of research results with the community studied so that corrections in the analysis and interpretation of the results can be made when needed (Madge, 2007). This kind of conduct might contribute to a more positive online environment where the researchers would be met with trust rather than with suspicion. We shared the results of our pilot study (Kantanen et al., 2014) with the national *Sometu* community and received positive feedback from the forum administrators.

4. Discussion

In the following, we discuss our case in light of the basic ethical principles of research defined in our country: respecting the autonomy of research subjects, avoiding harm, and protecting privacy and data (Finnish Advisory Board on Research Integrity, 2009).

Participation in research must be voluntary and based on informed consent. So far, we have not necessarily needed consent because we have been studying archived online discussion threads. When interviewing participants, we will need their consent, which we can gain electronically by using a form accepted by the Committee on Research Ethics of our university. The form includes the following information for the research subjects: project title, research team members, purpose of the study, research funding, information about what participation will involve, risks, benefits, costs and compensations, confidentiality, participant rights, and contact information (see also Kozinets, 2010, p. 194).

Our study has not at any stage included particularly vulnerable groups like minors, cognitively impaired people, survivors of abuse, or support groups for those with serious diseases. Groups of that kind are, of course, very vulnerable and deserve extra protection and careful ethical consideration.

In our country, some exemptions from informed consent are possible "if advance information would distort the results of the study" (Finnish Advisory Board on Research Integrity, 2009, p. 8). For example, power relationships can be studied without the consent of those in power, or there may be groups that can be a risk to the researcher's safety if he or she reveals his or her identity. In these cases, ethical review is always necessary. Research cultures differ from country to country and, therefore, global forums present challenges. For instance, many virtual communities and social media platforms are owned by and administered from the United States; therefore, it is not enough to take national guidelines of research ethics into account, but U.S. standards as well. Moreover, if the research results are to be published in one of the "international" languages, other nations' standards may also need to be taken into account.

We consider the question of protecting Internet researchers a very topical one, even though this has not been a problem in our study. What if a senior investigator sends a junior to study a hostile online forum and the research subjects trace his or her personal information and start verbal attacks with threats of off-line violence? Is this a question of research ethics? Or is it unethical to withdraw from studying risky issues and/or forums because of fear? Both Bruckman (2006) and Jane (2015) give terrifying examples of what impudent online hostility—Jane calls this "e-bile"—can involve. Therefore, we wish to include the aspect of protecting researchers, particularly inexperienced junior researchers, in our ethical considerations.

We have attempted to treat our research subjects with respect and dignity, which is not difficult because they (like us) are mostly experts within the field of education. Our study does not include elements that might cause mental, financial or social harm to the research subjects. If, however, we had studied synchronous interaction in online communities, our presence might have had negative consequences to the natural flow of conversations and could have provoked irritation or hostility—mental harm, that is.

The Terms of Service of different virtual platforms may have different views on privacy than those of their users (Markham & Buchanan, 2012). Moreno, Goniou and Moreno (2013) give examples of cases where courts have concluded that a person cannot expect privacy when posting on social networking sites. Often, ethical demands can be harder than legal ones. Extant laws set the ultimate limits, but do not necessarily determine what is ethical. In this article, our focus has been on ethical, not legal considerations (for a possible basis for legal liability of Internet researchers, see Lipinski, 2006).

Protecting privacy in research publications may be challenging because we use direct quotes from our data. However, as explained above, the issues discussed in our community are not very sensitive; therefore, a "light disguise" (Bruckman, 2002), where the names and other identifiers are hidden, should be enough. It is of course possible that if a quotation appears in a journal article, someone could track the original source of the quotation with the help of a search engine. Therefore, there is a slight risk that our study might cause some reputational harm to forum participants if, for example, original quotations with hostile and aggressive comments, "flames" can be tracked. However, this risk is low and, if we ever publish any flaming-related quotes, the focus will be on showing how moderators diffuse heated situations in a specific virtual community, not on the identities of those involved in them.

In our project, each researcher is responsible for safeguarding the research materials in his or her office and office computer. For ethical reasons, the materials may not be handed over to third parties—not even after the research project has been finished. After the project, the research data will be stored at the university for ten years according to the prevailing archive's regulations. Our data will not be available for secondary research, not even without identifiers, because this is the procedure accepted by our ethics committee. In this regard, the ethics committee may need to change their view because of increasing demand for openly accessible research data.

5. Conclusion

"Internet research ethics is complex, not impossible" (McKee & Porter, 2009b, p. 141). However, Bruckman (2006) maintains that studying online communities in an ethical fashion is a challenge, even for experienced researchers, and that the Internet continually raises novel ethical issues. If we are too lax in our ethics, we may violate the rights of individuals, or disrupt the communities we study; if we are too strict, we may not gain the knowledge needed to understand these communities (Bruckman, 2002, p. 218). She gives an example of how one student of hers was denied access to study an online group because someone else had studied the community earlier, "and left members feeling like their activities were disrupted and their privacy violated" (Bruckman, 2006, p. 217). Therefore, forgetting ethical conduct harms the whole academia.

Working with international forums can prove problematic. Researchers, forum owners and moderators, and research subjects may come from very different cultures, including research cultures with different views on research ethics. Therefore, we recommend consulting the ethical review board of one's own university. First, it is much easier to approach an international community with ethical approval, because in many countries it is always a part of any research process. Moreover, the process makes researchers seriously consider different ethical aspects of their projects. That said, we would like to add that, of course, it helps if the local ethics committee or review board has a supportive, advisory attitude towards its researcher clients. By delving into the complexities of Internet research, we have also tried to pay attention to the need for ethical considerations in fields where official reviews are not necessary. For us, the process that started with our local ethics committee has been very useful in the long run.

Acknowledging the ephemeral characteristics of Internet contexts, we argue that, in line with other authors (Markham & Buchanan, 2012; McKee & Porter, 2009b), ethical considerations should be more case-based and processual, rather than relying on one model for all solutions. We suggest that local ethics committees or institutional review boards could, with their expert knowledge of ethics, provide valuable support for researchers operating in the complex and dynamic terrain of Internet research, as well as in fields and research settings where an ethical review is not a standard part of the research process. There may also be a need for these review boards to revise their instructions and forms to better respond to the volatile research environments studied by Internet researchers (Dennen, 2012).

Acknowledgements

This article is one of the fruits of the Innovation Practice Project of the Business School of the University of Eastern Finland, funded as one of the Innovative Research Initiatives of the University during 2011–2014. It originated in a workshop on Ethical and Unethical Research of Internet Data, held by Helena Kantanen, at the International Doctoral Consortium on Management and Organization Studies at St. Mary's University, Halifax, in June 2014. The key points of this paper were presented at the Social Media Research Symposium at the University of Jyväskylä, Finland, on November 20, 2015. We thank our colleagues, Professor Päivi Eriksson and Professor Albert J. Mills, for their valuable insights on improving the manuscript.

Conflict of Interests

The authors declare no conflict of interests.

References

Bassett, E. H., & O'Riordan, K. (2002). Ethics of Internet research: Contesting the human subjects research model. *Ethics and Information Technology*, *4*(3), 233-247.

Bruckman, A. (2002). Studying the amateur artist: A perspective on disguising data collected in human subjects research on the Internet. *Ethics and Information Technology*, *4*(3), 217-231.

Bruckman, A. (2006). Teaching students to study online communities ethically. *Journal of Information Ethics, Fall 2006,* 82-95.

Buchanan, E., & Zimmer, M. (2013). Internet research ethics. In E. N. Zalta (Ed.), *The Stanford encyclopedia of philosophy* (Fall 2013 Edition). Retrieved from http://plato.stanford.edu/archives/fall2013/entries/ethics-Internet-research

Dennen, V. P. (2012). When public words are not data. Online authorship, consent, and reasonable expectations of privacy. In D. Heider & A. L. Massarini (Eds.), *Digital ethics* (pp. 21-38). New York: Peter Lang.

Eriksson, P., & Kovalainen, A. (2016). *Qualitative methods in business research. A practical guide to social research*. London: Sage.

Finnish Advisory Board on Research Integrity. (2009). *Ethical principles of research in the humanities and social and behavioural sciences and proposals for ethical review*. Retrieved from http://www.tenk.fi/sites/tenk.fi/files/ethicalprinciples.pdf

Flicker, S., Haans, D., & Skinner, H. (2004). Ethical dilemmas in research on Internet communities. *Qualitative Health Research*, *14*(1), 124-134.

Hine, C. (2000). *Virtual ethnography*. London: Sage.

Hine, C. (2005). Virtual methods and the sociology of cyber-social-scientific knowledge. In C. Hine (Ed.), *Virtual methods. Issues in social research on the Internet* (pp. 1-13). Oxford: Berg.

Hudson, J. M., & Bruckman, A. (2004). "Go away": Participant objections to being studied and the ethics of chatroom research. *The Information Society*, *20*(2), 127-139.

Jane, E. A. (2015). Flaming? What flaming? The pitfalls and potentials of researching online hostility. *Ethics and Information Technology*, *17*(1), 65-87.

Kantanen, H., & Manninen, J. (August, 2014). *Seeds, sprouts, weeds and blooms of innovation: Learning in professional virtual communities*. Paper presented at the 7th EARLI SIG 14. Learning and Professional Development Conference. Transformations in Knowledge and Professional Learning, Oslo, Norway.

Kantanen, H., Manninen, J., & Kontkanen, J. (2014). Emergent dialogue as a prerequisite of learning and innovation in professional virtual communities. *International Journal of Web Based Communities*, *10*(2), 211-231.

Korhonen, J., & Seppälä, N. (2005). The strength of a high–trust society. In A. Habisch, J. Jonker, M. Wegner, & R. Schmidpeter (Eds.), *Corporate social responsibility across Europe* (pp. 13-22). Berlin: Springer.

Kosonen, M. (2009). Knowledge sharing in virtual communities—A review of the empirical research. *International Journal of Web Based Communities*, *5*(2), 144-163.

Kozinets, R. V. (2010). *Netnography. Doing ethnographic research online*. Los Angeles: Sage.

Lakkala, M. (2010). How to design educational settings to promote collaborative inquiry: Pedagogical infrastructures for technology–enhanced progressive inquiry. (Doctoral dissertation). University of Helsinki, Helsinki, Finland. Retrieved from http://urn.fi/URN:ISBN:978-952-10-6178-3

Lipinski, T. A. (2006). Emerging tort issues in the collection and dissemination of Internet-based research data. *Journal of Information Ethics, Fall 2006*, 55-81.

Madge, C. (2007). Developing a geographers' agenda for online research ethics. *Progress in Human Geography, 31*(5), 654-674.

Manninen, J., & Nevgi, A. (2000). Opetus verkossa [Teaching in the Web]. In J. Matikainen & J. Manninen (Eds.), *Aikuiskoulutus verkossa: Verkkopohjaisten oppimisympäristöjen teoriaa ja käytäntöä*. [Adult Education in the Web—Theory and Practice of Web Based Learning Environments] (pp. 93-108). Helsinki: Palmenia-kustannus.

Markham, A. N. (2006). Ethic as method, method as ethic: A case for reflexivity in qualitative ICT research. *Journal of Information Ethics, Fall 2006*, pp. 37-54.

Markham, A., & Buchanan, E. (2012). *Ethical decision-making and Internet research. Recommendations from the AoIR ethics working committee (version 2.0).* Retrieved from http://aoir.org/reports/ethics2.pdf

McKee, H. A., & Porter, J. E. (2009a). Playing a good game: Ethical issues in researching MMOGs and virtual worlds. *International Journal of Internet Research Ethics*, *2*(1), 5-37.

McKee, H. A., & Porter, J. E. (2009b). *The ethics of internet research: A rhetorical, case-based process*. New York: Peter Lang.

Mikkonen, J. (2015, November 7). Tutkija sai tarpeekseen vihapuheesta—harkitsee tutkintapyyntöä [Researcher Fed Up with Hostile Messages—Considers request for investigation]. *Savon Sanomat*. Retrieved from http://www.savonsanomat.fi/uutiset/kotimaa/ita-suomen-yliopiston-tutkija-sai-tarpeekseen-vihapuheesta-harkitsee-tutkintapyyntoa/2164266

Moreno, M. A., Goniou, N., & Moreno, P. S. (2013). Ethics of social media research: Common concerns and practical considerations. *Cyberpsychology, Behavior, and Social Networking*, *16*(9), 708-713.

Rosenberg, Å. (2010). Virtual world research ethics and the private/public distinction. *International Journal of Internet Research Ethics*, *3*(12), 23-35.

Rutter, J., & Smith, G. W. H. (2005). Ethnographic presence in a nebulous setting. In C. Hine (Ed.), *Virtual methods. Issues in social research on the Internet* (pp. 81-92). Oxford: Berg.

Sanders, T. (2005). Researching the online sex work community. In C. Hine (Ed.), *Virtual methods. Issues in social research on the Internet* (pp. 67-79). Oxford: Berg.

Tavani, H. T. (2006). Cyberethics as an interdisciplinary field of applied ethics. Key concepts, perspectives, and methodological frameworks. *Journal of Information Ethics*, *Fall 2006*, 18-36.

Tiiliharju, P. (2015). *Yhteisöllinen oppiminen ja järkeistäminen virtuaalisissa käytäntöyhteisöissä* [Collective learning and sensemaking in virtual communities of practice] (Master Thesis). University of Eastern Finland, Joensuu, Finland.

Turtiainen, R., & Östman, S. (2013). Verkkotutkimuksen eettiset haasteet: Armi ja anoreksia [Ethical challenges of internet research: armi and anorexia]. In S. Laaksonen, J. Matikainen, & M. Tikka (Eds.), *Otteita verkosta. Verkon ja sosiaalisen median tutkimusmenetelmät* [Grips on the net. Internet and social media research methods] (pp. 49-67). Tampere: Vastapaino.

U.S. Department of Health & Human Services. (2009). *Code of federal regulations. Title 45. Public welfare department of health and human services*. Retrieved from http://www.hhs.gov/ohrp/humansubjects/guidance/45cfr46.html

Walther, J. B. (2002). Research ethics in Internet-enabled research: Human subjects issues and methodological myopia. *Ethics and Information Technology*, *4*(3), 205-216.

Wasko, M. M., & Faraj, S. (2005). Why should I share? Examining social capital and knowledge contribution in electronic networks of practice. *MIS Quarterly*, *29*(1), 35-57.

Wenger, E., Trayner, B., & de Laat, M. (2011) *Promoting and assessing value creation in communities and networks: A conceptual framework*. Retrieved from http://wenger-trayner.com/wp-content/uploads/2011/12/11-04-Wenger_Trayner_DeLaat_Value_creation.pdf

Zimmer, M. (2010). "But the data is already public": On the ethics of research in Facebook. *Ethics and Information Technology*, *12*(4), 313-325.

9

Social Movements and Political Agency in the Digital Age: A Communication Approach

Anastasia Kavada

Westminster School of Media, Arts and Design, University of Westminster, Middlesex, HA1 3TP, UK;
E-Mail: A.Kavada@westminster.ac.uk

Abstract

Digital media pose a dual challenge to conventional understandings of political agency. First, digital media destabilize long-held assumptions about the nature of collective action, about social movements and their capacity to effect change. This is because digital media are thought to facilitate more decentralized, dispersed, temporary and individualized forms of political action that subvert the notion of the collective as singular, unified, homogeneous, coherent, and mass. One way of resolving this challenge is to view the collective in looser terms, as a process rather than as a finished product, a conceptualization that can be influence our understanding not only of social movements, but also of other political actors and of society as a whole. Second, digital media highlight the need to take communication seriously in how we conceptualize both collective action and political agency. Placing communication at the centre allows us to develop this looser and more processual understanding of the collective by studying it as a process that is constituted in and through communication. Inspired by organizational communication and particularly the work of Taylor and van Every (2000), this essay proposes a conception of collective action as emerging in conversations and solidified in texts. This conceptualization allows for a more multiplex and variegated view of political agency that takes into account the specific context where agency is exercised and the power that different actors can exert in a communicative process of negotiation, persuasion and claim-making.

Keywords

collective action; communication; digital media; political agency; social media; social movement

Issue

This commentary is part of the issue "Political Agency in the Digital Age: Media, Participation and Democracy", edited by Anne Kaun (Södertörn University, Sweden), Maria Kyriakidou (University of East Anglia, UK) and Julie Uldam (Roskilde University, Denmark).

The digital age challenges conventional understandings of political agency. Within social movement research this challenge is, I would like to argue, two-fold. First, digital media destabilize long-held assumptions about the nature of collective action, about social movements and their capacity to effect change. Second, digital media highlight the need to take communication seriously in how we conceptualize both collective action and political agency. In what follows, I outline these two interrelated challenges and suggest how they can be addressed.

The emergence of digital media has led to an intense questioning of the meaning of collective action and of the collective in general. Digital media are thought to facilitate more decentralized, dispersed, temporary and individualized forms of political action that subvert the notion of the collective as singular, unified, homogeneous, coherent, and mass. This is evident, for instance, in the declining use of the collective identity concept in recent studies of social media and activism (Treré, 2015). Instead, scholars like Bennett and Segerberg (2013) are exploring how the coordination mechanisms of digital media platforms bring disparate individuals together without the need for a coherent collective identity or formal organization. Bennett and Segerberg consider such action to be 'connective' rather than collective and explicitly position their influential framework against 'earlier models that insisted on stable identities, ideologies and organizations as a prerequisite for civil society mobilization and action' (Bakardjieva, 2015, p. 986).

One way to address the debates around the nature of the collective and to navigate around controversies over categorisation (is it connective or collective action?) is to think of the collective in looser terms, as a process rather than as a finished product. This is a conceptual move that requires us to delve into theoretical work that has attempted to transcend the 'static and often structuralist or psychologically reductionist' (Bakardjieva, 2015, p. 986) models of collective action against which scholars like Bennett and Segerberg are reacting. The work of Alberto Melucci (1996) is very useful in this respect as it is based on a definition of the collective as an open-ended process that is always in a state of becoming. Melucci (1996) thus invites us to study the interactive processes through which an aggregation of individuals becomes a collective with its own distinct identity, a question that, as he notes, 'is apparently raised by no one' (p. 84). 'The theoretical problem for us today', he suggests, 'is this unity, the creation of a collective subject of action as process which needs to be subjected to explanation' (p. 84).

But once we embrace such a conceptualization of the collective, why stop at social movements? Why not consider the various institutions and organizations that social movements engage with, from the police to the state to the media, also as open-ended processes and not as finished products? Movements are by definition less formalized actors, their structures more uneven, their seams and stitches showing. By contrast, institutionalized actors have sophisticated procedures that render them seamless, smooth and opaque to the outside, their backstage operations and internal divisions safely tucked away from public view. Yet this does not mean that they aren't also actors in the making.

The same can be said for the social system itself. Macro-structures, and particularly the structures of domination that social movements attempt to challenge, are often perceived as rigid, monolithic, and all-encompassing and thus changed only through wholesale revolution. This does not leave enough space for considering the more gradual and partial kinds of social change, those that erode rather than smash the system and which unfold on multiple levels and at different times. Furthermore, and as Sewell (2005) puts it, 'many structural accounts of social transformation tend to introduce change from outside the system and then trace out the ensuing structurally shaped changes, rather than showing how change is generated by the operation of structures internal to a society' (p. 139). To address this issue, Sewell argues that 'a theory of change cannot be built into a theory of structure unless we adopt a far more multiple, contingent, and fractured conception of society—and of structure' (p. 140).

A focus on communication helps us to develop exactly this conception of society and structure since it allows us to study the collective as a process that is constituted in and through communication. In other words, resolving the second challenge that digital media pose—the need to take communication seriously in our understanding of social movements and political agency—can go some way towards addressing the first.

Communication is a spectre that haunts collective action theory: it is always lurking in the background but rarely placed at the centre of enquiry (Flanagin, Stohl, & Bimber, 2006). It can be found in the looming presence of Goffman and symbolic interactionism that has influenced work on framing (Benford & Snow, 2000). It underlies Melucci's (1996) conception of collective identity as a process of interaction. It is most evident in the work of Tilly (2005) who studies contentious politics as a conversation between claim-makers and their targets. Yet the emergence of digital media has brought communication into sharper relief within social movement studies, leading to a shift in how we view the role of communication in collective action: from focusing on how already existing collectives communicate with other actors to also considering how communication is involved in the construction itself of the collective.

Such a change in perspective amounts to a paradigm shift in recent studies of digital media and collective action. For instance, scholars like Gerbaudo (2012, p. 138) and Bennett and Segerberg (2013, p. 8) view *communication as organization*, while Flanagin, Stohl and Bimber (2006) assert that collective action is a communicative phenomenon, 'involving the crossing of boundaries between private and public life' (p. 32). The field is marked by conceptual creativity as evidenced by the introduction of new frameworks like connective action or by the increasing cross-fertilization between social movement theory and media studies, with concepts such as mediatization (Mattoni & Treré, 2014) and media ecologies (Treré & Mattoni, 2015) crossing into social movement theory, while collective action concepts like political opportunity structures travel in the opposite direction as in Cammaerts' (2012) analysis of the 'mediation opportunity structure' (see also Uldam, 2013).

The approach outlined in this essay belongs in this new wave of theorising. Based on organizational communication, and particularly the work of Taylor and van Every (2000), I propose a conception of collective action as emerging in conversations and solidified in texts. For Taylor and van Every, conversation involves the ordinary interactions in which people enact their world. In the case of social movements, this would involve conversations over objectives and the mission of the movement, its boundaries, resources and processes, as well as its targets and adversaries. These conversations are then recorded and codified in texts—from the minutes of meetings, to common statements, to videos and photographs, to shared scripts of behaviour in meetings—that then affect the conversations of the movement in other times and spaces. 'Text' can be thought in broader terms here and it can encompass any stable patterning and materialization of conversation, including for instance software code and architectural design. Texts and conversations mutually constitute each other in a dynamic process that shapes and reshapes the organization.

Within this framework, the media can be thought as sites of conversation that have different affordances for interaction and 'textualization', for recording and codifying the conversations that take place in and through them. The media also have different spatialities and temporalities in terms of how they arrange interaction in time and space. Conversation sites—which can also include the spaces of face-to-face communication—are overlapping and interconnected through flows of people and information. Their articulation, boundaries, norms and regulations affect the collectives created through them (for a more detailed analysis, see Kavada, 2015a).

This conceptualization provides a more grounded perspective of the processes through which social movements come to constitute themselves as collective actors. It allows us to trace the sites, conversations and texts that play a crucial role in the creation of the collective and to study social movements as a dynamic process. This framework can also be applied to our understanding of the institutions and organizations that social movements engage with, and of social structures in general, allowing us to think of the social system in terms of 'flexibility, adaptability, and evolutionary change emerging from the sum of social interactions' (Chadwick, 2013, p. 16), rather than as a monolithic structure.

Placing communication at the centre also has significant implications for how we understand political agency. A prevailing tendency within social movement research is to assess a movement's political agency based on the effectiveness of its contentious performance and claim-making in the public arena. Tilly's (2005) concept of WUNC—an acronym for Worthiness, Unity, Numbers and Commitment, the four characteristics that collective actions should exhibit in order to be effective—is exemplary in this regard. In this approach, '[c]ollective actors are mainly studied as "entities" appearing on a public stage and addressing themselves to other actors' while their internal processes 'remain essentially a black box' (van de Donk, Loader, Nixon, & Rucht, 2004, p. 10).

Embracing a processual view of the collective and of society in general provides a more multiplex and variegated view of political agency. First of all, it points to the fact that the constitution of the movement as a political actor can, in itself, be a political outcome. In fact, a movement's public performance may consist exactly of the process through which it creates unity. A central component of the Occupy movement, for instance, was the public assemblies where participants were taking decisions following the rules of participatory democracy. What was essentially an internal process was rendered into a kind of public claim-making that functioned both as an implicit critique of the representative system of democracy and an example of what democracy could look like (Kavada, 2015b). In other words, rather than projecting unity in the sense of uniformity, such performances make the backstage public by shedding light on the processes through which the collective becomes a collective.

Furthermore, analysing the changes that social movements can effect on other institutions, and on society in general, needs to take stock of the specific communication episodes and sites of conversation where these actors interact. This entails a fine-grained analysis of the participants in each communication episode, of which parts of the movement are engaging with which part of society. It also requires a better understanding of where these communication episodes fit in the institutional processes that social movements aim to influence. What is more, paying attention only to public performances means that we lose sight of how political agency also hinges on secrecy, on access to elite spaces of power and on the preservation of closed internal spaces. Instead of training our vision only on a central public stage, our understanding of political agency needs to take into account the multiple sites of variable publicness where movements effect change. Dispersion might be as important as unity in this respect as it allows the movement to access and engage with institutions in different sites and communication episodes.

Within such episodes of engagement and interaction, the political agency of social movements can be thought in relation to their communication capacities. These are not limited to the effective public performance of claims, as the WUNC model suggests, but include the control, creation and manipulation of the rules of communication themselves and of the sites where episodes of interaction take place. In this respect, we can consider the following capacities: the capacity to *access* and participate in the sites of targets, adversaries, and the mainstream media; the capacity to *manage* and regulate the conversations with targets and adversaries; the capacity to *persuade,* to make compelling arguments, texts, visuals that sway public opinion, targets and adversaries; the capacity to *articulate*, to link different sites, actors, conversations and create alliances and coalitions; and the capacity to *represent*—to speak on behalf of (at least a part of) society, to assume and define its collective voice. Most importantly, communication power encompasses the capacity to *create* new codes that shape how society interacts, new sites of conversation that operate differently, to provide models of living and being that change the world in a way that conforms to the movement's ideals and values.

The short length of this piece does not allow for an in-depth analysis of these forms of communication power. But what this essay points to is the need to understand how power and agency play out in specific communication sites and episodes where movements attempt to bring change. It thus allows us to 'focus on the diversity of mechanisms and behaviors that enable power to be exercised in discrete contexts' (Chadwick, 2013, p. 16). Yet, through the notion of 'text', we can also study how these communication episodes are shaped by macro-structures of domination that constrain the capacities of movements in different contexts. We can further develop a more grounded view of how movements influence and generate more enduring codes or texts that can be transferred to other contexts and thus lead to a more wide-ranging transformation of social structure.

New media have a disruptive effect on both social practice and the theoretical frameworks we use to study it. Resolving the dual conceptual challenge posed by digital media—the need to think of the collective as an open-ended process and the need to take communication seriously in how collectives constitute themselves—can advance our understanding of social movements and political agency. Placing communication at the centre can be a catalyst for much-needed conceptual innovation in an effort to not only understand the world but also to change it.

Acknowledgements

I would like to thank the editors for giving me the opportunity to publish in this thematic issue. The research referred to in this article has been supported by a British Academy Mid-Career Fellowship for the project 'Digital Communications Technologies and Protest Movements: The Case of Occupy' (Ref: MD130045).

Conflict of Interests

The author declares no conflict of interests.

References

Bakardjieva, M. (2015). Do clouds have politics? Collective actors in social media land. *Information, Communication & Society*, *18*(8), 983-990.

Benford, R. D., & Snow, D. A. (2000). Framing processes and social movements: An overview and assessment. *Annual Review of Sociology*, *26*, 611-639.

Bennett, W. L., & Segerberg, A. (2013). *The logic of connective action: Digital media and the personalization of collective action*. New York: Cambridge University Press.

Cammaerts, B. (2012). Protest logics and the mediation opportunity structure. *European Journal of Communication, 27*(2), 117-134.

Chadwick, A. (2013). *The hybrid media system: Politics and power*. Oxford and New York: Oxford University Press.

Flanagin, A. J., Stohl, C., & Bimber, B. (2006). Modeling the structure of collective action. *Communication Monographs*, *73*(1), 29-54.

Gerbaudo, P. (2012). *Tweets and the streets: Social media and contemporary activism*. London: Pluto Press.

Kavada, A. (2015a). *The communicative constitution of collective action*. Paper presented at the 65th Annual Conference of the International Communication Association, San Juan, Puerto Rico, 21–29 May 2015.

Kavada, A. (2015b). Creating the collective: Social media, the Occupy Movement and its constitution as a collective actor. *Information, Communication & Society*, 18(8), 872-886.

Mattoni, A., & Treré, E. (2014). Media practices, mediation processes, and mediatization in the study of social movements. *Communication Theory*, *24*(3), 252-271.

Melucci, A. (1996). *Challenging codes: Collective action in the information age*. Cambridge: Cambridge University Press.

Sewell, W. H. Jr (2005). *Logics of history: Social theory and social transformation*. Chicago and London: The University of Chicago Press.

Taylor, J. R., & van Every, E. J. (2000). *The emergent organisation: Communication as its site and surface*. Mahwah, NJ: Lawrence Elbaum Associates.

Tilly, C. (2005). *Identities, boundaries and social ties*. Boulder, CO: Paradigm Publishers.

Treré, E. (2015). Reclaiming, proclaiming, and maintaining collective identity in the #YoSoy132 movement in Mexico: An examination of digital frontstage and backstage activism through social media and instant messaging platforms. *Information, Communication & Society*, *18*(8), 901-915.

Treré, E., & Mattoni, A. (2015). Media ecologies and protest movements: Main perspectives and key lessons. *Information, Communication & Society*, Online First, doi:10.1080/1369118X.2015.1109699

Uldam, J. (2013). Activism and the online mediation opportunity structure: Attempts to impact global climate change policies? *Policy & Internet*, *5*(1), 56-71.

Van de Donk, W., Loader, B. D., Nixon, P.G., & Rucht, D. (2004). Introduction: Social movements and ICTs. In W. van de Donk, B. D. Loader, P. G. Nixon, & D. Rucht (Eds), *Cyberprotest: New media, citizens and social movements* (pp. 1-25). London and New York: Routledge.

10

Networked Authoritarianism and the Geopolitics of Information: Understanding Russian Internet Policy

Nathalie Maréchal

Annenberg School for Communication and Journalism, University of Southern California, Los Angeles, CA 90007, USA; E-Mail: marechal@usc.edu

Abstract

In the aftermath of the 2016 U.S. election, researchers, policymakers and the general public are grappling with the notion that the 45th president of the United States may very well owe his electoral victory to a sophisticated propaganda effort masterminded by the Kremlin. This article synthesizes existing research on Russia's domestic information controls, its internet policy at the global level (notably via internet governance processes), and the country's resurgence as a major geopolitical player to argue that policymakers as well as the general public should consider these themes holistically, particularly as they formulate responses to what many see as the Russian threat to Western liberal democracy. Russia may have lost the Cold War, but it is now waging information warfare against the liberal democracies of Europe and North America in a sophisticated bid to win the next round. Russia does not view internet governance, cybersecurity, and media policy as separate domains. Rather, all the areas covered by those disciplines fall under "information security" for Russian foreign policy. The paper begins by tracing the history of information controls within what is now the Russian Federation before discussing the role of information and internet policy in Russian foreign policy, drawing connections between the Russian government's control and manipulation of information—including its internet policy—in the domestic and international arenas. Next, it discusses the spread of networked authoritarianism and suggests that a "geopolitics of information" will become increasingly necessary in the coming years. Just as networked authoritarianism establishes strategic infrastructures to control the message domestically and intervene in global media systems, liberal democracies need to rethink media and communication infrastructures to ensure they foster pluralist, rights-respecting societies that are resilient to authoritarianism and extremism. In doing so, they should resist the temptation to respond to this threat in ways that will erode democracy even further, such as expanded surveillance and limits on free expression.

Keywords

2016 election; censorship; data localization; human rights; networked authoritarianism; propaganda; Russia; surveillance

Issue

This article is part of the issue "Post-Snowden Internet Policy", edited by Julia Pohle (WZB Berlin Social Science Center, Germany) and Leo Van Audenhove (Vrije Universiteit Brussel, Belgium).

---

1. Introduction

After a long and bitter electoral campaign, the results of the 2016 U.S. election have precipitated an ongoing constitutional crisis, and continued uncertainty about the role of Russia's government in Donald Trump's electoral victory has prompted renewed interest in Russia, a country that hadn't been at the forefront of the national agenda since the end of the Cold War. Several factors contribute to making the current situation a perfect storm of uncertainty and ambiguity, including: policymakers' and the public's comparative lack of knowledge about Russia; the difficulty of parsing out something resembling empirical truth from the jumble of official statements, leaks, speculations and claims made by the various actors involved; the tumultuous presidential transition; and the arcane nature of the empirical claims underlying the web of controversy surrounding the election and any role Russia might have had in influencing the result. It will take time and serious effort for the dust to settle; an analysis of the events leading up the 2016 election, or of the election's aftermath, would be premature. However, at this stage it is appropriate to consider what we do know about Russia's policies concerning information, the internet and international relations under Vladimir Putin.

There is a natural tendency in scholarship and policy to work within disciplinary silos, without sufficiently considering related developments that are better aligned with a different field of expertise. At a time when American interest in Russia is at perhaps its highest since the end of the Cold War, it is important to consider all of Russia's information and internet policy, both domestic and international, in order to properly situate current developments and formulate policy responses that defend and support democracy and human rights. The topic is a complex one, and it would be impossible to cover it entirely, with all its nuances and complexities, in an article-length piece. My aim here is twofold: to draw connections between the Russian government's control and manipulation of information—including its internet policy—both domestically and externally, and to theorize on the spread of networked authoritarianism and the future of the geopolitics of information.

This article was written for a thematic issue on "Internet Policy After Snowden", but it is broader than that in at least two ways. First, it goes beyond narrow definitions of internet policy to consider several aspects of Russian information and communication policy that are inextricably intertwined. And second, it has very little to say about Edward Snowden. At least in the Russian context, the 2013 Snowden revelations mainly serve as a temporal marker. They alerted global public opinion to mass surveillance and made possible a change in the Kremlin's rhetoric, but did not cause a shift in Russian policy. If there was a turning point in Russian internet policy, that moment was in 2011: the year of the Arab Spring, but also the year that Russian civil society used social media to organize protests of the legislative election, about which then-U.S. Secretary of State Hillary Clinton expressed "serious concerns" (Labott, 2011). It was also the year before Putin resumed the presidency, after swapping roles with Dmitri Medvedev for four years.

In this article, I synthesize existing research on Russia's domestic information controls policy, internet policy at the global level (notably via internet governance processes), and the country's resurgence as a major geopolitical player to argue that policymakers as well as the general public should consider these themes holistically, particularly as they formulate responses to what many see as the Russian threat to Western liberal democracy. In doing so, they should resist the temptation to respond to this threat in ways that will erode democracy even further, such as expanded surveillance and limits on free expression.

Methodologically, the article relies chiefly on secondary sources, including translations of Russian sources and sources written in English by Russian journalists, while drawing on my interactions with a variety of policy experts (both Russian and Western) in the course of other ongoing work, some of whom have asked to remain anonymous for their own safety. Throughout the article I consider information policy, media policy and internet policy holistically, as they are closely interrelated. The article begins by tracing the history of information controls (which predate the internet) within what is now the Russian Federation before discussing the role of information and internet policy in Russian foreign policy. Next, I discuss the spread of networked authoritarianism and suggest that a "geopolitics of information" will become increasingly necessary as the 21st century marches on, and theorize on what this might be, concluding with a call to defend, protect and improve Western liberal democracy.

2. Information in Russia Before the Internet

This section traces the history of the media and information controls in Russia, which is distinct from the history of the press and the media in the West. Media in Russia have always served as instruments of political propaganda, going back to the country's first newspaper. *Vedomosti* was founded in 1702 to disseminate the czar's wishes, plans, and priorities across the country, and to build popular support for the ruler (Rohlenko, 2007). Under the USSR, information was considered a dangerous commodity to be feared and controlled, rather than a right and a public good. Contrary to liberal conceptions of a free press serving as a fourth branch of governance and fostering a habermasian public sphere (Habermas, 1989), the Soviet regime saw the media as a danger to be tightly controlled, with only select elites permitted access to objective news or to foreign publications (Gorny, 2007; Soldatov & Borogan, 2015). For example, ownership and use of photocopiers were tightly restricted in an attempt to prevent the distribution of *samizdat*, photocopied pamphlets of "subversive" material (Hanson, 2008).

It is no accident of history that the collapse of the USSR coincided with the emergence of the information society in the West. Indeed, Castells and Kiselyova (1995) argue that this death grip on information was the primary reason for the USSR's implosion. The 1990s were a period of relative freedom for the press in post-Soviet Russia, albeit a short-lived one as the levers of power—recently relinquished by the Communist Party—were seized by the new oligarch class. The media were no longer beholden to a monolithic ideology, but instead answered to a variety of corporate backers whose interests didn't always align. Print media lost their state subsidies and saw their circulation and importance decline precipitously, leaving broadcast TV to take over as the country's predominant communication medium (Ognyanova, 2015).

Vladimir Vladimirovich Putin, Yeltsin's chosen successor, first assumed the presidency of the Russian Federation in 1999, and quickly restored the Kremlin's control over print and broadcast media—a move that he characterized as "liberating" news outlets from the oligarchs. For many Russia experts, understanding Putin is key to understanding Russia today. Putin served in the Soviet intelligence agency, the KGB, for 16 years, rising to the rank of colonel, and he spent much of the pivotal perestroika years outside of Russia. His views on governance, the rule of law, the role of information in society, and the Russian national interest are very much influenced by the KGB's authoritarian traditions, themselves grounded in the authoritarianism of imperial Russia. Putin switched posts with his prime minister, Dmitri Medvedev, in 2008 to circumvent constitutional term limits, and in 2012 Putin returned to the Kremlin and redoubled his efforts to control the internet (Ognyanova, 2015; Soldatov & Borogan, 2015).

The end of the Cold War, which also ended Russia's superpower status (as nominal as it might have been, particularly toward the end), was a sore spot for the Russian elite, which perceived the U.S.'s success in exporting its cultural products as a threat to national sovereignty. Elites also resented growing U.S. influence in Eastern Europe and Central Asia, which they saw as their rightful sphere of influence, and the European Union's eastward expansion. Over the course of his first presidency (2000–2008), during which time domestic internet access grew considerably, Putin came to see the information revolution as "one of the most pervasive components of U.S. expansionism in the post-Soviet sphere, most notably in Russia itself" (Nocetti, 2015, p. 129). Where others might have seen opportunities for innovation and growth, Putin saw threats to the status quo and his hold on power, thus following in the footsteps of his Soviet and pre-bolshevik predecessors alike.

3. The Russian Information Controls Regime

Ronald Deibert and his team at the University of Toronto's Citizen Lab coined the phrase "information controls" to describe the "techniques, practices, regulations or policies that strongly influence the availability of electronic information for social, political, ethical, or economic ends". These include technical means like "filtering, distributed denial of service attacks, electronic surveillance, malware, or other computer-based means of denying, shaping and monitoring information" and policies like "laws, social understandings of 'inappropriate' content, media licensing, content removal, defamation policies, slander laws, secretive sharing of data between public and private bodies, or strategic lawsuit actions" (Citizen Lab, 2015). As a field of inquiry, information controls can also include the means of circumventing or otherwise countering barriers to the free flow of information online. Importantly, the field is inherently multidisciplinary and transcends the barrier between academia and civil society, with many important advances coming from activists and nonprofits.

The Freedom on the Net Index classifies information controls under three broad categories: obstacles to access, limits to content, and violations of user rights (Karlekar & Cook, 2009). Compared to China, Russia rarely uses obstacles to access (which include infrastructural and economic barriers as well as shutdowns and application-level blocking), relying instead on censorship and intimidation. However, Russia is taking steps to create an internet "kill switch", allowing it to disconnect the RuNet from the global network "in case of crisis", without specifying what such a crisis might entail beyond vague allusions to the internet being shut off from the outside (Duffy, 2015; Nocetti, 2015). Internet shutdowns—whether of all connection to the outside world, or of specific applications and protocols like VOIP, Twitter or WhatsApp—are used by governments like Egypt, Uganda and Iran to control the flow of information around elections, protests, and other politically sensitive events (DeNardis, 2014). The advocacy organization Access Now has reported a marked increase in the number of network shutdowns worldwide in recent years (Access Now, 2016). The Russian "kill switch" system has yet to be put into effect, as of this writing.

Censorship and violations of user rights, then, have historically been the principal mechanisms for information control in Russia. Katherine Ognyanova (2015) identifies three mechanisms through which the Russian state asserts power over the media: censorship and resulting chilling effects, state control over mainstream (especially broadcast) media, and the selective application of unrelated laws (building codes, tax laws, criminal laws, and intellectual property laws have all been used for this purpose) to put pressure on media organizations as well as individual journalists, bloggers, and activists. Extrajudicial executions are not uncommon. This is in many ways a continuation of the mechanisms used by successive Russian and Soviet governments to control the traditional print and broadcast media (Ognyanova, 2015). One key difference from the Soviet era is that the domestic media has since been privatized, and foreign companies—notably internet intermediaries—now operate in Russia as well.

In Russia, as in most countries, the physical structure of the internet is built, owned and maintained by the private sector. Companies like internet companies, Internet Service Providers (ISPs), social networking sites (SNSs), search engines, blogging platforms, and more then exercise a form of de facto private governance over online activity (MacKinnon, 2012). This private rule-making can come into conflict with the law. Absent a strong rule of law, governments can use their power to constrain, influence and even coerce information and telecommunications (ICT) companies. As Laura DeNardis notes, "state control of Internet governance functions via private intermediaries has equipped states with new forms of sometimes unaccountable and nontransparent power over information flows" (DeNardis, 2014, p. 15). We now turn to an examination of how the Russian state practices censorship and surveillance with the assistance of the private sector.

4. Censorship

Media in the Russian Federation, including the internet, is regulated by a branch of the Ministry of Communications and Mass Media, the Federal Service for Supervision of Communications, Information Technology, and Mass Media, better known as Roskomnadzor. Unlike the UK's Ofcom or the U.S. Federal Communications Commission, which are independent agencies with no power of prior restraint (the main enforcement mechanism is to assess fines), Roskomnadzor can block certain types of content without a court order: calls for unsanctioned public actions (i.e. protests), so-called extremist content, materials that violate copyright, information about juvenile victims of crime, child abuse imagery, drug propaganda, and information about suicide—as can several other agencies, including the Federal Drug Control Service, the Federal Service for Surveillance on Consumer Rights and Human Wellbeing, and the Prosecutor General's Office (Freedom House, 2015). Other types of content can also be blocked, but a court order is required.

While the authority to censor rests with the state, the responsibility to implement censorship falls on the internet service providers, who are held legally responsible for any forbidden content that is accessible to their users, a legal construct known as intermediary liability (MacKinnon, Hickock, Bar, & Lim, 2014). Since 2014, the Russian media regulator Roskomnadzor has maintained a block list of websites featuring banned content, including child abuse imagery, drug-related content, and "suicide advocacy". ISPs must regularly consult this "blacklist" of verboten websites, and are incentivized to interpret blocking orders as widely as possible to avoid liability for under-censoring, which can result in heavy fines and even the loss of their state licenses. The "blacklist" itself is often vague as to which page within a website or service should be blocked, or only specifies an IP address—which can represent any number of websites. Crucially, the list itself is secret, leaving internet users in the dark as to what is actually prohibited (Freedom House, 2015, 2016).

Roskomnadzor's powers are even greater with respect to websites that are registered as mass media—a broader category than one might think, thanks to the "Bloggers' Law". As early as 2001, the then-press minister, Mikhail Lesin,[1] "called for legislation requiring the registration of Internet media outlets", which would have included any website registered with the .su or .ru top-level domain (TLD) (Ulmanu, 2001, as cited in Bowles, 2006). Lesin finally got his wish in 2014, when the so-called "Bloggers Law" was instituted, requiring all online outlets (including blogs and personal pages within social networking sites) with more than 3,000 daily page views to register with the government, while the "Law Against Retweets" punishes the dissemination or re-dissemination of "extremist content" with up to five years in prison. "Extremist content" is defined so vaguely that it can be interpreted to include many kinds of speech that would be considered innocuous in many other countries. Another 2014 law prohibits the use of public wifi without providing one's mobile phone number. Acquiring a SIM card, in turn, requires providing one's passport number, as does signing up for home internet access. It is all but impossible, then, to surf the "RuNet" (as the Russian-language internet is called) without linking one's online activity to one's identity and passport (Duffy, 2015).

Under Article 4 of the law "On Mass Media", the regulator can issue warnings to an outlet's editorial board about "abuse of freedom of mass media", a category that includes such infractions as obscene language, information about illegal drugs, extremism, incitement to terrorism, and propaganda and cruelty. Here again, the specific interpretation of these terms leads to censorship well beyond what a literal reading of the law might suggest. For example, news sites have received warnings for publishing stories about calls for greater local governance ("federalization") and for government reform, and about international news events related to freedom of expression such as the attack on the Charlie Hebdo offices in Paris in January 2015 (Freedom House, 2015).

In addition to legislative and technical controls, the flow of information on the Russian internet is limited by two "soft" factors: cultural norms and practices grounded in centuries of authoritarianism, and deliberate framing of the internet as dangerous (Ognyanova, 2015). The Russian political class and broadcast media work together to frame the internet as a dangerous place, and online content as "unreliable, biased, and dangerous" (Kratasjuk, 2006; Ognyanova, 2015). For example, the mayor of Moscow wrote that "propaganda of drugs and violence, human trafficking and child prostitution—that's the reality of today's internet", asserting that "the Internet is gradually being settled by unconcealed terrorists who turn the web, not only into their own mailbox, but into a real, underground, military infrastructure" (Ognyanova, 2015). The strategy seems to be effective. Indeed, the report "Benchmarking Public Dissent: Russia's Appetite for Internet Control" found that 49% of all Russians believe that information on the internet needs to be censored, while 42% of Russians believe foreign countries are using the internet against Russia and its interests, and 24% think the internet threatens political stability (Nisbet, 2015). Propaganda of the kind described above allows the Kremlin to present its restrictions on the free flow of information as responses to popular will.

Restrictions on free expression continue apace, as the 2016 Yarovaya laws place new restrictions on "proselytizing" (i.e. discussing one's religion with potential converts) and require anyone with knowledge that someone else is "planning" certain kinds of crimes, mainly offenses

[1] Lesin was found dead, seemingly of a blow to the head, in a Washington hotel in November 2015. See Smith and Walker (2016).

that involve expressing dissenting views, to notify the authorities (Lokshina, 2016).

5. Surveillance

Domestic surveillance in Russia predates the internet, of course. As with censorship, the current surveillance regime is historically grounded in the country's Soviet and imperial past. The KGB may have a new acronym, FSB (standing for Federal'naya sluzhba bezopasnosti, or Federal Security Service), but it casts a long shadow (Soldatov & Borogan, 2015).

The System of Operational-Investigatory Measures (SORM) was first implemented in 1995, requiring telecommunications operators to install FSB-provided hardware allowing the agency to monitor users' communications metadata and content—including phone calls, email traffic and web browsing activity, despite the low internet penetration rate at the time.

Coming in the final year of Yeltsin's presidency, the 1999 SORM-2 reform required the FSB to obtain a post-collection court warrant to access records (Bowles, 2006). This was an encouraging sign that the intelligence services of the new Russian Federation would be governed by the rule of the law. However, shortly after taking office, Putin authorized several additional agencies to access SORM's collected data, including the tax authorities, border patrol and customs agencies, and the Presidential Security Service. The warrant requirement remains in place, but is remarkably toothless: surveillance can begin before the warrant is granted (or even requested), the warrant need not be shown to anyone (whether the surveillance target or the telecom operator), and it is only required for the retrieval of collected communications content, and not for the metadata that is often just as revealing as content, if not more so. In 2012 SORM-2 was expanded to include social media platforms, though documentation of how this works in practice is scant (Paganini, 2014; Soldatov & Borogan, 2012, 2015). Nevertheless, the assumption among Russian digital rights activists is that any information shared on Russian social networks like Vkontakte or Odnoklassniki is collected by the intelligence services (author interviews, 2016).

The latest update to SORM came in 2014, when the Ministry of Communications ordered companies to install new equipment with Deep Packet Inspection (DPI) capability (Soldatov & Borogan, 2015). As DeNardis puts it, "DPI is a transformational technology that creates unprecedented regulatory possibilities for controlling the flow of content online" (2014, p. 206). Demonstrating why this is the case requires a basic understanding of the technology itself. Information (whether it's text, voice, or something else) is transmitted over the internet as packets, small bundles of data that are individually routed from the sender to the receiver, then put back together in the correct order. Packets consist of both payload (the actual content of the communication) and a header, which contains the packet's metadata: its origin, destination, and not much else. The header is analogous to an envelope, telling each piece of equipment along the way where the payload should be delivered. Until fairly recently, computing power limited the types of analyses that routers, switches and other network hardware could perform on passing traffic, but advances in this domain have made it possible for hardware to simultaneously process millions of packets, reading not just the headers but the payload as well. Unless the packet is encrypted, the only impediment to stopping a DPI-capable machine from reading the payload are social and legal norms against this type of surveillance—which are absent in Russia. From there it is possible to block or throttle back traffic based on its origin, destination, file type (text, voice, multimedia), protocol (P2P, FTP, HTML, SMTP) or the content of the message itself (DeNardis, 2014). Here again, there is little reliable, publicly available information on how SORM-3 works, as discussing the topic is against the law. The new, secret regulations came into effect in fall 2016, and apply to all ISPs in Russia. Noncompliance comes at a steep price: stern warnings from Roskomnadzor followed by revocation of the ISP's license. Extra-legal intimidation is common, and formal enforcement appears to be increasing. Indeed, investigative journalists Andrei Soldatov and Irina Borogan obtained internal Roskomnadzor statistics that showed that the number of warnings issued by the agency grew from 16 in 2010 to 30 in 2012 (Soldatov & Borogan, 2013).

Also in 2012, SORM was applied to social networking sites, a key area of concern for Russian authorities given the role of such sites in various "color revolutions" and the 2011 Arab Spring (Howard & Hussain, 2013). As Soldatov and Borogan note, the tools used to monitor social networking sites had a crucial flaw:

> These systems were developed for searching structured computer files, or databases, and only afterwards adapted, some more successfully than others, for semantic analysis of the Internet. Most of these systems were designed to work with open sources and are incapable of monitoring closed accounts such as Facebook.
>
> The FSB discovered early on that the only way to deal with the problem was to turn to SORM. The licenses require businesses that rent out site space on servers to give the security services access to these servers via SORM, without informing the site owners. With this provision, the FSB has had few problems monitoring closed groups and accounts on Russian social networks Vkontakte and Odnoklassniki. But Facebook and Twitter don't store their user data in Russia, keeping it out of SORM's reach. (Soldatov and Borogan, 2013, para. 20)

Edward Snowden's revelations about the U.S. National Security Agency's PRISM program, which tapped into American ICT companies' data centers to extract desired information, provided the perfect justification for requiring all data pertaining to Russian citizens to be stored within the Russian Federation. Brazil and several European countries have made announcements about eventual data localization requirements, as well, providing further legitimacy to the Russian plan in the eyes of public opinion. However, there is no evidence that data localization does much to protect user privacy (Sargsyan, 2016). Indeed, it is much easier (and more clearly within the bounds of U.S. law) for the U.S. intelligence apparatus to target data outside of the U.S., while locating data centers within Russia makes it easier for Russian agencies to access user content. Data localization serves to increase the Kremlin's access to citizen data under the guise of protecting the Russian public from American spies.

The 2016 Yarovaya laws further expanded the government's surveillance powers by increasing the mandatory data retention period to six months for content and three years for metadata and mandating cryptographic backdoors in all messaging applications (Lokshina, 2016).

6. Conscripting the Private Sector

Twenty-first century information controls in Russia distinguish themselves from earlier systems of repression in two key ways: the introduction of ICT technologies, and the irruption of the private sector in what was previously a totalitarian, state-controlled ecosystem. Moscow's appetite for surveillance has grown apace with the potential targets provided by widespread ICT adoption, and the FSB-oligarchic alliance that dominates both the state and the economy excels at finding ways to pressure ICT companies to provide the needed access to data flows.

A 2013 study by the now-defunct Center for the Study of Media and Society at the New Economic School in Moscow[2] sought to ascertain the policies and mechanisms used by domestic Russian ICT companies to protect the digital rights of their users. Conducted during a time of great uncertainty for the ICT sector in Russia, the study found that company representatives were hesitant to discuss issues of human rights (preferring the term "user rights"), the pressures they faced from the Kremlin, or the possibility of doing anything other than following the law. The majority of companies reported that they comply with all demands from the government, while only a few seemed to try to negotiate these demands. All of the companies surveyed reported being sensitive to government demands and having to contend with censorship issues, all the while insisting that they adhered to high standards of privacy and security (Maréchal et al., 2015; Petrova, Fossato, Indina, Dokuka, & Asmolov, 2013).

The Russian government ensures the compliance of domestic companies in particular by holding them liable for banned, copyrighted or otherwise illegal content accessible through their services or platforms. This intermediary liability strongly incentivizes ICT companies to block or remove any content that might plausibly be deemed illegal, lest they suffer grave repercussions (Petrova et al., 2013). Indeed, protection rackets and related thuggery are endemic in Russia, and business owners can find themselves targeted for prosecutions of dubious legal merit simply because they have upset the wrong oligarch or FSB operative (Pomerantsev, 2014). Legal remedies are nonexistent in these cases, leaving submission and exile as the only viable options. The current context of quick legislative reform and uneven enforcement keeps companies—and their staff—in a state of constant uncertainty about the rules and the penalties for breaking them.

Foreign companies operating in Russia typically have deeper pockets, greater technical and managerial knowhow, and reduced vulnerability to physical threats compared to their domestic counterparts. Google closed its Russian engineering offices in late 2014 (Luhn, 2014), and a number of former high-level executives have left the country (author interview, 2016). Neither Facebook nor Twitter have offices in Russia (Masnick, 2014), and without local staff who could face retaliation, the American platforms have greater leeway to push back against demands for censorship or for user information. According to Twitter's Transparency Report, the company refused to comply with any of the 233 requests for user information it received from Moscow in 2014–2015 (Twitter, 2015, 2016), and complied with only 5% of takedown requests received in the second half of 2015 (Twitter, 2016). Similarly, Google only produced user information for 5% of Russian government requests in the first half of 2015, though it complied with 62% of takedown requests during that period (Google, 2016). Facebook didn't comply with any Russian requests for user information, and restricted 56 pieces of content. The company does not disclose the number of requests for content restriction it received (Facebook, 2016).

Unlike domestic Russian companies, Google and Facebook (though not Twitter) are members of the Global Network Initiative, employ legal teams and other experts dedicated to advancing their users' digital rights, and engage in public transparency reporting about these issues. These efforts should be supported and encouraged. But if these companies comply with data localization laws, their users' data will fall into SORM's net, particularly given SORM-3's more powerful DPI capabilities. If they refuse, Roskomnadzor may very well block the sites entirely, as at least some of its officials have wanted to do for years (Masnick, 2014).

LinkedIn became the first foreign social media company to be banned from Russia, in part due to noncompliance with the data localization law. Roskomnadzor had sued the social networking site, which was ac-

[2] The Center received much of its funding from Western charitable foundations, which it is now prohibited from doing under the Russian law on "foreign agents". Unsurprisingly, the Center has not been able to identify domestic sources of funding, and much of its former staff is now living in the West (author interview, 2016).

quired by Microsoft earlier in 2016, for illegally sharing the personal data of non-users without obtaining prior consent—a claim that, if true, would indeed put LinkedIn afoul of data management best practices. The suit also argued that LinkedIn did not comply with data localization requirements. In its August 4, 2016, ruling, the court ordered Russian authorities to "take steps" to limit access to the site, though as of late October it remained accessible to most users (Rothrock, 2016). LinkedIn lost its appeal in November, and Roskomnadzor required Apple and Google to remove the LinkedIn app from the Russian versions of their respective app stores (Kang & Benner, 2017; Scott, 2016). With Roskomnadzor due to begin proactively enforcing foreign companies' compliance with data localization in 2017, the decisions of U.S. ICT companies like Google, Facebook and Twitter will be a test of the firms' commitment to user privacy and freedom of expression.

7. Russian Information and Internet Policy at the International Level

Russian internet policy—in both the domestic and foreign policy spheres—is rooted in the premise that Western countries (mainly the U.S.) use the internet to overthrow governments in "countries where the opposition is too weak to mobilize protests" (Nocetti, 2015, p. 114)—or, in other words, countries living under authoritarian regimes. Russian foreign policy hews to a strict interpretation of Westphalian nation-state sovereignty, at the core of which is the principle of non-intervention.[3] The free and open internet threatens that principle, allowing foreign and potentially subversive viewpoints to circulate across Russia. The "color revolutions" of the early 21st century and the Arab Spring have further fueled concerns that the internet represents a threat to the status quo and that it poses a threat to Russian political leaders (Nocetti, 2015). Indeed, opposition groups led by Alexei Navalny used Facebook to coordinate street protests in the aftermath of the 2011 legislative elections, and while the protests failed to coalesce into a lasting social movement, such an outcome was not completely outside the realm of possibility (Soldatov & Borogan, 2015; White & McAllister, 2014). Moreover, there is good reason to believe that Putin sees the U.S., and specifically then-Secretary of State Hillary Clinton, as directly responsible for fomenting these protests. Under this paradigm, such interference in Russia's domestic politics constitutes a violation of national sovereignty tantamount to information warfare. Likewise, U.S. policy initiatives like democracy promotion and the Internet Freedom Agenda are seen as promoting political projects that are aligned with U.S. interests, almost invariably at the expense of Russia's own interests (Nocetti, 2015).

Digital rights and the free flow of information are thus doubly threatening to the Kremlin. Not only does the internet embolden and empower the domestic opposition, it is (from Putin's perspective) closely associated with the U.S. government, which has historically played a unique role in internet governance and is a major funder of the global digital rights movement. In Russia's Westphalian view of the world, nation-states are the only actors that matter, and that should matter, and the actions of all other actors (be they individuals, civil society organizations, or corporations) can be imputed to a government motivated by the accumulation of power. That is the logic behind the 2012 law "On foreign agents", which stigmatizes internationally-funded NGOs that criticize the Kremlin by labelling them as "traitors" or "spies" (Human Rights Watch, 2017).

The Kremlin responded to what it sees as an existential threat by launching a campaign to reshape its near-abroad in its image, most dramatically in Estonia and Ukraine. The European and American response was tepid, and Putin grew bolder. Before long, the Kremlin was providing financial and ideological support to far-right parties and movement across the European Union, including Viktor Orbán in Hungary, the Brexit "Leave" campaign, and pro-Russian candidates in Bulgaria and Moldova (Eichenwald, 2017; Oliphant, 2016). A transnational, neo-fascist, authoritarian movement grounded in ethno-nationalism was taking shape. And then, of course, there is Donald Trump. Early analysis suggests that Trump was initially no more than a "useful fool" to be used to discredit Hillary Clinton and cast doubts on her legitimacy as president, but after a series of astounding events, the election, of course, went another way. The 2017 elections in France and Germany will be the next tests.

French Russia expert Julien Nocetti (2015) argues that "Moscow is crucially involved in the politicization of global cyber issues, to a large extent owing to the inextricable interweaving of the Russian Federation's domestic and external affairs" (p. 112). He stresses that:

> The slogan "content as threat" encapsulates the Russian perception that digital technologies can be used as tools *against* Russia. In Russian documentation it is expressed more fully as the "threat of the use of content for influence on the socio-humanitarian sphere". The notion of content as threat is reinforced by the projection onto foreign partners of Russia's own preconceptions of how international relations work, and by the presumption that a primary aim of western powers is to disrupt and undermine Russia. (p. 116)

For many years, Russia simultaneously sought to constrain the use of this powerful weapon (information) through international norms and treaties even as it developed its own offensive capabilities, echoing its Cold War approach to nuclear weapons. Since 1998—shortly before Putin became president—Russia has proposed

[3] A Westphalian paradigm doesn't mean that a country won't interfere in another country's affairs; it means that any such intervention is considered an act of war.

annual UN resolutions prohibiting "information aggression", which Nocetti interprets to mean the use of ideas or ideology to undermine regime stability (2015, p. 122). This is only one example of Russian attempts to regulate the use of information under international law. At the same time, Russia uses the Shanghai Coordination Organization (SCO) to provide technical assistance and knowledge transfer to other illiberal regimes eager to up their information controls game. This authoritarians' club further includes China, Kazakhstan, Kyrgyzstan, Tajikistan and Uzbekistan, with several other countries having observer or dialogue partner status. Russia and China use the SCO to share new advances in repression with one another, as well as with the less powerful member states whose regimes they want to bolster (Diamond, Plattner, & Walker, 2016; Nocetti, 2015).

8. Edward Snowden

More than three years after his initial revelations, Edward Snowden's continued asylum in Russia remains perplexing for many observers, some of whom speculate that the former NSA contractor must be a Russian agent, even if a reluctant one. The Snowden camp categorically denies this, and available evidence strongly suggests that Snowden's arrival in Moscow was not of his own making. Shortly after coming out to the world as the source for the Guardian and Washington Post stories about NSA surveillance, Snowden left Hong Kong for Latin America, with a layover in Moscow. He was accompanied by WikiLeaks's Sarah Harrison, who was apparently sent by Julian Assange to help escort Snowden to safety. There are only so many options for this route, and Moscow seemed to pose the fewest risks of being intercepted by U.S. officials. Unfortunately for Snowden, his passport was revoked while he was in the air, and he was stuck within the Moscow airport for 39 days while his asylum application was processed. Snowden was granted temporary asylum in Russia for a year, followed by a three-year residency permit in 2014 that was later extended to 2020 (Greenwald, 2014; Harding, 2014; Sharkov, 2016; Williams & Toropin, 2017).

As the world grappled with the unprecedented revelations of U.S. spying, and the key role played by internet platforms and telecommunications companies in collection programs like PRISM, governments explored ways to protect their citizens from the NSA's reach. Data localization schemes were proposed by countries as varied as Brazil, China, France, Germany, South Korea and Russia with the stated aim of ameliorating privacy risks from foreign surveillance. But in Russia at least, data localization laws "leveraged the public outrage and the heightened privacy concerns caused by the NSA spying to extend their control over data and their surveillance potential by data localization" (Sargsyan, 2016). The Kremlin thus seized the Snowden revelations, as well as his presence in Moscow, as an opportunity to craft a narrative that furthered its political objective: to portray the U.S. and its allies as the real adversaries of privacy and individual autonomy while continuing to intensify domestic censorship, surveillance, and the dismantling of Russian civil society. Meanwhile, Snowden has been an outspoken critic of Russian policy (Nechepurenko, 2016).

9. Analysis: Understanding Russia's Networked Authoritarianism

The key to understanding Russian internet policy is that it is part and parcel of an overall information control policy, the goal of which is the accumulation of power and wealth for Russia's kleptocratic elites. The global practice of information controls has undergone three generational shifts in rapid succession (Deibert, Palfrey, Rohozinski, & Zittrain, 2010). First generation controls prevent the population from accessing forbidden content, either through barriers to access or by blocking specific websites or pages. China's "Great Firewall" is a classic example of first generation information controls, and the Roskomnadzor blacklist is a poorly executed example of the same. The second generation involves creating legal and technical frameworks allowing public and private authorities to deny access to information on a case-by-case basis. "Just-in-time" blocking and sporadic internet shutdowns linked to specific political events exemplify this method. Third-generation controls combine legal and technical means with a proactive public relations (or propaganda) strategy: "it is less a matter of refusing access as of competing with potential threats through effective counter-information campaigns which discredit or demoralize the opponent" (Deibert et al., p. 16). The Kremlin's army of online trolls and use of broadcast and online media for domestic and external propaganda exemplify such third-generation controls. Deibert further identifies advocating for illiberal practices in internet governance arenas as a possible fourth generation of information controls (Deibert, 2016). This is already a core part of Russian foreign policy, as discussed above. The result is "networked authoritarianism" (MacKinnon, 2011), a political system that leverages ICTs and media regulation to carefully control the expression of dissent in a way that gives the impression of limited freedom of expression without allowing dissent to gain traction. Russia has long been "on the cutting edge of techniques aimed to control online speech with little or no direct filtering" (p. 43).

While historically Russia has indeed eschewed the more heavy-handed information controls in favor of second- and third-generation tactics, since Putin's 2012 return to the presidency—preceded by popular demonstrations that shared many characteristics of successful "color" revolutions (White & McAllister, 2014)—there have been increasing signs that the gloves are coming off. Google chairman Eric Schmidt worried as early as 2013 that Russia was beginning to copy China in internet censorship (Luhn, 2014), while SORM-3 and data localization requirements (including the LinkedIn ban) are further indications that the Kremlin is serious about controlling information within its borders. At the international level, Russia is normalizing and helping to spread networked authoritarianism through various strategies in internet governance fora, at the UN, and through the Shanghai Cooperation Organization "authoritarians' club" (see Pearce & Kendzior, 2012, for an examination of networked authoritarianism in Azerbaijan). At the same time, it has been waging a slow, covert campaign to dismantle the transatlantic alliance using "information weapons" honed in its near-abroad, most famously in Ukraine but also in Moldova. If information has always been political, today it is geopolitical and weaponized.

If true, the allegations of Russian interference in Western elections, including the 2016 U.S. presidential contest, would clearly constitute a pattern of "information aggression". Russia may be trying to give its adversaries a taste of as their own medicine (as the Kremlin sees it), or it may be teaching the world an object lesson on the dangers of the free flow of information. It is also possible that having failed to garner support for a norm against informational violations of state sovereignty, Russia decided to use that powerful weapon to reshape the international system to better fit its authoritarian, Westphalian worldview. Regardless of the grand strategy pursued by Putin, the tactics used insidiously turned open societies' strengths—pluralism, free expression, acceptance of diversity—against them at a time when they were especially vulnerable. Indeed, in the aftermath of the 2008 financial crisis the economic recovery has left too many behind, for which many Americans blame coastal elites and the incumbent Democrats. Populist contestations of capitalism, including the surveillance capitalism that powers the internet economy (Zuboff, 2015), open a door for competing political projects like the far-right ethno-nationalisms gaining ground across Europe and, of course, the Trump phenomenon—itself no stranger to xenophobia and white supremacist themes. Liberal democracies' policy responses must navigate between Scylla and Charibdis, facing down the threat of far-right extremism without developing our own version of networked authoritarianism.

10. Towards a Geopolitics of Information

As early as 2012, Rebecca MacKinnon predicted that "in the twenty-first century, many of the most acute political and geopolitical struggles will involve access to and control of information" (2012, p. XXV). Geopolitical debates about the flow of information typically pit champions of free expression and access to information against those who want to see state sovereignty replicated in cyberspace. There are shades of gray between those positions, of course, but it is nevertheless an ideological division that should be taken seriously. As Shawn Powers and Michael Jablonski note in their book about the Internet Freedom Agenda:

> The real cyber war is not over offensive capabilities or cybersecurity but rather about legitimizing existing institutions and norms governing Internet industries in order to assure their continued market dominance and profitability....While heavy-handed government controls over the Internet should be resisted, so should a system whereby Internet connectivity requires the systematic transfer of wealth from the developing world to the developed. (Powers & Jablonski, 2015, p. 24)

Powers and Jablonski thus identify two internet-mediated threats to human wellbeing: information controls (Crete-Nishihata, Deibert, & Senft, 2013) and surveillance capitalism (Zuboff, 2015). The former represents a threat from the state, while the latter is best understood as a threat from capitalism. This article has described a third threat: information warfare, a threat from external adversaries who strategically use information to achieve geopolitical goals—or, as defined by the former head of the Directorate for Electronic Warfare of the Russian Main Naval Staff, "securing national policy objectives both in peacetime and in wartime through means and techniques of influencing the information resources of the opposing side" (Pomerantsev, 2016, p. 181).

However, it is important not to succumb to false equivalencies that equate civic activities (like teaching people how to run elections) with the present moment—the stuff of dystopian science fiction. U.S. democracy promotion and the Internet Freedom Agenda undoubtedly support regime change in a number of countries by bolstering alternative political projects (author interview with Daniel Sepulveda, 2015), however that is far from being the only reason for supporting fair elections or the open internet. In many cases, the U.S. is less interested in supporting a specific alternative to the incumbent regime than it is in opening markets for U.S. companies, and many individual policymakers and bureaucrats genuinely embrace the ideals of access to information, free expression, and accountable democracy (Powers & Jablonski, 2015). Moreover, there is no evidence that domestic demands for free and fair elections, or a free and open internet, are anything other than genuine, including in Russia.

The past several years have seen a shift from a normative debate between the "free flow" and "online sovereignty" camps, to carefully plotted intervention. President Barack Obama noted in a 2009 speech that "the great irony of the information age" is that "those states that have most successfully adopted and exploited the opportunities afforded by the Internet are also the most vulnerable to range of threats that accompany it" (Carr, 2016, p. 2). Indeed, the Russian campaign's two greatest ostensible victories to date, the British "Brexit" vote and Donald Trump's victory, took place in deeply connected societies. If politics is war by other means, then we might call this terrorism by other means. Like terrorism, information warfare turns open societies against themselves, creating chaos and breeding suspicion. Without knowing friend from foe, or credible analysis from "fake news", societies become paralyzed, unable to coordinate against a shape-shifting enemy that many doubt is even there. For scholar Madeline Carr, "No previous technology has been regarded concurrently as a source of power and vulnerability in quite the way that the Internet has" (Carr, 2016, p. 2).

Monroe Price's (2015) examination of "the new strategic communication" provides a useful framework for understanding the new geopolitics of information. The concept almost seems tailor-made for the current crisis: strategic communication is a "consolidating relationship between information and power" that is "heavily subsidized, usually transnational, engineered and often deceptive" (p. 7), and it is "sensitive to the particular environment in which the information intervention takes place" (p. 9). This describes Russian intervention in Western elections perfectly. Price argues that the affordances of ICTs have "raised the consequences and possibilities of strategic communication to new levels" (p. 1), empowering states to "experiment with ways to 'move the needle' of public opinion among targeted populations utilizing advanced tools of communication and [to] integrate the consequences in their theories of speech and conduct" (p. 3). Having failed to secure an international agreement circumscribing transnational communication, Russia resolved to use "information weapons" first in the pursuit of its strategic objectives, with apparent success.

At least part of that success can be traced to the state of our media ecosystem. Before Facebook launched in 2005, "the often unstated assumption was that [information intermediaries like newspapers and television networks] would function (or would be obligated to function) as guardians of the public interest" (Price, 2015, p. 35). The system was far from perfect, but by and large media institutions took their gatekeeping role seriously, and followed a highly developed code of journalism ethics.

Today's intermediaries have no such ethical code, and some explicitly reject a sense of responsibility for their platforms' impact on society, as Facebook's Mark Zuckerberg did at several points during the 2016 U.S. presidential campaign (Zuckerberg, 2016). Further complicating matters, the most visible intermediaries have a global footprint: how does a profit-seeking corporation, lacking any appetite to perform journalistic functions, determine what is in the best interest of humanity?

Meanwhile, traditional media outlets have lost advertising revenues and audience shares to social media platforms, and in their weakened financial state have been absorbed by vertically integrated media conglomerates motivated by financial gain (McChesney, 2013; Pickard, 2014, 2017). The quality of discourse suffers, and the public struggles to parse truth from falsehood, opinion from fact. The "marketplace of ideas" is flooded with mediocre fare that anyone can access for free. Journalists struggle to make a living, and would-be members of the Fourth Estate flock to careers in public relations. The "quality control" on the public sphere erodes inexorably, leaving public discourse vulnerable to manipulation.

Price introduces the concept of "strategic architectures", which he defines as "large-scale efforts to fix or stabilize the relationship of states and other major players to information flows" (p. 9):

> These wholesale approaches include active rethinking of communications structures by powerful states so as to maintain control over their own narratives and affect relevant communications systems outside their borders. These are designs not only of government but of the corporate empires for whom communication is key and certainly for the media companies themselves. For those who seek to ensure a particular narrative—for example, of governmental legitimacy, religious authenticity, or the advantages of consumerism—establishing an infrastructure they can control is significant. (Price, 2015, pp. 9–10)

As John Gilmore said in 1993, the free and open global internet treats censorship as damage and routes around it, presenting a threat to networked authoritarianism. The threat would have been even greater if it had been embraced and promoted by a hegemonic power, as would doubtless have been the case under a Hillary Clinton presidency. The Kremlin saw undermining her presidency, and Americans' faith in democracy, as a geopolitical imperative, and established a strategic infrastructure to spread messages that would favor her opponent, Donald Trump, whose authoritarian predisposition, ignorance of global affairs, and business ties to Russia further increased his value as a "useful fool" (Davidson, 2016; Miller & Entous, 2017) The early days of the Trump presidency show no indication that the 45th president will respect, much less support, a free press or open internet.

11. Conclusion

The brewing conflict between Vladimir Putin's regime and the liberal democracies of Europe and North America appears to pit two conflicting paradigms about the role of information—distributed via the internet—in society (Zuboff, 2015). This article has described Russia's historical and contemporary approaches to controlling the flow of information, both domestically and at the international level, to argue that Russia does not view internet governance, cybersecurity, and media policy as separate domains. Rather, all the areas covered by those disciplines falls under "information security" for Russian foreign policy. Domestic surveillance, content censorship and illiberal internet governance reform are deeply connected to misinformation campaigns abroad, and are used strategically to achieve geopolitical goals.

Despite all its flaws, liberal democracy is still the best form of governance available if the goal is to ensure human rights and economic prosperity. Just as networked authoritarianism establishes strategic infrastructures to control the message domestically and intervene in global media systems, we need to rethink our media and communication infrastructures to ensure they foster a pluralist, rights-respecting society that is resilient to authoritarianism and extremism. Governments, corporations, civil society organizations and the public all have roles to play in this endeavor.

Moreover, the liberal democracies of Europe and North America need significant reforms to fulfill their promises to their citizens if they are to survive. In the U.S., Barack Obama's presidency was a solid, albeit imperfect, start that a majority of voters endorsed by voting for Hillary Clinton. Scholars of all disciplines should consider how their work can support the positive reforms that our democracies urgently need, counter the forces of authoritarianism, and actively participate in the shared work of governance.

Acknowledgements

The author gratefully acknowledges Griffin Boyce, Sergei Hovyadinov, Priya Kumar, Jeff Landale, Tanya Lokot, Rebecca MacKinnon, and Sarah Myers West for their comments at various stages of this manuscript, as well as the issue editors and anonymous reviewers.

Conflict of Interests

The author declares no conflict of interests.

References

Access Now. (2016). *#KeepItOn*. Retrieved from https://www.accessnow.org/keepiton

Bowles, A. (2006). The changing face of the RuNet. In H. Schmidt, K. Teubener, & N. Konradova (Eds.), *Control + shift. Public and private usages of the Russian internet* (pp. 21–33). Norderstedt: Books on Demand.

Carr, M. (2016). *US Power and the internet in international relations*. New York, NY: Palgrave Macmillan.

Castells, M., & Kiselyova, E. (1995). *The collapse of Soviet communism: A view from the information society*. Los Angeles, CA: Figueroa Press.

Citizen Lab. (2015). *Citizen Lab summer institute*. Retrieved from http://citizenlab.org/summerinstitute

Crete-Nishihata, M., Deibert, R., & Senft, A. (2013). Not by technical means alone: The multidisciplinary challenge of studying information controls. *IEEE Internet Computing*, *17*(3), 34–41. doi:10.1109/MIC.2013.29

Davidson, J. D. (2016, August 31). Russia's cyber warfare has bigger aims than electing Donald Trump. *The Federalist*. Retrieved from http://thefederalist.com/2016/08/31/russias-disinformation-operations-aim-to-undermine-american-democracy

Deibert, R., Palfrey, J., Rohozinski, R., & Zittrain, J. (Eds.). (2010). *Access controlled: The shaping of power, rights, and rule in cyberspace*. Cambridge, MA: MIT Press.

Deibert, R. (2016). Cyberspace under siege. In L. Diamond, M. F. Plattner, & C. Walker (Eds.), *Authoritarianism goes global: The challenge to democracy* (pp. 198–215). Baltimore, MD: Johns Hopkins University Press.

DeNardis, L. (2014). *The global war for internet governance*. New Haven, CT: Yale University Press.

Diamond, L. J., Plattner, M. F., & Walker, C. (Eds.). (2016). *Authoritarianism goes global: The challenge to democracy*. Baltimore, MD: Johns Hopkins University Press.

Duffy, N. (2015). *Internet freedom in Vladimir Putin's Russia: The noose tightens*. Washington, DC: American Enterprise Institute.

Eichenwald, K. (2017, January 10). Trump, Putin and the hidden history of how Russia interfered in the U.S. presidential election. *Newsweek*. Retrieved from http://www.newsweek.com/trump-putin-russia-interfered-presidential-election-541302

Facebook. (2016). *Global government requests report*. Retrieved from https://govtrequests.facebook.com

Freedom House. (2015). Freedom on the net. *Freedom House*. Retrieved from https://freedomhouse.org/report/freedom-net/freedom-net-2015

Freedom House. (2016). Freedom on the net. *Freedom House*. Retrieved from https://freedomhouse.org/report/freedom-net/freedom-net-2016

Google. (2016). *Transparency report*. Retrieved from https://www.google.com/transparencyreport/?authuser=1

Gorny, E. (2007). *The Russian internet: Between kitchen-table talks and the public sphere*. Boston, MA: Art Margins.

Greenwald, G. (2014). *No place to hide: Edward Snowden, the NSA, and the U.S. surveillance state*. New York, NY: Henry Holt and Co.

Habermas, J. (1989). *The structural transformation of the public sphere: An inquiry into a category of bourgeois society*. Cambridge, MA: MIT Press.

Hanson, E. C. (2008). *The information revolution and world politics*. Lanham, MD: Rowman & Littlefield.

Harding, L. (2014). *The Snowden files: The inside story of the world's most wanted man*. New York, NY: Vintage Books.

Howard, P. N., & Hussain, M. M. (2013). *Democracy's fourth wave? Digital media and the Arab Spring*. Oxford and New York, NY: Oxford University Press.

Human Rights Watch. (2017, January 17). Russia: Government vs. rights groups. *The Battle Chronicle*. Retrieved from https://www.hrw.org/russia-government-against-rights-groups-battle-chronicle

Kang, C., & Benner, K. (2017, January 6). Russia requires Apple and Google to remove LinkedIn from local App Stores. *The New York Times*. Retrieved from https://www.nytimes.com/2017/01/06/technology/linkedin-blocked-in-russia.html

Karlekar, K., & Cook, S. (2009). *Access and control: A growing diversity of threats to internet freedom*. Washington, DC: Freedom House.

Kratasjuk, E. (2006). Construction of "reality" in Russian mass media news on television and on the Internet. In H. Schmidt, K. Teubener, & N. Konradova (Eds.), *Control + shift. Public and private usages of the Russian internet* (pp. 34–50). Norderstedt: Books on Demand.

Labott, E. (2011, December 6). Clinton cites "serious concerns" about Russian election. *CNN*. Retrieved from http://www.cnn.com/2011/12/06/world/europe/russia-elections-clinton

Lokshina, T. (2016, July 7). Draconian law rammed through Russian parliament: Outrageous provisions to curb speech, privacy, freedom of conscience. *Human Rights Watch*. Retrieved from https://www.hrw.org/news/2016/06/23/draconian-law-rammed-through-russian-parliament

Luhn, A. (2014, December 12). Google to close engineering office in Russia as internet restrictions bite. *The Guardian*. Retrieved from http://www.theguardian.com/world/2014/dec/12/google-closes-engineering-office-russia

MacKinnon, R. (2011). China's "networked authoritarianism". *Journal of Democracy*, *22*(2), 32–46.

MacKinnon, R. (2012). *Consent of the networked: The world-wide struggle for Internet freedom*. New York, NY: Basic Books.

MacKinnon, R., Hickock, E., Bar, A., & Lim, H. (2014). *Fostering freedom online: The role of internet intermediaries*. Paris: UNESCO.

Maréchal, N., MacKinnon, R., Bar, A., Kumar, P., Mendes de Almeida Bottino, C. B., Micek, P., . . . Wanstreet, R. (2015). *Case study research: Laying the groundwork for the methodology*. Washington, DC: New America Open Technology Institute. Retrieved from https://rankingdigitalrights.org/wp-content/uploads/2015/02/RDR-Case-studies.pdf

Masnick, M. (2014, May 16). Russian official threatens to block Twitter and Facebook in Russia. *Tech Dirt*. Retrieved from https://www.techdirt.com/articles/20140516/06421727254/russian-official-threatens-to-block-twitter-facebook-russia.shtml

McChesney, R. W. (2013). *Digital disconnect: How capitalism is turning the Internet against democracy*. New York, NY: The New Press.

Miller, G., & Entous, A. (2017, January 6). Declassified report says Putin "ordered" effort to undermine faith in U.S. election and help Trump. *The Washington Post*. Retrieved from https://www.washingtonpost.com/world/national-security/intelligence-chiefs-expected-in-new-york-to-brief-trump-on-russian-hacking/2017/01/06/5f591416-d41a-11e6-9cb0-54ab630851e8_story.html?utm_term=.8ec13fc7ff94

Nechepurenko, I. (2016, June 27). Edward Snowden criticizes "Big Brother" measure in Russia. *The New York Times*. Retrieved from https://www.nytimes.com/2016/06/28/world/europe/edward-snowden-criticizes-big-brother-measure-in-russia.html

Nisbet, E. (2015). *Benchmarking public demand: Russia's appetite for Information control*. Philadelphia, PA: Center for Global Communication Studies.

Nocetti, J. (2015). Contest and conquest: Russia and global internet governance. *International Affairs*, *91*(1), 111–130.

Ognyanova, K. (2015). In Putin's Russia, information has you: Media control and internet censorship. In M. M. Merviö (Ed.), *Management and participation in the public sphere* (pp. 62–78). Hershey, PA: IGI Global.

Oliphant, R. (2016, November 14). Pro-Russian candidates win presidential votes in Bulgaria and Moldova. *The Telegraph*. Retrieved from http://www.telegraph.co.uk/news/2016/11/14/pro-russian-candidates-win-presidential-votes-in-bulgaria-and-mo

Paganini, P. (2014). New powers for the Russian surveillance system SORM-2. *Security Affairs*. Retrieved from http://securityaffairs.co/wordpress/27611/digital-id/new-powers-sorm-2.html

Pearce, K. E., & Kendzior, S. (2012). Networked authoritarianism and social media in Azerbaijan. *Journal of Communication*, *62*(2), 283–298. doi:10.1111/j.1460-2466.2012.01633.x

Petrova, M., Fossato, F., Indina, T., Dokuka, S., & Asmolov, G. (2013). *Ranking digital rights report: Russia* (Unpublished Report). Moscow: Center for the Study of New Media and Society.

Pickard, V. W. (2014). *America's battle for media democracy: The triumph of corporate libertarianism and the future of media reform*. New York, NY: Cambridge University Press.

Pickard, V. W. (2017, January 30). The problem with our media is extreme commercialism. *The Nation*. Retrieved from https://www.thenation.com/article/the-problem-with-our-media-is-extreme-commercialism

Pomerantsev, P. (2014). *Nothing is true and everything is possible: The surreal heart of the new Russia* (1st ed.). New York, NY: PublicAffairs.

Pomerantsev, P. (2016). The Kremlin's information war. In L. Diamond, M. F. Plattner, & C. Walker (Eds.), *Authoritarianism goes global: The challenge to democracy* (pp. 174–186). Baltimore, MD: Johns Hopkins University Press.

Powers, S. M., & Jablonski, M. (2015). *The real cyber war: The political economy of internet freedom*. Urbana, IL: University of Illinois Press.

Price, M. E. (2015). *Free expression, globalism, and the new strategic communication*. New York, NY: Cambridge University Press.

Rohlenko, D. (2007). *The first Russian printed newspaper*. Science and Life.

Rothrock, K. (2016, October 25). Russia is reportedly banning LinkedIn. *Global Voices*. Retrieved from https://globalvoices.org/2016/10/25/russia-is-reportedly-banning-linkedin

Sargsyan, T. (2016). Data localization and the role of infrastructure for surveillance, privacy, and security. *International Journal of Communication*, *10*, 2221–2237.

Scott, M. (2016, November 10). Russia prepares to block LinkedIn after court ruling. *The New York Times*. Retrieved from https://www.nytimes.com/2016/11/11/technology/russia-linkedin-data-court-blocked.html?_r=0

Sharkov, D. (2016, April 14). Kremlin rebuffs Donald Trump's Edward Snowden "spy" claims. *Newsweek*. Retrieved from http://www.newsweek.com/kremlin-rebuffs-donald-trumps-snowden-claims-433332

Smith, D., & Walker, S. (2016, March 10). Former Putin press minister died of blow to head in Washington hotel. *The Guardian*. Retrieved from http://www.theguardian.com/world/2016/mar/10/mikhail-lesin-blunt-force-trauma-death-washington-dc-vladimir-putin

Soldatov, A., & Borogan, I. (2012). The Kremlin's new internet surveillance plan goes live today. *Wired*. Retrieved from https://www.wired.com/2012/11/russia-surveillance

Soldatov, A., & Borogan, I. (2013). Russia's surveillance state. *World Policy Journal*. Retrieved from http://www.worldpolicy.org/journal/fall2013/Russia-surveillance

Soldatov, A., & Borogan, I. (2015). *The red web: The struggle between Russia's digital dictators and the new online revolutionaries* (1st ed.). New York, NY: PublicAffairs.

Twitter. (2015). *Transparency report*. Retrieved from https://transparency.twitter.com/en.html

Twitter. (2016). *Transparency report*. Retrieved from https://transparency.twitter.com/en.html

White, S., & McAllister, I. (2014). Did Russia (nearly) have a Facebook revolution in 2011? Social media's challenge to authoritarianism. *Politics*, *34*(1), 72–84. doi:10.1111/1467-9256.12037

Williams, J., & Toropin, K. (2017, January 18). Russia extends Edward Snowden's asylum to 2020. *CNN*. Retrieved from http://www.cnn.com/2017/01/18/europe/russia-snowden-asylum-extension

Zuboff, S. (2015). Big other: Surveillance capitalism and the prospects of an information civilization. *Journal of Information Technology*, *30*(1), 75–89. doi:10.1057/jit.2015.5

Zuckerberg, M. (2016, November 12). *Facebook post*. Retrieved from https://www.facebook.com/zuck/posts/10103253901916271

11

#JeSuisCharlie: Towards a Multi-Method Study of Hybrid Media Events

Johanna Sumiala [1], Minttu Tikka [1,*], Jukka Huhtamäki [2] and Katja Valaskivi [1]

[1] School of Communication, Media and Theatre, University of Tampere, 33014 Tampere, Finland; E-Mails: johanna.sumiala@helsinki.fi (J.S.), minttu.tikka@uta.fi (M.T.), katja.valaskivi@uta.fi (K.V.)
[2] Intelligent Information Systems Laboratory, Tampere University of Technology, 33720 Tampere, Finland; E-Mail: jukka.huhtamaki@tut.fi

* Corresponding author

Abstract
This article suggests a new methodological model for the study of hybrid media events with global appeal. This model, developed in the project on the 2015 *Charlie Hebdo* attacks in Paris, was created specifically for researching digital media—and in particular, Twitter. The article is structured as follows. Firstly, the methodological scope is discussed against the theoretical context, e.g. the theory of media events. In the theoretical discussion, special emphasis is given to i) disruptive, upsetting, or disintegrative media events and hybrid media events and ii) the conditions of today's heterogeneous and globalised media communication landscape. Secondly, the article introduces a multi-method approach developed for the analysis of hybrid media events. In this model, computational social science—namely, automated content analysis (ACA) and social network analytics (SNA)—are combined with a qualitative approach—specifically, digital ethnography. The article outlines three key phases for research in which the interplay between quantitative and qualitative approaches is played out. In the first phase, preliminary digital ethnography is applied to provide the outline of the event. In the second phase, quantitative social network analytics are applied to construct the digital field for research. In this phase, it is necessary to map a) what is circulating on the websites and b) where this circulation takes place. The third and final phase applies a qualitative approach and digital ethnography to provide a more nuanced, in-depth interpretation of what (substance/content) is circulating and how this material connects with the 'where' in the digital landscape, hence constituting links and connections in the hybrid media landscape. In conclusion, the article reflects on how this multi-method approach contributes to understanding the workings of today's hybrid media events: how they create and maintain symbolic battles over certain imagined constructs of social imaginaries of solidarity, belonging, contestation, and exclusion, a topic of core value for the theory of media events.

Keywords
automated content analysis; *Charlie Hebdo*; digital ethnography; hybrid media event; social network analytics; Twitter

Issue
This article is part of the issue "Successes and Failures in Studying Social Media: Issues of Methods and Ethics", edited by Epp Lauk and Niina Sormanen (University of Jyväskylä, Finland).

---

1. Introduction: *Charlie Hebdo* 2015, a Hybrid Media Event

On Wednesday, 7 January 2015, at 11:30 a.m., French–Algerian brothers Saïd and Chérif Kouachi attacked the headquarters of *Charlie Hebdo*. Eleven people were killed in the rampage. After the attack, the Kouachi brothers returned to their car and exchanged fire with the police officers blocking their escape route. A few minutes later, they executed an injured police officer named Ahmed Merabet at point-blank range. The perpetrators escaped from the building, and the shooting of the police officer was filmed from a nearby apartment. The event instantly exploded into a transnational media event, and the amateur video material that was filmed began to circulate rapidly. Newsrooms all over the world followed the massive security operation as the Kouachi brothers hijacked another car and fled north out of Paris. In the evening, tens of thousands of people took to the streets around Europe to show their solidarity with those killed by the gunmen. The next day, 8 January 2015, the attackers continued their escape, and thousands of security personnel were deployed to comb the area approximately 90 kilometres from Paris, where the two men were last seen. Meanwhile, in Paris, reports emerged that a policewoman had been shot and killed; however, the link with the *Charlie Hebdo* attack was not immediately apparent. As night fell, the Eiffel Tower's lights were switched off in memory of the victims. On Friday, 9 January 2015, the police located the attackers in the Dammartin-en-Goële area. The brothers were chased to an industrial complex 35 kilometres from Paris, where they seized a printworks and took a hostage. In east Paris, at around 12:30 p.m., a third gunman named Amedy Coulibaly seized a Jewish supermarket, killed four people, and took hostages. It emerged that Coulibaly was responsible for the killing of the Parisian policewoman, Clarissa Jean-Philippe, the day before. In his phone call to the French TV station BFM-TV, Coulibaly stated that his attack was synchronised with the attacks of the Kouachi brothers, and that they belonged to the same group of terrorists. He also threatened to kill his hostages unless the Kouachi brothers were allowed to go free. After several hours of this hostage situation, police special forces stormed the market and killed Coulibaly. The Kouachi brothers were killed by the special forces on the same day.

Over the course of these three days, new updates constantly appeared on websites, on YouTube, and on news broadcasts. Social media websites were inundated with comments, links, and images connected to the event, and these were shared and commented on by both journalists and ordinary citizens. The course of the events, as presented by professional journalists and international and national media houses, was intermixed with memes and comments that citizens from different countries shared via social media. In addition, various strategic and spontaneous (both political and religious) interest groups made use of the situation and competed for attention, tailoring and recycling details about the events with content aimed at different audiences.

One of the prominent features of the *Charlie Hebdo* event was the use of the slogan *Je Suis Charlie* ("I Am Charlie"), which became a symbol of solidarity and freedom of expression. The volume of communication around the event is well illustrated by the fact that the hashtag *#JeSuisCharlie* was—at least at the time of the event—the most popular tweet in the history of Twitter. The tag was tweeted 6,500 times per minute at its height and was featured in 3.4 million tweets in one 24-hour period (Whitehead, 2015). In addition to *#JeSuisCharlie*, there were many other expressions articulated and shared via Twitter. The slogan *Je ne suis pas Charlie* ("I am not Charlie") came to represent myriads of opinions opposed to or critical of the mass *Je Suis Charlie* declaration. Another perspective was highlighted by the slogan *Je Suis Ahmed* ("I am Ahmed"), which referred to the French police officer Ahmed Merabet, who was Muslim and who was shot on the street by terrorists shouting, "Allahu Akbar" and "We have avenged the prophet". The slogan *Je Suis Ahmed* brought forth the perspective of French Muslims, who opposed the association between Islam and terrorism, as victims of the terror attack. The slogans were used on social media, in the news, and in demonstrations, and they were also circulated in images and caricature drawings emblematic of the case of *Charlie Hebdo*.

This brief illustration of the media workings in the *Charlie Hebdo* attacks is given here to demonstrate the hybrid nature of communication around the events and how an event can be transformed into a hybrid media event (Vaccari, Chadwick, & O'Loughlin, 2015). The term hybrid refers to a complex intermedia dynamic between mainstream news media and social media, as well as the complex circulations between messages and actors and the recombination of media on a variety of media platforms (Chadwick, 2013; Kraidy, 2002). Vaccari, Chadwick and O'Loughlin (2015, p. 1044) describe hybrid media events as "media events whose significance for media professionals, politicians, and non-elites is being reconfigured by the growth of social media". When thinking about the *Charlie Hebdo* attacks as a hybrid media event, we may approach it as a constellation of fluid social intensifications that are most typically created in a complex network of Internet-based and mobile communication technologies. The *Charlie Hebdo* attacks comprise elements of ceremonial mass media communication, but these also converge with contemporary forms of vernacular mass self-communication (cf. Castells, 2009), occasionally also thought of as a form of citizen journalism (cf. Allan & Thorsen, 2009). The element of "liveness" in the Charlie Hebdo attacks as a hybrid media event is intensified in the real-time circulation of texts and images and the dispersion of the event in several locations simultaneously. The level of connectivity between the official and viral narratives of the event may vary greatly, depending on the nature of a message in circulation. Hence, the concept of the "whole world" watching Paris needs to be analysed as an experience that is scattered onto a multiplicity of screens. While people may be sharing *Charlie Hebdo* as a collective spectacle—to use Kellner's (2003) terminology—they are connected to it in different ways. That is, they use different communication media to follow the event, associate with different—and even conflicted—narratives circulating on the event, and feel connected with different groups and identities involved in the event. Consequently, a multiplicity of shared experiences is created in this hybrid media event. Thus, the question of power embedded in social integration as underlined in the classic theory of media events by Dayan and Katz (1992) needs to be addressed on several levels, including a variety of hybrid constellations of sociality (cf. Sumiala & Korpiola, 2016).

In the following sections, we suggest a multi-method approach for the empirical study of hybrid media events, using the *Charlie Hebdo* attacks as a case study. To meet this goal, we first provide a brief outline for our theoretical framework—the theory of media event—which is necessary to contextualise the methodological model. Secondly, we introduce a multi-method approach developed for the analysis of hybrid media events. In this approach, computational social science—or more specifically, a combination of automated content analysis (ACA) (Boumans & Trilling, 2016) and computational social network analytics (SNA) (Huhtamäki, Russell, Rubens, & Still, 2015)—is used in concert with a qualitative approach—specifically, digital ethnography. The article outlines three key phases for research in which the interplay between quantitative and qualitative approaches is played out. In the first phase a preliminary digital ethnography is applied to provide an initial sketch of the event. In the second phase, quantitative social network analytics is applied to construct the digital field for research. In this phase, it is necessary to map a) what is circulating on the websites and b) where this circulation takes place. In the third and final phase, a combination of the qualitative approach and digital ethnography is applied to provide a more nuanced, in-depth interpretation of what (substance/content) is circulating and how this material connects with the 'where' in the digital landscape, hence constituting links and connections in the hybrid media landscape. In conclusion, the article reflects on how this multi-method approach contributes to the understanding of the workings of today's hybrid media events—how they create and maintain symbolic battles over certain social imaginaries of solidarity, belonging, contestation, and exclusion. This is a topic of core value for the theory of media events.

2 Theoretical Framework: Re-Thinking Media Events

Since the birth of the modern mass media, many sociologists, cultural theorists, and communication scholars have examined the interplay between modern society and mass-media saturated gatherings (Bennet & Segerberg, 2012; Boorstin, 1973; Debord, 1967; Kellner, 2003; Rojek, 2013; Shils & Young, 1956). A key focal point in creating this tradition of thought in media studies is *Media events: The live broadcasting of history*, published by Daniel Dayan and Elihu Katz (1992). According to Dayan and Katz, a media event is a special genre that is powerful enough to interrupt everyday media flow, bring the viewer into touch with society's central values, and invite the audience to participate in the event (Dayan & Katz, 1992, pp. 5-9). In their lexicon, media events have their own grammar, their own meaning structure (story form or script), and their own practices, which are characterised by live broadcasting: the interruption of daily media rhythms and routines, the scripting and advance preparation of the event, a huge audience (the "whole world" is watching), social and normative expectations attached to viewing ("must see"), the ceremonial tone of media narration, and the intention to connect people.

As the story forms, media events can be divided into "conquests", "contests", and "coronations". According to Dayan and Katz (1992), these scripts constitute (i) the main narrative possibilities within the genre, (ii) the distribution of roles, (iii) and the ways in which these roles are enacted. In many cases, the three story forms are closely intertwined, and historical events correspond to and resonate with each other at different levels. One event may have certain features of each form; the form of an event may also change, transforming into another story form as the event develops. It is also important to acknowledge that all these scripts are embedded in deeper meaning structures in any given culture (Dayan & Katz, 1992, pp. 28-29). The common denominator for Dayan and Katz's (1992) original work is the ceremoniality associated with media performance. The authors indicate that the significance of media events is in their ability to reach a larger audience than any event that requires physical presence. The audience itself is well aware of this, as they follow the unfolding media event in different locations, which may be private, semi-public, or public.

Since its publication in the 1990s, the media events theory has stimulated vigorous scholarly debate, with its value believed to be in its theoretical and methodological innovation (Cottle, 2006; Couldry, 2003; Dayan, 2010; Fiske, 1994; Hepp & Couldry, 2010; Hepp & Krotz, 2008; Katz & Liebes, 2007; Kyriakidou, 2008; Liebes, 1998; Nossek, 2008; Roel, 2009; Rothenbuhler, 1998; Scannell, 1995, 2001; Sumiala, 2013). The main criticisms of Dayan and Katz's approach have addressed (i) the assumed ceremonial and integrative functions of media events, (ii) the attempt to exclude any disruptive or traumatic events from the focus of their theory, and (iii) the strong focus on television and broadcasting, which may result in inadequate study of global web-based media events.

In other words, many argue that Dayan and Katz's initial account of media events assumes too straightforward a relationship between media coverage and audience endorsement, thereby obscuring the ideological construction of social order, as well as the challenges and disruptive potential that are implicit in many media events (Cottle, 2006; Couldry, 2003; Fiske, 1994; Kellner, 2003; Kyriakdou, 2008; Rothenbuhler,

2010; Scanell, 1995, 2001). In addition, given the globalisation of communication through the Internet and social networking websites, critics have called for a re-contextualisation of the explicit focus on TV and broadcasting in the media events theory.

Hepp and Couldry (2010, p. 9) argue that in theorising media events today we should not perceive them as placed at a defined locality, but rather as disembedded, or even ubiquitous, communicative practices. Drawing from the work of Hepp and Couldry, we postulate that today's media events should be understood as multi-sited, multi-temporal, multi-actor and multi-voiced phenomena articulated by a simultaneous connectivity of a variety of communication processes. These media events may be simultaneously structured around relatively centralised power structures, such as national and global mainstream media—for example the BBC or CNN—and multi-centred power structures, such as social networking sites (Hepp & Couldry, 2010, p. 9). Hepp and Couldry (2010, p. 12) offer a new working definition for contemporary media events to better grasp their fluid nature:

> "Media events are certain situated, thickened, centring performances of mediated communication that are focused on a specific thematic core, cross different media products and reach a wide and diverse multiplicity of audiences and participants."

Dayan and Katz have responded to the criticism of their original theory of media events and have re-adjusted their ideas in different public forums. Katz and Liebes (2007, 2010) suggest that the focus of analysis should be shifted from conquests, contests, and coronations to disaster, terror, and war. According to Katz and Liebes (2007, p. 157):

> "We believe that cynicism, disenchantment, and segregation are undermining attention to ceremonial events, while the mobility and ubiquity of television technology, together with the downgrading of scheduled programming, provide ready access to disruption. If ceremonial events may be characterized as 'co-productions' of broadcasters and establishments, then disruptive events may be characterized as 'co-productions' of broadcasters and anti-establishment agencies, i.e. the perpetrators of disruption."

Furthermore, Katz and Liebes suggest that marathons of terror, natural disaster, and war—media disasters—should be distinguished from media events as a separate genre. These mediatized disasters of different kinds have become far removed from the ceremonial roots of the original media events (Cottle, 2006; Liebes, 1997; Liebes & Blonheim, 2005). Daniel Dayan (2010) has written extensively about the changing nature of media events. For him, the "macabre accoutrements to televised ordeals, punishments, and tortures" and the emphasis on "stigmatization and shaming" in today's mediatized public events have caused media events to lose their potential to reduce conflict; instead, they 'foster divides, and install and perpetuate schisms' (Dayan, 2010, pp. 26-27). As a result, media events tend to lose their distinct character and instead migrate towards other genres: new media events are no longer clearly differentiated entities, but exist on a continuum. Dayan (2010, p. 27) suggests this 'banalization of the format' produces what he calls "almost" media events. Dayan reminds us that the pragmatics of media events have changed as messages have become multiple, audiences selective, and social networks ubiquitous. Dayan (2010, p. 27) summarises the difference between original and current media events in the following manner:

> "Interpersonal networks and diffusion processes are active before and after the event, mobilizing attention to the event and fostering intensive hermeneutic attempts to identify its meaning. But during the liminal moments we described in 1992, totality and simultaneity were unbound; organizers and broadcasters resonated together; competing channels merged into one; viewers gathered at the same time and in every place. All eyes were fixed on the ceremonial centre, through which each nuclear cell was connected to all the rest."

Dayan leaves the reader in a state of scepticism. For him, in today's "contested territory of media events", disenchantment and the loss of the "we"—the most critical functions of media events—are the most likely consequences. Although it is reasonable to ask whether this "we" ever existed, it is nevertheless inevitable that the dimensions of media events have changed with the changing media environment and the contemporary multiplicity of the media.

The concept of hybrid media events is one attempt to respond to the criticism offered by Hepp and Couldry (2010) and the response offered by Dayan (2010) and Katz and Liebes (2010). The idea of hybrid media events acknowledges the situated nature of transnationally or even globally mediated communication of a certain thematic core (here, the killings and related public reactions), while underscoring the fluidity of the movement in the circulation of the related posts, memes, images, news, and reports. The concept of the hybrid media event highlights the complex intermedia dynamics between the different media platforms (namely, mainstream news media and social media) in communicating those solidarities, belongings, and controversies associated with the event.

One of the key challenges for the study of contemporary media events is a methodological one. As the media landscape changes and media events become more transnational and global, the right methodological tools need to be developed to better grasp these changing conditions. During the 1980s and 1990s in the empirical study of media events, the methodological focus was mainly on qualitative research. The empirical analysis focused on the study of national broadcast media, such as the BBC, or the national press, and the focus was on observation, textual analysis, and interviews related to the production, representation, and reception of media events (cf. Couldry, 2003; Couldry, Hepp, & Krotz, 2010; Eide, Kunelius, & Phillips, 2008).

While dividing the empirical focus between the production, representation, and reception of media events has proven a useful strategy for understanding national media events, this approach lacks the tools to analyse those communicative processes that go beyond the national frame and take place between and *betwixt* production, representation, and reception of media events. In these new conditions, messages, tweets, posts, memes, images, and symbols circulate and travel from one context to another. The categories between production, representation, and reception become blurred. It takes only one click to transform the person receiving a message into the one who produces it. As a result, new methodological approaches and tools need to be developed to capture these processes of communication that are crucial for today's hybrid media events. This suggests a new type of methodological dialogue between qualitative and quantitative approaches.

Here, the quantitative methods that make it possible to deal with a large amount of data circulating on a variety of media platforms are combined with more in-depth qualitative methods, such as digital ethnography, that enable researchers to go deeper into the data and trace pieces of meaning associated with symbolic battles carried out in the process of communicating about the events. In the following section, we introduce our methodological model for the study of hybrid media events with global appeal. This model, developed in the project on the 2015 *Charlie Hebdo* attacks in Paris, was created primarily for researching digital media—specifically Twitter.

3. Studying Hybrid Media Events on Twitter

Twitter is a micro-blogging website created in 2006 that enables users to send up to 140 character messages, commonly called "tweets". According to Twitter's own statistics from December 2015, the service has 320 million monthly active users (Twitter, 2016). Although the user growth has stalled in 2016—as Twitter is having its tenth birthday—it is still among the most popular social networking sites, along with Facebook and Instagram (Statista, 2016). On Twitter, messages are public by default, although the service also offers a feature called direct message (DM), which is private. On Twitter, the model of social relationships is directed and non-reciprocal, meaning that users can subscribe to other users' tweets in order to follow them. However, those they follow don't have to follow them back. When a user follows other users, the tweets of those followed will be visible on the user's main Twitter homepage, constituting a "tweet timeline" that appears in reverse chronological order. The characteristic practices for Twitter communication allow individual tweets to be liked and retweeted, which can increase the visibility and popularity of a single tweet. The retweet practice can also push a single tweet into a circulation that crosses the borders of different media platforms. Users can make a reference to other user with the @ symbol. With the prefix @ followed by a username, users can mention or reply to other users. An important feature is the hashtag—a word or phrase prefixed with the # symbol. Hashtags provide means for labelling tweets under certain topics, which gives structure to the communication on Twitter and enables users to find the information that interests them. Additionally, Twitter allows users to post images, videos, and hyperlinks.

As Twitter communication is limited to short messages that can be enriched with other communicative elements, such as images, videos, and hyperlinks, it is suitable for fast information sharing. Due to its public nature, it is popular among journalists, authorities, and organisations, as well as ordinary people. It is a prominent platform in the context and construction of different types of media events, varying from sports and politics to crises and disasters. A recent report on Twitter states that typical content on Twitter is twofold: either conversational, with thousands of people engaging with a particular topic for an extended period of time, or breaking news stories that drive large spikes in traffic over shorter periods of time (Parse.ly, 2016). Studies focusing on Twitter during political elections and sport events such as the Olympics give emphasis to idea of the audiences as co-producers of a media event, in addition to the traditional mass media (cf. Girginova, 2015; Kreiss, Meadows, & Remensperger, 2014). In the field of crisis communications, Twitter has been at the centre of many discussions. From the Arab Spring to the 2011 London riots, Twitter has been identified as a prominent platform for citizen communication in several revolutions, protests, and movements, as it connects people and bypasses the gatekeepers, whether they be the authorities or journalists (cf. Bennet & Segerberg, 2012; Procter, Vis, & Voss, 2013). From the journalistic viewpoint of crisis reporting, the 2010 Haiti earthquake has been called the first "Twitter disaster". This title underlines the fact that during the first 24 hours of the Haiti earthquake, news organisations were depending on social media, and especially the rapid and easily accessible flow of information provided by Twitter (Bruno, 2011). In times of crisis, ordinary people can actively produce information, and they can also link and share published news stories from mainstream news media (Utz, Schultz, & Glocka, 2013; Parse.ly, 2016). In this context, Twitter has been perceived as a symbol of change in the media landscape:

> "If we allow ourselves to paraphrase the CNN effect of the 1990s, this changeover in the media landscape could be called the Twitter effect. As was true for the CNN effect, which was caused by more than just the CNN organization, the Twitter effect must also be considered as a symbol of a much broader phenomenon, concerning several online tools oriented to the publication of user-generated, real-time content (Twitter, Facebook, YouTube, etc.)." (Bruno, 2011, p. 8)

For our research, Twitter offers a fruitful context for the study of a hybrid media event. First of all, in contrast to Facebook, Twitter provides an Application Programming Interface (API) that allows access to the majority of the data published through the service (cf. Vis, 2013). Secondly, although we fully acknowledge that Twitter is only one platform in the hybrid media system, we state that it played a key role as a prominent platform during the unfolding of the *Charlie Hebdo* attacks, through which information, images, videos, and links about the incident were circulated. Thirdly, Twitter has become a key platform for breaking news, and therefore events that draw attention tend to surface on the platform. Finally, Twitter offers rich data that also sheds light on other forms of media. Several media organisations, politicians, and authorities use Twitter, and the content and actors from other media platforms are also present through a hypermedia chain (cf. Kraidy & Mourad, 2010). To give an example, a tweet that contains an image taken of the TV screen showing the news is a common convention that constructs a chain of different media.

4. Towards a Multi-Method Model

4.1. Automated Content Analysis and Computational Social Network Analytics

In our multi-method model, we combine computational social science—more specifically, automated content analysis (ACA) (Boumans & Trilling, 2016) in concert with computational social network analytics (SNA)—with a qualitative approach—particularly, digital ethnography. The computational approach allows for analysing both what is being said and by whom. Moreover, the individual actors can be connected to each other through their interactions for richer context to content, and this allows, for example, the identification of densifications in interaction between actors. More specifically, methods of automated content analysis allow us to identify the content that is circulating in the context of the hybrid media event under investigation. Social network analytics give us the means to investigate the overall structure between the actors that discuss and share content related to the event.

Here, the computational approach is used primarily to support digital ethnographic investigations. In terms of content analysis, the computational approach allows us to identify the key topics that are discussed in the data collected on the event. Four main approaches exist for automated content analysis: counting and dictionary, unsupervised learning, semi-supervised learning, and supervised learning (Boumans & Trilling, 2016; Laaksonen, Nelimarkka, Tuokko, Marttila, & Kekkonen, 2015). In its simplest form, automated content analysis is implemented by counting the number of times individual keywords or, in Twitter's case, hashtags and usernames, are included in the data. Unsupervised learning allows, for example, the creation of content-based clusters from the data to identify topics and their combinations or, in other words, to "identify potentially significant fragments" (Procter et al., 2013). In supervised learning, part of the data is categorised manually, and this learning data is used to teach an algorithm to categorise the rest of the material according to its category. Examples of approaches for automated content analysis include keyword extraction, topic modelling, natural language processing (NLP), and entity recognition (Boumans & Trilling, 2016; Finkel, Grenager, & Manning, 2005).

Compared to the situation that Procter et al. (2013) faced when they started mining tweets and found that there was very little existing infrastructure to support them, the availability of tools supporting analysis has improved over the last few years. Online services and social media analysis platforms, including Pulsar and others, provide investigators with dashboards that are able to manage millions of tweets. Using such environments for research is, however, far from trivial. Transparency of data and analysis routines remains a key issue. For ethnographic research, this limitation is not as major, as the investigation is done first and foremost on a qualitative basis, and therefore representative sampling is not a major issue. It is, however, important for the ethnographic research to understand what, in fact, is "the field" where the research takes place. This can be a problem when using commercial analytics services, as, due to technical and business restrictions, it is not always possible to gain the necessary information on how the data has been obtained.

The key approach into the analysis of structure that emerges from the interaction between individual actors in the data is social network analysis (SNA). Here we follow the insight of Yang and Leskovec (2014, p. 1892) as they maintain that, "networks provide a powerful way to study complex systems of interacting objects". SNA supports investigators in observing latent structures and patterns in source data and in sharing their findings with others (Freeman, 2000). When analysing communication networks, actors are represented as network nodes and connected to each other through interactions. Network analysis allows us to quantify both structural properties of networks, as well as the structural positions of individual actors. Moreover, cluster identification can be used to identify groups of nodes that are interconnected to each other.

Network-level metrics come into play when individual network representations are compared to each other. Moreover, network metrics support the temporal analysis of network structure. Size, connection count, density, diameter, and average path length are examples of metrics that can be used as indicators as to which way a network under investigation is evolving. In investigating hybrid media events, one can, for example, create network representations of interactions that are related to a particular topic (identified using automated content analysis) and use network-level metrics to compare the properties of these topic networks.

Cluster identification is a particularly useful method for supporting early exploration of communication data. Clusters emerge from the topology of the network and challenge the investigators to make sense of why a particular cluster emerges. To support the sense-making process, the investigators can use the cluster membership to volumes of hashtags and other topic identifiers and therefore name or label the clusters according to their content signature.

Node-level metrics can be used for a number of purposes. Nodes with a high "betweenness" value, for example, are likely to act as bridges or boundary spanners (Hansen, Shneiderman, & Smith, 2011, "bridge scores for boundary spanners") connecting the different clusters of the overall network. Nodes with a high "in-degree", receive attention from the other actors. Nodes with a high "out-degree" are active in producing new content. Closeness centrality allows us to make a distinction between nodes with peripheral position and those close to the core of the network.

4.2. Digital Ethnography

Concepts such as digital ethnography, virtual ethnography, web ethnography, netnography, mobile ethnography, ICT ethnography, and virtual ethnography have emerged to describe fieldwork conducted in digital environments and landscapes (Boellstorff, 2008; Hine, 2015; Kozinets, 2015; Wittel, 2000). Online access to vast amounts of archived social interactions, along with live access to the human beings posting, changes the practice of ethnography. Researchers of the media are not dealing merely with words, but with images, drawings, photography, sound files, edited audiovisual presentations, website creations, and other digital artifacts (Kozinets, 2015, p. 4).

A characteristic of this qualitative methodological approach is that the researcher conducts fieldwork in the digital environment and applies participatory observation as a means to analyse human–technology interactions in the media and the social and cultural implications this interaction has for the present day digitalized life. In more practical terms, a digital ethnographer constructs his/her field by following ortracing the event, phenomenon, oractivity in question. The fieldworker makes notes, keeps field diary, takes screen shots, downloads material, and he or she may also interview informants by meeting them face-to-face or via digital communication media. It is not untypical that digital or online ethnography is combined with offline ethnography (cf. Postill & Pink, 2012).

Ethnographic understanding of the digital environment and its related interactions aims at in-depth, holistic, and situational understanding and knowledge of the studied event, phenomenon, activity and people (Hine, 2015, pp. 2-3). Considering the global, fluid, and continuously changing nature of the digital landscape, the issue of proximity and situational knowledge also needs re-framing. As Hine (2015, pp. 3-4) argues:

> "When we watch a fight break out on Twitter we cannot be sure whether any of the followers of those involved are seeing the same fight, at the same time, and understanding it in the same way that we do...The very notion of singular 'situation' as a pre-existing object breaks down when we look closely...An ethnographer in such circumstances must get used to a perpetual feeling of uncertainty, of wondering what has been missed, and attempting to build interpretations of events based on sketchy evidence."

In digital ethnography, the researcher has to deal with his/her limited human capacity to encompass the whole of the situation. For this challenge, computational social science offers valuable tools to map the digital landscape and provide a broader frame for the communicative and social processes taking place in that landscape. The value of ethnographic thick description and situational understanding lies in the depth, detail and the ability to grasp more profound layers of meaning in those actions and activities taking place in Twitter and elsewhere in digital media. To follow Hine (2015, p. 5):

> "Ethnography is highly necessary for understanding the Internet in all its depth and detail, and yet it can be challenging to develop way of conducting ethnographic studies which both embrace all that mediated communication offers and still provide us with robust, reliable insights into something in particular."

5. Three Phases

In the following, we will explain in more detail how the computational social science methods, automated content analysis (ACA) and social network analytics (SNA), can be combined with digital ethnography, and how this methodological interplay contributes to developing a new multi-method model for the study of such media events. This method has three phases:

1) Digital ethnography provides the first outline of the event;
2) Automated content analysis and social network analytics construct the digital field for research;
3) Digital ethnography provides an in-depth interpretation of what (substance/content) is circulating and how this material connects with the 'where' in the digital landscape, hence constituting links and connections in the hybrid media landscape necessary for the social meaning making of the event.

5.1. Digital Ethnography Sketches the Event

Like traditional media events, hybrid global media events interrupt the daily routines of the media and of the everyday. In the case of disruptive events, not only the mainstream news media, but also the social media environment turns to a disaster mode and begins to broadcast and circulate news, comments, tweets, posts, and images on the events as they unfold. This moment of massive media saturation and circulation of information produces the first methodological challenge for the study of hybrid media events. This first phase of chaotic information flow demands a digital ethnographic scope—a perspective in which the events are followed and structured into a timeline. In the case of *Charlie Hebdo* attacks, we started our pilot study immediately as the events unfolded. As digital ethnographers, we traced the news in the mainstream media, such as the *BBC*, the *New York Times*, the *Guardian* and *Le Monde*, as well as on Twitter, YouTube, and Facebook. Our personal media streams also included national news outlets, as well as friends and family members located in our native Finland and in different parts of the world, reporting and commenting on the events from different local perspectives. We identified certain prominent messages, hashtags, posts, memes, and images circulating in those media environments. To give one example, the hashtag #JeSuisCharlie was soon announced as the most-tweeted message in the history of Twitter, offering a simple and interesting lead to be followed in the course of the events. This first ethnographic phase of the analysis is best described as suggestive, and its findings may well be challenged in the later process of quantitative and qualitative analysis. Yet, it is a necessary stage for the process to follow, as it is this first stage of the project in which the chaotic information flow around the events is given its first suggestive sketch. This phase provided insight to what might be interesting, relevant, and peculiar in the events as they evolve and, thus, direct the analysis in the next phase. As a concrete way of gathering data, this phase results in many field notes, screenshots, memes, images, videos, and links, as well as a timeline of the events.

5.2. Using Automated Content Analysis and Social Network Analytics to Map the Field

In the next phase, social network analytics are applied to draw a more general overview of communication around the events with more data. In the case of the Charlie Hebdo attacks, the media platform analysed was Twitter. In this so-called "helicopter stage" of the analysis, social network analytics are used to construct the research field and give an overview of the data as well as map certain elements considered relevant based on the first phase of the pilot study. Prior to the analysis, the data needed to be collected. In this case, it was acquired through the social media analytics platform Pulsar using several search words[1]. The number of hits for #JeSuisCharlie totalled 2.3 million.

At the second stage, it is important to make a distinction between *what* is circulating in Twitter and *where* this circulation is taking place. In the *Charlie Hebdo* attacks project, we began with the hashtag #JeSuisCharlie and identified certain key groups: actors including ordinary media users, professional media houses; sites such as connected media platforms, countries and connections associated with it - both communication and non-communication between the different virtual communities created around this particular hashtag. As a result, this mapping can be further expanded to identify hashtags and actors that are related to #JeSuisCharlie. This mapping helps us to empirically illustrate communicative networks created around the events—where and when they take place and how they exist in relation to each other.

Human-in-the-loop analysis is particularly important when ethnographic and computational methods and approaches are used together. Therefore, we point to the Ostinato Model (Huhtamäki et al., 2015) for a structured process for data-driven visual network analytics that allows for balancing between exploration and automation (i.e. reproducibility) of analysis. This way, a multidisciplinary group of investigators can develop the rich description of a hybrid media event in an iterative and incremental fashion through a process that resembles peeling an onion and, thus, to begin to quan-

[1] The list of search words applied is the following: je suis charlie, #jesuischarlie, je ne suis pas charlie, #jenesuispas charlie, je suis ahmed, #jesuisahmed

titatively identify what is circulating (which hashtags) and in which digital media landscapes this circulation takes place. Starting with Twitter helps us to follow the circulation of certain hashtags and actors tweeting and re-tweeting onto new networks of communication (for example, Facebook, Instagram, or online media sites such as Huffington Post have been identified).

However, it must be noted that while collecting data from Twitter is relatively straightforward, given that the investigative team has the required technological capabilities, hybrid media introduce a major issue into data collection. The two public APIs that Twitter offers for developers, response-request based REST API and real-time streaming API, only allow data collection at the time it is published on Twitter. REST API allows the collection of limited amounts of data dating back to a number of days, and the streaming API operates in real-time by definition. The only way to collect extensive data on *Charlie Hebdo*, for example, is to acquire (buy) the data either directly from Twitter or through a social media listening service such as Pulsar. The data ecosystem has transformed since Procter et al. (2013) conducted their research regarding the 2011 London riots. Importantly, Twitter acquired Gnip[2] in 2014 that is currently the only company through which Twitter data can be purchased.

5.3. Applying Digital Ethnography in Tracing the Social

In the final stage of the empirical analysis, networks mapped by using quantitative analysis and social network analytics and its visual illustrations are taken into an ethnographic reconsideration. The quantitative analysis draws a map of the field and helps to orientate the ethnographic immersion. After choosing an interesting incident within the larger event, this case is followed in and through different media platforms. This phase aims to develop a holistic understanding of the chosen research object. Thus, the fieldwork in a digital landscape integrally involves a dense description of the observations in the form of field notes as well as documentation and recording of data by any means available, such as screenshots and prints (cf. Sumiala & Tikka, 2013). In order to capture the research object in a highly complex and dynamic landscape, it is useful to go back to the timeline of the events and re-evaluate the first sketch of the events against the quantitative framework and, consequently, make necessary re-orientations. In this phase, the researcher needs to re-evaluate the incident's relationship with the larger event and the key nodal points in this process. This can be carried out by searching for facts connected to the events and identifying certain key elements such as time, place, and people. In the digital landscape, this can be challenging as hybrid media events host and entice myriads of interpretations, misunderstandings, rumours as well as intentional misinformation. After re-locating the basic elements in the event, the researcher can begin to add layers of meanings to the event. This can be done in two overlapping ways; it is possible to conduct ethnographic fieldwork by following paths and trails of links, streams, and algorithmic suggestions offered by Twitter and other social media platforms, but it may also be useful to conduct digital ethnography by approaching the event simultaneously from different directions for example by making searches in search engines. In these overlapping processes digital ethnographer develops a more nuanced and in-depth understanding of the event and can begin to make interpretations of those more or less visible and hidden representations, discourses, actors and symbols and related communicative practices that contribute to creating and maintaining different types of social imaginaries of solidarities, belongings, and exclusions embedded with the events.

[2] https://blog.twitter.com/2014/twitter-welcomes-gnip-to-the-flock

6. Conclusions

In this article, we suggest a new multi-model methodological approach to the study of hybrid media events developed for the study of the *Charlie Hebdo* attacks. In this new condition of hybrid media, events, messages, tweets, posts, memes, images, and symbols spread simultaneously and are constantly on the move. Old hierarchies between the centre and peripheries in the media event need to be reconsidered as hybrid media events appear more horizontal and multi-sited, multi-temporal, multi-actor, and multi-voiced social phenomena.

As a result, new methodological approaches and tools need to be developed to capture these processes of communication and better understand the workings of today's hybrid media events. This multi-method model proposed in the article consists of combining quantitative automated content analysis (ACA) and social network analytics (SNA) with qualitative digital ethnography. The key for the model is a close interplay between the different approaches and their careful adaption in the different phases of the research. This offers a unique possibility to bridge the gap between situational, in-depth knowledge achieved by qualitative methods in the study of media events and their understanding in the more global communication context.

The theory of media events was first established to explain the social dynamics activated as people gathered together around their TV sets to watch national rituals as live history to be performed on the screen. As discussed earlier, later developments in this theory have challenged the assumed social cohesion created by these events and emphasised instead the disruptive nature of media events. This has implied a certain contested view on the issue of sociality. The hybrid character of contemporary global, disruptive media events such as the *Charlie Hebdo* attacks makes the issue of social integration even more complicated. The question of establishment and anti-establishment is also changed in the hybrid media system. A terrorist attack is as carefully crafted and designed as a coronation, despite aiming at disruption rather than integration. The hybridity of the media environment causes a situation where no individual actor is able to control the flows of information, attention and effect. Despite this, hybrid media events also represent and reproduce existing social solidarities and antagonisms. Continuity and change take place through the circulation of meanings. Twitter is a particular environment for the circulation to take place. Its specific properties contribute to a culture of circulation (Lee & LiPuma, 2002) that seems complex and dispersed. This complexity calls for the multi-method approach.

The question of social integration in media events is not only a theoretical one. It is important to ask how we should empirically study the social dynamics activated in hybrid media events. In this article we suggest a methodological model that has potential to move from one research scale to another. The wider scale observations of the *Charlie Hebdo* attacks as a hybrid media event suggest a multiplicity of social dynamics were activated during the events. Hence, it suggests an interpretation that emphasises the heterogeneity as well as the ephemerality of those social dynamics. To understand more profoundly what kind of meanings and interpretations are associated with those messages and actors circulating in the digital landscape, an ethnographic perspective is necessary. In the future, more empirical research is needed to grasp these complex dynamics of social imaginaries of solidarity, belonging, but also exclusion. The multi-method approach is one attempt to point to this direction.

Acknowledgements

This article is based on the research project *Je Suis Charlie*—The symbolic battle and struggle over attention, conducted in the School of Communication, Media and Theatre in the University of Tampere. This two-year-project (2015–2017) is funded by the Helsingin Sanomat Foundation. The writers wish to thank the anonymous reviewers for their insightful comments.

Conflicts of Interests

The authors declare no conflicts of interests.

References

Allan, S., & Thorsen, E. (Eds.) (2009). *Citizen journalism: Global perspectives*. New York: Peter Lang.

Bennett, L. W., & Segerberg, A. (2012). The logic of connective action. *Information, Communication & Society, 15*(5), 739-768.

Boellstorff, T. (2008). *Coming of age in second life. An anthropologist explores the virtually human*. Princeton: Princeton University Press.

Boorstin, D. J. (1973). *The image—A guide to pseudo-events in America*. New York: Atheneum.

Boumans, J. W., & Trilling, D. (2016). Taking stock of the toolkit. *Digital Journalism*, *4*(1), 8-23.

Bruno, N. (2011). *Tweet first, verify later? How real-time information is changing the coverage of worldwide crisis events*. Reuters Institute for the Study of Journalism. Oxford: University of Oxford.

Castells, M. (2009). *Communication power*. New York: Oxford University Press.

Chadwick, A. (2013). *The hybrid media system: Politics and power*. New York: Oxford University Press.

Cottle, S. (2006). Mediatized rituals: beyond manufacturing consent. *Media, Culture & Society*, *28*(3), 411-432.

Couldry, N. (2003). *Media rituals: A critical approach*. London: Routlegde.

Couldry, N., Hepp, A., & Krotz, F. (Eds.). (2010). *Media events in a global age*. Routledge: Abingdon.

Dayan, D. (2010). Beyond media events. Disenchantment, derailment, disruption. In N. Couldry, A. Hepp, & F. Krotz (Eds.), *Media events in a global age* (pp. 23-42). London: Routledge.

Dayan, D., & Katz, E. (1992). *Media events. The live broadcasting of history*. Cambridge, MA: Harvard University Press.

Debord, G. (1967). *Society of the spectacle*. Buchet-Chastel.

Eide, E., Kunelius, R., & Phillips, A. (Eds.), (2008). *Transnational media events: The Mohammed cartoons and the imagined clash of civilizations*. Göteborg, Sweden: Nordicom.

Finkel, J. R., Grenager, T., & Manning, C. (2005). *Incorporating non-local information into information extraction systems by Gibbs sampling* (pp. 363-370). Stroudsburg, PA: Association for Computational Linguistics.

Fiske, J. (1994). *Media matters: Everyday culture and political change*. Minneapolis: University of Minnesota Press.

Freeman, L. C. (2000). Visualizing social networks. *Journal of Social Structure*, *1*(1). Retrieved from http://www.cmu.edu/joss/content/articles/volume1/Freeman.html

Girginova, K. (2015). New media, creativity, and the Olympics: A case study into the use of #NBCFail during the Sochi winter games. *Communication & Sport*. doi:10.1177/2167479515576101

Hansen, D. L., Shneiderman, B., & Smith, M. A. (2011). *Analyzing social media networks with NodeXL: Insights from a connected world*. Burlington, MA: Morgan Kaufmann.

Hepp, A., & Couldry, N. (2010). Introduction: Media events in globalized media cultures. In N. Couldry, A. Hepp, & F. Krotz (Eds.), *Media events in a global age* (pp. 1-20). Abingdon: Routledge.

Hepp, A., & Krotz, F. (2008). Media events, globalization and cultural change: An introduction to the special issue. *Communications. The Journal of European Communication Research, 33*(3), 265-272.

Hine, C. (2015). *Ethnography for the internet: Embedded, embodied and everyday*. London: Bloomsbury.

Huhtamäki, J., Russell, M. G., Rubens, N., & Still, K. (2015). Ostinato: The exploration-automation cycle of user-centric, process-automated data-driven visual network analytics. In S. A. Matei, M. G. Russell, & E. Bertino (Eds.), *Transparency in social media: Tools, methods and algorithms for mediating online interactions* (pp. 197-222). Retrieved from http://link.springer.com/chapter/10.1007/978-3-319-18552-1_11

Katz, E., & Liebes, T. (2007). 'No more peace!' How disaster, terror and war have upstaged media events. *International Journal of Communication, 1,* 157-166.

Katz, E., & Liebes, T. (2010). 'No more peace!' How disaster, terror and war have upstaged media events. In N. Couldry, A. Hepp, & F. Krotz (Eds.), *Media events in a global age* (pp. 32-42). Abingdon: Routledge.

Kellner, D. (2003). *Media spectacle.* London: Routledge.

Kozinets, R. (2015). *Netnography: Redefined.* London: Sage.

Kraidy, M. M. (2002). Hybridity in cultural globalization. *Communication Theory, 12*(3), 316-339.

Kraidy, M., & Mourad, S. (2010). *Hypermedia space and global communication studies lessons from the Middle East.* Retrieved from http://repository.upenn.edu/cgi/viewcontent.cgi?article=1256&context=asc_papers

Kreiss, D., Meadows, L., & Remensperger, J. (2014). Political performance, boundary spaces, and active spectatorship: Media production at the 2012 Democratic National Convention. *Journalism, 16*(5), 677-595.

Kyriakidou, M. (2008). Rethinking media events in the context of a global public sphere: Exploring the audience of global disasters in Greece. *Communications. The Journal of European Communication Research, 33*(3), 273-291.

Laaksonen, S.-M., Nelimarkka, M., Tuokko, M., Marttila, M., & Kekkonen, A. (2015). Data augmented ethnography: using big data and ethnography to explore candidates' digital interactions. In *Proceedings of the Empiricist's Challenge: Asking Meaningful Questions in the Age of Big Data Conference.* Mannheim: University of Mannheim.

Lee, B., & LiPuma, E. (2002). Cultures of circulation: The imaginations of modernity. *Public Culture, 14*(1), 191-213.

Liebes, T. (1997). *Reporting the Arab Israeli conflict: How hegemony works*. London: Routledge.

Liebes, T. (1998). Television's disaster marathons. A danger for democratic processes? In T. Liebes & J. Curran (Eds.), *Media, ritual and identity*, (pp. 71-84). London: Routledge.

Liebes, T., & Blondheim, M. (2005). Myths to the rescue: How live television intervenes in history. In E.W. Rothenbuhler & M. Coman (Eds.), *Media anthropology*, (pp. 188-198). California: Sage.

Nossek, H. (2008). 'News media'—Media events: Terrorist acts as media events. *Communications. The Journal of European Communication Research, 33*(3), 313-330.

Parse.ly (2016). Does Twitter matter to news. The authority report. *Parsely.com* Retrieved from http://learn.parsely.com/rs/314-EBB-255/images/authority-report-10.pdf

Postill, J., & Pink, S. (2012). Social media ethnography. The digital researcher in a messy web. *Media International Australia, 145*, 123-134.

Procter, R., Vis, F., & Voss, A. (2013). Reading the riots on Twitter: Methodological innovation for the analysis of big data. *International Journal of Social Research Methodology, 16*(3), 197-214.

Roel, P. (2009). Intense media coverage. *Communications. The Journal of European Communication Research, 34*(1), 1-20.

Rojek, C. (2013*). Event power: How global events manage and manipulate.* London & Thousand Oaks: Sage.

Rothenbuhler, E. W. (1998). *Ritual communication: From everyday conversation to mediated ceremony*. Thousand Oaks: Sage.

Rothenbuhler, E. W. (2010). Media events in the age of terrorism and Internet. *The Romanian Review of Journalism and Communication, IV*(2), 34-41.

Scannell, P. (1995). Media events (review). *Media, Culture & Society, 17*(1), 151-157.

Scannell, P. (2001). Editorial. *Media, Culture & Society, 23*(6), 699-705.

Shils, E., & Young, M. (1956). The meaning of the coronation. *Sociological Review, 1*(2), 63-82.

Statista. (2016). Leading social networks worldwide as of April 2016, ranked by number of active users (in millions). *Statista.com.* Retrieved from http://www.statista.com/statistics/272014/global-social-networks-ranked-by-number-of-users

Sumiala, J. (2013). *Media and ritual. Death, community and everyday life*. London: Routledge.

Sumiala, J., & Korpiola, L. (2016). Tahrir 2011: Contested dynamics of a media event. In B. Mitu & S. Poulakidakos (Eds.), *Media events: A critical contemporary approach*. London: Palgrave McMillan.

Sumiala, J., & Tikka, M. (2013). Broadcast yourself—Global news! A netnography of the 'flotilla' news on YouTube. *Communication, Culture & Critique, 6*(2), 201-352.

Twitter. (2016). Twitter usage/company facts. *Twitter.*

Retrieved from https://about.twitter.com/company

Utz, S., Schultz, F., & Glocka, S. (2013). Crisis communication online: How medium, crisis type and emotions affected public reactions in the Fukushima Daiichi nuclear disaster. *Public Relations Review*, *39*, 40-46.

Vaccari, C., Chadwick, A., & O'Loughlin, B. (2015). Dual screening the political: Media events, social media, and citizen engagement. *Journal of Communication, 65*(6), 1041-1061.

Vis, F. (2013). A critical reflection on big data: Considering APIs, researchers and tools as data makers. *First Monday, 18*(10). doi:10.5210/fm.v18i10.4878

Whitehead, T. (2015, January 1) Paris Charlie Hebdo attack: Je Suis Charlie hashtag one of most popular in Twitter history. *Telegraph.* Retrieved from http://www.telegraph.co.uk/news/worldnews/europe/france/11336879/Paris-Charlie-Hebdo-attack-Je-Suis-Charlie-hashtag-one-of-most-popular-in-Twitter-history.html

Wittel, A. (2000). Ethnography on the move: from field to net to Internet. *Forum Qualitative Sozialforschung/Forum: Qualitative Social Research, 1*(1).

Yang, J., & Leskovec, J. (2014). Overlapping communities explain core-periphery organization of networks. *Proceedings of the IEEE*, *102*(12), 1892-1902.

12

Corporate Privacy Policy Changes during PRISM and the Rise of Surveillance Capitalism

Priya Kumar

College of Information Studies, University of Maryland, College Park, MD 20742, USA; E-Mail: pkumar12@umd.edu

Abstract

Disclosure of the NSA's PRISM program demonstrated that Internet companies have become prime targets of government surveillance. But what role do companies themselves play in putting users' privacy at risk? By comparing the changes in the privacy policies of ten companies—the nine in PRISM plus Twitter—I seek to understand how users' privacy shifted. Specifically, I study how company practices surrounding the life cycle of user information (e.g. collection, use, sharing, and retention) shifted between the times when companies joined PRISM and when PRISM news broke. A qualitative analysis of the changes in the privacy policies suggests that company disclosure of tracking for advertising purposes increased. I draw on business scholar Shoshana Zuboff's conceptualization of "surveillance capitalism" and legal scholar Joel Reidenberg's "transparent citizen" to explain the implications such changes hold for users' privacy. These findings underscore why public debates about post-Snowden privacy rights cannot ignore the role that companies play in legitimizing surveillance activities under the auspices of creating market value.

Keywords

Internet companies; PRISM; privacy policies; surveillance capitalism; targeted advertising; transparent citizen

Issue

This article is part of the issue "Post-Snowden Internet Policy", edited by Julia Pohle (WZB Berlin Social Science Center, Germany) and Leo Van Audenhove (Vrije Universiteit Brussel, Belgium).

---

1. Introduction: The Relationship between Government and Corporate Surveillance

In August 2016, New Zealander Tony Fullman became "the first person in the world to be publicly identified as a confirmed" target of the NSA's PRISM surveillance program (Gallagher & Hager, 2016). Intelligence officials in New Zealand believed Fullman and others were concocting a plot to violently overthrow Fiji's authoritarian leader. According to documents that Edward Snowden provided to The Intercept, an investigative news outlet, the U.S. National Security Agency (NSA) used PRISM to access Fullman's Gmail and Facebook accounts and turned over more than 190 pages of his communication and private information, such as bank statements, to New Zealand authorities. The information revealed no evidence of a plot, and ultimately, the government never brought charges against Fullman or others it investigated (Gallagher & Hager, 2016).

While governments are certainly justified in investigating credible threats of violence, The Intercept's investigation suggests that even before New Zealand's authorities received Fullman's communications from the NSA, they had scant evidence that the plot to assassinate Fiji's leader was, in fact, credible. Fullman exemplifies the "transparent citizen" (Reidenberg, 2015). By using networked digital technologies now common in everyday life, he becomes increasingly visible to institutional actors like governments and companies, yet those institutions' use of his personal information remains obscure. The rise of a transparent citizenry threatens privacy, undermines trust in rule of law, and challenges international norms and data flows (Reidenberg, 2015). PRISM targets non-U.S. persons located outside of the U.S., but a report from the U.S. Privacy and Civil Liberties Oversight Board ([PCLOB], 2014) found that aspects of the program also present privacy concerns for U.S. persons.

PRISM is a top-secret intelligence program in which the NSA can compel U.S.-based companies to provide information associated with certain "selectors", such as an email address or phone number. Selectors cannot include individual names or other key words (PCLOB, 2014). The Snowden disclosures name nine U.S.-based company partners: Microsoft, Yahoo, Google, Facebook, Paltalk, YouTube, Skype, AOL, and Apple (Gellman & Poitras, 2013). The program stems from legal authority Congress granted to the U.S. government under Section 702 of the Foreign Intelligence Surveillance Act Amendments Act of 2008. The PCLOB reviewed PRISM and other surveillance programs operating under the aegis of Section 702 and concluded, "PRISM collection is clearly authorized by the statute" (PCLOB, 2014, p. 9). Nevertheless, privacy and surveillance lawyers argue that Section 702's overbroad scope and insufficient protections, combined with the government's lack of transparency regarding the operations of surveillance programs authorized under Section 702, threaten the privacy and civil liberties of those within and beyond the U.S. (Butler & Granick, 2016). In 2015, the Court of Justice of the European Union invalidated the Safe Harbor agreement that permitted U.S. companies to transfer the personal data of E.U. citizens into the U.S. The court cited concerns with the U.S. surveillance programs described in Snowden's disclosures, including PRISM (Ni Loideain, 2016).

The Snowden disclosures re-ignited a public conversation about the extent to which governments should access data that people generate in the course of their daily lives. The act of governments obtaining data from third parties such as companies is nothing new. However, the rise of cloud computing and pervasive computing coupled with inexpensive data storage has enabled companies to store and retain increasing amounts of data, giving governments more data to pursue (Bellia, 2008). Indeed, "government and nongovernment surveillance support each other in a complex manner that is often impossible to disentangle" (Richards, 2013, p. 1940). Of course, companies do not collect and store user information with the goal of sharing it with the government. Rather, the allure of big data entices companies to collect and retain as much data as they can. Analyzing that data enables companies to predict and modify human behavior while also generating revenue and market control. Such is the logic of surveillance capitalism, "a new social relations and politics that have not yet been well delineated or theorized" (Zuboff, 2015, p. 76).

In the wake of Snowden's disclosures, several companies denied giving the U.S. government "direct access" to their servers, as PRISM was mistakenly first reported to entail (Blodget, 2013). However, companies are legally required to respond to national security demands, such as those the government makes under PRISM, and in some cases, companies facilitated this process (Miller, 2013). Important debate continues about the legality of Section 702, which authorizes PRISM and other surveillance programs (Butler & Granick, 2016). I argue that, in addition to interrogating the legality of surveillance frameworks, conversations regarding post-Snowden Internet policy must also examine the degree to which companies' own business practices can legitimate surveillance of Internet users around the world.

Why study these companies? The nine U.S. companies named in Snowden's PRISM disclosures are by no means the only ones who engage in and benefit from surveillance capitalism. And while disclosure of PRISM certainly spotlighted these companies, several companies had already attracted significant public and regulatory attention due to privacy concerns before the news broke. Nevertheless, the U.S. government's decision to explicitly include them in a secret surveillance program suggests that their data holds particular value and that their business practices related to that data deserve closer examination. These companies collectively serve billions of Internet users around the world, meaning they hold the power to respect or imperil the privacy rights of many (MacKinnon, 2012).

In this vein, I analyze the changes in company privacy policies over two time frames to understand how users' privacy rights shifted since companies entered PRISM. I focus on one aspect of privacy—the flow of user information across the "the informational life cycle", (Schwartz & Solove, 2014, p. 892), which includes the collection, use, sharing, and retention of user information (Kumar, 2016). This translates to the following research question:

> How did company practices surrounding the life cycle of user information (its collection, use, sharing, and retention) change in the time period spanning companies' entrance into PRISM and the program's disclosure to the public?

I don't contend that PRISM caused the companies to change their privacy policies. I suggest that while they were part of PRISM, companies undermined their users' privacy rights by expanding their use of targeted advertising, which is tantamount to tracking their users. This offers evidence of the rise of surveillance capitalism, where companies have business incentives to aggregate more and more user information, and governments gain an attractive trove of data to access for surveillance purposes. The next section of this paper describes the various stakeholders that influence company actions and outlines this paper's conception of users' privacy rights online. Section 3 explains the methods I used to locate and analyze company privacy policies. Section 4 reviews privacy policy changes related to the life cycle of user information, and sections 5 and 6 examine what this analysis contributes to debates about privacy rights in a post-Snowden world.

2. The Role of Companies in Respecting Users' Online Privacy Rights

Encouraging companies to act in ways that respect their users' privacy is a complex endeavor. Companies are accountable to several stakeholders: investors expect maximized returns and minimized risk; regulators expect adherence to law; consumers expect valuable, trustworthy products and services; civil society expects support for the public interest. Evaluating companies according to certain standards and comparing their performance can incentivize competition among companies. It can also provide valuable information to various stakeholders, who can likewise pressure companies to perform better. The Ranking Digital Rights project (RDR) developed criteria to evaluate companies in the information and communications technology (ICT) sector on their respect for free expression and privacy rights[1] (Maréchal, 2015).

RDR's criteria, which stem from nearly four years of consultation and testing, build on several existing human rights frameworks and principles and translate them into concrete, measurable indicators. While imperfect, this approach provides a mechanism to evaluate and compare companies (Maréchal, 2015). RDR's privacy indicators draw from the Fair Information Practice Principles, OECD Privacy Guidelines, European Union regulations, and other frameworks (Ranking Digital Rights, 2016a). The indicators related to company data practices focus on company disclosure related to the collection, sharing, use, and retention of user information as well as users' ability to access and control their own information (Ranking Digital Rights, 2016b). Often, company disclosure about these practices appears in a privacy policy.

Policy documents alone cannot reveal whether companies respect privacy rights, but they do represent company practice. Privacy policies notify the public, and regulators in particular, about a company's privacy practices. As such, they serve as an important source of information to understand how users' privacy rights fare online. Scholars, journalists, and those in civil society have studied privacy policies for this purpose, and some privacy policy research has taken a longitudinal approach (Jeong, 2016; Milne, Culnan, & Greene, 2006; Opsahl, 2010). In this paper, I draw on my experience studying privacy policies for RDR to evaluate how changes in the PRISM company privacy policies suggest shifts in users' privacy rights. I particularly focus on changes related to the life cycle of user information.

3. Locating and Analyzing Company Privacy Policies

This study compares versions of ten privacy policies in effect before and after two points in time:

1. The date the company entered PRISM, according to documents from Snowden (Gellman & Poitras, 2013). These dates range from September 2007 to October 2012.
2. June 6, 2013, the day the Washington Post published its story on PRISM, alerting the public to the program's existence (Gellman & Poitras, 2013).[2]

It includes the nine companies implicated in PRISM as well as Twitter, which attracted media attention for its absence from the list of PRISM companies (Martin, 2013). Since Twitter was not publicly named as a PRISM company, I only analyzed it for the second time frame.

Google and Twitter provide archives of their privacy policies. For the remaining companies, I used the Internet Archive's Wayback Machine to find previous versions of their privacy policies. Murphy, Hashim and O'Connor (2007) suggest the Wayback Machine is a valid source when examining website content and age. To check the Wayback Machine's validity for this study, I compared versions of Google and Twitter's policies from their company archives and the Wayback Machine. The text was identical in both versions, except the Wayback Machine version of one policy lacked a reference to Google's archive. This suggests the Wayback Machine provides adequate representations of previous versions of privacy policies.

Table 1 lists the policies used for each company. All companies except Paltalk included the date the policy was last updated or the date the policy went into effect, which made it easy to determine when the policies changed. The first time frame includes three policies for Paltalk because the first updated policy only contained a change in the company's mailing address. Paltalk's second updated version included one substantive change. Corporate oversight structures also influenced which policies were reviewed. Google has owned YouTube since 2006. During the first time frame, YouTube maintained a separate privacy policy, so changes in its policies are included in this analysis. By the second time frame, Google's privacy policy covered all of its services, including YouTube, so that period does not include an analysis of separate YouTube policies. Conversely, Microsoft bought Skype in 2011, but Skype maintained a separate privacy policy during both time frames and is included in both.

I used a difference-checking tool to identify the changes in each company's "before" and "after" policies. I logged each change in a spreadsheet. The addition or removal of an entire sentence represented one change. If one sentence included several distinct edits, I logged them separately. I looked at the original policies to determine whether the change was substantive, using an inductive approach to develop codes related to the substance of changes (Thomas, 2006). In the first pass, I developed the codes and assigned them to each change. I took a second pass through the entire dataset and checked for consistency. Table 2 contains examples of each code. These codes were mutually exclusive.

Overall, the policies included 814 changes, with Facebook accounting for 651, or 80 percent. Facebook overhauled its policy during the first time frame and made significant changes during the second time frame, far outpacing the number of changes from other companies. In

[1] Until August 2016, I was a research analyst with the RDR project.

[2] The Washington Post first reported the story on June 6, 2013 and updated its story on June 7, 2013 (Blodget, 2013).

Table 1. Privacy policies analyzed across two time frames.

Company	Date of Policy	Timeframe 1: Entered PRISM	Date of Policy	Date of Policy	Timeframe 2: PRISM News	Date of Policy
Microsoft	Jan. 2006	Sept. 11, 2007	Oct. 2007	April 2012	June 6, 2013	Aug. 2013
Yahoo	Nov. 22, 2006	Mar. 12, 2008	Oct. 28, 2008	May 31, 2013		Sept. 25, 2014
Google	Aug. 7, 2008	Jan. 14, 2009	Jan. 27, 2009	July 27, 2012		June 24, 2013
Facebook	Nov. 26, 2008	June 3, 2009	Nov. 19, 2009	Dec. 11, 2012		Nov. 15, 2013
Paltalk	Oct. 7, 2009 (crawled)	Dec. 7, 2009	Feb. 7, 2010; Dec. 4, 2010 (crawled)	May 19, 2013		No change
YouTube	Mar. 11, 2009	Sept. 24, 2010	Dec. 8, 2010	See Google		See Google
Skype	Nov. 2010	Feb. 6, 2011	June 2011	Dec. 2012		Aug. 2013
AOL	Feb. 14, 2011	Mar. 31, 2011	Mar. 30, 2012	May 14, 2013		June 28, 2013
Apple	May 21, 2012	Oct. 2012	No change	No change		Aug. 1, 2013
Twitter	N/A	N/A	N/A	May 17, 2012		July 3, 2013

Table 2. Examples of substantive and non-substantive changes in privacy policies.

Substantive Changes	Explanation or Example
Addition of information	Added sentence: "When we display personalized ads, we take a number of steps designed to protect your privacy."
Removal of information	Removed sentence: "You will only receive special offers via email from Paltalk if you have indicated in your account preferences, or at some other time, that you would like to receive them."
More precise information	Added the bold phrase: "If we learn that we have collected the personal information of a child under 13 **without first receiving verifiable parental consent** we will take steps to delete the information as soon as possible."
Less precise information	Changed the bolded phrase from: "If you are under 13, please do not attempt to register for Facebook or **send any information about yourself to us, including your name, address, telephone number, or email address**" to "If you are under age 13, please do not attempt to register for Facebook or **provide any personal information about yourself to us.**"
Non-Substantive Changes	
Simple fact change	Changed the "Last updated" date in a policy.
Position change	Moved a sentence from one paragraph in the policy to another.
Style change	Changed phrase from: "**NOTICE: Click here for practical tips from the federal government and the technology industry** to help you guard against Internet fraud, secure your computer and protect your personal information" to "**The federal government and technology industry have developed practical tips** to help you guard against Internet fraud, secure your computer and protect your personal information" [Hyperlink present in both sentences].
Fixing typos	Changed phrase from: "To protect your privacy and **security, may** use passwords to help verify your identity before granting access or making corrections to your AOL information" to "To protect your privacy and **security, we may** use passwords to help verify your identity before granting access or making corrections to your AOL information."

total, the policies showed 424 substantive changes, with Facebook accounting for 347, or 82 percent. This analysis focuses on the substantive changes. To answer the question of what these policy changes suggest with regard to the life cycle of user information, I again used an inductive approach to develop codes related to digital rights, as framed by RDR's indicators (Ranking Digital Rights, 2016b; Thomas, 2006). In a first pass, I developed and assigned the codes to each substantive change and in a second pass, I checked for consistency. This yielded 11 codes across four themes. These codes were not mutually exclusive, and 30 changes received two codes (25 of those changes applied to Facebook). Table 3 shows the themes and the codes present in each. It also states how many changes related to each theme appeared in Facebook's policies compared to other companies.

Table 3. Digital rights themes and codes.

Digital Rights Theme	Codes Included in Theme	Number of Changes (Not Mutually Exclusive)
Management of user information	Data collection, Use of data, Retention, Security	146 (Facebook: 133)
Data sharing and tracking	Third party, Data sharing, Tracking	149 (Facebook: 115)
User action	More information, Choice	115 (Facebook: 89)
Corporate governance	Accountability, Remedy	44 (Facebook: 35)

4. Policy Changes Related to the Life Cycle of User Information

Two of the four digital rights themes focused on the life cycle of user information: management of user information and data sharing and tracking. Together, these themes encompassed 70 percent of the substantive changes. The following analysis describes what the changes suggest for users' privacy.

4.1. Management of User Information

Over both time frames, Facebook's policies in particular included many changes related to the company's collection and use of information. Positively, changes during the first time frame clarified what information the company requires when new users join, and what additional information users can provide. The revised policy contained clear examples of what Facebook considers user content; the previous version of the policy told users to check the company's Terms of Use for a definition. However, the policy changes also disclose Facebook collecting more user information over both timeframes (see Annex Table A.1., rows 1–2, changes in bold).

Microsoft and Facebook included changes related to retention. In the first time frame, Microsoft positively added a sentence stating that it stores information about a user's behavior (e.g. page views, clicks, and search terms) separately from information that identifies the user (e.g., name, e-mail address) (see Table A.1., row 3). Somewhat positively, Facebook added a sentence describing a time frame in which it anonymizes data it receives from advertisers, but it applies only to information the company doesn't already have (see Table A.1., row 4). This suggests that some advertising-related user information is not subject to anonymization. In the second time frame, Facebook stated that apps connected to Facebook might retain user information after users delete the app (see Table A.1., row 5). Facebook also added a sentence saying users could contact the app directly and request deletion of their data.

Overall, changes across both timeframes suggest companies, primarily Facebook, provided additional detail regarding what they collect and how they manage it. In some cases, this can help users better understand company practices, for example what information they must provide and what is optional.

4.2. Data Sharing and Tracking

Yahoo and Facebook included changes related to sharing user information with governments, though the changes do not appear to be linked to PRISM (see Annex Table A.2., rows 1–2). Yahoo stated that it responds to law enforcement requests; PRISM requests fall under national security. Facebook added a sentence stating that it may disclose user information in response to requests from foreign jurisdictions; PRISM requests come from the U.S. government.

Several companies added information to policies related to their use of targeted advertising: Microsoft and YouTube in the first time frame; Skype, Yahoo, and Twitter in the second time frame; and Facebook across both timeframes. Changes in Facebook's policies appeared to give the company wider latitude in sharing user information, particularly with advertisers.

In the first time frame, Microsoft added more companies as advertising partners. It also listed the types of data it uses to target advertising (see Table A.2., row 3). Microsoft added that advertising networks compile information "over time" about where users click or see advertisements and may "associate this information with your subsequent visit, purchase or other activity on participating advertisers' websites in order to determine the effectiveness of the advertisements". Finally, Microsoft removed a sentence from its policy, raising questions about its access to advertising networks' cookies (see Table A.2., row 4). Changes in YouTube's policies state that it shows users advertising even when they are logged out, that advertisers can serve ads based on demographic categories inferred from users' behavior, and that they can serve ads based on user information obtained from other companies (see Table A.2., rows 5–7).

In the second time frame, Yahoo added two sentences to its policy that explain how it uses device identifiers to target advertising, framed in the parlance of personalization (see Table A.2., row 8). Twitter added two sentences about user information it may receive from advertising partners (see Table A.2., row 9). Skype added language suggesting that third-party advertisements would appear on its various sites and that Skype and its advertising partners would receive information (changes in bold) "about your relationship with **and use of** Skype's websites, software, and products…".

Changes in Facebook's policies over both time frames appeared to give the company wider latitude to share information, particularly with advertisers. In the first time frame, Facebook removed the phrase stating that it shares information with third parties "only in limited circumstances". The policy gained two sentences explaining what types of information Facebook uses when targeting advertising and how advertisers may interact with users. Facebook stated it only uses non-personally identifiable attributes but then stated that it may use sensitive, personal information to target advertising, and that advertisers may be able to discern that information (see Table A.2., row 10). In the second time frame, Facebook revised the following sentence about how it shares information with advertisers (changes in bold):

> 2012: We only provide data to our advertising partners or customers after we have removed your name or any other personally identifying information from it, or have combined it with other people's data in a way that it is no longer **associated** with you.
>
> 2013: We only provide data to our advertising partners or customers after we have removed your name **and** any other personally identifying information from it, or have combined it with other people's data in a way that it no longer **personally identifies** you.

While the shift from "or" to "and" seems to provide greater protection to users, the shift from the higher threshold of association to the lower threshold of "personally identifiable" seems to negate that protection, because information that does not personally identify a user can still be associated with a user and thus can identify the user. Facebook also revised its policy to more clearly state that it uses all user information to target advertising (see Table A.2., row 11).

While these additions provide more detail for users to understand company practices, the practices themselves appear to subject users to greater tracking for advertising purposes. They include examples of companies tracking users in more circumstances and using more information to target those ads. The disclosures also use jargon such as "non-personally identifiable information" and "device identifiers" and they reference the data processing techniques of inference and association, the nuances of which are likely unfamiliar to average users. This can make it difficult for anyone who actually reads privacy policies to fully understand what the policies mean.

5. Privacy Policy Changes Offer Evidence of Surveillance Capitalism

Collectively, these privacy policy changes offer evidence that suggests several of the world's largest Internet companies operate according to the logic surveillance capitalism. We cannot know whether these privacy policy changes reflected actual changes in company practice or if they provided more detail about practices in which companies already engaged. But the changes suggest that between the time the companies joined PRISM and the public learned of PRISM, companies disclosed that they managed more user information and, in particular, broadened their targeted advertising.

Targeted advertising is the dominant business model that powers most Internet companies today (Richards, 2013). This entails collecting data from individuals' digital interactions, however minor: "Facebook 'likes', Google searches, emails, texts, photos, songs, and videos, location, communication patterns, networks, purchases, movements, every click, misspelled word, page view, and more" (Zuboff, 2015, p. 79). Companies then employ advanced data analysis techniques to determine how to use such data to extract revenue from advertisers, transforming the data into what Zuboff calls "surveillance assets" (2015, p. 80).

As a condition for using such services, people must agree to terms such as those in privacy policies, whose narrow definitions and vague language prevent people from understanding how their data flows through the life cycle of user information (Kumar, 2016). This model, which puts the onus on users to manage their own privacy and hinges on whether they "consent" to such practices, does not meaningfully protect users' privacy (Solove, 2013).

Beyond disclosing their practices in policies, companies justify their big data activities by arguing that users gain something in return, for example, free services or personalized experiences. People pay for these benefits by foregoing their right to decide whether to disclose a given facto or keep it to themselves. As such, surveillance does not erode privacy rights; it redistributes them, enabling companies or governments to know information about people without their ever having a choice (Reidenberg, 2015; Zuboff, 2015).

PRISM is one example of "the blurring of public and private boundaries in surveillance activities...between state security authorities and high tech firms" (Zuboff, 2015, p. 86). Companies collect and retain massive amounts of data about their users—itself an act of surveillance (Richards, 2013)—and the NSA can compel companies to turn over that data for targeted surveillance. The PCLOB report (2014) reviewed the checks and balances under which the government's PRISM program operates. However, the surveillance activities of companies in PRISM do not operate with as much oversight. Debates about privacy rights in a post-Snowden world cannot ignore the fact that companies have business incentives to collect and retain the data that governments can obtain through surveillance activities.

6. Conclusion: Government Surveillance as a Symptom of Surveillance Capitalism

PRISM did not cause surveillance capitalism, but this analysis suggests that PRISM companies further enmeshed themselves in it over the past decade. They did so while belonging to a secret surveillance program in which the U.S. government could compel them to turn over all the information they had associated with a given user's email address or telephone number. The PRISM companies serve billions of users worldwide. They have the power to adopt business practices that significantly enhance the privacy of everyday users. This analysis of privacy policy changes that companies made between joining PRISM and PRISM's disclosure to the public suggests that companies went in the other direction by expanding their use of targeted advertising. It illustrates that public debates about people's privacy rights in the wake of the Snowden disclosures must not ignore the role that companies themselves play in legitimizing surveillance activities under the auspices of creating market value.

Acknowledgements

I thank Nathalie Maréchal, Katie Shilton, Karen Boyd, and Jessica Vitak for their input. I also thank the editors and three anonymous reviewers, whose feedback significantly strengthened this work.

Conflict of Interests

The author declares no conflict of interests.

References

Bellia, P. L. (2008). The memory gap in surveillance law. *University of Chicago Law Review*, *75*, 137–179.

Blodget, H. (2013, June 7). The Washington Post has now hedged its stunning claim about Google, Facebook, etc, giving the government direct access to their servers. *Business Insider*. Retrieved from http://www.businessinsider.com/washington-post-updates-spying-story-2013-6

Butler, J., & Granick, J. S. (2016). Correcting the record on section 702: A prerequisite for meaningful surveillance reform. *Just Security*. Retrieved from https://www.justsecurity.org/wp-content/uploads/2016/09/Butler-Granick-Correcting-the-Record-Scope-of-702.pdf

Gallagher, R., & Hager, N. (2016, August 14). In bungled spying operation, NSA targeted pro-democracy campaigner. *The Intercept*. Retrieved from https://theintercept.com/2016/08/14/nsa-gcsb-prism-surveillance-fullman-fiji

Gellman, B., & Poitras, L. (2013, June 7). U.S., British intelligence mining data from nine U.S. Internet companies in broad secret program. *The Washington Post*. Retrieved from https://www.washingtonpost.com/investigations/us-intelligence-mining-data-from-nine-us-internet-companies-in-broad-secret-program/2013/06/06/3a0c0da8-cebf-11e2-8845-d970ccb04497_story.html

Jeong, S. (2016, January 14). The history of Twitter's rules. *Vice Motherboard*. Retrieved from http://motherboard.vice.com/read/the-history-of-twitters-rules

Kumar, P. (2016). Privacy policies and their lack of clear disclosure regarding the life cycle of user information. *2016 AAAI Fall Symposium Series*. Retrieved from http://aaai.org/ocs/index.php/FSS/FSS16/paper/view/14089

MacKinnon, R. (2012). *Consent of the networked: The worldwide struggle for Internet freedom*. New York, NY: Basic Books.

Maréchal, N. (2015). Ranking digital rights: Human rights, the Internet and the fifth estate. *International Journal of Communication*, *9*, 3440–3449.

Martin, S. (2013, June 7). Twitter notably absent from NSA PRISM list. *USA Today*. Retrieved from http://www.usatoday.com/story/tech/2013/06/07/nsa-prism-twitter/2401605

Miller, C. C. (2013, June 7). Tech companies concede to surveillance program. *The New York Times*. Retrieved from http://www.nytimes.com/2013/06/08/technology/tech-companies-bristling-concede-to-government-surveillance-efforts.html

Milne, G. R., Culnan, M. J., & Greene, H. (2006). A longitudinal assessment of online privacy notice readability. *Journal of Public Policy & Marketing*, *25*(2), 238–249. doi:10.1509/jppm.25.2.238

Murphy, J., Hashim, N. H., & O'Connor, P. (2007). Take me back: Validating the Wayback Machine. *Journal of Computer-Mediated Communication*, *13*(1), 60–75. doi:10.1111/j.1083-6101.2007.00386.x

Ni Loideain, N. (2016). The end of safe harbor: Implications for EU digital privacy and data protection law. *Journal of Internet Law*, *19*(8), 7–14.

Opsahl, K. (2010, April 28). Facebook's eroding privacy policy: A timeline. *Electronic Frontier Foundation*. Retrieved from https://www.eff.org/deeplinks/2010/04/facebook-timeline

Privacy and Civil Liberties Oversight Board. (2014). *Report on the surveillance program operated pursuant to section 702 of the Foreign Intelligence Surveillance Act*. Washington, DC: Privacy and Civil Liberties Oversight Board.

Ranking Digital Rights. (2016a, September 14). *Methodology development*. Retrieved from https://rankingdigitalrights.org/methodology-development

Ranking Digital Rights. (2016b, September). *2017 corporate accountability index research indicators*. Retrieved from https://rankingdigitalrights.org/wp-content/uploads/2016/09/2017Indexmethodology.pdf

Reidenberg, J. R. (2015). The transparent citizen. *Loyola University Chicago Law Journal*, *47*, 437–463.

Richards, N. M. (2013). The dangers of surveillance. *Harvard Law Review*, *126*, 1934–1965.

Schwartz, P. M., & Solove, D. J. (2014). Reconciling personal information in the United States and European Union. *California Law Review*, *877*, 877–916.

Solove, D. J. (2013). Privacy self-management and the consent dilemma. *Harvard Law Review*, *126*, 1880–1903.

Thomas, D. R. (2006). A general inductive approach for analyzing qualitative evaluation data. *American Journal of Evaluation*, *27*(2), 237–246. doi:10.1177/1098214005283748

Zuboff, S. (2015). Big other: Surveillance capitalism and the prospects of an information civilization. *Journal of Information Technology*, *30*, 75–89. doi:10.1057/jit.2015.5

Annex

Table A.1. Privacy policy changes related to management of user information.

	Company	Timeframe 1		Timeframe 2	
		Pre-Join PRISM	Post-Join PRISM	Pre-PRISM Disclosed	Post-PRISM Disclosed
1	Facebook	2008: "When you enter Facebook, we collect your browser type and IP address."	2009: "When you **access** Facebook **from a computer, mobile phone, or other device**, we **may** collect **information from that device about** your browser type, **location**, and IP address, **as well as the pages you visit**."		
2	Facebook			2012: "This may include your IP address and other information about things like your Internet service, location, the type (including identifiers) of browser you use, or the pages you visit."	2013: "This may include **network and communication information, such as** your IP address **or mobile phone number**, and other information about things like your Internet service, **operating system**, location, the type (including identifiers) **of the device or** browser you use, or the pages you visit."
3	Microsoft		2007: **Added** "For example, we store page views, clicks and search terms used for ad personalization separately from your contact information or other data that directly identifies you (such as your name, e-mail address, etc.)."		
4	Facebook		2009: **Added** "If in any of these cases we receive data [from advertising partners] that we do not already have, we will 'anonymize' it within 180 days, meaning we will stop associating the information with any particular user."		
5	Facebook				2013: **Added** that when users delete an app connected to Facebook, "it [the app] may still hold the information you have already shared."

Table A.2. Privacy policy changes related to data sharing and tracking.

	Company	Timeframe 1		Timeframe 2	
		Pre-Join PRISM	Post-Join PRISM	Pre-PRISM Disclosed	Post-PRISM Disclosed
1	Yahoo			2013: "We respond to subpoenas, court orders, or legal process or to establish or exercise our legal rights or defend against legal claims."	2014: "We respond to subpoenas, court orders, or legal process **(such as law enforcement requests)**, or to establish or exercise our legal rights or defend against legal claims."
2	Facebook	2008: "We may **be required to** disclose user information pursuant **to lawful requests, such as subpoenas or court orders**, or in compliance with applicable laws. **We do not reveal information until** we have a good faith belief that **an information request by law enforcement or private litigants meets applicable legal standards**."	2009: "We may disclose information pursuant to **subpoenas, court orders, or other requests (including criminal and civil matters)** if we have a good faith belief that **the response is required by law. This may include respecting requests from jurisdictions outside of the United States where we have a good faith belief that the response is required by law under the local laws in that jurisdiction, apply to users from that jurisdiction, and are consistent with generally accepted international standards.**"		
3	Microsoft		2007: **Added** "For example, we may select the ads we display according to certain general interest categories or segments that we have inferred based on "(a) demographic data, including any you may have provided when creating an account (e.g. age, zip or postal code, gender), general demographic data acquired from other companies, and a general geographic location derived from your IP address, (b) the pages you view and links you click when using Microsoft's and its partners' web sites and		

Table A.2. Privacy policy changes related to data sharing and tracking. (Cont.)

	Company	Timeframe 1		Timeframe 2	
		Pre-Join PRISM	Post-Join PRISM	Pre-PRISM Disclosed	Post-PRISM Disclosed
3	Microsoft		services, and (c) the search terms you enter when using Microsoft's Internet search services, such as Live Search."		
4	Microsoft		2007: **Removed** "Microsoft does not have access to the cookies that may be placed by the third-party ad servers or ad networks."		
5	YouTube	2009: "**If** you are **logged into** your YouTube Account, we may also show you advertising based on **the information** you have provided to us in your YouTube Account."	2010: "**While** you are logged in **or logged out** of your YouTube Account, we may also show you advertising based on **non personally identifiable** information you have provided to us in your YouTube Account."		
6	YouTube	2009: "Advertisers may serve ads based on **interests** associated with non-personally identifiable online activity, such as videos viewed, frequency of uploading or activity on other AdSense partner sites."	2010: "Advertisers may serve ads based on interests **and demographic categories** associated with non-personally identifiable online activity, such as videos viewed, frequency of uploading or activity on other AdSense partner sites."		
7	YouTube	2009: "Advertisers may also serve ads to you based on previous activity on that advertiser's website."	2010: "Advertisers may also serve ads to you based on previous activity on that advertiser's website **or based on non-personally identifiable information from other companies**."		
8	Yahoo				2014: **Added** "We may also set and access device identifiers which could include IP address, user agent information (browser version, OS type and version), and device provided identifiers. Once you log into Yahoo on your device, Yahoo may recognize your device to provide you with a

Table A.2. Privacy policy changes related to data sharing and tracking. (Cont.)

	Company	Timeframe 1		Timeframe 2	
		Pre-Join PRISM	Post-Join PRISM	Pre-PRISM Disclosed	Post-PRISM Disclosed
8	Yahoo				personalized experience, independent of your device settings."
9	Twitter				2013: **Added** "Third-party ad partners may share information with us, like a browser cookie ID or cryptographic hash of a common account identifier (such as an email address), to help us measure ad quality and tailor ads. For example, this allows us to display ads about things you may have already shown interest in."
10	Facebook		2009: **Added** "We allow advertisers to choose the characteristics of users who will see their advertisements and we may use any of the non-personally identifiable attributes we have collected (including information you may have decided not to show to other users, such as your birth year or other sensitive personal information or preferences) to select the appropriate audience for those advertisements...Even though we do not share your Information with advertisers without your consent, when you click on or otherwise interact with an advertisement there is a possibility that the advertiser may place a cookie in your browser and note that it meets the criteria they selected."		

Table A.2. Privacy policy changes related to data sharing and tracking. (Cont.)

	Company	**Timeframe 1**		**Timeframe 2**	
		Pre-Join PRISM	Post-Join PRISM	Pre-PRISM Disclosed	Post-PRISM Disclosed
11	Facebook			2012: "We use the information we receive, including the **information you provide at registration or add to your account or timeline, to deliver** ads **and to make them** more relevant to you."	2013: "**So we can show you content that you may find interesting**, we **may** use all of the information we receive **about you** to serve ads that are more relevant to you."

13

Crises, Rumours and Reposts: Journalists' Social Media Content Gathering and Verification Practices in Breaking News Situations

Klas Backholm [1,*], Julian Ausserhofer [2,3], Elsebeth Frey [4], Anna Grøndahl Larsen [4], Harald Hornmoen [4], Joachim Högväg [5] and Gudrun Reimerth [6]

[1] Swedish School of Social Science, University of Helsinki, 00014 University of Helsinki, Finland;
E-Mail: klas.backholm@helsinki.fi
[2] Department of Communication, University of Vienna, 1090 Vienna, Austria; E-Mail: julian.ausserhofer@hiig.de
[3] Research Group Internet Policy & Governance, Alexander von Humboldt Institute for Internet and Society,
10117 Berlin, Germany
[4] Department of Journalism and Media Studies, Oslo and Akershus University College of Applied Sciences, 0130 Oslo, Norway; E-Mails: elsebeth.frey@hioa.no (E.F.), anna.larsen@hioa.no (A.G.L.), harald.hornmoen@hioa.no (H.H.)
[5] Experience Lab, Åbo Akademi University, 65100 Vaasa, Finland; E-Mail: joachim.hogvag@abo.fi
[6] Department of Media and Design, FH JOANNEUM University of Applied Sciences, 8020 Graz, Austria;
E-Mail: gudrun.reimerth@fh-joanneum.at

* Corresponding author

Abstract

Social media (SoMe) platforms provide potentially important information for news journalists during everyday work and in crisis-related contexts. The aims of this study were (a) to map central journalistic challenges and emerging practices related to using SoMe for collecting and validating newsworthy content; and (b) to investigate how practices may contribute to a user-friendly design of a web-based SoMe content validation toolset. Interviews were carried out with 22 journalists from three European countries. Information about journalistic work tasks was also collected during a crisis training scenario ($N = 5$). Results showed that participants experienced challenges with filtering and estimating trustworthiness of SoMe content. These challenges were especially due to the vast overall amount of information, and the need to monitor several platforms simultaneously. To support improved situational awareness in journalistic work during crises, a user-friendly tool should provide content search results representing several media formats and gathered from a diversity of platforms, presented in easy-to-approach visualizations. The final decision-making about content and source trustworthiness should, however, remain as a manual journalistic task, as the sample would not trust an automated estimation based on tool algorithms.

Keywords

crisis; journalism; situational awareness; social media; usability; user-centred design; verification

Issue

This article is part of a multidisciplinary issue of *Media and Communication*, edited by Epp Lauk (University of Jyväskylä, Finland) and Raul Reis (Emerson College, USA).

1. Introduction

Journalists use the same social media (SoMe) channels as the public to gather information about breaking news situations. Due to the vast amount of available information, filtering and validation is time-consuming and demanding (Diakopoulos, De Choudhury, & Naaman 2012; Schifferes et al., 2014; Silverman, 2014). A central challenge for crisis journalism is to find ways to simplify this process. As suggested by e.g. Brandtzæg, Luders, Spangenberg, Rath-Wiggins and Folstad (2016), part of the solution may be to introduce new technical innovations that support journalistic filtering and validation processes.

The general aim of this study is to add to current knowledge about how existing journalistic verification practices and needs can be applied to a changing information environment, and to map how practices could be adjusted. A second aim is to apply this knowledge to a product development framework, to provide valuable information for scholars and product developers aiming to design new technical innovations supporting verification processes. We employ two approaches: First, we map practical challenges news journalists currently face in their SoMe usage, and thus identify the main needs and emerging new practices. Second, we investigate how the needs may contribute to a user-friendly design of a content validation toolset for journalistic work in everyday and crisis-specific contexts. We aim to expand current knowledge by illustrating how journalistic needs could be implemented in a validation toolset, and by explaining why designing the tool in the suggested way will improve situational awareness (SA) when working in a high-stress environment.

In the literature review, we first elaborate on the challenges journalists face when gathering information from SoMe platforms, and on whether journalists use tools that can support their work. We then introduce two concepts that are relevant when designing innovations for journalistic work in emergencies—usability and SA.

1.1. Journalistic Challenges with Gathering and Verifying SoMe Information

Sourcing is an integral part of the journalistic news production process. For decades, journalists have tended to rely heavily on official and elite sources, such as government representatives, in their reporting (Hallin, Manoff, & Weddle, 1993), and have developed different methods to verify sources (Shapiro, Brin, Bédard-Brûlé, & Mychajlowycz, 2013). Journalists can apply established practices to social media content, but the structure and usage of the Internet and SoMe complicate journalistic information gathering and verification processes. First, online, users communicate "through complex networks that are bottom-up, top-down, as well as side-to-side" (Ito, 2008, p. 3). For journalists, these communication traces can be difficult to follow. Second, costs as a barrier to disseminating information have practically been eliminated (Benkler, 2006), leading to a situation of journalists online being confronted with an increasing number of sources. While greatly expanding the range of available sources, the digital environment thus confronts journalists with challenges related to filtering and assessing the authority, trustworthiness and veracity of sources. These challenges are accentuated during emergencies where the production pace is faster, SoMe activity increases, and trustworthy information is crucial (Diakopoulos et al., 2012).

Existing research on content gathering and validation strategies suggests that when journalists find interesting information via SoMe channels, the majority still turn to traditional verification methods, such as phone, e-mail or face-to-face contact (Brandtzæg et al., 2016). A small number of journalists make use of manual crowdsourcing techniques in social media (Hermida, Lewis, & Zamith, 2014). However, journalists are not dismissing new innovations, such as content validation tools, as long as functionality and design reflect established journalistic verification procedures and needs (Brandtzæg et al., 2016; Silverman, 2014).

There have been several examples of so-called hybrid techniques, i.e. trial-and-error attempts to combine new tools with well-established journalistic verification strategies (Schifferes et al., 2014). Guidelines and tip sheets such as the European Journalism Centre's "Verification Handbook" (Silverman, 2014) and the "Social Media Reporting Tools" by the Dart Center for Journalism and Trauma (Jenkins, 2013) include case examples of how hybrid techniques have been developed and tried out. These descriptions currently form a basis for what may become established practices. When scholars have previously mapped journalists' experiences and needs relating to the possible use of a tool, responses about identifying new content have usually overlapped with answers about verifying the trustworthiness of the information.

The importance of the following factors have commonly been emphasized. Tools should:

- be able to monitor SoMe content and identify newsworthy information, such as emerging events or trends, sudden turns during ongoing events, and key influencers affecting SoMe opinions about the event (Brandtzæg et al., 2016; Schwartz, Naaman, & Teodoro, 2015; Schifferes et al., 2014);
- be able to handle verification of varying forms of content, such as text or videos, and integrate content from several SoMe platforms into verification processes (Brandtzæg et al., 2016; Schifferes et al., 2014);
- offer the journalist a high level of control over, and possibilities to filter, what type of content is tracked or presented, e.g. being able to address both content and source verification in order to answer to individual journalistic needs (Diakopoulos et al., 2012; Schifferes et al., 2014);
- be able to identify the geographical location of a source (Diakopoulos et al., 2012);
- have an easy-to-use design and visualization of content to answer to the rapid content production requirement (Brandtzæg et al., 2016; Schwartz et al., 2015);
- have a user-friendly design regardless of the technical equipment used (Brandtzæg et al., 2016).

In addition to needs explicitly related to the tool, most studies have highlighted the importance of understanding how the tool has carried out included tasks and algorithm transparency, e.g. whether the tool uses crowdsourcing as a part of the validation process (Schwartz et al., 2015). If journalists do not understand how results reported by a tool are produced, it will be difficult to make a final journalistic decision regarding the trustworthiness of the content (Diakopoulos, 2014; Park, Sachar, Diakopoulos, & Elmqvist, 2016).

While previous works have produced several relevant findings, their results are also limited. Studies have cooperated with legacy newsrooms situated mainly in the United States and the UK (Diakopoulos et al., 2012; Schifferes et al., 2014; Schwartz et al., 2015). Their research has focused on experienced social media editors, e.g. "some of the best, most prominent, and leading-edge users of social media in journalism today" (Diakopoulos et al., 2012, p. 6), drawing from a male-dominated sample (Brandtzæg et al., 2016; Diakopoulos et al., 2012). Brandtzæg et al. (2016) suggest future research that better considers the perspective of young and female practitioners. Our study seeks to fill the research gaps outlined above by integrating the perspectives of young journalists of both sexes, with varying SoMe experience, and working in mid-sized media organizations in different European countries.

1.2. Usability and Situational Awareness

One of the aims with this study is to investigate how a SoMe validation tool should be designed to reach good usability and contribute to SA. Usability is the extent to which a product can be used by a specified user group to achieve goals with effectiveness, efficiency and satisfaction in a specified context of use (ISO 9241, 2010). Usability-focused developers try to optimize a product according to how users can, want, or need to use it, not to force users to change their behaviour according to the product's requirements (Hertzum & Clemmensen, 2012; Wallach & Scholz, 2012).

When investigating usability in a high-stress context, an understanding of factors affecting SA is central. SA addresses the challenges occupational groups face when working with information flows in high-stress surroundings including many actors and other moving parts (Endsley, 2009; Salmon et al., 2008). News work with SoMe content during an emergency is indeed such an event. A high level of SA is a state of experiencing that one is in control and understands what is happening in a situation (Yin, Lampert, Cameron, Robertson, & Power, 2012). Individuals are often a part of a team working in the same environment, and thus, SA includes individual and collaborative decision-making (Salmon et al., 2008).

Underlying cognitive mechanisms that affect the level of SA include information processing—such as collecting relevant information and interpreting it correctly—and decision-making. The cognitive mechanisms interact continuously with external factors and requirements. For instance, physical or psychological fatigue due to vast workloads may affect working memory and decision-making, while technical factors such as tool or system complexity may take away attention from the main functions necessary for carrying out tasks (Endsley, 2009; Salmon et al., 2008; Yin et al., 2012).

According to Brandtzæg et al. (2016), user-centred methods should be emphasized in future research on journalism innovations. Previous studies mapping journalistic validation needs have in some cases provided general suggestions for how to design a tool that could answer to these needs (Schifferes et al., 2014), but rarely included explanations of how the design would enhance SA. Thus, our study provides a valuable contribution to the literature, as we present strategies for turning journalistic needs into features relevant for tool design, and also clarify how such features will support better SA for individual users and teams during high-stress assignments.

2. Methods

Dataset 1 consisted of semi-structured interviews with news journalists (N = 22, females n = 8) from three European countries (see Table 1 for sample characteristics). Interviews were carried out in 2015, and recorded and transcribed by the authors. The following main themes were included: a) descriptive data related to work description and background; b) SoMe usage strategies in everyday work and during sudden crises; c) the usefulness of a SoMe content validation toolset for news work, and d) factors that would enhance usability when using a toolset. To enable a detailed mapping of points c) and d), a relatively broad sample of journalists was included.

Information for dataset 2 was gathered by shadowing work tasks and conducting subsequent contextual interviews with journalism students (N = 5, females n = 4; Table 1) during a crisis training scenario in 2015. Students were involved as news journalists covering the crisis. To protect the identity of participants, information about the region of the scenario is excluded. The scenario was a two-day event in a large city setting. Authorities, rescue personnel, hospitals and media workers participated, and the crises included various industrial accidents with casualties and injured. The personnel trained crisis management and how to communicate with mass media and the public. They communicated directly with participating media organizations, and informed via web pages and two SoMe platforms (Table 1). SoMe content included continuous posts from professional communicators, the public, and media organizations.

The authors observed a training scenario instead of an actual crisis due to the practical difficulties related to planning for shadowing newsrooms during ongoing crises. Three authors carried out the job shadowing. The observers followed work routines and developments on the journalist's computer screen. Observations were followed up with semi-structured interviews within two weeks to verify that the observer had understood developments during the training correctly.

Table 1. Study sample characteristics.

	Dataset 1. Interviews, news journalists ($N = 22$)	**Dataset 2.** Job shadowing during crisis scenario, journalism students ($N = 5$)
Country	Austria, Finland, and Norway	
Types of media	Newspaper, radio, television and web	Newspaper, television and web-based outlets during scenario
Types of work tasks	Management tasks, news production, news broadcasting	News production in the field or at a news desk during scenario
Number of SoMe platforms	1–5 used daily for work purposes	Two platforms used during scenario: Twitter and a platform reminiscent of Facebook, created for usage in scenarios
Years of work experience	3–35	0–4

We used conceptual frameworks as described in the transcendental realism approach (Miles, Huberman, & Saldana, 2014) to design interview/observation schemes and to analyse data. We applied ethical guidelines provided by the Ethics Board at Åbo Akademi University in the study, including e.g. informed consent, guaranteeing participant anonymity, and using secure servers for data storage.

3. Results and Discussion

First, we present results related to aim 1, mapping practical challenges news journalists face in their SoMe usage. We then present results focusing on aim 2, investigating factors that may enhance usability of a content validation toolset and user SA. These results are derived from dataset 1 only, as the crisis scenario did not focus on usability.

3.1. Current Challenges: Changing Practices and Lacking Guidelines

Journalists mainly used Facebook, Twitter and Instagram in their everyday information validation work. In the acute phase of an emergency, Twitter usage was accentuated due to the short content format and platform searchability, e.g. hashtags. Participants saw Facebook as not keeping up with developments during the acute phase, but as useful when crises calmed down. Instagram was rarely mentioned.

Participants also described an ongoing change when it comes to SoMe practices. While all organizations had clear strategies about publishing their own media products and monitoring the reach of such content, none had similar guidelines for gathering and verifying information in SoMe platforms. The latter was rather seen as something that a small group of journalists within the organization, often described as young reporters with good computer skills, were good at—while the rest lagged behind:

> We don't have a good system to verify social media content. We have several journalists who are really good at this, but what we manage to get done really depends on who happens to be working. (Social media editor, radio/television/web journalism)

The discrepancy between well-developed SoMe publication strategies and close to non-existent gathering and verification guidelines was explained in several ways. Some participants in the two datasets referred to limited financial resources or lack of interest to develop strategies among e.g. managers in the organization. This finding echoes previous research. Brandtzæg et al. (2016), for instance, point to how the current general newsroom context with financial restraints and a growing workload on journalists will affect the way in which SoMe validation strategies are developed. This context may take different concrete forms, such as managers' reluctance to promote strategies, or the "outsourcing" of validation tasks to a small subgroup of tech-savvy journalists.

Other participants described individualized and hybrid techniques (cf. Schifferes et al., 2014; Silverman, 2014) where, for instance, each journalist continuously modifies individual combinations of verification skills and tasks, but where general journalistic guidelines and golden standards apply. Here, traditional journalistic skills are combined with available technical innovations in order to construct relevant routines for individual journalists' work with SoMe content (Schifferes et al., 2014; Silverman, 2014). From this viewpoint, the need for specific SoMe strategies is limited.

> How you do this [SoMe content verification] should really be up to you to decide. Of course, there are general requirements about how to carry out your job that you need to follow, you need to act responsibly and so on. But...I do not see any need for specific regulations about this. (Editor-in-chief, radio/television/web journalism)

The lack of overall SoMe verification strategies was also reflected in the low number of participants who were familiar with and used existing tools designed for SoMe content handling. Figures on how common such tools are have seldom been provided in previous research (Brandtzæg et al., 2016). In this study, most participants did not use a tool themselves. One fourth of the journalists had heard about someone else at the workplace using a tool. Among these tools, Tweetdeck was the most common. However, while not currently using tools, virtually all participants considered a toolset as something that would be useful.

3.2. Current Challenges: Many Platforms and Vast Amounts of Information

Participants were asked to freely identify challenges with their current SoMe usage in everyday journalistic work as well as during crises. The most common challenge concerned filtering out interesting content and/or rapidly finding the original source among vast amounts of information (see also Brandtzæg et al., 2016; Schifferes et al., 2014). The issue of backtracking to the original source becomes especially relevant during unfolding crises or similar high-priority news events, where the production pace is faster, SoMe activity increases and verified information is crucial (cf. Diakopoulos et al., 2012). In our study, a majority of journalists highlighted challenges concerning information overload as a main problem that an automated validation tool could help to solve.

> To be able to quickly find the original source, who started writing about this?...What I see as a problem is the huge amount of information, to try to filter that, so that is the kind of help I need. (News journalist and anchor, radio/television/web journalism)

Journalism students participating in the crisis training scenario experienced similar problems. During the training, social media feeds included information from official communicators as well as from the public. Observed students seldom tried to contact potential eyewitnesses or other non-authority social media users directly to verify posted information. In post-scenario interviews, students explained that they were aware of the need to include eyewitnesses in crisis-related journalism, but they had chosen not to. They based their decisions on insecurity about how to carry out the actual verification process, and on time constraints, i.e. not having enough time to backtrack and verify the content.

Another challenge that emerged in the study was the need for simpler routines and innovations for information gathering across several SoMe platforms simultaneously. This would provide a better overview of social media activity and diminish the risk of overlooking relevant content. Again, this need becomes even more relevant during crises. For example, during the training scenario, one participant who was assigned to monitor SoMe platforms for a television outlet simultaneously followed over 20 SoMe and web channels on one screen. While this mostly worked well, the participant overlooked several pieces of vital information due to the vast number of monitored channels. In addition, requirements set by the physical surrounding, e.g. a hectic production pace, also contributed to increasing the risk of missing relevant content. In this specific case, the student disrupted the monitoring when asked to carry out unexpected tasks, such as booking interviews. Similar problems could be observed with other cases during the training, and were also familiar to the journalists interviewed.

Participants also sought for better strategies for identifying possibly interesting content gathered from these platforms. In practical terms, SoMe content should be channelled from several platforms into one, and presented according to the journalist's personal needs. Useful sorting functions mentioned by participants included features familiar from existing SoMe platforms, such as the time of content posting or trending topics in terms of reposts or comments, but also more specific features such as geolocation of sources or lists of most popular sub-trends within a trending story.

These needs reflect attempts at diminishing time pressure and supporting the quick choices required in journalistic work, and are consistent with other studies. For instance, Schifferes et al. (2014) reported that journalists need to monitor information across platforms as well as across content formats, while Diakopoulos et al. (2012) and Schwartz et al. (2015) stated that journalists want support with identifying possible hyperlocal news.

3.3. Usability of a Validation Toolset: The Importance of Insight into Automation

In this section, we shift focus from identifying journalistic challenges to discussing practical factors that should be addressed when designing a user-friendly information validation tool for everyday and crisis journalism. A central challenge related to implementing a tool was the risk of automation taking over. Most journalists were concerned that the level of automation in a tool might affect the quality of their journalistic work. Participants mentioned this in two ways.

Firstly, to be able to use a tool for verifying content trustworthiness, the user needs to be able to verify the tool itself. This includes factors such as understanding how central algorithms are constructed, and being able to follow chains of searches or other tasks carried out automatically by the tool (for more about suggested ways to do this, see below). This design-related risk is familiar from SA literature in general. E.g., Endsley and Jones (2011) refer to the "out-of-the-loop syndrome" as one of the main issues designers need to understand when building complex systems. The European ISO-standard for human-centred design (ISO 9241, 2010) underlines the importance of using a multi-faceted decision process based on several levels of comparisons when choosing which tasks to automate and which ones to assign to human performance.

The second automation risk focused on the possible automation of final decisions about what is labelled as useful or verified content (see also, Diakopoulos, 2014; Park et al., 2016; Schwartz et al., 2015). This was seen as something that cannot be outsourced or programmed, but rather has to remain a manual choice based on several layers of information, provided e.g. by a validation tool. In other words, the former type of risk related to automation is based on a practical sense of enhancing SA by understanding how the tool works, and thus avoiding the "out of the loop-syndrome". The latter risk is perhaps a more general reflection of the unique type of work and practical decisions included in day-to-day journalism.

> It would be good if something would take care of [verifying content] since this is a job you do not have time to do if you are in the midst of something. But this does not release us from our responsibility. (Social media editor, newspaper/web journalism)

> I am not sure that this is an entirely technical issue, I think it involves something of a real journalistic technique to know whether a source is credible or not. (News journalist, newspaper/web journalism)

3.4. Usability of a Validation Toolset: Using Visualizations to Explain Automation

Thus, the functions included in a SoMe validation tool should, according to the sample, be seen as supporting manual verification work rather than taking over work tasks. A crucial issue was the level of insight into tasks and algorithms carried out automatically. This was present in most discussions about the types of practical tasks that should be included in order to enhance usability and SA when designing the tool. Therefore, based on the interviews, we have extracted three main usability-promoting categories (see Table 2). The categories represent automatic features, manual tasks, and visualization of results. However, the reader is advised to bear in mind that listed features were those most commonly mentioned, e.g. a wish list, but not necessarily those that can all be integrated into a well-functioning tool. Listed functions often hovered across functions related to monitoring, filtering, and verifying SoMe content.

Automatic features (Table 2) are tasks that according to the sample should be carried out automatically by the tool, and that would provide solutions to some of the main SoMe challenges related to risk of information overload and fatigue among users. Central automatic features included: (1) identifying the original source who posted a piece of information, by collecting data from several SoMe platforms, using timestamps, and creating chains of posted and reposted content (regardless of content format) within as well as between SoMe platforms; (2) identifying the trustworthiness and quality of a source, by carrying out comparisons of the type, quality and quantity of the source's previous SoMe activity within and across platforms, and by carrying out comparisons based on geolocation information; and (3) finding new trending content as well as new developments within already identified content areas, by collecting data from within and across SoMe platforms.

The second subcategory, manual tasks (Table 2), includes settings within the tool that a user or team should be able to modify according to current needs. Commonly mentioned settings included familiar parameters, such as basic search (a Google across SoMe platforms) and sorting functions (fresh; top; trending), combined with more advanced settings. A key element here would be to allow for searches across platforms. Advanced search and sorting parameters should, for example, include geolocation and language of content settings as well as being able to set content publication timeframe limitations and to choose between formats (e.g. video only). The idea with a range of manual tasks was that since journalists have individual needs, a user-friendly tool should allow for a large degree of personalization. In addition, manual tasks enhance SA by allowing for more insight into the automatically carried out algorithms, as the user or team is able to create own parameters.

The third subgroup of features enhancing tool usability—visualization of results—represents factors that would further bridge the gap between functions automatically carried out and journalists' needs to (a) understand what the tool has done, and to (b) make well-judged manual decisions based on the information provided. By including clear visualizations of interesting content, the tool would enhance the level of SA by, again, addressing the need to understand tool algorithms, and by avoiding user fatigue. In addition to visualizations related to trending content in general, the tool should provide information focusing on areas of interest relevant to the specific assignment the journalist or team is carrying out (Table 2). Such parameters should be set by the user within the tool's "manual tasks" subcategory. Mentioned visualizations included: summaries of how content has been automatically compared and cross-referenced across SoMe platforms; visual chains of automatically identified steps between reposts and the original source of information; and summaries of content listed according to advanced search parameters, such as geolocated posts placed on a map of e.g. the media organization's distribution area.

In addition to the automatic/manual/visualization features, journalists mentioned some purely technical requirements to enhance usability. Requirements reflected central practical needs for journalists, as well as the need to be able to integrate a new tool into existing workplace software. The sample stressed the importance of tool functionality across screen sizes and equipment, as well as automatic and frequent updates of content feeds to enable rapid inclusion of the latest information. Moreover, participants wanted an easily accessible content saving function in a format compatible with existing publication formats.

The main features suggested by this sample for each tool subcategory (automatic; manual; visual; technical)

Table 2. Subcategories of features and main factors enhancing usability and SA in a social media information validation tool.

Automatic features	Manual tasks	Visualization of results
Include and save content from several SoMe platforms	Set which platforms to include	Overview of content from several SoMe platforms
Cross-reference content between platforms	Set content search/cross-referencing parameters	Cross-referenced content overview
Create chains of reposts back to original source across platforms	Set content presentation parameters	Chains of reposts back to original source overview
Track and gather trending content across platforms	Communicate tasks with colleagues	Trending content overview
		Source geographical location and similar advanced search parameter overviews
How the subcategory would enhance individual and team SA		
Avoid fatigue, by taking care of complex and time-consuming monitoring and validation tasks automatically	Diminish information overload and enhance understanding of tool algorithms, by allowing users to set parameters for areas of interest across several platforms in one tool	Diminish information overload and enhance understanding of tool algorithms, by providing visualizations of summarized content of interest
Diminish information overload, by compressing information seeking procedures from several platforms into one tool	Enhance team SA, by including communication into the tool and thus allowing team members to avoid repeating monitoring and validation tasks already carried out by other team members	Avoid fatigue and support journalistic choices, by providing summaries of content of interest visualized according to parameters of relevance (e.g. geolocation)

are roughly similar to functions mentioned in previous research (as listed in the introduction section). However, compared to other studies, factors such as the ability to monitor across several SoMe platforms simultaneously and the risks of automation taking over were more emphasized in this study, while the importance of finding content regardless of format (text; picture; video) was toned down.

3.5. Usability of a Validation Toolset: Enhancing Team-Level Usability

While many of the above-mentioned factors can be applied to enhancement of individual as well as team SA, one factor explicitly addressing team level SA also emerged. This factor was part of the manual tasks subcategory (Table 2), and reflected the need to communicate within the toolset with colleagues about e.g. search results/visualizations or tasks being carried out. By including a communication function, team SA would be enhanced as unnecessary repetitions of tasks already carried out by other team members could be avoided. This need has seldom been reported in previous attempts to map journalistic usability of validation tools, perhaps because team-level SA has rarely been overtly mentioned. However, as stated by Salmon et al. (2008), team level SA should be taken into account when designing user-friendly products, and this area should be integrated into future research about journalistic work, technical innovations, and SoMe.

4. Conclusions and Limitations

The first aim of this study was to map central challenges news journalists currently face and the new practices that are emerging in regard to using SoMe for validation of potentially newsworthy content. The second aim was to investigate how challenges and practices may contribute to a user-friendly design of a content validation toolset for journalistic work in everyday and crisis-specific contexts, and to improved SA. Journalists reported that they are in the midst of a change in applying traditional practices to SoMe content. However, news organizations lack formal guidelines concerning how to gather and validate content.

The most common challenges when carrying out validation of content included problems with simultaneously monitoring and filtering out content across vast amounts of information acquired from several platforms, and with backtracking across platforms and reposts to identify the original source. In order to approach the challenges and the ongoing redefinition of journalistic practices, journalists underlined the key role of senior managers. A positive attitude towards introducing new strategies and allocating appropriate resources are central contributing factors.

Journalists also saw a tool for SoMe content validation or similar technical innovations as useful means to support their work. To achieve a user-friendly design, a validation tool needs to support, but not fully automate, the journalist's work. The final decision about content trustworthiness has to remain a manual task. By designing the product according to an automatic-manual-visual feature dynamics, where several manual settings and clear visualizations allow the journalist to interpret automated content filtering results, the tool design would provide better SA during assignments, and allow for a high level of insight into automated tasks, but leave more control to the journalist.

This study has some limitations that need to be taken into account. Listed usability factors provide a wish list of possibly useful features for a SoMe information toolset, not features that have to be included for the tool to work. On the contrary, too many functions will affect usability and SA negatively, as the tool will become too complex and offer the user an overload of information. Most journalists in the sample addressed this concern. Also, study results should be interpreted with caution, as the data were gathered from a convenience sample. Results may not reflect all aspects of journalistic needs or represent other work contexts than those included in the study. Students were included in one dataset, and this subsample will naturally have a more limited work experience than seasoned journalists. On the other hand, this subsample may be more tech-savvy and have a better understanding of SoMe usage patterns. Also, the crisis training scenario does not reflect an actual crisis assignment, and comparisons between results gathered from this part with work in real-life crises should be made with caution.

A useful tool can be developed based on knowledge from this study, previous research on the subject, and functions provided by existing tools. However, tool content should be carefully weighed against tool complexity, and practical usability tests of tool prototypes should be carried out with journalists.

Acknowledgments

This work was supported by the Norwegian Research Council under Grant 233975/H20; The Högskolestiftelsen i Österbotten Foundation; and The Svensk-Österbottniska Samfundet Foundation.

Conflict of Interests

The authors declare no conflict of interests.

References

Benkler, Y. (2006). *The wealth of networks: How social production transforms markets and freedom*. New Haven, CT: Yale University Press.

Brandtzæg, P., Luders, M., Spangenberg, J., Rath-Wiggins, L., & Folstad, A. (2016). Emerging journalistic verification practices concerning social media. *Journalism Practice*, *10*(3), 323–342.

Diakopoulos, N. (2014). Algorithmic accountability. *Digital Journalism*, *3*(3), 398–415.

Diakopoulos, N., De Choudhury, M., & Naaman, M. (2012). Finding and assessing social media information sources in the context of journalism. In J. A. Konstan, E. H. Chi, & K. Höök (Eds.), *Proceedings of the SIGCHI Conference on Human Factors in Computing Systems* (pp 2451–2460). Austin, TX: ACM.

Endsley, M. R. (2009). Theoretical underpinnings of situation awareness: A critical review. In M. R. Endsley & D. J. Garland (Eds.), *Situational awareness analysis and measurement* (pp 3–29). Mahwah, NJ: Lawrence Erlbaum.

Endsley, M. R., & Jones, D. G. (2011). *Designing for situation awareness. An approach to user-centered design* (2nd ed.). Boca Raton, FL: CRC Press.

Hallin, D. C., Manoff, R. K., & Weddle, J. K. (1993). Sourcing patterns of national security reporters. *Journalism Quarterly*, *70*(4), 753–766.

Hermida, A., Lewis, S. C., & Zamith, R. (2014). Sourcing the Arab Spring: A case study of Andy Carvin's sources on Twitter during the Tunisian and Egyptian revolutions. *Journal of Computer-Mediated Communication*, *19*(3), 479–499.

Hertzum, M., & Clemmensen, T. (2012). How do usability professionals construe usability? *International Journal of Human-Computer Studies*, *70*(1), 26–42.

ISO 9241. (2010). *Ergonomics of human-system interaction—Part 210: Human-centered design for interactive systems*. Geneva: International Standard Organization.

Ito, M. (2008). Introduction. In K. Varnelis (Ed.), *Networked publics* (pp. 1–14). Cambridge, MA: MIT Press.

Jenkins, M. (2013). *Social media reporting tools*. Retrieved from https://dartcenter.org/content/social-media-reporting-tools

Miles, M. B., Huberman, A. M., & Saldana, J. (2014). *Qualitative data analysis. A methods sourcebook* (3rd ed.). Thousand Oaks, CA: Sage.

Park, D., Sachar, S., Diakopoulos, N., & Elmqvist, N. (2016). Supporting comment moderators in identifying high quality online news comments. In J. Kaye, A. Druin, C. Lampe, D. Morris, & J. P. Hourcade (Eds.), *Proceedings of the 2016 CHI Conference on Human Factors in Computing Systems* (pp. 1114–1125). San Jose, CA: ACM.

Salmon, P. M., Stanton, N. A., Walker, G. H., Baber, C., Jenkins, D. P., McMaster, R., & Young, M. S. (2008).

What really is going on? Review of situation awareness models for individuals and teams. *Theoretical Issues in Ergonomics Science*, *9*(4), 297–323.

Schifferes, S., Newman, N., Thurman, N., Corney, D., Goker, A. S. & Martin, C. (2014). Identifying and verifying news through social media: Developing a user-centred tool for professional journalists. *Digital Journalism*, *2*(3), 406–418.

Schwartz, R., Naaman, M., & Teodoro, R. (2015). *Editorial algorithms: Using social media to discover and report local news*. Paper presented at the Ninth International AAAI Conference on Web and Social Media, Oxford, UK.

Shapiro, I., Brin, C., Bédard-Brûlé, I., & Mychajlowycz, K. (2013). Verification as a strategic ritual: How journalists retrospectively describe processes for ensuring accuracy. *Journalism Practice*, *7*(6), 657–673.

Silverman, C. (Ed.). (2014). *Verification handbook. A definitive guide to verifying digital content for emergency coverage*. Maastricht: European Journalism Centre.

Wallach. D., & Scholz, S. C. (2012). User-centered design: Why and how to put users first in software development. In A. Maedche, A. Botzenhardt, & L. Neer (Eds.), *Software for people* (pp 11–38). Berlin: Springer.

Yin, J., Lampert, A., Cameron, M., Robinson B., & Power, R. (2012). Using social media to enhance emergency situation awareness. *IEEE Intelligent Systems*, *27*(6), 52–59.

14

No Digital "Castles in the Air": Online Non-Participation and the Radical Left

Linus Andersson

Media and Communication Studies, School of Health and Welfare, Halmstad University, 30118 Halmstad, Sweden; E-Mail: linus.andersson@hh.se

Abstract

This article presents results from a study of online presence in activist milieus associated with the radical left in Sweden discussed from a perspective of non-participation. With the aim to further the understanding of digital non-participation as communicative strategy in activism, it builds upon empirical findings and argues that the online practices and use of social media, as could be observed in milieus associated with the radical left, indicates active non-participation and that this, in turn, is related to the ambition to claim autonomy. The article draws from existing scholarship on critical perspectives on protest movements and social media as well as empirical examples of online content published by radical leftist groups. Furthermore, it analyses how these activities could be understood in terms of active and passive non-participation, abstention or adaptation to social media affordances, as well as implosion of the social in digital media. The findings suggest that much of the activities in the material could be described as active non-participation and that this media practice relates to ideological positioning and values in the milieu.

Keywords

activism; digital media; non-participation; online media; radical left

Issue

This article is part of the issue "Political Agency in the Digital Age: Media, Participation and Democracy", edited by Anne Kaun (Södertörn University, Sweden), Maria Kyriakidou (University of East Anglia, UK) and Julie Uldam (Roskilde University, Denmark).

---

1. Introduction

Ten years ago, "cyber-protest" usually meant active engagement with digital online media by protest- or activist groups (e.g. van de Donk, 2004). However, with the present development and proliferation of online digital media, the question of how to understand political agency in relation to online media practices has become less obvious. Following heady narratives about "Facebook revolutions" and "revolutions 2.0", there has emerged a literature where more critical perspectives on protest movements and social media are presented (e.g. Cammaerts, Mattoni, & McCurdy, 2013; Dencik & Leistert, 2015). This approach has turned its attention to a number of tensions and contradictions that come with the use of social media for social change, including issues such as surveillance and censorship (Hintz, 2015; Redden, 2015), affordances of individualism (Fenton & Barassi, 2011), commodification of users and systemic constraints (Fuchs, 2011; Leistert, 2015), and, affordances of connectivity versus the need for anonymity in activist groups (Treré, 2015).

This article is based on the findings from a previous study of online presence of the radical left in Sweden (Swedish Media Council, 2014). The ambition is to address some of the conflicts above and connect them to a recent discussion about online non-participation as a strategy (Casemajor, Couture, Delfin, Goerzen, & Delfanti, 2015), with the purpose to contribute to our understanding of non-participation. My argument is that the online practices and use of social media as could be observed in milieus associated with the radical left indicates active non-participation and that this, in turn, is related to a political ambition to claim autonomy.

The argument is structured as follows: After a brief background about the nature of the study I will discuss the theoretical concepts *participation*, *empowerment* and *autonomy* and present the analytical framework, followed by notes on method. The analytical part is structured from three themes: active and passive non-participation, abstention and adaptation, and implosion of the social. The paper ends with a discussion about the possibilities for the concept online non-participation and its implications for further, empirical studies.

1.1. Background

In contrast to much of what has been published about social movements and online media, the study from which the material in this article was taken could be described as a propaganda study (Jowett & O'Donell, 1999) designed to chart "anti-democratic and pro-violent messages on the internet" (Swedish Media Council, 2014). It was conducted by the Swedish Media Council and initiated by the Swedish government as part of an "Action Plan for Protecting Democracy against Pro-Violence Extremism". The task was to describe where and what type of messages could be found online that publicly propagated for ideologically motivated violent action, and what could be said about recruitment strategies in this material. The question was not what these groups do or why, but how they present their activity and cause publicly. Much of the aim, design, and scope of the study were defined by the commissioner, which meant that the findings are limited to a quite narrow area of investigation. It is not a study of social movements in general, but of a small autonomous or anarchist fraction of the radical left who publicly display an apologetic sentiment toward violence. Nor is it a study exclusively about corporate social media, but more broadly defined online media that includes organization web sites.

The findings showed that the radical left, at least in the sense as was defined by the assignment, were sparse users of online digital media for dissemination of propaganda; in contrast to the other groups included in the study, especially the extreme right. Instead, they seemed to be quite reluctant in adapting to online communication. While the original study did not include measures for examining non-participation, the results were of a kind that activates questions about participation/non-participation dynamics that motivates a review of these findings in a new theoretical context.

2. Online Non-Participation

Lately, the scholarly interest in the issue of online non-participation and disconnection has increased (Cammaerts, 2008; Kaun & Schwarzenegger, 2014; Portwood-Stacer, 2013; Selwyn, 2003). While much of the focus of these studies has been on individual motivations for abstention, attention has also been drawn to non-participation as a form of activism (Casemajor et al., 2015), as well as an interest in the decline of certain types of online radical politics (Wolfson, 2014). Still, the greater part of the literature that has surfaced since the Arabic spring, the Occupy-, and Los Indignados-movement tends to focus on connectivity, online presence and participation (Bennett & Segerberg, 2013; Gerbaudo, 2012; Hands, 2011). In this section I will look into some of the theories and models of participation and discuss theoretical foundations for understanding digital non-participation in terms of strategy or protest. Online media here refers to those channels and services where messages and content is made public on the web; either in the case with social networking sites, or in other forms of user-generated content, what used to be called web 2.0. Hence, forms of private or non-public online communication such as e-mail or direct messages are not included in this definition. The reason is that the original study focused on public messages that were easily accessible and published with the intent to reach an audience.

2.1. Social Implosion and Interpassivity

The idea of non-participation as empowering in relation to media has been part of what could be described as a postmodern critique of social theory, especially as articulated by Jean Baudrillard (1988). Even if Baudrillard's work does not present a scholarship that offers verifiable theories, some observations and concepts have proven useful figures of thought and Baudrillard was early to assess the affordances of an abundant information society. One such concept that he addressed both politically and philosophically was the issue of media-related non-participation. In the essay "The Masses: The implosion of the social in the media" (Baudrillard, 1988), Baudrillard introduced the idea that non-participation should be understood as a rational and effective response to a power structure that fostered a hypocritical form of non-communication:

> "I would no longer interpret in the same way the forced silence of the masses in the mass media. I would no longer see in it a sign of passivity and of alienation, but to the contrary an original strategy, an original response in the form of a challenge." (Baudrillard, 1988, p. 208)

Non-participation in this context is not understood as hampered citizenship, but as rational and empowering, a position that finds resonance in more recent accounts of non-participation (Casemajor et al., 2015). The challenge is directed toward a system that requires of its population a symbolic engagement: to have opinions, to be well-informed, to make conscious choices.

What Baudrillard opposes is the equation of participation with empowerment—a theory of empowerment that only acknowledges active participation is seen as hypocritical and quite useless; a more efficient form of opposition would be to refuse to participate. While Baudrillard's level of analysis makes grand claims with little-to-none empirical grounding, his change in perspective should also be added to the recent debate on strategic non-participation also when it comes to digital media.

The backdrop for Baudrillard's argument was a Marxist understanding of mass media as a tool for manipulation of the masses. In the digital era, manipulation and false consciousness may not hold the same position in critical thought, even if the notion of filter bubbles (Pariser, 2011), is an example of updated suspicion about media manipulation ("what the internet is hiding from you"). Its legacy is also present in discussions about involuntary participation where notions of social media's affordances of visibility and individualism have been commented on by scholars (Fenton & Barassi, 2011; Fuchs, 2014; Poell & van Dijck, 2015). Furthermore, the challenge in digital media can also be approached through the concept of interpassivity (Dean, 2009; Žižek, 1998), described as the opposite to interactivity. Originally developed as a critical term in order to explain how mediated quasi-interactivity functions as stand-in for real engagement, it has come to use in discussions about online engagement/disengagement and what is sometimes called "slacktivism" (Morozov, 2011), where taking part in online petitions and campaigns become stand-in for actual social engagement and activism.

2.2. Participation and Empowerment

Participation is a key feature of digital life (Kelty, 2015). The concept, however, is polysemous and it is quite difficult to define what qualifies as participation. This means that any attempt to build conceptual models for participation/non-participation has to be dynamic (Casemajor et al., 2015). In the field of media studies, at least two theoretical conceptualizations of participation co-exist. On the one hand, there is the tradition that understands participation as a term connected with the political, e.g. in form of democratic deliberation (Dahlgren, 2014). On the other hand, there is the notion theoretically based in cultural studies about active audiences and audience participation, which gained new status with the rise of digital, interactive media. Media studies harbor both these conceptual understandings that sometimes lead to tensions (as could be illustrated by the dialogue in Jenkins & Carpentier, 2013). But what brings them together is that they both address the notion of empowerment.

Definitions of empowerment are manifold and range from individual aspects such as psychological enhancement, and self-awareness, to more social and political where both individuals and groups achieve a status of autonomy (Freire, 2000; Rodriguez, 2001). Sometimes empowerment is described as a scale from self-awareness to political action (Higgins, 1999). In the context of this article, empowerment should be understood in relation to autonomy rather than self-awareness. Much of the literature on mediated participation has concentrated on the question of empowerment (Castells, 2009; Dahlgren, 2009) and participation (Carpentier, 2011; Jenkins, 2008). Some of these scholars have pointed to online social media's role in increasing civic engagement and political participation for citizens (Castells, 2009). One could say that the position taken by these scholars has equated empowerment with participation, and accordingly the idea that more participation equals more autonomy has taken hold.

Notions of empowerment and digital media have been connected with the problem of the unequal distribution of access to the internet, popularly referred to as the digital divide (e.g. Norris, 2001). Lately, with the expansion of internet access on a global scale, interests in various types of digital divides, in terms of social inequalities have gained ground in critical research (Danielsson, 2014; Livingstone & Helsper, 2007). This means that focus has changed from asking if people have the possibility to go online, to asking what they do when online. Here again, the question of empowerment becomes important since there are structural limitations to how digital media can be used. Along traditional lines of active and passive media use, online digital media can be used as a means for political participation (simulating the golden days of public sphere) or as mere passive consumption (the decline of the public sphere). However, there is yet another type of relation to digital media and empowerment that does not fit into these categories, namely the acts of deliberate non-participation.

2.3. Models of Non-Participation

An interesting paradox in relation to the discussion about participation and empowerment above is that much of the developments in today's digital media could be described in terms of forced or involuntary participation: online mainstream media invite us to "like" and share content with our social networks, while smartphones gathers data over our mobility and communication (Dahlgren, 2014). The idea of participation has been a central part of all theorization about the internet, in terms of affordances for interactivity or user-generated content (Kelty, 2015). One recurring critique from critical internet scholars has been that power relations have too easily been eradicated from theories on participation and that digital media participation creates new or reinforces existing structures of unequal distribution of power (Beer, 2009; Cammaerts, 2008; Goldberg, 2010).

One reason for taking an interest in non-participation is that it could (and should) be understood as a politically significant action (Casemajor et al., 2015, p. 851). This means that in an era of forced participation that serves the interest of existing power structures, one way of opposition is to refuse to participate. This insight is part of the dynamic model of online participation/non-participation proposed by Casemajor et al.: "The framework...is an attempt at going beyond the linear model of participation and showing that non-participation cannot just be considered as hampered citizen action or passivity; it can also be empowering" (2015, p. 863).

The model sketches four possible types of participation: active participation, passive participation, active non-participation, and passive non-participation. And in the case of active non-participation, three ideal types of action are defined. The first one is obfuscation which means to act in ways to diffuse data gathering online, through erratic behavior that renders collected data useless. The second type of active non-participation is called sabotage and includes strategies to disrupt digital platforms, for instance, denial of service-attacks on websites. The final ideal type is exodus and simply means withdrawal from digital platforms, sometimes in order to create own.

The model proposed by Casemajor et al. (2015) shows some resemblance to a model developed by Rucht (2004) called the "Quadruple 'A'"; a model that presented four ideal types of communicative strategies that social movements have developed in relation to unfavorable mainstream media coverage. Building on data dating back to the 1960s and onwards, Rucht identifies four strategies on an axis between inward- and outward oriented strategies; as well as strategies with low or high resource demands: abstention and attacks on mainstream media are not very resource-demanding. The former means avoiding publicity and "keeping to oneself" while the other allows interactions with mainstream media but voices mistrust. Alternatives and adaptation, on the other hand, are strategies with quite high resource demands where the former means creating own media outlets and the latter to enact events that might attract the attention of mass media (Rucht, 2004, p. 46). Two of these strategies, abstention and alternative are directed inwards, while attack and adaptation are outward-looking. Rucht (2011) has later commented on the implications of online digital media for his model, acknowledging the possibilities but warning about over-estimating the importance of digital media (p. 259).

2.4. Activism and Media Practice

The role of digital media in mobilization among radical groups is well-researched (Askanius, 2012; Neumayer, 2013). In a study of online counter publics associated with the extreme right and radical left, Neumayer (2013) argues that in order to understand how these groups make use of digital media, one has to look at three dimensions: technological affordances; strategies, tactics and media practices; as well as political positions and ideology. Consequently, media practices do not exist in a vacuum but should be understood in relation to both technology and ideology. Mattoni (2012, 2013) discusses media practice as part of wider repertoires of communication in social movements. In that context, repertoires include both participation and non-participation in terms of interactions with media technologies, media outlets and media professionals, what Mattoni refers to as "relational media practices" (Mattoni, 2013, p. 49).

When approaching media practices and repertoires of communication from the perspective of ideology, notions of empowerment and autonomy again become relevant. Langlois & Dubois (2005) discuss autonomous media strategies, as attempts to "bypass mainstream media through experimentation with new forms of democratic communication" (Langlois & Dubois, 2005, p. 23). On a similar note, Milan (2013) speaks of appropriation of means of communication by social movements in terms of "liberated technologies" and part of "emancipatory communication practices" (Milan, 2013, p. 2). This, in turn, is related to the practices of the autonomist leftist tradition of creating and claiming autonomous spaces in the social landscape (e.g. Katsiaficas, 2006). Following this, it is possible to understand ideologically motivated non-participation as part of the media practices and repertoires of communication in radical groups.

The perspectives outlined above constitute an analytical framework that turns attention to participation/non-participation dynamics, as well as issues of autonomy and empowerment in an ideological context.

3. Material and Method

As already mentioned, the original study was designed as a propaganda study, i.e. an investigation into modes of address and means of persuasion as employed by groups advocating violent means for an ideological cause. The method was a qualitative content analysis of digital media and online platforms, with a focus on text analysis (semiotics, discourse analysis). The material consisted of online content produced within three ideological milieus that were pre-defined by the assignment: the extreme right, militant jihadist and the autonomous left.[1] While there are many aspects that

[1] The governmental action plan and its use of terms such as "anti-democratic" and "pro-violent" have been contested by social activists and academics, especially because of a tendency to equate extra parliamentary activism and civil disobedience with extremism. For an overview of this debate, see Kaun (2015).

separate these types of movements, they had been targeted by officials as environments with a potential to propagate for violent actions for an ideological cause. It should be said that the sample was quite limited since the content up for analysis had to meet the criteria for voicing an extreme stand in favor of political violence. Few groups or online content did this and the material analyzed here was published in milieus in and around militant anti-fascist and militant animal rights groups. Needless to say, this is a marginal phenomenon in context of the radical left activist scene online, but it stood out in terms of communication strategies in comparison to what could be observed in the material published in the extreme right milieu where more aggressive discourses were present. In all, three websites associated with the militant fringe of the radical left were observed: antifa.se, revfront.org, and djurensbefrielsefront.org, and of these only revfront.org could be described as active. These are also strictly closed milieus that seldom engage in propaganda or open recruitment. "Act without being seen" has been a motto and this might be true also for how participation in digital media is organized.

The analysis consisted of three parts: first, a description of pro-violent communication as could be found in the online milieu associated with the radical left; thereafter followed a charting of the web presence of three groups that had been identified as groups who met the criteria of openly expressing themselves in favor of ideologically motivated violence. Finally, the report included a thematic analysis of online videos published on YouTube (for a full account, see Swedish Media Council, 2014, pp. 132-190).

In the review of these findings, it is important to acknowledge the communicative modalities and affordances provided by online, digital media. What qualifies as online content is not restricted to symbolic expressions in the form of words, images, video and audio, but could also include possibilities for interaction that are part of the communication practice and experience, or a social, or network media logic (Klinger & Svensson, 2015; Van Dijck & Poell, 2013). To like, link, share, and comment are activities that have become part of meaningful communication and by looking into how these activities are activated, one can get the sense of how digital media communication works in the studied environment. The study did not analyze user interaction, but paid attention to affordances for interactivity, and how these were used.

4. Analysis

The following argument is structured in order to address two sets of questions: what types of non-participation can be identified in the online activities of the radical left, and, how can this material be conceptualized in relation to theories on activist media practices? The analysis has been thematically divided into three categories: active and passive forms of non-participation; abstention and adaptation; as well as the implosion of the social online.

4.1. Active and Passive Non-Participation

The most visible form of non-participation that appears in the material is "exodus", i.e. instances of apparent withdrawal from online communication. The other types of active non-participation that are described in Casemajor's et al. (2015) model, obfuscation and sabotage, are not represented in the material. The withdrawals can come in different guises, either in terms of complete exodus, i.e. closing down web sites, or in semi-withdrawals as in turning off or limit communicative affordances. Both are result of active choice.

When it comes to complete exodus, this can be observed in the case with antifa.se, web site for a militant antifascist group Antifascist action (AFA). It had been on the web since the early 2000s but was apparently disconnected around 2010. Hence, the site was not in operation during the sample period. A similar case of probable exodus was *djurensbefrielsefront.org*, a web site by DBF, the Swedish branch of militant animal rights activists: Animal Liberation Front. The site was still accessible but gave the impression of having been abandoned, the last updates dated back to 2010.

Online communities and chat forums dedicated to the radical left were filled with speculations on whether AFA still exist at all, since they showed no presence online. The quote below is an example from this type of discussion on socialism.nu, a leftist online community, and is an answer to questions about the existence/non-existence of AFA:

> "Oh, yes. They're still here. Their activities haven't disappeared with the web site. That line of thinking originates from how the Nazis organize themselves. There, they have tons of Web sites but little or no activity IRL. It's a good thing that AFA does not spend time building digital "castles in the air". Those who need to know about AFA's existence will certainly see it =)" (https://www.socialism.nu/showthread.php?t=6164&page=8)

Even if we do not know how well-informed this commentator is regarding the issue, the response bears witness to a notion of active non-participation. Furthermore, the quote highlights another aspect apart from mere presence/absence, as it makes a clear distinction between online activities and activities in the "real" world. By describing online activity as "building digital castles in the air", the commentator gives voice to a view where "real" action is preferred over symbolic action. This could also be seen as an outcome of ideological positioning and an act of distinguishing themselves from political opponents by means of its view on and understanding of media practices. Haunss (2015) addresses the issue of online/offline-dynamics and notes that much of the recent literature on protest movement's social media practices stresses the role of preexisting social ties in mobilization (p. 26). This has been noted in previous studies on autonomous scenes, where personal interaction is preferred above mediated communication (Leach & Haunss, 2009).

The study focused on content that was accessible and could be observed; hence, it is not correct to speak of full non-participation. However, there are examples of what could be described as semi-withdrawals from online communication. One such example is the YouTube channels *RevFrontMedia* and *RevFrontMedia2*, both associated with the militant group Revolutionary Front (RF), who, at the time of the study had published in total 19 videos online depicting violent confrontations with neo-Nazis and the vandalizing of homes and properties of people claimed to be associated with the extreme right. While the publication of these videos arguably is an example of online participation, they also display a tension between active non-participation and passive participation. This manifested itself through the use of the comment function, which is pre-set by YouTube to be automatically attached to the published video. This comment function can however be deactivated, and this has been done for all of the videos published by *RevFrontMedia*. Since the deactivation requires an active choice, it is fair to argue that this also could be interpreted in line with the argument of active non-participation. At least, it does not invite viewers to participate or communicate through the means of the affordances of this type of digital media.

4.2. Abstention and Adaptation

While the exodus strategies described above could be filed under what Rucht (2004) named "abstention", i.e. to avoid attention from mass media and keep to oneself, there are examples in the material of strategies that rather meet the criteria of "adaptation". Rucht (2004) describes adaptation as an extrovert strategy with considerable high resource demands where activist groups plan their activities with (mass) media attention in mind. For the adaptation strategy, the distinction between "real" and symbolic action is less articulated which means that actions that are "unsuccessful" in meeting their concrete aims can still be deemed successful if they achieve the right media attention (e.g. DeLuca, 1999).

One example of adaptation to media attention in the material is the Facebook-account and logo that RF launched during the sample period. It could be added that this addition of a Facebook page in late 2012 does not make the group appear as early adopters when it comes to social media. This arguably late awakening does not lessen the enthusiasm; the launch was announced in quite high-flown manner on the website revfront.org:

> "[Revolutionary Front] is an organization that constantly strives for improvement and to take steps forward in our political work. We understand the importance of being seen in public space, both on the streets and on the Internet. We have therefore chosen to start a Facebook page. A page that, we hope, our readers will appreciate. The page will serve as a tool for spreading our news and to reach out to more people with our political message." (http://revfront.org/?p=5465)

With Mattoni's (2012, 2013) concept "relational media practices" it becomes possible to approach adaptation as not only an adaptation of activist groups to media logics in order to attract the attention of mainstream media professionals, as described by Rucht (2004), but to also understand adaptation in relation to technological affordances. The quote above could be seen as an example of adaptation where the group adapts its action to the requirements or logics of a media technology, in this case online social media. Milan (2015) writes about a "politics of visibility" (p. 63) brought about by social media, a politics that allows surveillance and mass scrutiny and makes activist groups vulnerable to political adversaries and the state. There are good reasons to abstain from using these services, but Milan's (2015) research has pointed to a sense of inevitability of corporate social media that leads protest groups and activists to a resignation to the unwanted consequences of being present in corporate social media. The Facebook page in itself could be seen as a form of adaptation.

However, the words by which this Facebook page was announced bear witness to an understanding of Facebook as, not primarily a means for reciprocal communication, but for broadcasting political messages. There are also formulations that declare that this move is partly motivated by the ambition to reach out to outsiders. However, the announcement says nothing about using the Facebook page as a platform for contact and communication, but seems to treat it more as a tool for broadcasting political messages. This tendency becomes even clearer as they describe political messages as "propaganda", a term probably more associated with totalitarian ambitions of manipulation through media than social and reciprocal communication:

> "After ten years as an organization we are also proud to present the [Revolutionary Front] logo! It will represent the organization and mark our propaganda." (http://revfront.org/?p=5465)

The mode of communication employed could be

described in terms of a complicated tension between secrecy and visibility. Communication is reduced to one-way channels of information rather than to share and create a sense of community. Comments-functions are turned off, and overall, the communication affordances provided for interaction and reciprocal communication are not put to use in any considerable extent. One way to approach this is to see it as "asocial" media practices.

4.3. Implosion of the Social Online

A common definition of social media is that it refers to media services that enable reciprocal communication between humans, and provides some sense of community (cf. Fuchs, 2014, p. 1). When observing the use of social networking sites and digital media in the sample, it appears as if the way that these services have been put to use renounces some of those modalities of communication and community-building that makes them "social". In accordance with the discussion about semi-withdrawal above, it is a complex act of being present without full participation, similar to passive forms of participations such as lurking (Crawford, 2011).

A first example of "asocial" online presence is RF who are active in publishing propaganda on the web and in social media, but seem more cautious when it comes to sociability online. The content that is published is not aimed at recruiting sympathizers; it does little to promote the positive and inspiring sides of being associated with RF or participating in their actions (perhaps it is not be necessary to advertise—potential followers might be attracted or motivated by other incentives than to seek for a social community). It might also be more important for various reasons to keep internal activities secret than it is to put themselves on display (other than through their actions). Anyone wishing to come in contact with the group is directed to e-mail or a pre-paid mobile phone number. There was a @revfront Twitter-account but it was closed for outsiders—only accepted followers could read its tweets and see the number of followers.

The asocial online presence is also true for the other groups; AFA and DBF are even more reclusive, the latter explicitly discouraging people from attempting to make contact with them. Leach and Haunss (2009) have noted how autonomist activist scenes build heavily on personal contacts and direct communication, which might help explain this desire to redirect users from the online platforms to other means of communication that are more direct and personal.

Secondly, many of the services for publishing content online are social per default, and hence set limits for the control over content. As has already been mentioned, *RevFrontMedia* had switched off the commenting-functions for their YouTube-videos, but the display of these videos is companied by a list of suggestions for similar videos presented in the right-hand margin on the YouTube web site. On many occasions during the sample period, the viewer was given suggestions for videos produced and published by right-wing extremist groups. Hence, when using YouTube as a tool for broadcasting propaganda, there is a risk that it provides unintentional attention to propaganda from political enemies.

Finally, articles and communiques published in the milieu are written by pseudonyms or unidentifiable collectives. This anonymity feeds into an overarching strategy of secrecy that is complemented by photographs depicting people in ski-masks or a casual custom of blurring out faces from photographs and videos. Who these individuals are remains a secret. One of the things that social networking sites brought to online culture was identity. Where previous forms of online communities had been characterized by a logic where identities were disconnected from physical reality ("On the internet, nobody knows you're a dog") (Turkle, 1995), My Space and Facebook brought back traditional modes of identification ("On the internet, everybody knows you're a dog") (see Gershon, 2011). Fenton and Barassi (2011) have noted how social media is built on a "politics of individuation" that stands in a contradictory position to collective action, solidarity and participation. For groups that traditionally have valued its secrecy, sometimes on good grounds regarding a history of surveillance and infiltration of groups on the marginal left, the priority to keep oneself hidden is in conflict with the visibility paradigm of digital media. Furthermore, Fenton and Barassi (2011) argue that the logic of self-centered participation promoted by social media can represent a threat for political groups rather than an opportunity. This tension reflects an ideological contradiction within autonomist tradition between individual liberty and collective solidarity. Autonomist politics have sometimes been described as a "politics in the first person" (Leach & Haunss, 2009, p. 262). Related to this, lifestyle politics and slacktivism has long been targeted as a problematic consequence of social media activism.

The process of de-socialization could be understood both as an extension of a tradition of secrecy within the milieu, but also a strategy of how to oppose a technical architecture that reduces the ability to control over content. Put another way, the conflict between control and emancipation as identified by Dencik and Leistert (2015) is relevant here as well. The groups that were included in the study constituted a very secluded milieu. They did not show much interest in using the web to attract new followers or recruit activists. Control over content appeared to be more important than sociability.

5. Discussion: Non-Participation and Empowerment

Previous research on militant groups associated with the radical left have pointed out that these groups seldom take an active part in designing propaganda or make efforts to reach out for new possible sympathizers (e.g. Peterson, 2001). Propaganda is understood as a means associated with the extreme right. It is therefore not surprising to find the type of active non-participation presented in the analysis. Theoretically, we can assume that there are numerous reasons for these kinds of groups to abstain from online communication and corporate social media (Dencik & Leistert, 2015). Still, as was shown in the empirical analysis, abstention is not total, but rather selective and partial. From these findings we can make the following observations:

First, empowerment is a complex term (and it is difficult to speak of empowerment without hearing the voice of those assumedly empowered). Still, if we understand empowerment partly as acts to claim autonomy, it is possible to review much of the online media practices described above as active non-participation with claims to autonomy. It is clear that much of the non-participation is a consequence of active choice. The groups are present online, but they have orchestrated their presence in a way that reduces the degree of participation, for instance by disabling possibilities for commenting and keeping strict directives of how to get contacted.

Following this, when these milieus are put in a historical context, it shows that they have a tradition of "acting without being seen" which collides with the affordances of connectivity and visibility of social media. This tradition, in turn, might help explain the tendency to treat online media as channels for the broadcasting of propaganda (rather than open it up for reciprocal communication) as a form of non-participation.

6. Conclusions

From what we have seen in this study, there are clear instances of active non-participation in digital media in the milieus included in the sample, which opens the field for further inquiries about activism and non-participation as media practice. Because this study was limited to analyses of online content, questions that concern intentions are beyond its scope. Hence, further research into the strategy and political implications of disconnection and non-participation would be instrumental to complement these findings, as well as would also efforts to put them in historical and geographical contexts. Such research would require a different methodological approach, preferably including interviews. In addition to this, the question of how a certain ideological position is associated with a media practice that builds on non-participation is worth elaboration, especially considering possible variations between different ideological groups. Given its limitations, the study shows how a non-participation-framework can provide a fresh perspective for understanding activism in the digital age.

Acknowledgements

The research and data that is considered in this article was collected in a study supported by the Swedish Media Council.

Conflict of Interests

The author declares no conflict of interests.

References

Askanius, T. (2012). *Radical online video: YouTube, video activism and social movement media practices* (Doctoral dissertation). Lund: Studies in Media and Communication 17.

Baudrillard, J. (1988). *Selected writings*. Cambridge: Polity.

Beer, D. (2009). Power through the algorithm? Participatory web cultures and the technological unconscious. *New Media & Society, 11*(6), 985-1002.

Bennett, W. L., & Segerberg, A. (2013). *The logic of connective action: Digital media and the personalization of contentious politics*. Cambridge: University Press.

Cammaerts, B. (2008). Critiques on the participatory potentials of Web 2.0. *Communication, Culture & Critique, 1*(4), 358-377.

Cammaerts, B., Mattoni, A., & McCurdy, P. (2013). *Mediation and protest movements*. Bristol: Intellect.

Carpentier, N. (2011). *Media and participation: A site of ideological-democratic struggle*. Bristol: Intellect.

Casemajor, N., Couture, S., Delfin, M., Goerzen, M., & Delfanti, A. (2015). Non-participation in digital media. Toward a framework of mediated political action. *Media, Culture & Society, 37*(6), 850-866.

Castells, M. (2009). *Communication power*. Oxford: Oxford University Press.

Crawford, K. (2011) Listening, not lurking: The neglected form of participation. In H. Greif, L. Hjorth, A. Lasen, & C. Lobet-Maris (Eds.), *Cultures of participation* (pp. 63-74). New York: Peter Lang.

Dahlgren, P. (2009). *Media and political engagement: Citizens, communication, and democracy*. New York: Cambridge University Press.

Dahlgren, P. (2014). Political participation via the web: Structural and subjective contingencies. *Interactions: Studies in Communication & Culture, 5*(3), 255-269.

Danielsson, M. (2014). *Digitala distinktioner: Klass och kontinuitet i unga mäns vardagliga mediepraktiker* [Digital distinctions: Class and continuity in young men's everyday media practices] (Doctoral dissertation). Jönköping University.

Dean, J. (2009). *Democracy and other neoliberal fantasies: Communicative capitalism & left politics*. Durham: Duke University Press.

DeLuca, K.M. (1999). *Image politics: The new rhetoric of environmental activism*. New York: Guilford Press.

Dencik, L., & Leistert, O. (Eds.) (2015). *Critical perspectives on social media and protest: Between control and emancipation*. London: Rowman & Littlefield.

Fenton, N., & Barassi, V. (2011). Alternative media and social networking sites: The politics of individuation and political participation. *The Communication Review, 14*(3), 179-196.

Freire, P. (2000). *Pedagogy of the oppressed*. New York: Bloomsbury.

Fuchs, C. (2011). *Foundations of critical media and information studies*. Abingdon: Routledge

Fuchs, C. (2014). *Social media: A critical introduction*. London: Sage.

Gerbaudo, P. (2012). *Tweets and the streets: Social media and contemporary activism*. London: Pluto Press.

Gershon, I. (2011). On the Internet, everyone knows you're a dog. A review essay. *Comparative Studies in Society and History, 53*, 997-1007.

Goldberg, G. (2010). Rethinking the public/virtual sphere: The problem with participation. *New Media & Society, 13*(5), 739-754.

Hands, J. (2011). *@ is for activism: Dissent, resistance and rebellion in a digital culture*. London: Pluto.

Haunss, S. (2015). Promise and practice in studies of social media and movements. In L. Dencik & O. Leistert (Eds.), *Critical perspectives on social media and protest: Between control and emancipation* (pp. 13-34). London: Rowman & Littlefield.

Higgins, J. W. (1999). Community television and the vision of media literacy, social action, and empowerment. *Journal of Broadcasting & Electronic Media, 43*(4), 624-644.

Hintz, A. (2015). Social media censorship, privatized regulation and new restrictions to protest and dissent. In L. Dencik & O. Leistert (Eds.), *Critical perspectives on social media and protest: Between control and emancipation* (pp. 109-126). London: Rowman & Littlefield.

Jenkins, H. (2008). *Convergence culture: Where old and new media collide*. New York: New York University Press.

Jenkins, H., & Carpentier, N. (2013). Theorizing participatory intensities: A conversation about participation and politics. *Convergence: The International Journal of Research into New Media Technologies, 19*(3), 265-286.

Jowett, G., & O'Donnell, V. (1999). *Propaganda and persuasion* (3rd ed.). Thousand Oaks: Sage.

Katsiaficas, G. N. (2006). *The subversion of politics: European autonomous social movements and the decolonization of everyday life* (2nd ed.). Oakland, CA: AK Press.

Kaun, A. (2015). Civil disobedience is not the same as violent extremism. *Open Democracy*. Retrieved from https://www.opendemocracy.net/anne-kaun/civil-disobedience-is-not-same-as-violent-extremism

Kaun, A., & Schwarzenegger, C. (2014). "No media, less life?" Online disconnection in mediatized worlds. *First Monday, 19*(11).

Kelty, C. M. (2015). Participation. *Digital Keywords*. Retrieved from: http://escholarship.org/uc/item/8z13p7g9

Klinger, U., & Svensson, J. (2015). The emergence of network media logic in political communication: A theoretical approach. *New Media & Society, 17*(8), 1241-1257.

Langlois, A., & Dubois, F. (Eds.). (2005). *Autonomous media: Activating resistance & dissent*. Montréal: Cumulus Press.

Leach, D. K., & Haunss, S. (2009). Scenes and social movements. In H. Johnson (Ed.), *Culture, social movements, and protest*. Aldershot: Ashgate.

Leistert, O. (2015). The revolution will not be liked: On the systemic constraints of corporate social media platforms for protests. In L. Dencik & O. Leistert (Eds.), *Critical perspectives on social media and protest: Between control and emancipation* (pp. 35-52). London: Rowman & Littlefield.

Livingstone, S., & Helsper, E. (2007). Gradations in digital inclusion: Children, young people and the digital divide. *New Media & Society, 9*(4), 671-696.

Mattoni, A. (2012). *Media practices and protest politics: How precarious workers mobilise*. Farnham: Ashgate.

Mattoni, A (2013). Repertoires of communication in social movement processes. In B. Cammaerts, A. Mattoni, & P. McCurdy (Eds.), *Mediation and protest movements* (pp. 39-56). Bristol: Intellect.

Milan, S. (2013). *Social movements and their technologies: Wiring social change*. Houndmills and Basingstoke: Palgrave Macmillan.

Milan, S. (2015). Mobilizing in times of social media: From a politics of identity to a politics of visibility. In L. Dencik & O. Leistert (Eds.), *Critical perspectives on social media and protest: Between control and emancipation* (pp. 53-72). London: Rowman & Littlefield.

Morozov, E. (2011). *The net delusion: How not to liberate the world*. London: Allen Lane.

Neumayer, C. (2013). *When neo-Nazis march and anti-fascists demonstrate: Protean counterpublics in the digital age* (Doctoral dissertation). Copenhagen: IT University.

Norris, P. (2001). *Digital divide? Civic engagement, information poverty, and the Internet worldwide*. Cambridge: Cambridge University Press.

Pariser, E. (2011). *The filter bubble: What the Internet is hiding from you*. London: Viking.

Peterson, A. (2001) *Contemporary political protest: Essays on Political militancy*. Aldershot: Ashgate.

Poell, T., & van Dijck, J. (2015). Social media and activist communication. In C. Atton (Ed.), *The Routledge companion to alternative and community media* (pp. 527-537). London: Routledge.

Portwood-Stacer, L. (2013). Media refusal and conspicuous non-consumption: The performative and political dimensions of Facebook abstention. *New Media & Society, 15*(7), 1041-1057.

Redden, J. (2015). Social media protest in context: Surveillance, information management, and neoliberal governance in Canada. In L. Dencik & O. Leistert (Eds.), *Critical perspectives on social media and protest: Between control and emancipation* (pp. 127-143). London: Rowman & Littlefield.

Rodríguez, C. (2001). *Fissures in the mediascape: An international study of citizens' media.* Cresskill, NJ: Hampton Press.

Rucht, D. (2004). The quadruple 'A': Media strategies of protest movements since the 1960s in W. v.d. Donk (Ed.), *Cyberprotest: New media, citizens and social movements*. London: Routledge.

Rucht, D. (2011). Protest movements and their media usages. In B. Cammaerts, A. Mattoni, & P. McCurdy (Eds.), *Mediation and protest movements* (pp. 249-268). Bristol: Intellect.

Selwyn, N. (2003). Apart from technology: Understanding people's non-use of information and communication technologies in everyday life. *Technology in Society, 25*(1), 99-116.

Swedish Media Council. (2014). *Pro-violence and anti-democratic messages on the Internet*. Stockholm: Swedish Media Council.

Treré, E. (2015). The struggle within: Discord, Conflict and paranoia in social media protest. In L. Dencik & O. Leistert (Eds.), *Critical perspectives on social media and protest: Between control and emancipation* (pp. 163-180). London: Rowman & Littlefield.

Turkle, S. (1995). *Life on the screen: Identity in the age of the Internet.* New York: Simon & Schuster.

van de Donk, W. (Ed.) (2004). *Cyberprotest: New media, citizens and social movements*. London: Routledge.

van Dijck, J., & Poell, T. (2013). Understanding social media logic. *Media and Communication, 1*(1), 2-14.

Wolfson, T. (2014). *Digital rebellion: The birth of the cyber left.* Springfield: University of Illinois Press.

Žižek, S. (1998). Cyberspace, or, how to traverse the fantasy in the age of the retreat of the big other. *Public Culture, 10*(3), 483-513.

15

Facebook's Emotional Contagion Experiment as a Challenge to Research Ethics

Jukka Jouhki [1,]*, Epp Lauk [2], Maija Penttinen [1], Niina Sormanen [2] and Turo Uskali [2]

[1] Department of History and Ethnology, University of Jyväskylä, 40014 Jyväskylä, Finland; E-Mails: jukka.jouhki@jyu.fi (J.J.), maija.s.penttinen@student.jyu.fi (M.P.)
[2] Department of Communication, University of Jyväskylä, 40014 Jyväskylä, Finland; E-Mails: epp.lauk@jyu.fi (E.L.), niina.sormanen@jyu.fi (N.S.), turo.uskali@jyu.fi (T.U.)

* Corresponding author

Abstract
This article analyzes the ethical discussion focusing on the Facebook emotional contagion experiment published by the *Proceedings of the National Academy of Sciences* in 2014. The massive-scale experiment manipulated the News Feeds of a large amount of Facebook users and was successful in proving that emotional contagion happens also in online environments. However, the experiment caused ethical concerns within and outside academia mainly for two intertwined reasons, the first revolving around the idea of research as manipulation, and the second focusing on the problematic definition of informed consent. The article concurs with recent research that the era of social media and big data research are posing a significant challenge to research ethics, the practice and views of which are grounded in the pre social media era, and reflect the classical ethical stances of utilitarianism and deontology.

Keywords
Big data; emotional contagion; Facebook; informed consent; manipulation; methodology; privacy; research ethics; social media; user data

Issue
This article is part of the issue "Successes and Failures in Studying Social Media: Issues of Methods and Ethics", edited by Epp Lauk and Niina Sormanen (University of Jyväskylä, Finland).

---

1. Introduction

In June 2014 the *Proceedings of the National Academy of Sciences* (*PNAS*) published an article entitled "Experimental Evidence of Massive-Scale Emotional Contagion Through Social Networks". It was about an experiment[1] conducted by Adam D. I. Kramer from Facebook's Core Data Science Team together with Jamie E. Guillory and Jeffrey T. Hancock from Cornell University. The article provided experimental evidence about emotional contagion, a phenomenon that has been widely studied before but mostly in offline environments. In January 2012, the research team manipulated the News Feeds of a massive number (N = 689,003) of Facebook users for a week, reducing the amount of emotional content in their feeds. After analyzing over three million posts and over 122 million words, the results showed that when the amount of positive status updates published in their News Feed was reduced, users published more negative status updates and fewer positive updates. Conversely, when the amount of negative status updates was reduced, users published more positive status updates and fewer negative updates. Moreover, the less emotional content the users were exposed to, the fewer words they used in their status updates. (Kramer, Guillory, & Hanckock, 2014).

The research suggested that emotional states "can be transferred to others via emotional contagion, lead-

[1] Henceforth, "the Facebook experiment" or "the experiment".

ing people to experience the same emotions without their awareness" (Kramer et al., 2014, p. 8788). Emotional contagion had been proved earlier (e.g. Barsade, 2002; Huntsinger, Lun, Sinclair, & Clore, 2009; Kramer et al., 2014, p. 8788 also refer to several other studies), but proving that it happens "outside of in-person interaction" and particularly in the increasingly popular social media was new (see e.g. Ferrara & Yang, 2015 for a similar but more recent study). Moreover, as there are common conceptions about positive social media postings making people sad or envious (e.g. Copeland, 2011), the experiment produced valuable information to the contrary. The experiment suggested that people's "hearts and minds", as Schroeder (2014, p. 3) puts it, can be manipulated online, for good or ill. (See also Shah, Capella, & Neuman, 2015; Summers-Effler, Van Ness, & Hausmann, 2015, p. 472; cf. Parkinson & Manstead 2015, p. 377.)

Academic and non-academic reactions to the study—defined as ethically controversial (Ananny, 2015, p. 101; Harriman & Patel, 2014; Pejovic & Musolesi, 2015, p. 18; Simon, 2014; Thorson & Wells, 2015, p. 10)—were mixed. On a broader view, the heterogeneity of the views on the ethics of the experiment is a sign of how contested and fluid the concept of privacy is (e.g. Ess, 2013, p. 260). Moreover, as Facebook cooperates with several universities such as Cornell, Stanford and Harvard (see e.g. Cheng, Adamic, Dow, Kleinberg, & Leskovec, 2014; Friggeri, Adamic, Eckles, & Cheng, 2014; Sun, Rosenn, Marlow, & Lento, 2009)[2] the experiment has raised debate about whose research ethics prevail in such joint ventures—those of a private company or those of an academic research institution. In this article, we focus on the academic but also look to some extent at the non-academic ethical commentary on the Facebook experiment, and ask what it tells us about ethical research issues in the current era of social media research.

The ethical discussion presented in this article is founded on an integrative literature review (see e.g. Card, 2010; Torraco, 2005) that we conducted by searching major journal databases such as Science Direct, Google Scholar, Sage Journals, and Ebsco Academic Search Elite for articles covering the experiment. As a result we obtained articles from journals such as *Research Ethics*; *Big Data & Society*; *Media, Culture & Society*; *Nature*; and *Information, Communication & Society*. In addition to journal articles, we searched for conference proceedings on the experiment as well as scholarly analyses of the issue published in blogs and other internet sites. Some news and magazine articles as well as blog posts were also included in order to offer some non-academic views on the issue.

Overall, our approach to the ethical discussion revolving around the Facebook experiment is essayistic in nature (see e.g. Ceserani, 2010; Cornelissen, Gajewskade, Piekkari, & Welch, 2012, pp. 198-199), which means that we prefer exploring and discussing the topic in a heuristic manner: we tend to concentrate on raising questions rather than put forward any definite results based on empirical research. However, we do argue that there are two crucial themes of debate which sum up the ethical discussion revolving around the experiment: *research as manipulation* (discussed in Section 3) and the related *informed consent* (discussed in Section 4). Moreover, we suggest that the debates about the ethics of human-subject big data research, while demanding a rethink of research ethics, still reflect the classical divide between the utilitarian and the deontological points of view. In the next section we will introduce some key questions of research ethics in the era of social media. Then we move on to present the Facebook experiment and the ensuing ethical discussion.[3]

2. Research Ethics and the Human Subject

The views on research ethics generally put into practice in any academic research can be seen as balancing between two classic moral philosophical stances. Utilitarianism attempts to calculate the morality of an act by estimating the total amount of happiness or suffering produced by the act, while deontology views certain actions as immoral or moral per se, regardless of their consequences. Both these stances are applied, for example, in social media research when scholars contemplate the effect of their study on the subjects' privacy: the utilitarian view of privacy might allow certain incursions into privacy if the result is the greater good, whereas from the deontological point of view, a certain level of privacy is a right that should not be violated, for example, by conducting a study without receiving the informed consent of the subjects of the study (Ess, 2013, pp. 256-262; Shrader-Frechette, 2000). Both stances are problematic, and neither of them is applied in research without any consideration of the other—or in moral decision-making outside of academia, for that matter. At any rate, the utilitarian emphasis on avoidance of harm and the more deontological value of receiving informed consent from research subjects are considered the two most significant imperatives of research ethics in studies with human participants (e.g. the British Psychological Society, 2010). Actual policies as to how exactly the imperatives are defined and in what situations they apply (e.g. in big data research) vary significantly.

[2] For Stanford's recent collaboration with Facebook, see www.sserg.org/new-collaboration-with-stanford-university-and-facebook. More about Facebook's partnerships at https://research.facebook.com. On Facebook's exclusive cooperation with a few universities that have been granted access to Facebook's data, see e.g. Paolillo, 2005, p. 50.

[3] This article is based on an unpublished conference paper by Jouhki et al. (2015).

One of the key ethical principles of the Association of Internet Researchers (AoIR)—that the greater the vulnerability of the subject of study, the greater the obligation of the researcher to protect the subject—is a good example of how challenging it is to formulate specific rules of ethical research (Markham & Buchanan, 2012, pp. 4-5). Obviously, protecting the research subject depends on how one defines both the harm that might be inflicted on the unprotected person and also a research subject. The context of any research setting means that ethical codes are not so much strict rules as incentives to individual researchers to reflect on the moral ground of their research and make ethical decisions using their own judgment of what is in fact practicable in the circumstances. Especially when informed consent cannot be obtained in human-subject research, the benefits of the study should outweigh the harm of any invasion of privacy.

Often anonymity is seen as enough to ensure the no-harm rule in cases of non-experimental (e.g. purely observational) research. In experiments that affect the participants' behavior, the rules are stricter (See e.g. Vainio, 2012; Vanderpool, 1996.). The level of sensitivity required for the decision-making to be ethically sufficient is a constant topic of debate. For example, a research institution or a commercial company engaging in research might hold the view that obeying the law is enough to make the research ethical (Hudson & Bruckman, 2004, pp. 132-133). If the participants are not harmed in any way during the data gathering, an ethically sensitive researcher—whether working in a private company or a university—might still take into account the hypothetical situation that a research participant at some point learns about his or her role in the research and is offended (i.e. harmed) by having been a participant without having given consent (e.g. Hudson & Bruckman, 2004, pp. 136-138). Moreover, an ethically sensitive researcher might treat public content on the internet (e.g. tweets, blog posts) as intimate parts of their creator's personhood. Most researchers, however, use this content without securing informed consent (Hesse, Moser, & Riley, 2015, p. 27).

The fact that data are accessible and public does not necessarily mean that using them is not jeopardizing privacy and is thus ethically justified (see e.g. boyd, 2010;[4] Marx, 2013; Tinati, Halford, Carr, & Pope, 2014, p. 673; Zimmer, 2010). The boundaries between private and public information—especially on the internet—are frustratingly ambiguous, contested and changing (Markham & Buchanan, 2012, p. 6; Ess, 2007, p. 499; see also Rooke, 2013; Rosenberg 2010; Weeden, 2012, pp. 42-43). Even when a researcher wants to have participants' informed consent to take part in a study, it might be impossible for him or her to obtain it if the research in question concerns, for example, massive data mining processes and projects. Moreover, big data researchers often ignore the whole question of informed consent because they define their data as either public or proprietary (Paolillo, 2015, p. 49). Also, when there is no direct contact between the researchers and their human subjects it is questionable whether the subjects should even be called participants. Besides, when experiments are made on them, it is unclear whether they are to be subject to the same ethical research scrutiny as human-subject study participants normally are (Hutton & Henderson, 2015, p. 178; Kahn, Vayena, & Mastroianni, 2014, p. 13677.). Even if a researcher did in such cases manage to obtain the participants' consent, there would be no real guarantee that it was indeed informed (Flick, 2016, p. 15-17).

To problematize the issue further, even if informed consent was verified and the researcher was allowed to use the participants' personal data, the data might also include information about people (e.g. contacts of the users) who had not given their informed consent (Phillips, 2011, p. 32). Thus it is no surprise that a large number of extensive data mining projects are carried out without informing the groups or individuals targeted by the researchers; the only measure taken to promote the ethicality of the research is making sure that the participants are anonymous, thus ensuring confidentiality (Lindsay & Goldring, 2010; Zwitter, 2014, p. 5; see also Sormanen et al., 2016).

In contrast, when conducting qualitative research like virtual ethnography or, more specifically, participant observation, in smaller internet forums, obtaining the consent of participants is technically relatively easy. However, it is rarely done because of the possibility that knowing that they are being observed might cause participants to act differently from usual, which would skew the data. Then again, in practice, many scholars do not seek informed consent because they are afraid it would be denied (e.g. Hine, 2000, pp. 23-24.). Sometimes participant observation even without consent is impossible (e.g. in the case of private discussion groups), so the researcher might engage in deception (e.g. an invented alias) in order to gain access to the group of participants. As Brotsky and Giles (2007, pp. 95-96) put what is indeed rather obvious, covert participant observation is "highly controversial from an ethical position", but as in most completed research projects with ethical research challenges, it is ultimately justified by reference to the benefits brought by the results. Sometimes even informed consent does not create an authentic consensual atmosphere, for example if the subjects of the research do not feel they have been treated fairly or if the purpose of the research is not felt to be morally valuable enough (Kennedy, Elgesem, & Miguel, 2015). Lastly, even if informed consent is received, there is the problem of the level of informedness. How can a researcher be sure that the

[4] The author danah boyd wants her name to be written in lower case.

research subject has sufficiently understood the purpose and the consequences of the research? (E.g. Escobedo, Guerrero, Lujan, Ramirez, & Serrano, 2007; Svanteson, 2007, p. 72.)

3. The Facebook Experiment as Manipulation

On Facebook, the News Feed is practically a list of status updates of the contacts in a user's network. The updates shown in or omitted from the News Feed depend on "a ranking algorithm that Facebook continually develops and tests in the interest of showing viewers the content they will find most relevant and engaging". Facebook is thus like any traditional media as it provides content to its users selectively, but where it differs from the old media is that the content is modified individually according to what the medium evaluates to be the optimally engaging experience. (Kramer et al., 2014, p. 8788.) Users accept this practice when signing up for Facebook.

In their massive-scale experiment, Kramer et al. (2014) tested the emotional engagement of Facebook users by modifying their News Feed. The "experiment on the manipulative power of Facebook feeds", as Peacock (2014, p. 8) described it, was criticized almost immediately upon publication of the article. Bloggers claimed Facebook made users "sad for a psych experiment" (Grimmelmann, 2014) or the company was using people as "lab rats" (a blogger quoted by Rushe, 2014). According to *The Guardian*'s poll (Fishwick, 2014), most people who read about the experiment were not surprised that Facebook would experiment on user data the way it did but, at the same time, they declared they had now "lost trust" in Facebook and were considering closing their account. The "secret" experiment, as *The Guardian* called it, "sparked outrage from people who felt manipulated by the company". It can be speculated that had Facebook known what the public reaction to their experiment was going to be, they would not have published it. danah boyd (2014; see also Paolillo, 2015, p. 49) suggests that the intended PR outcome of the experiment from Facebook's point of view was to show that Facebook can downplay negative content in their service and thus make customers happier. Presumably this was seen as better for users and better for Facebook, as experimentation is how websites make their services better (Halavais, 2015, pp. 689-690; Kahn et al., 2014, p. 13677).

It is possible that many people missed the benevolent intention of the research team and concentrated on the contestable ethics of their method. The criticism about the experiment reached such levels that Facebook's researcher and the first author of the article, Adam Kramer, defended the experiment in his own Facebook page, pointing to the minimal "actual impact on people". During the week of the experiment, he explained, the users who were affected "produced an average of one fewer emotional word, per thousand words". (Kramer, 2014.) The magnitude of the impact was perhaps unknown to many critics of the experiment, as many objected to it on the grounds that Facebook was "controlling the emotions" of its users. Moreover, regardless of the magnitude of the impact of the experiment, the user agreement of Facebook can be interpreted to mean that users of Facebook allow researchers to experiment on them.

Thus, many ethicists would agree with Meyer (2014), who published a statement with five co-authors and on behalf of 27 other ethicists "to disagree with these sweeping condemnations" of Facebook's ethics in the experiment. She wrote that "the experiment was controversial, but it was not an egregious breach of either ethics or law." If Facebook is permitted to mine user data and study users for personal profit but academics are not permitted to use that information and learn from it, it "makes no one better off" (Meyer, 2014). However, for many critics it was more a matter of ethical principle than actual impact. For example, Kleinsman and Buckley (2015, p. 180) rejected Meyer's statement and claimed that "[i]f an experiment is in 'breach of either ethics or law,' then whether it is an 'egregious' breach or not is irrelevant." In this view, there is no grey area in research ethics, and consequently, a person as a subject of research is—in a binary way—either harmed or not harmed.

Many scholars were even more critical than Kleinsman and Buckley (2015). Recuber (2016), for example, noted how quick scholars were to draw analogies between the Facebook experiment and the infamous Milgram's (1963) experiment analyzing obedience to authority, as well as to the Stanford Prison experiment, also known as the Zimbardo experiment (Haney, Banks, & Zimbardo, 1973; Zimbardo, 1973), that studied the psychological effects of becoming a prisoner or a guard. According to Recuber, there were indeed some similarities between the Facebook experiment and the two notorious experiments from the 1960s, one being the fact that all three studied the researchers' ability to manipulate change in the participants' behavior. However, the Facebook experiment was different in its failure to reflect on this aspect (Recuber, 2016, pp. 46-47). The user reactions studied in the Facebook experiment were caused by the observers but the power relations between the experimenters and the experimentees were downplayed or normalized, and not at all problematized. This, at least to Recuber, is a typical and insidious element of contemporary big data research. (Recuber, 2016.) When the number of research subjects is so high, individually they tend to vanish in the haze of the overarching term "big data". However, the "power" exerted per capita over the participants in the Facebook experiment can be viewed as rather minimal (albeit massive in scale). The experiments carried out by Milgram and Zimbardo, on the other hand, caused their participants to suffer severe physical and psychological stress.

The ethics of human-subject research is mainly about protecting the subject. In this sense, the Facebook experiment was found ethically questionable. Strict assessments of the experiment conclude that the study indeed "harmed" its participants (albeit almost unnoticeably), because it changed the participants' mood (e.g. Bryman & Bell, 2015, p. 141; Grimmelmann, 2014; Kleisman & Buckley, 2015, p. 181). However, if harming is defined as changing a participant's mood, then a vast quantity of empirical research on humans is harmful, especially research that requires face-to-face interaction. In general, big data studies or techniques to test or predict personality or actions might not be legally problematic but they do undermine a "sense of individuality on a personal level", claims Schroeder (2014, p. 7).

Facebook has experimented on its users before, and has published research about it (see e.g. Bond et al., 2012; Chan, 2015, p. 1081; Simonite, 2012). However, these experiments were explicit in their intention to influence users. For example, in 2010 on the day of the US congressional elections, Facebook encouraged randomly assigned users to vote, managed to increase voting activity, and afterwards published an article about it in *Nature* (Bond et al., 2012). Moreover, in 2012 Mark Zuckerberg, the CEO of Facebook, used Facebook to encourage people to register as organ donors, after which organ donor enrollment increased significantly in the US (Simonite, 2012). These forms of "manipulation" did not raise as much ethical debate as the experiment we discuss here did. The reason for this might be that people see explicit forms of intended manipulation as more acceptable than covert forms, even if the explicit manipulation attempts to elicit significantly greater change in the subject than the covert form.

Research ethics are often implemented more strictly in the academic world than in the corporate research environment. Then again, the ethical views of social media users might be quite flexible, and a lot of how users relate to being studied and experimented on by researchers depends on the application of the results (Kennedy et al. 2015, pp. 8-10). It seems like people do not want to be experimented on for the sake of an experiment but they are more likely to accept it if the experiment might result in some kind of benefit for themselves or others. Many people also do not mind commercials or other manipulations—even outright propaganda—as they are often part of the deal between users and service providers (cf. Searls 2015 on ad blockers). In the case of the Facebook experiment, even though scholars did not read any status updates, some people still felt that their privacy was violated. The problem in these kinds of cases is often the fact that one has a feeling of being private while actually being public (Kennedy et al., 2015, p. 13). According to Chan (2015, p. 1080), the fact that neither Facebook nor Cornell University—the two parties involved in conducting the study—apparently anticipated the public backlash they would face for the data manipulation shows "the vast disconnect between the research culture of big data (whether based in corporate or academic institutions) and the general public's cultural expectations."

4. The Problem of Informed Consent

It is the "informed" in informed consent that is the other major ethical research issue in the experiment that worried both the general public and academia (see e.g. Kahn et al., 2014, p. 13677). Cornell University researchers (Guillory and Hancock) analyzed the data after Facebook (Kramer) had collected them. The study therefore did not go through an ethical review at Cornell University, which might have been critical of how the informed consent of the participants was going to be secured (Paolillo, 2015, p. 50). In the article, research ethics is discussed in two sentences (Kramer et al., 2014, p. 8789). The first sentence states that the researchers themselves did not read any of the texts analyzed for the experiment as a linguistic software program was used to analyze the data. The other sentence declares that the data collection "was consistent with Facebook's Data Use Policy, to which all users agree prior to creating an account on Facebook, constituting informed consent for this research." In other words, the authors interpreted Facebook's user agreement to mean informed consent.

In that case, the level of informedness is highly debatable, as most users of Facebook do not read or completely understand the data use policy (Flick, 2016, p. 17; see also Kennedy et al., 2015, pp. 10-15). When a user accepts the terms and signs up for Facebook, he or she is informed that the service provider will use the personal data for all sorts of things (Facebook, 2015a). The user might give their consent but is most likely not well informed, since the description of the data use policy is not very precise (see e.g. Grady, 2015, p. 885; Sloan, Morgan, Burnap, & Williams, 2014, p. 16.). For example, at the time of the experiment, the research use of personal data was not mentioned although, following the wide publicity the experiment received, it has subsequently been added to the policy.

Kleisman and Buckley (2015; see also Bail, 2015, p. 23) hold the view that because the authors of the Facebook experiment could have asked for proper informed consent from the users, they should have done so. It does not matter whether the research is unlikely to cause harm or if it is beneficial or otherwise important: consent is always essential if it can be obtained. The scholars should at least have informed those users who were affected afterwards (Recuber, 2016, p. 54; see also McKelvey, Tiessen, & Simcoe, 2015, pp. 580-581). A month after the publication of the experiment, *PNAS*'s Editor-in-Chief, Inder M. Verma (2014), added a foreword to the contested article. It was entitled "Editorial Expression of Concern and Correction" and it defended the authors' ethical choices by separating Facebook's data collection process from the actions of Cornell University. Readers were reminded that it was a non-academic private company (= Facebook's Kramer) that gathered the data, and the academics (= Cornell's Guillory and Hancock) only analyzed them. However, as the responsibility fell partly on the journal (see e.g. Kahn et al., 2014, p. 13679), Verma (2014, p. 10779; see also Schroeder, 2014, pp. 2-3) did concede that perhaps everything was "not fully consistent with the principles of obtaining informed consent and allowing people to opt out."

Many human-subject big data scientists know that a strict interpretation of the opting-out option makes their research extremely difficult. The problem is further complicated by the fact that in many cases the data are not collected by academics but by third parties such as Facebook. Should the data collectors abide by the ethical research norms of academia? If they did, there would be a lot of ethical problems, particularly with data produced by third parties, such as filmed footage, photographs, Google Street View data, televised rock concert recordings, and so on. Even if participant anonymity was secured, the human subjects in these cases could not opt out. If scholars did not have to worry about opting out as an ethical norm, they could team up with someone outside of academia to do their "dirty work" (see e.g. Kahn et al., 2014, p. 13677; Wrzus & Mehl, 2015, p. 264; cf. boyd, 2014.). On the other hand, one could say that a person can opt out of any Facebook experiment by not signing up for Facebook in the first place—just like a potential participant in a psychology experiment can decide not to attend the experiment if he or she does not want to be manipulated.

In general, an ethically pragmatic social media user's informed consent is more like meta-informedness, or "implicit informed consent" (Bryman & Bell, 2015, p. 139), where the user knows that for example Facebook will do various known and unknown things with its user data but is unlikely to do anything that is morally too dubious—although it has been observed that users tend to underestimate the level of their privacy when they are excited about a social media application (Kehr, Kowatsch, Wentzel, & Fleisch, 2015). For most users, Facebook's data policy is thus a reasonably informed and fair trade-off between the user who gets to use the service without a fee, and the service provider who gets to sell the data to third parties such as advertisers (Kennedy et al., 2015, p. 12; see also Hutton & Henderson, 2015, p. 178). This is actually the common logic of commercial media, and the "ethical fig leaf" (O'Hara, Nguyen, & Haynes, 2014, p. 4) of a social media researcher.

As Chan (2015, p. 1080; see also Aiken & Mahon, 2014, p. 4) notes, Facebook's data use policy "enables any user to potentially become an experiment subject without need for prior consent". In the end, a scholar interested in research ethics might ask if there is anything ethically new in the Facebook experiment. People were studied without their knowing about it but they had allowed it by signing up for Facebook. (Schroeder, 2014, p. 3; see also Zwitter, 2014, p. 1.) Certainly companies have been doing experiments with only vaguely informed consent before, as have psychologists, so many people think the Facebook experiment is merely a recent example of an old ethical research issue (Schroeder, 2014, pp. 1-2; cf. Selinger & Hartzhog, 2016).

In a way, the Facebook user agreement is similar to the informed consent form the participants in most psychological experiments have to fill out. Participants are informed that they (and the data they will produce) will be used for scientific purposes but the participant might not know exactly what those purposes are. He or she might even be deceived about the real purpose of the study to which they have consented. The message of informed consent is, "I trust you. Do what is needed." Perhaps the only new aspect in this case is that there are over a billion people on Facebook every day. It is an essential networking tool for a large amount of people, many of whom are dependent (to a greater or lesser extent) on the service. This means that its user agreement is not necessarily an ethical act between two equal parties: opting out of an experiment becomes equal to opting out of a significant part of one's social life (see e.g. Gertz, 2016). One might therefore suggest that a participant might be sufficiently informed but the question of consent is more controversial.

After multiple critical reviews of the experiment, Mike Schroepfer, the Chief Technology Officer for Facebook, wrote an apologetic post for Facebook's Newsroom. According to him, they should have "considered non-experimental ways" to do the research. Also, the research would have "benefited from more extensive review by a wider and more senior group of people". Schroepher also notes that they did not inform the public about the experiment well enough (Schroepfer, 2014). Schroepher also introduced a new framework of research that Facebook is going to implement. It included clearer guidelines for researchers, a more extensive review stage, and training (including on privacy and security matters), as well as the establishment of a special research website (Facebook, 2015b).

Describing the new guidelines section, Schroepher announced that a more enhanced review process would be conducted prior to research if the intended research focused on "studying particular groups or populations (such as people of a certain age) or if it related to content that may be considered deeply personal (such as emotions)." Also, a further review would be conducted if there was any collaboration with the academic community. The statement ends with trying to convince the reader—supposedly a daily Facebook user—that Facebook wants to do research "in a way that honors the trust you put in us by using Facebook every day." (Schroepher, 2014.) This seems to be Facebook's way of admitting that the experiment lacked informed consent. Perhaps for PR reasons as well as due to potential legal issues, Schroepher could not say outright that the experiment failed to obtain informed consent (cf. Verma, 2014).

5. Discussion

In this article we have shown how the debate around the Facebook experiment brings up two crucial and interrelated themes of research ethics: research as manipulation, and the problem of informed consent. The debate around the experiment shows that the era of big data research demands some rethinking of research ethics. Although the two key issues presented here are not unique to contemporary research but had been debated for decades before big data research came in (see e.g. Faden & Beauchamp, 1986; Roelcke, 2004), the unprecedentedly large amount of human subjects that are called for in such research has led to a need for special scrutiny. At the same time, it seems that the ethical evaluation of such experiments is based on the classical ethical stances of utilitarianism or deontology. The proponent of the former sees little or no harm done in such an experiment and no loss of happiness caused by it, while the proponent of the latter considers that, regardless of the degree of actual harm, human integrity has been violated (see e.g. Ess, 2013, pp. 256-262; Harman & Cornelius, 2015, p. 58; Shrader-Frechette, 2000).

Reaching any ethical consensus about the Facebook experiment is further impeded by disagreements over the definition of key concepts such as the "harm" done to human subjects, and their "informed consent". When academic research ethics is so vague, it might seem simpler for scholars to leave it to the law and user agreements to define the ethics of the research. However, according to Chan (2015, p. 1082; see also Paolillo, 2015, p. 50; Burgess & Bruns, 2015, p. 99), commercial companies' ethical research standards should not be allowed to spread to the academic world. Flick (2016; see also Halavais, 2015, p. 592) agrees and thinks that the commercial and academic sectors should negotiate and agree on standards, but without making any concessions in the commercial companies' favor. However, as universities' opportunities to cooperate with private companies working with big data increase, the opportunities to leave the problematic ethics of data collection to companies increase likewise.

Mike Schroepher, the Chief Technology Officer of Facebook, stated that Facebook should have communicated "clearly why and how" they did the experiment (Schroepfer, 2014). The statement implies that a person is deprived of optimal well-being if the reasons and methods of any actions carried out on him or her are not properly communicated. On the other hand, one could easily claim the opposite: a person suffers less when he or she does not know or notice anything about such actions. As Stilgoe (2015, pp. 46-47) observes, the Facebook experiment was rare in being openly published and publicly scrutinized, since most such experiments are conducted in secret. We can wonder if people were outraged about the experiment because Facebook altered its users' states of mind or because it reminded them that their states of mind are being altered all the time by all kinds of things, people and organizations (see e.g. boyd, 2016; see also Kehr et al., 2015).

At the same time, Kennedy et al. (2015, p. 2) observe that there has been little research about what social media users themselves actually think about being observed, studied and—we would add—experimented on. This is rather disconcerting, given the massive number of people that use social media and are in some form or other observed and experimented on by researchers. Perhaps surprisingly, the social media users Kennedy et al. (2015, pp. 3-4) studied seemed to be concerned about privacy, but mainly about social privacy. That is, they wanted to be sure that they could choose which individuals in their network have access to their personal information. They were not so worried about institutional privacy, or "the mining of personal information by social media platforms, commercial companies and governments". Although we are talking about only one study, there is reason to suggest that the ethical criticism of the Facebook experiment made by academics might not reflect users' worries. This is a topic that should be further studied, as it would be relevant for research ethics in the era of social media to be more grounded in the user level. A more holistic and inclusive ethical research study would ensure that researchers do more than define what is morally optimal in big data research; or, as Tama Leaver (2013) states, "Big Data needs Big Ethics, and we don't have them yet."

If we go further into the ethical implications of social media experiments that aim to enhance user experience, we are faced with a more profound ethical challenge than a discussion of manipulation and informed consent reveals. If in Facebook we are fed imagery that further filters our experiences of the "real" world, then what are the ethical ramifications of researchers teaming up with companies that aim to give people "the experience they want" (Simonite, 2012)? Would the companies be in charge of the "hard ethical choice...of what content to show...without oversight, transparency, or informed consent" (boyd, 2014)? The way media and new media influence our perceptions of reality has already been widely studied (e.g. Fairclough, 1995; Macey, Ryan, & Springer, 2014) but there has been little consideration so far of the ethics of academics taking part in these kinds of studies.

The way big data is "all at once essential, valuable, difficult to control, and ubiquitous" seems to be reflected in our complex, context-dependent attitudes toward it (Pushcmann & Burgess, 2014, p. 1695). Gertz (2016, p. 56) notes that despite the Facebook controversy, the number of Facebook users is still growing. At the same time, users' autonomy seems to be diminishing. From this it can be concluded that many users do not mind the asymmetrical relationship they have with the service provider. As Ess (2013, p. 254) notes, "our engagements with new digital media appear to bring in their wake important transformations in our sense of self and identity." Our "foundational conception of autonomous self" that has legitimated concepts of privacy that "modern liberal-democratic" states respect seems to be changing. Perhaps the question we should ask is primarily existential rather than ethical, as Gertz (2016, p. 61) suggests. According to him, we should first think about the increasingly significant role technology plays in our lives. If we accept it, then we can have a more meaningful discussion on the ethics of scholars experimenting with it.

Conflict of Interests

The authors declare no conflict of interests.

References

Aiken, M., & McMahon, C. (2014). A primer of research in mediated environments: Reflections on cybermethodology. *SSRN Working Papers*. Retrieved from http://papers.ssrn.com/sol3/Papers.cfm?abstract_id=2462700

Ananny, M. (2015). Toward an ethics of algorithms: Convening, observation, probability, and timeliness. *Science, Technology, and Human Values*, *4*(1), 93-117.

Bail, C. A. (2015). Taming big data: Using app technology to study organizational behavior on social media. *Sociological Methods & Research*. Retrieved from http://smr.sagepub.com/content/early/2015/05/15/0049124115587825.full

Barsade, S. (2002). The ripple effect. Emotional contagion and its influence on group behavior. *Administrative Science Quarterly, 47*(4), 644-675.

Bond, R. M., Fariss, C. J., Jones, J. J., Kramer, A. D. I., Marlow, C., Settle, J. E., & Fowler, J. H. (2012). A 61-million-person experiment in social influence and political mobilization. *Nature*, *489*(7415), 295-298.

boyd, d. (2010, April). *Publicity and privacy in web 2.0.* Keynote speech at WWW2010, Raleigh, USA. Retrieved from www.danah.org/papers/talks/2010/SXSW2010.html

boyd, d. (2014). What does the Facebook experiment teach us? Growing anxiety about data manipulation. *The Message*. Retrieved from https://medium.com/message/what-does-the-facebook-experiment-teach-us-c858c08e287f

boyd, d. (2016). Untangling research and practice: What Facebook's "emotional contagion" study teaches us. *Research Ethics*, *12*(1), 4-13.

The British Psychological Society (2010). *Code of human research ethics.* Leicester: The British Psychological Society. Retrieved from www.bps.org.uk/sites/default/files/documents/code_of_human_research_ethics.pdf

Brotsky, S. R., & Giles, D. (2007). Inside the "Pro-ana" community: A covert online participant observation. *Eating Disorders: The Journal of Treatment & Prevention*, *15*(2), 93-109.

Bryman, A., & Bell, E. (2015). *Business research methods*. Oxford: Oxford University Press.

Burgess, J., & Bruns, A. (2015). Easy data, hard data: The politics and pragmatics of Twitter research after the computational turn. In G. Langlois, J. Redden, & G. Elmer (Eds.), *Compromised data: From social media to big data* (pp. 93-111). New York: Bloomsbury Academic.

Card, N. A. (2010). Literature review. In N. J. Salkind (Ed.), *Encyclopedia of research design* (pp. 726-729). Thousand Oaks: Sage.

Ceserani, R. (2010). The essayistic style of Walter Benjamin. *Primerjalna književnost*, *33*(1), 83-92.

Chan, A. (2015). Big data interfaces and the problem of inclusion. *Media, Culture & Society*, *37*(7), 1078-1083.

Cheng, J., Adamic, L. A., Dow, P. A., Kleinberg, J., & Leskovec, J. (2014). Can cascades be predicted? *Proceedings of the 23rd International Conference on World Wide Web* (pp. 925-936). New York: ACM. Retrieved from http://dl.acm.org/citation.cfm?id=2567997

Copeland, L. (2011). The anti-social network. *Slate.* Retrieved from www.slate.com/articles/double_x/doublex/2011/01/the_antisocial_network.html

Cornelissen, J., Gajewskade, M., Piekkari, R., & Welch, C. (2012). Writing up as a legitimacy seeking process: Alternative publishing recipes for qualitative research. In S. Gillian & C. Cassel (Eds.), *Qualitative organizational research: Core methods and current challenges* (pp. 185-203). London: Sage.

Escobedo, C., Guerrero, J., Lujan, G., Ramirez, A., & Serrano, D. (2007). Ethical issues with informed consent. *Bio-Ethics*, *1*, 1-8. Retrieved from http://cstep.cs.utep.edu/research/ezine/Ezine-ethicalIssueswithInformedConsent.pdf

Ess, C. M. (2007). Internet research ethics. In A. Joinson (Ed.), *Oxford handbook of internet psychology* (pp. 481-502). Oxford: Oxford University Press.

Ess, C. M. (2013). Global media ethics? Issues, requirements, challenges, resolutions. In S. J. A. Ward (Ed.), *Global media ethics: Problems and perspectives* (pp. 253-271). West Sussex: Wiley-Blackwell.

Facebook (2015a). *Terms of service*. Retrieved from www.facebook.com/terms.php

Facebook (2015b). *Research at Facebook*. Retrieved from https://research.facebook.com

Faden, R. R., & Beauchamp, T. L. (1986). *A History and theory of informed consent*. Oxford: Oxford University Press.

Fairclough, N. 1995. *Media discourse*. London: Bloomsbury.

Ferrara, E., & Yang, Z. (2015). Measuring emotional contagion in social media. *PloS ONE*, *10*(11). Retrieved from http://journals.plos.org/plosone/article?id=10.1371/journal.pone.0142390

Fishwick, C. (2014, June 30). Facebook's secret mood experiment: Have you lost trust in the social network? *The Guardian*. Retrieved from www.theguardian.com/technology/poll/2014/jun/30/facebook-secret-mood-experiment-social-network

Flick, C. (2016). Informed consent and the Facebook emotional manipulation study. *Research Ethics*, *12*(1), 14-28.

Friggeri, A., Adamic, L. A., Eckles, D., & Cheng, J. (2014). Rumor cascades. *Proceedings of the Eighth International AAAI Conference on Weblogs and Social Media (ICWSM)* (pp. 101-110). Palo Alto, CA: AAAI Press. Retrieved from www.aaai.org/ocs/index.php/ICWSM/ICWSM14/paper/view/8122

Gertz, N. (2016). Autonomy online: Jacques Ellul and the Facebook emotional manipulation study. *Research Ethics*, *12*(1), 55-61.

Grady, C. (2015). Enduring and emerging challenges of informed consent. *The New England Journal of Medicine*, *372*(9), 855-862.

Grimmelmann, J. (2014). As flies to wanton boys. *The Laboratorium*. Retrieved from http://laboratorium.net/archive/2014/06/28/as_flies_to_wanton_boys

Halavais, A. (2015). Bigger sociological imaginations: Framing big social data theory and methods. *Information, Communication & Society*, *18*(5), 583-594.

Haney, C., Banks, C., & Zimbardo, P. (1973). A study of prisoners and guards in a simulated prison. *Naval Research Reviews*, *30*(9), 4-17.

Harman, L. B., & Cornelius, F. (2015). *Ethical health informatics*. Burlington, MA: Jones & Bartlett.

Harriman, S., & Patel, J. (2014). The ethics and editorial challenges of internet-based research. *MBC Medicine*, *12*, 124-127.

Hesse, B. W., Moser, R. P., & Riley, W. T. (2015). From big data to knowledge in the social sciences. *The Annals of American Academy of Political and Social Science*, *659*(1), 16-32.

Hine, C. (2000). *Virtual ethnography*. London: Sage.

Hudson, J. M., & Bruckman, A. (2004). Go away: Participant objections to being studied and the ethics of chatroom research. *The Information Society*, *20*(2), 127-139.

Huntsinger, J. R., Lun, J., Sinclair, S., & Clore, G. L. (2009). Contagion without contact: Anticipatory mood matching in response to affiliative motivation. *Personality and Social Psychology Bulletin*, *35*(7), 909-922.

Hutton, L., & Henderson, T. (2015). "I didn't sign up for this!": Informed consent in social network research. *Proceedings of the Ninth International AAAI Conference on Web and Social Media (ICWSM)* (pp. 178-187). Palo Alto, CA: AAAI Publications. Retrieved from www.aaai.org/ocs/index.php/ICWSM/ICWSM15/paper/view/10493

Jouhki, J., Lauk, E., Penttinen, M., Rohila, J., Sormanen, N., & Uskali, T. (2015, November). *Social media personhood as a challenge to research ethics: Exploring the case of the Facebook experiment*. Paper presented at the Social Media Research Symposium, Jyväskylä, Finland.

Kahn, J. P., Vayena, E., & Mastroianni, A. C. (2014). Opinion: Learning as we go: Lessons from the publication of Facebook's social-computing research. *Proceedings of the National Academy of Sciences of the United States of America*, *111*(38), 13677-13679.

Kehr, F., Kowatsch, T., Wentzel, D., & Fleisch, E. (2015). Blissfully ignorant: The effects of general privacy concerns, general institutional trust, and affect in the privacy calculus. *Information Systems Journal*, *25*, 607-635.

Kennedy, H., Elgesem, D., & Miguel, C. (2015). On fairness: User perspectives on social media data mining. *Convergence: The International Journal of Research into New Media Technologies*. Retrieved from http://con.sagepub.com/content/early/2015/06/26/1354856515592507.full

Kleinsman, J., & Buckley, S. (2015). Facebook study. A little bit unethical but worth it? *Journal of Bioethical Inquiry*, *12*(2), 179-182.

Kramer, A. (2014). A post on 29.6.2014. *Facebook*. Retrieved from www.facebook.com/akramer/posts/10152987150867796

Kramer, A. D. I., Guillory, J. E., & Hancock, J. T. (2014). Experimental evidence of massive-scale emotional contagion through social networks. *Proceedings of the National Academy of Sciences of the United States of America*, *111*(24), 8788-8790.

Leaver, T. (2013, September). *Birth, death and Facebook*. Paper presented at Adventures in Culture in Technology (ACAT) Seminar Series, Perth. Retrieved from www.tamaleaver.net/2013/10/03/birth-death-and-facebook

Lindsay, S., & Goldring, J. (2010). Anonymizing data for secondary use. In A. J. Mills, G. Durepos, & E. Wiebe (Eds.), *Encyclopedia of case study research* (pp. 25-27). London: Sage.

Macey, D. A., Ryan, K. M., & Springer, N. J. (Eds.). (2014). *How television shapes our worldview: Media representations of social trends and change*. New York: Lexington Books.

Markham, A., & Buchanan, E. (2012). *Ethical decision-making and Internet research. Recommendations from the AoIR ethics working committee (version 2.0).* Chicago: Association of Internet Researchers. Retrieved from http://aoir.org/reports/ethics2.pdf

Marx, G. T. (2013). An ethics for the new (and old) surveillance. In F. Flammini, R. Stola, & G. Franceschetti (Eds.), *Effective surveillance for homeland security: Balancing technology and social issues* (pp. 2-20). Boca Raton, FL: Taylor & Francis.

McKelvey, F., Tiessen, M., & Simcoe, L. (2015). A consensual hallucination no more? The Internet as simulation machine. *European Journal of Cultural Studies, 18*(4-5), 577-594.

Meyer, M. N. (2014). Misjudgments will drive social trials underground. *Nature, 511*(7509), 265.

Milgram, S. (1963). Behavioral study of obedience. *Journal of Abnormal and Social Psychology, 67*(4), 371-378.

O'Hara, K., Nguyen, M.-H. C., & Haynes, P. (2014). Introduction. In K. O'Hara, M.-H. C. Nguyen, & P. Haynes (Eds.), *Digital enlightenment yearbook 2014: Social networks and social machines, surveillance and empowerment* (pp. 3-24). Amsterdam: IOS Press.

Paolillo, J. C. (2015). Network analysis. In A. Georgakopoulou & T. Spilioti (Eds.), *The Routledge handbook of language and digital communication* (pp. 36-54). London: Routledge.

Parkinson, B., & Manstead, A. S. R. (2015). Current emotion research in social psychology: Thinking about emotions and other people. *Emotion Review, 7*(4), 371-380.

Peacock, S. E. (2014). How web tracking changes user agency in the age of Big Data: The used user. *Big Data & Society, 1*(2), 1-11. Retrieved from http://bds.sagepub.com/content/1/2/2053951714564228

Pejovic, V., & Musolesi, M. (2015). Anticipatory mobile computing. A survey of the state of the art and research challenges. *ACM Computing Surveys, 47*(3), 1-29.

Phillips, M. L. (2011). Using social media in your research. Experts explore the practicalities of observing human behavior through Facebook and Twitter. *gradPSYCH, 9*(4), 32.

Recuber, T. (2016). From obedience to contagion: Discourses of power in Milgram, Zimbardo, and the Facebook experiment. *Research Ethics, 12*(1), 44-54.

Roelcke, V. (2004). Introduction: Historical perspectives on human subjects research during the 20th century, and some implications for present day issues in bioethics. In V. Roelcke & G. Maio (Eds.), *Twentieth century ethics of human subjects research: Historical perspectives on values, practices, and regulations* (pp. 11-18). Stuttgart: Franz Steiner Verlag.

Rooke, B. (2013). Four pillars of internet research ethics with Web 2.0. *Journal of Academic Ethics, 11*(4), 265-268.

Rosenberg, Å. (2010). Virtual world research ethics and the private/public distinction. *International Journal of Internet Research Ethics, 3*(1), 23-37.

Rushe, D. (2014, October 2) Facebook sorry—almost—for secret psychological experiment on users. *The Guardian.* Retrieved from www.theguardian.com/technology/2014/oct/02/facebook-sorry-secret-psychological-experiment-users

Schroeder, R. (2014). Big Data and the brave new world of social media research. *Big Data & Society, 1*(2), 1-11.

Searls, D. (2015, November 6). Ad blockers and the next chapter of the Internet. *Harvard Business Review.* Retrieved from https://hbr.org/2015/11/ad-blockers-and-the-next-chapter-of-the-internet

Selinger, E., & Hartzog, W. (2016). Facebook's emotional contagion study and the ethical problem of co-opted identity in mediated environments where users lack control. *Research Ethics, 12*(1), 35-43.

Shah, D. V., Cappella, J. N., & Neuman, W. R. (2015). Big data, digital media, and computational social science: Possibilities and perils. *The Annals of the American Academy of Political and Social Science, 659*(1), 6-13.

Shrader-Frechette, K. (2000). *Ethics of scientific research.* London: Rowman & Littlefield.

Simon, J. R. (2014). Corporate research ethics: Whose responsibility? *Annals of Internal Medicine, 161*(12), 917-918.

Simonite, T. (2012, June 13). What Facebook knows. *MIT Technology Review.* Retrieved from www.technologyreview.com/s/428150/what-facebook-knows

Sloan, L., Morgan, J., Burnap, P., & Williams, M. (2014). Who tweets? Deriving the demographic characteristics of age, occupation and social class from Twitter user meta-data. *LloS ONE*, 10(3), 1-20.

Sormanen, N., Rohila J., Lauk, E., Uskali T., Jouhki J., & Penttinen M. (2016). Chances and challenges of computational data gathering and analysis: The case of issue-attention cycles on Facebook. *Digital Journalism, 4*(1), 55-74.

Stilgoe, J. (2015). *Experiment earth: Responsible innovation in Geoengineering.* London: Routledge.

Summers-Effler, E., Van Ness, J., & Hausmann, C. (2015). Peeking in the black box: Studying, theorizing, and representing the micro-foundations of day-to-day interactions. *Journal of Contemporary Ethnography, 44* (4), 450-479.

Sun, E., Rosenn, I., Marlow, C., & Lento, T. (2009). Gesundheit! Modeling contagion through Facebook news feed. *Proceedings of the Third International ICWSM Conference* (pp. 146-153). Palo Alto, CA: AAAI Publications. Retrieved from http://aaai.org/ocs/index.php/ICWSM/09/paper/view/185

Svanteson, D. J. B. (2007). *Private international law and the Internet.* Alphen aan den Rijn: Kluwer Law International.

Thorson, K., & Wells, C. (2015). Curated flows: A framework for mapping media exposure in the digital age. *Communication Theory*. Retrieved from http://ssc.sagepub.com/content/early/2015/10/19/0894439315609528.refs

Tinati, R., Halford, S., Carr, L., & Pope, C. 2014. Big data: Methodological challenges and approaches for sociological analysis. *Sociology*, *48*(4), 663-681.

Torraco, R. J. (2005). Writing integrative literature reviews: Guidelines and examples. *Human Resource Development Review*, *4*(3), 356-367.

Vainio, A. (2012). Beyond research ethics: Anonymity as 'ontology', 'analysis' and 'independence'. *Qualitative Research*, *13*(6), 685-698.

Vanderpool, H. Y. (1996). *The ethics of research involving human subjects: Facing the 21st century.* Frederick: University Publishing Group.

Verma, I. M. (2014). Editorial expression of concern and correction. *Proceedings of the National Academy of Sciences*, *111*(29), 10779.

Weeden, M. R. (2012). Ethics and on-line research methodology. *Journal of Social Work Values and Ethics*, *9*(1), 40-51.

Wrzus, C., & Mehl, M. R. (2015). Lab and/or field? Measuring personality processes and their social consequences. *European Journal of Personality*, *29*(2), 250-271.

Zimbardo, P. (1973). On the ethics of intervention in human psychological research: With special reference to the Stanford prison experiment. *Cognition*, *2*(2), 243-256.

Zimmer, M. (2010). "But the data is already public": On the ethics of research in Facebook. *Ethics and Information Technology*, *12*(4), 313-325.

Zwitter, A. (2014). Big Data ethics. *Big Data & Society*, *1*(2), 1-6.

16

From Research Ethics to Researching Ethics in an Online Specific Context

Sari Östman * and Riikka Turtiainen

School of History, Culture and Arts Studies, Faculty of Humanities, University of Turku, 28100 Pori, Finland;
E-Mails: sari.ostman@utu.fi (S.Ö.), riikka.turtiainen@utu.fi (R.T.)

* Corresponding author

Abstract

Along with the rise of a research field called digital humanities, online specific research ethics plays an especially significant role. Research on the same (Internet related) topic is usually multidisciplinary, and understanding research ethics even inside the same research community may vary essentially. It is important to recognise and pay attention to online specific contexts as well as the researcher's own disciplinary background. In this empirical research paper, we will first sum up our previous work. Currently, we are working on a model which will help in positioning multidisciplinary researchers as ethical actors based on their research topics and backgrounds. In this article, we will present this model with a demonstration of the empirical data collected as part of a Finnish research project called *Citizen Mindscapes*, which concerns the cultures and history of Finnish discussion forums. We argue that in Finland, and probably also worldwide, online research ethics is in a phase where the focus should be moving from defining the ethical guidelines to studying research ethics as such. We will also discuss how the model will be further developed in an in-depth empirical process.

Keywords

digital culture; digital humanities; Internet; online specific research ethics; online studies; research ethics

Issue

This review is part of the issue "Successes and Failures in Studying Social Media: Issues of Methods and Ethics", edited by Epp Lauk and Niina Sormanen (University of Jyväskylä, Finland).

---

1. Introduction

As an online researcher, how do you understand the ethical research process? Do you work in a field where research ethics is being taught starting the first years of your university studies? Or did you, as a junior researcher, have to stumble your way through your first online specific research process trying to recognise and solve the ethical questions by yourself? Or, maybe you are from a discipline in which ethical questions are not a major concern?

We have worked with research ethics for years; teaching, publishing, developing Finnish understanding about *online specific research ethics* (see Turtiainen & Östman, 2013). In Finland, research ethics and online studies are both quite novel objects to academic interest (Pekkala, 2000). Until now, the ethical interest in Finland has mainly concerned creating guidelines for conducting online-related research. However, such guidelines have existed internationally for at least 15 years (Ess, 2002; Baym & Markham, 2009; Markham & Buchanan, 2012) and the Finnish ones have not differed from those significantly (Kuula, 2006; Turtiainen & Östman, 2009).

In the rise of *digital humanities,* online specific research ethics has also come to a situation where these basic principles become as important as ever. Simultaneously, we need to pay attention to new ethical aspects: digital humanities bring together researchers from multiple various disciplinary backgrounds, which means multiple ethical backgrounds. We work in the project *Citizen Mindscapes* (*CM24*)[1], which brings together researchers, among others, from the following disciplines: sociology, psychology, digital culture, computer science, language technologies, statistics, anthropology and history. All of these researchers have rather varied opinions about which kind of ethics should be followed when studying *Suomi24*, Finland's oldest and largest online discussion forum. Östman is the responsible researcher in a work package, which concerns research ethics. Among the project, we have noticed that in order to create new, multidisciplinary understanding about online specific research ethics, we need to make it so that ethics is the actual object of research. Therefore, we are moving on from our previous work with developing online specific research ethics to *researching online research ethics*. In this report, we question: *Which kind of variety of ethical viewpoints exists in a multidisciplinary, online specific research project?* With this question, we will start mapping the field out for *how the ethics can be studied.*

Our current data is preliminary and comprises 16 answers to an open-answer survey in a project consortium seminar in May 2016. We asked the participants about their disciplinary background, their understanding and experiences of research ethics and the ethical challenges and questions in their current research situation.

While teaching and publishing about research ethics, we have developed certain self-reflexive methods for (novice) online researchers. We understand ethics as passing through the entire research process from choosing the subject to reporting and societal discussion. Therefore, it is also combined with every stage of the process and, in our opinion, especially with source criticism. In this report, we will present one of these methods which combines ethics with source criticism. This is an important aspect in qualitative online research (Baym & Markham, 2009, pp. xii–xv). At the end of the report, we will tie the benefits of this method to our current findings.

First, however, we will discuss the understanding of research ethics among digital humanities. We will consider the linkage between ethics and methodology, especially source criticism. Then, we will present the story-method and 'room board' which reminds one of certain basic principles in online specific research ethics. At the end, we present a model for organising and pre-analysing the data collected from the *CM24* participants. Finally, we will briefly discuss how these findings seem to lead us towards a new ethical paradigm—studying the ethical processes themselves.

[1] The project is funded by the Academy of Finland's Digital Humanities Programme. About this, see: *Academy of Finland grants funding for Citizen Mindscapes in a Social Media project*: https://www.uef.fi/en/-/suomen-akatemia-rahoittaa-kansakunnan-mielenliikkeet-sosiaalisessa-mediassa-tutkimusta

2. Digital Humanities

First, we will briefly introduce the concept of *digital humanities*. The term has gained extensive visibility in the academic societies in the Northern countries during the last couple for years. It was coined in the early 2000s, although it has not been possible to pinpoint it to any specific researcher or discipline. In 2010, however, the Professor of English Literature, William Pannapacker, announced digital humanities to be 'the next big thing' in research, since the digital technology had affected every possible discipline. A year later, he continued this argument on his blog in *The Chronicle of Higher Education* by writing that actually there is no 'next' to that; and, that very soon digital humanities will only be 'the humanities'. (Pannapacker, 2011; see also Spiro, 2012, p. 16). A mere year after that, media and communication researcher David Parry (2010) blogged about how digital humanities would fundamentally challenge all of the current humanistic research.

According to the researchers of digital culture, Jaakko Suominen and Anna Haverinen, holistic change was strongly linked to the discourse about the digital revolution at the end of the 1990s. At that time, several projects were started which, for example, aimed at digitalising humanistic research material. In addition, tools for computer-assisted production and handling of data were developed. (Suominen & Haverinen, 2015).

Digital humanities was evolved in a situation where Western societies have been changing rapidly. It does not have centuries or even decades of tradition, which would have given it a stabilised definition. As Suominen and Haverinen write, it is a discipline—or an era of research—which has been actively developed by researchers. Digital humanities lives and further evolves along with the technologies applied in the current societies. (Suominen & Haverinen, 2015).

There are at least two separate ways of defining digital humanities: for example media theorist Gary Hall as well as media and technology researchers Leighton Evans and Sian Rees see it as humanistic research appropriating information technological methods, which in their opinion is not necessarily a good thing (Evans & Rees, 2012, p. 29; Hall, 2013, pp. 2-3, 133-134; see also Suominen & Haverinen, 2015). The other orientation emphasises a wider understanding about the current, digitalised culture; it includes theorising the digital world more than just applying computer-assisted methods in producing and analysing the materials. (Suominen & Haverinen, 2015). Our understanding follows the latter orientation. In positioning ourselves in the field of digital humanities, we have utilised Suominen and Haverinen's model (Figure 1) for evaluating the relationship of the researcher/research project with digitality. The model is based on the two orientations mentioned above, and on whether the research in question emphasises digitality itself as making and developing things or as a theoretical understanding about the digitalised world.

According to Suominen and Haverinen, this coordination might help to define any researcher's or project's, even networks' or consortiums' (e.g. *CM24*), internal relationships concerning digitality. This would be of significant help especially in multi-/interdisciplinary research. (Suominen & Haverinen, 2015). As researchers of digital culture, we would position ourselves quite far on the right, more in the top than the lower corner; however, the vertical position depends extensively on every current research topic and may, therefore, vary a lot. It is also possible for us to move up and down as well as left and right on the axels according to the stage of research, even inside an individual project. After all, the division between the practical and theoretical digital humanities is not biased as much as a moving line.

With our main focus more on the understanding end, we are conducting research which quite often involves human beings either as subjects or informants of the study. In addition, we see the Internet and digitality as a *research environment* that ethnologists might call *the field*. Ethnographical methods are often applied to these kinds of studies. It is especially in these cases, but also with other kinds of methods, that ethics is extensively intertwined with methodology. Next, we will discuss what we mean by this.

3. Self-Reflexive Ethical Tools for Digital Humanities

In the English-speaking academic world, online studies have existed since the early 1990s, and less than a decade later, online specific research ethics was also taken into account (see Baym & Markham 2009, pp. viii-ix). In Finland, however, research ethics in general only became an object of interest in the 1980s, but it did not get much attention until the 1990s (Pekkala, 2000). The Internet generalised in Finland since c. 1995, and only started to appear in research more widely a decade later. Since it is becoming increasingly more common to Finnish scholars to publish internationally, we need to update our late-born understanding of the online research ethics and further develop it. This is what we are aiming at in the *CM24*'s ethics-related work-package. This further work, reaching for studying ethical processes as such, will also be generalisable more widely; we find this approach beneficial for multiple disciplinary backgrounds in international academic cultures.

The challenges that the traditional Finnish disciplines had to face due to this novelty, the Internet where people shared and lived their lives, became clearly visible to us around 2008. At that time, we were working on our online-related doctoral theses in Digital Culture. In 2008 and the coming years, we got several

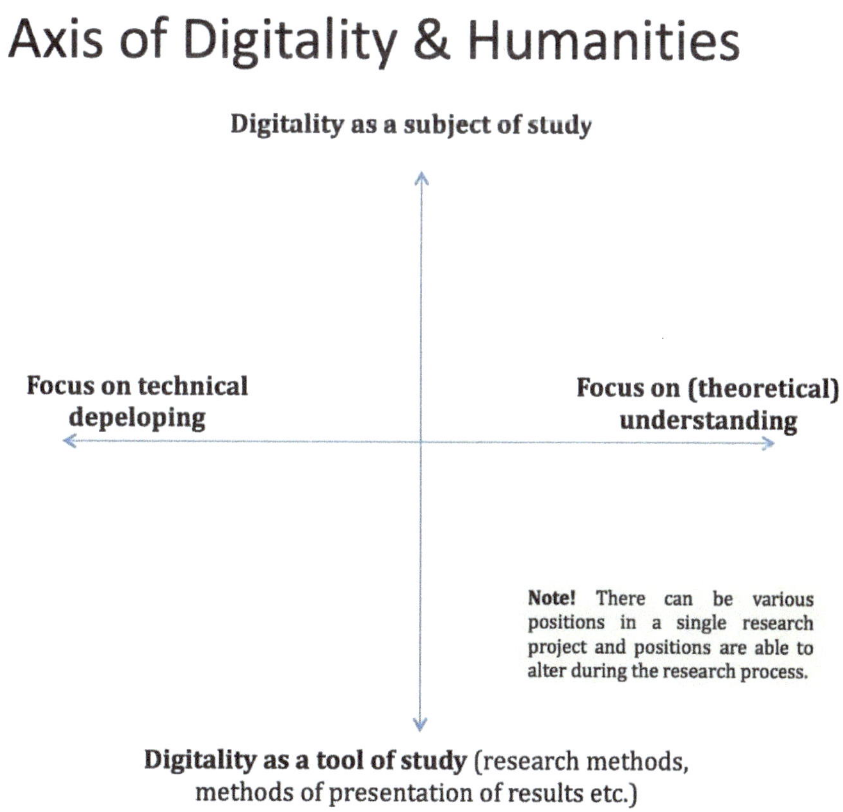

Figure 1. Model for positioning yourself among Digital Humanities research. Source: Suominen & Haverinen, 2015 (S. Östman & R. Turtiainen, Transl.).

questions from doctoral students, lecturers and researchers from other disciplines (for example ethnology, anthropology etc.) concerning online studies. We were asked, for example, on what conditions we could trust our informants to be what they claimed to be; we were confronted about asking people's permission for studying them. It seemed to be a common idea that when people voluntarily published pieces of their lives online, these lives could be used for research without questioning their publicity and authors' right for the contents they had created.

On the Web, everything builds to the context: how the sites are built, what they are used for, who uses them, how the users communicate, how they feel about their contents...these elements vary a lot. Not knowing enough might lead to misinterpretations or (unintended) disrespectful usage of material (see Aull Davies, 2008; Ess, 2002). We have created a tool with certain basic principles for online researchers: 'a Room Board of Ethics' (Figure 2): in it, we ask whether the Internet is your *tool, source* or *subject*; are you conducting research *with, on* or *about* the Internet. Depending on your relationship to the Internet as a researcher, the Internet might be your *research environment* in a way which in ethnographic studies might be called *the field*. In these cases, it should also be seen as any other ethnographical field: you need to get hands-on experience in order to understand its mechanisms.

There are some tools for essential ethical consideration. The question of whether something can be used freely or more carefully lies at the bottom. Asking for permission, rights for citing, identities of informants/subjects to research and so on seem to be important ethical matters even still in 2016. Malin Sveningsson and others have presented in *Att fånga nätet. Kvalitativa metoder för Internetforsking* (*To Study the Web. Qualitative Methods for Internet Studies*, Sveningsson, Lövheim, & Bergquist, 2003) a coordination system (Figure 3) to which researchers may position their subject, informants, material and so on,

BOARD OF ETHICS FOR ONLINE RESEARCHER
(R. Turtiainen & S. Östman 2013,
see also partial transl. A. Haverinen 2014, 61)

Is the internet your	**in other words, is your research**
tool	*with the internet*
source ***or***	*on the internet* ***or***
subject	*about the internet*

To an internet researcher, the web is often a combination of all the abovementioned, in which case the internet (or a piece of it) is ***the research environment***, where the researcher must inter alia:

* remember that ethics is related to **source criticism**
* appropriate the **cultural conventions** of the particular research environment
* understand the **contextualities** of how the research material is being created in the environment
* consider the **intimacy or publicity** of the content from the point of view of the informants (or the members of the community, if you just examine the texts)
* **respect** the people being researched and the contents they produce
* remember that online environments are not static, but constantly changing, which is why all research ethics are to be considered **case-by-case**

The researcher should also remember that the responsibility and freedom of science always walk hand in hand. You need to be able to stand for your choices: you need to **reason your every choice.**

Figure 2. The Roomboard of Ethics: Some guidelines and basic principles for online research (See also Turtiainen & Östman, 2013).

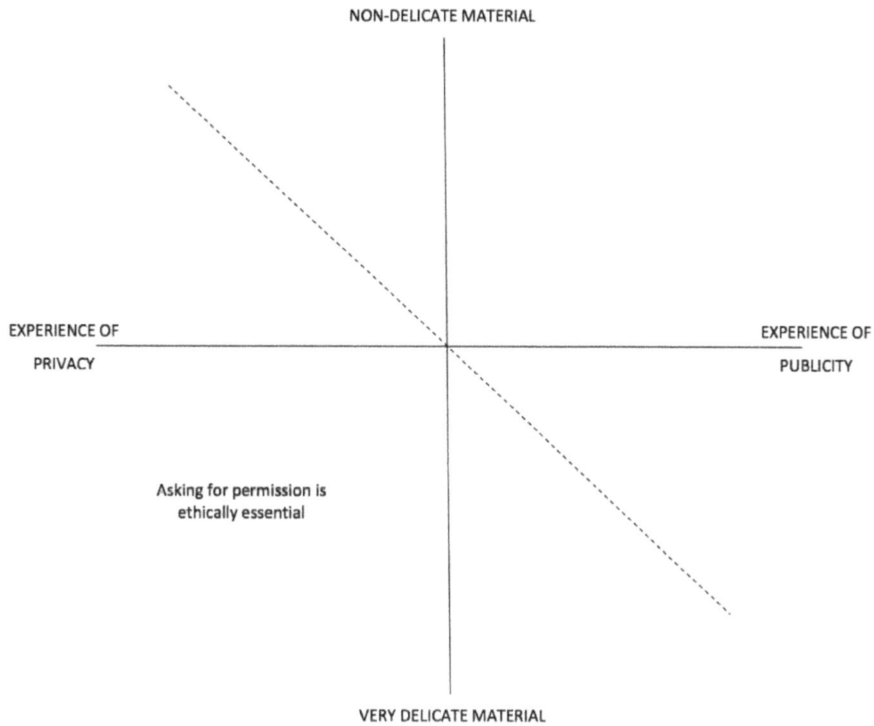

Figure 3. Delicacy of the material. Source: Sveningsson, Lövheim and Bergquist, 2003, p. 186 (the figure has been applied for example by: McKee & Porter, 2008, p. 73, 2009, p. 11; Turtiainen, 2012, p. 52; Östman, 2015, p. 74).

according to how delicate the material is (to a reader) and how private or public the creators consider it. This most probably requires contact with the authors—or at least an extensively thorough reading by the researcher in order to learn the authors' understanding about their actions and culture: this understanding might only exist implicitly in their media texts. Either way, Sveningsson's method is very useful.

We recommend Sveningsson's model for any researcher whose data consist of users' personal online contents. This tool, however, does not offer a practical walk-through of the ethical decision-making process as an entity. For that, we have developed a story-method which has proved useful among Digital Culture undergraduates as well as graduated, but still novice online researchers.

4. 'Mary's Mistakes'—A Method for Recognising Online Specific Ethical Matters

'Mary's mistakes' is a method that we have built for recognising ethical challenges in online specific studies. It is a story with as many ethical dilemmas as possible, for which Östman invented a prototype some years ago for teaching. We developed this idea further in our Finnish article in 2013, and Turtiainen has been using the final version of the story in her teaching ever since. We find Mary's story internationally useful, since it can be applied to any individual case of research, at least in digitally oriented cultural studies. It is our further aim to find out whether or not a similar tool would work in other contexts among Digital Humanities as well (such as extremely theoretical or strictly quantitative/statistical disciplines).

Mary[2] is writing her master's thesis in psychology. She wants to study eating disorders with girls. Her research question is: 'Which body images do 13–15 year old girls with an eating disorder have?' The subject is delicate, and Mary fears that volunteers are hard to find. She studies Digital Culture as a minor, and by linking her study to that, she finds a solution: Mary decides to use some pro-ana[3] discussions and blogs she found on a random discussion site. Mary has had an eating disorder, but has never participated in any Internet activity about it. Actually, she does not use social media almost at all. For her study, she creates a fake profile to the site, with the nickname 'Thinspy-98'. 98 in a nickname usually refers to the birth year—Mary was born in 1991. With this nickname, she starts discussions, asking and commenting, wishing that this way she would get material for her study.

'Mary' has built for herself a great number of traps in the story: for example, her question does not quite

[2] Mary is a fictional character to whom and whose study we have gathered as many ethical problems as we could think of on the basis of the questions we obtained from researchers from other disciplines.

[3] 'Pro-ana' refers to culture in which people with anorexia nervosa consider themselves not ill, but rather willingly choose this life-threatening lifestyle.

match her chosen material; the subject is very delicate as well as the informants, who are teenagers with a severe illness; she has not thought her methods through thoroughly enough (online material is not necessarily the best choice for studying experience); she plans on cheating her informants with the fake profile; she is not going to ask for their permission; she is studying a subject very close to her; yet, she does not know anything about the environment in which she is going to produce her material.

An experienced online researcher might easily recognise all of Mary's traps. For example, in online environments, it is essential to know something about the context: who is using the site, what was it built for, which kind of conventions and habits are there (e.g. are old users and 'newbies'[4] equally allowed to speak up—usually they are not), which kind of tone of voice is usual there, which aims and needs do the users have (e.g. peer support, encouraging others, asking for help, sharing own experiences...) and so on. All these aspects affect the discourse, which is unique on every site, even if they cover the same subject. Knowing the field you are working; knowing who is speaking, what they are saying, to whom, how and why they say it the way they do is basic source criticism, especially in ethnographically emphasised research.

Moreover, every case of research is unique and includes multiple different ethical dilemmas. Writing down your intended research process—for example into a story like this—may help to recognise the case-bounded ethical matters. Mary's story has proved useful for the students in Turtiainen's yearly ethics class for digital culture students, and we also used it in a workshop for an ethnography course at the University of Turku in 2015. The learning process proceeds as followed:

1. Students read Mary's story;
2. The class analyses the story in the lecturer's guidance piece by piece until the class has recognised every ethical risk in the story;
3. The students write their own stories about their bachelor's/master's/doctoral theses;
4. In the course exam, they are given back their own stories for analysis, similar to which the class did together earlier with Mary's story.

The story method has several benefits. It forces the researchers to be self-reflective, which helps them in positioning themselves in relation to the subject as well as practising sustainable source criticism. The doctoral students in our ethnography workshop found this method very useful: in their feedback, they described it as practical, illustrative and eye-opening. Some of the students had not recognised the current challenges, but also understood why certain earlier processes or phases had not succeeded. A doctoral student wrote:

'I found the workshop really useful considering my doctoral studies and future career as a researcher. Especially, I'm thankful for the concrete examples with which both the lecture and the workshop demonstrated the ethical questions that we might face in the research process.'

Next, we will move on from online specific research ethical tools for researchers; we will proceed to discussing the possible tools for actually studying these ethics. By applying our model to preliminary *CM24* data, we will aim at finding out how ethical viewpoints vary among a multidisciplinary project. The next steps after this pilot study will lead us towards creating some commonly applicable guidelines for such widely multidisciplinary projects.

5. Towards Studying Research Ethics

The coordinate system that we presented in the beginning (Suominen & Haverinen, 2015), was suggested to be utilised for scholars to position themselves according to their research focus and motives. This model is a great start for positioning yourself on the field of online studies. It also has inspired us in developing a tool for studying various ethical approaches (Figure 4). We collected some preliminary data in a *CM24* consortium seminar in May 2016. Östman asked the seminar participants to answer the following questions:

1. Disciplinary background and current research;
2. Describe your understanding about research ethics and/or ethically conducted research; which matters do you find the most essential; what kinds of things have affected your understanding?
3. Which ethical questions and/or practices do you expect to face during your current research; how do you plan to proceed with them?

We obtained 16 answers, one of which could not be integrated to our model. We have coded the answers as P1–P15 (P = Participant). The participants came from multiple disciplinary backgrounds, and they integrate into our model (see Figure 4).

The basic idea of this fourfold table is based on Suominen and Haverinen's figure. We have further developed it on the basis of our roomboard: in it, we defined a researchers' relationship with the online environment as being threefold: it may be a tool, a subject or a source for the study. In this example (Figure 4), we have specified 'online environment' as the Suomi24 discussion forum, which is the focus of the whole *CM24* project. Our former studies have shown that the more focal the online environment is and the more understanding the manner of research, the more

[4] New users.

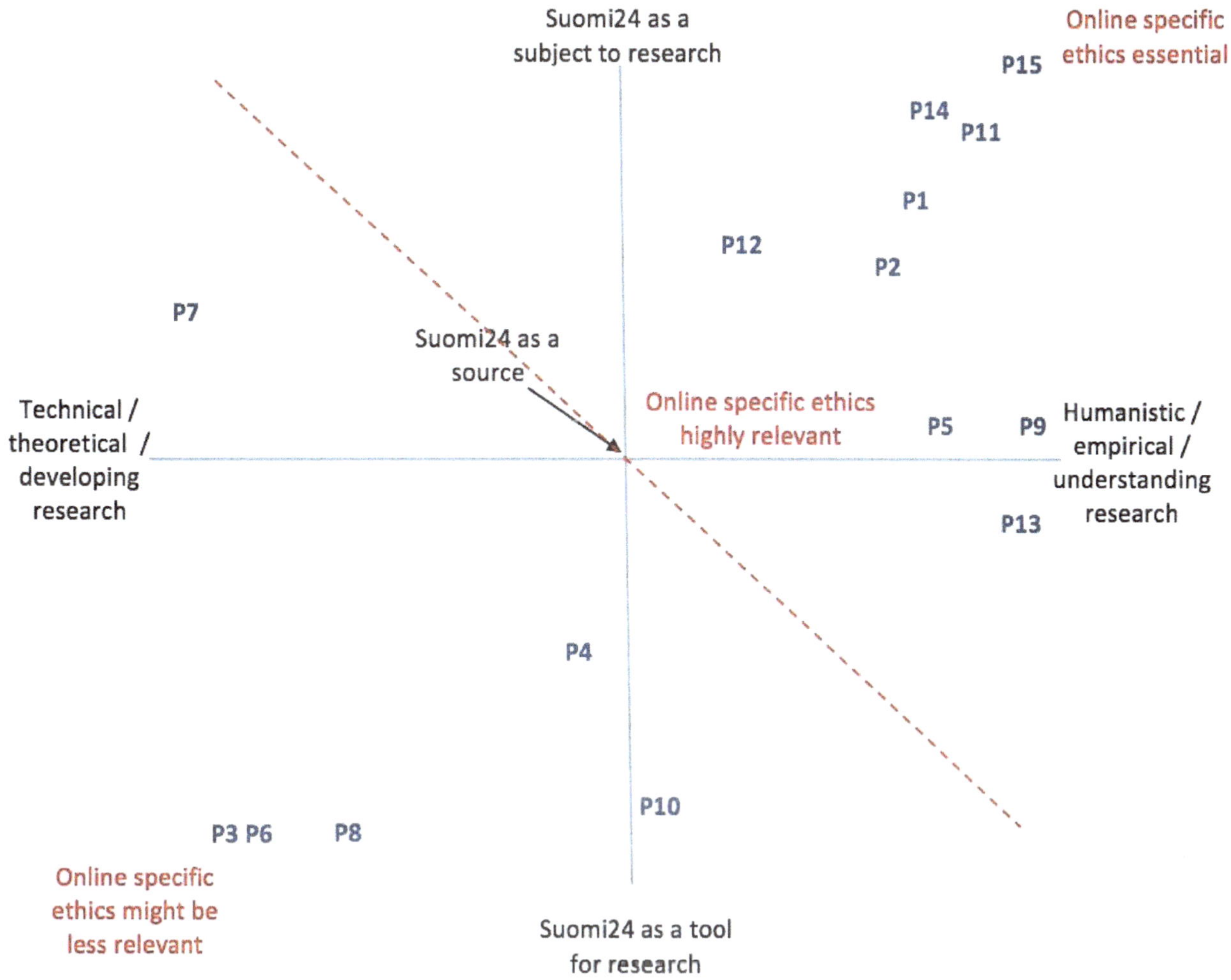

Figure 4. Online environment (Suomi24 discussion forum) in multidisciplinary research.

relevant, even essential, it is to take online specific ethics into account (Östman & Turtiainen, in press).

In Figure 4, the participants P3, P4, P6, P7, P8 and P10 represent quantitatively and statistically oriented disciplines and backgrounds[5]. According to their survey answers, they are situated below the line, which defines the relevance of online specific ethics. Among those, an online specific take to ethics might not be that necessary, which was well articulated in their answers. With their background, ethics mostly have to do with such matters as copyright laws (P3, P7) and open access to the data: 'Privacy protection might be in contradiction with what could be learned from the data' (P4).

Participants P1, P2, P5, P9, P11–P15 are situated above the relevance-defining line. They come from humanistic backgrounds and tend to have human-related, understanding and in several cases, culturally oriented research take: 'Will my analysis do justice to the data; that is, will it give a right kind of a voice to the participants?' (P5). They answered the survey more thoroughly and seemed to have a wider understanding about the research ethical processes; some of them had been taught ethics in their university studies, whereas the first group (below the line) had not been educated about ethics and tended to see it more as legal points rather than decision-processes. However, multidisciplinary research environments helped the participants to appropriate a more reflexive, process-oriented ethical take. P12 had their background in information technology. However, he/she saw their multidisciplinary experience and discussions as an ethically evolving actor, which had led to a reflexive ethical approach.

To be able to consider all the facts needed for ethical decision-making in a multidisciplinary process, the researcher needs to understand at least these three things; the contexts, the research environment and their own background (of importance of recognising the contextual specificities see also Nielsen, Paasonen, & Spisak, 2015, p. 11). Doing this, we suggest that indi-

[5] In order to keep answers anonymised, we cannot specify the individual disciplines.

vidual researchers, even those situated in the low left corner of our tool, might benefit from a case-based self-reflexive ethical analysis such as 'Mary's mistakes' method. The next step of our study will include engaging these participants to apply Mary-method in their own case studies. This will be done in the next consortium seminar in fall 2016. By analysing the results of that step, we will find out whether the ethical co-understanding of a multidisciplinary project will benefit from this kind of case-based learning. Simultaneously, we will further proceed in this new field of studying online specific research ethics as its own entity. Based on this process, we would like to suggest that in Finland, possibly also worldwide, a shift of paradigm from research ethics to researching ethics is about to appear.

6. Summary

In this article, we have presented a) a tool to researchers for positioning themselves in the field of Digital Humanities (Suominen & Haverinen, 2015), b) a method for contextually reflexive ethical decision-making and certain basic principles for that, and finally c) a tool for studying the actual ethical decision-making processes. By leading researchers to actively consider their ethical approaches, we will be able to study research ethics and its practical applying-processes in multiple disciplines. By doing this, we aim at creating a commonly functional and effective guideline for online specific, widely multidisciplinary research. The follow-up for this preliminary study will be carried out in fall 2016 (Step 2: Mary-method) and 2017 (Steps 3 and 4: undefined[6]).

Acknowledgements

The article is part of the *Citizen Mindscapes* project which is funded by the Academy of Finland.

Conflict of Interests

The authors declare no conflict of interests.

References

Aull Davies, C. (2008). *Reflexive ethnography. A guide to researching selves and others*. London and New York: Routledge. (Original work published 1998)

Baym, N. K., & Markham, A. N. (2009). Introduction: Making smart choices on shifting ground. In A. N. Markham & N. K. Baym (Eds.), *Internet inquiry. Conversations about method* (pp. viii-xix). Los Angeles: Sage Publications.

Ess, C. (2002). *Ethical decision-making and Internet research. Recommendations from the AoIR ethics working committee*. Retrieved from http://aoir.org/reports/ethics.pdf

Evans, L., & Rees, S. (2012). An interpretation of digital humanities. In M. B. David (Ed.), *Understanding digital humanities* (pp. 21-41). New York: Palgrave Macmillan.

Hall, G. (2013). Towards a postdigital humanities: Cultural analytics and the computational turn to data-driven scholarship. *American Literature*, *85*(4), 781-809.

Kuula, A. (2006). *Tutkimusetiikka: aineistojen hankinta, käyttö ja säilytys*. Tampere: Vastapaino.

Markham, A., & Buchanan, E. (2012). *Ethical decision-making ad internet research*. Retrieved from aoir.org/reports/ethics2.pdf

McKee, H., & Porter, J. (2008). The ethics of digital writing research: A rhetorical approach. *College Composition and Communication*, *59*(4), 711-749.

McKee, H., & Porter, J. (2009). Playing a good game: Ethical issues in researching MMOGs and virtual worlds. *International Journal of Internet Research Ethics*, *2*(1), 5-37.

Nielsen, S., Paasonen, S., & Spisak, S. (2015). 'Pervy role-play and such': Girls' experiences of sexual messaging online. *Sex Education: Sexuality, Society and Learning*, *15*(5), 472-485.

Östman, S. (2015). *'Millasen päivityksen tästä sais?' Elämäjulkaisijuuden kulttuurinen omaksuminen* (Published Doctoral dissertation). University of Turku, Pori, Finland.

Östman, S., & Turtiainen, R. (in press). How to position yourself as an ethical researcher? Analytical viewpoints to online research ethics. In P. Hakamies & A. Heimo (Eds.), *Doing folkloristics in the digital age*. Turku: Folklore Fellows Communications.

Pannapacker, W. (2011, January 8). Pannapacker at MLA: Digital humanities triumphant? *The Chronicle of Higher Education*. Retrieved from http://www.chronicle.com/blogs/brainstorm/pannapacker-at-mla-digital-humanities-triumphant/30915

Parry, D. (2010). The MLA, @briancroxall, and the non-rise of the Digital Humanities. *AcademicHack*. Retrieved from http://academhack.outsidethetext.com/home/2010/the-mla-briancroxall-and-the-non-rise-of-the-digital-humanities

Pekkala, A. (2000). Tutkijan eettiset ongelmat. In P. Laaksonen, S. Knuuttila, & U. Piela (Eds.), *Tutkijat kentällä* (pp. 85-110). Helsinki: SKS.

Spiro, L. (2012). "This is why we fight": Defining the values of digital humanities. In M. K. Gold (Ed.), *Debates in the digital humanities* (pp. 16-34). Minnesota: University of Minnesota Press.

Suominen, J., & Haverinen, A. (2015). Koodaamisen ja kirjoittamisen vuoropuhelu?—Mitä on digitaalinen humanistinen tutkimus. *Ennen ja nyt*. Retrieved from http://www.ennenjanyt.net/2015/02/koodaamisen-ja-kirjoittamisen-vuoropuhelu-mita-on-digitaalinen-humanistinen-tutkimus/#identifier_14_1502

[6] In order to protect the novelty of our research.

Sveningsson, M., Lövheim, M., & Bergquist, M. (2003). *Att fånga Nätet. Kvalitativa metoder för Internet-forskning*. Lund: Studentlitteratur.

Turtiainen, R. (2012). *Nopeammin, laajemmalle, monipuolisemmin. Digitalisoituminen mediaurheilun seuraamisen muutoksessa*. (Published Doctoral dissertation). University of Turku, Pori, Finland.

Turtiainen, R., & Östman, S. (2009). Tavistaidetta ja verkkoviihdettä. Omaehtoisten verkkosisältöjen tutkimusetiikkaa. In M. Grahn & M. Häyrynen (Eds.), *Kulttuurituotanto. Kehykset, käytäntö ja prosessit* (pp. 336-358). Helsinki: SKS.

Turtiainen, R., & Östman, S. (2013). Verkkotutkimuksen eettiset haasteet: Armi ja anoreksia. In J. Matikainen & M. Tikka (Eds.), *Otteita verkosta. Verkon ja sosiaalisen median tutkimusmenetelmät* (pp. 49-67). Helsinki: Gaudeamus.

17

The New Visual Testimonial: Narrative, Authenticity, and Subjectivity in Emerging Commercial Photographic Practice

Heather Morton

Photography Department, Sheridan College, Oakville, L6H 2L1, Canada: E-Mail: heather.morton@sheridancollege.ca

Abstract

By studying the cultural and aesthetic impact of increasingly pervasive digital technologies and mass amateurization, this paper examines the ramifications of the networked information economy on professional photographic practice and considers the concomitant implications for the photographic classroom. Using the framework of convergence culture as per the writings of Yochai Benkler, Henry Jenkins, Mark Deuze, and Axel Bruns, the impact of accessible and instantaneous image creation and dispersal are explored. Given the rise of consumer engagement in brand co-creation on social media platforms, we can observe massive changes to professional practice in areas such as aesthetics, and the erosion of previous sustainable business models. Indeed, as traditional notions of "expertise" shift from technological prowess to narrative and disseminative abilities, the effects on commercial practice and photographic education need to be addressed. This paper argues that there are three emerging priorities for commercial image use: narrative ability, authenticity, and subjectivity and suggests initial steps in their pedagogical application. By acknowledging these transformations, this paper explores the idea that students need to harness technique, social media influence, adaptability, subjectivity, and storytelling power in order to better serve emerging image-based needs in commercial spaces.

Keywords

brand co-creation; commercial photography; convergent culture; Instagram; marketing; post-secondary education; social media; user generated content

Issue

This article is part of a multidisciplinary issue of *Media and Communication*, edited by Mark Cocks (University of Wales Trinity Saint David, UK) and Michelle Bogre (The New School, USA).

---

1. Introduction

In the summer of 2010, Domino's Pizza launched an advertising campaign called *Show Us Your Pizza* in which they pledged to forego the traditional tools and tricks of commercial food photography and would instead "shoot their pizzas just the way they come out of the oven" (Lincoln, 2013). This was part of a larger "Turnaround" campaign in which Domino's acknowledged (and indeed showcased) consumer dissatisfaction with their product and subsequently revamped the recipe. In order to engage the consumer in this rebranding strategy, Domino's encouraged customers to photograph their own pizza exactly as it arrived at their door and upload the photos to a dedicated URL. These images populated a curated, but not manipulated, website of user generated pizza pictures.

This aspect of the *Show Us Your Pizza* campaign was part of a bigger strategy that integrated online and mass-market motion spots, online games, and a social media strategy. The goal was to get the consumer engaged with the improved Domino's pizza in what could be perceived as an experiential and authentic way. The campaign resulted in a 14% increased market share, a slew of press coverage, and various coveted marketing awards (Lincoln, 2013; Litz, 2010). For Domino's, *Show Us Your Pizza* heralded the beginning of what would be a continued commitment to consumer engagement through a number of marketing channels and has resulted in consistent growth for the brand; increasing their market share most recently from 9 to 12.3% between 2014 and 2016 (Derousseau, 2016; He, Zha, & Li, 2013).

Although by no means unique in this respect, the *Show Us Your Pizza* campaign represents the culmination of the possibilities for consumer engagement and the threat to established protocols and priorities in the networked information economy. Acting as an unwitting harbinger, a Domino's chef insists: "We know that [the consumer is] the *authentic* source for great Domino's pizza pictures [emphasis added]" (Litz, 2010).

This essay considers the effects on the commercial photography industry endemic to the massive changes in the way culture is now created and consumed. As this paper will show, the framework of convergence culture has lead to a climate in which previous barriers to entry have been negated, lines delineating professional and amateur engagement with photography have been blurred, and new opportunities for consumer involvement have been introduced. As such, new priorities have emerged which privilege authenticity, subjectivity, and narrative ability. This essay will explore these three key attributes that are increasingly integral to image use in commercial contexts, and will consider appropriate opportunities for their integration in post secondary commercially focused photography programs.

To fully appreciate the cultural changes of the last two decades, it is necessary to understand the framework in which the public is consuming (and producing) media in the networked information economy. Though the theorists I reference are preoccupied with a variety of content creation (from citizen journalism to Wikipedia to Flickr and gaming), their prosumption critiques can also be applied singularly to the sphere of commercial media.

2. Consumer Engagement and Convergence Culture

The related concepts of produsage, the prosumer, and convergence culture have attracted attention from a range of theorists working from a political economy and critical perspective. Not surprisingly, this scholarship has also garnered interest from marketing industry strategists, who are eager to adopt new models of consumer engagement. This shifting interest, which has resulted in the widespread inclusion of non-professionals in content creation, has serious ramifications on heretofore predictable and sustainable photography-based careers. It is important therefore to understand the consumptive and productive atmosphere as identified in the writings of Bruns, Benkler, Jenkins, and Deuze after starting with Alvin Toffler to provide a bit of early and prescient context to our current state of commercial image use.

The prosumer was first named by Toffler and described in his book *The Third Wave* published in 1980. Toffler suggests that in the next stage of human innovation, culture would be typified by, among other things, a demassification of the media (p. 165) and the rise of the prosumer. The name prosumer describes the phenomenon in which we are increasingly active in the production of things that we then consume (p. 265). In a produsage paradigm, not only should marketing be tailored to the consumer's interests but she should also have agency in creating the things with which she is surrounded (if not creating the actual marketing itself as per user generated content in general and the Domino's example in particular). Due to the advent of digital technology and the concomitant rise of instant, targeted communication, these desires can be accomplished to an increasingly satisfactory degree. Axel Bruns' 2008 book *Blogs, Wikipedia, Second Life, and Beyond: From Production to Produsage*, elaborates on Toffler's thesis by outlining the major characteristics of produsage as "the collaborative, iterative, and user-led production of content by participants in a hybrid user-producer, or produser role" (p. 1). In a review of the book, David Karpf (2009) outlines the four main tenets of produsage as: "(a) open participation, communal evaluation, (b) fluid heterarchy, ad hoc meritocracy, (c) unfinished artefacts, continuing process, and (d) common property, individual rewards" (p. 81). That the characteristics of produsage themselves are anathema to a "professional" practice should be obvious but it will be discussed further below.

Yochai Benkler is optimistic about the potential for change inherent in this new approach to content creation. In his book *The Wealth of Networks* (2006), he situates our current media landscape in its historical context and suggests that we might consider mass culture as having been democratized because its creative potential is now in the hands of the individual. He writes: "The networked information economy also allows for the emergence of a more critical and self-reflective culture" (p. 15) and this has "made human creativity and the economics of information itself the core structuring facts in the new networked information economy" (p. 4).

In an editorial written by Henry Jenkins and Mark Deuze (2008) on the idea of convergence culture, they consider Benkler's theory of hybrid media ecology which acts in a transformative way on all content producers including those working in commercial, political, activism, and journalism contexts (p. 5). Taking it a step further, Jenkins and Deuze (2008) claim that individuated content is less important than the actual collaborative experience of building the content in shared spaces. They suggest the pre-eminence of this "socialized media" of which the photo sharing site Flickr is named as an example (p. 5). So again, we see that collaboration and creativity is crucial to our engagement with culture.

In his earlier essay *The Cultural Logic of Media Convergence*, Henry Jenkins (2004) catalogues the myriad of ways the consumer is engaged with established and remixed media across multiple channels. He hints at the overall effect of these shifting relationships, explaining convergence culture as "a reconfiguration of media power and a reshaping of media aesthetics and economics" (p. 35). Note the care he takes to name aesthetics as an area worthy of consideration. To put it another way, Jenkins and Deuze (2008) explain, "the flow of media content is shaped as much by the decisions made in teenagers' bedrooms as it is by decisions made in corporate boardrooms" (p. 7).

Clearly there are some common themes across these theoretical frameworks which are useful in identifying the key attributes of convergence culture: a desire to be creative, a desire for customized content, a desire to collaborate with others, and a desire for shared spaces in which collaboration might take place. Turning back for a moment to the Domino's example used at the beginning of this essay, we can see that *Show Us Your Pizza* successfully harnesses and fulfills these desires while simultaneously eroding the prospects for professional photographers.

Certainly an analysis of contemporary marketing priorities illustrates the increasing value of collaborative spaces and user generated content (UGC). Not surprisingly, the corollary is also true; traditional marketing approaches are experiencing a retraction in their use and value, and a concomitant reallocation of their media budgets (Banet-Weiser, 2011; Gotter, 2016; Lyngsfeldt, 2015; Moore, 2015). In an aggregate analysis of 2014 and 2015 marketing data, London agency Freely cites a study which suggests that by 2019, mobile advertising will represent 72% of all US digital ad spending (Moore, 2015). Quoting the *Social Media Examiner*, the analysis includes this finding: "Figuring out how to best connect with people remains high on the list of questions marketers want answered (89%). As more businesses become social, those that best engage will stand out" (Moore, 2015).

UGC consistently outperforms traditional media in areas of "trust" and "helpfulness" (Gotter, 2016) so much so that in a directed analysis on attitudes towards visual-based UGC, Olapic found that consumers trusted user generated visual content almost twice as much as professional images created by brands (Olapic, 2016) and more than half of those surveyed said that they "were more likely to click on an ad employing UGC than one using stock photography" (Leggatt, 2016).

Hence, as a result of the technical, aesthetic, and disseminative abilities of the networked information economy expressed in the bundling of the camera phone, social media, and the internet, we find a systematic erosion of traditional sustainable photographic practice. The accompanying democratizing shifts in aesthetic ambitions and access, coupled with an engagement hungry public vis a vis convergence culture, may have led to a schism between what we teach and the image-making skills required in commercial spaces. This essay will illuminate what brands want from their imagery, and consider how we can deliver industry ready practitioners given these findings.

3. "Professional" as a Questionable Distinction

To begin it is important to understand the erosion of traditional and long-standing notions of what constitutes professional practice. According to the membership guidelines found on the website of the American Society of Media Photographers (ASMP), professional membership is reserved for photographers working in either still or motion who have been "actively and consistently engaged in professional practice for at least 3 years" (ASMP, 2016). This definition is considerably more vague than the stipulations found on the website in 2013 which used concrete achievements to signal professionalism, prioritized publication, and required its members to be earning at least 50% of their primary income from licensing their photography (ASMP, 2013). This shift away from a quantitative approach is telling. The Professional Photographers of Canada (PPoC) uses similarly vague language, welcoming "photographers of all genres", and suggesting that membership will help attain accreditation as a "professional", without ever specifying what that entails (PPoC, 2016). In the case of the Canadian Association of Professional Image Creators (CAPIC), the eligibility for membership requires meeting several criteria, and puts emphasis on having an appropriate portfolio and business documentation in addition to proof of publication (CAPIC, 2016).

Despite the ambiguities, there remains a loose collection of characteristics which seem to constitute professionalism from an industry standard perspective: a sustained record of successful jobs (having been published), the use of professional business documents (which may indicate whether the prospective member considers maintaining a sustainable fee structure important), that there is an existing body of work which corresponds to some agreed upon presentation standards (the portfolio), and that the majority of income is made from photography.

These defining features stand in contrast to the trends of mass amateurization which problematize the traditional distinction between professional photographer and everyone else with a camera. Further to the collaborative, creative and consumptive desires of convergence culture, non-professional image makers are eager to participate in the creation of mass marketing campaigns like *Show Us Your Pizza*, so much so that one 2016 consumer trend study claims that over 50% of respondents actually want more opportunities and direction from brands on what content to create (Gotter, 2016). Likewise, the platforms that are so heavily foundational to convergence culture (Instagram, Flickr, Facebook, Twitter, Snapchat) facilitate the process by which advertisers can utilize the branded work being done by the public to their own promotional and disseminative ends. This newly "commercial" work includes everything from UGC, to sponsored hashtags, to working with "influencers" (Kolm, 2015). This illuminates the false distinction between professional and non (Duffy, 2010; San Cornelio & Gomez Cruz, 2014; Schroeder, 2013) and nullifies the need for proof of professional practice. Referencing Prahalad and Ramaswamy, Banks and Deuze (2009) state that in fact "value is increasingly *co-created* by both the firm and the consumer. Today, media consumers, fans and audiences are redefined as 'the drivers of wealth production within the new digital economy'" (p. 420), resulting in diminished opportunities for professional creative practitioners overall.

In the end, non-professionals want to create work for brands, they have the ability to do so and to spread this work around, and brands are happy to receive and use this work on their own disseminative media platforms. In addition, the technical and aesthetic barriers to entry have been dismantled: camera technology has gained precision and image capture has advanced to include ever-larger digital sensors, having the gradual effect that images taken with smaller cameras can more accurately retain their integrity when reproduced at bigger sizes (the recent *Shot on an iPhone* campaign is a relevant example). Plus, aesthetic banality delivers its own branding benefits as will be shown below.

Thus there is an emerging strata of non-professional image-makers who are engaging with brands for a variety of reasons that sit outside of the typical sustainability goals of professional practice. Instead, they report that their participation delivers the following: an increase in social capital, pleasure in being part of brand co-creation, a creative challenge, an outlet for self-expression, and a sense of empowerment. (Brabham, 2008; Duffy, 2010; Marcus Reker, 2016; Nava, Blake, MacRury, & Richards, 2013; San Cornelio & Gomez Cruz, 2014). Certainly in these emerging marketing contexts, there is no inherent need for a "professional" approach as defined by the ASMP, PPoC and CAPIC above: business documents and portfolios don't apply and proof of prior paid remuneration is beside the point. Furthermore, as we will see below, the authenticity aspect of these ads also leaves any aesthetic or technical professionalism out of the picture by necessity.

Certainly, our presumptions about photographic "work" need to change. Speaking recently at the *Image Truth/Story Truth* symposium, conference panelists Stephen Mayes and Fred Ritchin reject the hand-wringing fixation on recompense, suggesting that in fact there are numerous emerging revenue streams for photographers, many of them non-traditional and some necessitating collaboration with non-professionals (Tow Centre, 2015). Ritchin goes further to call for a change in the way professionalism is defined, arguing for example, that the citizen journalist may be better equipped (mostly from an access perspective) to provide the most appropriate images from a conflict (Tow Centre, 2015). Similarly, referencing the quote used above from Jenkins and Deuze (2008), one could certainly argue that the proverbial teenager in the bedroom is indeed a more appropriate mediator of visual identity for many brands eager to engage with exactly that demographic.

Without a doubt, given the erosion of traditionally stable revenue streams, commercial photographic education at the post secondary level has a responsibility to ensure that our students become fully cognizant of the field in which they are entering—one that is crowded with powerfully engaged, connected, and able consumers and one that is susceptible to influence from the aesthetic approach that these consumers bring.

4. New Priorities: Storytelling, Subjectivity, and Authenticity

This essay identifies three key emerging priorities that are critical components of contemporary commercial image culture as:

A. Storytelling or narrative abilities;
B. The importance of authenticity;
C. Expressions of subjectivity.

As this essay will show, these priorities can give direction to emerging image creators and should prompt educators in commercially focused programs to ensure that our pedagogical approach enables our students to understand, and execute along these shifting priorities.

5. The Persistence of Storytelling

Though convergence culture encourages the micro and diverse participation of consumers in brand co-creation, the sophistication of a marketing strategy considered as a whole also requires rich storytelling which can engage the audience at an emotional and experiential level (Olapic, 2016; Scoblete, 2015). When brands pursue UGC, this can take the form of co-created narratives (Deuze, 2005) enabled by accessible and transformative technology (Harper, 2016). However, there is also an increasing need for intentional affect, which triggers emotional responses using implicit associations.

In her case analysis of the Instagram presence of Nike and Starbucks, Chia Yu Chang (2014) contrasts hard and soft sell tactics, finding that in the case of the latter: "These appeals tend to be subtle and indirect; an image or atmosphere may be conveyed through a beautiful scene or the development of an emotional story" (pp. 21–22). In Chang's analysis, she characterizes UGC as most often simple and direct, and explicit in its support for the brand. On the other hand, the intentional posts generated by Nike and Starbucks worked at the implicit level, leveraging visual messages designed to "delight and inspire" (p. 37). Arguably this ability to tell a complex story and seed an emotional experience in a single image is a challenge which requires skill beyond the ease of the snap/filter/hashtag/post/repeat cycle. Iterative and reflective practice is appropriate and necessary to this goal.

Though Eric T. Meyer's (2015) study considers the pedagogical ramifications in a motion context, his assessment of the use of iPad's in a filmmaking classroom is related and applicable for our purposes. He finds that "the expertise being taught is no longer necessarily in the technical areas of manipulating filming equipment and editing suites, but in the area of storytelling and teaching students collaborative and creative working techniques" (p. 311). Note the shift away from technical concerns in favour of collaborative and narrative development as an area of differentiation vis a vis non professional image makers. Though this is in some ways a false dichotomy, the perceived valuation shift is noteworthy. Certainly in low-resolution, social media spaces, technical skill isn't privileged nor is it even differentiated (San Cornelio & Gomez Cruz, 2104). In fact, in Lawrence, Fournier, and Brunel's (2013) study of the effectiveness of consumer generated advertising, they found that "authenticity and creativity judgments figure prominently in people's attitudes towards consumer generated advertising and that executional quality may be traded off for these benefits" (p. 297). This isn't to suggest that technical prowess and "quality" are not important parts of commercial photographic education but rather that they shouldn't be of singular focus.

Given the above, I would argue that this prioritizing of narrative abilities must be addressed explicitly and persistently in the curriculum throughout the post-secondary education experience. Emphasis must be placed on understanding the relationship between semiotics, composition, and rhetorical emotional cues. As per Chang's point, this is a subtle and ephemeral expectation, but rich in conceptual opportunity. Undoubtedly this is already part of most commercial photographic curricula but I would argue that we need to integrate narrative goals into even the most technical and/or foundational assignments. An appropriate question to ask our students might be "How is the brand illuminated figuratively as well as literally through each particular lighting choice?

This also requires an understanding of the brand story in and of itself in order to provide an application of technique that fits the brand (rather then a dependence on default rules of product lighting for example). Studying the stories that brands tell about themselves and understanding the subtleties between differentiating identities of competitors in crowded sectors is crucial in order to anticipate the look and feel that might be most appropriate. There is value then in an historic understanding of the complexities of visual messaging changes and their progression through time. Lessons in the history of the use of photography in commercial contexts helps enmesh this understanding as a crucial part of brand partnerships on the part of working photographers. As an author of such a course, I find it is useful to track the changes in our collective approach to the use of applied visuals throughout the last century and to acknowledge that advertising "works on us" in different ways over time. As a result of this study, students begin to appreciate the impact of larger socio-economic trends on commercial expression and can start to anticipate the ways in which aspects of current culture and values are being articulated in the type of imagery we use and how we use it. Through specific case studies, they begin to understand how brands variously deal with growing product parity, product diversification, and increasing media differentiation and dispersion. Students are thusly enabled to apply a critical framework to speculative, future work, and emerging areas of image use.

There is value too in participating in social media spaces and experimenting with the inherent and differentiated narrative attributes which these spaces provide (certainly as opposed to only lamenting the loss of traditional media). Plus, social media platforms are being constantly innovated by artists wanting to use these new mediums to tell stories in unique ways. Two foundational examples are Rachel Hulin's Instagram novel *Hey Henry Hey Matilda* (Dewey, 2015) and Amalia Ulman's 2104 Instagram Art Project (Sooke, 2016). An awareness of innovation and experimentation in various realms of image use is crucial and informative, and will well situate our students for future innovations.

Indeed, this might also be a matter of clearly deconstructing a perceived and sometimes entrenched separation between "types" of photography within the structure and rhetoric of our programs. I would argue that keeping documentary, fine art, and advertising photography siloed (never mind the problematic division between moving and still images), is not appropriate given the increasing porousness of these areas and our need to pull from the persuasive approaches of each. This is echoed in the marketplace; newly formed agencies like NAMARA Reps and Getty's Verbatim agency (Laurent, 2016) are catering to the interest corporations have in telling authentic stories using narrative techniques inherent to the professional practice of photojournalists. Speaking about a recent project, Jane Mackie, Vice President of the Fairmont Hotel Brand mused: "Working with NAMARA has given us an opportunity to capture some of [our employee's] incredible stories and showcase them in a way that is authentic and meaningful" (Marketwired, 2016). Developments like these represent new opportunities for innovative image-makers who are willing to look beyond traditional professional barriers and reject the biases contained therein.

6. Authenticity and Aesthetic Creep

The desire for authenticity as voiced in the quote above from Fairmont Hotels is reminiscent of the Domino's chef's insistence that the consumer is really the best source of authentic photographs. Considered together, the underlying assumption is clear: the polish of a traditional commercial image is misleading and untrustworthy. This distrust has important but not unprecedented aesthetic consequences.

A vernacular photographic style began to appear in advertising in the 1990's due in part to the influence of the visual tropes of post-modernism (Schroeder, 2013). This had the effect of privileging real, authentic, snapshot-type images in mass-market contexts as more truthful to a marketing-weary and skeptical public (Berger, 2011; Schroeder, 2008). At the time, these "snapshots" were produced by professional commercial photographers like Terry Richardson, who reported preferring small, compact, point-and-shoot cameras for their ability to capture spontaneity and realness (Schroeder, 2008, pp. 284–285). In these cases, photographers were adopting and recreating the aesthetic qualities of the vernacular (to varying degrees: skewed composition, directional and harsh lighting, unflattering poses, image grain, over or underexposure, etc.) while still engaging multiple production elements and intentionally applied technical skill.

Meanwhile, in the early 2000's the rise of participation in online image sharing spaces begins to reinforce a similar vernacular aesthetic. These platforms privileged the mundane and the everyday experiences of life (Chang, 2014; Frey, 2012; Hjorth, 2008; Wagner, 2011). As a result, the banal visual tropes that were endemic to this type of diaristic image-making became associated with inherently authentic and real, in-between moments (Hjorth, 2008; Schroeder, 2013). As the desires of convergence culture became doubly encouraged and fulfilled by this online visual engagement and expression, marketers began to participate. By harnessing content created in these spaces, brands are able to borrow authenticity from the presumed aesthetic neutrality of these types of images. Indeed, authenticity is seen increasingly as a competitive advantage (Frey, 2012; Scoblete, 2015) and gives the brand more credibility in the marketplace (Deuze, 2005; Duffy, 2010; Lyngsfeldt, 2015; Uzunoğlu, 2011). As such, user generated ads are proving to be more successful than brand initiated campaigns by several metrics (Gotter, 2016; Lawrence et al., 2013; Lyngsfeldt, 2015; Olapic, 2016). As Schroeder (2013) explains: "This imagery serves to distance the brand from corporate control, associating it instead with consumer cocreation". Uzunoğlu (2011) elaborates: "as [it] is peer-created, it may have higher credibility and trustworthiness than company provided messages" (p. 148). And in Schroeder's (2013) research, he found "Thus, from the point of view of the brand manager, snapshot aesthetics offers a way into a *participatory* (consumer generated images), *sincere* and *less directive* (more ambiguous and flexible, perhaps) strategic style".

However, the rise of Instagram and the wide use of filters on that platform belie the snapshot aspect of these images. Indeed, the filters act to mediate these "banal" moments and as such, it is important to acknowledge the creeping aesthetic engagement of consumers in online image sharing spaces. Frey (2012) emphasizes the communicative usefulness of these capabilities and hints at the challenge for aspiring "professional" photographers: "These image processing features further enable the extension of photographic practice by reducing the threshold of competence required to produce appealing images with what were hitherto expensive professional, and difficult to master effects" (p. 27). In many cases then, there is a consistent effort to improve technique, develop a personal style and to engage in a practice that is more deliberate (Zappavigna, 2016, p. 3).

With this in mind, it is important to note that broad amateur photo expression has a duality: it is both banal and tries to look professional. Likewise for aspiring image-makers, desired visual expressions on social media are authentic but mediated, and participate in a mutually reinforcing loop of influence. More research is warranted in parsing the figurative layers and trade-offs contained in these images; analyzing, among other things, aesthetic engagement, access to brands and products, and the influence of dispersive communities.

Regardless, established photographers are competing with actual brand users whose visual testimonials are mostly unquestioned as authentically (more) pure, freely given, and shot without artifice. Plus, they are happening in real time in a way that can be organized and reconstituted through hashtags, likes, and reposts by the brand or others. From a photographic education perspective then, a brand approach that is "less directive" has some serious ramifications. Indeed, if brand-heavy mass-market communication is waning in favour of interactive social media and experiential based campaigns (Moore, 2015) there might be less opportunity for stylized, technique-rich imagery. Arguably, technical "mastery" as a singular or primary focus has been devalued. Having said this, there will always be a need for well-crafted lighting, considered tone and mood, and innovative aesthetic approaches on some marketing platforms (and certainly in terms of narrative ability as discussed above) but the prevailing trend towards "authenticity" has unquestionably empowered non professional image-makers who are already active in many brand enabled spaces. Is it necessary then to shift our learning outcomes to consider the possibility that technical skill is not the ultimate differentiator anymore?

Indeed, it is instructive to consider which aesthetic qualities can signal authenticity and understand how and when they might be engaged. Though technical skill and mastery is important in theory, students need to be taught to parse the particular client needs as they might align with context: where will this image appear, how long will it last, what is the experience it is designed to provoke? And after mastery is achieved, students need to be able to understand the importance of occasionally and thoughtfully "breaking the rules" of commercial lighting and composition and that "bad" photography delivers its own set of connotations which may be useful in certain marketing scenarios (as an example: Viviane Sassen's 2013 campaign for Carven in which the focus lies in the deep background landscape, leaving the foregrounded dress and model, presumably the point of the ad, very soft, the details of the dress having been completely obscured. KesselsKramer's long running work for the Hans Brinker Budget Hotel is another notable example). Also, it is important to review the visual tropes of the vernacular and their value from an historic perspective in order to appreciate the legacy of our ambiguous relationship with reality and fantasy in commercial imagery. How does a brand's shifting interest or engagement in "reality" challenge our assumptions about proper commercial work?

Furthermore, can instructed image-makers also participate in authentic brand experiences and reflect that back in non-traditional advertising spaces? This again suggests that there is value in understanding what the central brand qualities are in order to then capture and reflect those attributes. I would argue that our students need to go beyond the cliché "shoot in the style of your favourite brand" assignment and parse the platforms that pair with a particular visual approach for a specific client. They should be able to defend their aesthetic choices based on their understanding of the medium as well as the brand guidelines. In fact, there may well be untapped opportunity here. There is reason to believe that marketers are struggling to keep up with the demands of content hungry, multi-channel platforms. Considering advertorials in particular, a Photo District News article asserts "The hard part for agencies may be getting their heads around the type of content that best reflects their clients" (Ahearn, 2013). It will be to their advantage if our students can add value by applying an understanding of the medium coupled with an ability to execute across various narrative needs.

Similarly, the image-maker's own brand needs to be perceived as authentic as well. As we will see below, expressions of subjectivity can help deliver this message of authenticity; social media provides an ideal promotional space for this exploration and it can be harnessed to showcase all manner of image-based work, personal relationships, preferences, and experiences. As per a report from a 2015 PhotoPlus panel on this topic: "the route to success in social media doesn't follow a neat script and has far less to do with a given tactic and far more to do with honesty, positivity and having something of value to share with the world" (Scoblete, 2015).

7. Subjectivity and the Visual Testimonial

Imbedded in the attributes and desires of convergent culture is a preoccupation with subjectivity; processes of self-creation, re-inventing and performance have been encouraged and indulged by mobile media and the cameraphone (Gómez Cruz & Meyer, 2012). At the same time, social media platforms which allow individuated and targeted messaging, are becoming more central to brand communications as outlined above. As a result, brands are able to engage in value co-creation with their consumers, in part by highlighting their customer's subjective experiences with their products (Chang, 2014; Schroeder, 2013). This can in turn influence the brand's own visual approach (Gillett, 2014), exacerbating the divide between mass marketing, top-down approaches and organic, subjective and spontaneous expressions of brand engagement. In addition, consumers are also exploring their own identities in online spaces with reference to the established narratives of products, brands and corporate messages (Frey, 2012).

In her consideration of the use of Instagram, Zappavigna (2016) characterizes the personal expressions of subjectivity therein as an "unfolding construal of identity" (p. 3). In this way, subjectivity, authenticity and aesthetic choices are co-dependent. When brands pursue UGC, they engage the desires of convergence culture to have one's subjectivity indulged and included in brand performance, and one's individuated experience shared (Deuze, 2005; Keep, 2014). For this reason, the subjective (in the case of peer to peer marketing) message is more personally resonant. In essence, Instagram posts act as visual testimonials for the brand delivered instantaneously from trusted sources via social networks.

Of course there is both an acceptance and celebration of the aesthetic ramification of this subjectivity. Further to the discussion of the patina of authenticity delivered by non-professional image creation, Jonathan Schroeder (2013) explains: "Snapshot aesthetics signal a step away from corporate control and staging, expanding consumers' role to become both subjects and producers of strategic imagery" and Aaron Frey (2012) finds expression of self-hood and subjectivity in social media as a cycle of remaking, in part as a reaction to "packaged narratives and identities of a globalized consumer culture" (p. 8). In addition, we have seen a rising skepticism of the widespread use of photoshop which has come to be considered a misleading market tool (Leggatt, 2016; Olapic, 2016). This has hastened the preference for user generated imagery which can show, for example, an article of clothing on a real person who may more closely resemble the prospective buyer than an undoubtedly photoshopped model. So again we encounter a distrust and disavowal of mediated imagery as symptomatic of a brand's disinterest in a relationship with eager consumer partners.

How might students engage with this proclivity towards subjectivity? As was discussed above, this can nudge an aesthetic approach towards the everyday or the banal, but this could also work in a very different way, influencing the development and expression of the photographer's own brand. In a business or marketing context, it is increasingly important for students to explore expressions of self, personality, opinion, and personal perspective and understand the ways in which those can be executed in social media spaces. An understanding of the place of the "influencer" in the contemporary media landscape is one area of knowledge that would benefit our students and indeed a study and familiarity with social media as a promotional and expressive tool should be a requirement of any contemporary curriculum.

In another way, though the open and participatory nature of subjective engagement with brands in social media spaces might sidestep aesthetic ambitions or barriers to entry, there might also be an opportunity to exploit this preference for subjective experience by exploring deeply particular stylistic choices. Certainly it might allow expression for one's own particular photographic perspective when engaging with brands in social media, especially knowing that marketers are paying attention and willing to be influenced aesthetically themselves (Gillett, 2014). Without a doubt, individual consumer testimonials are compelling regardless of their aesthetic make up but there are clues that subjective experience can be considered, mediated, and even stylized. This is another rich area for study and application by our students in the context of understanding the opportunities inherent in new platforms.

8. Conclusion

This paper has attempted to chronicle the massive shifts in contemporary commercial image use and has named three main areas of emerging interest: narrative ability, authenticity, and subjectivity. With these three qualities in mind, this paper seeks to begin a discussion on how post secondary commercial photographic education might meet these needs and rewrite inappropriate and outdated "professional" ambitions for our students. My research suggests that we should focus on the experiential, affective and emotional power of not only a subjective and authentic photographic approach but also within the narrative strength of the image. I have made several suggestions as to how commercial programs might reorganize our priorities to meet the emerging challenges and opportunities posed by the technological and cultural shifts of convergent culture. There are clearly some ambiguities contained herein regarding the juxtaposition of technical skill in storytelling and the authenticity inherent to a seemingly snapshot approach. These ambiguities might pose the most vexing challenge, the answer to which can only be a deep commitment to understanding these new spaces of commercial engagement and experimenting with the tools these spaces provide.

In terms of the limits of this paper, this seeks to be an illumination of important trends and an introduction to the path forward. More research is required to find models of pedagogical approaches that are already addressing these shifts; there are undoubtedly educators who are engaged in a responsive practice with their students. Furthermore, though beyond the scope of this paper, there are opportunities for platform development work—helping brands capture user contributions and creating networks for citizen collaboration in brand initiatives (both commercial and within a mandate of social responsibility). Broadening the scope of what we teach our students to reach into the realms of programming, app development, and technical partnerships will undoubtedly be fruitful.

Without question, there are many interesting avenues of exploration for those committed to a sustained photographic practice. Though the consumer-generated content of which the Domino's campaign was typical seven years ago is still prevalent, there are signs that social media is also creating more space for deliberate image creation and use. Speaking about Instagram's latest Snapchat-like feature "Stories", Hugh Pile, L'Oréal's Chief Marketing Officer for Western Europe, explains that the appeal of this new approach comes from a duality: "Within the same platform now we've got this lovely juxtaposition that allows you to tell a richer story, but maybe [providing] a more authentic, or more earthy experience alongside the more polished core visuals" (Handley, 2016). It is crucial then to unlock the possibilities in our students to find these opportunities on platforms that will continue to engage the consumer as brand co-creators.

Acknowledgements

Thanks to Catherine Jones for early research help and to my co-faculty members for their commitment to providing robust educational opportunities for our students. Also many thanks to my Associate Dean, Donna Braggins and Sheridan College for their support of this paper.

Conflict of Interests

The author declares no conflict of interests.

References

American Society of Media Photographers. (2016). Membership categories. *ASMP*. Retrieved from http://www.asmp.org/join/membership-categories

Ahearn, M. (2013, June). 21 reasons to love photography now. *Photo District News*, 46. Retrieved from http://www.pdnonline.com/features/reasons-to-love-photography-now-part-1

Banet-Weiser, S. (2011). Convergence on the street: Rethinking the authentic/commercial binary. *Cultural Studies*, *25*(4/5), 641–658.

Banks, J., & Deuze, M. (2009). Co-creative labour. *International Journal of Cultural Studies*, *12*(5), 419–431.

Benkler, Y. (2006). *The wealth of networks: How social production transforms markets and freedom*. New Haven, CT: Yale University Press.

Berger, L. (2011). Snapshots, or: Visual culture's clichés. *Photographies*, *4*(2), 175–190.

Brabham, D. C. (2008). Crowdsourcing as a model for problem solving: An introduction and cases. *Convergence: The International Journal of Research into New Media Technologies*, *14*(1), 75–90.

Bruns, A. (2008). *Blogs, Wikipedia, Second Life, and beyond: From production to produsage* (Vol. 45). Bern: Peter Lang.

Canadian Association of Professional Image Creators. (2016). Membership categories. *CAPIC*. Retrieved from http://capic.org/membership-categories/

Chang, C. Y. (2014). *Visualizing brand personality and personal branding: Case analysis on Starbucks and Nike's brand value co-creation on Instagram*. (Master Thesis). University of Iowa, Iowa, USA.

Derousseau, R. (2016). 4 Reasons Domino's Pizza (DPZ)

keeps delivering growth. *U.S. News*. Retrieved http://money.usnews.com/investing/articles/2016-03-08/4-reasons-dominos-pizza-dpz-keeps-delivering-growth

Deuze, M. (2005). Towards professional participatory storytelling in journalism and advertising. *First Monday*, *10*(7). Retrieved from http://firstmonday.org/ojs/index.php/fm/article/view/1257/1177Beyond

Dewey, C. (2015). Behind the scenes of the world's first true Instagram novel. *Washington Post*. Retrieved https://www.washingtonpost.com/news/the-intersect/wp/2015/10/12/behind-the-scenes-of-the-worlds-first-true-instagram-novel

Duffy, B. E. (2010). Empowerment through endorsement? Polysemic meaning in Dove's user-generated advertising. *Communication, Culture & Critique*, *3*(1), 26–43.

Frey, A. (2012). *Pics or it didn't happen: Instagram in prosumer capitalism and reflexive modernity*. (Master Thesis). Lund University, Lund, Sweden.

Gillett, R. (2014). How the most successful brands dominate Instagram, and you can too. *Fast Company*. Retrieved from https://www.fastcompany.com/3029395/bottom-line/how-the-most-successful-brands-dominate-instagram-and-you-can-too

Gómez Cruz, E., & Meyer, E. T. (2012). Creation and control in the photographic process: iPhones and the emerging fifth moment of photography. *Photographies*, *5*(2), 203–221.

Gotter, A. (2016). 38 mind-blowing stats about user generated content. *Tint*. Retrieved from http://www.tintup.com/blog/38-mind-blowing-stats-effectiveness-user-generated-content

Handley, L. (2016). What does Instagram stories mean for brand engagement? *The Guardian*. Retrieved from https://www.theguardian.com/media-network/2016/sep/22/instagram-stories-brand-engagement-loreal-ted-baker

Harper, S. P. (2016). The commercial elephant in the room: The curious silence in the discussions on digital. *Take on Art*, *2*(1), 1–8.

He, W., Zha, S., & Li, L. (2013). Social media competitive analysis and text mining: A case study in the pizza industry. *International Journal of Information Management*, *33*(3), 464–472.

Hjorth, L. (2008). Being real in the mobile reel: A case study on convergent mobile media as domesticated new media in Seoul, South Korea. *Convergence: The International Journal of Research into New Media Technologies*, *14*(1), 91–104.

Jenkins, H. (2004). The cultural logic of media convergence. *International Journal of Cultural Studies*, *7*(1), 33–43.

Jenkins, H., & Deuze, M. (2008). Convergence culture. *Convergence-London*, *14*(1), 5–12.

Karpf, D. (2009). Blogs, Wikipedia, Second Life, and Beyond: From production to produsage, by Axel Bruns. *Journal of Information Technology & Politics*, *6*(1), 81–83.

Keep, D. (2014). The liquid aesthetic of the cameraphone: Re-imagining photography in the mobile age. *Journal of Creative Tecnhologies*, *4*, 128–146.

Kolm, J. (2015). Shine influencers launch in Toronto. *Strategy*. Retrieved from http://strategyonline.ca/2015/11/12/shine-influencers-launches-in-toronto

Laurent, O. (2016). Exclusive: New Getty image subsidiary to focus on commercial work. *Time*. Retrieved from: http://time.com/4473759/getty-images-subsidiary-news

Lawrence, B., Fournier, S., & Brunel, F. (2013). When companies don't make the ad: A multimethod inquiry into the differential effectiveness of consumer-generated advertising. *Journal of Advertising*, *42*(4), 292–307.

Leggatt, H. (2016). Consumers more likely to click on ads featuring user-generated photography. *BizReport*. Retrieved from http://www.bizreport.com/2016/12/consumers-more-likely-to-click-on-ads-featuring-user-generate.html

Lincoln, A. (2013, March 29) *"Domino's 'Show Us Your Pizza' integrated"*. Retrieved from https://vimeo.com/52483368

Litz, J. (2010) "Domino's launches 'Show us Your Pizza' campaign." *Pizza Market Place*. Retrieved from https://www.pizzamarketplace.com/news/dominos-launches-show-us-your-pizza-campaign

Lyngsfeldt, T. (2015). User generated content beats traditional advertising. *AdNews*. Retrieved from http://www.adnews.com.au/opinion/user-generated-content-beats-traditional-advertising

Marcus Reker, K. B. (2016). *"Why can't run 'like a girl' also mean win the race?": Commodity feminism and participatory branding as forms of self-therapy in the neoliberal advertising space*. (Senior Thesis). Scripps College, Claremont, USA.

Marketwired. (2016). Fairmont Hotels & Resorts partners with NAMARA represents on first-of-its kind photojournalism project. *Marketwired*. Retrieved from http://www.marketwired.com/press-release/fairmont-hotels-resorts-partners-with-namara-represents-on-first-its-kind-photojournalism-2121777.htm

Meyer, E. T. (2015). The expert and the machine: Competition or convergence? *Convergence: The International Journal of Research into New Media Technologies*, *21*(3), 306–313.

Moore, L. (2015). The ultimate list of marketing statistics for 2015. *Freely*. Retrieved from https://freely.net/marketing-statistics

Nava, M., Blake, A., MacRury, I., & Richards, B. (2013). *Buy this book: Studies in advertising and consumption*. London: Routledge.

Olapic. (2016). Consumer trust: Keeping it real. *Olapic*. Retrieved from http://www.olapic.com/consumer-trust

Professional Photographers of Canada. (2016). Member benefits. *PPoC*. Retrieved from https://www.ppoc.ca/en/membership

San Cornelio, G., & Gomez Cruz, E. (2014). Co-creation and participation as a means of innovation in new media: An analysis of creativity in the photographic field. *International Journal of Communication, 8*, 1–20.

Schroeder, J. E. (2008). Visual analysis of images in brand culture. In B. J. Phillips & E. McQuarrie (Eds.), *Go figure: New directions in advertising rhetoric* (pp. 277–296). Reference Press.

Schroeder, J. E. (2013). Snapshot aesthetics and the strategic imagination. *Invisible Culture, 18*. Retrieved from https://papers.ssrn.com/sol3/papers.cfm?abstract_id=2377848

Scoblete, G. (2105). How photographers with huge followings grew their social networks. *PDNPulse*. Retrieved from http://pdnpulse.pdnonline.com/2015/10/how-to-grow-your-social-network-photography.html

Sooke, A. (2016). Is this the first Instagram masterpiece? *Telegraph*. Retrieved from: http://www.telegraph.co.uk/photography/what-to-see/is-this-the-first-instagram-masterpiece

Toffler, A. (1980). *The third wave—The classic study of tomorrow*. New York, NY: Bantam Books.

Tow Centre. (2015). *Image truth/story truth (5/5): What is a photography? The future of photography and the professional image-maker*. Retrieved from https://vimeo.com/146125101

Uzunoğlu, E. (2011). Consumer as advertiser: A conceptual perspective. *Global Media Journal: Turkish Edition*, *2*(3), 138–159.

Wagner, K. (2011). Moblogging, remediation and the new vernacular. *Photographies*, *4*(2), 209–228.

Zappavigna, M. (2016). Social media photography: Construing subjectivity in Instagram images. *Visual Communication*, *15*(3) 271–292.

Migrating Servers, Elusive Users: Reconfigurations of the Russian Internet in the Post-Snowden Era

Ksenia Ermoshina and Francesca Musiani *

Institute for Communication Sciences, 75013 Paris, France; E-Mails: ksenia.ermoshina@cnrs.fr (K.E.), francesca.musiani@cnrs.fr (F.M.)

* Corresponding author

Abstract
In response to the growing censorship of their national Internet, Russian users, content producers and service providers have developed several resistance tactics. This paper analyzes these tactics with particular attention paid to their materiality. It first addresses the different levels of Internet "governance by infrastructure" in Russia, then focuses on the different tactics of individual and collective resistance and concludes by discussing how forms of control enacted at different levels of infrastructure are reconfiguring the geopolitics of the Russian Internet.

Keywords
digital sovereignty; Edward Snowden; Internet geopolitics; Internet governance; Internet infrastructure; resistance; Russian Internet

Issue
This article is part of the issue "Post-Snowden Internet Policy", edited by Julia Pohle (WZB Berlin Social Science Center, Germany) and Leo Van Audenhove (Vrije Universiteit Brussel, Belgium).

---

1. Introduction

The last two decades of Russian Internet (RuNet)'s development have showed a paradoxical situation where a rapidly developing[1] Internet coexisted with a state-centered Internet governance. A "half-freedom of speech" (Gelman, 2010) was associated with the hope of a democratization of the country (Elting et al., 2010; Lonkila, 2012). However, after the defeat of the protest movement "For Fair Elections" (2011–2012), these democratic expectations were questioned. The Kremlin started seeing the Internet "as politically disruptive because it enables citizens to circumvent government-controlled 'traditional' media" (Nocetti, 2015, p. 113).

Recent developments in RuNet regulation demonstrate the government's will to establish national control of the digital sphere (Freiberg, 2014; Nocetti, 2015). The presidential administration organized an "Internet + Sovereignty" forum in May 2016 around issues of national governance of the Internet of Things (IoT) and Big Data, promoting a project of Russian standards and the possibility of building a closed national network in the field of IoT. The intention to develop a "sovereign Internet" was also proposed as a double response to the terrorist threat and the domination of American web services.

However, the laws that frame online activities of Russian users are diverse and constantly evolving as a patchwork of incomplete measures that overlap and sometimes contradict each other. Each of these measures challenges IT professionals, e.g. Internet service providers, hosting providers, developers, journalists, bloggers and NGOs. Simultaneously, a set of individual practices, know-how, or *arts de faire*, is being developed by RuNet users to bypass access restrictions or protect their communications from governmental surveillance.

[1] 75% of population are said to have Internet access in 2016.

Emerging NGOs and associations promote and institutionalize some of these hacks and launch large-scale campaigns for RuNet freedom.

In light of this context, the central research aim of this paper is to understand the connection between the "State-centered" style of Russian Internet governance and the local tactics of *détournement* and bricolage (Akrich, 1998). Our hypothesis is that in the Russian case, resistance to Internet control and surveillance happens not only and not *primarily* at the political and legal levels (e.g. lobbying or negotiations with governmental structures, class action or collective mobilizations) but at the level of everyday individual practices of usage, such as anonymization of users or migration of people and infrastructures. A specific body of research dedicated to local social movements in contemporary Russia (Erpyleva & Magun, 2014; Kharkhordin, 2011; Prozorov, 2012; Zhuravlev, Savelyeva, & Yerpylova, 2014) is helpful to analyze this style of contention: indeed, this research analyzes post-Soviet de-politicization as the consequence of an "exodus" from the public sphere to the private sphere. It shows that Russian civil society tends to mobilize around local problems, often related to the materiality of the city (Ceruzzi, 2006) rather than to support global challenges; for example, bottom-up activities of repair and maintenance of a particular district or equipment in the city will be favored over a protest against the Mayor of the same city. In this sense, and along the lines of recent scholarship such as Klyueva's (2016), the article is also an attempt to understand the specificities of the response of Russian civil society—with its mix of collective and individual tactics of resistance—to restrictive Internet policies.

The structure of the paper is as follows. First, it addresses the different levels of Internet "governance by infrastructure" (DeNardis & Musiani, 2016), in Russia—showing how the Russian State is increasingly leveraging, co-opting and on occasion "tampering with", Internet infrastructure in order to fulfill political aims that, in some instances, are sensibly different than the objectives the infrastructure was originally meant for. Then, the paper focuses on the different tactics of individual and collective resistance, and concludes with a discussion of how the forms of control enacted at different levels of RuNet infrastructure are reconfiguring its geopolitics.

The paper builds upon observations of "cryptoparties", on original interviews with Russian IT-specialists, Internet service providers (ISPs) and expatriate journalists and developers, and situates this material by means of a brief analysis of Russian Internet legislation. More specifically, the empirical part of the research combined several methods: observation of three cryptoparties in 2012, 2015 and 2016—the purpose of these observations being to analyze different tools used in order to protect anonymity and bypass censorship, as well as the discourse organizers and participants were developing about Internet regulations in Russia; interviews with 3 internet service providers, 4 expatriated developers, 1 NGO organizer and a dozen users. The interviews were semi-structured with grids adapted to providers, developers and users, and lasted between 40 minutes and 2 hours. Qualitative analyses of relevant press materials and Web ethnographies analyzing professional forums of ISPs as well as the biggest Internet resources dedicated to Internet Freedom in Russia (such as Moskovskiy Libertarium or Rublacklist) were also conducted.

2. Surveillance, Data Storage and Filtering: Levels of Infrastructure-Based Internet Control in Russia

RuNet governance has developed upon several layers, with three main types of measures adopted since 1998:

a) Surveillance measures of 'lawful interception', called System of Operative Investigative Measures (SORM), aimed at giving governmental services such as FSB (former KGB) access to private communications both by telephone and on the Internet;[2]
b) Regulation of data storage, restricting important data flows to national borders;
c) Filtering measures, restricting access to a growing list of websites (blacklist)[3] considered as extremist. These three layers are interconnected and show a global tendency towards a RuNet "balkanization"—hyper-localization and nation-state regulation of data and communication flows.

2.1. "SORMisation" of Russia: Surveillance Measures and ISP Markets

The SORM was first implemented in Russia in 1998. SORM provides an architecture by which law enforcement and intelligence agencies can obtain direct access to data on commercial networks. During the past eight years, SORM has given rise to new configurations of sociotechnical "actants" (Latour, 1988) with long-term consequences on the market of ISPs. Three generations of SORM measures have seen the light. SORM-1 allows FSB to access telephone traffic, including mobile networks. SORM-2, implemented in 2005, is responsible for inter-

[2] Apart from FSB and Roskomnadzor, MVD (Ministry of Internal Affairs), FSO (Federal Service of Security), FSKN (Federal Service for Control of Drug Traffic), FTS (Federal Customs Service) and FSIN (Federal Penitentiary Service) also participate in online surveillance in Russia. However, while MVD, FSB and FSKN both possess the equipment and have the right to use it for lawful interception, FSO and FTS depend on FSB to have an access to the equipment, while FSIN has the equipment but does not have the right to use it for investigative activities. Apart from state actors regulating online surveillance, a market of surveillance equipment has been developing in recent years (especially since the adoption of SORM-3 measures). Several private companies seem to play the most important role in this field: "Special technologies" and "MFI-Soft" (who earn 5–6 billion rubles a year on SORM equipment) and smaller manufacturers (Reanet, Norsi-Trans and TechArgos each earning 1 billion rubles a year). The most recent player on the market is the State corporation RosTech, supposed to produce the necessary equipment to implement Yarovaya law.

[3] Officially called "Unified Register of Domain Names, Internet Website Page Locators, and Network Addresses that Allow to Identify Internet Websites Containing Information Prohibited for Distribution in the Russian Federation" (or Unified Register).

cepting IP traffic, including VoIP. SORM-3, implemented in 2014, gathers information from all communication media, and offers long-term and comprehensive storage of subscriber data (Privacy International, 2016).

Compared to international Lawful Interception standards, SORM gives great autonomy to surveillance actors. In most Western countries, law enforcement agencies seek a warrant from a court and then issue an order for lawful interception to a network operator or ISP, which is obliged to intercept and deliver the requested information. The FSB does not need to contact the ISP because of the very architecture of SORM, containing two main elements: the "extractor" (the equipment—software and hardware—that performs data extraction) and the "remote control station". The control station is localized in the FSB regional office and enables remote control of the extractor without the provider's permission: the provider may not know which data, and how, is intercepted, analyzed and transferred. No court decision is necessary in order to activate the interception of the metadata. However, in order to access the actual telephone recordings, FSB has to ask for a court permission. In 2012, there were 372,144 orders distributed, according to the official data provided by the Supreme Court.[4]

The most expensive component of SORM is the circular buffer for data storage. However, each new generation of SORM measures has changed the technical requirements: while for SORM-2 providers needed to store all the traffic for 12 hours, SORM-3 obliged them to store all the metadata for three years. Thus, the providers have to change all their equipment as the implementation of SORM systems completely relies on them: "We pay for it", remarks internet provider Michael I. "If you do not put this equipment, you do not have license and you lose state clients".

When the local FSB or prosecutor's office identifies shortcomings, they send the information to Roskomnadzor (the Federal Service for Supervision of Communications, Information Technology and Mass Media).[5] The ISP is warned, first fined, then if violations persist, its license may be revoked (Borogan & Soldatov, 2013). Roskomnadzor statistics show that in 2010, there were 16 warnings, 13 in 2011, and 30 in 2012.[6]

Providers have to renew SORM equipment by themselves as no certified standards exist on the market and there is no consensus among manufacturers. As a result, providers have to adapt to the new technical demands, sometimes via DIY tinkering with old equipment: "Adapt the parts of your system, first of all...because when they will finally publish the certificates...we will have to spend tons of bucks again, and we will have to do it, because that's the Law",[7] notes user Andrei on 14 November 2015.

An inquiry led by Leonid Volkov, activist, blogger and programmer, claims that "a small provider has to give about 20%–30% of his annual income to buy SORM equipment" (Volkov, 2016). The two biggest manufacturers of SORM equipment earn 5–6 billion rubles per year on SORM, while three other small manufacturers earn about 1 billion. To reduce their costs, smaller providers buy SORM-as-a-service from their upstream providers. The implementation of SORM-1 in Russia sparked a protest campaign by IT-professionals, human rights organizations and Internet freedom defenders. The first anti-SORM movement was launched in the late 1990s in the form of a DDoS attack on FSB semantic analysis tools. Activists were adding specific keywords to every mail, such as "bomb", "explosion", "terrorist attack", triggering constant alerts to the control station and overloading it. Moscovskiy Libertarium,[8] with Russian and international partners, launched an international solidarity campaign against SORM. A public petition was sent to the Supreme Court and former Russian president Boris Yeltsin, asking him to "use his authority in order to stop the implementation of SORM", an "unprecedented example of violation of the rights to privacy and human rights convention".[9] While this campaign did not produce immediate results, fifteen years later the European Court of Human Rights has recognized that SORM was a violation to the European Convention of Human Rights, because its technical infrastructure enabled interception of communications without court permission, thus bypassing legal procedures.

The early-2000s anti-SORM campaign was mostly led by journalists, NGO activists and programmers, while providers were almost absent from the controversy, with the exception of "Bayard-Slaviya Communications". As Sergey Smirnov, activist of Pravozashitnaya Set (Human Rights Network), notes: "Internet service providers have come to the conclusion that the perspective to lose their license is much worse than the necessity to collaborate with FSB. In one of the recent publications about SORM, an FSB officer noticed that in the majority of cases providers apply all the requirements without any pressure and even demonstrate an understanding".[10] The

[4] According to the official statistics provided by the Supreme Court, in 2012, 372,144 orders were distributed, compared to 326,105 in 2011, 276,682 in 2010, 245,645 in 2009, 229,144 in 2008 and 189,591 in 2007: https://ria.ru/infografika/20130815/956535235.html

[5] Roskomnadzor is a Federal Executive Authority of the Russian Federation, performing the following functions: control and supervision of mass media (including electronic mass media), mass communications, information technology, and telecommunications; supervision and statutory compliance control of personal data processing; managing the Radio Frequency Service activities; supervision of production of copies of audiovisual works, computer software, databases and audio recordings on any media; accreditation of experts and expert organizations for content evaluation in order to ensure child information security. It is affiliated to the Ministry of Communications and Mass Media of the Russian Federation. The role of Roskomnadzor has recently expanded. The list of all its functions may be found on its official website: http://eng.rkn.gov.ru/about

[6] Available at https://rkn.gov.ru/press/annual_reports

[7] Available at http://forum.nag.ru/forum/index.php?showtopic=47641&st=560

[8] Available at http://www.libertarium.ru, created by Anatoliy Leventchuk in 1994.

[9] Available at http://www.libertarium.ru/l_sormact_gilc

[10] Available at http://www.libertarium.ru/l_sormact_conf6aprd

lack of providers in the anti-SORM movement made any civil disobedience movement technically impossible. In order to create a precedent, Leonid Volkov launched a campaign against SORM-3 in 2015; he started the so-called "Attack on SORM", a legal and political project of collective appeal to court by operators and providers, to demand better regulation of SORM and state-funded certified equipment.

2.1.1. Yarovaya Law: When Law (Unusually) Pre-Dates Technology

Nonetheless, the development of SORM legal and technical requirements created tensions in the ISP community. In June 2016, a new set of surveillance measures was proposed by Representative Irina Yarovaya: Russian telecom operators will have to store all traffic (including calls, letters, documents, images and video) for six months, and related metadata for three years. The importance of this case lies in its revealing a "reverse gap" between legal measures and financial and technical resources: while "governments are struggling to keep up with the pace of technological change, with technology evolving faster than law-making efforts" (Nocetti, 2015, p. 111), in the Yarovaya law case, law-making has outpaced the actual technological development of the country. Indeed, such surveillance needs a complex and multilayered technical infrastructure (including servers, the network itself, data storage systems and software), with far-reaching implications for the ways Internet and telecommunications work in Russia, including quality of connection, the speed at which and the amounts of data the network is able to transfer and the price of Internet services. Vladimir K., ISP, says: "Yarovaya law is technically absurd. Firstly, there is no necessary equipment on the market. Secondly, it is useless to store encrypted data. With the same success, we can code a random numbers generator and send this data to FSB pretending it is our users' traffic".

The problem is both technical and geopolitical, as it questions the limits of the Russian nation-state and its capabilities to implement a new infrastructure independently from the Western market. Within embargo, due to the Western sanctions imposed on Russia following the annexation of Crimea in 2014, the Russian government turns to national companies to produce the necessary equipment. The politics of "substitution of imports" coupled with the new series of surveillance laws have an important impact on the Russian IT-industry. The CEO of MGTS (Moscow State Telecom Network), Andrey Ershov, states: "Today we do not have any equipment in order to be able to put the 'Yarovaya law' into practice....So, the biggest concern that all telecom operators publicly express, is related to the cost of such solutions. [The equipment] is about tens of billion rubles". Even the emerging set of firms specialized in SORM equipment cannot satisfy Yarovaya law requirements in terms of equipment, estimated at 10.3 billion rubles (Kantyshev, 2016). Providers and telecom operators have publicly expressed their skepticism of the new surveillance law, pointing out that new solutions risk becoming obsolete within a few years and will demand further investment (Schepin, 2016). Press and specialized websites show a rise in disapproval of the Yarovaya law among IT professionals, for similar reasons. Among the actors criticizing the law are the biggest Russian IT companies, Mail.ru and Yandex, as well as professional associations Russian Association of Electronic Communications and Russian Civic Organization Center for Informational Technologies and even a pro-governmental working group "Communications and IT" ("Svyaz i IT"). The most popular professional forum of Russian providers, Nag.ru, creatively reacted to the law by developing a "Yarculator"[11], a software enabling providers to calculate the prices for the necessary equipment and the cost of Internet services for end users.

The law was largely contested by civil society. A petition on Change.org gathered 623,465 signatures as of 8 January 2017. A demonstration against the law was held in Moscow in August 2016 and gathered between 2,400 to 4,000 people (Kozlov & Filipenok, 2016). On his end, Edward Snowden publicly asked Putin not to sign the Yarovaya law, emphasizing its nefarious economic consequences and pointing out that a six-month storage of data is dangerous, unfeasible and expensive[12] (Figures 1 and 2).

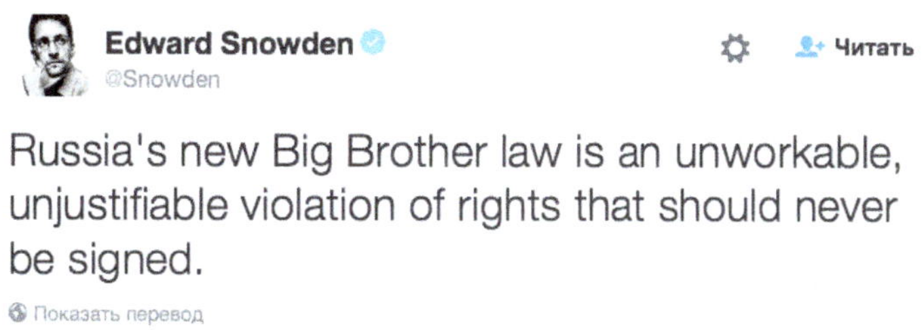

Figure 1. Edward Snowden's critical tweet on the Yarovaya law.

[11] Available at http://nag.ru/articles/article/29513/-yarkulyator-kalkulyator-yarovoy.html#comments

[12] Available at http://www.macdigger.ru/iphone-ipod/snouden-raskritikoval-zakon-yarovoj-on-otnimet-u-rossiyan-dengi-i-svobodu.html

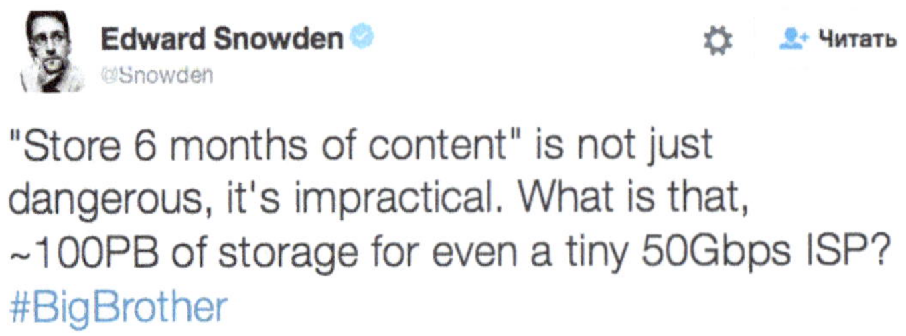

Figure 2. Edward Snowden's critical tweet on the duration of data storage outlined in the Yarovaya law.

While SORM and Yarovaya law give FSB access to data stored on Russian servers without informing site owners or providers, it is more difficult to get access to foreign services, e.g. Facebook and Twitter. Thus, a set of new measures has been adopted to reconfigure data storage and transfer.

2.2. "Snowden Effect" on RuNet: Migrations of Personal Data

Snowden's revelations had a considerable effect on IT markets. The leaks "changed the way people perceive their personal data, and will cost internet corporations, especially American ones, millions of dollars" (Filonov, 2014). Indeed, in January 2014, Canadian provider Peer1 showed that 75 British and Canadian companies did not want to store their data in the US because of the fear of being tracked down by the surveillance services.[13] Internet companies started creating servers outside US territory.

Russian Internet users—particularly specific groups including developers and activists—were seemingly not caught unprepared by Snowden's revelations. SORM being well-known since the late 1990s to all active Internet users, it was not news for Russians that governments could track their communications without a court order. Maxim I., hosting provider with Komtet, notes: "His revelations were not a surprise for specialists....In Russia, and I am sure, in any country, it is possible to get whatever information about a user or his websites. Some RuNet users even joked about the role Snowden played in RuNet regulation: 'Why have they kept Snowden here?' Very simple. They just asked him about the downsides of the American system of surveillance and made a better one".[14]

Snowden's revelations attracted attention to existing surveillance practices and made it possible to compare SORM with the US system. However, the revelations' most important impact concerned the role of US cloud services and internet corporations. In response, the Russian government modified the "Law on storage and protection of personal data" and reconsidered data geopolitics to allegedly guarantee the "protection of Russian citizens' data from US government surveillance". Researcher-journalists Andrei Soldatov and Irina Borogan insist on the role that Snowden played in this: "Right on time, Edward Snowden appeared on the world stage. The NSA scandal made a perfect excuse for Russian authorities to launch a campaign to bring global web platforms such as Gmail and Facebook under Russian law—either requiring them to be accessible in Russia by the domain extension .ru, or obliging them to be hosted on Russian territory" (Borogan & Soldatov, 2013).

The law #242-FZ was adopted on 1 September 2014. It obliges providers to "store personal data of Russian citizens, used by internet services, on the territory of the Russian Federation". Providers must guarantee recording, systematization, accumulation, storage, updates, modifications and extraction of personal data using databases located on Russian territory.[15] Noncompliance with this new law may result in total blockage of the service. Thus, for example, in November 2016 LinkedIn was blocked in Russia (including mobile apps) for the violation of the new data storage policies. Web services are also required to build backdoors for Russian secret services to access stored data. Another way to put pressure on western companies is to block entire web services because they store "forbidden information". Thus, YouTube was blocked in Russia for hosting a video judged as extremist. Facebook removed a page called Club Suicide rather than seeing its entire network blacklisted. The repatriation of data illustrates the tendency of Russian internet governance towards "digital sovereignty" (Nocetti, 2015, p. 112).

Several resistance tactics have developed in response to these balkanization measures. A petition addressed to Google, Facebook and Twitter asks them not to oblige: "We don't trust the domestic security services that are in charge of data security once the data is in Russia. We're asking internet companies to withstand this pressure using all possible legal means and we are ready to support them".[16] Developers were immediately concerned, as the law attacked the instruments they were constantly using, such as GitHub, as well as their data storage practices. Another tactic deployed was a reorientation towards new products that would avoid storage of personal

[13] Available at http://go.peer1.com/rs/peer1/images/Peer1-Report-NSA-Survey-NA.pdf
[14] Available at http://www.yaplakal.com/forum1/st/75/topic1086610.html
[15] Available at http://www.garant.ru/news/648095/#ixzz4LqmT7iT8
[16] Available at https://www.change.org/p/facebook-google-twitter-don-t-move-personal-data-to-russia

data: "We try to make services that do not store user data, so that we do not have to store it on our servers", remarks Alexey P., developer, CTO of Progress Engine; "We have some apps that we make for TV, or for electronic wallets, where the data is stored on the servers of our clients". These are specific resistance tactics which we could call tactics of "evasion". In fact, instead of contesting the law #242-FZ by communicating directly with the Russian government, citizens either try to communicate with western IT companies (addressing petitions to Google and Facebook), or modify their own practices and professional activities in order to find legal gaps or grey zones (e.g. using APIs for authorization or third parties for user data storage, or repositioning their product in order to use no personal data at all).

Another step towards digital sovereignty was made in spring 2016 with an ambitious project of "state-in-the-middle": during the forum "IT + Sovereignty", the intended creation of state-owned SSL-certification was announced. Forum member Natalya Kasperskaya explains: "Roskomnadzor and FSB are lobbying the delegation of SSL certificates to governmental organizations....Now we have a piece of the Internet that is completely out of control by our own country, and it is not good. Because the data is being gathered globally, by someone who is beyond the borders of our state, and it is totally wrong".[17] According to our interviewees, this project is actually a response to the inefficient Yarovaya law and the growing popularity of encryption among RuNet users. Alexey P. emphasizes: "They understood that storing gigabytes of data will give no results, especially because it is encrypted....So the project to build a Man-in-the-middle attack on the governmental level is scary".

2.3. Error 451: Filtering Websites, Restricting Access to the Content

```
HTTP/1.1 451 Unavailable For Legal Reasons
<h1>Unavailable For Legal Reasons</h1>
<p>This request may not be serviced in the
Roman Province of Judea due to the Lex Julia
Majestatis, which disallows access to
resources hosted on servers deemed to be
operated by the People's Front of Judea.</p>
</body>
</html>
```
[18]

A third set of measures, based on filtering, seeks to control user access to the content of websites judged as extremist or criminal. Since 2007, regional prosecutors have implemented court decisions requiring ISPs to block access to banned sites accused of extremism, but this has not been done systematically. In order to centralize these different materials, a "Single register of Internet resources containing information whose distribution is forbidden in Russia" was created in 2012: any websites that enter this blacklist have to be blocked and three governmental agencies participate in the constitution of this blacklist. Since the adoption of the "Lugovoy law" on 1 February 2014, the list includes websites that "appeal to extremism", e.g. mass disorders, religious or interethnic discord, participation in terrorist attacks or some types of public mass events.

On 13 March 2014, Roskomnadzor blocked access to four webpages: Grani.ru (a liberal online media platform), Kasparov.ru (the website of Garry Kasparov, chess-player and a leader of the liberal opposition), Ezhednevniy Zhurnal (liberal media platform) and the blog of Alexey Navalny (anti-Putin movement leader in 2011–2012 and reputable blogger). Roskomnadzor stated that "these websites contain appeals to illegal activities and participation in mass demonstrations that violate the law".[19]

The list of forbidden webpages is accessible online.[20] As of 30 September 2016, 41,064 pages—mostly concerning prostitution, gambling, black markets, gaming and torrents—are blocked. However, NGO websites are also present, such as the site of Mirotvorets,[21] a pro-Ukrainian organization that informs about the conflict in Ukraine, in particular on the location of Russian troops.

The blocking happens in three ways: by DNS, by IP address or by URL, using Deep Packet Inspection. Administratively, hosting providers are responsible for keeping the blacklist up-to-date and communicating with the owners of forbidden sites and end-users. Maxim I. notes that "The blocking is very easy. We receive and update regularly the black list, twice in a day, and we block those of our clients who are not lucky....We inform our client that his site has been added to the blacklist. Then we listen to everything that the client wants to say about Roskomnadzor but we can't help them or ignore the demand of Roskomnadzor because in this case they can block the IP address of the server, or even an address pool. I am not even speaking about administrative consequences for the company".

While providers have very little possibility to resist the blocking of the blacklisted resources, they choose other forms of action to express their critique of Internet censorship. Vladimir K., director of the ISP CLN, says: "When users try to access to a blocked page, we show them the error message that starts with a phrase: "The struggle against evil is almost never a struggle for good". Thus, the error message itself becomes a space of expression where providers can symbolically communicate with their users by showing their attitude towards the Lugovoy law.

However, Russian filtering and blocking systems are applied unevenly from one region to another, from one

[17] Available at https://rublacklist.net/21509
[18] Available at https://tools.ietf.org/html/rfc7725
[19] Available at http://www.newsru.com/russia/13mar2014/block.html
[20] Available at https://reestr.rublacklist.net
[21] Available at www.myrotvorets.center

provider to another. For example, several employees of ISPs of big companies/monopolists, such as Russian Railways, confirm that they have not been blocked, as Dmitry M. in 2014: "We have this provider in our company, and all the blacklisted websites can be opened. However this seems quite logical, because Roskomnadzor can't give any orders to Russian Railways, who own this provider" (Nossik, 2014). Also, filtering works only partially, depending on the region, the provider and its position on the market, its connections with western providers (e.g. providers who had a peering agreement with Stockholm could access blacklisted websites).

The paradox of filtering consists in the double digital divide that it creates. The more "politicized" users, familiar with the forbidden online resources, will keep on accessing them, using specific tools to bypass censorship. However, the majority of the population will be unable to access this content, lacking the necessary knowledge, resources and technologies to do so. Search engines are also impacted by filtering, so reinforcing the divide: before the blockage, users could accidentally discover some websites (e.g. Navalny's blog) through search engines, but after the blockage these sites "disappeared" (were dereferenced) from the search results. This consequently reduces considerably any potential audience and reinforces the echo-chamber effect by regrouping users who already agree, as mentioned by user popados: "These blockages are not for those who read and will bypass no matter how. It is for random visitors that come from the search or other casual channels that actually constitute the majority. They will just go to another website. In this sense, the blockage is rather efficient" (Nossik, 2014). The same phenomenon touches blacklisted torrent websites, such as Rutracker, that demonstrate a significant decrease in traffic: "the majority of users are just lazy, they are finding new open sources of content. So the goal of the filtering is not to close for everyone, but for an important part", says Maxim I.

Still, access restrictions are not especially difficult to bypass. The IETF notes that "in many cases clients can still access the denied resource by using technical countermeasures such as a VPN or the Tor network" (RFC 7725). Indeed, users deploy manifold technical practices, bricolages and *arts de faire*.

3. Elusive Users: Countermeasures for Bypass and Anonymity

> "Long ago, when GSM connection was not very high quality, there was a trick: you just need to say 'bomb, president, terrorism' and the connection would become much better" Fedor, ISP

Users recently gathered in associations to denounce RuNet censorship and surveillance and promote countermeasures: these include but are not limited to the Russian Pirate Party, *Roskomsvoboda* (Association for the Freedom of Communications), a website for monitoring and analytics of the blockages (Rublacklist), and the project Openrunet promoting countermeasures. While some of these are focused on political campaigning against access restrictions, others concentrate on promoting countermeasures and do not focus on the government but on RuNet users.

Different resistance tactics circulate on forums, blogging platforms and social networks, in the form of comments, posts or specific tutorials. Dedicated "offline" workshops, called "cryptoparties", are organized to present privacy-enhancing tools, and draw from an international cryptoparty movement launched in 2012. Pre-Snowden, in 2012, we participated in such workshops in Saint-Petersburg. They were aimed at left activists (anarchists and antifascists). After 2013, seminars were aimed at a wider audience including NGO workers, journalists, rights defenders and RuNet users seeking to adapt their habits to new realities. The event name was also adapted, the marked word "cryptoparty" being replaced by "seminars on information security".

A wide range of bypass and anonymization tactics and tools exist, circulating both on the Web and during thematic seminars. The organizers themselves attempt to classify existing tools and practices, to build tutorials and construct a coherent presentation, for which several strategies have been observed. Classification occurred, for example, based on the question "Who is your enemy?" Thus Igor, moderator of a cryptoparty for an audience of NGO workers in April 2016, Saint-Petersburg, constructed his presentation around two "big enemies": the state and corporations. He presented the tools that can help bypass state censorship and some devices that would help resist targeted advertising and data tracking. A different format was observed in the *Roskomsvoboda* tutorials, which organize materials according to the tasks users want to perform: "access to a blocked website", "communicate in privacy", "protect your metadata while surfing the web".

On our end, we distinguish such practices here according to the laws they intend to challenge, whether it is SORM or filtering practices and access to blacklisted content. Some of the tools are used in both cases.

As SORM is aimed at intercepting communications, bypassing techniques consist in encrypting them. Encryption tools are used at both the application and network layers. At the application layer, cryptography has been promoted since the first campaigns against SORM launched in 1998 by Moscovskiy Libertarium.[22] Back then, activists were promoting PGP or GnuPG over a mail client, all the while understanding the limits of cryptography: "These countermeasures can't *exclude* the possibility to intercept your communications, but our goal is to make this access extremely hard and *expensive*" (Otstavnov, 1998, our emphasis). Moskovskiy Libertarium was promoting massive usage of these tools

[22] Available at http://www.libertarium.ru/sorm_crypto_esc

as collective action to make surveillance hard and economically disadvantageous for the state: "If the Internet community used these technical means at least in half of the cases, it would become almost immunized against all these dirty tricks such as SORM. However, even occasional usage of strong crypto (especially for fun) will make our opponents' work very hard" (Otstavnov, 1998).

Nowadays, usage of PGP has increased, while remaining far from the ambitious goal of 50% or 100% of users; however, mobile apps for encrypted messaging are gaining popularity. The market for encrypted messaging and mailing clients being in expansion (Ermoshina, Musiani, & Halpin, 2016), cryptoparty organizers and specialized NGOs (e.g. Roskomsvoboda) elaborate several sets of criteria to rate and compare the apps. For example, Igor, the moderator mentioned above, presented a set of criteria including open source, end-to-end, group chat and calls, synchronization between devices, self-destroying messages, notifications about logins from different devices, logging history and multi-layered authentication.

For the time being, alongside WhatsApp,[23] Telegram remains the most popular secure messaging app among Russian users. The usage of Telegram varies according to users' goals and threat models. Several functionalities of the app make it convenient for different user groups: chats, secret chats, group chats, bots and channel broadcasting. Users faced with a low level of threat, not associated with any political activities, tend to adopt Telegram as an alternative to WhatsApp and SMS for everyday conversations with their peer groups. Many activists and privacy-concerned users are aware of the absence of "privacy by default" in Telegram chats (client to-server encryption) and opt for a "secret chat" option that offers end-to-end encryption. This user group also adopts two-step authentication and self-destruct timer options. Functions such as "Group chat" are used for group conversations between up to 200 users and are popular among activists, journalists or researchers for organizational purposes, as an alternative to Google Groups or mailing lists. For example, one of our use-cases, a group of researchers working in Eastern Ukraine, use Telegram on a daily basis to coordinate research activities, discuss fieldwork, materials and other organizational information. However, they do not rely on Telegram for very sensitive discussions and prefer face-to-face offline meetings.

The popularity of Telegram in Russia can be partly explained by the reputation of its founders, Nicolai and Pavel Durov, Russian-born developers and entrepreneurs. Pavel Durov, the founder of Vkontakte, the most famous Russian social network, is colloquially referred to as the "Russian Zuckerberg" and became *persona non grata* in Russia after his refusal to collaborate with the FSB.[24] Telegram's quick rise on the market of messaging apps is of particular interest as it tells us a lot about the socio-economic factors that influence the success of an innovation in the field: it was when Facebook bought WhatsApp (followed by a several hours blackout for the latter), that the Telegram download rate exploded. As opposed to WhatsApp, Telegram can publicly underline its non-for-profit character and lack of ties with any commercial or governmental services.

While the Russian version of Telegram was released in 2012, before the Snowden revelations, Durov claims that the international version of his tool was inspired by the whistleblower: "In 2012 my brother and I built an encrypted messaging app for our personal use—we wanted to be able to securely pass on information to each other, in an environment where WhatsApp and other tools were easily monitored by the authorities. After Edward Snowden's revelations in 2013 we understood the problem was not unique to our situation and existed in other countries. So we released the encrypted messaging app for the general public".[25]

As Telegram servers are located in five different countries around the world, outside Russia, its broadcasting function is used by censored media as a way to bypass the blockage, and by bloggers as an alternative to Facebook and traditional blogging platforms (for example, Alexey Navalny's popular bot on Telegram and the Grani.ru channel and bot, amongst others). However, unlike private communications on Telegram, public channels may be read and blocked by ISPs and by the Telegram technical team. As of January 2016, 660 channels attributed to ISIS were blocked.

While the "broadcasting channel" function made Telegram an alternative to other news sources and social networks, political activists prefer either the "secret chat" function, or Signal. The Signal application, which Snowden recommended, is used for a specific and limited set of functions—SMS and phonecalls. However, at recent cryptoparties Signal has been criticized for the absence of functions such as automatic synchronization among different devices, time-settings and search.

The technologies used to bypass the Lugovoy law and access censored websites mostly employ the practice of IP address-switching. Therefore one of the most popular and easy-to-use tools is an online proxy server,such as hideme.ru or cameleo.ru. However, this system was criticized by our IT-security activist interviewees for its lack of traffic encryption: a proxy is only useful for by-

---

[23] We do not examine WhatsApp here, as it was not initially designed as a secure messaging app with end-to-end encryption. Our research and interviews with developers of secure messaging apps (especially with Peter Sunde from Heml.is, who had been contacted by WhatsApp before they decided to purchase the Signal protocol) also show that WhatsApp's motivation to adopt encryption was a market-driven choice, not an ideological decision. Even though the consequences of WhatsApp's decision are very important for the overall "passive" adoption of encryption in Russia, what interests us in this paper is the deliberate and intentional choice of a secure tool. We also do not have data measuring the explicit adoption of WhatsApp consequent of its turn to end-to-end encryption.

[24] Available at http://www.reuters.com/article/idUS74722569420130830

[25] http://www.dazeddigital.com/artsandculture/article/24279/1/pavel-durov

passing the blockage to access content from a blacklisted website, but it does not hide the content that a user is reading. Users are also creatively adapting existing tools to achieve the bypassing goal. For instance, Russians actively use Net archives (archives.org, archive.is or cached versions of websites stored by Google), or activate the "turbo" mode in Opera or Yandex browsers, enabling a very high speed of data transfer. However, once again these tools merely give access to the blocked page, but do not guarantee any anonymity. Moreover, in November 2016, Roskomnadzor started negotiations with Opera representatives about the possibility of blocking access to forbidden content even in "turbo" mode. As of January 2017 no agreement has yet been reached, due to Opera having recently been sold to Golden Brick Capital, a Chinese investment consortium.

As users can be tracked and eventually persecuted for their search of forbidden materials, a set of anonymizing network-layer tools is promoted through cryptoparties and online tutorials, starting with Tor. However, this popular tool is increasingly criticized. Snowden's revelations proved the importance of metadata protection and exposed the vulnerability of Tor. While seminars on informational security observed before 2013 in Saint-Petersburg were promoting widespread use of Tor with almost no attendant criticisms, more recent observations (2015 and 2016) show a growing skepticism and loss of trust. Igor explained the vulnerability of Tor at a workshop organized by Teplitsa Sotsialnih Technologiy: "First of all, your internet service provider will see that you use Tor. That gives him, and the people behind him, a reason to be attentive to you: who is this person who is constantly using Tor? Snowden said that the NSA is tracking everybody who uses Tor, automatically. There are only 7,000 exit nodes in the Tor network, it is not that complicated to track them all".

Another type of network layer tools is a Virtual Private Network (VPN), which adds a supplementary layer of traffic protection. Some of our interviewees pointed out that VPN usage "has become a norm" for them after the GitHub blocking incident in Russia. Among the trusted VPN plugins, activists prefer "zenmate"[26] and "tunnelbear",[27] as they do not need to access user data, while other apps demand the right to access the memory card, photos and contacts. Another popular VPN is offered by Riseup.net,[28] which has a good reputation among politically engaged users ("done by activists for activists"). However, along the lines of Ethan Zuckerman's "cute cat theory of digital activism" (2008), users point out that activist-oriented tools are more vulnerable to targeted attacks than are general public-oriented tools.

Snowden's revelations had a pedagogical effect on Russian activist communities: during observed cryptoparties they were repeatedly heard to emphasize the global character of the surveillance phenomenon. Information security advocates insisted on the necessity for users to change their whole "lifestyle", including interaction with different devices and publishing on social networks. Igor remarks: "You can encrypt your traffic as you wish, you can hide, but if you go to Vkontakte and publish your photo, or talk about revolution, you must understand that it is extremely easy to de-anonymize you and track your network of friends. So start by using your brains, before using Tor and VPN". Thus, after Snowden revealed the interests of big corporations in collecting user-generated data, cryptoparties began to focus not only on activist use cases but on everyday life habits, "unboxing" mobile devices and laptops to demonstrate customization of privacy settings.

On their end, activists are learning how to program message self-destruction or deactivate the tracking of search history and location. Encryption of mobile devices and usage of pass-paragraphs and double or triple authentication methods (combining fingerprints, password and a figure) are becoming popular alongside the use of anonymous search engines such as StartPage or DuckDuckGo, adblocking plugins and cookie controls. Activists advocate multilayered protection and encryption by combining virtual machines, VPN, TOR and encrypted mail and messaging clients.

Finally, Snowden's revelations on NSA surveillance enabled a comparison of the Russian SORM and US intelligence strategies, showing common points and important differences between the two surveillance systems. Activists describe the Russian system as less efficient than its US counterpart, pointing to the geopolitical reasons behind this gap. Not only is Russian surveillance less effective, but the diplomatic context and IT-market configuration also make it harder for Russian surveillance services to be as omnipresent as US ones. Yuriy, an activist, developer and participant in the April 2016 workshop, notes: "As we now know from Edward Snowden's leaks, Americans have their own kind of SORM deployed by the NSA. But it is much more expanded than SORM, it has lots of subdivisions, some of them really crack servers, some others do cryptoanalytics. Snowden claims American services have managed to somehow survey even the Tor traffic, by taking control over the exit nodes. But well...I am really not sure whether it is possible for Russian services to control exit nodes, because sometimes they are located, I don't know, in Panama. And the NSA has much more power to control exit nodes in different countries than Russia. No one likes Russia, and Russia likes no one. It is much more complicated for the FSB to negotiate the access". Therefore it is the controversial position of Russia within the international political arena that makes it harder to negotiate with Western companies to control the traffic of Russian citizens who use anonymizers and Tor.

[26] Available at https://zenmate.com
[27] Available at https://www.tunnelbear.com
[28] Available at https://riseup.net/en/vpn

4. Migrating Servers (and People): A Geopolitical Countermeasure

Due to this geopolitical aspect of RuNet governance, another effective protection tactic is the physical migration of servers and people. Indeed, the legal and technical constraints of RuNet result not only in individual strategies for bypassing and collective action and campaigning, but also in a significant exodus of Web professionals, especially journalists of online media.

The emigration of Russian journalists is not new. In the USSR a significant number of journalists left the country as a result of political persecution (De Tinguy, 2004). However, in the 2010s these exiles are paradoxical, because even if they leave the country they remain connected to Russian cyberspace and actively contribute to its development (Bronnikova, 2016).

Media websites Grani.ru and Meduza were shut down by Roskomnadzor in 2014, making it extremely hard for their editors and owners to survive economically. Despite bypassing tools, their audience decreased. This resulted in the migration of infrastructure and of some journalists out of the Russian Federation. Yuliya Berezovskaya, from Grani.ru, left for France, while Meduza was dislocated to Riga. The cases of Grani.ru and Meduza are interesting for reconsidering the notion of "brain drain". Indeed, the Internet connects migrant and non-migrant populations in their transnational online engagement (Diminescu, 2008; Nedelcu, 2010): online journalists and bloggers expatriated in the European Union, the US or Israel are not excluded from Russian political life but remain important actors in the RuNet freedom quest. For example, Meduza actively informs its readers about recent updates in Russian Internet governance.

Such expatriation also takes shape in a diaspora of infrastructures. In particular, what are called "mirrors" of forbidden websites are created, using platforms such as Amazon.[29] An increasing number of NGOs and other associations opt to transfer their hosting to outside of Russia. As Maxim I., a hosting provider, observes: "Such websites as Children 404[30] or oppositional websites are progressively transferred to foreign servers and start using non-Russian gTLDs (generic top-level domains, such as .ORG). The reason for this is simple: without any court decision your page or the entire website can be blocked, sometimes even by mistake, as it happened with Google or GitHub. I remember also a mass exodus of clients in Belarus, after they have been obliged to work only in Byelorussian data-centers". The tactic of domain zone migration was also adopted by Grani.ru which moved to the .org domain zone on 27 May 2016, two years after its chief editor physically left Russia. Another tactic of "exodus" concerns the kinds of platforms used to disseminate content: more and more of Russia's liberal online media are abandoning the traditional format of websites or blogs in favor of social media pages or Telegram broadcasting channels.

Interestingly, this exodus had begun even before the "Law on Personal Data Storage": Alexey Sidorenko, director of the NGO *Teplitsa Sotsialnih Technologiy*,[31] dates the first wave of infrastructure migration back to 2010. The second wave of digital migration can be attributed to the "Foreign Agent" law: Teplitsa itself had to move from Moscow to Warsaw after the clampdown on foreign aid agencies. IT specialists have seldom been using Russian data-centers because of their technical drawbacks: "People have been actively using western platforms, just because it is more useful and efficient", says Russian-born, Turkey-adopted developer Timofey. However, recent regulation of the Internet has modified the practices of developers and reconfigured the markets. Alexey, CTO of Progress Engine, concludes: "If GitHub is closed, this will enforce brain-drain. And it has already started, several of my colleagues have left to Germany. Folks prefer to work with foreign markets and foreign services. First of all, it's the quality of technological solutions. And also, when you work with a western client, there's a possibility to move. If there's more control from the government, you have a chance to leave".

5. Conclusions

As Edward Snowden is currently on (temporary) asylum in Russia, numerous scholars and journalists insist on the geopolitical significance of this act and emphasize its importance within the global context of a "Cold War 2.0". Yet, far from supporting Snowden's fight for transparency of government data and Internet users' freedom, the Russian government is gradually centralizing its surveillance over the RuNet. However, the direct and indirect influence of the Snowden revelations is making itself visible in a number of other ways, by exposing censorship and surveillance at an unprecedented scale and encouraging creative responses to it. This article has explored how, in response to growing censorship, a variety of tactics are being developed and deployed by Russian users and content producers, ranging from infrastructure-based countermeasures and *détournements* to geopolitical reconfigurations involving the migration of hardware and people.

Although it is not within the scope of this paper to estimate the long-term impact of recent mobilizations (as we do not have enough data to measure this), we can conclude that Russian civic mobilization may be analyzed at two levels. The first is public and collective, for example the "anti-SORM" movement or petitions against Yarovaya law. Such movements appear to have limited impact beyond encouraging visibility and draw-

[29] *Reporters without Borders*, having experimented this technique with Chinese bloggers, helped Russian blacklisted media to put it in practice. Thus, mobilizations for RuNet freedom are integrated in transnational campaigns.

[30] NGO defending the rights of LGBTQI-children.

[31] Teplitsa Sotsialnih Technologiy is an NGO specialized in IT-education of social workers and activists and in development of collaboration between Russian non-profit organizations and IT-specialists. Available at https://te-st.ru

ing public attention to the problem, and even so they remain limited to a small section of the population (with only around 600,000 signatures on Change.org and 2,000 people in attendance at the anti-Yarovaya law meeting), namely IT professionals, journalists, bloggers and Internet freedom activists. However, at the second level, that of so-called "evasion" tactics, mobilisation is far more successful: far from being a contentious means to criticize government or affect changes in legislation and Internet policy, these invisible or elusive techniques have a direct and immediate impact on the everyday practices of users and IT professionals. Evasion techniques are based on an ingenious and constantly changing set of tools and *arts de faire*, and can help to access or broadcast forbidden content as well as to continue IT-related business.

This article shows that Russian Internet governance increasingly takes shape as an "infrastructural battle", a dialectic between the government, who use and co-opt infrastructure, and users, developers and providers who hijack and reconfigure it, in a constant co-shaping of law and technology. This speaks to the "turn to infrastructure" we have recently explored as an increasing tendency in Internet governance (Musiani, Cogburn, DeNardis, & Levinson, 2016). If the Snowden revelations have constituted the 'perfect excuse' for the Russian government to try to enforce a radical approach of "digital sovereignty" (Nocetti, 2015), they have also become on the one hand a catalyst of freedom activists' mobilization, not only for "power users" but for the everyday situated practices of lambda users, and on the other hand an opportunity for Russian businesses working with Western companies to fight both from within and from outside the country. Moreover, the specific geopolitical and economic conditions of embargo can be understood as an important obstacle for Roskomnadzor. It is not civil society but rather Russia's lack of resources, infrastructure, expertise and technologies that make it impossible, at least for now, to apply this law in practice. Despite the current escalation of surveillance, could Russia's controversial position on the international chessboard turn into a paradoxical opportunity for the RuNet?

Acknowledgements

This work is supported by the European Union's Horizon 2020 Framework Programme for Research and Innovation (H2020-ICT-2015, ICT-10-2015) under grant agreement nº 688722—NEXTLEAP.

Conflict of Interests

The authors declare no conflict of interests.

References

Akrich, M. (1998). Les utilisateurs, acteurs de l'innovation, *Education Permanente*, *134*, 78–89.

Borogan, I., & Soldatov, A. (2013). Russian surveillance state. *World Policy*. Retrieved from http://www.worldpolicy.org/journal/fall2013/Russia-surveillance

Bronnikova, O. (2016). Publikovat dlya Rossii iz-za granitsi. Internet—prostranstvo bez granits? [Publishing for Russia from abroad. Is internet a borderless space?]. In F. Daucé, B., Ostromooukhova, O., Bronnikova, & A. Zaytseva (Eds.), *Nezavisimye ot kogo? Alternativnye SMI, malye izdatelstva i bloggery v sovremennoy Rossii [Independent from whom? Alternative mass-media, small editors and bloggers in contemporary Russia]*. Moscow: NLO. Book in preparation.

Ceruzzi, P. (2006). The materiality of the Internet. *IEEE Annals of the History of Computing*, *28*(3), 96–97.

De Tinguy, A. (2004). *La Russie et les Russes depuis l'ouverture du rideau de fer*. Paris: Plon.

DeNardis, L., & Musiani, F. (2016). Governance by infrastructure. In F. Musiani, D. Cogburn, L. DeNardis, & N. Levinson (Eds.), *The turn to infrastructure in Internet governance* (pp. 3–21) New York, NY: Palgrave-Macmillan.

Diminescu, D. (2008). The connected migrant: An epistemological manifesto. *Social Science Information*, *47*(4), 565–579.

Elting, B., Alexanyan, K., Kelly, J., Faris, R., Palfrey, J., & Gasser, U. (2010). *Public discourse in the Russian blogosphere: Mapping RuNet politics and mobilization* (Report no. 2010–11, October 19, 2010). Cambridge, MA: Berkman Center for Internet and Society.

Ermoshina, K., Musiani, F., & Halpin, H. (2016). End-to-end encrypted messaging protocols: An overview. *Proceedings of Internet Science Conference 2016* (pp. 244–254). Florence, Italy: University of Florence.

Erpyleva, S., & Magun, A. (Eds.). (2014). *Politika Apolitchnyh: Grazhdanskie Dvizheniya V Rossii 2011–2013 Godov. [Politics of apolitical: Civic movements in Russia in 2011–2013]*. Moscow: Novoe Literaturnoye Obozrenie.

Filonov, D. (2014, August 12). Otlozhennyi effekt. Kak Snowden zastavil Acronis potratitsya na servery [Postponed effect. How Snowden made Acronis spend money for the servers]. *Forbes.ru*. Retrieved from http://www.forbes.ru/tekhnologii/tekhnika-i-biznes/265017-otlozhennyi-effekt-kak-snouden-zastavil-acronis-potratitsya-na

Freiberg, P. (2014). *Putin's Russia—On a path to cyber sovereignty?* Retrieved from http://www.academia.edu/10762446/Future_of_Internet_Freedom_in_Russia

Gelman, V. (2010, March 9). Lovushka polusvobody: The trap of a half-freedom. *Slon.ru*. Retrieved from http://slon.ru/russia/lovushka_polusvobody-310531.xhtml

Kantyshev, P. (2016, September 4). Rostehu Nuzhno 10,3 Milliarda Rubley na Razrabotky Paketa Yarovoj [Rostech needs 10.3 mlrds of Rubles to develop Yarovaya Law]. *Vedemosti*. Retrieved from http://www.

vedomosti.ru/technology/articles/2016/09/05/655653-rostehu-zakona-yarovoi

Kharkhordin, O. (2011). *Ot obshchestvennogo k publichnomu: kollektivnaia monografiia [From social to public: Collective monograph]*. Berlin: EUSP Press.

Klyueva, A. (2016). Taming online political engagement in Russia: Disempowered publics, empowered state and challenges of the fully functioning society. *International Journal of Communication, 10*, 4661–4680.

Kozlov, V., & Filipenok, A. (2016, August 9). Miting protiv zakona Yarovoy v Moskve sobral neskolko tysyach chelovek [Meeting against Yarovaya law gathered several thousand people]. *RBC*. Retrieved from http://www.rbc.ru/politics/09/08/2016/57aa0a259a79470ed51332fd

Latour, B. (1988). *The pasteurization of France*. Cambridge, MA: Harvard University Press.

Lonkila, M. (2012). *Russian protest on- and offline. The role of social media in the Moscow opposition demonstrations in December 2011* (FIIA Briefing Paper 98). Helsinki: The Finnish Institute of International Affairs.

Musiani, F., Cogburn, D., DeNardis, L., & Levinson, N. (Eds.). (2016). *The turn to infrastructure in internet governance*. New York, NY: Palgrave-Macmillan.

Nedelcu, M. (2009). Du brain drain à l'e-diaspora: Vers une nouvelle culture du lien à l'ère du numérique? *TIC et Sociétés*, *3*(1). Retrieved from http://ticetsociete.revues.org/675

Nocetti, J. (2015). Russia's "dictatorship-of-the-law" approach to internet policy. *Internet Policy Review*, *4*(4). doi:10.14763/2015.4.380

Nossik, A. (2014, March 19). *Dyryavoe sito censury [Leaky strainer of censorship]*. Retrieved from http://dolboeb.livejournal.com/2652283.html

Otstavnov, M. (1998, June 26). *Chifrovaniye I SORM—Tchastnoye mnenie [Encryption and SORM"—A personal opinion]*. Retrieved from http://www.libertarium.ru/l_sorm_cryptsorm

Prozorov, S. (2012). Vtoroj konec istorii: Politika bezdejatelnosti ot perestrojki do Putina [The second end of History: The politics of inactivity from Perestroika to Putin]. *Neprikosnovennyj zapas*, *2*(82), 169–191.

Schepin, A. (2016, August 1). Irkutskie Operatory Svyazi O Nedostatkah Paketa Yarovoy [ISPs from Irkutsk: On the drawbacks of Yarovaya Package]. *IRK*. Retrieved from https://www.irk.ru/news/articles/20160801/package

Volkov, L. (2016, March 24). *Pedofil Na Slujbe FSB: Kto Sledit Za Nami v Internete? [A pedophile that serves FSB: Who is surveilling us in the internet?"]*. Retrieved from https://www.leonidvolkov.ru/p/119

Zhuravlev, O., Savelyeva, N., & Yerpylova, S. (2014). Individualizm I solidarnost v Novyh Rossijskyh Grazhdanskih Dvizheniyah [Individualism and solidarity in new Russian civic movements]. *Journal of Social Policy Studies*, *12*(2), 185–200.

Zuckerman, E. (2008, March 8). *The cute cat theory talk at ETech*. Retrieved from http://www.ethanzuckerman.com/blog/2008/03/08/the-cute-cat-theory-talk-at-etech

19

Narrative Agency in Hashtag Activism: The Case of #BlackLivesMatter

Guobin Yang [1,2]

[1] Annenberg School for Communication, University of Pennsylvania, Philadelphia, PA 19104, USA;
E-Mail: guobin.yang@asc.upenn.edu
[2] Department of Sociology, University of Pennsylvania, Philadelphia, PA 19104, USA

Abstract

Hashtag activism happens when large numbers of postings appear on social media under a common hashtagged word, phrase or sentence with a social or political claim. The temporal unfolding of these mutually connected postings in networked spaces gives them a narrative form and agency. Applying Karlyn Campbell's propositions about rhetorical agency to the case of #BlackLivesMatter, this essay shows that narrative agency in hashtag activism derives from its narrative form as well as from its contents and social context. Narrative agency is communal, invented, skillful, and protean.

Keywords

#BlackLivesMatter; agency; hashtag activism; narrative

Issue

This commentary is part of the issue "Political Agency in the Digital Age: Media, Participation and Democracy", edited by Anne Kaun (Södertörn University, Sweden), Maria Kyriakidou (University of East Anglia, UK) and Julie Uldam (Roskilde University, Denmark).

---

1. Introduction

One of the most interesting developments in digital activism in recent years is the rise of hashtag activism, meaning discursive protest on social media united through a hashtagged word, phrase or sentence. #BlackLivesMatter, for example, was a protest movement that happened both in the streets and on social media in response to the acquittal of George Zimmerman in July 2013 in the shooting death of African-American teen Trayvon Martin. Another example is #Ferguson, which happened in response to the shooting to death of Michael Brown on August 9, 2014 by a police officer in Ferguson, Missouri. Within the first week of Brown's death, millions of posts with the hashtagged #Ferguson appeared on Twitter alone (Bonila & Rosa, 2015).

These important cases of online protest brought renewed attention to the power of digital activism in shaping public discourse. Research on digital activism has focused on its networked and connective character (Bennett & Segerberg, 2013) and debated about the question of organization and leadership (Gerbaudo, 2012). This essay argues that a neglected form of agency in the study of digital activism is its narrative form.

2. The Narrative Analysis of Social Movements

Narrative forms are an essential element of human existence (Polkinghorne, 1988, p. 1). Scholars have argued that "the nature of daily action and self-construction lends an essentially narrative character to life" (Steinmetz, 1992, p.496). Carr, for example, claims that "Narrative is not merely a possibly successful way of describing events; its structure inheres in the events themselves" (1986, p. 117). Bruner (2004, p. 708) similarly states that "a life as led is inseparable from a life as told."

The most distinct feature of the narrative form is its temporal sequence. In literary representations, narrative form accounts for the progression from beginning through middle to an end. Thus Kenneth Burke states that a literary work has form "in so far as one part of it leads a reader to anticipate another part, to be gratified by the sequence" (1968, p. 124). The form of detective fiction, for example, often centers on a quest, adventure, or mystery. As the protagonist (the detective) goes in search of solutions, the plot generates curiosity, surprise, and suspense (Sternberg, 2003).

Like works of literature, social movements have narrative forms. In his study of working-class formation, sociologist Steinmetz notes that "Narrative thus has a beginning, a middle, and an end, and the movement toward the end is accounted for by conflicts, causal explanations, and the sequence of events" (Steinmetz, 1992, p. 497). Focusing on the rhetorical form of social movements, Griffin (1952, 1969, 2003) and Cathcart (1978) underscore the processual nature of social movements. Cathcart (1978, p. 234) argues that movements are "a kind of ritual conflict whose most distinguishing form is confrontation." Griffin (1969, p. 461) maintains that all social movements have forms: "Every movement...has form....It is a progression...from suffering, misfortune, passive condition, state of mind."

Social movement scholars have long recognized the power of narratives (Polletta, 2006; Selbin, 2010), but the question of narrative agency has received relatively little attention in studies of digital activism (but see Clark, 2016; Kaun, 2015). In contrast to "traditional" forms of digital activism such as distributed denial-of-service actions (DDoS) or signing online petitions, hashtag activism has a distinctly narrative character. An incidence of hashtag activism takes place when large numbers of comments and retweets appear on social media in response to a hashtagged word, phrase, or sentence. Because these comments and retweets consist of numerous personal stories and appear in temporal order, they assume a narrative form. Narrative agency is thus central to hashtag activism.

Rhetorical theorist Karlyn Campbell defines rhetorical agency as "the capacity to act, that is, to have the competence to speak or write in a way that will be recognized or heeded by others in one's community" (Campbell, 2005, p. 3). Adapting this definition, I consider narrative agency in hashtag activism as the capacity to create stories on social media by using hashtags in a way that is collective and recognized by the public. Illustrated with an analysis of a historical text (a speech allegedly delivered by Sojourner Truth at the 1851 woman's rights convention in Akron, Ohio), Campbell's five propositions about rhetorical agency are useful for analyzing narrative agency in hashtag activism.

First, she argues that "agency is communal, social, cooperative, and participatory and, simultaneously, constituted and constrained by the material and symbolic elements of context and culture" (p. 3). Second, agency is both "invented" and invention. Because authors and rhetors "are materially limited, linguistically constrained, historically situated subjects" (p. 5), they have to find and invent ways of expression. Agency is thus invention. Third, agency emerges in artistry or craft. It is a set of heuristic skills and includes "stratagem, flair, subtlety, and the like as well as the habits of mind learned through practice" (p. 7)

Fourth, agency is achieved through form. The agency of form is realized through generic conventions and textual and rhetorical devices. Narrative forms have agency because they "invite" audiences, readers or listeners to participate in the co-production of stories (also see Polletta, 2006). As Campbell puts it, "Textual agency is linked to audiences and begins with the signals that guide the process of "uptake" for readers or listeners enabling them to categorize, to understand how a symbolic act is to be framed" (Campbell, 2005, p. 7).

Fifth, Campbell warns that "agency can be malign, divisive, and destructive" (2005, p. 7). It is "protean, ambiguous, open to reversal" (p. 1). The openness of the narrative form makes it susceptible to perversion.

Below, I will discuss each of these five propositions as they are applied to the analysis of #BlackLivesMatter. One modification I will make to Campbell's framework is that I consider form as the most fundamental feature of the narrative agency of digital activism and will discuss it first.

3. The Power of Narrative Form

Digital activism on social media has different narrative forms because narrative conventions may differ from platform to platform. Earlier digital protests, for example, took place in electronic bulletin boards or newsgroups (Gurak, 1999), which allowed the posting and cross-positing of longer narratives. The wide circulation of several such narratives could create an online protest event, but the number of participating voices may be significantly more limited than on Twitter. A unique feature of hashtag activism on Twitter is that it starts, well, with a hashtag. Adding the hashtag sign # to a word, such as #change or #climate, makes it easier for other users on Twitter to search, link, and interact with one another via the hashtagged word and to share stories related to it. Indeed, such hashtags are a common practice on Twitter. They are routine hashtags.

These everyday hashtags, however, do not usually evolve into contentious collective events online. The most influential cases of hashtag activism, as opposed to routine hashtags, have a recognizable narrative form with a beginning, a crisis/conflict, and an end (Clark, 2016). Within this temporal framework, individuals contribute to the co-production of narratives by hashtagging their personal thoughts, emotions, and stories.

The hashtags in many influential cases of hashtag activism have complete sentence structures rather than single words like #change. The following is a random list of examples: #BlackLivesMatter, #BringBackOurGirls, #StopGamerGate, #WhyIStayed, #JeNeSuisPasCharlie, #OccupyEverywhere, #CancelColbert, #ThisIsACoup, #IcantBreathe, #MuslimsAreNotTerrorist.

As the above examples show, these hashtags contain verbs expressing a strong sense of action and force. The actions are petitioning, demanding, appealing, and protesting. They express refusals, objections, and imperatives to take immediate action. They often challenge narratives in mainstream media. In all these ways, activist hashtags embody what Cathcart (1978, p. 234), in his rhetorical study of social movement forms, refers to as "a kind of ritual conflict whose most distinguishing form is confrontation."

The narrative forms of hashtag activism are not limited to the syntactical structures of the hashtags. They also consist of the generic conventions and rhetorical devices used in the hashtagged postings. An incidence of hashtag activism typically spans days, weeks, and even months. During this period, textual signals and rhetorical devices "guide the process of 'uptake' for readers or listeners enabling them to categorize, to understand how a symbolic act is to be framed." (Campbell, 2005, p.7) They encourage audience participation. People participate by reading, retweeting, commenting on others' tweets or posting their own with the same hashtag. The temporal unfolding of such an incident is a process of people interacting with one another and collectively creating a larger narrative. To understand the narrative agency in this process, I will now turn to the other four dimensions of narrative agency as outlined by Karlyn Campbell and use the example of #BlackLivesMatter as an illustration.

4. Communal, Invented, Skillful, and Protean

According to a *USA Today* story (Guynn, 2015), the statement "Black lives matter" initially appeared in a Facebook post by Alicia Garza in July 2013 after Garza saw from television news the acquittal of George Zimmerman in the shooting death of African-American teen Trayvon Martin. Garza's friend Patrisse Cullors added the hashtag sign to the statement after she read it. The rest is history. #BlackLivesMatter quickly spread on social media and spawned not only an online protest event, but also a social movement organization headed by none other than Garza and Cullors.

At 8:45am Eastern Time on February 25, 2016, I searched the #BlackLivesMatter hashtag using my personal Twitter account. As I scrolled down the screen, the results expanded. I saved a 74-page pdf document of the search results. These 74 pages are only a small slice of the much longer temporality of the #BlackLivesMatter, but still show clearly #BlackLivesMatter as a case of narrative agency.

My Twitter's search results are shown in reverse chronological order, with the most recent postings at the top. The 74-page document is thus a narrative in reverse chronological order. My experience of reading it was like reading a live narrative about an unfolding event, one that is at the same time created by the narrative form.

At the top of the search results was a HuffPost Politics story showing a photograph of Hillary Clinton making a speech. The title of the story is "Black Lives Matter Activists Interrupt Hillary Clinton At Private Event In South Carolina: They wanted her to account for some of her past statements on racial justice." As I scroll down the results, I begin to see the key aspects of narrative agency at work.

First, the communal and participatory feature of agency is evident from the many likes and retweets of individual postings. Some postings have hundreds of "favorites" and "retweets." Individuals in these communal spaces may or may not know one another. They are like dramatic personae in what Campbell refers to, citing Sartre, as "a serial relationship": "Individuals in a serial relationship have no set of attributes in common except their shared relationship to an external object, event, or, in other cases, to a law, an institution, a norm, a stereotype and so on." (Campbell, 2005, p. 4) In this case, since they all tweeted with the #BlackLivesMatter hashtag, their relationship is primarily to the hashtag with all its moral, political, and social implications.

As I read on, the story grows, expands, and becomes richer and more complex. Texts are mixed with photos. One hashtag is used in combination with another, such that #BlackLivesMatter becomes intertwined with multiple other hashtags. Again, in reverse chronological order, I saw the following hashtags used together with #BlackLivesMatter: #blackish, #WhichHillary, #notasuperpredator, #ChicagoPD, #alwaysshavealwayswill, #Apple, #FeeltheBern, #Trump, #abff, #blacktwitter, #OscaSoWhite, and so on and so forth. Each of these hashtags tells a new story, but all are linked to #BlackLivesMatter. #BlackLivesMatter becomes a unifying theme of multiple stories about racial justice.

Second, Campbell writes that agency is invention and authors and rhetors are "inventors" in the rhetorical sense. They "link past and present, and find means to express those strata that connect the psyche, society, and world, the forms of feeling that encapsulate moments in time" (p. 5). This process of invention depends on artistry, craft, stratagem, flair, subtlety, and skill.

#BlackLivesMatter is the result of such a process of skillful invention. In a simple sense, all Twitter postings have to have some degree of artistry in order to meet the 140-character exigency of the Twitter platform. To create a collective story of struggles for racial justice, such as through #BlackLivesMatter, requires individual users to mobilize additional artistry and flair. One particularly powerful method is the sharing of personal stories. For example, one posting on February 22 goes: "In 2015, dozens of African American's [sic] were killed by police. I put 84 of their names on my shirt. #BlackLivesMatter pic.twitter.com/cOHOltrgEO." Such personal stories are linked to broader social issues and shared with the public through the use of the hashtag, thus giving hashtag activism a communal and collective character.

Part of the artistry of a collective hashtag narrative derives from its versatility of expressive forms. Besides the common practices of tweeting and retweeting, the posting itself takes different forms. There are photographs, jokes, slogans, curses, and cartoons. There are links to news, videos, music and songs. In the middle of these personalized but artful story-telling, a protest narrative is created and carried forward.

Finally, as Campbell notes, rhetorical agency is protean and promiscuous with a "malign, divisive, and destructive" side. In the case of #BlackLivesMatter, this malign side is seen in the racist language and remarks that appear in my search results. Considering the open nature of the Twitter platform, this is not surprising. The presence of such racist remarks vindicates the urgency of struggles for racial justice and the challenges facing activists and citizens. To those involved in the online narrating of #BlackLivesMatter, they are concrete evidence of the necessity of taking personal action. Thus, in response to a racist posting, one person tweeted on February 16: "I support #BlackLivesMatter because there's people like this."

5. The Social Context of Narrative Form

In Campbell's study of rhetorical agency, the capacity to act is "constituted and constrained by the material and symbolic elements of context and culture" (p. 3). In other words, agency responds to social conditions and articulates social issues. In the same way, the narrative forms of hashtag activism are not independent of culture and society. It is not a coincidence that hashtag activism has been especially notable in recent struggles for racial justice and gender equality (Berridge & Portwood-Stacer, 2015; Clark, 2016). As Bonnia and Rosa (2015, p. 8) write in their study of #Ferguson, "it is important to examine how and why digital activism has become salient to particular populations. It is surely not coincidental that the groups most likely to experience police brutality, to have their protests disparaged as acts of 'rioting' or 'looting,' and to be misrepresented in the media are precisely those turning to digital activism at the highest rates."

Because hashtag activism happens in social and political context, its forms may vary when contexts change. For example, does it take different narrative forms in a different language, say #JeNeSuisPasCharlie in French? Are confrontational forms more prevalent in the U.S than in China? Are some forms more effective than others? These are some of the questions for future research.

Acknowledgments

I would like to thank Anne Kaun, Maria Kyriakidou, and Julie Uldam for inviting me to give a keynote speech at the conference on "Political Agency in the Digital Age: Media, Participation and Democracy" in October 2015, which inspired this essay.

Conflict of Interests

The author declares no conflict of interests.

References

Bennett, P. W. L., & Segerberg, D. A. (2013). *The logic of connective action: Digital media and the personalization of contentious politics*. Cambridge: Cambridge University Press.

Berridge, S., & Portwood-Stacer, L. (2015). Introduction: Feminism, hashtags and violence against women and girls. *Feminist Media Studies*, *15*(2), 341-341. doi:10.1080/14680777.2015.1008743

Bonilla, Y., & Rosa, J. (2015). #Ferguson: Digital protest, hashtag ethnography, and the racial politics of social media in the United States. *American Ethnologist*, *42*(1), 4-17. doi:10.1111/amet.12112

Bruner, J. (2004). Life as narrative. *Social Research*, *71*(3), 691-710.

Burke, K. (1968). *Counter-statement.* Berkeley: University of California Press.

Campbell, K. K. (2005). Agency: Promiscuous and protean. *Communication and Critical/Cultural Studies*, *2*(1), 1-19. doi:10.1080/1479142042000332134

Carr, D. (1986). Narratives and the real world. *History and Theory*, *25*, 117-131.

Cathcart, R. (1978). Movements: Confrontation as rhetorical form. *Southern Speech Journal*, *43*, 233-247.

Clark, R. (2016). "Hope in a hashtag": The discursive activism of #WhyIStayed. *Feminist Media Studies.* doi:10.1080/14680777.2016.1138235

Gerbaudo, P. (2012). *Tweets and the streets: Social media and contemporary activism*. London: Pluto Press.

Griffin, L. M. (1952). The rhetoric of historical movements. *Quarterly Journal of Speech*, *38*, 184-188.

Griffin, L. M. (1969). A dramatistic theory of the rhetoric of movements. In W. H. Rueckert (Ed.), *Critical responses to Kenneth Burke* (pp. 456-477). Minneapolis: University of Minnesota Press.

Griffin, C. J. G. (2003). Movement as memory: Significant form in eyes on the prize. *Communication Studies*, *54*(2), 196-210.

Gurak, L. J. (1999). *Persuasion and privacy in cyberspace: The online protests over lotus marketplace and the clipper chip* (Revised edition). New Haven: Yale University Press.

Guynn, J. (2015, March 4). Meet the woman who coined #BlackLivesMatter. Retrieved from http://www.usatoday.com/story/tech/2015/03/04/alicia-garza-black-lives-matter/24341593

Kaun, A. (2015). When narratives travel: The Occupy

Movement in Latvia and Sweden. In J. Uldam & A. Vestergaard (Eds.), *Civic engagement and social media* (pp. 111-130). London: Palgrave Macmillan UK. Retrieved from http://link.springer.com/chapter/10.1057/9781137434166_6

Polkinghorne, D. (1988). *Narrative knowing and the human sciences*. Albany: State University of New York Press.

Polletta, F. (2006). *It was like a fever: Storytelling in protest and politics*. Chicago: University of Chicago Press.

Selbin, E. (2010). *Revolution, rebellion, resistance: The power of story*. London and New York: Zed Books.

Steinmetz, G. (1992). Reflections on the role of social narratives in working-class formation: Narrative theory in the social sciences. *Social Science History, 16*(3), 489-516.

Sternberg, M. (2003). Universals of narrative and their cognitivist fortunes. *Poetics Today, 24*(2), 297-395.

Outrage without Consequences? Post-Snowden Discourses and Governmental Practice in Germany

Stefan Steiger [1,*], Wolf J. Schünemann [2] and Katharina Dimmroth [3]

[1] Institute of Political Science, Heidelberg University, 69115 Heidelberg, Germany;
E-Mail: stefan.steiger@ipw.uni-heidelberg.de
[2] Institute of Social Sciences, Hildesheim University, 31141 Hildesheim, Germany;
E-Mail: wolf.schuenemann@uni-hildesheim.de
[3] Institute of Political Science, Rheinisch-Westfälische Technische Hochschule Aachen, 52074 Aachen, Germany;
E-Mail: katharina.dimmroth@ipw.rwth-aachen.de

* Corresponding author

Abstract
In 2013 Edward Snowden's disclosures of mass surveillance performed by US intelligence agencies seriously irritated politicians and citizens around the globe. This holds particularly true for privacy-sensitive communities in Germany. However, while the public was outraged, intelligence and security cooperation between the United States and Germany has been marked by continuity instead of disruption. The rather insubstantial debate over a so-called "No-Spy-Agreement" between the United States and Germany is just one telling example of the disconnect between public discourse and governmental action, as is the recent intelligence service regulation. This article considers why and where the "Snowden effect" has been lost on different discursive levels. We analyze and compare parliamentary and governmental discourses in the two years after the Snowden revelations by using the Sociology of Knowledge Approach to Discourse (SKAD) to dissect the group-specific statements and interpretive schemes in 287 official documents by the German Bundestag, selected ministries and agencies within the policy subsystem. These will be analyzed in reference to actual governmental practice.

Keywords
cyber security; discourse analysis; dispositive analysis; German–US intelligence cooperation; surveillance

Issue
This article is part of the issue "Post-Snowden Internet Policy", edited by Julia Pohle (WZB Berlin Social Science Center, Germany) and Leo Van Audenhove (Vrije Universiteit Brussel, Belgium).

---

1. Introduction

When the Snowden revelations exposed the extensive surveillance practices established by the US National Security Agency (NSA) and the British Government Communications Headquarters (GCHQ) in June 2013, international criticism loomed large. Among US allies, Germany has been one of the most vocal critics of the revealed surveillance measures. Chancellor Angela Merkel most prominently expressed German discomfort in October 2013, when she said "spying among friends is completely unacceptable" (Troianovski, Gorman, & Torry, 2013). While criticism was also expressed in parliament and a commission of inquiry was set up in early 2014, actual cooperation with the US remained relatively stable. Furthermore, in 2016 the federal government proposed a new legislative framework for the German foreign intelligence agency Bundesnachrichtendienst (BND) that was approved by the German Bundestag in October of the same year. The new law, according to many experts (Bäcker, 2016; Papier, 2016; Wetzling, 2016), legalizes extensive governmental surveillance practices and may even be unconstitutional.

It is this seemingly paradoxical mismatch between harsh criticism and stable cooperation that we are going to analyze within the scope of this article. Our main research questions are therefore: How is it possible that Germany was a vocal critic of the revealed spy practices and nevertheless maintained a stable cooperation with the US? As even a superficial look into the public and political debates in Germany reveals, there has clearly been a "Snowden effect" in Germany, which has brought the issue of mass surveillance to the fore of public policy. Why has it not led to a significant change in regulation or the practices of governmental agencies? Where and why did the Snowden effect get lost within different discourse formations (parliamentary, governmental)?

Up to now, research on governmental reactions to the Snowden revelations has been published only scarcely. When discussed, German government reactions have been covered with a focus on arguments legitimizing surveillance measures (Schulze, 2015). We will go further by also analyzing the parliamentary debate and investigating the practical implications of possible discursive shifts with a deeper look into the dispositives (institutions, regulations and practices). In the existing literature, one can identify slightly different perspectives on the German reaction to the disclosed practices. These views seem to be facilitated by an emphasis on either practical consequences or rhetoric. Emphasizing the harsh criticism following the revelations, Bersick, Christou and Yi (2016, pp. 176–177) state that:

> In the case of Germany, the Snowden affair even undermined the general belief in the normative foundations of the US–German relationship and gave rise to previously unheard-of criticism of the United States by German members of the federal cabinet.

Other scholars emphasized that practical relations (especially security cooperation) between the US and Germany remained stable in the aftermath of the revelations. Segal (2016, p. 150) concludes that "even at the zenith of the public backlash, cooperation between the US and German intelligence agencies never stopped". Segal tentatively argues that this reaction was motivated by the German "dependence on US intelligence capabilities" (Segal, 2016, p. 143), but his claim is not built on significant empirical data from the German administration or parliament. We would like to substantiate this debate and take those findings as a starting point for our analysis. We agree with Bersick et al. (2016) that leading politicians in Germany voiced strong criticism against the US (and the UK) regarding the revelations, and we also acknowledge in concurrence with Segal (2016) that practical implications remained marginal, as is clearly underlined by the latest developments. But together, both observations set the puzzle that we are investigating.

In order to provide an answer to our research questions, the article will proceed in four steps. The next section lays out our framework for discourse analysis and specifies our methodological approach. To illustrate the reluctant German reactions, the third section presents a short analysis of the most important practical events following the Snowden revelations; this part sheds light on the measures the German government has actually taken to deal with the revelations. Our empirical analysis of governmental and parliamentary discourse is then presented in the fourth section. A final conclusion sums up our findings.

2. Discourses, Dispositives and What Happens in between: Theory and Methodology

Discourse research has gained ground in political science in recent years (pars pro toto: Hajer, 2002; Howarth, Norval, & Stavrakakis, 2000; Wodak & Krzyzanowski, 2008). Even in international relations and security studies, discourse analysis (DA) has become more popular, and the scope of DA methodology has considerably broadened (for cyber security and online communication issues see for instance: Balzacq, 2011; Gorr & Schünemann, 2013; Xiao Wu, 2012). First of all, we adhere to a Foucauldian discourse theory (Foucault, 2002), which makes the discourse a socio-historically specific knowledge formation that appears materially manifested in social communication. Moreover, we apply an approach developed from the combination of Foucauldian discourse theory and the Sociology of Knowledge tradition in sociology. The Sociology of Knowledge Approach to Discourse ([SKAD] Keller, 2008) has been developed by German sociologist Reiner Keller since the late 1990s. One crucial advantage of SKAD in relation to other discourse analytical approaches is that it brings the actor back into focus. SKAD furthermore provides the analyst with a research framework encompassing a set of basic interpretive schemes, which complement the interpretive analytics otherwise adopted from Foucault.

Corpus-building is one of the first and most important steps of any solid discourse research. For this study, we chose an actor-oriented approach. This was relatively easy for the parliamentary debate, as we selected all Bundestag protocols dealing with cyber security issues by using the search function of the official Bundestag database, entering the search terms "cyber security" and "cyber attack". We cut and parsed the resulting protocols to include only the sections that dealt with the relevant issue, since a single Bundestag debate may deal with a variety of topics. For governmental actors and agencies, we identified ministries and investigative authorities as the key actors in German cyber security policy, i.e. the policy subsystem (Sabatier, 1988). The identified actors were the Federal Government, the Federal Foreign Office, the Federal Ministry of the Interior, the Federal Ministry of Defense, the Federal Ministry for Economic Affairs and Energy, the Federal Ministry of Justice and Consumer Protection and the Federal Office for Information Security. We continued our document-gathering by entering the same query terms of "cyber security"

("Cybersicherheit") and "cyber attack" ("Cyberangriff") using the search functions provided by the ministries' websites. The query terms had been intuitively selected and then validated using the "relative query term relevance" (RQTR) method proposed by Costas Gabrielatos (2007). The period of analysis spans the two years following the Snowden revelations, i.e. June 1, 2013, to May 31, 2015. The governmental documents we identified by using our query terms ranged from official ministry reports, interviews and speeches to press releases. Our final corpus for analysis consisted of 287 documents in total, 156 of which came from government offices and 131 from parliament.

As to our interpretive analysis, we analyze our corpus first for the recurrent statements and then look, in accordance with SKAD methodology, for all sorts of interpretive schemes (some call them frames) included therein. These patterns of interpretation can again be divided into subtypes such as narratives, classifications or subject positions (Keller, 2008). While statements are thus the basic analytical unit for a discourse analysis, being based on the social actors' worldview, i.e. how people make sense of the world around them, the interpretive scheme is the overarching analytical category towards which the more concrete and specific interpretive codes of the researcher are oriented. Our case, for example, raises the question of whether the newly disclosed surveillance activities amount to illegal espionage and a breach of trust, or whether they are seen and justified as a legitimate part of a protective role and, thus, an example of successful intelligence cooperation.

In addition to SKAD, the Foucauldian term of the dispositive is also of particular importance for this study. The dispositive—in the Foucauldian sense and as adopted by Keller—is an umbrella term for all sorts of power-effects through which a discourse leaves its lasting mark on the world and/or the organization of a given society. While the discourse is a practice itself and it appears as materialized practice as well, it is still necessarily transient as knowledge elements are being processed all the time and never reach a fixed state. However, they do have long lasting effects on the world and the ordered living of a society through established practices, regulations, and institutions. The dispositive thus includes "material objects (buildings, technologies, etc.), practices (such as the execution of punishments) and elements in the form of texts (such as the adoption of laws)" (Keller, 2013, pp. 78–79). Changes in regulatory discourses on public security will likely lead to institutionalization and intervention into the material world or into the rulebook of a society. The same can be expected of data protection or cyber security issues. The "privacy by design" guideline, for instance, which has become almost common sense in many regulatory discourses, is increasingly being institutionalized in laws or guidelines that could be labeled as a data protection dispositive. The sequential and causal logic is not as clear-cut as the examples so far suggest. Of course, dispositives have repercussions for discourses as well. The concept of the dispositive encompasses not only the effects discourses have on the world but also the very infrastructure of discourse production: "The concept of dispositive means the bundle of measures that carries a discourse and transposes it into real-world consequences" (Keller, 2007, p. 50, translation by the authors). This also makes sense and can be illustrated with reference to the cyber security subsystem. The dispositive includes privileged speaker positions (such as the ministers of the interior or the chancellery) as well as fora of discourse production (such as the "NSA-Untersuchungsausschuss" or the Parliamentary Control Committee).

3. German Reactions to the Snowden Revelations

In one of her first public reactions to the revelations in July 2013, Chancellor Merkel already expressed her concerns by highlighting that not all technical possibilities should actually be used to facilitate surveillance, but she also expressed sympathy for different needs for security in the US and Germany (Federal Government, 2013). In this statement, she also announced a program to enhance privacy in order to deal with the new situation. One of the program's key elements took shape in cooperation with the Brazilian government. Both Chancellor Merkel and then President Dilma Rousseff were among the most prominent surveillance targets and were therefore very critical of the practices revealed by Snowden. Together both governments drafted a UN-resolution to ensure privacy in the digital age. Resolution 68/167 was passed by the United Nations General Assembly after some debate in December 2013 (UN, 2013). The resolution emphasized:

> that unlawful or arbitrary surveillance and/or interception of communications, as well as unlawful or arbitrary collection of personal data, as highly intrusive acts, violate the rights to privacy and to freedom of expression and may contradict the tenets of a democratic society. (UN, 2013, p. 2)

The passing of the resolution also closely coincided with a new embarrassment for the German government when surveillance of Angela Merkel's cell phone was disclosed in October (Smale, 2013). While this reaction is connected to privacy concerns frequently articulated in public and parliamentary discourses, it is remarkable that the intergovernmental UN General Assembly was selected as a regulatory forum. Given the non-binding character of UN resolutions, it does not imply any change in practice, not even by the German government as one of the initiators of the resolution.

In contrast, the establishment of a commission of inquiry (the "NSA-Untersuchungsausschuss") by the German Bundestag in January 2014 can be seen as a concrete step to re-evaluate the established intelligence cooperation. Its task is not only to further investigate accusations against the US and British intelligence agencies but to also clarify the activities of German agencies. Another concrete measure, which even entailed a change of practices, came when the federal government, after negotiations on a "no-spy-agreement" had failed, changed its practice of contracting a foreign provider by recalling contracts with Verizon in June 2014. Until then the government had tasked the US-based enterprise with providing services for its telecommunications infrastructure. Consequently, Verizon was replaced by Deutsche Telekom (Hudson, 2014). The decision to replace a US-based company by a German competitor can be seen as clearly rooted in the pursuit of digital sovereignty (see DA below).

In contrast, the temporal and partial disruptions of the German–US intelligence cooperation that started in May 2015 (Connolly, 2015), while being an obvious change in the practices of information sharing, were more of symbolic value. Information sharing was halted when it became public that the NSA had used its cooperation with the German BND to spy on targets within Germany and the European Union (EU). But the change only affected the cooperation in Bad Aibling and, following an investigation, cooperation was re-established in January 2016 (Mascolo, 2016).

Finally, in June 2016 the German government presented a new legal framework for the foreign surveillance activities of the BND (Federal Chancellery, 2016). Since the draft enabled easier information sharing between intelligence agencies and weakened previously established limitations on data collection (Papier, 2016), it was met with considerable criticism. NGOs and journalists argued that the government had legalized previously illegal activities and thereby enhanced the surveillance capabilities of the German intelligence agency (Deutscher Journalisten-Verband, 2016; Meister, 2016). Furthermore, critique was also expressed by representatives of the Organization for Security and Co-operation in Europe (OSCE) and the UN (OSCE, 2016; UN, 2016). Nevertheless, the government remained committed to the new legislative framework and parliament finally passed the new law in October 2016.

As this short summary clearly shows, the German government responded quite reluctantly to the revelations and resorted to more symbolic reactions. In 2016 the government even began to enhance surveillance capabilities. These developments were enabled by different governmental and parliamentary discourses that will be analyzed in the following section.

4. Post-Snowden Discourses Compared: The Debates in the German Bundestag and the Governmental Discourse

In the course of our discourse analysis in the wake of the Snowden revelations, we identified five recurrent discursive elements that seem particularly important for understanding what happened to the Snowden effect in German policy-making. Therefore, we compare how the respective discursive elements differ between the statements of parliamentary and governmental speakers. What is modified and in what way? What gets lost? What is added? How does all this influence the (un)likelihood of a change in practices?

4.1. Reduced Need to Act—The Parliamentary Discourse

4.1.1. The Fundamental Problem—The Tense Relation between Freedom and Security

One of the prevalent discursive trends in parliament after the Snowden revelations strikes at the very heart of the matter, explicitly addressing the tension between freedom and security, which most speakers agree needs to be re-balanced either towards security (with regard to terrorism and potential attacks) or towards freedom. Determining the measures necessary to balance the security and physical wellbeing of the citizens with their right to freedom and privacy is of course the key issue for politicians of all affiliations in the context of the NSA affair.

Most parliamentary speakers tend to come down on the side of freedom:

> These rights to freedom must be protected—against an overly powerful surveillance state, for example—because the quest for complete security leads to tyranny and a lack of freedom. To quote an American, Benjamin Franklin: Those who would give up essential Liberty, to purchase a little temporary Safety, deserve neither Liberty nor Safety. Manfred Grund, CDU/CSU (Deutscher Bundestag, 2014)

This speaker stands out in particular as his statements provide one of the few explanations for the emphasis on one societal good over another:

> Freedom is a very important good. It is in fact the most important good of our constitution. There's a reason the enumeration of civil liberties is at the very beginning of our constitution. Manfred Grund, CDU/CSU (Deutscher Bundestag, 2014)

This is one of the clearest examples of a parliamentarian explaining the prioritization of freedom over security. The Grundgesetz serves as a point of reference, since the rights ensuring freedom for the average German citizen are the first to be documented in the constitution. Additionally, a notable moment in parliamentary discourse is brought about when one of the members references the "super fundamental right of security", a term coined by Interior Minister Friedrich, to make the opposing argument:

> In our negotiations and discussions we'll now make it very clear that there is a super fundamental right

> to freedom in the United States as well as here at home, and we'll make it clear that the Federal Government [of Germany] isn't perceiving this affair as being concluded by a long shot. Michael Hartmann, SPD (Deutscher Bundestag, 2014)

The call for freedom isn't particularly surprising given the massive privacy invasions the Snowden revelations brought to light. Nonetheless, while the importance of freedom is invoked, in many cases its absolute value is diluted by mentioning its close relationship with security concerns. The very existence of the freedom v. security framing points to the fact that none of the speakers are disregarding the importance of security as a societal good. This implies a preparedness for concessions and may indicate parliamentary tolerance for non-action on the part of the government.

4.1.2. Digital Sovereignty—The Struggle for Digital Autonomy

With digital sovereignty, we coded one remarkable interpretive scheme through which the current distribution of power in cyberspace and the German dependence on other forces (above all the US) is vehemently challenged. The respective demand is made quite often in parliamentary debate. It is almost always rooted in the context of the EU regulatory framework, in which higher autonomy seems achievable. Hence, speakers mostly call to develop a European digital strategy:

> Ladies and Gentlemen, in light of the excessive data-gathering by the NSA, it is our central task in Germany and Europe to reclaim sovereignty over what is done with our data. We need legal and technical means to do that. Günter Krings, CDU/CSU (Deutscher Bundestag, 2014)

The argument for a renewed sovereignty in the digital realm also points to the problem of the asymmetrical dependence on the US. This dependence is stated explicitly in the following example:

> This is not about IT-nationalism, but if we take an honest look at the situation, we have to admit that we're dependent on US or Asian software and hardware in many instances. We need our own initiatives in the areas of research and development. Lars Klingbeil, SPD (Deutscher Bundestag, 2014)

It is acknowledged that other state actors such as the US and Asian countries possess more resources in the area of digital development, something Germany isn't able to compete with, at least at the moment. Developing the ability to counter these dependencies is given high importance in the wake of the Snowden revelations. The text sequences coded with the digital sovereignty scheme are the ones that most clearly challenge the current relations and practices between Germany and the US regarding security issues and intelligence.

4.1.3. Cyber Angst—The New Level of Threat in the Digital Age

A frequently appearing narrative in both discourses underscores the elevated need for security in reaction to a higher threat level in the digital age affecting both states and citizens. This narrative, which we coded with the term "cyber angst", explores the many potential threats cyberspace poses to a state's security. This includes possible terrorist attacks on critical infrastructure as well as criminal activity in the cyber realm. The narrative serves a securitization logic (Buzan, Waever, & de Wilde, 1998), as it is prone to justifying extraordinary surveillance measures. So-called cyber angst, particularly regarding critical infrastructure, is a crucial narrative in the governmental discourse. It is also found in the parliamentary debate:

> We need online security, especially within the area that's important for our society and country. Communication on a state level must be safe. If we want to uphold critical infrastructure it has to be safe from hacking, attacks and espionage. Hans-Peter Uhl, CDU/CSU (Deutscher Bundestag, 2013a)

4.1.4. Post Privacy—It's a New World

There is another narrative that might serve to reduce the severity and thus lessen the impact of the Snowden revelations within the parliamentary debate. Like cyber angst, it is also rooted in the newness and paradigm-shifts that are ascribed to internet development and the digital era. Cyberspace is depicted by some advocates as such a new and foreign world that some normative prescriptions, as central as they may be, cannot fully apply. This narrative implies that modern societies have moved towards a post-privacy age. Following that argument, the actions of the US government are not justified per se, but the societal norm of privacy that is in danger is depicted as already compromised:

> We shouldn't let citizens believe that they're still safe from espionage if they disclose private matters online. We have to make that clear, especially to young people using Facebook and Twitter among other things. We have to tell them that everything they put online stays there and that there's no digital eraser. That's an illusion. We have to tell people that. Hans-Peter Uhl, CDU/CSU (Deutscher Bundestag, 2013a)

The post-privacy narrative comes with another important implication: the blame for a privacy breach is put not only on firms or state agencies that conduct surveillance, but is also attributed to online users who freely share private information on the internet. The responsibility shifts to citizens, as they are expected to know that information shared online at any time might be the target of corporate or government espionage. Given the overwhelming regulatory demands that internet communication confronts us with, the best line of defense is seen in self-regulation instead of government intervention.

4.1.5. Asymmetrical Dependence in the Security Realm

An effective interpretive scheme that potentially reduces any activism supporting a path-breaking turn in security cooperation with the US is the continued reminder that Germany is highly dependent on US intelligence in security matters. This asymmetrical dependence is brought up many times:

> Every single one of us knows that attacks in Germany were prevented by US intelligence, that's part of the truth of this debate. But we also have to think about how we'll prevent future surveillance. Michael Grosse-Brömer, CDU/CSU (Deutscher Bundestag, 2013b)

This statement addresses a need to prevent surveillance in Germany, while at the same time stating the absolute necessity of US–German cooperation in the security realm to prevent terrorist attacks. This discursive element is the most overt in explaining Germany's continued intelligence and security cooperation with the United States in spite of the Snowden revelations. The bottom line of this logic seems to be that while Germany condemns the surveillance, there simply is no other option to safeguard domestic security apart from cooperating with the US. Additionally, there is an element of gratefulness towards the US for its role in preventing attacks in Germany, which may inhibit harsh criticism of their surveillance activities. One speaker addresses the impossibility of truly faulting the US for its actions while at the same time relying on them for intelligence:

> It won't impress the Americans if we rightly and legitimately criticize their actions in the NSA affair, but at the same time, in Germany and Europe, allow our own defense efforts to erode to the point that we always have to ask for data and insights from the US agencies when things get serious. Günter Krings, CDU (Deutscher Bundestag, 2013b)

If we follow this argument, German officials are in no position to criticize the US for its surveillance activities as they provide the very same intelligence that has kept German citizens safe in the past. The speaker states that even the legitimate criticism will more than likely fall on deaf ears in the US if its allies in Europe take few measures to ensure their own safety and are thus reliant on their partner overseas. The implied solution is the development of intelligence capabilities by Germany and other European states to lessen the dependence on US intelligence and gain some equality in the security relationship and open a dialogue on these matters.

4.2. Refused Need to Act—The Governmental Discourse

4.2.1. The Fundamental Problem—The Tense Relation between Freedom and Security

Explicit reflections on the relationship between security and freedom are even more frequent in the governmental discourse. There are distinct differences to the way parliamentarians discussed it. Representatives in the Bundestag mainly prioritize freedom over security, while government officials talk about security as a transcendental good, i.e. a good without which other goals, including freedom, cannot be achieved:

> Security is the prerequisite for freedom. Hans-Dieter Heumann (Federal Academy for Security Policy, 2015)

When even freedom is seen and depicted as dependent on security, it is not far to the statement of then Minister of the Interior Hans-Peter Friedrich emphasizing security as a "super fundamental law" (Bewarder & Jungholt, 2013). If there can be no freedom without security, the mass surveillance by the US government could even be portrayed as a way of ensuring freedom instead of endangering it. While this is not uttered explicitly, the implications help to understand why meaningful change in cooperative practices with the US is not only regarded as not feasible, but also as not necessary in the end. Furthermore, one governmental document addresses the varying response to the freedom v. security struggle in different countries and puts this down to different historical experiences:

> The balance of freedom and security takes various shapes in different states for historical reasons. (Ministry of the Interior, 2013)

Even though it is only implied here, the idea is that the US surveillance is rooted in historical experiences that make them more likely to come down on the side of security, particularly the terrorist attacks of 9/11. This is a sympathetic view that seeks to somewhat justify US intelligence activities, as they have been employed after a traumatic event that would cause a state to be hypervigilant in security matters.

4.2.2. Digital Sovereignty—The Struggle for Digital Autonomy

Standing in contrast to the other recurrent elements, demands for digital autonomy or sovereignty are articulated in a clearer fashion within the governmental discourse than in the parliamentary debate. The idea that Germany must achieve a sort of digital sovereignty—

mostly in cooperation with the EU—to break free of US influence was supported even by the German Minister for the Interior de Maizière:

> Our political leverage is significantly defined by our technological capabilities. Therefore, we have to do everything possible to maintain IT capabilities in order to keep and further build our own technological platforms....The government is going to develop a strategy to secure national competitiveness. I've already said that this is a modern form of patriotism. Thomas de Maizière (Ministry of the Interior, 2014a)

In this speech, de Maizière also emphasized that the EU is crucial to achieving this goal. This also shows that even though the need for independence from US cooperation is acknowledged, Germany is not seen as being capable of achieving this goal alone, i.e. outside of the cooperative framework of the EU. The idea of building a European counterbalance to US hegemony in digital matters is one of the few ways in which the Snowden revelations seem to have had a disruptive effect on US–German cooperation.

4.2.3. Cyber Angst—The New Level of Threat in the Digital Age

The narrative that cyberspace is exposing states and their citizens to a higher level of risk is much more frequently used in the governmental discourse than in parliament. There are also differences in the way how it is told. Moreover, the implied claims are presented with much more certainty as are the derived solutions:

> A stable, secure, open and free internet offers great opportunities: for economic growth and development, for good governance and democracy, as well as for social exchange between people around the world. At the same time, it confronts us with new threats: Numerous states are pursuing military cyber-capabilities, which might lead to an atmosphere of mutual distrust and conflict. Private actors have shown great skill in abusing the net for criminal purposes. Terrorists have been using the internet for their means. Norbert Riedel (Ministry of Foreign Affairs, 2015a)

This quote offers insight into the way this particular narrative unfolds. While some positive effects of the cyber age are acknowledged, the dangers posed by this new way of dealing with the world are exposed at the same time. In this instance, two different kinds of threats are addressed: the atmosphere of distrust created by this new way states can attack each other and the possibility of terrorists and criminals using the internet for their own purposes. In its entirety, this narrative creates an atmosphere of fear and implicitly justifies using extraordinary means—e.g. mass surveillance—to ensure the security of a state or society. This comes down to a securitization logic with government officials as the prime securitizing agents (Buzan et al., 1998).

4.2.4. Post Privacy—It's a New World

While the cyber angst narrative is more important for the governmental discourse than for the parliamentary one, the opposite is true of the narrative according to which cyberspace has brought about a kind of post privacy era, as it is much less prominently represented in governmental discourse than it is in the parliamentary debate. Nevertheless, the narrative is employed as well:

> In a changing world that requires answers for the continued digitalization of our society and newly developing areas of organization, we cannot simply fall back on our ordinary patterns of behavior and keep rigid systems that don't live up to the challenges of this day and age. Norbert Riedel (Ministry of Foreign Affairs, 2015b)

In this instance, the narrative of cyberspace as a new frontier is used to challenge the outdated strategies used to deal with these new circumstances. From this perspective, a more extreme argument would be possible by which the revealed mass surveillance of the NSA is seen as a coping technique employed to deal with the new challenges cyberspace poses to states and their governments.

4.2.5. Asymmetrical Dependence in the Security Realm

In contrast to the previous example, there is not much difference in how the idea of an asymmetrical security relationship between Germany and the US appears in governmental and parliamentary discourses. Rather, this seems to be more or less common sense:

> The United States is our most important partner and our closest ally. The security cooperation with our US partners is irreplaceable in regards to our domestic and external security. That's especially true for the fight against terrorism. This is the reason we want to continue and deepen our cooperation. Thomas de Maizière (Ministry of the Interior, 2014b)

The demand in this quote from Minister of the Interior de Maizière is very clear: given the high dependence of German security on US intelligence information, there is no other option to guarantee the security of Germany than to continue the close security cooperation with the US. He even goes further by expressing a desire to deepen the already existing cooperation instead of reducing it. The way de Maizière frames the cooperation doesn't imply that it is a necessary evil brought about by Germany's own lack of intelligence capabilities in certain areas. On the contrary, he explicitly names the US as the closest partner and ally, a role that German government officials apparently take no objection to even in the wake of the Snowden revelations. Considering how the actions of the US government have widely been interpreted as a betrayal of its allies, this hints at a relationship that runs very deeply indeed.

5. Conclusion

Considering the outrage the Snowden revelations provoked in German public discourse, one could have expected that politicians would react to it with a bundle of measures to reform policies, institutions and practices in the security realm. From this perspective, it seemed likely that especially the close security cooperation with the US would be restrained by more privacy-sensitive regulation in this field. However, as we all know by now, the consequences of the Snowden revelations for the German–US intelligence collaboration have been few and far between. Security cooperation with the US remained stable most of the time, and the government even extended the capabilities of German intelligence agencies with a new legal framework for foreign surveillance. The reforms that have been carried out are rather symbolic in nature, but some even legalize the revealed practices instead of trying to forbid them. This discrepancy between public statements and government action is the puzzle that our research started with. We approached the problem with a discourse analytical framework. Relying on the Sociology of Knowledge Approach to Discourse, we comparatively analyzed parliamentary and governmental discourses in Germany after the Snowden revelations.

In our empirical sections, we identified five recurrent elements that could be found in parliamentary and governmental discourses that facilitated the reluctant reactions in different ways. The first one included all general and/or explicit reflections on the tense fundamental relationship between freedom and security and is thus rather indifferent regarding the expected consequences; the debate seems to favor neither side overwhelmingly and an absolute call for security is rarely made. Additionally, we found a push for digital sovereignty or autonomy which clearly effected a change of practice with the German government canceling its contract with Verizon. While this element certainly influenced the move away from a contractor based in the US, the dependencies addressed also include concerns about Asian companies, therefore leading to more nuanced thoughts about which dependencies might be less problematic and how to avoid them altogether.

While the two elements mentioned above can potentially either increase or decrease cooperation with the US, we also found three recurrent elements which all serve to reduce the perceived severity of the NSA scandal and thus prevent more resolute efforts to reduce cooperation with the US. The first one we called cyber angst. This element expresses a diffuse anxiety about the new threats in our increasingly digital world. Fears are stoked about state and non-state actors using cyberspace to forward their (malicious) goals at the expense of German society, leading to calls for a more active state response and more cooperation among trusted allies. The second element consists of post-privacy narratives. These focus on the distinct newness of cyberspace and argue that standards established in the offline world might not be suitable for the digital world; far reaching surveillance measures may eventually be normal conduct in the new medium. Furthermore, the state might not be the most dangerous actor in this field after all, since big companies are also engaged in extensive data collection. A reluctant response was further facilitated by the argument of asymmetrical dependence. This element emphasizes the German dependence on the US in the realm of security policy. Proponents of this argument stress the fact that cooperation with US intelligence agencies helps to protect German citizens. This is often combined with a reference to the important role the US has played in German history. It is argued that even if surveillance might be problematic, the US is not the most dangerous threat to Germany, since there are far more problematic actors that need to be countered. This argument thereby also seamlessly connects to the cyber angst narratives.

All in all, given the initial public outrage, the alleged Snowden effect seems to have diminished over time through an apparent cascade in sequential logic in the public discussions examined here. We could identify a considerable difference between the discourses in parliament and government. The need for change or stronger regulation seems reduced already by what is said and argued in the parliamentary debates. Any call for a considerable regulation that might cause a disruption in German–US security cooperation is almost completely disregarded in the governmental discourse.

Acknowledgements

We acknowledge financial support by Deutsche Forschungsgemeinschaft and Ruprecht-Karls-Universität Heidelberg within the funding programme Open Access Publishing.

Conflict of Interests

The authors declare no conflict of interests.

References

Bäcker, M. (2016). Stellungnahme zu dem Entwurf eines Gesetzes zur Ausland-Ausland-Fernmeldeaufklärung des Bundesnachrichtendienstes. *Deutscher Bundestag*. Retrieved from http://www.bundestag.de/blob/459630/1ddfe2451c0fd067872976d0f0467882/18-4-653-g-data.pdf

Balzacq, T. (2011). A theory of securitization. Origins, core assumptions, and variants. In T. Balzacq (Ed.), *Securitization theory. How security problems emerge and dissolve* (pp. 1–30). London: Routledge.

Bersick, S., Christou, G., & Yi, S. (2016). Cybersecurity and EU–China relations. In. E. J. Kirchner, T. Christiansen, & H. Dorussen (Eds.), *Security relations between China and the European Union* (pp. 167–186). Cambridge: Cambridge University Press.

Bewarder, M., & Jungholt, T. (2013, July 16). Friedrich erklärt Sicherheit zum "Supergrundrecht". *Welt*. Retrieved from https://www.welt.de/politik/deutschland/article118110002/Friedrich-erklaert-Sicherheit-zum-Supergrundrecht.html

Buzan, B., Waever, O., & de Wilde, J. (1998). *Security: A new framework for analysis*. Boulder, CO: Rienner.

Connolly, K. (2015, May 7). German secret service BND reduces cooperation with NSA. *The Guardian*. Retrieved from https://www.theguardian.com/world/2015/may/07/german-secret-service-bnd-restricts-cooperation-nsa-us-online-surveillance-spy

Deutscher Bundestag. (2013a). Stenografischer Bericht 249. Sitzung Berlin, Mittwoch, den 26. Juni 2013. *Deutscher Bundestag*. Retrieved from http://dip21.bundestag.de/dip21/btp/17/17249.pdf

Deutscher Bundestag. (2013b). Stenografischer Bericht 2. Sitzung Berlin, Montag, den 18. November 2013. *Deutscher Bundestag*. Retrieved from http://dip21.bundestag.de/dip21/btp/18/18002.pdf

Deutscher Bundestag. (2014). Stenografischer Bericht 7. Sitzung Berlin, Mittwoch, den 15. Januar 2014. *Deutscher Bundestag*. Retrieved from http://dip21.bundestag.de/dip21/btp/18/18007.pdf

Deutscher Journalisten-Verband. (2016, September 16). BND-Gesetz. Kein Schutz für Journalisten. *Deutscher Journalisten-Verband*. Retrieved from http://www.djv.de/startseite/profil/der-djv/pressebereich-download/pressemitteilungen/detail/article/kein-schutz-fuer-journalisten.html?cHash=cad80f8c0f4108ced1be30a704676f24&type=500

Federal Academy for Security Policy. (2015). Cyber-Realität zwischen Freiheit und Sicherheit. *Federal Academy for Security Policy*. Retrieved from https://www.baks.bund.de/en/node/513

Federal Chancellery. (2016). Entwurf eines Gesetzes zur Ausland-Ausland-Fernmeldeaufklärung des Bundesnachrichtendienstes. *Bundeskanzleramt*. Retrieved from https://www.bundesregierung.de/Content/DE/_Anlagen/2016/06/2016-06-28-entwurf-bnd-gesetz.pdf?__blob=publicationFile&v=1

Federal Government. (2013). Deutschland ist ein Land der Freiheit. *Bundesregierung*. Retrieved from https://www.bundesregierung.de/ContentArchiv/DE/Archiv17/Artikel/2013/07/2013-07-19-bkin-nsa-sommerpk.html;jsessionid=FA5B3F77DAD45E2755C7E47F46DED066.s7t2?nn=437032#Start

Foucault, M. (2002). *Archaeology of knowledge*. London and New York, NY: Routledge.

Gabrielatos, C. (2007). Selecting query terms to build a specialized corpus from a restricted-access database. *ICAME Journal*, *31*, 5–43.

Gorr, D., & Schünemann, W. J. (2013). Creating a secure cyberspace: Securitization in Internet governance discourses and dispositives in Germany and Russia. *International Review of Information Ethics*, *20*(12), 37–51.

Hajer, M. A. (2002). Discourse analysis and the study of policy making. *European Political Science*, *2*(1). Retrieved from http://www.maartenhajer.nl/upload/Hajer%20EPS.pdf

Howarth, D., Norval, A. J., & Stavrakakis, Y. (Eds.). (2000). *Discourse theory and political analysis. Identities, hegemonies and social change*. Manchester: Manchester University Press.

Hudson, A. (2014, June 26). German government cancels Verizon contract in wake of U.S. spying row. *Reuters*. Retrieved from http://www.reuters.com/article/us-germany-security-verizon-idUSKBN0F11WJ20140626

Keller, R. (2007). *Diskursforschung. Eine Einführung für SozialwissenschaftlerInnen*. Wiesbaden: VS Verlag für Sozialwissenschaften.

Keller, R. (2008). *Wissenssoziologische Diskursanalyse. Grundlegung eines Forschungsprogramms*. Wiesbaden: VS Verlag für Sozialwissenschaften.

Keller, R. (2013). *Doing discourse research: An introduction for social scientists*. London: SAGE Publications.

Mascolo, G. (2016, January 8). BND und NSA kooperieren wieder in Bad Aibling. *Süddeutsche Zeitung*. Retrieved from http://www.sueddeutsche.de/politik/abhoerskandal-bnd-und-nsa-kooperieren-wieder-in-bad-aibling-1.2810828

Meister, A. (2016, June 30). Das neue BND-Gesetz—Alles, was der BND macht, wird einfach legalisiert und sogar noch ausgeweitet. *Netzpolitik.org*. Retrieved from https://netzpolitik.org/2016/das-neue-bnd-gesetz-alles-was-der-bnd-macht-wird-einfach-legalisiert-und-sogar-noch-ausgeweitet/

Ministry of Foreign Affairs (2015a). Rede des Beauftragten für Cyber-Außenpolitik, Botschafter Dr. Norbert Riedel, bei der Tagung der Freedom Online Coalition in Ulan Bator (Mongolei). *Ministry of Foreign Affairs*. Retrieved from http://www.auswaertiges-amt.de/DE/Infoservice/Presse/Reden/2015/150504-Riedel_Freedom_Online_Coalition_Conference.html

Ministry of Foreign Affairs (2015b). Es braucht neue Regeln fürs Internet—Deutschland und Brasilien im Einsatz für Privatsphäre und Sicherheit. *Ministry of Foreign Affairs*. Retrieved from http://www.auswaertiges-amt.de/DE/Infoservice/Presse/Interviews/2015/150330_Cyber_Privatsphaere.html

Ministry of the Interior. (2013, August). Maßnahmen für einen besseren Schutz der Privatsphäre. Fortschrittsbericht vom 14. August 2013. *Ministry of the Interior*. Retrieved from http://www.bmwi.de/BMWi/Redaktion/PDF/ST/massnahmen-fuer-einen-besseren-schutz-derprivatsphaere,property=pdf,bereich=bmwi2012,sprache=de,rwb=true.pdf

Ministry of the Interior. (2014a). Schutz—Sicherheit—Vertrauen Auftrag der Politik im digitalen Zeitalter. *Ministry of the Interior*. Retrieved from http://www.

protokoll-inland.de/SharedDocs/Reden/DE/2014/06/dud.html

Ministry of the Interior. (2014b). Rede von Bundesinnenminister de Maizière anlässlich des 11. Symposiums des Bundesamtes für Verfassungsschutz am 8. Mai 2014 in Berlin. *Ministry of the Interior*. Retrieved from http://www.bmi.bund.de/SharedDocs/Reden/DE/2014/05/bfv-symposium.html

Organization for Security and Co-operation in Europe. (2016). Surveillance amendments in new law in Germany pose a threat to media freedom, OSCE Representative says, asks Bundestag to reconsider bill. *Organization for Security and Co-operation in Europe*. Retrieved from http://www.osce.org/fom/252076

Papier, H.-J. (2016). Beschränkungen der Telekommunikationsfreiheit durch den BND an Datenaustauschpunkten. *Neue Zeitschrift für Verwaltungsrecht*, *35*(15), 1–15.

Sabatier, P. A. (1988). An advocacy coalition framework of policy change and the role of policy-oriented learning therein. *Policy Sciences*, *21*(2/3), 129–168.

Schulze, M. (2015). Patterns of surveillance legitimization. The German discourse on the NSA scandal. *Surveillance & Society*, *13*(2), 197–217.

Segal, A. M. (2016). *The hacked world order: How nations fight, trade, maneuver, and manipulate in the digital age*. New York, NY: PublicAffairs.

Smale, A. (2013, October 23). Anger growing among allies on U.S. spying. *New York Times*. Retrieved from http://www.nytimes.com/2013/10/24/world/europe/united-states-disputes-reports-of-wiretapping-in-Europe.html?_r=0

Troianovski, A., Gorman, S., & Torry, H. (2013, October 24). European leaders accuse U.S. of violating trust. *Wall Street Journal*. Retrieved from http://www.wsj.com/articles/SB100014240527023047994045791950188871722

United Nations. (2013). Resolution 68/167. *United Nations*. Retrieved from. http://www.un.org/ga/search/view_doc.asp?symbol=A/RES/68/167

United Nations. (2016). *Stellungnahme*. Retrieved from https://netzpolitik.org//wp-upload/2016/09/160829_Stellungnahme_UN-Sonderbeauftragte_zur_BND-Reform.pdf

Wetzling T. (2016). Stellungnahme zum Entwurf eines Gesetzes zur Ausland-Ausland-Fernmeldeaufklärung des Bundesnachrichtendienstes (BND) sowie weiterer Vorlagen. *Deutscher Bundestag*. http://www.bundestag.de/blob/459622/a6a22e212bb9c777028554ed1ba4bbfc/18-4-653-c-data.pdf

Wodak, R., & Krzyzanowski, M. (Eds.). (2008). *Qualitative discourse analysis in the social sciences*. Basingstoke: Palgrave Macmillan.

Xiao Wu, A. (2012). Hail the independent thinker. The emergence of public debate culture on the Chinese internet. *International Journal of Communication*, *6*, 2220–2244.

21

Under the Influence: Advertisers' Impact on the Content of Swiss Free Newspapers

Colin Porlezza

IPMZ—Institute of Mass Communication and Media Research, University of Zurich, 8050 Zurich, Switzerland;
E-Mail: c.porlezza@ipmz.uzh.ch

Abstract

The study focuses on whether and to what extent advertisers influence the editorial content of free newspapers in the German part of Switzerland. The contribution analyzes, grounded on an historic approach, the most competitive period in Switzerland, 2008, when not less than five freesheets were competing for advertisers and public attention. By using Altmeppen's (2006) organizational theory, the paper offers a theoretical frame able to describe the vanishing co orientation between the media management and the newsroom, a trend that aggravates commercialization processes in news organizations. In a situation of economic turmoil, so the hypothesis, newsrooms are more inclined to positively adapt the valence of their coverage about their main advertisers in order to keep them in the portfolio. Using a content analysis, the author examined the editorial coverage of six among the most important advertisers of Swiss free newspapers, carrying out an aggregated statistical analysis based on logistic regression. The study revealed that free newspapers with a strong market orientation display a higher chance to publish positive facts and evaluations about advertisers with a high advertising expenditure.

Keywords

advertising; commercialization; free newspapers; journalism; media accountability

Issue

This article is part of a multidisciplinary issue of *Media and Communication*, edited by Epp Lauk (University of Jyväskylä, Finland) and Raul Reis (Emerson College, USA).

---

1. Introduction

Newspapers are confronted with massive financial problems due to their business model still mostly grounded on advertising, which in the present context seems no longer viable. Several scholars argue in fact that newspaper organizations have experienced "severe difficulties because of their historical dependence on advertising notably classified ads as a source of revenue" (Siles & Boczkowski, 2012, p. 1379; see also Meyer, 2009). The intensifying pressures on media enterprises lead to the assumption that decisions concerning the publication of editorial content are much more frequently taken under the influence of economic principles and not under the perspective of journalistic news values (Esser & Brüggemann, 2010)—with the risk that media firms may orientate their strategic decisions, also with regard to the selection of the editorial content, more on the needs and requests of the advertising industry rather than leave them to journalists. These economic pressures may well tear down the "Chinese Wall" that usually separates the editorial from the commercial part (Schudson, 1978).

This dysfunctional trend is reflected by the increasing use of hybrid advertising formats in newspapers such as advertorials, brand journalism, sponsored content, promotional news and other terms used to describe different marketing tools (Siegert & Brecheis, 2005). The current issues with regard to hybrid advertising formats are aggravated by the increased use of native advertising in digital news outlets (Porlezza, 2017). However, the redefinition of the rising advertising-editorial divide (Carlson, 2015) is not limited to hybrid forms of advertising. The commercial influence goes well beyond formal aspects and visuals. This leads to what McChesney (2004) has labeled as "hyper-commercialization", that is the specific impact of advertisers' pressures and interests onto the journalistic production process in terms of coverage and tone. Although there are some case studies, mostly based on anecdotal evidence, quantitative data on specific markets such as freesheets are rare.

This study aims to go beyond the predominant discourse about hybrid advertising. It wants to shed light on whether and to what extent advertisers influence the editorial content by focusing on free newspapers in the German part of Switzerland. The contribution analyzes, grounded on an historic approach, the most competitive period in the Swiss print media market, 2008, when not less than five free newspapers were competing for advertisers and public attention. This was an exceptional and unique era in the history of the Swiss media market, also because today, only two free newspapers are left. At the time, the enormous economic difficulties due to the financial crisis led not only to a massive decline of advertising revenues, it also increased the competition for advertising between the main media conglomerates.

In this grieve economic situation, so the main hypothesis, newsrooms are more inclined to positively adapt the tone of their coverage about their main advertisers in order to keep them in their portfolio, with dysfunctional consequences for their independence, the transparency as well as the quality of their journalistic content. As a result, the traditional separation between editorial and commercial content is abolished, leading to a biased coverage. Using a quantitative content analysis, the author examined the editorial coverage of six among the most important advertisers (in terms of advertising expenditures) of the free newspapers, carrying out an aggregated statistical analysis based on logistic regression. The study revealed that free newspapers with a strong market orientation display a higher chance to publish positive facts and evaluations about advertisers with a higher advertising expenditure. This phenomenon constitutes a serious challenge for the future of (free) newspapers, because it undermines their credibility and threatens journalistic autonomy in general. The shrinking financial resources that favor the trend to tear down the "Chinese Wall" needs a close scrutiny as well as a critical stance in terms of journalistic norm construction and the development of accountability practices in order to allow journalists to operate independently of commercial pressures and to avoid market-driven information.

2. The Impact of Advertising on Journalism

Although in the 1920s scholars like Max Weber and Karl Bücher already condemned the risk of commercialization of the press due to advertising (Kiefer, 2005, p. 20ff.), the discussion about the crumbling "Chinese Wall" was launched in the Anglo–American world between the 1980s and early 1990s by critical scholars such as Herman and Chomsky (1988), Underwood (1993) or McManus (1994), all of whom referred to different forms of market-driven journalism. However, particularly during the 2000s, researchers such as McChesney (2004) and Croteau and Hoynes criticized the newspaper industry for having followed an economic oriented approach, which "certainly challenges the belief that the unregulated marketplace adequately responds to the public's needs" (2006, p. 30).

The increasing commercialization of the news media is also reflected by a continuous shift in the organizational structures of the news media that favor the implementation of an economic logic in the newsroom. Particularly useful in this regard is the theory presented by Altmeppen (2006), which shows how the partnership between the media management and the newsroom becomes increasingly unbalanced. Ever more often, the management applies pressure on the newsroom by adopting threats such as budget cuts in order to influence the editorial content. This way, the co-orientation between the management and the newsroom becomes uneven, which is why the economic logic of the management overlaps the normative orientation of journalists towards the public interest. Advertising income becomes therefore a dominant factor, as the media management passes on the requests from the advertisers to the newsroom.

Although most empirical research on the interweaving of journalism and advertising concentrates on hybrid advertising formats (see e.g. Bærug & Harro-Loit, 2012; Carlson, 2015; Eckman & Lindlof, 2003; Erjavec, 2004; Ferrer Conill, 2016; Harro-Loit & Saks, 2006; Lewis, Williams, & Franklin, 2008) or on their effects on consumers (see e.g. Austin & Newman, 2015; Howe & Teufel, 2014), a few empirical studies confirm in fact that advertisers' demands are passed on to the newsrooms. Hays and Reisner (1990) discovered that journalists are regularly exposed to the pressure of advertisers. Soley and Craig (1992) endorsed these findings since about 90% of the surveyed journalists reported that some pressure had been applied to them. In addition, most editors said that the pressure was not coming from the advertisers but directly from within their newspapers, which reflects also Altmeppen's theoretical model presented above. An and Bergen (2007) as well as Nyilasy and Reid (2011) both confirm this impression, demonstrating that advertising directors "are willing to appease their advertisers, and are also willing to positively respond to advertisers requests" (An & Bergen, 2007, p. 118). This occurs more frequently at smaller, chain owned newspapers than in big and independent papers.

Other studies show that advertising pressure can also cause different forms of complacent journalism. Reuter and Zitzewitz (2006), looking at fund recommendations in financial publications, reveal that they are in fact correlated with advertising expenditures. Rinallo and Basuroy (2009) discover similar relationships, demonstrating that advertising spending influences the media coverage of advertisers. They examined the coverage of 291 Italian fashion companies in 123 publications from Italy, France,

Germany, the UK and the US. The two authors found that advertising has a strong positive influence on coverage and that publishers, which depend more on a specific industry for their advertising revenues, are susceptible to a higher degree of influence from their corporate advertisers. Gambaro and Puglisi (2009) draw similar conclusions in a study on the daily coverage of listed companies in the Italian press. The two researchers illustrate that newspaper coverage of a given company is positively correlated to the amount of ads purchased by that company.

When it comes to the impact of advertisers on the coverage about them, research is often limited to case studies, frequently based on indirect evidence due to methods such as interviews or surveys (see e.g. Siegert & Eberle, 2004; or Fassihi, 2008). In addition, results are not always consistent among the different studies, bearing either contradicting findings or small effects. Andresen (2008), analyzing the German magazine *Der Spiegel* and the newspaper *Süddeutsche Zeitung*, investigated whether the amount of ad spending was correlated to a more favorable coverage of four advertisers and their products. He found only weak correlations between the two variables. Kolb and Woelke (2010) carried out a study on two Swiss free newspapers and their coverage of a Swiss bank, which advertised only in one of the two papers. The results show that the newspaper without any ads reported more often about the bank and the tenor was far more critical. Based on the previous two analyses, Lagetar and Mühlbauer (2012) did a similar case study scrutinizing the coverage of German and Austrian news outlets about a supermarket chain. In their case, however, the findings were inconsistent, as there were no clear-cut differences between the coverage of those newspapers with and those without advertising from the supermarket.

Based on these reflections, this study poses the following general research question:

> RQ: What kind of impact does the ad volume exert on the editorial coverage of advertisers?

Two different premises are related to this question: the higher the advertising volume of an advertising company, the greater the likelihood that they will be able to control the reporting thanks to the interventions of the media management. Large advertising customers are central to the survival of a free newspaper. For this reason, it can be assumed that the newspapers report more positively about important advertisers. On the other hand, print media, in which a company buys little to no advertising, pay less attention to their interests and report more critically, which means that:

> H1: The larger the ad volume of an advertiser, the greater the chance of a positive coverage with regard to the presented facts.

Likewise, it is possible that the coverage yields positive effects on the judgments made by journalists (and on the selection of quotes from other actors), which may ultimately help to establish a positive frame around advertisers:

> H2: The larger the ad volume of an advertiser, the greater the probability of positive judgments by journalists and other actors in the articles.

3. The Swiss Media Market in 2008: The Climax of the Free Newspapers War

After a very positive decade in the 1980s in terms of profits, in the 1990s in the Swiss press market the number of titles started to shrink dramatically. About a third of all independent newspaper titles disappeared (Fög, 2010). At the same time, the mergers between media companies started to increase. The concentration processes in the print media market continued unimpeded after the turn of the millennium, with the result that the competition between the larger publishing houses grew steadily. In 2001 and particularly in 2002, the economic crisis led to a collapse in display prices, in addition to falling circulation figures, which added up to the pressure on newspapers.

On December 13, 1999, the Norwegian publisher Schibsted launched the first free newspaper, *20 Minuten*, in Zurich. For the first time, a free newspaper offered also journalistic content, aiming at the "unproductive" time of commuters between their home and the workplace. While there had already been free newspapers, their structure as well as the news they offered corresponded more to an official house gazette. The launch of daily free newspapers thus marked the beginning of new era in the Swiss press market.

On January 31, 2000, only four weeks after the start of *20 Minuten*, the Swedish company Metro International launched *Metropol*. However, the ill-designed project was doomed to a quick end, and shortly after its second anniversary, the newspaper ceased its publication in 2002. In the meantime, the most important Swiss publisher, Tamedia, acquired *20 Minuten* from Schibsted. Over the next three years, *20 Minuten* further strengthened its market position. Tamedia also expanded the website and launched a weekend edition of *20 Minuten*.

In 2006, another important publishing house, Ringier, entered the free newspaper market, but with a differed concept: *Heute*[1] was launched as an evening paper, intended to attract commuters on their way home—avoiding direct competition with Tamedia's *20 Minuten*, which was published early in the morning. Parallel to this project, Ringier launched a free special interest newspaper in 2006, *Cash Daily*, which was oriented at finance and business reporting. However, the distribution was organized differently, because *Cash Daily* was available at newsstands only, while *20 Minuten* and *Heute/Blick am Abend* had their own newspaper boxes in the streets.

[1] In 2007 Ringier wanted to relaunch *Heute* to strengthen the brand of their main tabloid newspaper *Blick*. At the end of May 2008, just before the start of the European Football Championship, Ringier published *Heute* under its new name *Blick am Abend*.

In September 2007, the competition in the free-market market was even further intensified when an independent PR consultant launched another free newspaper called *.ch*. The new competitor provoked reactions especially at Tamedia. The publisher immediately increased the circulation of *20 Minuten*. Shortly thereafter, in December 2007, Tamedia launched another free newspaper called *NEWS*, which should be distributed in the same areas as *.ch*. Although *NEWS* appeared as a sober journalistic product, it was clearly a product used to assure the dominance of Tamedia in the free commuter newspaper market. 2008 was therefore the culmination point of the free newspaper competition in the Swiss print media market.

Although *.ch* underwent a re-launch in October 2008, the financial problems of the title did not cease. Hence, the project was abandoned after only one and a half years of existence in May 2009. Seven months later, in December 2009, Tamedia withdrew *NEWS* from the market. A couple of months before, in March, they had already closed down *Cash Daily* following a steady decline in advertisement income. This marked the end of a long and hard competition for the free newspaper market in the German-speaking part of Switzerland, which consolidated the image of Switzerland as a stronghold for freesheets. It was by far one of the fiercest battles for market shares on the Swiss print media market and characterized a unique era. Today, with *20 Minuten* and *Blick am Abend*, only two free newspapers survived. By sharing the commuter streams in the morning and during the evening, they do not get in the way of each other, which allows for an apparent peaceful cohabitation. After the free newspaper war ended nearly ten years ago, the print media markets in urban areas such as Zurich continued to be consolidated, also because *20 Minuten* and *Blick am Abend* have become cash cows for the two publishing companies, given that they absorb a considerable amount of advertising within the press market.[2]

4. Method

The research design to determine an advertiser influence on the journalistic coverage included a two-step methodological process on a sample of five freesheets (*20 Minuten, Heute*, *Cash Daily*, *.ch* and *NEWS*) and, as an object of comparison, one paid-for newspaper (*Tages-Anzeiger*): (1) a content analysis that was necessary to determine the advertising volume for each advertiser, (2) another content analysis in order to investigate the journalistic coverage of selected advertisers in terms of the valence.

Since it was not possible to obtain specific advertising data for each newspaper it was necessary to carry out a content analysis to establish the advertising volume of each major advertiser. The analysis included three natural weeks between February 18, 2008 and March 7, 2008. The analysis included advertisements out of the five most ad-intensive markets with regard to the newspaper sector: retailers, car/automotive business, banks/insurances, telecommunication/mobile and electronics/IT.[3] Besides that, four more sub-markets were included, where the hybridization between the editorial and commercial content was expected to be strong: cosmetics, jewelry/watches/accessories, clothing, tourism, and public transport. The study included a total of 912 advertisements.

In order to avoid distortions due to the different page sizes of the newspapers, the study converted the aggregated advertising area into an index, so that the advertising volumes are directly comparable. This advertising index (*AI*) is calculated as follows:

$$AI = \Sigma F_A / F_{PS}$$

ΣF_A designates the total surface of a company's advertising, while F_{PS} indicates the page size of a newspaper. This is calculated from the height and width of the printable surface. By dividing the entire advertising surface of a company through the page size, one gets an advertising index *AI*. This index served not only as a basis for comparisons in terms of advertising volumes between the newspapers, but also as a starting point for the calculations regarding the influence of advertisers.

The second content analysis focused on a different unit of analysis: articles about selected advertisers. All kinds of editorial contributions such as news reports, comments or features were included, but not letters from the readers or other contributions from third parties. The analysis focused on the valence, which was assessed on the basis of a five-step scale ranging from 1 (unrestricted negative) to 5 (unrestricted positive). The intermediate expression (= 3) stands for a balanced, but also for an ambivalent reporting, in which both negative and positive arguments occur in the same way. According to the method of Kolb and Woelke (2010), balanced or ambivalent articles were omitted for the statistical calculations. Only articles that do express either a positive or a negative valence are included. The evaluative aspects play a decisive role not only in the overall assessment of the companies. They are also relevant when it comes to the specific statistical analysis of logistic regression, which requires a dichotomous dependent variable such as positive and negative facts or evaluations.

The period of analysis corresponds to the three weeks from the first content analysis. In order to include reporting that preceded as well as succeeded the advertising campaigns recorded during the period of observation, the analysis of the editorial coverage added another week before and one after the period of the advertising

[2] *20 Minuten*, with a circulation of 442,994, is the most read newspaper in Switzerland, *Blick am Abend* with a circulation of 270,894 is ranked number two (Schweizer Medien, 2016).

[3] The selection of the different industries was made on the grounds of Nielsen Media/Media Focus that publishes data about the most important advertising industries in Switzerland.

analysis. This means that the period of investigation for the second content analysis covers five weeks and ranges from February 11, 2008, to March 14, 2008. The reason to use natural weeks instead of artificial weeks is relevant, because it allows a continuous observation of advertising campaigns as well as the reporting. This might result in an overrepresentation of certain companies in the coverage due to specific events, but the synchronous analysis of different news outlets allows to control for biases in the coverage, since all newspapers are confronted with the same events (Andresen, 2006).

The second content analysis included companies from the following sectors only: retailers, banks, the telecommunications and mobile industry as well as public transport. The selection was made on the data collected in the first study. The selected companies were the ones with the highest advertising volumes. Table 1 shows the specific companies.

It has to be said that the chosen method does not allow to make any statements as to whether the presumed influence from the advertisers occurs directly or indirectly. The results only show whether there is an influence, not how it comes about. Consequently, the results cannot serve as a response to the question of whether there are any collusions between the management and the journalistic staff regarding the overall reporting strategy.

5. Results

The data set of the content analysis with regard to the coverage of the advertisers includes a total of 889 articles. In the five weeks under review, 227 articles belong to the *Tages-Anzeiger*, 193 to *Cash Daily*, 152 to *NEWS*, 120 to *20 Minuten*, 105 to *Heute* and 92 to *.ch*. The differences in the number of articles are mainly due to three factors. First, the *Tages-Anzeiger* has a larger page size than the freesheets and offers therefore room for more contributions. In addition, it also offers the highest number of pages, which makes it possible to report more extensively about a company. The second reason is related to *Cash Daily*: as a newspaper specialized in financial and business news, the paper focuses more often on the companies in the sample, particularly on the two banks, and reports more frequently about events that do not end up in the other newspapers. A third reason is related to the different market orientation of the newspapers: Particularly *20 Minuten* and *Heute* apply a tabloid style of journalism, which emphasizes subjects like entertainment, sports, style, fashion, celebrities and gossip. The clear focus on soft news rather than on traditional journalistic themes like politics and economy lets both paper appear as more market-driven compared to the other papers in the sample. Moreover, *20 Minuten* did not produce its own business section at that particular time, but they got the content from and external agency.

Table 2 shows that the newspapers often reported on the two banks UBS (282 articles) and Credit Suisse (165). The high number of articles on the two Swiss banks is related to the banking and economic crisis at that time. At the beginning of 2008, both banks were under public scrutiny due to the turmoil on the American mortgage market.

In order to analyze the relationship between the ad volume and the valence of the coverage about certain advertisers, logistic regression was chosen as a means of statistical analysis. Unlike linear regression, it does not provide estimates of expected values, but attempts to determine the probability of a specific outcome (Backhaus, Erichson, Plinke, & Weiber, 2003; Hosmer & Lemeshow, 2000). The logistic regression considers therefore the so-called odds. These reflect the probability for an event to happen, relative to the probability that the event does not occur. With regard to the presented study, the logistic regression considers the probability of a positive coverage compared to a negative outcome. The interpretation of the data is based on the odds ratio, which

Table 1. Sample of most important advertisers.

Retail	Banks	Telecommunications	Public transport
Migros	UBS	Swisscom	SBB
Coop	Credit Suisse		

Table 2. Number of articles about the selected advertisers.

	Migros	Coop	UBS	CS	Swisscom	SBB	Total
20 Minuten	7	9	46	20	9	29	120
Heute	16	13	17	13	22	24	105
.ch	10	3	29	21	5	24	92
Cash Daily	16	16	71	51	21	18	193
NEWS	11	10	57	28	6	40	152
Tages-Anzeiger	37	21	62	32	13	62	227
Total	97	72	282	165	76	197	889

Notes: Basis: February 11, 2008–March 14, 2008, n = 889.

indicates how much more likely a particular event occurs based on the degree of the independent variable. In other words: the odds ratio in this particular study indicates the chance of a positive coverage to the extent to which the advertising pages are increased by one unit. Obviously, this is only true if all other variables are kept constant. The study also controls for potentially interfering variables, such as the revenue of the advertiser or the penetration of the news outlet.

5.1. The Influence of Advertisers on Presented Facts

The central hypothesis of the study states that advertisers with a high advertising volume influence the reporting on their companies in a positive way. In other words, the higher the advertising expenditure of an advertiser, the greater the chance that the coverage will be positive. The analysis of the reporting took place on the grounds of two different dimensions: presented facts and evaluations from journalists and other actors.

The first dimension focuses on the valence of the presented facts. The coding is based on the presented facts only, not the judgements, allowing thus for a general assessment of the reporting. The balance between the number of positive and the negative facts determines how the general factual situation in the article is to be coded. For example, if an article contains the information that a bank has lost money due to an erroneous investment strategy, the element is coded as a negative fact. If an article contains for instance one positive fact and three negative facts, the article will be coded as overall negative. Table 3 shows the aggregated analysis for all free newspapers, for the two market-oriented papers *20 Minuten* and *Heute*, and for the paid-for newspaper *Tages-Anzeiger*.

In the aggregated analysis the results reveal that there is a small but nonetheless significant chance that free newspapers in general, and the two market-oriented papers in particular, offer more positive facts if the ad volume grows. However, there is basically no difference between the aggregated free newspapers and the two market-oriented newspapers, which might imply that the two free newspapers that offer more soft news are having a specific effect on the aggregated analysis. The paid-for newspaper does not show any significant relation between the ad volume and the valence of the coverage about the advertisers. Neither the revenue of the advertisers nor the penetration of the newspapers have an impact on the presented facts.

When it comes to the analysis of the individual titles, there are clear differences (see Table 4): particularly *Heute* with an odds ratio of 2.16 and *20 Minuten* with 1.08 show a higher chance of a positive coverage of their main advertisers. In other words: advertisers in *Heute* have more than twice the chance of getting related to positive facts if they increase their ad volume by one page. No other free paper shows significant results. This actually confirms the above mentioned thesis that the probability to get a positive coverage is so high for *Heute*—and to a lesser degree for *20 Minuten*—that the two market-oriented papers alone determine the aggregated analysis for all free newspapers.

5.2. The Influence of Advertisers on Journalists' Evaluations

The second dimension is based on the statements and evaluations of journalists and other actors mentioned in the articles about the companies in the sample. This dimension is used in order to shed light on how journalists personally—and through quotes of other people—assess the events. The coding process is carried out the exact same way as for the first dimension of the presented facts. While the selection of the presented facts may be more strongly influenced by the actual event, for instance due to a chronological narration of the different events that happened up to that particular moment, the judgements made by journalists and other people allow for a clearer account of the journalistic production process in relation to an advertiser.

The aggregated analysis of the evaluations made by journalists reveals that free newspapers in general, and

Table 3. Aggregated model for presented facts.

	All free newspapers			**Market oriented newspapers 20 Minuten & Heute**			**Paid-for newspaper Tages-Anzeiger**		
Predictor	*B*	*SE B*	e^B	*B*	*SE B*	e^B	*B*	*SE B*	e^B
Ad volume	0.11**	0.01	1.11	0.10**	0.03	1.11	0.01	0.01	1.11
News media (penetration)	0.00	0.00	1.00	−0.01**	0.00	0.99	−0.12	0.15	0.89
Advertiser (revenue)	0.00	0.00	1.00	0.00	0.00	1.00	0.00	0.00	1.00
Constant	−0.41	0.28		0.56	0.49		55.21	71.71	
Nagelkerke R^2		0.07			0.22			0.16	
n		372			133			115	
% correct predicted cases		68.8			69.9			73.9	

Notes: *B* = Regression coefficient, *SE B* = Standard error, e^B = Odds Ratio (95% confidence interval), Nagelkerke R^2 = explained variance, ** $p < .01$.

Table 4. Individual model with regard to the presented facts.

	20 Minuten			Heute			.ch			Cash Daily			NEWS		
Predictor	*B*	*SE B*	e^B	*B*	*SE B*	e^B	*B*	*SE B*	e^B	*B*	*SE B*	e^B	*B*	*SE B*	e^B
Ad volume	0.08**	0.04	1.08	0.77**	0.63	2.16	−2.37	1.46	0.09	−0.67	0.37	0.51	−0.31	0.26	0.74
Advertiser (revenue)	0.00	0.00	1.00	0.00	0.00	1.00	0.00	0.00	1.00	0.00	0.00	1.00	0.00	0.00	1.00
Constant	−0.29	0.58		−2.01	2.06		1.28	1.65		0.72	0.65		−0.49	0.91	
Nagelkerke R^2		0.17			0.29			0.09			0.07			0.03	
n		74			59			49			98			92	
% correct predicted cases		71.6			69.0			79.6			65.3			72.8	

Notes: *B* = Regression coefficient, *SE B* = Standard error, e^B = Odds Ratio (95% confidence interval), Nagelkerke R^2 = explained variance, ** $p < .01$. The penetration is missing because in the individual analysis it becomes a constant.

market-oriented freesheets in particular, show a significant chance to offer more favorable judgements about advertisers with higher ad volumes (see Table 5). On the other hand, the revenue of the advertiser, which is an indicator of its absolute market power, exerts no influence on the probability of a positive evaluation. However, the results with regard to the paid-for newspaper *Tages-Anzeiger* are surprising: the penetration seems to be a significant determining factor of the reporting. An odds ratio of 0.62 means that with a higher penetration of the newspaper, the likelihood of positive evaluations decreases. Accordingly, the probability of a positive evaluation of a company decreases by 38%, per thousand readers. This result—which is in line with what Reimann and Kreibe (2012) found out in a similar case study—could be explained by the fact that newspapers with a different business model based on advertising *and* subscriptions, are more resistant to pressures from the advertisers. Although the relation is flagged as significant, the result has to be interpreted with caution, since the standard error with respect to the parameter estimate is very large.

The individual media analysis shows one clear result: that chance to be positively judged by journalists in *Heute* is more than three times higher for an additional ad page ($e^B = 3.43$) than in any other newspaper (see Table 6). The likelihood of a positive assessment is so high that it influences the aggregated analysis for the two market-oriented newspapers ($e^B = 1.79$). However, in the case of journalistic evaluations, there are no other factors that might significantly influence the chances to improve the evaluations.

Overall it can be said that additional ad pages for free newspapers increase the chance for a positive rating. However, this effect is limited to freesheets like *20 Minuten* and *Heute* with a strong market orientation and with a tabloid style of journalism that strongly focuses on topics of human interest such as entertainment, sports, celebrities and gossip. In the paid-for newspaper, no effect could be observed, which means that the advertising volume in news outlets such as the *Tages-Anzeiger* does not seem to have any impact on the journalistic production process at all. Due to the fact that both analyses display a significant influence of the advertising vol-

Table 5. Aggregated model for journalists' evaluations.

	All free newspapers			Market oriented newspapers 20 Minuten & Heute			Paid-for newspaper Tages-Anzeiger		
Predictor	*B*	*SE B*	e^B	*B*	*SE B*	e^B	*B*	*SE B*	e^B
Ad volume	0.24**	0.10	1.27	0.58**	0.31	1.79	−0.01	0.19	0.99
News media (penetration)	0.00	0.00	1.00	0.00	0.00	0.99	−0.48*	0.21	0.62
Advertiser (revenue)	0.00	0.00	1.00	0.00	0.00	1.00	0.00	0.00	1.00
Constant	−1.49	0.46		−2.34	1.38		231.88	102.96	
Nagelkerke R^2		0.08			0.27			0.53	
n		220			67			75	
s% correct predicted cases		71.8			71.6			89.3	

Notes: *B* = Regression coefficient, *SE B* = Standard error, e^B = Odds Ratio (95% confidence interval), Nagelkerke R^2 = explained variance, ** $p < .01$.

Table 6. Individual model with regard to journalists' and quoted evaluations.

	20 Minuten			Heute			.ch			Cash Daily			NEWS		
Predictor	*B*	*SE B*	e^B	*B*	*SE B*	e^B	*B*	*SE B*	e^B	*B*	*SE B*	e^B	*B*	*SE B*	e^B
Ad volume	0.05	0.05	1.05	1.23*	1.00	3.43	−8.43	7.58	0.00	0.35	0.46	1.42	−0.27	0.50	0.77
Advertiser (revenue)	0.00	0.00	1.00	0.00	0.00	1.00	0.00	0.00	1.00	0.00	0.00	1.00	0.00	0.00	1.00
Constant	−0.75	0.87		−4.66	3.55		8.67	9.90		−1.05	0.80		−1.56	1.98	
Nagelkerke R^2		0.04			0.33			0.31			0.01			0.05	
n		40			28			33			69			51	
% correct predicted cases		70.0			67.9			84.8			65.2			80.4	

Notes: *SE B* = Standard error, e^B = Odds Ratio (95% confidence interval), Nagelkerke R^2 = explained variance, ** $p < .05$. The penetration is missing because in the individual analysis it becomes a constant.

ume on the chance of a positive reporting in terms of facts and evaluations, both hypotheses H1 and H2 are—at least in relation to market-oriented freesheets such as *20 Minuten* and *Heute*—partially confirmed.

6. Discussion and Conclusion

The trend towards profitability and efficiency is related to a wide-ranging commercialization process in the media. As a result, there is a growing tension between economic and journalistic interests. Market relations exert a greater pressure on media firms, in particular the advertising industry, as it remains the main financial source for most news outlets—especially for freesheets. The study's central finding is therefore sobering: market-oriented free newspapers, financed exclusively by advertising, display a higher chance to positively report about advertisers if their ad volume increases.

The increasing focus on the interests of advertisers and the hybridization between advertising and editorial content are additional signs of commercialization, because they show that business-related factors rule over journalistic autonomy. If free newspapers—like in Switzerland—belong to larger media conglomerates that publish traditional paid-for newspapers as well, the two papers must be positioned in different market segments in order to reduce the risk of cannibalization. This means, that (the remaining) free newspapers may evolve even further into journals that favor topics of human interest. Newspaper content, especially in free sheets, is designed to appeal to specific target groups—young commuters—whose attention can be sold to advertisers. This leads not only to a homogenization of the content, but it favors a continuous hybridization between advertising and editorial content—not surprisingly *Blick am Abend* was the first newspaper outlet to offer native advertising on its webpage. The co-orientation between journalists and the management described by Altmeppen (2006) becomes therefore increasingly undermined, with consequences that point directly to the heart of journalistic professionalism: younger journalists working in Swiss free newspapers are not primarily interested in the public interest, but in the economic wellbeing of the news outlet they are working for (Keel, 2011, p. 242).

Despite all the indicators, which point to a certain impact of the advertising expenditures, there are clear limits to it. The results of the individual analyses underscore this conclusion, since there is no general effect on newspapers. News outlets, which are committed to quality journalism, such as .ch or the *Tages-Anzeiger*, show no signs of influence. However, the prerequisite for such a result is an ongoing discourse on topics related to journalistic standards and professionalism within the news organization (both in the newsroom and the management). This might well increase the awareness of the positive effects of self-regulatory practices such as codes of ethics, guidelines or ombudsmen (Eberwein & Porlezza, 2016). The association of private Swiss media companies, Swiss Media, together with different associations from the advertising industry, have thus established a Code of Conduct, declaring that all actors—editors, publishers and advertisers—abide to the principle of transparency. All actors have to make it clear what kind of content is paid for (Swiss Media, 2016).

However, setting up self-regulating practices guaranteeing transparency is not enough. While (self-) regulatory practices may be able to uphold the "Chinese Wall" between editorial and commercial contents on a formal or visual basis, it becomes difficult to oppose economic influences that permeate the journalistic production process as presented in this study: "what strength do the judicial and self-regulatory systems have to maintain journalism as independent and as controller of both political and economic power?" (Svensson, 2016, p. 116). It takes both journalists and the media management to establish a new culture of accountability within the newsrooms. This is essential, as newsrooms are the main place where accountability and self-regulatory measures do have an impact, especially in countries where journalists' unions are not as strong as in Central and Northern Europe: "If media managers actively implemented accountability and transparency mechanisms, they could clearly demonstrate that they care for media accountability...." (Fengler, Eberwein, Mazzoleni, Porlezza, & Russ-Mohl, 2014, p. 268). By doing so, news organizations would also show that they actually care about their credibility, particularly in times when public trust in the media is waning in the wake of fake news and alternative news media outlets popping up everywhere.

This study helps to establish a broader approach to assessing the advertising pressure on (free) newspapers and expanding the scope of inquiry beyond a single case study and the discourse of hybrid advertising. However, this study also presents some limitations, which in turn are opportunities for further research. First, the content analysis was carried out in relation to a very specific moment in the history of the Swiss print media market. It would be interesting to see whether the impact of the advertisers, with only the two market-oriented free newspapers still on the market, is still intact. Over the last nearly ten years, the structure of the media system has changed and the market has become even more concentrated. Second, a follow-up study could focus on the question whether there are any differences between free sheets and traditional newspapers. Future research should also include other countries. Third, advertising expenditures had to be calculated by way of advertising space, as media organizations did not provide the relevant data.

In conclusion, more is at stake than the credibility of the media. As economic pressures become stronger and shape media content, will journalism still be capable of holding the powerful to account if the public service mission is no longer a central notion of journalism? Is journalism still able to legitimize its own work if journalists' professional role-conception shifts towards commercial interests, producing continuously ethical issues? If the answer is no, it will be rather difficult for journalism to rethink itself (see Peters & Broersma, 2016) bearing in mind the massive economic and digital challenges awaiting to be tackled.

Conflict of Interests

The author declares no conflict of interests.

References

Altmeppen, K.-D. (2006). *Journalismus und Medien als Organisationen. Leistungen, Strukturen und Management*. Wiesbaden: VS Verlag für Sozialwissenschaften.

An, S., & Bergen, L. (2007). Advertiser pressure on daily newspapers. A survey of advertising sales executives. *Journal of Advertising*, *36*(2), 111–121.

Andresen, N. (2008). Der Einfluss von Anzeigenkunden auf die redaktionelle Berichterstattung in der Qualitätspresse. Alles Lüge oder offenes Geheimnis? *Fachjournalist*, *4*, 21–26.

Austin, S., & Newman, N. (2015). *Attitudes to sponsored and branded content (native advertising)* (Digital News Report 2015). Oxford: Reuters Institute for the Study of Journalism.

Backhaus, K., Erichson, B., Plinke, W., & Weiber, R. (2003). *Multivariate Analysemethoden. Eine anwendungsorientierte Einführung*. Berlin and Heidelberg: Springer.

Bærug, J. R., & Harro-Loit, H. (2012). Journalism embracing advertising as traditional journalism discourse becomes marginal. *Journalism Practice*, *6*(2), 172–186.

Carlson, M. (2015). When news sites go native: Redefining the advertising–editorial divide in response to native advertising. *Journalism*, *16*(7), 849–865.

Croteau, D., & Hoynes, W. (2006). *The business of media. Corporate media and the public interest*. Thousand Oaks, CA: Pine Forge Press.

Eberwein, T., & Porlezza, C. (2016). Both sides of the story. Communication ethics in mediatized worlds. *Journal of Communication*, *66*(2), 328–342.

Eckman, A., & Lindlof, T. (2003). Negotiating the gray lines: An ethnographic case study of organizational conflict between advertorials and news. *Journalism Studies*, *4*(1), 65–77.

Erjavec, K. (2004). Beyond advertising and journalism: Hybrid promotional news discourse. *Discourse & Society*, *15*(5), 553–578.

Esser, F., & Brüggemann, M. (2010). The strategic crisis of German newspapers. In D. Levy & R. Nielsen (Eds.), *The changing business of journalism and its impact on democracy* (pp. 39–54). Oxford: Reuters Institute for the Study of Journalism.

Fassihi, F. F. (2008). *Werbebotschaften aus der Redaktion? Journalismus im Spannungsfeld zwischen Instrumentalisierung und Informationsauftrag*. Konstanz: UVK.

Fengler, S., Eberwein, T., Mazzoleni, G., Porlezza, C., & Russ-Mohl, S. (2014). Summary: Perspectives for newsrooms, policy-makers and journalism educators. In S. Fengler, T. Eberwein, G. Mazzoleni, C. Porlezza, & S. Russ-Mohl (Eds.), *Journalists and media accountability: An international study of news people in the digital age* (pp. 265–288). New York, NY: Peter Lang.

Ferrer Conill, R. (2016). Camouflaging church as state: An exploratory study of journalism's native advertising. *Journalism Studies*, *17*(7), 1–11.

Fög. (2010). Jahrbuch 2010—Qualität der Medien. *Fög—Research Institute for the Public Sphere and Society*. Basel: Schwabe.

Gambaro, M., & Puglisi, R. (2009). *What do ads buy? Daily coverage of listed companies on the Italian press* (Working Paper n. 2009-36). Milan: University of Milan.

Harro-Loit, H., & Saks, K. (2006). The diminishing border between advertising and journalism in Estonia. *Journalism Studies*, *7*(2), 312–322.

Hays, R. G., & Reisner, A. E. (1990). Feeling the heat from advertisers: Farm magazine writers and ethical pressure. *Journalism Quarterly*, *67*(4), 936–942.

Herman, E. S., & Chomsky, N. (1988). *Manufacturing consent. The political economy of the mass media*. New York, NY: Vintage Books.

Hosmer, D. W., & Lemeshow, S. (2000). *Applied logistic regression*. New York, NY: John Wiley.

Howe, P., & Teufel, B. (2014). Native advertising and digital natives: The effects of age and advertisement format on news website credibility judgments. *International Symposium on Online Journalism #ISOJ*, *4*(1), 78–90.

Keel, G. (2011). *Journalisten in der Schweiz: eine Berufsfeldstudie im Zeitverlauf*. Konstanz: UVK.

Kiefer, M.-L. (2005). *Medienökonomik. Einführung in eine ökonomische Theorie der Medien*. Munich and Vienna: Oldenbourg.

Kolb, S., & Woelke, J. (2010). Einfluss von Werbekunden auf redaktionelle Inhalte—Quasi-experimentelle Modellierung und empirische Erhebung. *Studies in Communication Sciences*, *10*(2), 51–77.

Lagetar, M., & Mühlbauer, C. (2012). Skandalös zurückgehalten? Berichterstattung über Werbekunden am Beispiel des Lidl-Bespitzelungsfalles. In S. Gadringer, S. Kweton, J. Trappel, & T. Vieth (Eds.), *Journalismus und Werbung* (pp. 167–189). Wiesbaden: Springer VS.

Lewis, J., Williams, A., & Franklin, B. (2008). A compromised fourth estate? *Journalism Studies*, *9*(1), 1–20.

McChesney, R. (2004). *The problem of the media: U.S. communication politics in the 21st century*. New York, NY: Monthly Review Process.

McManus, J. H. (1994). *Market-driven journalism. Let the citizen beware?* Thousand Oaks, CA: Sage.

Meyer, P. (2009). *The vanishing newspaper: Saving journalism in the information age*. Columbia, MO: University of Missouri Press.

Nyilasy, G., & Reid, L. N. (2011). Advertiser pressure and the personal ethical norms of newspaper editors and ad directors. *Journal of Advertising Research*, *51*(3), 538–551.

Peters, C., & Broersma, M. (Ed.). (2016). *Rethinking journalism again: Societal role and public relevance in a digital age*. London: Routledge.

Porlezza, C. (2017). Digitaler Journalismus zwischen News und Native Advertising. Risiken und Nebenwirkungen einer heiklen Beziehung. In W. A. Meier (Ed.), *Abbruch—Umbruch—Aufbruch: Globaler Medienwandel und lokale Medienkrisen* (pp. 249–270). Baden-Baden: Nomos.

Reimann, A., & Kreibe, F. (2012). Mass genommen! Das Volumenverhältnis von Redaktion & Werbung in Zeitungen. In S. Gadringer, S. Kweton, J. Trappel, & T. Vieth (Eds.), *Journalismus und Werbung* (pp. 101–121). Wiesbaden: Springer VS.

Reuter, J., & Zitzewitz, E. (2006). Do ads influence editors? Advertising and bias in the financial media. *Quarterly Journal of Economics*, *121*, 197–227.

Rinallo, D., & Basuroy, S. (2009). Does advertising spending influence media coverage of the advertiser? *Journal of Marketing*, *73*, 3–46.

Schudson, M. (1978). *Discovering the news*. New York, NY: Basic Books.

Schweizer Medien. (2016). *Tageszeitungen und Sonntagszeitungen 2016*. Retrieved from http://www.schweizermedien.ch/SCHM/media/SCHMMediaLibrary/Statistiken/Statistiken%202016_1/16_Tageszeitungen-Sonntagszeitungen-2016_1.pdf

Siegert, G., & Brecheis, D. (2005). *Werbung in der Medien- und Informationsgesellschaft*. Wiesbaden: VS Verlag für Sozialwissenschaften.

Siegert, G., & Eberle, S. (2004). Kommerzialisierung der Kommunikation: Die Werbebranche der Schweiz und die Hybridisierung der Kommunikationsangebote. *Medienwissenschaft Schweiz*, *2*, 13–18.

Siles, I., & Boczkowski, P. J. (2012). Making sense of the newspaper crisis: A critical assessment of existing research and an agenda for future work. *New Media and Society*, *14*(8), 1375–1394.

Soley, L. C., & Craig, R. L. (1992). Advertising pressures on newspapers: A survey. *Journal of Advertising*, *21*(4), 1–10.

Svensson, E.-M. (2016). Upholding the legislation between editorial and commercial content in legislation and self-regulation. In M. Edström, A. T. Kenyon, & E.-M. Svensson (Eds.), *Blurring the lines* (pp. 109–119). Göteborg: Nordicom.

Swiss Media. (2016). *Code of conduct*. Retrieved from http://www.schweizermedien.ch/getattachment/Medien/Code-of-Conduct/Code_of_Coduct_Unterzeichnet.pdf.aspx

Underwood, D. (1993). *When MBAs rule the newsroom*. New York, NY: Columbia University Press.

22

Subjective Evaluation of Media Content as a Moderator of Media Effects on European Identity: Mere Exposure and the Hostile Media Phenomenon

Waqas Ejaz [1,*], Marco Bräuer [2] and Jens Wolling [1]

[1] Empirical Media Research and Political Communication Department, Technical University of Ilmenau, 98693 Ilmenau, Germany; E-Mails: mian-waqas.ejaz@tu-ilmenau.de (W.E.), jens.wolling@tu-ilmenau.de (J.W.)
[2] Federal Office for the Family and Civil Society, 02959 Schleife, Germany; E-Mail: marcobraeuer@me.com

* Corresponding author

Abstract

This paper posits that the concept of European identity is an important indicator of the legitimacy of the European Union (EU). It further assumes that the exposure to EU related media content can influence the feeling of European identity. In order to verify this assumption, we combined the mere-exposure-theory and the hostile media phenomenon. We assume that these theoretical concepts could help to understand the influence of media on people's levels of attachment to the EU. Regression analyses are performed on secondary data that were collected in a Eurobarometer survey in 2013. Our findings revealed that media exposure affected the respondents' identification with Europe, as well as the modifications of this effect based on their assessments of EU media coverage. The results of the current study not only validate assumptions about the mere-exposure effects on identity but also confirm the theoretical assumption that perceived hostility reduces such effects, whereas exposure to information that is perceived as neutral promotes the effects of media exposure on the feeling of European identity.

Keywords

collective identity; European identity; hostile media; mere-exposure effect

Issue

This article is part of a multidisciplinary issue of *Media and Communication*, edited by Epp Lauk (University of Jyväskylä, Finland) and Raul Reis (Emerson College, USA).

---

1. Introduction

The idea that European polity requires a collective identity of the European citizens in order to support the process of European integration is not new. Already in 1973 a normative concept of identity was introduced into the European political discourse during the Copenhagen European Commission Summit (European Commission, 1973). Today, it is often argued by scholars that developing and strengthening European identity is necessary to bolster the achievements of the integration process (De Vreese & Boomgaarden, 2006; Triga & Vadratsikas, 2016) and that it might even help to legitimize further European integration (Bruter, 2005). This assumed capacity of European identity prompted many political scholars to investigate the relationship of identity with several key political concepts such as democracy and citizenship (Habermas & Derrida, 2005), Europeanisation (Harmsen & Wilson, 2000; Risse, 2010), European Union (EU) foreign policy (Manners, 2002), Euroscepticism (Hooghe & Marks, 2005; Szczerbiak & Taggart, 2008), and migration (Favell & Recchi, 2009).

Despite being rigorously investigated, a unanimous definition of European identity is still not available, because the concept is used in varied contexts and for different purposes. That is why the term European identity is described in various ways such as "flexible" (Walkenhorst, 2008, p. 4), "abstract" (Stråth, 2002) and "hybrid"

(Maier & Risse, 2003, p. 29). Studying and researching European identity is particularly problematic because as an idea, European identity leaves open a myriad of options for interpretation. In parts of the literature, European identity is interpreted as a necessary precondition, for political integration, because at citizen's level it promises to foster solidarity and active participation (Walkenhorst, 2009). On the other hand, it is also considered vital because it promotes legitimacy and increase effectiveness of the political system (Kaina & Karolewski, 2013). Contrary to the positive connotation of identity, the literature also highlights the contested characteristics of identity (Brubaker & Cooper, 2000, p. 1; Gandemer, 2014), and such contestation does not only exist in the interpretation of the concept, but it is also present in the debate of how it can be developed (Stone Sweet, Sandholtz, & Fligstein, 2001; Wendt, 1999) along with its complementary (Agirdag, Phalet, & Van Houtte, 2016; Delanty, 2014) or tense relationship with national identity (Carey, 2002).

Regardless the divergent interpretations of European identity, it remains a key-concept for the investigation of the future of EU. That is why researchers from diverse fields continue to investigate the topic and reveal its varied manifestations. Besides political and social scientists, also communication scholars are involved in investigations related to European identity. Because citizens become involved in European politics mainly through the media, it is reasonable to expect that European identity— understood as a political concept—is influenced by the exposure to EU-related media coverage. The "Brexit" might be considered as a recent example of the influence media may have on identity. At least it was intensely debated in the media whether the coverage on "Brexit" was biased (Reuters Institute for the Study of Journalism, 2016) and cultivated national boundaries rather than a common European identity (Corbett, 2016). In spite of the widespread assumption that media impact identity, the research on the effects of media on European identity is still rare, with view exceptions (for overviews see, Bruter, 2005; De Vreese & Boomgaarden, 2006; De Vreese, Boomgaarden, & Semetko, 2011; Olausson, 2010; Staehelin, 2016; Triga & Vadratsikas, 2016). Therefore, the purpose of this paper is to broaden this field of research.

In the light of above arguments, the main goal of this study is to clarify the influence of the exposure to European political news on identification with the EU. Consequently, we first define the concept of European identity and then examine the current research that explores the effects of media on European identity. In addition, we highlight the research gaps in the field. In the subsequent section, we focus on two theoretical concepts—mere exposure and hostile media perceptions—both of which have not been employed within the context of European identity. Based on these theoretical approaches, we develop hypotheses concerning the effects of media exposure on identity and the intervening effects of media perception and tested them with the help of a secondary data analysis. The results of this analysis reveal a connection between mere-exposure effects and hostile media perceptions with regard to European identity. In the final section, the results are discussed, the limitations of the research are considered, and recommendations for future research are specified.

2. Conceptualizing European Collective Identity

Collective identity is a broad concept and not restricted to any particular aspect. Among others gender, culture, ethnicity, religion, and nationality have been considered as basis of people's identity (Irimie, 2014). With regard to the origins of such collective identities, different theoretical arguments offer contested views. One theoretical standpoint argues that identity is essentially primordial, i.e. it is constructed from kinship, cultural or historical ties that are enshrined in the collective memory of the culture (Smith, 1992). In addition, there are postmodernist scholars who posited that individuals perceive that they have something in common on the basis of which they form an "imagined ommunity". For these scholars cultural and geographical constraints do not really matter (Anderson, 1991). Contrary to the aforementioned understandings, a third theoretical approach draws inspiration from modernist school of thought which argues that European identity is an elusive, socially constructed and negotiated reality, something that has a different meaning for each individual and does not really rely on common past (Gellner, 1983).

Within the context of this paper, European identity is considered as a form of socially constructed collective identity of the Europeans. This sense of collective identity is not developed separately within each individual, but is socially constructed, which means it emerges as the intentional or unintentional consequence of social interactions (Fligstein, Polyakova, & Sandholtz, 2012, p. 108). European identity is based on the subjective feeling and sense of belonging together as Europeans. However, this paper is focused only on the political nature of European collective identity.

In the political science literature, Easton (1965, p. 185) termed collective identity as the "we-feeling" and regarded it as a necessary condition for individuals who want to cooperate politically and authorize certain representatives to act and rule on their behalf. Hence, identity is the primary source of the legitimization of any political community and structure. Thus, in the context of this paper, it can be argued that Europeans are required to have such sense of community and belonging to EU, which consequently foster European collective identity.

Without such an attachment, any governmental regime could be considered illegitimate. In a similar vein, John Stuart Mill (1861, p. 391) argued that collective identity is a necessary aspect of democratic decision-making. Consequently, the legitimacy of a new political structure depends on an explicit and implicit agreement that links the political community to its citizens and gives it fundamental institutional acceptability (Bruter, 2003). In this context it is of high importance to understand that different forms of collective identities do not have to be in a conflictual relationship (for overviews see Delanty & Rumford, 2005, p. 51; Risse, 2003; Ruiz, et al., 2004, p. 2). For example, it is possible to have a very strong national identity and at the same time to be strongly attached to Europe (e.g. Ruiz et al., 2004, p. 8). This fact is taken into account by various models of the relationship among national and European identities, e.g. models of nested identities, concentric circles, layer cake, crosscutting identities or marble cake (Risse, 2010).

Despite these divergent views, scholars neither concede that collective identity is not significant. Consequently, researchers are interested in the factors influencing the development of collective identities. The following section of the paper narrows the scope and outlines the impact of media on European identity.

2.1. The Nature and Impact of EU Media Coverage

In the debate on the development of European identity, it is imperative to understand the role of media, because primarily media serve at the heart of (re)construction process of European identity (Schneeberger, 2009). Due to the lack of first-hand experiences of politics, whether domestic, European, or international, citizens depend heavily on the mass media to obtain information about political matters (Ball-Rokeach & Defleur, 1976), which in turn affects their political attitudes (Rittberger & Maier, 2008).

Outlining the pre-requisites of identity formation, Thompson (1995, p. 186) argued that "identity requires symbolic material for its maintenance, growth and transformation". In the processes of identity formation, the news media play a relevant role because of their ability to (re)produce symbolically certain perspectives on the world and our place in it (Olausson, 2010). They "have become organised mechanisms of great significance for constructing identities in local, national and transnational contexts within modernity" (Georgiou, 2006, p. 11). A second precondition for European identity to take root is its establishment as a conversational "habit", within general public discourses, and media play a crucial role in this regard (Gripsrud, 2007, p. 490) by continuously placing certain issue on its agenda.

To understand the role of the media for European integration and European identity much research is done on the characteristics of the European media system and on media coverage related to the EU. Results show the absence of an influential pan-European media outlet. This indicates that "the EU as a political structure lacks a corresponding communication system" (Kaitatzi-Whitlock, 2007, p. 687). Consequently, the representation of the EU in the media depends on national media outlets, which are not always Brussels' "best friends" (Gerhards, Odfferhaus, & Roose, 2009; Hillje, 2013). This deficiency significantly affects the provided image of the EU. Kaitatzi-Whitlock (2007) characterized the reportage of EU affairs in national media as scattered, offering only minimal visibility, and having national biases; moreover, the coverage usually has a focus on personalization and "ethno-controversial" issues.

Norris (2000) found that coverage of EU affairs in TV news between 1995 and 1997 was with mostly neutral or negative tone. Similarly, De Vreese (2004) reported findings that EU actors were often not evaluated in the news; but, when they were judged, the tone was negative. Findings from Peter, Semetko and De Vreese (2003) showed that most of the national TV coverage of the EU is neutral. Another analysis on media representation of EU in selected member states reported mixed media coverage (Alarcón, 2010). More positive accounts concerning the evaluation of the EU were obtained by some studies on the quality press (Koopmans & Statham, 2010; Trenz, 2007). Consequently, Schuck et al. (2011) summarized the state of research saying that all in all there is negative bias toward the EU albeit most of the news media coverage is neutral.

But, how this kind of coverage might influence the "we" feeling among Europeans, still remains somehow an open question. On the one hand, there is widespread confirmation of a "crucial role of media for collective identities" (Hillje, 2013, p. 7). On the other hand, it is unclear how this role looks like and what effects might appear. Because of this uncertainty one would expect intense research efforts to clarify the role of the media. But in fact media effects research on public opinion about the EU is still an "embryonic" field of study (De Vreese & Boomgaarden, 2006, p. 421). Similarly, Rittberger and Maier (2008) stated that the literature on public opinion and EU integration has thus far neglected the role of media effects on attitudes towards feeling European.

In the literature, the few exceptions that investigate the effects of media on European identity and integration primarily focus on agenda setting, priming, and framing effects (see Semetko, 2004) or conduct *elite communication discourse analysis* (see Suszycki, 2006; Wodak, 2004). Elite communication discourse analyses revealed that promoting and constructing a specific identity is a "top-down" affair (Shore, 2000). However, this paradigm has shifted, and scholars now assume that identity formation is not the exclusive task of elites because it also can be constructed from the "bottom up" (Bruter, 2005). Thus, analyses should not be limited to the discourse of the elites, but the broad public also should be considered. Therefore, other methods such as surveys should also be applied in order to study "bottom-up" European identity construction.

Although there is not much research on media effects, one important finding revealed the ability of negative news to have stronger influence on political support, and European integration and identity than positive news (De Vreese et al., 2011). The stronger influence of negative news does not mean that positive news has no effect, "but overall, negative arguments win the day" (De Vreese et al., 2011, p. 194). Based on the findings of a more negative tendency in the coverage and the stronger effects of negative coverage on people´s attitude, it seems plausible to expect that the exposure to media information about the EU would have a negative effect on European identity. In the following chapter we will unfold theoretical considerations that challenge this expectation.

3. Theoretical Reorientation: Mere-Exposure and Hostile Media Effects

The mere-exposure-theory suggests that people tend to develop positive attitudes towards objects merely because of the repeated exposure to these objects. No further elaboration by the individual is required (Zajonc, 2001, p. 225). The mere-exposure effect can occur without any cognitive processing, even if people are not aware that they are exposed to a specific stimulus. Therefore, recipients are not required to feel familiarity with the object (Zajonc, 2001, p. 225). The only condition is that the first experience with that object is not an explicitly negative one. These premises fit the situation of the consumption of news about European issues. Even though the general tendency of the coverage on the EU is negative, the overwhelming majority of media content is neutral. Following this argumentation, the mere-exposure-theory calls into question the prospect of negative effects.

Research on the attitudes towards foreign countries has shown that the mere-exposure effect can be triggered by media use (Perry, 1990). Some evidence also supports the applicability of the idea to European identity. Studies that measured the frequency of appearance of EU topics in various national media demonstrated that the more frequently EU topics appeared the better was the breeding-ground for a sense of community and the development of "Europeanized national public spheres" (e.g., D'Haenens, 2005; De Vreese, 2007). Continuous exposure to news coverage about the EU makes people feel familiar with the EU. According to the mere-exposure effect, this perception of familiarity will lead to a stronger identification with the EU. Furthermore, this effect might be strengthened by the tendency of selected exposure (Slater, 2007).

It is evident that the assumption of a linear relationship oversimplifies the connection between media and identity because it ignores the role of the recipients´ perceptions and interpretations of the media content. Studies dealing with the perceptions of news slant or bias showed that recipients, especially partisans, critically assess the news with regard to the issue of interest and claim frequently that the news media are hostile towards their own party. Therefore, a close examination of the mechanism of the perception of media biases is necessary.

The observation that partisans frequently perceive the media coverage on relevant issues as biased against their own position is called the *hostile media phenomenon*. In a seminal experimental study, Vallone, Ross and Lepper (1985) showed that the media coverage of the Beirut massacre in Lebanon was perceived as biased by both, the pro-Israeli group and the pro-Arab group. Moreover, experimental and survey studies have continuously replicated previous findings on hostile media perceptions. Hence, it can be taken for granted that there is a "tendency for individuals with a strong existing attitude on an issue to perceive that ostensibly neutral, even-handed media coverage of the topic is biased against their side and in favor of the antagonist's view" (Perloff, 2015, p. 707). Recently, a meta-analysis of 34 hostile media studies concluded that stronger partisanship leads to higher perceptions of media bias, but even at moderate partisanship levels (low involvement), hostile media perceptions are detectable (Hansen & Kim, 2011).

Studies that investigated the hostile media phenomenon predominantly dealt with the identification of the mechanisms that cause the perception of bias (Giner-Sorolla & Chaiken, 1994; Gunther & Liebhart, 2006; Vallone et al., 1985). Only a few studies have dealt with the potential effects of hostile media perceptions, such as of the support of democracy (Tsfati & Cohen, 2005), the estimation of the opinion climate (Gunther, Christen, Liebhart, & Chih-Yun Chia, 2001), and the willingness to engage in discussions (Hart, Feldman, Leiserowitz, & Maibach, 2015; Hwang, Pan, & Sun, 2008). But none of the studies directly related to hostile media perceptions link effects of media on (political) identity, therefore, the insights contributed by this research provide some inspiring ideas for the research on the effects of media on European identity.

It could be argued that European citizens generally evaluate the performance of the EU with regard to the functioning of its institutions and the outcome of its policies. Consequently, they develop attitudes towards the EU polity. Obviously the concept of "attitudes" is not identical with concept of "partisanship", however they are related. From the body of hostile media research we can conclude that it is likely, that citizens who perceive the overall performance of the EU as (very) good would claim that the representation of the EU by news media is too negative. Furthermore, citizens who perceive the overall performance of the EU as quite negative would blame the news media for portraying the EU in an overly positive light. However, because the evaluation of an object is not the same as partisanship, it is also possible that citizens with a negative attitude towards the performance of the EU could perceive that the media draws an overly negative picture of the EU. Correspondingly, people with a positive image of EU institutions and policies might observe that news media providing an overly positive representation of the EU.

Based on these theoretical elaborations we assume that the evaluation of the performance of the object (EU) in connection with the evaluation of the representation of the object (EU) in the media would probably moderate the strength of the mere-exposure effect. Even if according to the mere-exposure-theory, no further elaboration of the individual is necessary, recipients will always make judgments about the sources of information (e.g. if they perceive the media to be hostile towards an object). We assume that these judgments modify the mere-exposure effect.

4. Research Questions and Hypotheses

Following the foregoing theoretical elaboration, two research questions are posed:

(1) Does the intensity of the exposure to news about the EU have an effect on the development of a European identity?
(2) Is this effect modified by the perception of media hostility?

The *mere-exposure-theory* postulates that the amount of exposure to information about the object (EU) leads to an individual's familiarization with it and hence, supports the creation of identity:

H1: The higher the exposure to news about the EU, the stronger the European identity.

Based on the theoretical assumptions and findings from hostile media research, it might be possible that hostile media perceptions modify the strength of the mere exposure effect on European identity (see Figure 1). Although the mere-exposure effect works subconsciously, it is plausible that the conscious evaluation of the representation of the stimulus could reinforce or attenuate the mere-exposure effect. If persons perceive the media as hostile, it is probable that the mere-exposure effect is weakened thus we hypothesize:

H2: The mere-exposure effect is weaker in persons who perceive the media as hostile, than in persons who perceive the media as not hostile.

Furthermore, we argue that within the group of persons who perceive the media as not hostile, some might be particularly susceptible to the mere-exposure effect. We assume that among those who are not partisans and perceive the media coverage as neutral, the mere-exposure effect is even more present than among all the others without hostile media perceptions:

H3: The mere-exposure effect is strongest in non-partisan persons who perceive the media as objective.

Taken together we assume that the weakest mere-exposure effect appears in persons with hostile media perceptions, while the strongest effect appears in non-partisans who perceive the media as objective. The strength of the mere-exposure effect for the others is in between.

Furthermore, we assume that other factors also influence European identity. First of all, we assume that the evaluation of the performance of the EU has a strong direct effect on identity; those who evaluate the performance of the EU more positively will identify themselves more with Europe as others. Besides that, we will control for several socio-demographic variables like age, education or social status, which might influence identity as well. The complete model is depicted in Figure 1.

5. Method

To test the four hypotheses, a secondary data analysis was conducted on surveys in the Eurobarometer 80.1 series that were carried out in November 2013. The data collection was executed by TNS OPINION (Brussels) as re-

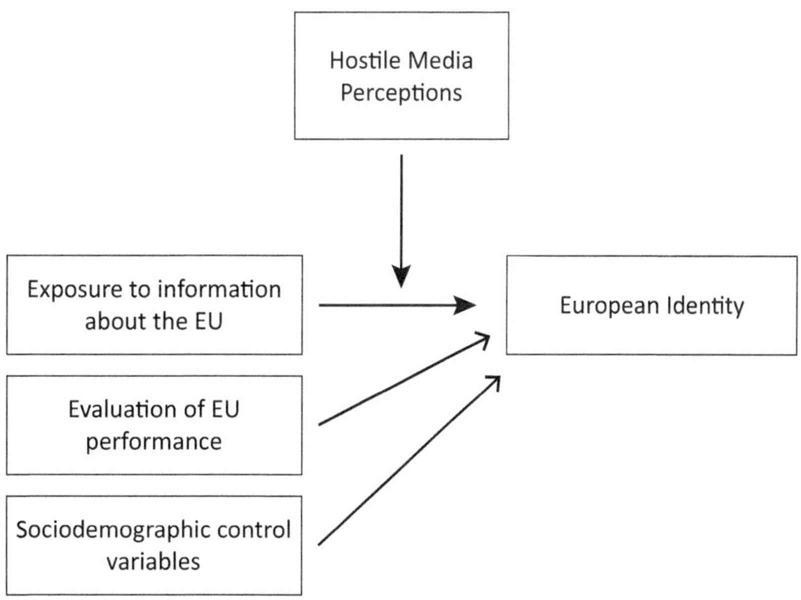

Figure 1. The variable model.

quested by the European Commission. It consists of survey data collected from the 28 member states of the EU. Overall, data gathered from 27,829 persons were analyzed. The data were weighted before the analysis. The weighting factors adjusted the national samples for sex, age, and region according to the share in the total population aged 15 years and older in the EU.

The dependent variable (identity) was operationalized by two indicators: Citizens were asked to answer the following question: "Please tell me how attached you feel to the European Union" by using a scale from 1 (not attached at all) to 4 (very attached). Furthermore, the item "You feel you are a citizen of the EU" was used in index-building. The participants were asked to indicate the extent to which this item corresponded to their own opinion. Possible answers were 1 (no, definitely not), 2 (no, not really), 3 (yes, to some extent), and 4 (yes, definitely). The two items were highly correlated (r = .67), and the scale reliability was good (Alpha = .80). Thus, they were deemed suitable for index-building. Based on this index, the mean level of European identity was about 2.6, which was almost exactly in the middle of the scale (1–4). However, there were some differences in the level of European identity between the countries. The average identity in most countries was somewhere between 2.3 and 2.7. The negative outliers were Greece (2.1), Great Britain (2.2) and Cyprus (2.2) while the positive exceptions were Luxembourg (3.0), Germany (2.8) and Belgium (2.8).

The independent variable was operationalized by a combination of several items: The participants were first asked the following question: "Could you tell me to what extent you...a) watch television on a TV set or via the Internet, b) listen to the radio, c) read the written press d) use the Internet?" Possible answers were: 5 (every day/almost every day), 4 (two or three times a week), 3 (about once a week), 2 (two or three times a month), 1 (less often), 0 (never/no access to this medium). Later they were questioned: "Where do you get most of your news on European political matters? Firstly? And then?" Possible answers were respectively: Television, the Press, Radio, and the Internet. Out of these two measurements a new variable for every medium was calculated indicating if the respective medium was the first source for EU news (2), a less relevant one (1), or if the medium was not a source for EU news at all (0). Afterwards each of the four variables was multiplied with the respective media-use variable. By doing so, four variables (on a scale from 0 to 10) were obtained, each indicating the amount of EU specific input from the respective media (TV, Newspaper, Radio, Internet). Finally, an index out of these four variables was calculated indicating the overall exposure to EU-news.

To operationalize the hostile media perceptions as the intervening variable, two measurements were required. First, the perceived bias in the coverage was registered, and the evaluation of the performance of EU was traced to identify the individual standpoints of the respondents.

The perceived bias was operationalized by three items. The respondents were asked, "Do you think that the [national] television present(s) the EU too positively, objectively, or too negatively?" The same question was repeated regarding the radio and the press. The answers were coded for each variable as 1 (too negatively), 2 (objectively), and 3 (too positively). The three variables were highly correlated (between r = .68 and r = .75), and the scale reliability was also good (Alpha = .88); thus, the items could be used in index building. Therefore, the three variables were summed and afterwards recoded into three groups. The values 3, 4, and 5 were recoded into 1 (too negatively), value 6 was recoded into 2 (objectively), and the values 7, 8, and 9 were recoded into 3 (too positively).

In the operationalization of the individual's evaluation of the performance of EU, two items were applied for index building. The first item operationalized satisfaction "with the way democracy works in in the EU". The responses were measured on a 4-point scale: 1 (not at all satisfied), 2 (not very satisfied), 4 (fairly satisfied), and 5 (very satisfied). The second item referred to the expected future development of the EU: "At the present time, would you say that, in general, things are going in the right direction or in the wrong direction in EU?" The variable consisted of three values: 1 (things are going in the wrong direction), 3 (neither the one nor the other), and 5 (things are going in the right direction). Because the two variables were positively correlated (r = .42), they were combined in an index. On the one hand this variable was introduced in the model as indicator for the "Evaluation of EU Performance" and on the other hand it was used to operationalize hostile media perceptions. Therefore, the index was recoded into three groups: 1 (negative evaluation of the EU; 1.0–2.4), 2 (neutral evaluation of the EU; 2.5–3.5), and 3 (positive evaluation of the EU; 3.6–5.0).

To identify persons with hostile media perceptions, the individual standpoint concerning the evaluation of the performance of the EU must be combined with the perceived media bias. Figure 2 shows several possible combinations of individual standpoints and media-bias perceptions. In the upper part of the figure, the combinations, which indicate a hostile media perception, are illustrated. The two other examples are of biased media perceptions, but they do not indicate the hostile media phenomenon. The evaluation of a hostile media perception requires that the person has a clear standpoint on the issue (i.e., is a partisan) and perceives the media as biased in a direction against his or her own opinion. Both requirements were met in the upper example but not in the other two examples.

Table 1 shows the combinations of the values of the two variables that indicate the different types of hostile and non-hostile media perceptions. The respective numbers of cases of the groups are shown in brackets. As Table 1 shows, the group of persons who have hostile media perceptions consists of roughly 3,900 persons (group 1). The group with a neutral standpoint and an ob-

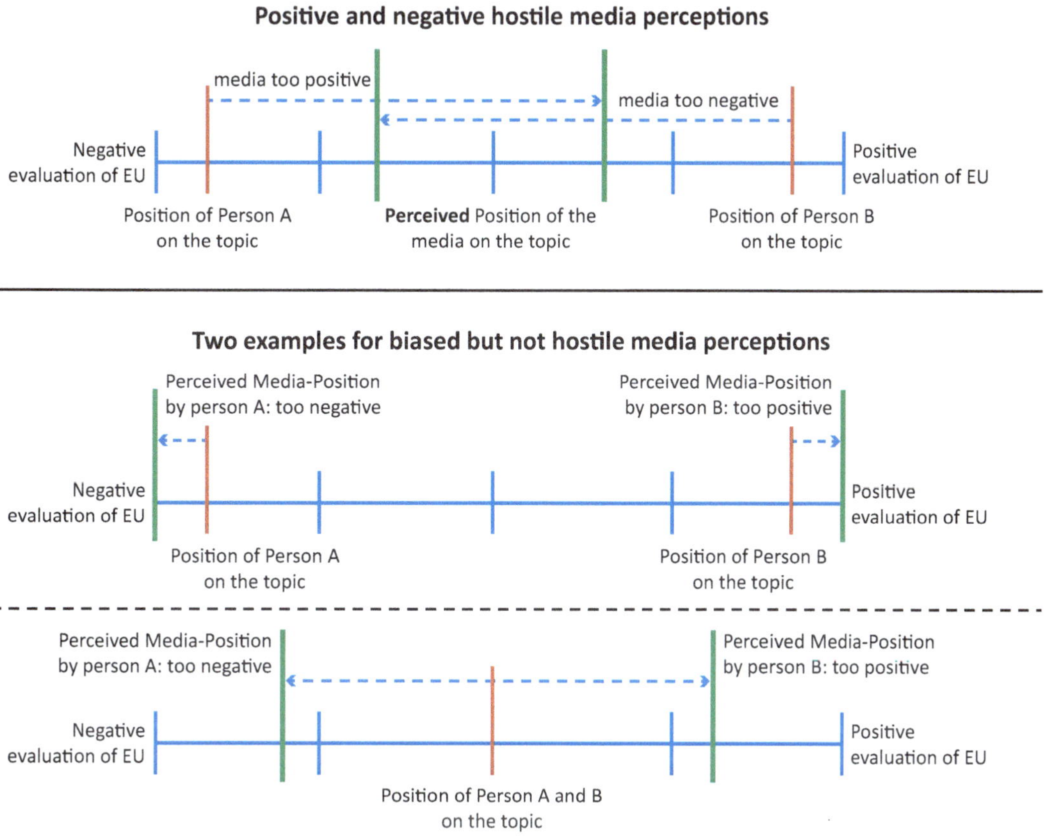

Figure 2. Hostile media perceptions vs. biased media perceptions.

Table 1. Hostile media perception (typology and number of cases).

		Evaluation of EU		
		negative	neutral	positive
Evaluation of the way the national media present the EU	too negatively	2 (n = 2,156)	2 (n = 1,928)	1 (n = 1,099)
	objectively	2 (n = 3,990)	3 (n = 5,163)	2 (n = 3,997)
	too positively	1 (n = 2,810)	2 (n = 1,725)	2 (n = 924)

Note: 1 = hostility perception, 2 = no hostility perception, 3 = objective media perception by non-partisans (neutrality perception).

jective perception (group 3) is somewhat larger (approx. 5,200). Because this group contrasts the groups with hostile media perceptions, their perspective is designated as a neutrality perception.

6. Findings

Regression analyses were conducted to test the three hypotheses. In each analysis European Identity (mean = 2.6; on a scale from 1 = low to 4 = high; SD = 0.8) was the dependent variable and the media use index (mean = 3.4; on a scale from 0 = no to 10 = high; SD = 1.3) was the independent variable. Besides media use the evaluation of the performance of the EU (mean = 2.9 on a scale from 1 = negative to 5 = positive; SD = 1.3), age (mean = 48.9 years; SD = 17.8), sex (female = 52%), education (mean = 19.3 age, when formal education was finished on a scale from 10 to 40; SD = 4.5), and social level (mean = 5.5 on a scale from 1 = lowest, to 10 = highest; SD =1.6) were introduced as control variables in the model.

In all models, the five control variables: EU-performance, societal level, education, age and sex were controlled, but the effects are not displayed in Table 3.

H1 refers to the general mere-exposure effect: The higher the exposure to news about the EU, the stronger the European identity. The hypothesis was confirmed by the results of the regression analysis (see Table 2). Despite rigorous control of further factors, a small but highly significant positive effect (beta = .12) was observed, indicating that people who have a higher exposure to EU related news have also a stronger EU iden-

Table 2. Regression analysis: Hypothesis testing.

Hypothesis	H1	H2		H3
Sample	Whole Sample	Persons who perceive media as hostile	Persons who perceive media *not* as hostile	*Non Partisans* who perceive media *not* as hostile
n =	20,456	3,384	17,072	4,472
R^2 =	.20	.28	.16	.05
		beta coefficients		
Exposure to EU-News	.12 ***	.09 ***	.14 ***	.15 ***
EU- performance	.37 ***	.44 ***	.32 ***	.08 ***
Social level	.08 ***	.09 ***	.07 ***	.03 (n.s.)
Education	.08 ***	.10 ***	.09 ***	.11 ***
Age	−.01 (n.s.)	−.04 **	−.01 (n.s.)	.01 (n.s.)
Sex	−.02 **	.02 (n.s.)	−.03 ***	−.05 **

Note: *** = $p < .001$; ** = $p < .01$; * = $p < .05$

tity. This positive relationship between media use and identity was observed in all European countries, and in 26 of 28 countries the effect was significant (only in the Netherlands and Hungary it was not). Among the other countries the strength of the effect varied: In Ireland and Estonia, the effects were the lowest (beta = .07/.08) while in Germany and Malta the effects were the highest (beta = .18/.18).

H2 introduces the perceived hostility as an intervening variable: The mere-exposure effect is weaker in persons who perceive the media as hostile, than in persons who perceive the media as not hostile. To test this hypothesis, the sample was divided into two parts, and the same regression was conducted in both subsamples. The first subsample consisted of those who perceived the media as hostile (group 1 in Table 1); the other groups (2 and 3) constituted the comparison sample. H2 was also supported by the results (see Table 2). The beta coefficient in the group of those who perceived the media as hostile was smaller (beta = .09) than in the comparison group (beta = .14).

H3 considers differential effects within the group of people without hostile media perception, positing that the mere-exposure effect is stronger in non-partisans who perceive the media as objective as in non-partisans who perceive the media as biased. To test H3, the sample of people without hostile media perception was divided into two parts and the regression analysis was conducted just for group 3 (see table 1 the group in the center). H3 was also supported by the results. The results show that the mere-exposure effect on non-partisans who perceived the media as objective (neutrality media perception) was (at least slightly) stronger than on all other groups (beta = .15).

To verify whether these results could be replicated in all parts of Europe, the sample was divided into three parts: seven countries with citizens having a low European identity were merged in the first group (n = 8,094); 14 countries with a medium level of European identity were pooled in the second group (n = 6,994); the remaining seven countries, with citizens having the highest European identity, were combined in the third group (n = 8,704). The regression analyses (including the five control variables) were repeated in these three country groups. The findings show that the general structure of the results remained the same. Table 3 depicts the relevant effects of the exposure to EU news (beta coefficients). In each subsample the effects were lowest in the hostile subgroup, while the non-partisan group, whose members perceive the media as objective, showed the strongest effect. This finding was consistent in all subsamples. On the other hand, the effect-strengths var-

Table 3. Mere-exposure effects modified by hostile media perceptions. Replications in different national subsamples.

	Countries with low European identity	Countries with medium European identity	Countries with high European identity
n =	1,388/4,329/1,097	1,004/3,798/1,323	990/4,470/2,050
		beta coefficients	
Hostility	.04 (n.s.)	.08 **	.12 ***
Non-Hostility	.08 ***	.12 ***	.15 ***
Neutrality Perception	.09 **	.13 ***	.16 ***

Note: *** = $p < .001$; ** = $p < .01$; * = $p < .05$

ied noticeably between the three country groups. The mere-exposure effect is much lower in countries where the citizens showed lower European identity while it is much more noticeable in countries with high European identity.

7. Discussion

Based on the results of several content analyses (De Vreese et al., 2011; Peter et al., 2003) of media coverage about the EU, one might expect that higher exposure to media content about EU affairs might lead to a lower European identity. However, the results obtained in this study consistently showed the opposite. In almost all subsamples, we found (at least slight) significant positive effects. These findings support our theoretical assumption, that frequent contact with predominantly neutral information provokes mere-exposure effects, which promote the feeling of European identity. Even the unintended, casual contact with news on the EU provided by the media fostered European identity. These findings illustrate the importance of a continuous coverage on EU topics by the mass media for the development of a common European identity.

The results obtained also support our theoretical assumptions based on the hostile media theory, confirming both hypotheses. Nevertheless, it must be considered that the differences in effect-strength were just moderate. Particularly in countries in which the citizens had a higher European identity, the discrepancies were slight. If the citizens of a certain country predominantly felt attached to Europe (at least somewhat), the mere-exposure effect was always relatively high, regardless of whether they perceived the media as hostile or not. This result was not obtained in countries where the majority of the citizens felt a low attachment to Europe. In these societies, the mere-exposure effect was just existent in people *without* hostile media perceptions. The effect disappeared in citizens who perceived the media as hostile. This finding points to the important role of media perception in media effects on European identity. Therefore, if European institutions aim to foster a common identity in countries with low levels of European identity, it is not enough that the citizens feel motivated to use the news about European issues provided by the media. It is even more important that media are perceived as neutral.

Finally, the results of the study also offer some room to speculate about the effects of media coverage on European identity, particularly in times of crisis. In the light of the results it can be reasoned that it is not necessary that a disintegrating event such as the Brexit or the Eurozone financial crisis immediately garner negative feelings about EU despite the excessive on-going negative media coverage. The reason for such an attribute is that identities are not constructed in a short period of time, rather it is a long term process (Cinpoes, 2008). Thus, a crisis that either remains in the media or lasts for short time may not affect people's feelings of attachment with the respective political system. Much more important seems to be how the media coverage is evaluated by the people in the respective countries. If people lose faith in the neutrality of media this could also affect the identification with the political collective. Thus, recent attacks from populists on the media´s independency in many European countries might be an even more serious threat to European democracy than any critical comment of journalists about the performance of the EU.

7.1. Limitations and Suggestions for Future Research

In the present study, a secondary data analysis was applied, which has its own typical problems. The most significant limitation was that the analyses were confined within the boundaries of variables that could be deemed too imperfect to measure identity. Additionally, the available indicators of media use combined with the perceived relevance of these sources for news on the EU might be considered of questionable appropriateness in measuring the amount of contact with European issues. It might be argued that the respondents were not aware from which media they obtained news about EU affairs. Thus, the indicator did not measure an EU specific media use but instead indicated the general use of news on public affairs. If the available indicators did not measure EU-specific media use but political media use in general, it is arguable that the observed variable relationships could be interpreted as mere-exposure effects. Thus, to address this potential limitation, the dependent variable (EU identity) was replaced by indicators of national and local identity. The findings showed that in both cases, the effects almost disappeared. The beta-coefficients of the media use variable on national identity and local identity were quite small (beta = .04) respectively. Thus, it is reasonable to state that we observed a mere-exposure effect.

To operationalize media hostility, this study dealt with the evaluation of the performance of the EU. However, the evaluation of the EU is not necessarily the best indicator of partisanship. Better indicators of partisanship towards the EU would be highly desirable, such as political party (pro-Europe or Euroskeptic) affiliations of respondents, but they were not available in the Eurobarometer data. Furthermore, the hostility of the media towards the EU was measured by using only one indicator (the overall estimation of bias). In general, the hostile media research applies a fine-grained measurement of media hostility, including, for example, the individual estimation of the percentage of favorable or non-favorable references to one's position or the perception of the personal views of the journalists.

Despite this critique, the presented results show the relevance of media coverage on European issues for European identity even for those who are not intentionally searching for information and news on the EU. But the results also highlight which problems the EU will face if peopleś reliance on a neutral coverage of the media erodes or even disappears.

Acknowledgments

We acknowledge support for the Article Processing Charge by the German Research Foundation and the Open Access Publication Fund of the Technische Universität Ilmenau.

Conflict of Interests

The authors declare no conflict of interests.

References

Agirdag, O., Phalet, K., & Van Houtte, M. (2016). European identity as a unifying category: National vs. European identification among native and immigrant pupils. *European Union Politics*, *17*(2), 285–302.

Alarcón, A. (2010). Media representation of the European Union: Comparing newspaper coverage in France, Spain and the United Kingdom. *International Journal of Communication*, *4*, 398–415.

Anderson, B. (1991). *Imagined communities: Reflections on the origin and spread of Nationalism*. London: Verso.

Ball-Rokeach, S., & Defleur, M. L. (1976). A dependency model of mass-media effects. *Communication Research*, *3*(1), 3–21.

Brubaker, R., & Cooper, F. (2000). Beyond "identity". *Theory and Society*, *29*, 1–47.

Bruter, M. (2003). On what citizens mean by feeling 'European' : Perceptions of news, symbols and borderlessness. *Journal of Ethnic and Migration Studies*, *30*(1), 21–39.

Bruter, M. (2005). *Citizens of Europe? The emergence of a mass European identity*. New York, NY: Palgrave Macmillan.

Carey, S. (2002). Undivided loyalties. Is national identity an obstacle to European integration? *European Union Politics*, *3*(4), 387–413.

Cinpoes, R. (2008). Thematic articles—National and European identity. *Journal of Identity and Migration Studies*, *2*(1), 1–14.

Corbett, S. (2016). The social consequences of Brexit for the UK and Europe: Euroscepticism, populism, nationalism, and societal division. *International Journal of Social Quality*, *6*(1), 11–31.

D'Haenens, L. (2005). Euro-vision: The portrayal of Europe in the quality press. *Gazette*, *67*(5), 419–440.

De Vreese, C. (2004). Primed by the Euro: The impact of a referendum campaign on public opinion and evaluations of government and political leaders. *Scandinavian Political Studies*, *27*(1), 45–64.

De Vreese, C. (2007). *The EU as a public sphere*. Retrieved from http://www.europeangovernance-livingreviews.org/Articles/lreg-2007-3/download/lreg-2007-3BW.pdf

De Vreese, C. H., & Boomgaarden, H. G. (2006). Media effects on public opinion about the enlargement of the European Union. *Journal of Common Market Studies*, *44*, 419–436.

De Vreese, C., Boomgaarden, H. G., & Semetko, H. A. (2011). (In)direct framing effects: The effects of news media framing on public support for Turkish membership in the European Union. *Communication Research*, *38*(2), 179–205.

Delanty, G. (2014, February 28). *European election specials*. Retrieved from http://en.theeuropean.eu/gerard-delanty/8002-the-europeanization-of-national-identity

Delanty, G., & Rumford, C. (2005). *Rethinking Europe: Social theory and the implications of Europeanization*. London: Routledge.

Easton, D. (1965). *A framework for political analysis*. Englewood Cliffs, NJ: Prentice-Hall.

European Commission. (1973). *Declaration on European identity*. Brussels: European Commission.

Favell, A., & Recchi, E. (2009). *Pioneers of European integration*. Northampton: Edward Elgar.

Fligstein, N., Polyakova, A., & Sandholtz, W. (2012). European integration, nationalism and European identity. *JCMS: Journal of Common Market Studies*, *50*(1), 106–122.

Gandemer, W. (2014). *Prospects for European identity: A case study of third culture kids in Strasbourg*. Groningen: University of Groningen.

Gellner, E. (1983). *Nations and nationalism*. Oxford: Blackwell.

Georgiou, M. (2006). *Diaspora, identity and the media: Diasporic transnationalism and mediated spacialities*. New York, NY: Hampton Press.

Gerhards, J., Odfferhaus, A., & Roose, J. (2009). Wer ist verantwortlich? Die Europäische Union, ihre Nationalstaaten und die massenmediale Attribution von Verantwortung für Erfolge und Misserfolge. In F. Marcinkowski & B. Pfetsch (Eds.), *Politik in der Mediendemokratie: Politische Vierteljahresschrift Sonderheft* (pp. 529–558). Wiesbaden: Verlag fuer Sozialwissenschaften.

Giner-Sorolla, R., & Chaiken, S. (1994). The causes of hostile media judgements. *Journal of Experimental Social Psychology*, *30*, 165–180.

Gripsrud, J. (2007). Television and the European public sphere. *European Journal of Communication*, *22*(4), 479–92.

Gunther, A. C., & Liebhart, J. L. (2006). Broad reach or biased source? Decomposing the hostile media effect. *Journal of Communication*, *56*(3), 449–466.

Gunther, A. C., Christen, C. T., Liebhart, J. L., & Chih-Yun Chia, S. (2001). Congenial public, contrary press, and biased estimates of climiate of opinion. *Public Opinion Quarterly*, *65*(3), 295–320.

Habermas, J., & Derrida, J. (2005). February 15, or what binds Europeans together: A plea for a common foreign policy, beginning in the core of Europe. *Constellations*, *10*(3), 291–297.

Hansen, G. J., & Kim, H. (2011). Is the media biased

against me? A meta-analysis of the hostile media effect research. *Communication Research Report, 28*(2), 169–179.

Harmsen, R., & Wilson, T. (2000). *Europeanization: Institution, identities and citizenship*. Amsterdam: Editions Rodopi.

Hart, P. S., Feldman, L., Leiserowitz, A., & Maibach, E. (2015). Extending the impacts of hostile media perceptions: Influences on discussion and opinion polarization in the context of climate change. *Science Communication, 37*(4), 506–532.

Hillje, J. (2013). *Saving Europe online? European identity and the European Union's Facebook communication during the eurozone crisis*. London: Media @ LSE.

Hooghe, L., & Marks, G. (2005). Calculation, community and cues: Public opinion on European integration. *European Union Politics, 6*(4), 419–443.

Hwang, H., Pan, Z., & Sun, Y. (2008). Influence of hostile media perception on willingness to engage in discursive activities: An examination of mediating role of media indignation. *Media Psychology, 11*(1), 76–97.

Irimie, R. (2014). *European identity vs national identity? The crisis of identification in the European Union*. Târgu Mureș: University of Târgu Mureș.

John, M. (1861). Considerations on representative government. In G. William (Ed.), *Utilitarism, on liberty, considerations on representative government* (pp. 188–410). London: J. M. Dent.

Kaina, V., & Karolewski, I. P. (2013). EU governance and European identity. *Living Reviews in European Governance, 8*(1), 1–59.

Kaitatzi-Whitlock, S. (2007). The missing European public sphere and the absence of imagined European citizenship. *European Societies, 9*(5), 685–704.

Koopmans, R., & Statham, P. (2010). *The making of a European public sphere: Media discourse and political contention*. New York, NY: Cambridge University Press.

Maier, M., & Risse, T. (2003). *Europeanization, collective identitis and public discourses*. Retrieved from http://cordis.europa.eu/documents/documentlibrary/82608121EN6.pdf

Manners, I. (2002). Normative power Europe: A contradiction in terms. *Journal of Common Market Studies, 40*(2), 235–258.

Norris, P. (2000). *A virtuous circle? The impact of political communications in post-industrial democracies*. Cambridge: Cambridge University Press.

Olausson, U. (2010, June 14). Towards a European identity? The news media and the case of climate change. *European Journal of Communication, 25*(2), 138–152.

Perloff, R. M. (2015). A three-decade retrospective on the hostile media effect. *Mass Communication and Society, 18*, 701–729.

Perry, D. K. (1990). News reading, knowledge about, and attitudes toward foreign countries. *Journalism Quarterly, 67*, 353–358.

Peter, J., Semetko, H., & de Vreese, C. (2003). EU Politics on television news. *European Union of Politics, 4*(3), 305–327.

Reuters Institute for the Study of Journalism. (2016, May 20). *Study shows that majority of press coverage in EU referendum campaign was heavily skewed in favour of Brexit in first two months of campaign*. Retrieved from http://reutersinstitute.politics.ox.ac.uk/news/study-shows-majority-press-coverage-eu-referendum-campaign-was-heavily-skewed-favour-brexit

Risse, T. (2003). The Euro between national and European identity. *Journal of European Public Policy, 4*, 487–505.

Risse, T. (2010). *A community of Europeans? Transnational identities and public spheres*. Ithaca, NY: Cornell University.

Rittberger, B., & Maier, J. (2008). Shifting Europe's boundaries: Mass media, public opinion and the enlargement of the EU. *European Union Politics, 9*(2), 243–267.

Ruiz, J., Antonia, M., Górniak, J., Kosic, A., Kiss, P., & Kandulla, M. (2004, July 29). *European and national identities in EU's old and new member states: Ethnic, civic, instrumental and symbolic components*. Retrieved from http://eiop.or.at/eiop/pdf/2004-011.pdf

Schneeberger, A. (2009, July). Constructing European identity through mediated difference: A content analysis of Turkey's EU accession process in the British press. *PLATFORM: Journal of Media and Communication, 1*, 83–102.

Schuck, A. R., Azrout, R., Boomgaarden, H., Elenbaas, M., van Spanje, J., Vliegenthart, R., & de Vreese, C. (2011). Media visibility and framing of the European Parliamentary elections 2009: A media content analysis in 27 countries. In M. Maier, J. Strömbäck, & L. L. Kaid (Eds.), *Political communication in European parliamentary elections* (pp. 175–198). Oxford: Routledge.

Semetko, H. A. (2004). Media, public opinion and political action. In J. Downing, D. McQuail, P. Schlesinger, & E. A. Wartella (Eds.), *The SAGE handbook of media studies* (pp. 351–374). Thousand Oaks, CA: SAGE.

Shore, C. (2000). *Building Europe. The cultural politics of European integration*. London: Routledge.

Slater, M. D. (2007). Reinforcing spirals: The mutual influence of media selectivity and media effects and their impact on individual behavior and social identity. *Communication Theory, 17*(3), 281–303.

Smith, A. (1992). *National identity and the idea of European identity*. Oxford: Blackwell.

Staehelin, K. P. (2016). *Drivers of change? Media effects on the identity and utilitarian EU attitude dimensions*. Amsterdam: University of Amsterdam.

Stone Sweet, A., Sandholtz, W., & Fligstein, N. (2001). *The institutionalization of Europe*. Oxford: Oxford University Press.

Stråth, B. (2002). A European identity: To the historical limits of a concept. *European Journal of Social Theory, 5*(4), 387–401.

Suszycki, A. M. (2006). European identity in Sweden. In I. P. Karolewski & V. Kaina (Eds.), *European identity: Theoretical perspectives and empirical insights* (pp. 179–208). Berlin: LIT Verlag.

Szczerbiak, A., & Taggart, P. (2008). *Opposing Europe?*. Oxford: Oxford University Press.

Thompson, J. (1995). *The media and modernity: A social theory of the media*. Cambridge: Polity Press.

Trenz, J. H. (2007). 'Quo vadis Europe?' Quality newspapers struggling for European unity. In J. Fossum & P. Schlesinger (Eds.), *The European Union and the public sphere* (pp. 89–109). London: Routledge.

Triga, V., & Vadratsikas, K. (2016). *The impact of media representations of the EU and its policies on European identity*. Limassol: COHESIFY Project.

Tsfati, Y., & Cohen, J. (2005). Democratic consequences of hostile media perceptions: The case of Gaza settlers. *The Harvard International Journal of Press/Politics*, *10*(4), 28–51.

Vallone, R. P., Ross, L., & Lepper, M. R. (1985). The hostile media phenomenon: Biased perception and perceptions of media bias in coverage of Beirut massacre. *Journal of Personality and Social Psychology*, *49*(3), 577–85.

Walkenhorst, H. (2008). *Constructing the European identity—Trap or gap? European integration between community-building and path-dependency*. Retrieved from http://www.ul.ie/ppa/content/files/Walkenhorst_constructing.pdf

Walkenhorst, H. (2009). *The conceptual spectrum of European identity: From missing link to unnecessary evil*. Limerick: University of Limerick.

Wendt, A. (1999). *Social theory of international politics*. Cambridge: Cambridge University Press.

Wodak, R. (2004). National transnational identities: European and other identities constructed in interviews with EU officials. In R. K. Herrmann, T. Risse, & M. B. Brewer (Eds.), *Transnational identities: Becoming European in the EU* (pp. 97–128). Lanham: Rowman & Littlefield.

Zajonc, R. B. (2001). Mere exposure: A gateaway to the subliminal. *Current Directions in Psychological Science*, *10*(6), 224–228.

Permissions

All chapters in this book were first published in Media and communication, by Cogitatio Press; hereby published with permission under the Creative Commons Attribution License or equivalent. Every chapter published in this book has been scrutinized by our experts. Their significance has been extensively debated. The topics covered herein carry significant findings which will fuel the growth of the discipline. They may even be implemented as practical applications or may be referred to as a beginning point for another development.

The contributors of this book come from diverse backgrounds, making this book a truly international effort. This book will bring forth new frontiers with its revolutionizing research information and detailed analysis of the nascent developments around the world.

We would like to thank all the contributing authors for lending their expertise to make the book truly unique. They have played a crucial role in the development of this book. Without their invaluable contributions this book wouldn't have been possible. They have made vital efforts to compile up to date information on the varied aspects of this subject to make this book a valuable addition to the collection of many professionals and students.

This book was conceptualized with the vision of imparting up-to-date information and advanced data in this field. To ensure the same, a matchless editorial board was set up. Every individual on the board went through rigorous rounds of assessment to prove their worth. After which they invested a large part of their time researching and compiling the most relevant data for our readers.

The editorial board has been involved in producing this book since its inception. They have spent rigorous hours researching and exploring the diverse topics which have resulted in the successful publishing of this book. They have passed on their knowledge of decades through this book. To expedite this challenging task, the publisher supported the team at every step. A small team of assistant editors was also appointed to further simplify the editing procedure and attain best results for the readers.

Apart from the editorial board, the designing team has also invested a significant amount of their time in understanding the subject and creating the most relevant covers. They scrutinized every image to scout for the most suitable representation of the subject and create an appropriate cover for the book.

The publishing team has been an ardent support to the editorial, designing and production team. Their endless efforts to recruit the best for this project, has resulted in the accomplishment of this book. They are a veteran in the field of academics and their pool of knowledge is as vast as their experience in printing. Their expertise and guidance has proved useful at every step. Their uncompromising quality standards have made this book an exceptional effort. Their encouragement from time to time has been an inspiration for everyone.

The publisher and the editorial board hope that this book will prove to be a valuable piece of knowledge for researchers, students, practitioners and scholars across the globe.

List of Contributors

Juha Herkman
Department of Social Research, University of Helsinki, 00014 Helsinki, Finland

Matthias Schulze
International Relations Department, Friedrich-Schiller University Jena, 07743 Jena, Germany

Benedetta Brevini
Department of Media and Communication, The University of Sydney, Sydney, NSW 2006, Australia

Mikko Villi
Department of Communication, University of Jyväskylä, 40014 Jyväskylä, Finland

Janne Matikainen
Department of Social Research, University of Helsinki, 00014 Helsinki, Finland

Julia Velkova
Department of Media and Communication Studies, Södertörn University, 14189 Huddinge, Sweden

Kerry McCallum
News and Media Research Centre, Faculty of Arts and Design, University of Canberra, Bruce, ACT 2600, Australia

Lisa Waller
Faculty of Arts and Education, Deakin University, Burwood, VIC 3125, Australia

Tanja Dreher
School of Arts, English and Media, Wollongong University, Wollongong, NSW 2522, Australia

Mostafa Shehata
Department of Communication and Arts, Roskilde University, 4000 Roskilde, Denmark

Helena Kantanen
Business School, University of Eastern Finland, 70211 Kuopio, Finland

Jyri Manninen
School of Educational Sciences and Psychology, University of Eastern Finland, 80101 Joensuu, Finland

Anastasia Kavada
Westminster School of Media, Arts and Design, University of Westminster, Middlesex, HA1 3TP, UK

Nathalie Maréchal
Annenberg School for Communication and Journalism, University of Southern California, Los Angeles, CA 90007, USA

Johanna Sumiala, Minttu Tikka and Katja Valaskivi
School of Communication, Media and Theatre, University of Tampere, 33014 Tampere, Finland

Jukka Huhtamäki
Intelligent Information Systems Laboratory, Tampere University of Technology, 33720 Tampere, Finland

Priya Kumar
College of Information Studies, University of Maryland, College Park, MD 20742, USA

Klas Backholm
Swedish School of Social Science, University of Helsinki, 00014 University of Helsinki, Finland

Julian Ausserhofer
Department of Communication, University of Vienna, 1090 Vienna, Austria
Research Group Internet Policy & Governance, Alexander von Humboldt Institute for Internet and Society, 10117 Berlin, Germany

Elsebeth Frey, Anna Grøndahl Larsen and Harald Hornmoen
Department of Journalism and Media Studies, Oslo and Akershus University College of Applied Sciences, 0130 Oslo, Norway

Joachim Högväg
Experience Lab, Åbo Akademi University, 65100 Vaasa, Finland

Gudrun Reimerth
Department of Media and Design, FH JOANNEUM University of Applied Sciences, 8020 Graz, Austria

Linus Andersson
Media and Communication Studies, School of Health and Welfare, Halmstad University, 30118 Halmstad, Sweden

Jukka Jouhki and Maija Penttinen
Department of History and Ethnology, University of Jyväskylä, 40014 Jyväskylä, Finland

Epp Lauk, Niina Sormanen and Turo Uskali
Department of Communication, University of Jyväskylä, 40014 Jyväskylä, Finland

Sari Östman and Riikka Turtiainen
School of History, Culture and Arts Studies, Faculty of Humanities, University of Turku, 28100 Pori, Finland

Heather Morton
Photography Department, Sheridan College, Oakville, L6H 2L1, Canada

Ksenia Ermoshina and Francesca Musiani
Institute for Communication Sciences, 75013 Paris, France

Guobin Yang
Annenberg School for Communication, University of Pennsylvania, Philadelphia, PA 19104, USA
Department of Sociology, University of Pennsylvania, Philadelphia, PA 19104, USA

Stefan Steiger
Institute of Political Science, Heidelberg University, 69115 Heidelberg, Germany

Wolf J. Schünemann
Institute of Social Sciences, Hildesheim University, 31141 Hildesheim, Germany

Katharina Dimmroth
Institute of Political Science, Rheinisch-Westfälische Technische Hochschule Aachen, 52074 Aachen, Germany

Colin Porlezza
IPMZ—Institute of Mass Communication and Media Research, University of Zurich, 8050 Zurich, Switzerland

Waqas Ejaz and Jens Wolling
Empirical Media Research and Political Communication Department, Technical University of Ilmenau, 98693 Ilmenau, Germany

Marco Bräuer
Federal Office for the Family and Civil Society, 02959 Schleife, Germany

Index